D0980290

CHRISTIANITY ON TRIAL

COLIN CHAPMAN

Tyndale
House
Publishers, INC.
Wheaton,
Illinois

CONTENTS

The three sections of
Christianity on Trial were
first published as three
separate books in Great
Britain by Lion Publishing,
Berkhamsted, Herts.
Book One, copyright ©
1972 Lion Publishing;
Book Two, copyright ©
1974 Lion Publishing;
Book Three, copyright ©
1974 Lion Publishing.

This combined edition is
published by Tyndale
House Publishers, Inc.,
Wheaton, Illinois 60187,
by arrangement with, and
permission of, Lion Pub-
lishing. All rights reserved.

Library of Congress Catalog
Card Number 74-19644
ISBN 8423-0246-8
Second printing, American
edition, November 1975
Printed in the United
States of America

GENERAL INTRODUCTION

Is Christianity *true* or isn't it?

How can we possibly *know* whether it is true or not?

These are the basic questions before us in putting Christianity on trial. We are dealing primarily with Christian beliefs about God and Jesus Christ, about man and the universe. We are asking whether they tell us "the truth" about ourselves and about the universe in which we live.

But how can Christian beliefs be put on trial?

QUESTIONS ABOUT JESUS CHRIST

There was a time when it seemed very simple to prove the truth of Christianity. A Christian could stage a trial that ended like this:

> Judge: Gentlemen of the Jury, I have laid before you the Substance of what has been said on both Sides. You are now to consider of it, and give your Verdict.
>
> Foreman: My Lord, we are ready to give our Verdict.

Judge: Are you all agreed?

Jury: Yes.

Judge: Who shall speak for you?

Jury: Our Foreman.

Judge: What say you? Are the Apostles guilty of giving false Evidence in the Case of the Resurrection of Jesus, or not guilty?

Foreman: Not guilty.

This happened in England in 1729.

Recently a similar trial was staged in a youth club in Scotland, but with significant differences. This time a Christian was put on trial, and the charges against him were these:

1. That your faith is based on a myth—the resurrection;

2. That your faith is irrelevant to life in the twentieth century.

All who took part in this trial were speaking for themselves and expressing their own beliefs. They were not role-playing. A few were Christians, but most were not. The audience was the jury, but there was no vote at the end. The judge in his summing up simply explained that each person must decide for himself whether or not he thought the Christian was guilty on these two charges.

If the idea of this second trial appeals to you, or at least makes some sense to you, you may want to go straight to Part 3 of this book, which deals with the evidence for Jesus Christ, the meaning of his death, and the question of his resurrection.

QUESTIONS ABOUT GOD, MAN, AND THE UNIVERSE

To many, however, this second trial sounds just as strange or absurd as the first. If you cannot understand or accept Christian beliefs about Jesus, it may be because you do not accept some of the most fundamental Christian assumptions about God, man, and the universe, and not simply because you are not convinced by the evidence about Jesus.

Bishop Butler, writing in 1736:

It has come, I know not how, to be taken for granted, by many persons, that Christianity is not so much a subject for inquiry but that it is, now at length, discovered to be fictitious. And accordingly they treat it as if in the present age this were an agreed point among all people of discernment, and nothing remained, but to set it up as a principal subject of mirth and ridicule, as it were by way of reprisals, for its having so long interrupted the pleasures of the world.

J. S. Mill:

I am . . . one of the very few examples, in this country, of one who has not thrown off religious belief, but never had it: I grew up in a negative state with regard to it. I looked upon the modern exactly as I did upon the ancient religion, as something which in no way concerned me.

Nietzsche, writing in 1865 at the age of 21:

If Christianity means belief in a historical person or event, I have nothing to do with it. But if it means the need for salvation, then I can treasure it.

Mahatma Gandhi:

I may say that I have never been interested in an historical Jesus. I should not care if it was proved by someone that the man called Jesus never lived, and that what was narrated in the Gospels was a figment of the writer's imagination. For the Sermon on the Mount would still be true for me.

Colin Wilson:

The need for God I could understand, and the need for religion; I could even sympathize with the devotees like Suso or St. Francis, who weave fantasies around the Cross, the nails and all the other traditional symbols. But ultimately I could not accept the need for redemption by a Savior. To pin down the idea of salvation to one point in time seemed to me a naive kind of anthropomorphism.

If, therefore, your questions and objections about Christianity are about fundamental assumptions about God, man, and the universe, there will be little point in making Jesus the starting point of the discussion. You ought to begin with one or more of the questions in Part 2 of this book. Who or what is "God"? Does "he" exist? What is man? Who am I? What kind of universe do we live in?

QUESTIONS
ABOUT
DEFINITION
AND TRUTH

But what if you are not sure what Christianity is?

James Mitchell:

> I used to be a convinced Christian: I am no longer a
> convinced Christian: I am no longer convinced. In fact like
> many others of my generation I am profoundly uncertain
> as to what "being a Christian" actually means any more.

C. E. M. Joad:

> If you will forgive me for mixing my metaphors, to criticize
> Christianity is like assaulting a feather bed with the consist-
> ency of a jelly and the colors of a chameleon.

And what if the idea of putting *any* ideas or beliefs on trial
sounds absurd?

The hero in Henri Barbusse's novel *L'Enfer:*

> As to philosophical discussions, they seem to me altogether
> meaningless. *Nothing can be tested, nothing verified.* Truth—
> what do they mean by it?

Michael Harrington:

> The contemporary spiritual crisis is the result of this simul-
> taneous loss of faith and anti-faith . . . Its unique character-
> istic is that no one really seems to believe in anything.

C. E. M. Joad writing about the war of 1914–18:

> Then came the war . . . When it came to the point, the
> ethics of Christianity were, it seemed, as incapable of practi-
> cal application as its history and biology of scientific verifi-
> cation. The whole religion as it is taught and preached
> today thus came to seem a gigantic swindle . . .

Margaret Cole:

> It is partly because I care for verification that I cannot
> believe in any "revealed religion" . . . When the question of
> the *truth* of Christianity was raised in my mind . . . I per-
> ceived almost immediately that it was not true, and that it
> could not possibly be proved to be true; and the burden of
> religious belief fell from my back as easily as did the bur-

den of Christian in *The Pilgrim's Progress,* and has never shown any sign of returning to its perch.

If you share these feelings, or have a strong sympathy with those who feel this way, you will probably have to begin with the questions about definition and truth in Part 1.

THE METHOD AND MATERIAL USED

Each of the main sections has an introduction outlining the general approach and defining the question being tackled in that section.

Then, possible answers to the question are suggested and each answer is examined in detail.

Much of the book consists of quotations from different writers, because it is important that we try to feel the full force of what they are saying. Where there is merely a summary of a person's position, the summary is in most cases taken from a writer who has no particular axe to grind or does not share the outlook of this book. For this reason much use has been made of, for example, Paul Hazard's books *The European Mind 1680– 1715* and *European Thought in the Eighteenth Century.* Where italics have been used they are the italics of the original author.

Quotations have been chosen from the philosophers, tracing the history and progression of their thought; from the arts, because this is often the area where beliefs can be worked out and carried to their logical conclusions; from other religions, because East and West are becoming more aware of each other's ways of thinking and no approach to Christianity should leave them out of account; and from modern theology, which has been profoundly affected by the history of ideas.

Finally, some problems and questions about the Christian answers are dealt with.

THE STARTING POINT

What is "Christianity"? There are so many definitions that it is necessary, before we begin, to say something about the starting point of this book.

There are three possible ways of answering this question:

Try to find the lowest common denominator in all the different definitions of Christianity that are offered. Limit the definition to include only those items that all Christians or the vast majority of Christians would accept without question.

Refuse to define Christianity at all. Allow each person to have his own understanding of Christianity, and show maximum tolerance toward anything described as "Christian."

State your own understanding of what Christianity is, at least as a starting point. Further discussion will show to what extent it is consistent with the mind of Christ.

This third approach is the one I have adopted. I shall take as my starting point what is generally called biblical Christianity; *i.e.,* dependent solely on what we know of God and Christ from the basic documents of the Bible, both Old and New Testaments. This understanding of Christianity is not that of any one church or denomination.

No discussion is held from a purely neutral position. Therefore the aim in stating my own position is not to be sectarian and doctrinaire, but simply to declare the book's starting point openly and clearly.

The position of this book, then, is basically a committed one. But its method is open. It is for the reader to start where he will, at the point where he is. He can examine the options, follow up any that interest him in any order he wants. It may mean going back to an earlier question to be settled first.

Then it is for the reader to make up his own mind, to follow up the evidence—and act accordingly.

LIVING WITH YOUR BELIEFS

It is not enough simply to outline different answers and coldly consider them as possible theories for discussion. We have to ask: *What does it feel like* to live with a belief about God, to go through life with a particular understanding of man, or to live in that kind of universe?

For this reason the quotations (including those from the Bible) are intended not simply to convey the answers in a theoretical way, but to help us enter into the experience of those who hold these particular beliefs.

We follow up the different answers to see where they lead, applying the "simple but profound test of fact": i.e., *Does this*

concept really work; do its consequences fit our experience? (Bronowski,
see Part 1, pp. 23, 24). In each case we need to ask questions
such as these:
—What would happen if we were to be thoroughly consistent
and take this belief to its logical conclusion?
—What would happen if we were to live as if this belief were
really true?
And for *"What would happen if . . . ?"* we can usually substitute
"What has happened when . . . ?" —because there have always been
people who have tried to be consistent in their search for the
truth, and have explored all the possible answers and their
consequences.

In many cases we shall discover what Francis Schaeffer calls
the "point of tension" between what a person believes and the
real world in which he has to live. If a belief leads to disastrous
consequences, or if we can only hold it by not being totally
consistent, then it is highly likely that our belief is not true. We
are then faced with a choice:

Either we accept the full consequences of what we believe

Or we look for a different belief which stands up better to the
test of truth.

A change of mind of this kind is bound to have profound
effect on all our attitudes. If Christianity is true—and if we are
prepared to consider this possibility—we have to be willing to
change our minds, to open them to the truth which God has
revealed, and see where this leads us. This process of change
involves the heart and will as much as the intellect. Jesus said:
"Whoever has the will to do the will of God shall know whether
my teaching comes from him or is merely my own."

PART ONE HOW CAN WE KNOW IF CHRISTIANITY IS TRUE?

The question is not: *Does Christianity contain* truths? *Does it contain individual truths that can be combined with truths from other religions and philosophies?*

The question is rather: *Is Christianity itself* the truth? *Is the whole system of Christian beliefs consistent within itself, and consistent with every thing else we know? Do Christian beliefs, when taken together as a whole, teach "the truth" about man, the universe, and God?*

The question is not simply: *How can I know if Christianity is true* for me? *Is it true to my experience, true to my understanding of myself (regardless of whether or not it expresses the truth about all men)? Is it true "existentially"? Does it express the existential truth of my own experience (whether or not it is true objectively)?*

The question is rather: *Is Christianity objectively true? Does it give a true account of what is there? Is it true objectively* and *true existentially at the same time? Can it be true in my own experience simply because it is the truth about the way things are?*

QUESTION ONE:
HOW CAN WE KNOW
IF CHRISTIANITY IS TRUE?

William Koechling

INTRODUCTION

Many (if not most) people today have already concluded that
Christianity cannot be true in the above sense, or that it is
impossible to know for certain. But we must ask the question in
its simplest and most direct form. Is Christianity true or isn't it?
Is it true or false, or partly true and partly false? Or what?

The moment we put the question in this way, we are involved
in the more fundamental question of how we can "know" anything—the ways of knowing. Broadly speaking we may say that
there are six different approaches to knowledge and belief:

The way of verification. We observe certain things through our
senses, and we assume that they give us reliable knowledge about
what is there. We then draw certain conclusions about what we
perceive. Where we can, we carry out certain tests to eliminate
false or inadequate theories, and to find the best and most
convincing way of accounting for all that we observe.

The way of authority. We accept someone else's authority—the
authority of an individual, group, consensus, or tradition. For
example, most of what we believe about science is accepted on
the authority of others, since we are not in a position to carry
out the experiments ourselves.

The way of abstract reasoning. We start with certain assumptions in
our minds, and then demonstrate that once we accept these
assumptions, certain things must necessarily follow and be true.

The way of agnosticism. Many reach the point at which they say
that the other ways of knowing do not give us certain or even
adequate knowledge. We must simply accept the fact that we do
not know and cannot know anything for certain. There are no
fool-proof ways of knowing.

The way of intuition or blind faith. We believe certain things
because we "feel" that they are true. We cannot give rational
arguments for them, but deep down we feel that they must be
true. And sometimes we believe *against* the evidence; we find
that there are good reasons for *not* believing, and yet we believe
in spite of this. In this case we believe by a leap of blind faith.

5

The way of mysticism. This way, it is claimed, gives us direct and immediate knowledge of what the universe is all about. It can be acquired in many different ways, but it cannot be communicated adequately in words.

These six different approaches correspond roughly to the six basic answers that have been given about the truth of Christianity. Some people combine elements from several of the answers. But it is necessary and helpful to try to distinguish them.

Choose the one that appeals to you most. Then turn to the page shown. See whether the answer satisfies you or whether you then want to turn to one of the others.

HOW CAN WE KNOW IF CHRISTIANITY IS TRUE?

God has revealed the truth to man and it is open to verification.
PAGE 9

We can prove some Christian beliefs to be true by reason; the others we must accept on authority.
PAGE 37

Christian beliefs are true only if they accord with human reason and/or feeling.
PAGE 51

We can never know for certain whether or not Christianity is true.
PAGE 64

We can know Christianity is true only by a leap of faith.
PAGE 86

We can know Christianity is true only through mystical experience.
PAGE 110

ANSWER ONE:
BIBLICAL CHRISTIANITY

God has revealed
the truth to man
and it is open to
verification.

The Christianity of the Bible claims that:

☐ *God has revealed the truth about himself, the universe, and man.*

☐ *The truth he has revealed is open to verification.*
These two parts of the answer need to be taken very closely together.

GOD HAS REVEALED THE TRUTH

The Bible points to four different ways in which God has revealed truth to men: through the universe; through the nature of man; through the written word of God in the Bible; and above all through Jesus Christ.

Revelation through the universe

The universe tells us something about the God who made it. The character of the universe—its size, complexity, order, and beauty—tell us something about the Creator. It is not a revelation in words, but the universe does, as the psalmist says, "say" something about God.

> The heavens are telling the glory of God;
>   and the firmament proclaims his handiwork.
> Day to day pours forth speech,
>   and night to night declares knowledge.
> There is no speech, nor are there words;
>   their voice is not heard;
> yet their voice goes out through all the earth,
>   and their words to the end of the world.

This kind of revelation is limited. It tells us only certain things about God. Job, for example, is very conscious of the limitations of this kind of revelation.

> He binds up the waters in his thick clouds,
>   and the cloud is not rent under them.
> He covers the face of the moon,
>   and spreads over it his cloud . . .
> Lo, these are but the outskirts of his ways;
>   and how small a whisper do we hear of him!

But despite the incompleteness of this revelation, it leaves men with no excuse when they reject and suppress the amount of truth that is clearly revealed. Paul writes:

> For the wrath of God is revealed from heaven against all ungodliness and wickedness of men who by their wickedness suppress the truth. For what can be known about God is plain to them, because God has shown it to them. Ever since the creation of the world his invisible nature, namely, his eternal power and deity, has been clearly perceived in the things that have been made. So they are without excuse . . .

Richard Wurmbrand tells the story of how this kind of thinking about the universe occurred to a Russian couple who were both sculptors and had been brought up to believe that there is no God.

Once, we worked on a statue of Stalin. During the work, my wife asked me: "Husband, how about the thumb? If we could not oppose the thumb to the other fingers—if the fingers of the hands were like toes—we could not hold a hammer, a mallet, any tool, a book, a piece of bread. Human life would be impossible without this little thumb. Now, who has made the thumb? We both learned Marxism in school and know that heaven and earth exist by themselves. They are not created by God. So I have learned and so I believe. But if God did not create heaven and earth, if he created only the thumb, he would be praiseworthy for this little thing.

"We praise Edison and Bell and Stephenson who have invented the electric bulb, the telephone and the railway and other things. But why should we not praise the one who has invented the thumb? If Edison had not had a thumb he would have invented nothing. It is only right to worship God who has made the thumb."

The husband became very angry . . . "Don't speak stupidities! You have learned that there is no God. And you can never know if the house is not bugged and if we will not fall into trouble. Get into your mind *once and for all* that there is no God. In heaven there is *nobody*!"

She replied: "This is an even greater wonder. If in heaven there were the Almighty God in whom in stupidity our forefathers believed, it would be only natural that we should have thumbs. An Almighty God can do everything, so he can make a thumb, too. But if in heaven there is nobody, I, from my side, am decided to worship from all my heart the 'Nobody' who had made the thumb."

Revelation through the nature of man

Everyone in certain situations has feelings that are described by the word *ought*:

"You ought to do this" or "You ought not to do that."

"I ought to do this" or "I ought not to do that."

None of us is so completely amoral that we feel that anything can be allowed and nothing discouraged.

Different societies have different social codes and different laws, but there is a large measure of agreement between them. The moral codes of the great religions have much in common.

According to Christian beliefs, man is a fallen creature, and his conscience therefore does not invariably reflect the will of God. But at many points his own instincts correspond very closely with what God has revealed in a fuller way through the written word in the Bible through Jesus Christ.

Christianity says that these basic instincts reveal something, however dimly, of the character of the God who has made man in his likeness. They are not simply the product of the society and the culture in which man lives. Further, when we expect others to accept our standards, or judge others by our standards, we are assuming that these standards are right, consistent with the way things are. This in itself points to the existence of a personal God who has made things this way. Paul's letter to the Romans puts it like this:

> Therefore you have no excuse, O man, whoever you are, when you judge another; for in passing judgment upon him you condemn yourself, because you, the judge, are doing the very same things . . .

> When the Gentiles who have not the law do by nature what the law requires, they are a law to themselves, even though they do not have the law. They show that what the law requires is written on their hearts, while their conscience also bears witness and their conflicting thoughts accuse or perhaps excuse them . . .

These two kinds of revelation, however, are limited. The universe does not tell us anything about the moral character of God, whether he is a loving God or a cruel God. And man's sinfulness frequently blinds him to the limited amount of truth he knows from his own nature.

Revelation through the written word of God in the Bible

Belief in the Bible as a revelation of God is based on three things:

The claims of parts of the Old Testament. Many of the Old Testament writers speak of God revealing himself both through his actions and through his words, *i.e.,* by what he does in history, and by what he reveals in words communicated to the minds of the prophets.

> The Lord used to speak to Moses face to face, as a man speaks to his friend.

> Surely the Lord God does nothing, without revealing his
> secret to his servants the prophets.

Sometimes we are told that those who received this revelation
wrote down what had been revealed.

> Moses came and told the people all the words of the Lord
> and all the ordinances; and all the people answered with
> one voice, and said, "All the words which the Lord has
> spoken we will do." And Moses wrote all the words of the
> Lord.

> Then the Lord put forth his hand and touched my mouth;
> and the Lord said to me, "Behold, I have put my words in
> your mouth. See, I have set you this day over nations and
> over kingdoms . . ." And the word of the Lord came to me,
> saying, "Jeremiah, . . ."

> Then Jeremiah called Baruch the son of Neriah, and
> Baruch wrote upon a scroll at the dictation of Jeremiah all
> the words of the Lord which he had spoken to him.

This is how the writer of Psalm 119 speaks about the writings
of the scriptures he had at that time:

> thy precepts (verse 4)
> thy statutes (verse 5)
> thy commandments (verse 6)
> thy righteous ordinances (verse 7)
> thy word (verse 9)
> the ordinances of thy mouth (verse 13)
> thy testimonies (verse 14)
> thy law (verse 18)
> thy promise (verse 38)
> thy words (verse 57)

The New Testament writers believed that the Old Testament
had the highest possible authority.

> In many and various ways God spoke of old to our fathers
> by the prophets . . .

> No prophecy ever came by the impulse of man, but men
> moved by the Holy Spirit spoke from God.

*The claims of Jesus for parts of the Old Testament and for the Old
Testament as a whole.* While Jesus himself claimed to be a fuller
revelation of God, he did not question the truth or the authority

of what had already been revealed through the Old Testament. He assumed it had the highest possible authority and used it to explain his own authority.

> Think not that I have come to abolish the law and the prophets; I have come not to abolish them but to fulfill them. For truly, I say to you, till heaven and earth pass away, not an iota, not a dot, will pass from the law until all is accomplished. Whoever then relaxes one of the least of these commandments and teaches men so, shall be called least in the kingdom of heaven; but he who does them and teaches them shall be called great in the kingdom of heaven.

> Jesus answered them, "Is it not written in your law, 'I said, you are gods'? If he called them gods to whom the word of God came (and scripture cannot be broken), do you say of him whom the Father consecrated and sent into the world, 'You are blaspheming,' because I said, 'I am the Son of God'?"

> You search the scriptures, because you think that in them you have eternal life; and it is they that bear witness to me.

This is how Jesus speaks about the authority of certain specific parts of the Old Testament:

> And as Jesus taught in the temple, he said, "How can the scribes say that the Christ is the son of David? David himself, inspired by the Holy Spirit, declared,
>
> 'The Lord said to my Lord,
> Sit at my right hand,
> till I put thy enemies under thy feet.'"

> And Pharisees came up to him and tested him by asking, "Is it lawful to divorce one's wife for any cause?" He answered, "Have you not read that he who made them from the beginning made them male and female, and said, 'For this reason a man shall leave his father and mother and be joined to his wife, and the two shall become one'?"

> Then he said to them, "These are my words which I spoke to you, while I was still with you, that everything written about me in the law of Moses and the prophets and the psalms must be fulfilled." Then he opened their minds to understand the scriptures.

The authority Jesus gave the apostles. Jesus promised his disciples that the Holy Spirit would enable them to give a reliable account

of his teaching, and would show them more of the truth which
would be revealed later. This promise was primarily for the
apostles themselves.

> The Counselor, the Holy Spirit, whom the Father will send
> in my name, he will teach you all things, and bring to your
> remembrance all that I have said to you.

> I have yet many things to say to you, but you cannot bear
> them now. When the Spirit of truth comes, he will guide
> you into all the truth; for he will not speak on his own
> authority, but whatever he hears he will speak, and he will
> declare to you the things that are to·come.

Paul claimed that he too had been commissioned as an apostle—in his case, through the exceptional circumstances of his
conversion. He believed that the Holy Spirit had revealed the
truth to him in specific words.

> Now we have received not the spirit of the world, but the
> Spirit which is from God, that we might understand the
> gifts bestowed on us by God. And we impart this in words
> not taught by human wisdom but taught by the Spirit,
> interpreting spiritual truths to those who possess the Spirit.

Any claim to a new revelation must be tested by the standard
of what he and the other apostles taught. If it conflicted with
this, it must be rejected.

> I am astonished that you are so quickly deserting him who
> called you in the grace of Christ and turning to a different
> gospel—not that there is another gospel, but there are some
> who trouble you and want to pervert the gospel of Christ.
> But even if we, or an angel from heaven, should preach to
> you a gospel contrary to that which we preached to you, let
> him be accursed. As we have said before, so now I say
> again, If any one is preaching to you a gospel contrary to
> that which you received, let him be accursed.

> Follow the pattern of the sound words which you have
> heard from me, in the faith and love which are in Christ
> Jesus; guard the truth that has been entrusted to you by
> the Holy Spirit who dwells within us.

Revelation through Jesus Christ

Jesus spoke of himself as the one who reveals the Father.

> All things have been delivered to me by my Father; and no

one knows the Son except the Father, and no one knows
the Father except the Son and any one to whom the Son
chooses to reveal him.

Jesus said to him, "I am the way, and the truth, and the
life; no one comes to the Father, but by me. If you had
known me, you would have known my Father also; henceforth you know him and have seen him."

Philip said to him, "Lord, show us the Father, and we shall
be satisfied." Jesus said to him, "Have I been with you so
long, and yet you do not know me, Philip? He who has
seen me has seen the Father; how can you say, Show us the
Father? Do you not believe that I am in the Father and the
Father in me? . . ."

This is the comment of one of the disciples who knew Jesus:
Grace and truth came through Jesus Christ. No one has
ever seen God; the only Son, who is in the bosom of the
Father, he has made him known.

The writer of the letter to the Hebrews links together God's
revelation of himself through the prophets in the Old Testament
with his revelation of himself in Jesus Christ.

In many and various ways God spoke of old to our fathers
by the prophets; but in these last days he has spoken to us
by a Son.

To say that God has revealed the truth does not mean that he
has revealed everything there is to be known. The revelation he
has given in these four ways is not exhaustive but it is adequate.
We can be sure that what has *not* been revealed is not inconsistent in any way with what has been revealed. What we still have
to learn about God will not contradict what we already know
about him.

Moses, for example, makes a distinction between what has
been revealed and what has not been revealed. What has been
revealed provides an adequate basis for living both here and
now, and in the future.

The secret things belong to the Lord our God; but the
things that are revealed belong to us and to our children
for ever, that we may do all the words of this law.

Similarly, Paul contrasts his present knowledge of God with
the knowledge he will have in heaven.

Now we see in a mirror dimly, but then face to face. Now I

know in part; then I shall understand fully, even as I have
been fully understood.

The incompleteness of his knowledge in this life, however,
does not make Paul skeptical or agnostic. He believes that the
truth which has already been revealed is absolutely reliable and
trustworthy.

We have received . . . the Spirit which is from God, that we
might understand the gifts bestowed on us by God. And we
impart this in words not taught by human wisdom but
taught by the Spirit.

If anyone thinks that he is a prophet, or spiritual, he
should acknowledge that what I am writing to you is a
command of the Lord.

THE TRUTH GOD HAS REVEALED
IS OPEN TO VERIFICATION

In the course of the revelation, there were certain vital points
where the people involved were able to verify what came to them
as a revelation from God. If the word *verification* sounds very
modern, this does not mean that the idea is modern. All through
the Bible we find that men are concerned with the basic question: how can I *know* if this is true? They were not prepared to
believe any and every miracle or revelation that purported to be
from God.

Abraham is promised by God that he will be the ancestor of a
great nation, and that his descendants will inherit the land of
Canaan. At first he simply believes the promise; he takes it on
trust. But then he asks for more definite assurance that the
promise will be fulfilled.

He (God) brought him outside and said, "Look toward
heaven, and number the stars, if you are able to number
them." Then he said to him, "So shall your descendants
be." And he *believed* the Lord; and he reckoned it to him as
righteousness. And he said to him, "I am the Lord who
brought you from Ur of the Chaldeans to give you this
land to possess." But he said, "O Lord God, *how am I to
know* that I shall possess it?" . . .

The account then goes on to describe something God did
before Abraham's eyes.

Then the Lord said to Abram, "*Know of a surety* that your
descendants will be sojourners in a land that is not theirs

> . . . And they shall come back here in the fourth gen-
> eration . . ."

When *Moses* meets God in the wilderness, he is commissioned to
lead his people out of slavery in Egypt. Moses' reply has a
contemporary ring to it:

> Then Moses answered, "But behold, they *will not believe me*
> or listen to my voice, for they will say, 'The Lord did not
> appear to you.'" The Lord said to him, "What is that in
> your hand?" He said, "A rod." . . .

God then performs a miracle with the rod in Moses' hand.
The purpose of the miracle is:

> that they may *believe* that the Lord, the God of their
> fathers, the God of Abraham, the God of Isaac, and the
> God of Jacob, has appeared to you . . . If they will not
> believe you . . . or heed the first sign, they may believe the
> latter sign. If they will not believe even these two signs or
> heed your voice, you shall take some water from the Nile
> and pour it upon the dry ground; and the water which you
> shall take from the Nile will become blood upon the dry
> ground.

When *Pharaoh* refuses to let the people go, Moses prophesies
that there will be various plagues and then points to these as
evidence for his claims about God's revelation to him.

> Thus says the Lord, "By this you shall *know* that I am the
> Lord . . ."

Each of the subsequent plagues is prophesied with this intention:

> that you may *know* that there is no one like the Lord our
> God . . .
> that you may *know* that I am the Lord in the midst of the
> earth.

The record of the events at *Mount Sinai* includes several miracles
which were witnessed by all the people. This is how Moses
reminds the people, at a later stage, of the events at Mount
Sinai:

> Take heed . . . lest you forget the things which your eyes
> have *seen* . . . how on the day that you stood before the
> Lord your God at Horeb, the Lord said to me, "Gather the

people to me, that I may let them *hear* my words, so that
they may learn to fear me all the days that they live upon
the earth, and that they may teach their children so." And
you came near and stood at the foot of the mountain . . .
wrapped in darkness, cloud and gloom. Then the Lord
spoke to you out of the midst of the fire; you heard the
sound of words, but saw no form; there was only a voice.
And he declared to you his covenant, which he commanded
you to perform, that is, the ten commandments; and he
wrote them upon two tables of stone.

Elijah and the priests of Baal witness one of the most striking
examples of verification in the Old Testament. It comes at a time
of crisis in the history of the children of Israel, when false ideas
of God associated with Baal have become very popular. Elijah,
the prophet of God, issues a challenge to the prophets of Baal.

And Elijah came near to all the people, and said, "How
long will you go limping with two different opinions? If the
Lord is God, follow him; but if Baal, then follow him . . .
Let two bulls be given to us; and let them choose one bull
for themselves, and cut it in pieces and lay it on the wood,
but put no fire to it; and I will prepare the other bull and
lay it on the wood, and put no fire to it. And you call on
the name of your god and I will call on the name of the
Lord; and the God who answers by fire, he is God." And all
the people answered, "It is well spoken". . .

The prophets of Baal perform their rituals and call on Baal,
but nothing happens. Then:

Elijah the prophet came near and said, "O Lord, God of
Abraham, Isaac, and Israel, *let it be known this day that thou
art God* in Israel, and that I am thy servant . . . Answer me,
O Lord, answer me, that this people may know that thou,
O Lord, art God . . ." Then the fire of the Lord fell, and
consumed the burnt offering . . . And when all the people
saw it, they fell on their faces; and they said, "The Lord, he
is God; the Lord, he is God."

The *prophets* could never simply assume that everyone would
automatically accept every word they said as a revelation from
God. This is the test that Moses says should be applied to
messages claiming to come from God:

If you say in your heart, "How may we know the word
which the Lord has not spoken?"—when a prophet speaks

in the name of the Lord, if the word does not come to pass
or come true, that is a word which the Lord has not
spoken; the prophet has spoken it presumptuously, you
need not be afraid of him.

The prophet Isaiah prophesies about what God is going to do
in history. He says that God is telling them what will happen in
advance, so that they can be quite certain that he has done it and
that he has given the message to the prophet:

...that men may *see* and *know*,
   may consider and understand together,
that the hand of the Lord has done this,
   the Holy One of Israel has created it.
The former things I declared of old,
   they went forth from my mouth and I made
     them known;
   then suddenly I did them and they came to pass.
Because I know that you are obstinate,
   and your neck is an iron sinew,
   and your forehead brass,
I declared them to you from of old,
   before they came to pass I announced them
     to you,
   lest you should say, "My idol did them . . ."

Ezekiel, similarly, predicts what is to happen at different periods of the future; and in each case the intention is that through
the prediction and the event following, men may *know*.
   . . . and you shall *know* that I am the Lord.

The first disciples came to believe in Jesus gradually, through
being with him and working with him over a period of three
years. There was no sudden surrender or blind commitment.
They did not believe through the private illumination of any one
individual. They were persuaded by the combined evidence of
the character, teaching, and miracles of Jesus.
   They had ample opportunity to get to know almost every side
of his *character*. They could observe whether his life was consistent with what he taught.
   They were able to test his *teaching* against what they already
knew about God from the Old Testament. They came to see that
Jesus' claims about himself were consistent with what God had
already revealed.

Lord, to whom shall we go? You have the words of eternal life; and we have *believed*, and have come to *know*, that you are the Holy One of God.

His *miracles* provided further evidence of his unique relationship with God and confirmed the claims he made for himself.

This, the first of his signs, Jesus did at Cana in Galilee, and manifested his glory; and his disciples *believed* in him.

The climax of this evidence was the resurrection. When Thomas refused to accept the word of the other disciples that they had seen the risen Christ, when he insisted on being able to verify the story before he believed, the risen Christ appeared to him and invited him to touch him, to assure himself that Christ really had been raised from death.

Eight days later, his disciples were again in the house, and Thomas was with them. The doors were shut, but Jesus came and stood among them, and said, "Peace be with you." Then he said to Thomas, "Put your finger here, and see my hands; and put out your hand, and place it in my side; do not be faithless, but believing." Thomas answered him, "My Lord and my God!"

The early preaching about Jesus. Peter first preached about Jesus in Jerusalem, seven weeks after the resurrection. He could assume that his audience had heard the reports of what had happened and, if they wanted to, could check them for themselves by questioning those involved. All he need do therefore was to remind them of what had happened and to interpret its meaning.

Men of Israel, hear these words: Jesus of Nazareth, a man attested to you by God with mighty works and wonders and signs which God did through him in your midst, as you yourselves know—this Jesus, delivered up according to the definite plan and foreknowledge of God, you crucified and killed by the hands of lawless men . . . This Jesus God raised up, and of that we all are witnesses . . . Let all the house of Israel therefore know assuredly that God has made him both Lord and Christ, this Jesus whom you crucified.

Paul, in one of the earliest parts of the New Testament to be written, reminds the Corinthians in simple outline of the events of the resurrection:

> I delivered to you as of first importance what I also received, that Christ died for our sins in accordance with the scriptures, that he was buried, that he was raised on the third day in accordance with the scriptures, and that he appeared to Cephas, then to the twelve. Then he appeared to more than five hundred brethren at one time, most of whom are still alive, though some have fallen asleep. Then he appeared to James, then to all the apostles. Last of all . . . he appeared also to me.

In this context Paul is in effect saying, "If you want to check up on the facts, go and ask any of the eyewitnesses for yourselves. There are many still alive who claim to have seen what happened. Go and verify the story for yourself."

Luke explains his purpose in writing his Gospel in this way:

> Inasmuch as many have undertaken to compile a narrative of the things which have been accomplished among us, just as they were delivered to us by those who from the beginning were eyewitnesses and ministers of the word, it seemed good to me also, having followed all things closely for some time past, to write an orderly account for you, most excellent Theophilus, that you may know the truth concerning the things of which you have been informed.

From this carefully worded introduction, we learn several significant things:

☐ Many people before Luke had attempted to make some kind of record or narrative about the life of Jesus. They were not writing exhaustive records, but they were interested in recording what had happened.

☐ Luke does not claim to have been an eyewitness himself, but he does claim to have been in close touch with those who were.

☐ Luke wants his reader, Theophilus, to know the truth about the reports he has heard. In his companion volume, the Acts of the Apostles, Luke describes for Theophilus the beginnings of the Christian church after the resurrection. The last part of the book describes in detail the arrest of Paul and his various trials; and it ends with Paul in Rome on trial for his life.

If Theophilus was not actually involved in Paul's trial in some way, he must at least have been interested in it for some reason. And it seems that Luke is simply trying to explain the facts about the origin of Christianity and of how Paul came to be arrested and brought to Rome for trial. He is writing for a contemporary, and much of what he says would be open to verification. If Theophilus wanted to, he could check up on the details: the various Roman authorities Luke mentions, and so on.

CAN CHRISTIAN BELIEFS BE VERIFIED TODAY?

We are no longer in a position to carry out the same tests that people involved in the biblical events were able to carry out. But if we are familiar with what verification means in science, history, and philosophy, and even in personal relationships, we can see how the approach to establishing truth in each of these areas can be applied to Christian beliefs.

Scientific verification

This is how *Jacob Bronowski* describes the principle of verification in science:

> We cannot shirk the historic question, What is truth? On the contrary: the civilization we take pride in took a new strength on the day the question was asked. It took its greatest strength later from Renaissance men like Leonardo, in whom truth to fact became a passion. The sanction of experienced fact as a face of truth is . . . the mainspring which has moved our civilization since the Renaissance.
>
> The first step is the collection of data . . . Next comes the creative step . . . which finds an order in the data by exploring likenesses . . . and the third step is to create this concept (the central concept) . . . This sequence is characteristic of science. It begins with a set of appearances. It organizes these into laws. And at the center of the laws it finds a knot, a point at which several laws cross: a symbol which gives unity to the laws themselves. Mass, time, magnetic moment, the unconscious . . . And we test the concept, as we test the thing, by its implications. That is, when the concept has been built up from some experiences, we reason what behavior in other experiences should logically flow from it. If we find this behavior, we go on holding the concept as it is. If we do not find the behavior which the concept logically implies, then we must go back and correct it. In this way logic and experiment are locked together in the scientific method, in a constant to and fro in which each follows the other.

Science is the creation of concepts and their exploration in the facts. It has no other test of the concept than its empirical truth to fact. Truth is the drive at the center of science; it must have the habit of truth, not as a dogma but as a process.

The test of truth is the known factual evidence . . .

We must be careful, however, not to make exaggerated claims about verification in science. Scientists in recent years have become much more modest in their claims for the experimental method. Karl Popper, for example, has suggested that we should think of the experimental method as a method of *disproof* rather than proof.

John Wren-Lewis summarizes Karl Popper's views in this way:

It does *not* mean "proving your theories by experimental test." It is a commonplace in philosophy that nothing can ever be proved by experimental test, because an infinite number of tests would be required. What you *can* do is to *disprove* theories, and the essential feature of the experimental method is that it sets up artificial situations especially designed to disprove the chosen theory if possible . . .

The experimental method involves treating theories as *formulae for communicating possible innovations* rather than as intuitions of deeper truth.

Historic Christianity has always believed that the universe was created by God and is sustained by God; and that man is different from the animals in that he bears "the image of God." These beliefs must inevitably have some point of contact with the theories of various sciences, and especially about the origin of the universe and man.

If we accept biblical Christianity's answer to the question "How can we know if Christianity is true?" we also accept the challenge of the scientist. We have to reply, "What you say about the scientific method *is* relevant in considering the truth of Christianity. What we must do is to approach Christian beliefs about the origin and nature of man and the universe as one possible theory among many. And then we simply try to find out which of these theories accounts best for all that we know about man and the universe."

It can hardly be emphasized strongly enough that the question here is not simply: Did man evolve from the apes? This question is important, but it is not the only question. It must be

considered in the context of the much larger question: which of
these two ways of thinking about the universe fits the facts
better:

> that the universe is a completely closed system of cause and
> effect; that there is no supernatural God; that all there is is
> what can be seen; that the universe is the product of chance
> which has somehow produced purpose;

> or that the universe was created by God and depends for its
> existence on God; that man is what he is because he is
> stamped with God's likeness?

These two ways of thinking are completely incompatible. We
are forced to make a decisive choice between them. And this
choice is far more fundamental than the choice we make about
the specific question of the evolution of man.

The process of choosing between these two hypotheses can
follow the scientific method closely, step by step. Just as the
scientific method depends on presuppositions, observation, theory, and experiment, so in the same way in verifying Christian
beliefs, presuppositions, observation, theory, and experiment all
play their part.

PRESUPPOSITIONS
Just as the scientist has presuppositions which he accepts but cannot
prove with complete certainty . . .

So in the same way we are bound
to approach Christian beliefs with our
own presuppositions; *e.g,* that miracles can or cannot happen.

OBSERVATION
Just as the scientist must consider all
the possible evidence (or as much of
it as possible) . . .

So in the same way we must consider all the relevant evidence for
Christian beliefs (or as much of it as
possible)—and this will include the
evidence about the origin of the universe and of man, and also the total
experience of others and ourselves.

THEORY
Just as the scientist considers all the
possible theories and tries to find the
theory or hypothesis that best accounts for all he observes; *e.g.,* which
theory makes the best sense of the
data we observe:
  —that the sun goes round the
    earth?
  —*or* that the earth goes around
    the sun? . . .

So in the same way we must try to
find the theory that best fits the facts;
i.e., which theory makes the best
sense of what we observe in the universe and in man:
  —that the universe is a completely
    closed system of cause and ef-
    fect, the product of impersonal
    energy, time and chance?
  —*or* that the universe was created
    by an infinite, personal God?

EXPERIMENT
Just as the scientist must conduct the necessary experiments to test all the possible theories, and to eliminate false theories . . .

So in the same way we can test these rival beliefs by the test of fact; *i.e.,* by observing what happens when one lives consistently on the basis of one or other of these beliefs.

As an example of a non-Christian who accepts this method of discussing beliefs about man and the universe, we may again quote *Bronowski (Science and Human Values).* The Christian will not agree with the conclusion at which he arrives, but his method is precisely the same as that which has been outlined here:

> . . . Does this [concept] really work . . . without force, without corruption, and without another arbitrary superstructure of laws which do not derive from the central concept? Do its consequences fit our experience; do men in such a society live so or not so? This is the simple but profound test of fact by which we have come to judge the large words of the makers of states and systems. . . .
>
> There have always been two ways of looking for truth. One is to find concepts which are beyond challenge, because they are held by faith or by authority or the conviction that they are self-evident. This is the mystic submission to truth which the East has chosen, and which dominated the axiomatic thought of the scholars of the Middle Ages. So St. Thomas Aquinas holds that faith is a higher guide to truth than knowledge is; the master of medieval science puts science firmly into second place.
>
> But long before Aquinas wrote, Peter Abelard had already challenged the whole notion that there are concepts which can only be felt by faith or authority. All truth, even the highest, is accessible to test, said Abelard: "By doubting we are led to inquire, and by inquiry we perceive the truth" . . . .
>
> The habit of testing and correcting the concept by its consequences in experience has been the spring within the movement of our civilization ever since. In science and in art and in self-knowledge we explore and move constantly by turning to the world of sense to ask, Is this so? This is the habit of truth . . .
>
> Science is indeed a truthful activity. And whether we look at facts, at things, or at concepts, we cannot disentangle truth from meaning—that is, from an inner order. Truth therefore is not different in science and in the arts; the

facts of the heart, the bases of personality, are merely more difficult to communicate. Truth to fact is the same habit in both, and has the same importance for both, because facts are the only raw material from which we can derive a change of mind. In science, the appeal to fact is the exploration of the concept in its logical consequences. In the arts, the emotional facts fix the limits of experience which can be shared in their language.

This approach is worked out in greater detail in question three, "Man," and four, "The Universe," in Part 2.

Historical verification

When we think of verification in historical inquiry, we soon realize that there are many different levels or degrees of certainty. For instance, we cannot reach the same kind of certainty in history as in mathematics. We can illustrate some of these different levels of certainty in this way:

CERTAIN—that Winston Churchill is dead.
—that there was a Second World War.
PROBABLE—that Hitler committed suicide in 1945.
—that in 1700 the population of Scotland was just over one million.
POSSIBLE—that James IV was not killed at the battle of Flodden.
—that Queen Elizabeth was really a man (a recent theory).
—that Richard III did not murder the Princes in the Tower.
—that Conan Doyle was Jack the Ripper (a recent suggestion).
IMPROBABLE—that Jesus visited the south of England (an old tradition).
—that Bacon wrote Shakespeare's plays.

The modern historian is not so confident as his predecessors about his ability to reconstruct "what really happened." And even assuming that he has the facts right, he is much more conscious of the difficulty of interpreting them objectively.

Aldous Huxley:

Alas! There is no such thing as Historical Truth—there are only more or less probable opinions about the past, opinions which change from generation to generation. History is a function, mathematically speaking, of the degree of ignorance and of the personal prejudices of historians. The history of any epoch which has left very few documents is at the mercy of archaeological research; a happy discovery may necessitate its radical revision from one day to the next.

Pieter Geyl:

To expect from history those final conclusions, which may perhaps be obtained in other disciplines, is, in my opinion, to misunderstand its nature . . . The scientific method serves above all to establish facts; there is a great deal about which we can reach agreement by its use. But as soon as there is a question of explanation, of interpretation, of appreciation, though the special method of the historian remains valuable, the personal element can no longer be ruled out—that point of view which is determined by the circumstances of his time and by his own preconceptions. No human intelligence can hope to bring together the over-whelming multiplicity of dates and of factors, of forces and movements, and from them establish the true, one might almost say the divine balance. This is literally a superhuman task. A man's judgement—for however solemnly some peo-ple may talk about the lessons of History, the historian is after all only a man sitting at his desk—a historian's judge-ment, then, may seem to him the only possible conclusion to draw from the facts, he may feel himself sustained and comforted by his sense of kinship with the past, and yet that judgement will have no finality. Its truth will be rela-tive, it will be partial. Truth, though for God it may be One, assumes many shapes to men. Thus it is that the analysis of so many conflicting opinions concerning one historical phenomenon is not just a means of whiling away the time, nor need it lead to discouraging conclusions con-cerning the untrustworthiness of historical study. The study, even of contradictory conceptions can be fruitful . . . History is indeed an argument without end.

Some of the beliefs of Christianity are beliefs that certain events happened at particular places and at particular times. These beliefs therefore must be open to the ordinary methods of historical inquiry. Thus:

Just as the historian asks questions about events; *e.g.*, did the Battle of Hastings take place or did it not? And if it did happen, did it happen in the way in which the different accounts suggest?	**So in the same way** we can and must ask questions about the events recorded in the Bible; *e.g.*, Did Jesus rise from the dead or did he not? And if he did, did it happen in the way that the documents suggest?
Just as the historian is concerned about the interpretation of events, and asks such questions as: what were the causes of the Second World War? . . .	**So in the same way** we can ask such questions as: how are we to account for the origin and growth of Christianity?
Just as in attempting to answer these questions, the historian can never be 100 percent objective, but is inevitably influenced by his presuppositions; *e.g.*, Marxist theory . . .	**So in the same way** in considering the biblical documents we are bound to be influenced by our presuppositions; *e.g.*, that miracles can or cannot happen.
Just as the historian realizes that he cannot arrive at 100 percent certainty about the past but is content to accept lesser degrees of certainty . . .	**So in the same way** while we may not be 100 percent certain about the events in the Bible, we need not therefore be completely skeptical, discounting the possibility of knowing anything about what happened.
Just as historical events and theories are open to falsification; *i.e.*, they can be shown to be highly unlikely or improbable . . .	**So in the same way** the events recorded in the Bible are open to falsification; they are not immune from historical inquiry.

The Christian does not claim to be able to prove with 100 percent certainty that Jesus rose from the dead. What he can say is that there are good historical reasons for believing that he did. He can point out that the documentary evidence for the resurrection is at least as good as the evidence for other events of the period that are never questioned, and very much better than some.

We must therefore examine the evidence for the resurrection and decide where we would place it on the scale of the different degrees of certainty: certain, probable, possible, improbable . . . This approach is worked out in question seven (Part 3)—"Did Jesus rise from the dead?"

The following quotations from three Christian writers show the place historical verification has played or still plays in their faith.

C. S. Lewis, speaking about one stage in his conversion:

Early in 1926 the hardest boiled of all the atheists I ever

knew sat in my room on the other side of the fire and remarked that the evidence for the historicity of the Gospels was really surprisingly good. "Rum thing," he went on. "All that stuff of Frazer's about the Dying God. Rum thing. It almost looks as if it had really happened once!"

Frank Morison set out to prove that the resurrection did not happen, but through his study of the evidence was forced to change his mind:

I wanted to take this Last Phase of the life of Jesus, with all its quick and pulsating drama, its sharp, clear-cut, background of antiquity, and its tremendous psychological and human interest—to strip it of its overgrowth of primitive beliefs and dogmatic suppositions, and to see this supremely great Person as He really was. . . . Fully ten years later, the opportunity came to study the life of Christ as I had long wanted to study it, to investigate the origins of its literature, to sift some of the evidence at first hand, and to form my own judgement on the problem which it presents. I will only say that it effected a revolution in my thought. Things emerged from that old-world story which previously I should have thought impossible. Slowly but very definitely the conviction grew that the drama of those unforgettable weeks of human history was stranger and deeper than it seemed. It was the *strangeness* of many notable things in the story which first arrested and held my interest. It was only later that the irresistible logic of their meaning came into view.

A. R. Vidler refers to *N. P. Williams'* extreme statement of the vulnerability of his faith:

If an ostrakon were unearthed at Nazareth which showed conclusively that Joseph was the father of Jesus, he would abandon the Christian faith and look round for some other theory of the universe.

This approach is worked out in Part 3 in the questions about Jesus Christ.

Philosophical verification

Philosophy in the past has generally been concerned with the search for truth. This is how *C. E. M. Joad* sums up the aims of traditional philosophy:

The object of philosophy, as I conceive it, is not to help

people, but to discover truth. I want to know *qua* philosopher what the universe is like.

It is the business of philosophy, as I conceive it, to seek to understand the nature of the universe as a whole, not, as do the sciences, some special department of it, but the whole bag of tricks to which the moral feelings of the Puritan, the herd instinct of the man in the street, the religious consciousness of the saint, the aesthetic enjoyment of the artist, the history of the human race and its contemporary follies, no less than the latest discoveries of science contribute. Reflecting upon this mass of data, the philosopher seeks to interpret it. He looks for a clue to guide him through the labyrinth, for a system wherewith to classify, or a purpose in terms of which to make meaningful.

Bertrand Russell:

Is there any knowledge in the world which is so certain that no reasonable man could doubt it? This question, which at first sight might not seem difficult, is really one of the most difficult that can be asked. When we have realized the obstacles in the way of a straightforward and confident answer, we shall be well launched on the study of philosophy—for philosophy is merely the attempt to answer such ultimate questions, not carelessly and dogmatically, as we do in ordinary life and even in the sciences, but critically, after exploring all that makes such questions puzzling, and after realizing all the vagueness and confusion that underlie our ordinary ideas.

In philosophy, a belief is considered to be "true" if it corresponds to the facts. There are two stages in the process of verification:

First, does it make sense? Does it contradict itself in any way? Does it violate the basic rule of logic, the law of non-contradiction (that *a* cannot be *non-a*)?

Alasdair MacIntyre:

It is of the essence of assertions that they declare one state of affairs to hold at the expense of others: to assert that an object is one colour is to exclude it from being all other colours; to assert that someone is kind and good is to exclude their being cruel or countenancing cruelty. Thus it is a condition of a given utterance being an assertion that there are certain states of affairs which it excludes: and if

31

we find that such a state of affairs does in fact hold, the assertion will be false. So in order for an utterance to be an assertion and to be understood as one, it must be capable of falsity. A meaningful assertion must be falsifiable.

(The original form of the Verification Principle put forward by the Vienna Circle of Linguistic Philosophers, stated that a proposition is meaningful *only* if it is open to verification. If it is not open to any kind of verification, then it does not make sense, and we cannot even begin to ask whether it is true or not. This principle can hardly be applied consistently, because the principle itself is not open to verification; and therefore on its own terms cannot make sense, let alone be true.)

Second, does it fit the facts? Does it correspond to our experience, our knowledge?

Bertrand Russell:

Philosophical knowledge . . . does not differ essentially from scientific knowledge; there is no special source of wisdom which is open to philosophy but not to science . . .
Philosophy, like all other studies, aims primarily at knowledge.

It is customary to say that a general proposition is "verified" when all of its consequences which it has been possible to test have been found to be true.

Truth is a property of beliefs, and derivatively of sentences which express beliefs. Truth consists in a certain relation between a belief and one or more facts other than the belief. When this relation is absent, the belief is false. A sentence may be called "true" or "false" even if no one believes it, provided that if it were to be believed, the belief would be true or false as the case may be.

To say, therefore, that Christian beliefs are open to verification means that Christian beliefs can be discussed on the same level as philosophical beliefs. Therefore:

Just as philosophers ask "Does this theory make sense? Is it consistent with itself? Does it contradict itself?" . . .

So in the same way we can and must ask "Does this Christian belief make sense? Is it consistent with itself? Does it contradict itself?"

Just as the philosopher asks "Is this theory consistent with everything else that I know?" . . .

So in the same way we ask "Is this Christian belief consistent with everything else that I know?"

Just as the philosopher has to use as his data all his own experience and knowledge, and the experience and knowledge of others . . .	**So in the same way** in putting Christian beliefs on trial we can use as evidence all our own experience and knowledge, and the experience and knowledge of others.
Just as a philosophical belief is open to verification and is also open to falsification . . .	**So in the same way** Christian beliefs are open to falsification.

This does not mean that Christian beliefs can be reduced permanently to the level of an abstract hypothetical system. But it does mean that we can at least begin in this way. We have to ask ourselves whether this system fits the facts better than other beliefs claim to. If we consider them at all seriously, we will soon realize that we cannot remain forever in the position of the armchair philosopher or the disinterested spectator. For if Christian beliefs *are* true, we have to come to terms with our Creator, and this will have a profound effect on the way we think and feel and behave.

It was through following this approach that *C. E. M. Joad* eventually abandoned his agnosticism and became a Christian. In his book *The Recovery of Belief* he writes:

> The following book is an account of some of the reasons which have converted me to the religious view of the universe in its Christian version. They are predominantly arguments designed to appeal to the intellect . . .

> While I admit that intellect cannot go all the way, there can, for me, be no believing which the intellect cannot, so far as its writ runs, defend and justify. I must, as a matter of psychological compulsion, adopt the most rational hypothesis, the most rational being that which seems to cover most of the facts and to offer the most plausible explanation of our experience as a whole . . .

> It is because . . . the religious view of the universe seems to me to cover more of the facts of experience than any other that I have been gradually led to embrace it . . .

> What I have to record is a changed view of the nature of man, which in due course led to a changed view of the nature of the world . . .

> This view of human evil (that evil is merely the product of heredity and environment and can be eradicated through progress) which I adopted unthinkingly as a young man I have come fundamentally to disbelieve. Plausible, perhaps,

during the first fourteen years of this century when . . . the state of mankind seemed to be improving—though the most cursory reading of human history should even then have been sufficient to dispose of it—it has been rendered utterly unplausible by the events of the last forty years. To me, at any rate, the view of evil implied by Marxism, expressed by Shaw and maintained by psychotherapy, a view which regards evil as a by-product of circumstances, which circumstances can, therefore, alter and even eliminate, has come to seem intolerably shallow and the contrary view of it as endemic in man, more particularly in its Christian form, the doctrine of original sin, to express a deep and essential insight into human nature.

This approach is worked out in questions two, "God," three, "Man," and four, "The Universe" (Part 2).

Verification in personal relationships

We are not in the habit of associating verification with personal relationships. And many are inclined to drive a wedge between *scientific* knowledge and *personal* knowledge. But we can say that a kind of testing is going on all the time in our relationships with others. Without this testing, there would soon be a breakdown of understanding or of trust between people. Unless we are incredibly gullible, we do not believe everything that people say, and we do not accept people at their face value without ever raising any questions in our minds. Consciously (or perhaps unconsciously) we notice how people speak and behave, and in this way our estimate of them is either confirmed or revised. One dishonest or cruel action could be quite enough to make us change our mind about someone so that we cease to trust him in the same way.

This means that our faith in people cannot be separated from our knowledge of them. Our belief in them is closely tied up with what we believe about them. Trust and even love are therefore open to a kind of testing.

The process of finding out about Jesus Christ and coming to trust and love him can be basically the same as the process by which we come to trust and love another person. Thus:

Just as we can ask: can I trust *x*? Is he genuine? Is he the kind of person he claims to be? Can he do what he claims to be able to do? . . .

So in the same way we can ask: can I trust Jesus Christ? Is he genuine? Is he the person he claims to be? Can he really do what he claims to be able to do for me?

Just as we receive impressions about a person through observing his behavior and hearing his words, and through hearing what others say about him . . .	**So in the same way** we can receive impressions about Jesus through reading about his life and his words, and by hearing the testimony of those who trust him today.
Just as we are hesitant about trusting a person in big things unless we have good reasons for trusting him and have some basis for our confidence in him . . .	**So in the same way** we are not likely to trust Jesus and enter into a relationship with him unless we have good reasons for trusting him and have some good basis for our confidence.
Just as we cannot expect 100 percent certainty *before* we trust or love someone, but our trust and love are nonetheless constantly open to various kinds of tests (since a person's behavior toward us gives us some indication of his trust or love) . . .	**So in the same way** we cannot expect 100 percent certainty *before* we experience the love of Christ for ourselves and come to trust him; but we are not taking a leap in the dark, because at each stage we can test whether his words are genuine and whether he means what he says.

The Bible contains many invitations to put the character and promises of God to the test.

> O taste and see that the Lord is good!
>   Happy is the man who takes refuge in him!

> Offer to God a sacrifice of thanksgiving,
>   and pay your vows to the Most High;
> and call upon me in the day of trouble;
>   I will deliver you, and you shall glorify me.

> Bring the full tithes into the storehouse, that there may be food in my house; and thereby put me to the test, says the Lord of hosts, if I will not open the windows of heaven for you and pour down for you an overflowing blessing.

The invitation of Jesus:

> Come to me, all who labor and are heavy laden, and I will give you rest. Take my yoke upon you, and learn from me; for I am gentle and lowly in heart, and you will find rest for your souls. For my yoke is easy, and my burden is light.

The Bible also contains the testimony of many who tested the promises of God and verified the truth of his revelation for themselves.

> I sought the Lord, and he answered me,
>   and delivered me from all my fears.

35

I love the Lord, because he has heard
   my voice and my supplications.
Because he inclined his ear to me,
   therefore I will call on him as long as I live.

After this many of his disciples drew back and no longer
went about with him. Jesus said to the twelve, "Will you also
go away?" Simon Peter answered him, "Lord, to whom shall
we go? You have the words of eternal life; and we have
believed, and have come to know, that you are the Holy
One of God."

And the Word became flesh and dwelt among us, full of
grace and truth; we have beheld his glory, glory as of the
only Son from the Father . . . And from his fullness have
we all received, grace upon grace.

Then he said to Thomas, "Put your finger here, and see my
hands; and put out your hand, and place it in my side; do
not be faithless, but believing." Thomas answered him, "My
Lord and my God!"

That which was from the beginning, which we have heard,
which we have seen with our eyes, which we have looked
upon and touched with our hands, concerning the word of
life—the life was made manifest, and we saw it, and testify
to it, and proclaim to you the eternal life which was with
the Father and was made manifest to us—that which we
have seen and heard we proclaim also to you, so that you
may have fellowship with us; and our fellowship is with the
Father and with his Son Jesus Christ. And we are writing
this that our joy may be complete.

*Problems and questions arising out of
biblical Christianity's answer to the
question "How can we know if Christianity is true?" are taken up on p.
119. First we must look at some other
answers given to the basic question.*

ANSWER TWO:
AUTHORITARIANISM

We can prove some Christian beliefs to be true by reason; the others we must accept on authority.

Scholasticism and traditional Roman Catholic orthodoxy gives a two-part answer:

☐ *Man can find out some Christian beliefs by his own reason;*

☐ *The other Christian beliefs are beyond reason; they have been revealed by God, and must be accepted by faith.*

Thomas Aquinas (1225–1274):

It was necessary for man's salvation that there should be a doctrine revealed by God, besides the philosophical disciplines investigated by human reason . . . Hence it was necessary for the salvation of man that certain truths which exceed human reason should be made known to him by divine revelation . . .

Therefore, in order that the salvation of men might be brought about more fitly and more surely, it was necessary that they should be taught divine truths by divine revelation. It was therefore necessary that, besides the philosophical disciplines investigated by reason, there should be a sacred doctrine by way of revelation.

Although those things which are beyond man's knowledge may not be sought for by man through his reason, nevertheless, what is revealed by God must be accepted through faith.

MAN CAN FIND OUT SOME CHRISTIAN BELIEFS BY HIS OWN REASON

Man is finite, and he is a fallen creature; but he is still able to arrive at some of the truth about God and the universe simply by using his own reason. In this way, for example, he can know:

the existence of God: reason can prove *that* God exists, though it cannot tell us everything we need to know about God.

the existence of the moral law, or natural law, in the conscience.

This answer has led to the way in which the traditional arguments for the existence of God have been formulated. The three basic arguments in their simplest form can be formulated in this way:

The ontological argument

I have an idea of God as the Perfect Being, or as "that than which nothing greater can be conceived."
If the idea exists, then the thing itself must exist; the idea must correspond to something which is there outside my mind.
Therefore God must exist.

The cosmological argument

Every effect has a cause.
Therefore there must be a First Cause to create the universe, and God is by definition the First Cause.
Therefore God must exist.

The teleological argument

Anything that shows traces of design must have been designed by some intelligent being.

The universe shows signs of order and design; therefore there must be a Designer; and God is, by definition, the Creator and Designer.

Therefore God exists.

These arguments for the existence of God are still an official part of Roman Catholic teaching:

> If anyone says that the one true God, our Creator and Lord, cannot be known with certainty by the natural light of human reason through those things which are made: let him be anathema.

TRUTHS THAT ARE BEYOND REASON HAVE BEEN REVEALED BY GOD AND MUST BE RECEIVED BY FAITH

The knowledge we can gain by the use of reason is not complete. We cannot, for example, deduce the Trinity or belief in salvation through Christ simply by reason.

If these beliefs are beyond reason, we cannot test them in any way by reason. We can ask questions to test the authority that teaches us these truths, but once we have accepted that authority we accept the truth of what it teaches.

For example, Roman Catholicism gives certain reasons for the infallible authority of the church as the teaching institution: *e.g.,* the words of Jesus to Peter; the development of the papacy at Rome. Once we have accepted this authority, we accept what it tells us.

Cardinal Heenan:

> This secret of this wonderful unity of our Church is Christ's promise that the Church will never fail to teach the truth. Once we know what the Church teaches we accept it. For we know it must be true . . . All Catholic priests teach the same doctrine because they all obey the Vicar of Christ. The word "vicar" means "one who takes the place of another." The Pope is the Vicar of Christ because he takes the place of Christ as Head of the Church on earth.
>
> The Church remains one because all her members believe the same Faith. They believe it because the Church cannot teach what is false. This is what we mean when we say that the Church is infallible. Christ promised to guide his Church. One of the ways Christ chose to guide the Church

was by leaving his Vicar on earth to speak for him. That is why we say the Pope is infallible. He is the Head of the infallible Church. God could not allow him to lead it into error.

ISLAM

This answer is also the one Muslims give to the question "How can I know if Islam is true?" The Muslim believes that God has revealed something of himself in the universe and in the nature of man. But if one asks, "How can I know if the Qur'an is the word of God, a true revelation from God?" the *Qur'an* itself gives this kind of answer:

> This book is not to be doubted. It is a guide to the righteous, who have faith in the unseen and are steadfast in prayer; who bestow in charity a part of what We give them; who trust what has been revealed to you and to others before you, and firmly believe in the life to come . . .

☐ Mohammed performed no miracles to prove the truth of his claim to be a prophet. When challenged to produce his credentials, he simply pointed to the unique character of the Qur'an itself. The very fact of the Qur'an itself is therefore sufficient evidence that it is a true revelation from God.

> They ask: "Why has no sign been given him by his Lord?" Say: "Signs are in the hands of Allah. My mission is only to give plain warning."

> It is not enough for them that We have revealed to you the Book for their instruction? Surely in this there is a blessing and an admonition to true believers.

> If you doubt what We have revealed to Our Servant, produce one chapter comparable to this book. Call upon your idols to assist you, if what you say be true. But if you fail (as you are sure to fail) then guard yourselves against that fire whose fuel is men and stones prepared for the unbelievers.

☐ Belief and unbelief depend so entirely upon the will of Allah that if he wills a person to believe, he will believe, without any signs. The Qur'an does not seem to admit the possibility that the unbeliever, or even the believer, may have honest doubts and want to ask, "How can I be sure if it is true?"

> The unbelievers ask: "Why has no sign been given him by his Lord?"

Say: "Allah leaves in error whom He will, and guides those who repent and have faith; whose hearts find comfort in the remembrance of Allah. Surely in the remembrance of Allah all hearts are comforted."

☐ The punishment for unbelief is hell. The threat of hell should bring us to our senses and persuade us to believe.

Those who dispute our revelations shall know that they have no escape.

He has revealed to you the Book with the truth, confirming the scriptures which preceded it; for He has already revealed the Torah and the Gospel for the guidance of men, and the distinction between right and wrong.

Those that deny Allah's revelations shall be sternly punished; Allah is mighty and capable of revenge.

When Our clear revelations are recited to them, the unbelievers say: "This is plain magic." Such is their description of the truth when it is declared to them.

Do they say: "He has invented it himself"?

Say: "If I have indeed invented it, then there is nothing that you can do to save me from Allah's wrath. He well knows what you say about it. He is our all-sufficient witness. He is the Benignant One, the Merciful."

Say: "I am no prodigy among the apostles; nor do I know what will be done with me or you. I follow only what is revealed to me, and my only duty is to give plain warning."

Say: "Think if this Koran is indeed from Allah and you reject it; if an Israelite has vouched for its divinity and accepted Islam, while you yourselves deny it with scorn. Truly Allah does not guide the wrongdoers."

The appropriate response, therefore, is simply to listen and obey.

When you do not recite to them a revelation they say: "Have you not yet invented one?" Say: "I follow only what is revealed to me by my Lord. This Book is a veritable proof from your Lord, a guide and a blessing to true believers."

When the Koran is recited, listen to it in silence so that Allah may show you mercy.

It is He who has revealed to you the Koran. Some of its verses are precise in meaning—they are the foundation of the Book—and others ambiguous. Those whose hearts are infected with disbelief follow the ambiguous part, so as to create dissension by seeking to explain it. But no one knows its meaning except Allah. Those who are well-grounded in knowledge say: "We believe in it: it is from our Lord. But none takes heed except the wise. Lord, do not cause our hearts to go astray after You have guided us."

PROBLEMS AND QUESTIONS

The traditional arguments for the existence of God are no longer convincing.

While Thomas Aquinas's proofs may carry some conviction to those who already believe, they mean little to *the real* unbeliever.

The conclusion is implied in the premise. If you accept the first assumption (*e.g.*, every effect must have a cause), then the conclusion must follow of necessity. But this is a circular argument. It is similar to this kind of syllogism:

All men are mortal.
Socrates was a man.
Therefore Socrates must be mortal.

The arguments do not prove enough. The cosmological argument, for example, would only prove the existence of a First Cause. But it is far too big a jump to move from the First Cause to the God of the Bible. Similarly, the teleological argument points to the existence of a Creator God; but it cannot possibly prove that this Creator must be one God or that he is loving or infinite. The argument does not exclude the possibility that there could be many creator gods, or that God is finite or evil.

Many people today no longer accept even the premise. Many people today have the vaguest possible idea of "God," or have never seriously believed that he exists. For them therefore the idea of a Perfect Being is not obvious or self-evident. Similarly the principle of causality (that every effect has a cause) has been seriously questioned by many philosophers since Hume, and for them this premise is not self-evident. And while some say that they see little or no evidence of order or design in the universe, many others are convinced that evolution by natural selection gives a satisfactory account of the apparent order in nature. Others again do not think of the universe as being ordered; to them it is a product of chance and is basically chaotic and absurd. To them therefore the argument from design does not make sense.

Bronowski sums up the widespread rejection of this approach:

> These debates are scholastic exercises in absolute logic. They begin from concepts which are held to be fixed absolutely; they then proceed by deduction; and what is found in this way is subject to no further test. The deductions are true because the first concepts were true: that is the scholastic system.

The two-part answer of Scholasticism and orthodox Catholicism involves a division of truth.

It holds that there are two completely different kinds of truth: truths of reason and truths of revelation. Francis Schaeffer pictures this as a dividing line, with supernatural, religious truth—revealed by God and received by faith—above it, and natural, scientific truth—discovered by man and tested by reason—below:

$$\frac{\text{GRACE}}{\text{NATURE}}$$

This dichotomy of truth became widely accepted by both Protestants and Catholics.

Francis Bacon:

> It is therefore most wise soberly to render unto faith the things that are faith's.

> Sacred theology must be drawn from the word and oracles of God, not from the light of nature, or the dictates of reason.

> [To study theology] we must quit the small vessel of human reason, and put ourselves on board the ship of the Church, which alone possesses the divine needle for justly shaping the course.

> We are obliged to believe the word of God, though our reason be shocked at it. For if we should believe only such things as are agreeable to our reason, we assent to the matter, and not to the author.

> And therefore, the more absurd and incredible any divine mystery is, the greater honor we do to God in believing it; and so much the more noble the victory of faith.

43

Thomas Browne:

It is no vulgar part of Faith to believe a thing not only above but contrary to Reason, and against the arguments of our proper senses.

I can answer all the Objections of Satan and my rebellious reason with that odd resolution I learned of Tertullian, *certum est quia impossibile est.*

John Locke:

Reason is the discovery of the certainty or probability of such propositions or truths, which the mind arrives at by deduction made from such *ideas*, which it has got by the use of its natural faculties, *viz.*, by sensation or reflection. *Faith* on the other side, is the assent to any proposition not thus made out by the deductions of reason, but upon the credit of the proposer, as coming from God, in some extraordinary way of communication. This way of discovering truths to men we call *Revelation.*

Many who adopted this approach did so with the best of motives. As *Basil Willey* says of Francis Bacon:

What can be asserted with confidence, I think, is that Bacon's desire to separate religious truth and scientific truth was in the interests of science, not of religion. He wished to *keep science pure from religion*; the opposite parts of the process—keeping religion pure from science—did not interest him nearly so much . . . Bacon was pleading for science in an age dominated by religion. Religious truth, then, must be "skied," elevated far out of reach, not in order that so it may be more devoutly approached, but in order to keep it out of mischief.

In the long run, however, the results were disastrous. The guide and arbiter of truth from now on would be "natural instinct" and "common notions," which all men would accept.

Lord Herbert of Cherbury:

Universal consent will be the sovereign test of truth, and there is nothing of so great importance as to seek out these common notions, and to put them each in their place as indubitable truths.

These were some of Herbert's "common notions":

1. That there is a supreme power.

2. That this sovereign power must be worshiped.

3. That the good ordering or disposition of the faculties of man constitutes the principal or best part of divine worship, and that this has always been believed.

4. That all vices and crimes should be expiated and effaced by repentance.

5. That there are rewards and punishments after this life.

It was not long, therefore, before others began to make greater claims for man's reason, and dispensed with revelation altogether. This kind of answer thus eventually led to the answer of the Rationalists. (See Part 2, "Man.")

Authoritarianism is an offense to the questioning mind.

This approach encourages us to use our minds to prove the existence of God—and to establish the supreme authority of the church which guarantees the truth of God's revelation. And once we have accepted this authority, everything else follows. We can ask questions about what the revelation means, and in certain matters there may be liberty in interpretation. But we cannot question the truth of the revelation.

In practice this kind of authoritarian approach has often led to:

either   a blind and unquestioning acceptance of what the church teaches;

or   a rebellion against the authoritative teaching of the church (even among those who stay within the church) and a refusal to accept all its teachings;

or   a total rejection of the church as an authoritative teacher of the truth;

or   a mysticism that allows the individual to hold loosely to the accepted credos of the church, and at the same time to remain within the church.

The following extracts are from writers who explain why they reject this kind of authoritarianism:

A Roman Catholic Modernist, writing in 1905:

The very idea of dogma is now repugnant, and a source of scandal.

These are the reasons he gives, as summarized by Alec Vidler:

1. A dogma appeared to be a proposition that was said to be intrinsically true, neither proved nor provable. But now-

adays men rightly want to be shown that there are reasonable grounds for belief.

2. If reasons for accepting dogmatic propositions are forthcoming, they take the form of an appeal to a transcendent authority that is supposed, as it were, to introduce the truth into us from outside. A dogma thus seems to be an external fetter, a limit to thought, a sort of intellectual tyranny, denying man's need to be autonomous and sincere.

3. Allowing for the sake of argument that dogmas could be simply taught by a doctrinal authority, they would in that case have to be intelligible and unambiguous. But the trouble with traditional Christian dogmas was that they were expressed in philosophical terminology. "In short, the first difficulty which numbers of people today find when confronted with dogmas is that they do not convey to them any intelligible meaning. These statements say nothing to them, or rather seem to them to be indissolubly bound up with a state of mind which is no longer theirs . . . Many believers are implicitly of the same opinion and so prefer to abstain from reflecting on their faith."

4. There is the grave objection that dogmas do not cohere with the rest of knowledge. Dogmas too are supposed to be immutable while thought is always progressive. Dogmas do not throw any light on scientific or philosophical problems. They do not connect.

H. J. Blackham:

An open mind is vulnerable to evidence.
By comparison a religious faith may not be vulnerable. If the believer will not allow that any experience could falsify his belief, he does not have an open mind about it because it is not founded on rational grounds. His faith rests in something other than the reliability of tested evidence. His trust is likely to be in God, who is then at once the author and the object of the faith.

George Harrison:

When you're young you get taken to church by your parents and you get pushed into religion at school. They're trying to put something into your mind. But it's wrong you know. Obviously because nobody goes to church and nobody believes in God. Why? Because religious teachers don't know what they're teaching. They haven't interpreted the Bible as it was intended.

This is the thing that led me into the Indian scene, that I didn't really believe in God as I'd been taught it. It was just like something out of a science fiction novel . . . You're taught just to have faith, you don't have to worry about it, just believe what we're telling you.

Fyodor Dostoievsky protests vigorously against authoritarian Christianity and is very well aware of the connection between authoritarian religion and authoritarian government. In his imaginary account of the Grand Inquisitor, the Inquisitor represents the authoritarianism of the Roman Catholic Church at the time of the Inquisition in the sixteenth century. This is how the Inquisitor speaks to Christ when he meets him face to face:

Why . . . did you come to meddle with us? . . . Tomorrow I shall condemn you and burn you at the stake as the vilest of heretics . . . Have you the right to reveal to us even one of the mysteries of the world you have come from? . . . No, you have not. So that you may not add anything to what has been said before and so as not to deprive men of the freedom which you upheld so strongly when you were here on earth. All that you might reveal anew would encroach on men's freedom of faith, for it would come as a miracle, and their freedom of faith was dearer to you than anything even in those days, fifteen hundred years ago. Was it not you who said so often in those days, "I shall make you free"? But now you have seen those "free" men . . . Yes, this business has cost us a great deal . . . but we've completed it at last in your name. For fifteen centuries we've been troubled by this freedom, but now it's over and done with for good . . . These men are more than ever convinced that they are absolutely free, and yet they themselves have brought their freedom to us and humbly laid it at our feet . . .

You did not come down from the cross when they shouted to you, mocking and deriding you: "If you be the Son of God, come down from the cross." You did not come down because . . . you did not want to enslave man by miracles and because you hungered for a faith based on free will and not on miracles. You hungered for freely given love and not for the servile rapture of the slave before the might that has terrified him once and for all . . .

There is a mystery here and we cannot understand it. And if it is a mystery, then we, too, were entitled to preach a mystery and to teach them that it is neither the free verdict of their hearts nor that love that matters, but the mystery which they must obey blindly, even against their own consciences. So we have done. We have corrected your great work and have based it on *miracle, mystery,* and *authority.* And men rejoiced that they were once more led like sheep and that the terrible gift which had brought them so much suffering had at last been lifted from their hearts . . . Why, then, have you come to meddle with us now? And why are you looking at me silently and so penetratingly with your gentle eyes?

Authoritarianism, however, is not by any means confined to one church, and it is not necessarily associated with the view that some truths can be proved by reason. Sometimes those who regard the Bible as the supreme authority (*i.e.,* they believe the first part of answer 1, pp. 9–36) use the authority of the Bible in the same way as the Catholic uses the authority of church. They make frequent use of the phrase "the Bible says . . . ," usually with the implication "what the Bible says must, by definition, be true; and you have no alternative but to accept what it says."

Emil Brunner links together these two approaches in this way:

From the outset it is assumed that the Christian Faith is the true Faith, because this faith is taught either in the Bible or by the Church. But the fact that the doctrine of the Church, or of the Bible, is "the truth," must be accepted as axiomatic. We believe in Jesus Christ, because we believe first of all either in the doctrinal authority of the Church, or in that of the Bible.

The resulting dilemma is well expressed by this *cri de coeur* written by the 24-year-old daughter of missionary parents:

I have been taught the Christian faith from childhood. I attended a Christian high school and college. According to the accepted pattern I should now be a stable, vibrant Christian . . . I wish I could conform to that pattern. But I cannot . . . I grew up praying, attending church, reading my Bible, witnessing and giving testimonies . . .

Then came a series of events that stopped me cold. I began to wonder if I really owned all that I claimed. I started to ask the meaning of faith in Christ, salvation by grace, and many other phrases that I had tossed around all my life . . . Realizing my faith was not truly my own, I then refused to give intellectual assent to forms of belief that I did not feel within myself. I could no longer accept without examination that which is supposed to meet man's deepest needs.

As I now stand facing adulthood, I am overwhelmed by the incomprehensibility of life. I often see myself as an unwelcome guest in a seemingly impersonal, deterministic universe. And I ask "Why am I here anyway?" I am like many other twentieth-century young people whose "blazing optimism" is tainted and dulled by fear.

I long to know God through an intimate relationship with Jesus Christ. I have gone through the act of accepting Christ as my personal Savior, but how can he meet my deepest needs? The simple statement of "Just trust the Lord" does not satisfy my intellectual restlessness nor my emotional turmoil. Such statements and phrases I have heard so often that they are trite and meaningless in the complexity of my individual context. I cannot accept "pat" answers, for to me they are dead clichés and platitudes that do not meet my feelings . . .

Occasionally I have suggested to my parents and evangelical friends that I must have opportunity to think and discover for my own satisfaction the form of faith that is to satisfy me. My parents accuse me of "going away from the Lord," of backsliding. They say my thinking is dangerous to my spiritual life. Perhaps so, but is it any less dangerous to be a robot responding to mechanical instructions?

I am putting this down on paper because I have found that I am not alone in the struggle. Others are searching, too, for a personal and satisfying relationship with God. I have talked with many other young people who have a deep desire for meaningful communication with Jesus Christ, though they have known "the answers" all their lives. We wonder how can parents and other adults help us?

I believe you can help by giving us sympathy and understanding . . . Most young people in this situation are in the process of trying to discover themselves as well, and we tend to rebel against any ideas that seem to be offered to us as a substitute for our thinking for ourselves . . .

Even quoting Scripture to us can be infuriating, because usually we are just as aware of these verses as you are, and we tend to wonder if they actually meet your needs any more than they meet ours . . . Your concern for me as an individual will have far deeper effects than if you try to offer answers . . . Parents will do well to try to understand the effects that modern psychological pressures have on the emotions of youth and why we are reacting in this manner, instead of throwing up their hands in horror at the attitudes we express. Patiently encourage us and give us the freedom to search for a meaningful relationship to God and to find a real expression for that relationship.

Muslims in the past have assumed that the Qur'an is the word of God. The impact of modern ways of thinking, however, is likely to make more and more people ask the question, "How can I *know* if the Qur'an is the word of God?"

Wilfred Cantwell Smith:

Muslims do not read the Qur'an and conclude that it is divine; rather, they believe that it is divine, and then they read it.

The Muslim world, also, is moving into what may possibly become a profound crisis, too; in that it also is just beginning to ask this question, instead of being content only with answering it. Young people in Lahore and Cairo, labour leaders in Jakarta and Istanbul, are beginning to ask their religious thinkers, and beginning to ask themselves, "Is the Qur'an the word of God?" Answering this question has been the business of the Muslim world for over thirteen centuries. Asking it is a different matter altogether, haunting and ominous.

When these questions are asked, the authoritarianism of Islam leads in practice to the same kind of reactions as the authoritarianism of Roman Catholicism:

either a blind and unquestioning acceptance of the Qur'an;
or an intellectual skepticism about God, combined with a limited practice of the Muslim way of life;
or a total rejection of Islamic beliefs about God and the supernatural;
or a mysticism that enables the Muslim to bypass or transcend certain intellectual problems.

ANSWER THREE:
RATIONALISM AND ROMANTICISM

Christian beliefs are
true only if they accord
with human reason
and/or feeling.

> *Rationalism and Romanticism both hold that Christian beliefs can only be accepted as true if they accord with reason and/or the heart. This answer varies according to where the emphasis is placed:*
>
> ☐ *Man can find the truth through his reason alone; there is no need for any revelation from God;*
>
> ☐ *Man can find the truth through reason and the heart.*

MAN CAN FIND THE TRUTH
THROUGH HIS REASON ALONE

It is important to stress that most of the philosophers who
thought in this way were not atheists. They did not deny the
existence of God. They simply said that God had little or nothing to do with man's search after the truth.

Ernst Cassirer says that the early Italian Renaissance included
three major currents of philosophical thought: Humanism
(which was largely interested in classical studies, and was not
opposed to Christianity or the church), Platonism, and Aristote-
lianism (which looked to Averroes as a guide, and eventually
came to inspire the free-thinkers of the seventeenth century,
especially in France). The following are some of the ideas of this
third group:

> The supremacy of natural reason, the denial of creation
> and personal immortality, with their theological conse-
> quences, and the unity of the intellect were taught in the
> universities and, we are told, accepted by many Venetian
> gentlemen. Such a philosophy expressed with precision the
> stage of skepticism toward the religious system, of anti-
> supernaturalism rather than of positive naturalism and hu-
> manism, which had been reached by the northern Italian
> cities in the fourteenth century.

Paul Hazard describes the more advanced stage reached by the
end of the seventeenth century:

> What men craved to know was what they were to believe,
> and what they were not to believe. Was tradition still to
> command their allegiance, or was it to go by the board?
> Were they to continue plodding along the same old road,
> trusting to the same old guides, or were they to obey new
> leaders who bade them turn their back on all those outworn
> things and follow them to other lands of promise. The
> champions of Reason and the champions of Religion were
> . . . fighting desperately for the possession of men's souls,
> confronting each other in a contest at which the whole of
> thoughtful Europe was looking on.

He describes the attitudes of the seventeenth- and eighteenth-
century Rationalists in this way:

> And now Reason breaks loose and there's no holding her
> any longer. Tradition, authority are nothing to her; "What
> harm," she says, "in wiping the slate clean and beginning

things all over again?" . . . Heaven was theirs, and earth
was theirs; theirs was the whole domain of the knowable.
There was nothing, they thought, nothing in the whole
universe which the geometrical mind could not grasp. Theology, too, was their business . . .

Descartes the geometrician had called the tune for the new
era. But what if the geometrical mind collides head on with
religion? What will happen if it is applied wholesale to
matters of faith? It would mean putting the sponge over
the religious slate; every religion would be wiped out.

Hazard traces the connection between the seventeenth century
and the Renaissance in this way:

This critical urge, whence came it? Who fostered it? What
made it at once so daring and so strong? Where, in a word,
did it originate? The answer is that it came from afar, from
very far indeed: it came from ancient Greece; from this,
that, or another heretical doctor of the Middle Ages; from
many other distant sources, but beyond all doubt or question it came from the Renaissance. Between the Renaissance
and the period we have just been studying (*i.e.*, 1680–
1715), the family likeness is unmistakable. There is the
same refusal on the part of the more daring spirits to
subordinate the human to the divine. In both cases a like
importance is assigned to man, to man who has no rival,
man who limits the boundary of the knowable, resolves all
problems that admit of solution, regarding the rest as null
and void, man the source and center of the hopes of the
world. Now and then, Nature comes in, not very clearly
defined, but powerful, Nature no longer regarded as the
work of a Creator, but as the upsurge of life as a whole,
and of human life in particular . . . This age bears upon it
all the characteristics of a second Renaissance but a Renaissance sterner, more austere, and, in a measure, disillusion-
ed, a Renaissance without a Rabelais, a Renaissance without
a smile . . .

And so the trend of modern thought can be charted more
or less accurately as follows: starting from the Renaissance,
an eagerness for invention, a passion for discovery, an urge
to play the critic, traits all so manifest that we may call them
the dominant elements in the European mentality. Somewhere about the middle of the seventeenth century there
was a temporary pause, when a truce, wholly unlooked for,

was entered into by the opposing forces, an entirely un-
predictable reconciliation. This phenomenon, which was
nothing short of miraculous, was what is called the Revival
of Learning, the revival of the classical spirit, and the fruit
of it was peace and tranquil strength . . .

As soon as the classical ideal ceased to be a thing to aim at,
a deliberated goal, a conscious choice, and began to degenerate into a mere habit, and an irksome one at that, the
innovators, all ready for action, set to work with all the old
zest and energy. And so, yet once again, the mind of
Europe set out on the unending quest. Then came a crisis
so swift and so sudden, so at least it seemed, that it took
men completely by surprise; yet it had long been stirring in
the womb of Time, and, so far from being a new thing, was
in reality a very old one.

Two formative thinkers

René Descartes (1596–1650):

☐ His basic principle was that of systematic doubt:

My first rule was to accept nothing as true which I did not
clearly recognize to be so; to accept nothing more than
what was presented to my mind so clearly and distinctly
that I could have no occasion to doubt it.

☐ One thing, however, he could not doubt was his own existence:
Cogito, ergo sum. I think, therefore I am.

☐ He was also aware that he was finite. And if he was finite, this
implied that there must be an infinite Being. He himself was
aware that he was imperfect, and this awareness implied that a
perfect Being must exist.

It is inconceivable that God should deceive us by giving us
ideas of this kind if they are not true. Therefore God must
exist.

John Locke (1632–1704):

The following are the basic ideas of Locke's philosophy that are
relevant here:

☐ The mind is like a blank piece of paper which receives all its
impressions from outside. It is like "white paper void of all
characters, without any ideas."

In bare naked perception the mind is, for the most part,
merely passive.

☐ All human knowledge is either *"ideas"* (which are impressions on
the mind from external objects—such as yellow, white, heat,
cold, soft, hard, bitter, sweet, and all we call sensible qualities) or
the *reflection* of the mind on these ideas.

> Human knowledge therefore hath no other immediate ob-
> ject but its own ideas.

☐ Reason and faith are totally different.

> *Reason* is the discovery of the certainty or probability of
> such propositions or truths, which the mind arrives at by
> deduction made from such *ideas*, which it has got by the use
> of its natural faculties, *viz.*, by sensation or reflection.

> *Faith*, on the other hand, is the assent to any proposition
> not thus made out by the deductions of reason, but upon
> the credit of the proposer, as coming from God, in some
> extraordinary way of communication. This way of discover-
> ing truths to men we call *Revelation*.

As an example of a truth of reason, he gives the existence of
God.

> The works of nature everywhere sufficiently evidence a
> Deity.

The existence of God is "the most obvious truth that reason
discovers"; "its evidence," he says, is "equal to mathematical
certainty."

Any truth of revelation must be tested by truths of reason. If
it does not contradict what we know by reason, then it can be
accepted. But if it does, it must be rejected.

> *Revelation* is natural *reason* enlarged by a new set of dis-
> coveries communicated by God immediately, which *reason*
> vouches the truth of by the testimony and proofs that they
> come from God.

> No principle can be received for divine revelation, or obtain
> the assent due to such, if it be contrary to our clear intui-
> tive knowledge.

This is how *Paul Hazard* describes the revolutionary impact of
Locke's philosophy:

> Locke it was who turned the attention of thinkers to psy-
> chological truths, truths present in the mind, living, con-
> stant, and indefectible . . .

An Essay concerning Human Understanding. Whatever may be said of it by those who care only for the high flights of philosophy, the date marks a definite change, a new orientation. Henceforth man's sphere of exploration was the mind of man and its unfathomable riches. Let us have done, said Locke, with these metaphysical conjectures; do we not realize how fruitless they are? Are we not tired of asking and always asking in vain? . . .

The certitude which we need resides in the mind. Let us look therein and cease to probe those infinite spaces which do but breed deceiving visions; thereon let us concentrate our attention. Clearly recognizing that our understanding is limited, let us accept its limitations . . . Putting aside the hope of attaining any perfect and absolute knowledge of the things around us as something beyond the range of finite beings, let us content ourselves with being what we are, with doing what we can, and with knowing what we can know.

This is *G. R. Cragg*'s estimate of his influence:

John Locke epitomized the intellectual outlook of his own age and shaped that of the next. For over a century he dominated European thought . . . The spirit in which he dealt with Christianity is more important than what he actually said about it. He made a certain attitude to religious faith almost universal.

The influence of ideas of this kind are clearly seen in the American *Declaration of Independence* of 1776:

We hold these truths to be self-evident; that all men are created equal, and that they are endowed by their Creator with certain inalienable rights . . .

MAN CAN FIND THE TRUTH THROUGH REASON AND THE HEART.

As men became conscious of the one-sided emphasis on reason in the eighteenth century, or as they became aware of the inability of reason to find convincing answers by itself, they began to feel that truth must be sought through reason *and* the heart working together.

By the 1760s the scientific and philosophical speculation of the Enlightenment seemed to have ended in an impasse. Chance, or the blind determinism of matter in regular but

aimless motion, appeared to regulate the operations of the
universe and the destiny of man. If metaphysical speculation had any meaning at all—which the skeptics denied—it
served merely to open a window on to the blank wall of
necessity. A brilliant and inquisitive age was not likely to be
content for long with such a prospect, and in response to
the challenge new attitudes were evolved that transformed
the terms in which men thought of themselves and of the
order of the universe. One of the most significant of these
attitudes . . . was the acceptance of the heart as legitimate
consort of the head. It is important . . . to realize what this
new assumption did *not* imply. To present it as a revolt
against an age of arid intellectualism seems to me to betray
extraordinary insensitivity toward the vigor of eighteenth-
century life and the excitement of its speculative thought.
What happened was not that the artist usurped the position
formerly occupied by the scholar, but that both turned to
the emotions for the guidance they had previously expected
of their reason. Sentiment came to be accepted as the
source of a kind of knowledge to which intelligence could
not aspire, and as the arbiter of action. But if feeling
became pilot, reason remained in command, except for a
few extremists whose shipwreck discouraged imitation. The
definition of their respective roles could never be established with finality but there was no question of the elimi-
nation of reason. However dramatically this new attitude
may have seemed to challenge the urbanity of the Enlightenment, both grew from a common stock and both were
rooted in the same intellectual soil . . .

In so far as one can ascribe a definite starting-point to a
change in attitude, the most appropriate date would be
1749, when Rousseau wrote his prize essay on the subject
set by the Dijon Academy: *Whether the restoration of the arts
and sciences has contributed to the refinement of morals.* In other
words, the "reaction" against the Enlightenment preceded
most of the major works of the Enlightenment itself!
(Hampson)

Two formative thinkers

Jean Jacques Rousseau (1712–1778):
As the eighteenth century wore on, it was discovered that
the "Nature" of man was not his "reason" at all, but his
instincts, emotions, and "sensibilities," and what was more,

57

people began to glory in this discovery, and to regard reason itself as an aberration from "Nature." *Cogito ergo sum* is superseded by *je sens, donc je suis* associated with Rousseau. Shaftesbury, Hutcheson, and Hume had prepared the way by proclaiming that our moral judgements, like our aesthetic judgements, are not the offspring of Reason at all but proceed from an inner sentiment or feeling which is unanalysable. (Basil Willey)

He stressed the part played by the emotions, not only in religion, but in literature, politics, and philosophy. He offered a broad and original treatment of all fields on the basis of his new sensibility. The result to a large extent of his work was the so-called Romantic Movement. This is the essential content of Rousseau, the "outsider," who fathered the romantic sensibility and opposed it to the dominant rationalism of his time. (Bronowski and Mazlish)

S. T. Coleridge (1772–1834):
Coleridge was well aware of the challenge to Christian faith from the philosophers Hume and Kant. His response was to emphasize the difference between reason and faith, and to associate faith with the conscience, or moral consciousness. In this way he made faith immune from refutation by reason. Faith cannot be proved rationally, and even if it could it would produce a compulsory assent.

Yet there had dawned upon me, even before I had met with the *Critique of Pure Reason*, a certain guiding light. If the mere intellect could make no certain discovery of a holy and intelligent first cause, it might yet supply a demonstration, that no legitimate argument could be drawn from the intellect *against* its truth. And what is this more than St. Paul's assertion that by wisdom (more perfectly translated by the powers of reasoning) no man ever arrived at the knowledge of God? . . . I became convinced that religion as both the corner-stone and the key-stone of morality, must have a *moral* origin; so far at least, that the evidence of its doctrines could not, like the truths of abstract science, be wholly independent of the will. It was therefore to be expected, that its *fundamental* truth would be such as *might* be denied; though only by the fool, and even by the fool from the madness of the heart alone.

This kind of answer, with the stress on reason or feeling or on both together, is still expressed today.

James Thurber:

> It may be that the finer mysteries of life and death can be comprehended only through pure instinct; the cat, for example, appears to Know (I don't say that he does, but he appears to). Man, on the other hand, is surely farther away from the Answer than any other animal this side of the ladybug. His mistaken selection of reasoning as an instrument of perception has put him into a fine quandary.

H. J. Blackham:

> . . . there is no immemorial tradition, no revelation, no authority, no privileged knowledge (first principles, intuitions, axioms) which is beyond question because beyond experience and which can be used as a standard by which to interpret experience. There is only experience to be interpreted in the light of further experience, the sole source of all standards of reason and value, forever open to question.

> Humanism is rooted in two historical quests of universal import: free inquiry and social agreement.

PROBLEMS
AND QUESTIONS

Man's reason becomes the ultimate arbiter.

Man starts with the assumptions that his reason approves, and if a so-called revelation does not fit in with these assumptions, so much the worse for the revelation. This subordination is seen, e.g., in Locke and Newton.

> Locke's strong emphasis on reason naturally raised the question of the status of revelation. He did not doubt its reality or its importance, but he reinterpreted it in conformity with his general picture of the religious life. What revelation confirms is the essentially reasonable character of Christianity. It shows that few dogmas are necessary; they are simple, and intelligible to ordinary men. Christianity has one essential doctrine: Jesus is the Messiah. Locke thus carried simplification to its extreme limits; most of the structure of traditional theology was casually dismissed as irrelevant. (G. R. Cragg)

> Sir Isaac Newton had of course no intention of repudiating Christianity; he merely proposed to reinterpret its truths,

but his rationalistic restatement left few of its traditional doctrines untouched. (G. R. Cragg)

Locke's approach determined the main thrust of Christian apologetics during the following century.

The title of Locke's treatise, *The Reasonableness of Christianity*, may be said to have been the solitary thesis of Christian theology in England for the greater part of a century. (Mark Pattison)

The very titles of the main works of the period indicate the extent to which the Christian revelation was subordinated to Reason:

Christianity Not Mysterious, Showing that there is Nothing in the Gospel contrary to Reason nor above it, and that no Christian Doctrine can properly be called a Mystery, by John Toland, 1696.

Christianity as Old as the Creation; or, the Gospel a Republication of the Religion of Nature, by Matthew Tindal, 1730.

The Analogy of Religion, Natural and Revealed, to the Constitution and Course of Nature, by Joseph Butler, 1736.

Butler's work is the high-water mark of this approach. He argues that Nature is full of mysteries and obscurities; and "Probability" is the best guide in life. If this is the case in the "natural" world, he says, surely we should be prepared to expect the same mysteries, obscurities, and probabilities in what claims to be a "supernatural" revelation.

Toward the close of the seventeenth century the prestige of Scripture, though outwardly unchanged, had actually diminished appreciably. It was not so much that men had rejected it as "false"; it was rather that as "natural religion" came more and more to seem all-sufficient, "revelation" began to appear, if not superfluous, at least secondary, and perhaps even slightly inconvenient. An age which discovered God effortlessly in the starry heavens above, and in the moral law within, could not but be embarrassed by having to acknowledge dependence upon the annals and legends of an unenlightened Semitic tribe . . . By the time we reach Joseph Butler, Nature, instead of being a valuable supplement to Revelation as it was with Bacon, has virtually become the standard against which Revelation itself is to be tested. (Basil Willey)

Tertullian of old could say *credo quia impossibile*; now an eighteenth-century saint asks us to believe Revelation to be authentic *because* it is as bewildering as an admittedly divine Nature. In this paradoxical defence Butler may seem to have virtually wiped out the distinction between Revelation and Nature. (Basil Willey)

Christian beliefs are whittled down.

If revelation is completely subordinate to reason, then reason must be free to reject any Christian beliefs that it finds unreasonable or offensive.

☐ *Locke* reduced the essential content of the Christian faith to faith in Christ, and in the doctrine of repentance; the only conditions of salvation were belief in the mission of Jesus and living a good life.

☐ *Friedrich Schleiermacher*, the German theologian (1768–1834), reduced the essence of Christianity to "a feeling of absolute dependence."

☐ *Adolph von Harnack*, the German theologian (1851–1930), reduced the essence of the teaching of Jesus to these three themes: the Kingdom of God and its coming; God the Father and the infinite value of the human soul; the higher righteousness and the commandment of love.

☐ *D. F. Strauss* in his *Life of Jesus* (written in 1835–36) entirely denied the supernatural element in the Gospels:

> All things are linked together by a chain of causes and effects, which suffers no interruption . . . This conviction is so much a habit of thought with the modern world, that in actual life, the belief in a supernatural manifestation, an immediate divine agency, is at once attributed to ignorance or imposture.

> In the person and acts of Jesus no supernaturalism shall be allowed to remain. He who would banish priests from the Church must first banish miracles from religion.

Skepticism—the logical conclusion

What happens when "Reason" and "Nature" are unable to point unambiguously to the truth? What happens when the heart and the mind give different answers?

> The famous eighteenth-century alliance between Nature and Reason had begun to crumble; Reason, it was found, could lead one way, and Nature another. Or, putting it

another way, the "Nature" to which the century had so confidently appealed could have two main sets of meanings: it could mean the head or it could mean the heart; ideas or facts; theories or history; what is congenial to abstract reason, or what is dear to the heart. The nineteenth century went on believing in "Nature," but not without misgivings due to the inherent contradictions of the creed. Was Nature best expressed in the "march of the mind," or in the heart's affections . . . These, it was found, could conflict. (Basil Willey)

The logical conclusion to which this answer pointed, therefore, was a position of complete skepticism. Having denied certain beliefs of Christianity, the critic begins to feel, "Why stop here? Why reject this, but accept that?" But many who saw that their questioning should lead them to a position of total doubt were unwilling to be utterly consistent.

This is how Paul Hazard describes the position of *Pierre Bayle*, one of the most radical of the French free-thinkers (1647–1706):

Did he reach the point of absolute skepticism? He would have done so had he suffered his mind to follow its natural bent. Nothing ever pleased him better than that interplay of *pro* and *con*. He would have floated away into that far-off void, where actions lose their significance and life its purpose, had he followed logic to its final term, and taken cognizance only of his human experience, which day by day impressed him more and more. He might, nay, he must, have arrived at last at what Le Clerc calls metaphysical and historical skepticism, at universal doubt.

But this he resisted. His intrepid spirit, the feeling that he had a mission to fulfill, an abhorrence of error, more potent than any doubt he might have entertained about truth, a reasoning mind that would not willingly accept defeat, and above all his strength of will enabled him to stop short of the final step.

The most advanced unbelievers among the thinkers with whom we have been dealing called a halt when they came face to face with the Nihilism to which their skepticism seemed about to lead them.

The irrational leap of faith

Some found it possible to hold on to some form of Christian beliefs by taking a leap of faith. Having already accepted that

Christian faith is in a different category from all that is investigated by the reason, it was not hard for them to feel that it was immune from the questioning of the reason.

Coleridge, for example, made a distinction between the "understanding" (*i.e.*, the intellect, the mind) and what he called "the reason" (meaning an inward intuitive faculty, not the intellect). This distinction enabled him to feel that his faith was not vulnerable to the challenges of reason. But there were others like *Thomas Carlyle* who pointed out the irrationality that seemed to be implied in this approach:

> What the light of your mind, which is the direct inspiration of the Almighty, pronounces incredible,—that, in God's name, leave uncredited; at your peril do not try believing that. No subtlest hocus-pocus of "reason" *versus* "understanding" will avail for that feat . . .!

> To *steal* into heaven, by the modern method, of sticking ostrich-like your head into fallacies on Earth, . . . is forever forbidden. High treason is the name of that attempt . . .

> What can it profit any mortal to adopt locutions and imaginations which do *not* correspond to fact; which no sane mortal can deliberately adopt in his soul as true; which the most orthodox of mortals can only, and this after infinite essentially *impious* effort to put out the eyes of his mind, persuade himself to "believe that he believes." Away with it; in the name of God, come out of it, all true men!

ANSWER FOUR:
AGNOSTICISM

We can never know
for certain whether or
not Christianity is true.

> *The agnostic says: no matter how hard*
> *we try to find the truth through reason*
> *or the heart, we cannot hope to find it.*
> *Our minds are finite, and we cannot*
> *solve the mysteries of the universe. We*
> *must be content to recognize the limits*
> *of our knowledge, and not hope to*
> *know anything beyond these limits.*

SOME TWENTIETH-CENTURY EXAMPLES

A. J. Ayer:

While I believe that there can be an explanation in mundane terms for anything that happens within the world, I do not think it makes sense to ask for an explanation of the existence or the characteristics of the world as a whole. In this sense, it is a matter of brute fact that the universe exhibits the patterns which it does.

Aldous Huxley:

The only facts of which we have direct knowledge are psychological facts. The Nature of Things presents us with them. There is no getting round them, or behind them, or outside of them. They are there, given.

One fact cannot be more of a fact than another. Our psychological experiences are all equally facts. There is nothing to choose between them. No psychological experience is "truer," so far as we are concerned, than any other. For even if one should correspond more closely to things in themselves as perceived by some hypothetical non-human being, it would be impossible for us to discover what it was.

No man has a right to speak for any one except himself and those who happen to resemble him . . . Every man has as good a right to his own particular world-view as to his own particular kidneys . . .

I have no desire to impose my particular brand of life-worship on any one else . . . We admit that every man has a right in these matters to his own tastes. "I like lobsters; you don't. And there's an end of it." Such is the argument of gastronomers. In time, perhaps, philosophers will learn to treat one another with the same politeness and forbearance.

The life-worshiper's philosophy is comprehensive. As a manifold and discontinuous being, he is in a position to accept all the partial and apparently contradictory syntheses constructed by other philosophers . . . Each belief is the rationalization of the prevailing mood . . . There is really no question of any of these philosophies being true or false . . . And since one psychological state cannot be truer than another, since all are equally facts, it follows that the rationalization of one state cannot be truer than the rationalization of another . . . The only branches of philosophy in regard to which it is permissible to talk of truth and falsehood are logic and the theory of knowledge.

Jacquetta Hawkes:

In all this realm of ultimate meaning there is only one thing I believe with certainty—that we live in an impenetrable mystery. The more that we find out about the Universe, the greater this mystery becomes. Our discoveries inspire us with unending wonder, but not with final understanding.

Rebecca West:

I have no faith in the sense of comforting beliefs which persuade me that all my troubles are blessings in disguise. I do not believe that any facts exist, or, rather, are accessible to me, which give any assurance that my life has served an eternal purpose.

Albert Einstein:

To ponder interminably over the reason for one's own existence or the meaning of life in general seems to me, from an objective point of view, to be sheer folly.

Barbara Wooton:

The universe in general must, I think, simply be accepted as a totally inexplicable mystery.

H. J. Blackham:

Scientific inquiry presupposes the situation of human beings confronting objects in this world. Anything supposed outside these conditions is not open to its inquiry. Anything totally transcendent, encompassing both subject and object, for example, is beyond such inquiry, and beyond conceptual thought . . . Ultimately, everything as given is equally inscrutable and mysterious; there is nothing privileged in terms of which all the rest can be explained. This is what is meant by renunciation of "God-like knowledge." Agnosticism, which is more fundamental and radical than atheism, is the only position warranted by experience: recognition of the permanent nature and conditions of human knowledge, with its open horizon of continuous progressive investigation.

THREE FORMATIVE THINKERS

David Hume (1711–1776)

The basic points in his philosophy that concern us are these:

☐ We perceive the data of our senses; and we cannot hope to go beyond our senses or to know anything beyond what they tell us.

Let us fix our attention out of ourselves as much as possible: let us chase our imagination to the heavens, or to the utmost limits of the universe; we never really advance a step beyond ourselves, nor can we conceive any kind of existence, but those perceptions, which have appear'd in that narrow compass. This is the universe of the imagination, nor have we any idea by what is there produc'd.

☐ The idea that every like cause produces a like effect is a product of our own thinking. It cannot be inferred from the data of our senses. If cause *a* always seems to produce effect *b*, we have no justification for saying that *a* has *caused b*. It is only habit or custom that makes us think this is so. All that we are entitled to say is that *a* generally seems to be followed by *b*.

There is nothing in any object, considered by itself, which can afford us a reason for drawing a conclusion beyond it.

'Tis not, therefore, reason, which is the guide of life, but custom. That alone determines the mind, in all instances, to suppose the future conformable to the past. However easy this step may seem, reason would never, to all eternity, be able to make it.

☐ Hume also held that the idea of miracles violates the principle of the uniformity of natural causes, and must therefore be ruled out as impossible.

Immanuel Kant (1724–1804)

The following are the main points of his philosophy that concern us here:

☐ He agreed with Hume and the empiricists in saying that "all knowledge begins with experience." He acknowledged his debt to Hume and said that it was the reading of his works that awoke him from his dogmatic slumbers.

☐ But at the same time, "it does not follow that it all arises out of experience." The mind also plays a part, and is therefore not a complete *tabula rasa*. In this he disagrees with Locke. The mind does not perceive things precisely as they are: it conditions everything it perceives.

☐ He then asks: if this is the case, what are the proper limits of human thought and knowledge? And his answer is to make a distinction between *knowledge* which has to do with *phenomena* (everything that can be seen) and *faith* which has to do with *noumena* (truths beyond space and time). These are two completely different ways of knowing. They are another example of the dichotomy we have already seen in Locke and others (compare the diagram on p. 43):

FAITH

KNOWLEDGE

Faith is concerned with *noumena* above the line, truths beyond space and time, things "in themselves," reality as it is, the truths of religion (such as the existence of God, free will, immortality). Knowledge, *phenomena*, is truth that can be perceived by the senses, *i.e.*, through science, truth about the external world of space and time.

Because of this distinction, therefore, we must accept the fact that we cannot *know* anything for certain beyond our direct experience of this world. Religious beliefs have their origin in the moral consciousness, but they cannot be classed as knowledge. This limitation of knowledge insures the possibility of religious faith, because it makes it impervious to the attacks of skeptics.

> I have therefore found it necessary to deny *knowledge* to make room for *faith*.

George Frederick Hegel (1770–1831)

☐ Hegel accepted Kant's distinction between faith and knowledge.

☐ He thought of truth as the "synthesis of opposing viewpoints." Nothing is true in any absolute sense. All that we can expect is that one idea (*thesis*) will be challenged by an opposite idea (*antithesis*), and that this will in turn be superseded by an idea that transcends the two contradictory ideas (*synthesis*). This means that in discussions about truth, the basic rule of logic no longer applies. For in the dialectical process, views that are mutually incompatible can be held together.

HINDUISM AND BUDDHISM

Both Hinduism and Buddhism are based on a profound agnosticism.

W. Cantwell Smith:

> Hindus are so cheerfully diverse, so insistent that religious ways are many, that only vast and distorting oversimplification could predicate that their diversity and their ways is (I

say "ways is" to enforce my point) true or false. No Hindu has said anything that some other Hindu has not contradicted.

Radhakrishnan, writing about Hinduism:

While it gives absolute liberty in the world of thought, it enjoins a strict code of practice. The theist, the skeptic and the agnostic may all be Hindus if they accept the Hindu system of culture and life . . . what counts is conduct, not belief.

K. M. Sen:

The religious beliefs of different schools of Hindu thought vary and their religious practices also differ; there is in it monism, dualism, monotheism, polytheism, pantheism, and indeed Hinduism is a great storehouse of all kinds of religious experiments.

Christmas Humphreys, writing about Buddhism:

The antitheses of cause and effect, substance and attribute, good and evil, truth and error, are due to the tendency of man to separate terms which are related. Fichte's puzzle of self and not-self, Kant's antinomies, and Hume's opposition of facts and laws, can all be got over if we recognize that the opposing factors are mutually complementary elements based on one identity!

PROBLEMS AND QUESTIONS

The laws of logic can be set aside

It is no longer necessary to say that *a* cannot be *non-a*. There need be no ideas that are incompatible. They can somehow be reconciled with each other and held together in such a way that both are held to be true.

Leopold Senghor underlines the fundamental difference that Hegel's philosophy created:

What, then, is dialectics? . . . Today, we define dialectics by opposing it to logic. Classical logic rests on three principles: identity (A is A); non-contradiction (A is not non-A); and exclusion (A cannot be A and not be A at the same time). Hegel, with Marx following in his footsteps, opposes these principles, and proposes in their stead the principles of dialectics, which are: contradiction, reciprocal action, and change. For Hegel, the dialectical process is composed of three steps: affirmation, negation, and conciliation. For Marx, it consists of "position, opposition, composition . . . We have thesis, antithesis, and synthesis . . . (or) affirmation, negation, and negation of the negation." But that is only the beginning. The synthesis or "new idea" is developed "in two contradictory thoughts that blend in turn into a new synthesis" or "groups of thoughts." This group, continuing the process and developing into two groups of contradictory thoughts, ends in a "series of thoughts." The entire series of ideas forms the "system" or body of doctrine.

In classical philosophy, which used logic, things and their concepts are objective realities placed one beside the other without any link or communication, fixed once and for all, immutable essences. They oppose each other in irreducible antitheses. Modern philosophy is quite different, for dialectics is its favorite instrument.

The dialectician can say at the same time: "A is A" and "A is not A," or "A is not B" and "A is B."

Bronowski believes that when we are speaking about the meaning of human existence, we are in the realm of poetry. This realm has no place for logic:

If logic asserts the proposition *P*, then it denies the proposition *not-P*. We are free in logic to say, if we believe it true, that love is simple, or blissful, or carnal; but we cannot then logically say of the same love that it is complex, or anguished, or spiritual. Even if we have a more sophisticated logic, in which there is a third alternative to *P* and *not-P*, that alternative asserts that they are both meaningless. But in poetry, to assert *P* and *not-P* together is not meaningless: it is not meaningless to say that love is ordinary and extraordinary at the same time. On the contrary, poetry claims that it contains the very meaning of the experience of living.

Aldous Huxley's agnosticism leads him to believe that God can be both one and many. Both monotheism and polytheism can be true:

One psychological fact is as good as another; there is no

conceivable method of demonstrating that God is either one or many. So far as human beings are concerned, he is both; monotheism and polytheism are equally true. But are they equally useful? Do they tend to the quickening and enhancement of human life?

Monotheism and polytheism are doctrines equally necessary and equally true. Man can and does conceive of himself and of the world as being, now essentially many, and now essentially one. Therefore—since God, for our human purposes, is simply Life in so far as men can conceive it as a whole—the Divine is both one and many. A purely monotheistic religion is thus seen to be inadequate and unrealistic.

When this procedure is carried over into theology, there are no longer any of the same distinctions or contradictions.

Paul Tillich believes that all religions must be subject to two ultimate criteria of religion:

. . . the criterion of a faith which transcends every finite symbol of faith and the criterion of a love which unconditionally affirms, judges, and receives the other person.

Eastern wisdom, like every other wisdom, certainly belongs to the self-manifestation of the Logos and must be included in the interpretation of Jesus as the Christ, if he is rightly to be called the incarnation of the Logos.

Teilhard de Chardin:

As I like to say, the synthesis of the Christian "God" on high and the Marxist "God" of the future is the only God we can henceforth adore in spirit and in truth.

John Robinson:

There is a powerful and perennial tradition—in philosophy, in mysticism, in Oriental religion—which refuses to remain content with this situation, and constantly yearns to break through to a non-duality, to a *coincidence* of opposites, to a higher all-embracing unity . . .

God for Nicholas (of Cusa) is to be seen always "beyond the coincidence of contradictories . . . and nowhere this side thereof." In other words, God is not *one* of the poles of traditional theism, but transcends these inevitable finite distinctions. To express this within the logic of non-contradiction is of course finally impossible.

Wilfred Cantwell Smith believes that we must give up asking the question "Is Christianity true or false?" because it cannot be answered. Instead we should ask the question "Is *my* Christianity true? Can this belief *become true* to me?" What we must search for is:

> . . . a new type of answer; neither a simple "yes" nor a simple "no" but some *tertium quid*, more subtle, more complex, tentative, yet to be hammered out.

> There is so much diversity and clash, so much chaos, in the Christian Church today that the old ideal of a unified or systematic Christian truth has gone. For this, the ecumenical movement is too late. What has happened . . . is that the Christian world has moved into that situation where the Hindu has long been: of open variety, of optional alternatives. It would seem no longer possible for anyone to be told, or even to imagine that he can be told, what it means or should mean, formally and generically, to be a Christian. He must decide for himself—and only for himself.

He even makes the breath-taking assertion that Christians in the past never really claimed that Christianity was *true*:

> I have urged the personalist quality of religious life as of ultimate significance, over against the abstract system . . . It is a surprisingly modern aberration for anyone to think that Christianity is true or that Islam is—since the Enlightenment, basically, when Europe began to postulate religions as intellectualist systems, patterns of doctrine, so that they could for the first time be labelled "Christianity" and "Buddhism," and could be called true or false. Earlier this was not so. No classical Christian theologian, I have discovered, ever said that Christianity is true.

This abandonment of the search for objective truth in religion leads Cantwell Smith to accept the existentialist concept of faith (see p. 88).

This general approach is rapidly becoming established dogma in theology. But there are those who realize that this approach means the abandonment of any search for truth in the original sense.

Alasdair MacIntyre:

> To introduce a contradiction is to introduce into one's system of thought a license to say anything.

Lewis Carroll, author of *Alice in Wonderland*, was a professor of mathematics at Oxford between 1855 and 1881. Although he could not have any idea of what the philosophical and theological debates of the twentieth century would be, he was well aware of what it means for the ordinary man to live in a world in which the laws of logic go by the board. It becomes like the game of Wonderland croquet:

> Alice soon came to the conclusion that it was a very difficult game indeed.
>
> The players all played at once without waiting for turns, quarrelling all the while, and fighting for the hedgehogs; and in a very short time the Queen was in a furious passion, and went stamping about, and shouting, "Off with his head!" or "Off with her head!" about once a minute . . .
>
> "I don't think they play at all fairly," Alice began, in a rather complaining tone, "and they all quarrel so dreadfully one can't hear oneself speak—and they don't seem to have any rules in particular; at least, if there are, nobody attends to them . . . and I should have croqueted the Queen's hedgehog just now, only it ran away when it saw mine coming!"

Or it is like a world in which words no longer define or describe anything with any accuracy:

> Alice . . . went on: "—and I thought I'd try and find my way to the top of that hill—"
>
> "When you say 'hill,'" the Queen interrupted, "*I* could show you hills, in comparison with which you'd call that a valley."
>
> "No, I shouldn't," said Alice, surprised into contradicting her at last; "a hill *can't* be a valley, you know. That would be nonsense—"
>
> The Red Queen shook her head. "You may call it 'nonsense' if you like," she said, "but *I've* heard nonsense, compared with which that would be as sensible as a dictionary!"
>
> Alice curtseyed again, as she was afraid from the Queen's tone of voice that she was a *little* offended; and they walked on in silence till they got to the top of the little hill.

It is also like wandering into the wood where things have no names:

> "This must be the wood," she said thoughtfully to herself,

"where things have no names. I wonder what'll become of
my name when I go in? I shouldn't like to lose it at all—
because they'd have to give me another, and it would almost certainly be an ugly one . . ."

She was rambling on in this way when she reached the
wood: it looked very cool and shady. "Well, at any rate it's a
great comfort," she said as she stepped under the trees,
"after being so hot, to get into the—into the—into *what?*"
she went on, rather surprised at not being able to think of
the word. "I mean to get under the—under the—under
this, you know!" putting her hand on the trunk of the tree.
"What *does* it call itself? I do believe it's got no name—why,
to be sure it hasn't!"

She stood silent for a minute, thinking: then she suddenly
began again. "Then it really *has* happened, after all! And
now who am I? I *will* remember, if I can! I'm determined
to do it!" But being determined didn't help her much, and
all she could say, after a great deal of puzzling, was "L, I
know it begins with L!"

Doubt extends even to the natural world—
with far-reaching effects.

Agnosticism begins by doubting whether we can ever know anything for certain about the meaning of the universe or about the
truth of Christianity. But sooner or later it leads to doubt as to
whether we can know anything for certain even about the physical world we can see.

Voltaire (1694–1778):

> From the stars to the earth's center, in the external world
> and within ourselves, every substance is unknown to us. We
> see appearances only; we are in a dream.

Hannah Arendt sums up the agnostic's dilemma in this way:

> Descartes' philosophy is haunted by two nightmares which
> in a sense became the nightmares of the whole modern age,
> not because this age was so deeply influenced by Cartesian
> philosophy, but because their emergence was almost ines-
> capable once the true implications of the modern world
> view were understood. These nightmares are very simple
> and very well known. In the one, reality, the reality of the
> world as well as of human life, is doubted; if neither the
> senses nor common sense nor reason can be trusted, then it

may well be that all that we take for reality is only a dream. The other concerns the general human condition as it was revealed by the new discoveries and the impossibility for man to trust his senses and his reason.

Colin Wilson says of the atmosphere of Sartre's novel *Nausea*:

In the Journal, we watch the breaking-down of all Roquentin's values. Exhaustion limits him more and more to the present, the here-now. The work of memory, which gives events sequence and coherence, is failing, leaving him more and more dependent for meaning on what he can see and touch. It is Hume's skepticism becoming instinctive, all destroying. All he can see and touch is unrecognizable, unaided by memory; like a photograph of a familiar object taken from an unfamiliar angle. He looks at a seat, and fails to recognize it: "I murmur: It's a seat, but the word stays on my lips. It refuses to go and put itself on the thing . . . Things are divorced from their names. They are there, grotesque, stubborn, huge, and it seems ridiculous to call them seats, or to say anything at all about them. I am in the midst of things—nameless things."

Thomas Mann's novels have something of the same atmosphere:

The entire world has become a sort of dialectical nightmare. There are no more certitudes. (Michael Harrington)

This kind of attitude to the natural world can have far-reaching consequences.
Bronowski:

The cultures of the East still differ from ours as they did then. They still belittle man as individual man. Under this runs an indifference to the world of the senses, of which the indifference to experienced fact is one face. Anyone who has worked in the East knows how hard it is there to get an answer to a question of fact. When I had to study the casualties from the atomic bombs in Japan at the end of the war, I was dogged and perplexed by this difficulty. The man I asked, whatever man one asks, does not really understand what one wants to know: or rather, he does not understand that one wants to know. He wants to do what is fitting, he is not unwilling to be candied, but at bottom he does not know the facts because they are not his language.

These cultures of the East have remained fixed because
they lack the language and the very habit of fact.

The fatal flaw in this kind of skepticism, however, is that you
cannot consistently *live* with it. *Hume,* for example, was well
aware of the logical conclusion of his skepticism. But these were
ideas that he thought about in his study. He realized he could
not actually live as if they were true:

> Carelessness and inattention alone can afford us any reme-
> dy. For this reason I rely entirely upon them; and take it
> for granted, whatever may be the reader's opinion at this
> present moment, that an hour hence he will be persuaded
> there is both an external and an internal world.

> Most fortunately it happens, that since reason is incapable
> of dispelling these clouds, Nature herself suffices to that
> purpose, and cures me of this philosophical melancholy and
> delirium, either by relaxing this bent of mind, or by some
> avocation and lively impression of my senses, which obliter-
> ate all these chimeras. I dine, I play a game of backgam-
> mon, I converse, and am merry with my friends; and when,
> after three or four hours' amusement, I would return to
> these speculations, they appear so cold and strained and
> ridiculous, that I cannot find in my heart to enter into them
> any further.

Skepticism about others; self-doubt

When agnosticism is linked with psychological determinism, we
question every motivation in ourselves and in others to such an
extent that we cannot be sure about the "real self" any longer.

Maurice Friedman quotes some words of Martin Buber about
these consequences:

> This unmasking begins in the service of truth . . . Yet it
> ends, paradoxically, by making all truth questionable and
> by undermining the foundations of existence between men.
> "One no longer fears that the other will voluntarily dissem-
> ble," writes Martin Buber in a statement on "existential
> mistrust." One simply takes it for granted that he cannot do
> otherwise.

> "I do not really take cognizance of his communication as
> knowledge . . . Rather I listen for what drives the other to
> say what he says, for an unconscious motive, say, or a
> 'complex' . . . My main task in my intercourse with my fel-
> low-man becomes more and more, whether in terms of

individual psychology or sociology, to see through and un-mask him. In the classical case this in no wise means a mask he has put on to deceive me, but a mask that has, without his knowing it, been put on him, indeed positively im-printed on him, so that what is really deceived is his own consciousness."

C. E. M. Joad writes about the practical effect of this ap-proach:

> The belief that men's views reflect their desires rather than their reason, has a number of harmful effects in practice. For example, it is destructive of good talk and inimical to fruitful discussion. Owing to the influence of psycho-analysis there prevails in modern society a refusal to discuss any view on its merits. If X expresses an opinion Y, the question discussed is not whether Y is true or at least reasonable, but the considerations which led X to believe it to be true. Objective truth being regarded as unobtainable, what alone is thought interesting are the reasons which led people to formulate their particular brand of error.

Bunuel's film *Belle de Jour* portrays both the real world and a world of fantasy at the same time, in such a way that one can never be sure what is going on:

> Most audiences will not find anything visually shocking about *Belle de Jour*. They will find instead a cumulative mystery: What is really happening and what is not? . . . The film continues—switching back and forth between Sever-ine's real and fantasy worlds so smoothly that after a while it becomes impossible to say which is which . . . There is no way of knowing—and this seems to be the point of the film with which Bunuel says he is winding up his 40-year career. Fantasy, he seems to be saying, is nothing but the human dimension of reality that makes life tolerable, and some-times even fun.

Harold Pinter in his plays portrays this kind of world. Certain-ties about people have dissolved:

> The desire for verification is understandable, but cannot always be satisfied. There are no hard distinctions between what is real and what is unreal, nor between what is true and what is false. The thing is not necessarily either true or

false; it can be both true and false. The assumption that to verify what has happened and what is happening presents few problems, I take to be inaccurate. A character on the stage who can present no convincing argument or information as to his past experiences, his present behavior or his aspirations, nor give a comprehensive analysis of his motives is as legitimate and as worthy of attention as one who, alarmingly, can do all these things. The more acute the experience the less articulate its expression.

Loss of content and direction in the arts

If we cannot be sure that we know anything about ourselves, others, or the external world, this is bound to affect the content of what the artist is communicating. The content is going to become thinner and thinner.

Eric Rhode:

> During the past decade a revolution has taken place in the arts, and nowhere more decisively than in the cinema. You could describe it crudely by saying that the distinction between high and lowbrow culture has been abandoned. Someone making movies now doesn't have to limit himself to serious subjects in order to be taken seriously. He isn't expected to explore the implications of his theme, or to have an emotional or intellectual commitment to it. The reign of Mindlessness has begun. Susan Sontag says that she's "against interpretation," against content. Our attention, she believes, should be mainly directed to questions of form and technique. This notion appears to be widely accepted, and examples of it can be found almost everywhere. In a letter recently published in the *Listener*, Allan King praises Robert Flaherty's *Louisiana Story* because it has "no intellectual or verbal information content to speak of": an assumption that would have shocked Flaherty.

Simon Hoggart, writing about a Conference on Broadcasting:

> The greater danger is, and this was amply illustrated by the conference, that we are reaching a stage in which television is only assessed in terms of either ratings or "suitability to the medium." The latter is a dropping from McLuhan; if the medium is the message, then the message becomes irrelevant, and we can only discuss quality in terms of how well a production fits the arrangement of light pulses we see on our screens. Baverstock was reduced to calling excel-

lence "the best talent with the best technical facilities," a statement which tells us nothing at all.

Science modifies its claim to discover "truth"

In the early period of modern science, it was confidently believed that the scientist was engaged in the pursuit of "the truth" about the universe. He believed that by observation and experiment he would eventually be able to formulate reliable theories about how the universe works. Scientists today, however, make a much more limited claim about what they are doing.

Bronowski:

> It is not possible for the brain to arrive at *certain* knowledge. All those formal systems, in mathematics and physics and the philosophy of science, which claim to give foundations for certain truth are surely mistaken. I am tempted to say that we do not look for truth, but for knowledge. But I dislike this form of words, for two reasons. First of all, we do *look* for truth, however we define it; it is what we *find* that is knowledge. And second, what we fail to find is not truth but certainty; the nature of truth is exactly the knowledge that we do find . . . No knowledge can be certain that continues to expand with us as we live inside the growing flesh of our experience.

Wren-Lewis:

> The modern theories are never more than models to suggest new lines of practical action, and therefore capable of being discarded at any time in favor of radically new models in a way which would be impossible if they were attempts to express the hidden truth behind phenomena. Experimental science succeeds by finding truth in experience, in action, and this is utterly incompatible with the traditional outlook on the world both logically and psychologically.

The following extract is from a review by Douglas Spanner of the book *The Survival of God in the Scientific Age* by Alan Isaacs:

> Dr. Isaac's humanism has no place for Truth . . . Science has often been regarded as "the disinterested search for Truth." To express it thus is simply to imply that in some sense truth is an absolute, already existent and awaiting the searcher; but this is too near to being a concession to the theologians to be acceptable to the rationalist. Science has

been held to seek truth in two respects at least; with regard to its *facts*, and with regard to its *theories*.

However, as Dr. Isaacs rightly points out, "the scientist no longer talks about facts as if there were fragments of the truth. The word *fact*, the scientist now sees, involves highly emotional ideas which are of much greater use to lawyers and theologians." Instead, "science deals not with facts but with observations." The difference? Simply facts are things conceived of as true in themselves, *i.e.*, *absolutely*; observations, on the other hand, are *relative* to the observer, and the relationship conditions their validity. Thus we slip our moorings!

Dr. Isaacs reveals by the whole tenor of his argument, that truth is no longer his goal; what he seeks for is rather *validity for the moment*.

This is how *C. S. Lewis* interpreted some of these developments in modern science:

Men became scientific because they expected Law in nature, and they expected Law in nature because they believed in a Legislator. In most modern scientists this belief has died: it will be interesting to see how their confidence in uniformity survives it. Two significant developments have already appeared—the hypothesis of a lawless subnature, and the surrender of the claim that science is true. We may be living nearer than we suppose to the end of the Scientific Age.

Professional philosophy abandons its search for truth.

Traditional philosophy has always been concerned with the pursuit of the truth. Now, however, philosophers generally have abandoned the search for truth in the older sense, and have been forced to limit the field of their inquiries to, for example, the study of concepts and the meaning of words.

G. J. Warnock in *English Philosophy since 1900* writes:

The proper concern of philosophy is with concepts, with the ways and means by which we think and communicate.

Ernest Gellner writes with scorn and despair over this betrayal of philosophy. This is how his attitude is summed up by Leslie Paul:

This has given rise to a paradox worthy of *Beyond the*

Fringe, that not a few philosophers disbelieve in philosophy: they believe that philosophy is the pathology of language and that their own role, as diagnosticians and therapists of linguistic mistakes, is to catch out the chaps who indulge in it. It is as if, the sociologist Ernest Gellner said, . . . swimming instructors no longer believed it possible to swim. In an epigram not easily forgotten he wrote, "A cleric who loses his faith abandons his calling, a philosopher who loses his, redefines his subject."

"The view that the needle *must* be in the haystack is extremely powerful, and operative in making philosophers seek it. The needle has not turned up. But the burrowing in this haystack has become habitual and established, and a cessation of it would leave men in a bewildered state. Some have no other skills. So, some alternative positions have emerged and are to be found: there *may* be needles in the haystack. Haystacks are interesting. We like hay."

"Truth-substitutes" fill the vacuum

People would like to know the truth. Life seems to work better when we know something of the true facts of our condition. But what if we reach the position when we feel that we cannot hope to know the truth about ourselves and the universe?

One answer is to say that what really matters is not so much the truth of what we believe, but the *sincerity* with which we believe it.

George Eliot:

I have too profound a conviction of the efficacy that lies in all sincere faith, and the spiritual blight that comes with no faith, to have any negative propagandism in me . . . I care only to know, if possible, the lasting meaning that lies in all religious doctrine from the beginning till now.

Another answer is to say that we should simply live *as if* what we believe is true. We cannot be sure that it is "the truth"; and we must therefore simply live on the assumption that it *is* true.

Lessing's Parable of the Three Rings:

There was once an ancient ring which had the power to bestow upon its owner the gift of being loved by God and man. This was passed on down many generations until it came into the possession of a father who had three sons equally dear to him. To resolve the dilemma, he had two replicas made and gave a ring to each son. After his death all three claimed to possess the true ring. But as with religion, the original cannot be traced. Historical investigation is of no avail. But a wise judge counsels each son to behave as if he had the true ring and prove it by deeds of love. Thus in the end it will not matter who had the original.

Another possible answer is to say that we should stop asking the question "Is it true?" and ask instead "Does it work?"
William James:

If the hypothesis of God works satisfactorily in the widest sense of the word, it is true.

Thomas Arnold:

All societies of men, whether we call them states or churches, should make their bond to consist in a common object and a common practice rather than in a common belief; in other words, their end should be good rather than truth.

J. B. Priestley:

We can try to feel and think and behave, to some extent, *as if* our society were already beginning to be contained by religion, as if we were certain that Man cannot even remain Man unless he looks beyond himself, as if we were finding our way home again in the universe.

Up to this point we have been thinking in terms of private and personal beliefs of individuals. If we cannot hope to find the truth, then we must leave each individual to reconcile himself to the situation as best he can. But what if some individual or some group comes into a position of power and then proceeds to *tell* the people what the truth is, and what is good and right? This is precisely what has happened in communism.
André Gide:

In Marxist doctrine there is no such thing as truth—at least not in the absolute sense—there is only relative truth.

George Orwell in *1984:*

Doublethink means the power of holding two contradictory beliefs simultaneously, and accepting both of them. The party intellectual knows that he is playing tricks with reality, but by the exercise of doublethink he also satisfies himself that reality is not violated.

Arthur Koestler, writing about "the comforts of double-think":

> Behind the curtain there is the magic world of double-think. "Ugly is beautiful, false is true, and also conversely." This is not Orwell; it was written in all seriousness by the late Professor Suzuki, the foremost propounder of modern Zen, to illustrate the principle of the identity of opposites . . . Facts and arguments which succeed in penetrating the outer defenses are processed by the dialectical method until "false" becomes "true," tyranny the true democracy, and a herring a racehorse.

This approach to truth in communism has practical consequences. It means, for example, that authorities feel perfectly free to tell any lies they want if it serves their purpose. *Ignazio Silone*, who was for many years a member of the Italian Communist Party, describes an incident that took place at a meeting of the International in Moscow:

> They were discussing one day, in a special commission of the Executive, the ultimatum issued by the central committee of the British trade unions, ordering its local branches not to support the Communist-led minority movement, on pain of expulsion. After the representative of the British Communist Party had explained the serious disadvantages of both solutions, because one meant the liquidation of the minority movement and the other the exit of the minority from the trade unions, the Russian delegate Piatnisky put forward a suggestion which seemed as obvious to him as Columbus' egg: "The branches," he suggested, "should declare that they submit to the discipline demanded, and then, in practice, should do exactly the contrary." The English Communist interrupted: "But that would be a lie." Loud laughter greeted this ingenuous objection, frank, cordial, interminable laughter, the like of which the gloomy offices of the Communist International had perhaps never heard before. The joke quickly spread all over Moscow, for the Englishman's entertaining and incredible reply was telephoned at once to Stalin and to the most important offices of State, provoking new waves of mirth everywhere.

Nikita Struve, writing about contemporary Russia and its attitude to Christianity:

> What impresses me . . . is that atheism today seems to have
> given up the search for truth. Facts and arguments which
> tell against it are dismissed in silence.

This answer to the question of truth, therefore, opens up the
frightening possibility that the horrors of Alice's dream world
can be enacted in history.

> At this moment the King, who had been for some time
> busily writing in his notebook, called out, "Silence!" and
> read out from his book, "Rule Forty-two: *All persons more
> than a mile high to leave the court.*"
>
> Everybody looked at Alice.
>
> "I'm not a mile high," said Alice.
>
> "You are," said the King.
>
> "Nearly two miles high," added the Queen.
>
> "Well, I shan't go, at any rate," said Alice: "besides, that's
> not a regular rule; you invented it just now."
>
> "It's the oldest rule in the book," said the King.
>
> "Then it ought to be Number One," said Alice.
>
> The King turned pale, and shut his notebook hastily. "Consider your verdict," he said to the jury in a low trembling
> voice . . .
>
> . . . said the Queen. "Sentence first—verdict afterwards."

John Lehmann, writing about the relevance of *Alice* in today's
world:

> This procedure, I suggest, though meant as a joke, was
> uncannily prophetic, and has become too painfully actual in
> our own age to be treated entirely as a joke.

Truth is sought through some "experience"

Many who have reached the position of agnosticism have taken
to drugs, for example, not simply for excitement and release, but
in the hope of being able to find out through this experience
what the universe is all about.

Aldous Huxley, in his earlier writings (e.g., *Do What You Will*,
1936), expresses his profound skepticism about the possibility of
finding the truth about the universe. (See p. 27.)

In his book *The Doors of Perception* (1954), he advocates the
use of drugs such as mescaline:

What happens to the majority of the few who have taken mescaline under supervision can be summarized as follows:

1. The ability to remember and to "think straight" is little if at all reduced . . .

2. Visual impressions are greatly intensified and the eye recovers some of the perceptual innocence of childhood, when the sensum was not immediately and automatically subordinated to the concept . . .

3. Though the intellect remains unimpaired and though perception is enormously improved, the will suffers a profound change for the worse. The mescaline taker sees no reason for doing anything in particular and finds most of the causes for which, at ordinary times, he was prepared to act and suffer, profoundly uninteresting. He can't be bothered with them, for the good reason that he has better things to think about.

4. These better things may be experienced (as I experienced them) "out there," or "in here," or in both worlds, the inner and the outer, simultaneously or successively. That they *are* better seems to be self-evident to all mescaline takers who come to the drug with a sound liver and an untroubled mind . . .

Other persons discover a world of visionary beauty. To others again is revealed the glory, the infinite value and meaningfulness of naked existence, of the given, unconceptualized event. In the final stage of ego-lessness there is an "obscure knowledge" that All is in all—that All is actually each. This is as near, I take it, as a finite mind can ever come to "perceiving everything that is happening everywhere in the universe" . . .

From this . . . excursion into the realm of theory we may now return to the miraculous facts—four bamboo chair legs in the middle of a room. Like Wordsworth's daffodils, they brought all manner of wealth—the gift beyond price, of a new direct insight into the very Nature of Things, together with a more modest treasure of understanding in the field, especially, of the arts.

Toward the end of his life he was still advocating the use of drugs as a way of "knowing."

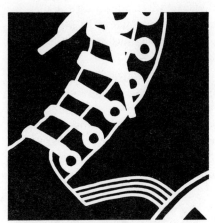

ANSWER FIVE:
CHRISTIAN EXISTENTIALISM

We can know
Christianity is true only
by a leap of faith.

The answer of most modern theologians has been that Christian claims to the truth are at best improbable and at worst absurd; they are an offense to the intellect. Christian beliefs are not so much beyond the understanding (as in Answer 2); they are against the understanding. Reason and feeling are not able to find the truth; rationalism leads to a dead end. Faith and scientific knowledge have little or nothing in common; they belong to two different worlds. If we are to find the truth,

*therefore, we will find it only by com-
mitting ourselves to the truth in a
"leap of faith." We cannot hope to
think out the truth and analyze it rationally. We can only experience it in
all its absurdity and contradiction.*

This answer was formulated by Soren Kierkegaard (see p. 93) and was first introduced into theology by Karl Barth (p. 96). The following quotations are from theologians who have accepted, to a greater or lesser extent, Kierkegaard's understanding of faith. It may well be objected that it is grossly unfair and misleading to group these writers together in one category. Barth and Brunner, for example, have very different attitudes to natural theology, and have been openly and fiercely critical of each other's writing. Some of these writers would call the resurrection a "myth," while others would insist that it was a historical event. The crucial point at issue here, however, is the answer to the question "How can I know if Christianity is true?" And however much these writers may differ from one another in certain areas of theology, they all share a common starting point because they give similar answers to this basic question.

SOME TWENTIETH-CENTURY VIEWS

Emil Brunner:

> When a believer is asked: Why do you believe that Jesus is the Christ? he can only answer: Why should I not believe, since Jesus confronts me as the Christ, when He meets me in the story and the witness of the Apostles as the Christ? It is not the believer who needs to give reasons, but the unbeliever . . . It is not the one who accepts this claim of Jesus, and obeys it, who has to give "reasons" for his faith; on the contrary, those who do not accept this claim ought to state the "reasons" for their decision . . . These reasons . . . do not belong to the sphere of academic knowledge, but to the sphere of one's philosophy of life, of self-knowledge, of faith.

Paul Tillich:

> Sometimes . . . a wave of light breaks into our darkness, and it is as though a voice were saying: "You are accepted.

You are accepted, accepted by that which is greater than you,
and the name of which you do not know. Do not ask for
the name now; perhaps you will find it later. Do not try to
do anything now; perhaps you will do much. Do not seek
for anything; do not perform anything; do not intend anything. *Simply accept the fact that you are accepted.*"

Absolute faith is "the accepting of the acceptance without
somebody or something that accepts."

Rudolph Bultmann:

Christ meets us in the preaching as one crucified and risen.
He meets us in the word of preaching and nowhere else.
The faith of Easter is just this—the faith in the word of
preaching. It would be wrong for us at this point to raise
again the problem of how this preaching arose historically,
as though that could vindicate its truth. That would be to
tie our faith in the word of God to the results of historical
research. The word of preaching confronts us as the Word
of God. It is not for us to question its credentials. It is we
who are questioned, we who are asked whether we will
believe the word or reject it.

It is precisely its immunity from proof which secures the
Christian proclamation against the charge of being mythological.

The real purpose of myth is not to present an objective
picture of the world as it is, but to express man's understanding of himself in the world in which he lives. Myth
should be interpreted not cosmologically, but anthropologi-
cally, or better still, existentially.

Wilfred Cantwell Smith:

To say that Christianity is true is to say nothing significant;
the only question that concerns either God, or me, or my
neighbor is whether *my* Christianity is true, and whether
yours is. And to that question, a truly cosmic one, in my
case the only valid answer is a sorrowful "not very." By my
Christianity I mean my actual, living Christianity, my Chris-
tianness, the specific religion of my personal life. . .

Furthermore, my Christianity may be more true this morning than it was yesterday afternoon. It may collapse altogether in some crisis tomorrow morning . . . Again, one
man's Christianity may be (must be) more false than an-

other's. Your Christianity may be truer than the Christianity of your next-door neighbor.

Teilhard de Chardin believes that evolution faces us with a choice between absolute optimism and absolute pessimism. Our choice between them amounts to a leap of faith, because there is no tangible evidence that points one way or the other:

> What makes the world in which we live specifically modern is our discovery in it and around it of evolution. And I can now add that what disconcerts the modern world at its very roots is not being sure, and not seeing how it ever could be sure, that there is an outcome—*a suitable outcome*—to that evolution.

> Either nature is closed to our demands for futurity, in which case thought, the fruit of millions of years of effort, is stifled, stillborn in a self-abortive and absurd universe. Or else an opening exists—that of the super-soul above our souls; but in that case the way out, if we are to agree to embark on it, must open out freely on to limitless psychic spaces in a universe to which we can unhesitatingly entrust ourselves.

> Between these two alternatives of absolute optimism or absolute pessimism, there is no middle way because by its very nature progress is all or nothing. We are confronted accordingly with two directions and two only: one upward and the other downward, and there is no possibility of finding a half-way house.

> On neither side is there any tangible evidence to produce. Only, in support of hope, there are rational invitations to an act of faith.

John Robinson asserts that to say "God is love" is an act of faith in the face of all the evidence:

> For this way of thinking, to say that "God is personal" is to say that "reality at its very deepest level is personal," that personality is of *ultimate* significance in the constitution of the universe, that in personal relationships we touch the final meaning of existence as nowhere else . . . To believe in God as love means to believe that in pure personal relationship we encounter, not merely what ought to be, but what is, the deepest, veriest truth about the structure of reality. This, in face of all the evidence, is a tremendous act

of faith. But it is not the feat of persuading oneself of the existence of a super-Being beyond this world endowed with personal qualities. Belief in God is the trust, the well-nigh incredible trust, that to give ourselves to the uttermost in love is not to be confounded but to be "accepted," that Love is the ground of our being, to which ultimately we "come home."

Statements of faith, to his mind, cannot be proved or disproved:

To affirm belief in God is indeed to assert a faith in how things are . . . It is to say that we can trust the universe not only at the level of certain mathematical regularities but at the level of utterly personal reliability that Jesus indicated by the word "Abba, Father!" It is the faith that this is as true and objective a picture of reality as that described by the natural sciences, and more fundamental . . .

God-statements are statements about the veracity of this relationship. They cannot be proved or disproved, any more than human trust or love can finally be proved or disproved. In that sense there is nothing that might occur, as Anthony Flew has demanded there should be, which would show conclusively that there is no God.

Alan Richardson is basically committed to Kierkegaard's leap of faith:

Subjectivity becomes the key to certitude when we take what Kierkegaard called "the leap of faith," when we learn to trust, to obey, and worship. Thus belief or faith in the true biblical and religious sense is not temporary acceptance of a hypothesis until proof or disproof is forthcoming. Belief in God is altogether misrepresented by being given the status of an explanatory hypothesis . . . Faith in God is essentially a relationship between persons, and therefore is no more susceptible of scientific proof or disproof than is a woman's trusting, obedient, and respecting love for her husband . . . The escape from subjectivity in the sense of self-imprisonment is therefore not by argument but by commitment, obedience, and worship . . . The "verification principle" of existential truth is commitment to it in faith, obedience and worship . . . In the last analysis the verification principle of existential truth is a subjective one.

But he adds certain important qualifications:

We do not suppose that there are ultimately two kinds of
knowledge or two kinds of truth. In the final analysis truth
is one and every particular truth coheres with all other
truth . . . Truth is a unity . . . Thus when we speak of two
kinds of knowledge we must not be understood to imply
that there is any fundamental contradiction between scientific and other ways of knowing.

This does not mean that there is no place for rational
intellect and scientific investigation in the sphere of religious truth . . . There are criteria of Christian truths
(namely, truths of history as recited in the creed) which
acquit Christianity from being "merely" subjective.

Rosemary Haughton wants to draw the attention of the questioner away from questions about presuppositions to consider the
character of Jesus himself. It is assumed that what Jesus was and
did will be self-authenticating and commend itself as true, quite
independently of other assumptions about God and man.

We do not know and cannot know in any ordinary sense
what is the reality to which we refer by the great symbolic
opening phrases of the creed. If all the rest depended on
answering the question "What is God?" we would not get
much further. But what we often fail to notice is the fact
that these very phrases do not refer to a being as such but
rather to a series of relationships. It is in the relationships
that we discover the reality, whatever it may be. Christ
himself never answered the question, "What is God?" When
Philip asked him, "Lord, show us the Father," the answer
he got was, "He who has seen me has seen the Father."

Leslie Paul:

It cannot be said that what emerges from my survey is a
"proved" Christianity and a "disproved" humanism, or vice
versa. This has not been the object of the exercise. In any
case, one is not moving in the realm of proof or disproof,
adding up lists of pros and cons for this view of that and
striking a credit balance here and a debit there, but in a
dimension of reflection and contemplation upon public and
private experience which thrusts us deeper and deeper into
the human dilemma. It is a spiritual enterprise bound to be
anguished as we grope for meanings given to the heart and
the poetic intuition as much as to the head.

The New Dutch Catechism, while it insists on a real historical resurrection, interprets the first eleven chapters of Genesis as "myth" in the sense that Bultmann uses the word (see p. 88). "These chapters have nothing to do with history, and our acceptance of the Christian assumptions they teach therefore becomes a leap of faith. We accept this outlook not because we have good reason to believe that it is true, but because it appeals to us."

> The first eleven chapters of Genesis tell of the origins of mankind—Adam, Cain, Noah, and Babel. We know that they are not descriptions of disconnected historical facts. They go deeper. The narratives are symbols in which the kernel of all human history is described, including that which is still to come. Adam is man. Cain is to be found in the newspapers and may be seen within our own heart. Noah and the builders of Babel—they are ourselves. Chapters 1–11 of Genesis describe the basic elements of all human encounter with God. It is only with Chapter 12, where Abraham appears, that we begin to make out historical figures in the past.

> We have seen what the story of paradise and the fall intended to convey: the purpose of God, as realized in the whole, and above all in the end. We really know nothing of the actual beginnings.

THREE KEY FIGURES

Blaise Pascal (1623–1662)

Pascal shows traces of this kind of answer in his approach.

☐ He makes a distinction between "the heart" and "the reason":

> The heart has its reasons which are unknown to reason . . . It is the heart which is aware of God and not reason. This is what faith is: God perceived intuitively by the heart, not by reason.

In making this distinction, he is continuing the dichotomy which we have noticed in Aquinas, Locke, and others:

The heart = "the intuitive spirit"
The Reason, Mind = "the geometric spirit"

What he did was to erect a dualism of his own in which two realms existed: one of the heart and one of the mind. In religion, unlike Descartes, he applied the logic of the heart. In mathematics and physics, however, Pascal used the same geometry as did Descartes. (Bronowski and Mazlish)

☐ He puts forward the idea of "The Wager": Christianity cannot be proved conclusively by the reason, but neither can it be disproved. If it turns out that Christianity is true, we have everything to gain; but if it turns out to be false, we have nothing to lose. We should accept the inevitable risk of faith, and gamble on the truth of Christianity.

> This was the essential step of Pascal: that doubt leads to faith, because doubt makes it certain that there is no answer to the question of self-consciousness. The view of Pascal was that the answer to the epistemological question is—that there is no rational answer. We must simply place our bet on faith. (Bronowski and Mazlish)

Soren Kierkegaard (1813–1855)

Pascal was an isolated philosopher and had no following. Kierkegaard, similarly, was an individualist in his philosophy, and had no following during his lifetime. But during this century he has suddenly become popular, and has become the source not only of Secular Existentialism, but also of Christian Existentialism.

He built his position on the position reached by Hume and Kant; i.e., he accepted the impossibility of finding certain knowledge through the senses. And he accepted Kant's distinction between *noumena* and *phenomena*. He is conscious, however, that he is breaking completely new ground.

> My task is so new that there is literally no one in the 1800 years of Christianity from whom I can learn how I should proceed.

His position and the direction his views have taken can be summed up as follows:

☐ There is no point in asking "What is 'the truth?'" because it is impossible to know the truth objectively. The question we must ask is "What is the truth *for me*? How am *I* to live my life?"

> The thing is to understand myself, to see what God really wishes *me* to do; the thing is to find a truth which is true *for me*, to find *the idea for which I can live and die.*

☐ Reasoning will lead us only to paradox; and historical inquiry leads only to probability, which is without value for faith.

If from such a point of view we enquire about the truth objectively, then we see that truth is a *paradox*.

If the contemporary generation had left nothing behind them but these words: "We believed that in such and such a year God appeared among us in our community, and finally died," it would be more than enough. The contemporary generation would have done all that was necessary: for this little advertisement, this *nota bene* on a page of universal history, would be sufficient to afford an occasion for a successor, and the most voluminous account can in all eternity do nothing more.

On the title page of *Philosophical Fragments or a Fragment of Philosophy* he puts the question:

Is a historical point of departure possible for an eternal consciousness; how can such a point of departure have any other than a merely historical interest; is it possible to base an eternal happiness upon historical knowledge?

☐ Christian beliefs are absurd; they are an offense to the reason. Christian faith, therefore, means believing *against* the reason, *against* the understanding.

. . . the paradox (of the Christian faith) cannot and shall not be understood . . . the task is to hold fast to this and to endure the crucifixion of the understanding.

A believer who believes, *i.e.*, believes against the understanding, takes the mystery of faith seriously and is not duped by the pretence of understanding.

Here is such a definition of truth: *objective incertitude, clung to and appropriated with passionate inwardness, is truth,* the highest truth that there can be, *for one who exists.*

The emphasis in faith is on the *will* rather than on the intellect.

Christianity, . . . or becoming a Christian, has nothing to do with a change in the intellect—but in the will. But this change is the most painful of all operations, comparable to vivisection . . . And because it is so terrible, becoming a Christian in Christendom has long since . . . been transformed into a change of the intellect.

Faith therefore depends entirely on the choice of the will. It is a huge risk.

And so I say to myself: I choose; that historical fact means
so much to me that I decide to stake my whole life upon it.
Then he lives; lives entirely full of the idea of risking his
life for it: and his life is the proof that he believes. He did
not have a few proofs, and so believed and then began to
live. No, the very reverse.

That is called risking; and without risk faith is an impossibility. *To be related to spirit means to undergo a test*; to
believe, to wish to believe, is to change one's life into a trial;
daily test is the trial of faith.

Faith must be existential faith.

From the Christian point of view faith belongs to the existential; God did not appear in the character of a professor
who has some doctrines which must first be believed and
then understood.

No, faith belongs to and has its home in the existential, and
in all eternity it has nothing to do with knowledge as a
comparative or a superlative.

Faith expresses a relation from personality to personality.

Personality is not a sum of doctrines, nor is it something
directly accessible . . . Personality is that which is within
. . . it is that which is within to which a man, himself in turn
a personality, may be related in faith. Between person and
person no other relation is possible. Take the two most
passionate lovers who have ever lived, and even if they are,
as is said, one soul in two bodies, this can never come to
anything more than that the one believes that the other
loves him or her.

In this purely personal relation between God as personal
being and the believer as personal being, in *existence*, is to
be found the concept of faith.

(Hence the apostolic formula, "the obedience of faith" (*e.g.,*
Romans 1:5), so that faith tends to the will and personality,
not to intellectuality—*marginal note.*)

This is how *Herbert Read* sums up Kierkegaard's position on
the nature of Christian faith:

"Faith expresses a relation from personality to personality
. . . In this purely personal relation between God as personal being and the believer as personal being, in *existence*,

is to be found the concept of faith." The whole of Kierkegaard's philosophy revolves around this axiom . . .

What one realizes, in reading these late extracts from the
Journals, is the absolute intransigence of the egoism which
Kierkegaard made the basis of his faith.

Karl Barth (1886–1968)

Karl Barth first introduced Kierkegaard's ideas into theology,
and he has been a major—if not *the* major—influence in theology in the first half of the twentieth century. We shall therefore
examine his thinking in some detail. The quotations summarizing his position are from T. F. Torrance, *Karl Barth: An Introduction to his Early Theology, 1910–1931.*

His debt to liberalism. Barth grew up within the tradition of the
liberal theology of the nineteenth century, and he admits that he
was at one stage a liberal theologian. However, in August 1914
he was appalled to find that many of his theological teachers had
joined other German intellectuals in a manifesto supporting
Kaiser Wilhelm II's war policy:

> Disillusioned by their conduct, I perceived that I should not
> be able any longer to accept their ethics and dogmatics,
> their biblical exegesis, their interpretation of history, that at
> least for me the theology of the nineteenth century had no
> future.

He detected two fatal weaknesses in nineteenth-century theology:

☐ It accommodated Christianity to the assumptions of the nineteenth century, which were basically the assumptions inherited
from the Enlightenment.

☐ This meant in practice that theology suffered from a cancerous
subjectivism. Schleiermacher could only speak of God by speaking of man in a loud voice. Thus since God was so reduced,
Christianity tended toward humanism or pantheism.

In spite of this, however, Barth continued to accept many of
the methods and conclusions of liberal scholars about the Bible.

His debt to Kierkegaard. In setting out to make a new beginning,
he drew certain important ideas from Kierkegaard:

☐ He thought of God as "Wholly Other," in reaction against the
liberal tendency to make God so like man that he is hardly

distinguishable from him. He maintained that there is an "infinite qualitative difference between God and man":

> The Gospel falls upon man as God's own mighty Word,
> questioning him down to the bottom of his being, uproot-
> ing him from his securities and satisfactions, and therefore
> tearing clean asunder all the relations that keep him prison-
> er within his own ideals in order that he may be genuinely
> free for God and for his wonderful new work of grace in
> Jesus Christ. The emphasis was quite definitely upon what
> became known as *diastasis*, the distance, the separation, be-
> tween God's ways and man's ways, God's thoughts and
> man's thoughts, between Christianity and culture, between
> Gospel and humanism, between Word of God and word of
> man.

☐ The concept of "indirect communication" between God and
man:

> In Jesus the communication of God begins with a rebuff,
> with the exposure of a vast chasm, with the clear revelation
> of a great stumbling-block. Remove from the Christian Re-
> ligion, as Christendom has done, its ability to shock, and
> Christianity, by becoming a direct communication, is al-
> together destroyed. It then becomes a tiny, superficial
> thing, capable of neither inflicting deep wounds nor of
> healing them; by discovering an unreal and merely human
> compassion, it forgets the qualitative distinction between
> God and man. (Kierkegaard)

Barth acknowledged his debt to Kierkegaard's existentialism
and his responsibility for introducing it into theology.

> For its introduction into theology, I myself must bear a
> good deal of unwitting responsibility, for I paid tribute to it
> in my commentary on the Epistle to the Romans (1921) and
> even in my well-known false start, the *Christliche Dogmatik
> im Entwurf* (1927). In the light of these works, and in
> respect of certain features of my theological thinking in its
> later development, I must admit that I have learned some-
> thing from what Kierkegaard and his modern followers
> teach.

In later years, particularly from 1931 onward, Barth changed
his position considerably. He confessed that he might have been
somewhat extreme in the way he had stated his case in his early

years. But Kierkegaard's influence had already determined many of his fundamental assumptions. Much of this influence Barth sought later to tone down and sometimes to cut out altogether.

It is certainly true, therefore, to say that the later Barth is different from the earlier Barth. But on this particular question about the truth of Christianity, he did not fundamentally alter his position, and his earlier writings were very influential in the development of modern theology.

His concept of the Word of God. He emphasizes that the Word of God is utterly rational. But at the same time it cannot be identified or equated with any particular form of words, even the words of the Bible. Its rationality is so unique that it cannot be related to any kind of rationality as *we* know it.

> In Revelation God gives himself to us as the object of our faith and knowledge, but because he remains God the Lord, he does not give himself into our hands, as it were; he does not resign himself to our mastery or our control as if he were a dead object. He remains the living Lord, unqualified in his freedom, whom we can only know in accordance with his acts upon us, by following his movement of grace, and by renouncing on our part any attempt to master him by adapting him to our own schemes of thought or structures of existence; that is, whom we can know only by knowing him out of himself as an objective reality (*Gegenstand*) standing over against us, as the divine Partner and Lord of our knowing of him. A favorite term that Barth uses to describe this unique object of knowledge, which we cannot bring under our own control, is *mystery.* By "mystery" Barth does not refer to anything a-logical or irrational, but on the contrary to full, complete, and self-sufficient rationality, the rationality of God, who is so fully rational that he does not need to be interpreted in terms of anything outside of himself. That is the supreme rationality that confronts us when God gives himself to us to be known as a reality whose possibility resides absolutely within himself, and whom we cannot understand, far less derive or substantiate, except out of himself. He reveals himself to us in such a way that we can know him only if our thinking begins with his revelation, and follows it through, if it is grounded entirely upon it, and never subjected to any other truth or criterion outside of it.

Even Jesus himself, therefore, is not an unambiguous revelation of God.

> In Jesus, God becomes veritably a secret: He is made
> known as the Unknown, speaking in eternal silence . . .

The Bible is not a means of direct communication between God and man; all it can do is to point beyond itself and bear witness to the Word of God.

> The Word of God comes to us in the Bible through the
> speech of sinful, fallible men to whom God has spoken and
> who bear witness to his speaking. We do not have here a
> direct speaking of God from heaven, but a speaking
> through a transient and imperfect human medium. No
> doubt the human word we hear in the Scriptures is not
> always appropriate or adequate to the Word of God which
> its authors have heard and to which they bear testimony,
> but nevertheless it is the human word which God has freely
> chosen and decided to use as the form in which he speaks
> his Word to us.

> This does not mean that the Revelation of God can be read
> directly off the pages of the historical Scriptures, for the
> actuality of Revelation is only indirectly identical with the
> actuality of the Bible . . . It is because we cannot speak of a
> direct identity of the Scripture as such with Revelation,
> although we cannot separate the Scripture from that Reve-
> lation, that our knowledge of the Bible as the Word of God
> is itself an event, an ever-new breaking-through to Revela-
> tion of faith and obedience.

> It is important, then, to recognize that in the Bible there is
> this "wall" between us and divine Revelation, namely, the
> man-conditioned and time-conditioned character of the wit-
> ness. If we deny or ignore it, then we turn the Bible into an
> organ of direct and immediate oracular communication,
> and, in point of fact, deny Revelation itself, that is, deny
> God himself in his Revelation whom we hear and know
> only in decisive encounter and to whom we respond in faith
> and obedience.

Moreover, the word of the Christian to the non-Christian is nothing more than an indirect witness. It is impossible to give direct and unambiguous answers.

The Word of God itself cannot be broken or retracted. But

our human word about God *is* broken, and only in this
"brokenness"—this absence of limpidly clear self-evidencing
terms—can it bear witness to the truth of God. "We know
that we are unable to comprehend except by means of
dialectical dualism, in which one must become two in order
that it may be veritably one" . . . "If you ask me about
God," Barth once wrote, "If you ask me about *God,* and if I
am ready to tell about him, dialectic is all that can be
expected of *me.* Neither my affirmation nor my denial lays
claim to being God's truth. Neither is more than a *witness* to
that Truth which stands in the center between every Yes
and No." (H. R. Mackintosh)

His answer to questions about truth. How can we *know* the Word of
God? How can we *know* what God is saying to us? How can we
be sure that it is *true*?

Barth's answer rules out the possibility of any kind of verification that is carried over from the sciences:

In the knowledge of God, we are concerned with an incom-
parable object (the Lord, God), and therefore it cannot be
scientific to carry over from our knowledge of other objects
the specific form of rationality or the specific method of
knowledge science has had to develop in accordance with
their (creaturely) nature. (T. F. Torrance)

He therefore refuses to discuss the presuppositions of the
non-Christian. The following passages are from Barth's Exposi-
tion of Anselm's work *Fides Quaerens Intellectum*:

And the other possibility, the possibility of a discussion on
the "unbeliever's" ground, was for Anselm, be it "easy" or
"difficult," excluded and forbidden—it was no possibility at all.

Thus it is concluded that his statement ("there is no God")
is nonsense, must be nonsense, and is debarred from serious theological debate.

Perhaps Anselm did not know any other way of speaking of
the Christian *Credo* except by addressing the sinner as one
who had not sinned, the non-Christian as a Christian, the
unbeliever as believer, on the basis of the great "as if"
which is really not an "as if" at all, but which at all times
has been the final and decisive means whereby the believer
could speak to the unbeliever. Perhaps, desiring to prove,
he did not really remain standing on this side of the gulf
between the believer and non-believer but crossed it,

though on this occasion not in search of a truce as has been said of him and has often happened, but . . . as conqueror whose weapon was the fact that he met the unbelievers as one of them and accepted them as his equal.

The approach that Barth derived from this study of Anselm determined his approach from that time onward. Thus, writing a new preface to his work on Anselm in 1958, he explains:

> . . . in this book (*Fides Quaerens Intellectum*) on Anselm I am working with a vital key, if not the key, to an understanding of that whole process of thought that has impressed me more and more in my *Church Dogmatics* as the only one proper to theology.

In his *Dogmatics*, therefore, he refuses to discuss basic presuppositions like the existence of God and the possibility of revelation.

> Really responsible, up-to-date theological thought, in genuine rapprochement with its contemporaries, will reveal itself to be such even today . . . by refusing to discuss the basis of its ground, questions such as whether God is, whether there is such a thing as revelation, *etc.*

Thus, if we asked Barth, "How can I know if Christianity is true?" his answer would be "through *obedience*," through complete surrender to the Word of God.

> If faith is indeed the knowledge of the Creator then it cannot understand itself as acting creatively, but only as acting obediently. It is knowledge of the truth solely in virtue of the fact that the truth is *spoken* to us to which we respond in pure obedience.

All that man can do therefore is listen and be informed, and then say Yes.

> In his dialectical thinking Barth was faced with a fundamental problem of all theology and all thinking about God. It is *man* who thinks, *man* who asks searching questions about God, *man* who is hungry to know God, to speak about him, and make judgments about him; but when that man stands face to face with God, he discovers that he stands at the bar of *God's* judgment and it is *God* who speaks to him and questions him. Man begins by investigating God but discovers that God is all the time investigating

him—and when he tries to express that, theologically, he finds that all his grammar gets upset—for God is always indissolubly Subject—and all he can do is to stammer "yes" and "no" in very fragmentary utterances. "I believe; help thou my unbelief."

Barth recognizes that there is an element of question-begging in this approach. But he believes that the method of theology is such that we have no alternative to this procedure.

We know God only through God and in God, or in that we are known by him, and therefore we cannot offer any proof of our knowledge of God outside of our actual knowledge of him, that is, outside of our acknowledgment of his self-revelation. We cannot offer any evidence of our knowledge of God's Word, except in that we recognize that Word in its self-evidence to us and participate in its communication. But does that not mean that we both start from God as our presupposition and end with him as our conclusion, that we are really moving in a circle?

Barth admits that, looked at from the point of view of logical form, that is a *petitio principii* . . . but the question must be asked whether in a genuine *theo*-logy we are not shut up to this kind of movement by the very nature of the subject-matter, that is, by the very nature of God himself? That is indeed the case, for in the knowledge of God we are concerned with One who is his own ground and his own evidence, and knowledge of this God can take place only as he breaks into the midst of our knowing of this world, to give us knowledge of himself beyond any possibility of our own.

This is how three writers (who are not Christians) sum up Kierkegaard's position on the nature of Christian faith:

In rejecting Christianity, Kierkegaard has perceived the discontinuity between faith and reason, and in rejecting speculative philosophy he retained this perception and built his position upon it. He made it the effort of his life to renew the meaning of Christianity by compelling recognition of the permanent cleavage between faith and reason . . .

Kierkegaard's argument deals with the object of Christian faith and the manner of apprehending it.

That a man born and living in history says that he is God

and dies in humiliation plunges into a dilemma those who would build their lives on him and his word. Nothing has happened since to enlighten by one scruple the strain on belief. The historical success of Christianity is worthless evidence. The present generation is exactly in the position of the contemporaries of Christ who witnessed his humiliation on the cross. Faith today, unless it is faith in the faith of the Apostles, is not other than their faith in the man who makes the most absurd of claims. The truth of this claim cannot in the nature of the case be made objectively certain, or even investigated; on the contrary the absolute discontinuity between the human and the divine which inheres in the conception of God makes it unthinkable, so that it cannot by any human mind be recognized as true, cannot be entertained as a possibility . . . If a man claims to be God, then all that reason can do is to take notice of this claim and give special attention to all the circumstances attending to it. Inquiry into the authenticity of the evidence (itself never finally conclusive) is beside the point, however, for if the historical facts were established beyond cavil the inquirer would be no nearer to making up his mind what to make of them. The incarnation is a paradox which can never be thought nor accepted by reason, and therefore the claim that it is the supreme truth imposes a limit on thought and throws the inquirer into a passion of uncertainty. If, by the grace of God he sets reason and experience aside and joins himself to the paradox in the passion of faith, he is "out upon the deep, over 70,000 fathoms of water" and risks everything. The decision to take the risk cannot bring certainty. The intelligibility of the paradox remains absolute, incapable of being reduced or got round. Its acceptance by faith does nothing to reduce its offense to reason; it is a perpetual tension with the intelligence, a cause of suffering and passion, reducing the most powerful understanding to the level of the most simple, and both to nothing; for it poses itself as the limit of all thought, and the question at issue is eternal happiness.

PROBLEMS
AND QUESTIONS

One can never be sure the words
mean what they say.

Both Christians and non-Christians have pointed out that one basic problem with this answer is that one can never be sure one

can take any form of words about Christian beliefs at their face
value.

Stephen Neill:

> One of the more valid criticisms of the Barthian position is
> that Barth has never succeeded in making quite clear what
> he does mean by the phrase "the Word of God."

William Warren Bartley, writing about Barth's approach:

> All theological statements . . . are for ever *conjectures* about
> the Word of God. We can never know whether or not our
> statements do in fact express the truth about the Word of
> God or whether they are mixed with error stemming from
> our misinterpretations, from our conscious or unconscious
> imposition of our own presuppositions on the historical
> event.

About Bultmann he says:

> . . . is this existentialism more than nominally theistic? Bult-
> mann's pupil Kamlah took the final step of pointing out
> that what Bultmann takes the life of faith to be makes its
> possibility logically independent of the occurrence of any
> event in Palestine in the first century and, indeed, of the
> existence of a supernatural being. Christianity is secularized
> by stages into an atheistic philosophy. Bultmann's own re-
> tention of some elements of traditional Christian theism
> appears to have no rational jurisdiction within the frame-
> work of his own thought.

The non-Christian has every right to protest if he is conscious
of any dishonesty or calculated ambiguity.

C. E. M. Joad, writing to Arnold Lunn about Christian interpretations of the Genesis account of creation and his own loss of
faith:

> The process of disillusionment once begun went far and
> fast. I discovered that many of the Bible stories were un-
> true, and that science, supported by an impressive weight
> of evidence and backed up by the plain facts of experience,
> required us to suppose that many events had taken place
> quite otherwise than the Bible recorded. I saw that the
> Church treated this evidence dishonestly, first denying it
> and, when it could deny it no longer, affirming that it had
> no bearing upon the truths of Christianity, which being

spiritual, belonged to a sphere other than that of science. The statements once presented to me in "Scripture" as constituting a record of historical facts were, it now appeared, of spiritual significance only. Or weren't they? To this day I do not know. But perhaps you will enlighten me affirming on what principle you know the story of the Resurrection to be history and of the Creation myth.

Beatrice Webb:

I am aware that these dogmas (*e.g.,* of the virgin birth and the resurrection of Jesus) are considered by some practicing Christians to be not statements of fact at all, but merely symbols of some invisible truth—appeals to the emotion and not to the intellect. This gloss on the creed of Christendom seems to me lacking in candor.

When we compare the statements of some theologians with the statements of those who make no profession of Christian faith, it often turns out that they are saying precisely the same thing.

Colin Wilson sees no objection to using Christian language to convey his own kind of humanism:

Of Christianity, the Outsider would state that every one of its doctrines has two meanings: the idea of Christ the Redeemer, Heaven and Hell, original sin, can be understood in the obvious physical sense—the sense in which most Christians have always understood them—and a spiritual sense, which is as elusive to the ordinary person as the Invisible man. The obvious physical sense appears to the Outsider as no better than a fabrication of myths and fairy-tales; but the spiritual sense remains true.

. . . Jesus' aim was the aim of every prophet and artist—to make men *more alive,* more conscious; a desire to get more life and more Will out of a great sea of half-dead monsters . . . This, then, is the essence of Christ's teaching: it is the will of the life-force that men should strive for more consciousness and life (or, as Jesus would have expressed it, it is God's will that men strive to become more like him).

If the language of the Christian does not mean what it says, then the ordinary man can be forgiven if he reacts as Alice reacts to the word-juggling and evasiveness of Humpty Dumpty:

"When *I* use a word," Humpty Dumpty said in rather a scornful tone, "it means just what I choose it to mean—neither more nor less."

"The question is," said Alice, "whether you *can* make words mean different things."

"The question is," said Humpty Dumpty, "which is to be master—that's all . . ."

"When I make a word do a lot of work like that," said Humpty Dumpty, "I always pay it extra" . . .

Alice waited a minute to see if he would speak again, but as he never opened his eyes or took any further notice of her, she said "Good-bye!" once more, and, on getting no answer to this, she quietly walked away: but she could not help saying to herself as she went "Of all the unsatisfactory— . . . of all the unsatisfactory people I *ever* met—" She never finished the sentence . . .

Faith is not open to verification in the ordinary sense

This kind of answer amounts to an invitation to take a blind leap of faith. For when the Christian is challenged by the unbeliever, he seems to retreat into a private stronghold, putting up a notice saying, FAITH—PRIVATE. He seems to be saying, "You can't catch me! My faith is purely personal and inward. It has nothing to do with reason or science. You cannot prove or disprove it."

If the Christian is more positive and tries to persuade the non-Christian to believe on the basis of this kind of answer, his invitation sounds in effect like this: "I can't point to any evidence to convince you that Christian beliefs are true. You simply have to believe them by an act of faith. You must have the experience of faith yourself. Simply commit yourself. Launch out in faith. There is no completely convincing evidence I can offer you, and in any case, evidence is unnecessary or irrelevant. Simply believe! The only certainty that is possible will be found after you have committed yourself in faith."

T. W. Fowle (writing in 1881):

The time is then, I think, rapidly drawing on when modern thought will demand of theology, and that with some excusable peremptoriness of tone, to state once for all upon which footing it elects to stand. At present the tone of many scientific minds seems to be somewhat as follows: "We really cannot occupy ourselves in serious discussion, because we never quite know where we have you. You always seem to us to assume a supernatural standpoint, and then, when confronted with obvious difficulties involved in this, to fly elsewhere for refuge. Adopt the alternative that it is only a framework for moral ideas and spiritual truths, and that too we can make shift to estimate. But to halt uneasily between the two, and to say that so tremendous an event as the resurrection of a dead man may have happened or may not, but that on the whole it does not much matter, is to impose a fatal barrier to sincere discussion with minds that have been trained to estimate the nature and consequences of fact. If this story be true, then every conception that man can form of himself and his surroundings must be carefully modified; if it be false, then it should not be allowed to intrude itself upon a religion which, as more than half seem to assure us, having first succeeded in convincing themselves, was not founded upon it, does not need it, and would be better without it."

Colin Wilson, writing about an illustration from Jean-Paul Sartre:

If the phone rang, and a voice at the other end said: "This is God speaking. Believe and you are saved; doubt and you are damned," the man holding the receiver would be justified in answering: "Very well, in that case, I'm damned." He would be justified because all men have a right to withhold belief in something they cannot know.

Marghanita Laski:

It is thoroughly depressing to learn . . . that some people can argue that "man is part of an evolving consciousness in Nature," and that in death the "hallmark" of evolution is carried into another dimension. What conceivable sense or use could stem from such propositions, and in any case how could they be shown to be true or false?

William Warren Bartley:

The leading Protestant theologians of the twentieth century have . . . embraced as fact the philosophical contention that rationality is logically limited, that every man—wil he, nil he, makes some ultimately irrational commitment; and they have used this contention to excuse rationally their own irrational commitment to Christ. Thereby, they have

been able in principle, although not in practice, to avoid
loss of intellectual integrity.

My basic objection to Barth's thought . . . involves the absolute irrational commitment on which he bases his
theory . . .

For many of us the difficulty lies in the initial irrational assumption. We wish to question the truth of the Word of God.
And that in itself puts us outside Barth's Church.

Leslie Newbigin writing about John Oman and Barth:

He (Oman) was more aware than many theologians are of
the ease with which theology can become dishonest. He
insisted on asking at every point the question: "How do you
know?" It is one of the accidents of history that his greatest
book, *The Natural and the Supernatural* . . . appeared just at
the time when the rise of Barthian theology was sweeping
that question under the carpet.

J. S. Bezzant, writing about Bultmann:

No intelligent person desires to substitute prudent acceptance of the demonstrable for faith; but when I am told
that it is precisely its immunity from proof which secures
the Christian proclamation from the charge of being
mythological, I reply that immunity from proof can "secure" nothing whatever except immunity from proof, and
call nonsense by its proper name. Nor do I think that
anything like historical Christianity can be relieved of objections by making the validity of assertions depend upon the
therapeutic function it plays in healing fractures in the
souls of believers, or understand how it can ever have this
healing function unless it can be believed to be true.

The approach which suggests that one should simply preach
Christ and leave questions about presuppositions on one side in
the hope that the proclamation of Christ will lead to faith in
God, is likely to become more and more unrealistic and ineffec-
tive in the agnostic world of today, where the Christian is surrounded by a non-Christian majority. The mere preaching of
Christ is no substitute for talking about questions of truth, God
and man, and the universe.

Altizer:

Christ cannot appear as God at the time in which God is
dead.

Ninian Smart:

> Christ's claims are not self-authenticating. There are . . .
> certain presuppositions which have to be accepted before
> the claims can be substituted as they stand. And these
> presuppositions will be repudiated by Jews and Muslims, to
> mention no others.

This exchange between *Alice* and the Queen reminds us of the
natural reaction to any invitation to believe what is unreasonable
or impossible:

> "Let's consider your age to begin with—how old are you?"

> "I'm seven and a half exactly."

> "You needn't say 'exactly,'" the Queen remarked: "I can
> believe it without that. Now I'll give *you* something to be-
> lieve. I'm just one hundred and one, five months and a
> day."

> "I can't believe *that!*" said Alice.

> "Can't you?" the Queen said in a pitying voice. "Try again:
> draw a long breath, and shut your eyes."

> Alice laughed. "There's no use trying," she said: "one *can't*
> believe impossible things."

> "I daresay you haven't had much practice," said the Queen.
> "When I was your age, I always did it for half-an-hour
> every day. Why, sometimes I've believed as many as six
> impossible things before breakfast!"

ANSWER SIX:
MYSTICISM
We can know
Christianity is true only
through mystical
experience.

> *The mystical approach to truth holds
> that we cannot hope to be able to verify
> Christian beliefs, or to demonstrate by
> reason that they are true, or simply to
> feel in the heart that they are true. We
> can only hope to know through mystical
> experience.*

David Knowles writes that mystical theology claims to be:

an incommunicable and inexpressible knowledge and love
of God or of religious truth received in the spirit without
precedent, effort, or reasoning.

F. C. Happold gives this summary of the main characteristics
of mystical states:

1. They defy expression in terms which are fully intelligible to those who have not had some analogous experience.

2. Though states of feeling, they are also states of knowledge, resulting in a deeper insight into the nature of things.

3. Except in the case of true contemplatives, when they can result in a permanent shift of consciousness, they are infrequent and of short duration.

4. They convey the sense of something "given," not dependent on one's own volition.

5. There is a consciousness of the oneness of everything.

6. They also have a sense of timelessness.

7. There is forced on one the conviction that the familiar phenomenal *ego* is not the real *I*.

The same writer believes that the religion of the future must be a mystical religion:

> The whole of our analysis more and more forces us to the conclusion that the *only possible religion for twentieth-century man is a mystical religion and that all theological language must be recognized as a language of symbols.*

H. R. Rookmaaker in his book *Modern Art and the Death of a Culture* says:

> There is no age as mystical as ours. Yet it is mysticism with a difference: it is a nihilistic mysticism, for God is dead. Very old ideas are being revived: gnosticism, neo-platonic ideas of reality emanating from and returning to God, and Eastern religion, a religion with a god that is not a god but impersonal and universalist, a god which (not who!) is everything and therefore nothing, with a salvation that is in the end self-annihilation. In the quest for humanity man is even willing to lose his identity, his personality. It is like the creed that the Beatles sing (on their Sergeant Pepper Lonely Hearts Club Band record): "When you've seen beyond yourself . . . the time will come when you see we're all one and life flows on within you and without you."

Mystical experience is said to lead to a real knowledge of "the truth" about the universe. This truth is inexpressible in words, but it can be felt. The medium can be music, drugs, meditation, or the traditional observance of eastern religious faiths.

Albert Ayler, a leader of the new wave in jazz of 1965:

Music is a prayer, a message from God, it is freedom, beyond the material.

Brian Wilson, the Beach Boys:

My experience of God came from Acid; it's the most important thing that's ever happened to me.

A member of the Divine Light Mission, followers of 15-year-old *Guru Maharaj Ji*:

When your mind is still, then this truth will come up inside you. And really stillness of mind, which brings peace, is what everybody's looking for . . . when you stop thinking and just start experiencing . . . It's not a bad thing to think, but really if you want the eternal truth you reach a state of thoughtlessness . . . There's only one proof with spiritual truth: you'll know when you've got what you want.

Aldous Huxley:

Meditation is more than a method of self-education; it has also been used, in every part of the world and from the remotest periods, as a method for acquiring knowledge about the essential nature of things, a method for establishing communion between the soul and the integrating principle of the universe. Meditation, in other words, is the technique of mysticism . . . Properly practiced . . . meditation may result in a state of what has been called "transcendental consciousness"—the direct intuition of, and union with an ultimate spiritual reality that is perceived as simultaneously beyond the self and in some way within it.

Many of those involved in the world of the popular arts are expressing the change such experiences have made to their whole generation's view of reality:

Brian Wilson, the Beach Boys:

Then things began changing in my personal life. A whole tide of miracles was basically altering my whole generation. I completely blew my mind. For a while I wasn't myself at all. It was good. I started approaching my music-making as an art-form—something pure from the spirit to which I could add dynamics and marketable reality. I'm very aware of the value and power of speaking through a song. Not messages—just what you can say through music itself.

Larry Ramos, of the Association:

> And you know this awareness you were talking about, well,
> I know a lot of people who are involved in various forms of
> mysticism at various levels . . . and it's all part of the same
> thing. We're going through fantastic changes. Like me, I
> thought I was a real atheist . . . But, believe me, it's some-
> thing else now. It's like we created our own church; the
> church of kids.

Peter Townsend, the Who:

> The simple point is that I believe in the probability of
> anything, including flying saucers. That's only possible if
> you believe in cosmic power.

BUDDHISM

Buddhism, especially in the school of Zen, aims at a mystical
experience which, it is claimed, brings real knowledge.

Christmas Humphreys:

> The purpose of Zen is to pass beyond the intellect. All that
> we know, we know but about. The expert, a wit has said,
> learns more and more about less and less; Zen wearies of
> learning about it and about, and strives to *know*. For this a
> new faculty is needed, the power of immediate perception,
> the intuitive awareness which comes when the perceiver
> and the perceived are merged in one. All mystics use this
> faculty, and all alike are unable to make their knowledge
> known. But he who knows can only say that he knows: to
> communicate what he knows he has to descend to the realm
> of concepts, counters of agreed and common meaning.
> Such are words, but they are fallible means of making our
> knowledge known . . . What *knows*? The answer is Buddhi,
> the faculty of direct awareness, as present in every human
> mind as the intellect which all possess but few have yet
> developed to the full.
>
> All phrases, dogmas, formulas; all schools and codes; all
> systems of thought and philosophy, all "isms," including
> Buddhism, all these are means to the end of *knowing*, and
> easily become and are not perceived as obstacles in the way.
> Zen technique is designed to develop the mind to the limits
> of thought and then to drive it to the verge of the preci-
> pice, where thought can go no further. And then? As Dr.
> Graham Howe, the psychiatrist, often says to his patients,

"When you come to a precipice, why stop, or go round, or go back? Why not go over?" For only then can we go on, and progress is a walking on and on to the Goal. It is true that at a later stage one learns that there is no walking and no Goal, but that is Zen . . . Meanwhile, until we achieve the goal of purposelessness, let us have this purpose: Said the Master Ummon to his monks, "If you walk, just walk; if you sit, just sit, but don't wobble!" . . .

The vision may come quite suddenly or slowly arise. It is in no way to be confused with a psychic trance or the phantasy of the schizophrenic. Nor is it concerned with morality or any man-made code. It is a foretaste of the Absolute Moment, of Cosmic Consciousness, of the condition in which I and my Father are one . . .

. . . Others who have tried to describe the reward of their years of tremendous effort speak of a sense of certainty, of serenity, of clarity, and of unity with nature and the universe around. Hui-neng described the serenity:

> Imperturbable and serene the ideal man
>   practises no virtue;
> Self-possessed and dispassionate he commits
>   no sin;
> Calm and silent he gives up seeing and hearing;
> Even and upright his mind abides nowhere.

PROBLEMS
AND QUESTIONS

Mysticism is founded on extreme agnosticism and is open to all the same objections.

The mystic seeks for his experience because he has despaired of finding truth through other approaches. He believes that all other approaches lead not to knowledge but to profound ignorance.

Dionysius the Areopagite:

> . . . neither does anything that is, know Him as He is; . . . neither can the reason attain to Him, nor name Him, nor know Him; neither is He darkness, nor light, nor the false, nor the true; nor can any affirmation or negation be applied to Him, for though we may affirm or deny the things below Him, we can neither affirm nor deny Him, inasmuch as the all-perfect and unique Cause of all things transcends

all affirmation, and the simple pre-eminence of His absolute nature is outside of every negation—free from every limitation beyond them all.

Aldous Huxley:

To the mystics who are generally regarded as the best of their kind, ultimate reality . . . appears as a spiritual reality so far beyond particular form or personality that nothing can be predicated of it.

"The atman is silence" is what the Hindus say of ultimate spiritual reality. The only language that can convey any idea about the nature of this reality is the language of negation, of paradox, of extravagant exaggeration. The pseudo-Dionysius speaks of the "ray of the divine darkness" of "the super-lucent darkness of silence," and of the necessity to "leave behind the senses and the intellectual operations and all things known by sense and intellect." "If anyone," he writes, "seing God, understands what he has seen, he has not seen God." "Nescio, nescio," was what St. Bernard wrote of the ultimate reality; "neti, neti," was Yajnavalkya's verdict at the other side of the world. "I know not, I know not: not so, not so."

The mystical approach is therefore open to the same objections as the approach of agnosticism. (See pp. 69–85)

For example, the mystic is prepared to hold together opposites. His utterances are not subject to the laws of logic. He can hold two contradictory beliefs at the same time.

Nicholas of Cusa:

I have learnt that the place where Thou (*i.e.,* God) art found unveiled is girt round with the coincidence of contradictories, and this is the wall of Paradise wherein Thou dost abide, the door whereof is guarded by the proud spirit of Reason, and, unless he is vanquished, the way will not be open. Thus 'tis beyond the coincidence of contradictories Thou mayest be seen and nowhere this side thereof.

Simone Weil:

The mysteries of the faith are not a proper object of the intelligence, permitting affirmation or denial. They are not of the order of truth, but are above it. The only part of the human soul which is capable of any real contact with them

is the faculty of supernatural Love. It alone therefore is
capable of an adherence in regard to them.

This can lead, therefore, to a synthesis of contradictory ideas
and of religious beliefs of many different religions and philosophies:

> F. C. Happold:
>
> We are thus led on to draw a distinction between *Truth* and
> *truths.* Each partial *truth* may be true within its own sphere,
> but be only a fragment of *Truth* in its fullness; and, owing
> to the limitations of human perception, there is not seldom
> a conflict between different *truths.*
>
> To India was given the vision of the spiritual foundation of
> the universe and the immanence of God in it; to Palestine
> the vision of the significance of the material world and of
> the historical process; to Greece the vision of order and
> reason.
>
> Each of these visions of reality can be seen as complementa-
> ry, each as a fragment of the full truth, each supplementing
> the other. All are necessary if one is to grasp the full
> significance of the Christ. . . .
>
> If you have stood in a Buddhist temple and gazed up at a
> beautiful statue of the Buddha above the flower-decked
> altar, you cannot, if you are spiritually sensitive, but have
> been impressed by the calm serenity of the face gazing
> down on you. This was the teacher who taught the way of
> the ending of the world's sorrow and an all-embracing
> compassion toward every sentient being. Here before you is
> the Buddhist "God-image." And, as you gazed, there may
> have come before you another symbol, another God-image,
> the image of the Man of Sorrows who took upon himself
> the world's sorrow and showed forth the love of God on a
> cross on a desolate hill. Are the two images incompatible;
> or are they complementary; two sides of the face of the
> Divine Totality?

The knowledge gained through mystical experience can only be expressed in symbol and myth.

> F. C. Happold:
>
> We are . . . compelled to use the only language available, a
> language of symbol and paradox, which may be alien and

incomprehensible to one not accustomed to it. The Divine Ground can be spoken of only in a language of polarity, a language of opposites, as non-personal and personal, supra-natural, and transnatural, other and not-other, without and within, transcendent and immanent, as Eternal Rest and yet evolving activity. All these descriptions are true in their different spheres and at their different levels of significance and awareness. None, alone, expresses the complete truth.

But there can never be a "true" interpretation of what a symbol means. It can mean different things to different people, and no one is in a position to say whether one person has grasped the truth more clearly than another. Symbols are pro-foundly ambiguous.

F. C. Happold:

We can feel that a symbol has meaning, indeed most pro-found meaning, yet we cannot hope to put into words exactly how or why. Not only that, symbols are ambivalent, they act differently on and convey different meanings to different people. A symbol acts on the hearer or seer in such a way that it arouses in him feelings of awe or fear or love; it shifts his center of awareness, so that things are perceived in a different light; it changes his values. It has thus a dynamic quality.

Those who do not begin with the same assumption of extreme agnosticism are bound to react to the language of symbols with indifference or impatience.

C. E. M. Joad:

I have never been able to make anything of symbolism. A symbol I understand to be a sign for something else. Either the symbolist knows what the something else is, in which case I cannot see why he should not tell us what it is straight out, instead of obscurely hinting at it in symbols, or he does not, in which case not knowing what the symbols stand for he cannot expect his readers to find out for him. Usually, I suspect, he does not, and his symbolism is merely a device to conceal his muddled thinking.

Mystical knowledge is incommunicable apart from mystical experience

We cannot hope to know the truth until we have experienced the truth through some kind of mystical experience. And until and unless we have the experience, we cannot hope to know the truth. We cannot investigate anything with our minds first, and then decide whether we think it is true and whether we are going to commit ourselves to it. We cannot really begin to know what we are talking about until we have had the experience. And even when we ourselves have had the experience, we cannot hope to be able to describe or explain it adequately to others.

F. C. Happold, writing about mystical states:

> They defy expression in terms which are fully intelligible to those who have not had some analogous experience.

C. E. M. Joad:

> . . . what, after all, is the nature of the distinction between knowledge and feeling? It is that knowledge is essentially communicable, while feeling is not, precisely because knowledge is of the intellect, and reason is public and common, whereas feeling is personal and private . . . It is for precisely this reason that the testimony of mystical experience in religion carries so little weight with non-mystics, for the mystics, in seeking to convey the nature of the reality which their experience reports to them are conveying something which is strictly meaningless to those who have not themselves had experience of that reality . . .

> Now the reason why knowledge is communicable and feeling is not is to be found in the fact that knowledge is of something other than and external to itself, whereas feeling reports nothing but the fact of the feeling. Knowledge, in short, involves a reference to something else, namely, that which is known; feeling does not.

BACK TO ANSWER ONE

God has revealed the truth to man, and it is open to verification.

**PROBLEMS
AND QUESTIONS**

Having examined other possible answers to the basic question, we must now return to the option one, the biblical Christian answer, and look at some of the main questions and objections raised.

This approach makes no appeal to the heart or the feelings or the imagination. It presents a cold, abstract, and impersonal orthodoxy.

Renan:

A religion as clear as geometry arouses no love or hate.

S. T. Coleridge:

> *Evidences* of Christianity! I am weary of the word. Make a
> man feel the *want* of it; rouse him, if you can, to the
> self-knowledge of his *need* of it; and you may safely trust it
> to its own Evidence.

Ronald Knox, the Roman Catholic apologist, suggests that the
task of the Christian apologist is to:

> suggest to the reader that in approaching Christian theolo-
> gy he is approaching something that is alive, not a series of
> diagrams. The hardest part of the author's task . . . will be
> to introduce some human element into natural theology; to
> prove that God is, and what God is, not merely with the
> effect of intellectual satisfaction, but with a glow of assent
> that springs from the whole being; "Did not our hearts
> burn within us when he talked with us by the way?" But his
> task will not end there . . . He will prove the divineness of
> our Lord's mission, not by presenting us with a series of
> logical dilemmas, but by trying to reconstruct the picture of
> our Lord himself, what it was that met the gaze of the
> Apostles, and the touch of their hands. He will read the
> New Testament not as a set of "passages" which must some-
> how be reconciled with one another, but as the breathless
> confidences of living men, reacting to human situations,
> and inflamed with zeal for their Master . . . Everything will
> come alive at his touch; he will not merely know what he is
> talking about, but feel what he is talking about.

☐ If we are prepared to accept the biblical understanding of truth,
there is no need to drive a wedge between "the logical dilemmas"
and the "human element" in the way Knox does. They need not
be mutually exclusive. It need not be a case of *either/or*. One way
to introduce "some human element" into natural theology is to
show real awareness of what it *feels* like to live consistently in a
universe without God. And in contrast to this, one can then
reconsider what it *feels* like to live in the Christian universe on
the basis of what God has revealed.

H. E. Root:

> If the gospel is to be communicated in any form, it must be
> commended by those with an imaginative awareness of its
> alternatives.

☐ Some Christian apologists have made great appeal to the imagination: e.g., George MacDonald and C. S. Lewis.

Alec Vidler sums up the strength of C. S. Lewis as an apologist in this way:

> As a Christian apologist, Lewis was primarily an imaginative writer. In the midst of a culture dominated by science, technology, and a secular outlook, he somehow managed to convey a sense of the reality of an invisible, eternal realm of being to which this world is subordinate. Words like heaven and hell, glory and guilt, redemption and miracle, the transcendent and the supernatural, which have become dead or archaic for most people nowadays, and to which it often seems that Christians pay no more than lip-service, in his hands acquire substance and fascination.

But there is a vast difference between the world of C. S. Lewis's books and the fantasy world of, for example, the Beatles' film *The Yellow Submarine*:

> Roll up, roll up! Come for a magical mystery ride with the Beautiful Beatles, far, far away to Pepperland . . . Travel with Old Fred and the Beatles as they journey in their yellow submarine through strange seas, peopled with dream characters, and find the realms beyond reality. Enter the colorful cartoon world of the Beatle's newest journey into fantasy . . .

> They have to sail through eight seas until they eventually reach the underwater Pepperland. Each sea has a name and different hazards to be encountered. There are the Seas of Time, Music, Science, Consumer Products, Nowhere, Monsters, Green Phrenology, and Holes, and the weird assortment of characters encountered including Shakespeare, Queen Elizabeth, the U.S. Cavalry, Napoleon, Einstein, Freud, King Kong, Paul's clean old grandad . . . cowboys, Indians, Father MacKenzie from "Eleanor Rigby," the Sheik, Cicero, Lucy (In the Sky with Diamonds, of course) and the Boob, who is a sheep-like creature with a large nose, and who represents "Nowhere Man" . . .

The outlook behind a film of this kind takes as its starting point answers 4 or 6 to the question of truth (see pp. 64 and 110). The books of C. S. Lewis are therefore not likely to communicate the Christian message to a person who accepts the outlook of this kind of film, unless he realizes that Lewis uses his imaginary world not only to entertain but to say things about the *real* world. Anyone who knows Lewis's beliefs from his straight-forward apologetic books can understand without much difficulty what the different stories hint at in terms of the real world.

☐ It is certainly true that the Christian faith is often presented in a coldly orthodox and abstract way. But there is no reason why it should be.

The following extract from *Constance Padwick's* biography of Temple Gairdner of Cairo shows how one Christian apologist in the world of Islam was aware of the problem and how he tried to solve it:

> Gairdner . . . found that the literature by which the Christian Church had set forth her living truth to Moslems was a curiously arid, machine-made literature. It was as though the compilers, holy men though they were, had been caught into the argumentative machinery of the schoolmen, and had expended all their vital strength in meeting Moslem arguments with juster arguments. The objector himself might be left on the field prostrate but cursing. The books were starved of personality and of appeal to aught save logic and justice. Moreover he saw, and it was one of his most fruitful perceptions, that the converts made by this literature were often born in its image—with the spirit of disputation rather than worship and of love, and apt to hammer rather than to woo and win.

> Gairdner believed . . . that there must needs be an apologetic literature, unafraid of controversial points. Silence, he felt, was tantamount to denial of the truth he knew and lived. But the literature must be humanized and written for fellowmen, not only for the defeat or argufiers. Moreover, to Gairdner, stories, history, drama, music, poetry, pictures, all that could bear the impress of the Spirit of Christ, was a reasonable part of the Christian apologetic to the whole man. . . .

> "We need the *song* note in our message to the Moslems . . . not the dry cracked note of disputation, but the song of joyous witness, tender invitation."

☐ This objection is sometimes based on a fundamentally different understanding of truth—e.g., that truth can be discerned only by the heart or the feelings, or by a leap of faith. This assumption is specially evident, for example, in Coleridge, who makes Reason and Faith totally different from each other.

This approach makes no appeal to the conscience; there is no challenge to repentance

This is how *Emil Brunner* voices his protest against the perversion of the Christian message into "sterile orthodoxy":

> Faith has become doctrine, a matter for the intellect, a play of thought, scholasticism . . . Dogma, the merely intellectual expression of the divine truth in Christ has itself become deified. The fact that God's Word is not a static theory, that it is not a Word which man can manipulate as he chooses, but that it is a living personal challenge has become forgotten . . . The word is no longer a challenge; it has become an object for consideration, a theory.

☐ The biblical approach we have outlined should not involve any softening down of the ultimate challenge to repentance. But the crucial point at issue is: what do we say when the unbeliever (or the believer) asks, "How can I *know* if this gospel is true? How can I repent before God if I cannot be sure that he is there or that Jesus is the person he claims to be?" According to Brunner, however, when the Christian is asked questions of this kind, he is under no obligation to answer them. It is the unbeliever who should be putting forward reasons for not believing.

The approach we have outlined is based on the assumption that we have every right to ask questions of this kind *and* to expect substantial answers. If we are in earnest in asking our questions, we will soon realize that we are not simply doing intellectual exercises or playing games with words.

People are not so rational as they think they are.

This objection, at least in its modern form, can be traced back primarily to Freud's psychological determinism, which says that all our "rational" thinking is little more than rationalizations of what is hidden in the subconscious mind. All our reasoning is determined by factors of which we are hardly aware. Our decisions are influenced by instinct and feeling rather than by reason and logic.

Freud sums up his attitude to religion in these words:

> While the different religions wrangle with one another as to which of them is in possession of the truth, in our view the truth of religion may be altogether disregarded. Religion is an attempt to get control over the sensory world, in which we are placed, by means of the wish-world, which we have developed inside us as a result of biological and psychologi-

123

cal necessities. But it cannot achieve its end. Its doctrines carry with them the stamp of the times in which they originated, the ignorant childhood days of the human race. Its consolations deserve no trust. Experience teaches us that the world is not a nursery. The ethical commands, to which religion seeks to lend its weight, require some other foundation instead, for human society cannot do without them, and it is dangerous to link up obedience to them with religious beliefs. If one attempts to assign to religion its place in man's evolution, it seems not so much to be a lasting acquisition as a parallel to the neurosis which the civilized individual must pass through on his way from childhood to maturity.

Leslie Paul writes about the effect of Freud's teaching in this way:

Freud's concept of the unconscious is probably the most revolutionary change in thought which this century has produced . . . The acceptance of the existence of the unconscious struck a blow at a fundamental humanist principle—the rationality of the mind. If the mind was subject to occult influences, never properly exposed to reason, let alone controlled by it, and if these occult influences determined to some extent the structure of the mind—what indeed became of the supremacy of human reason and therefore of the sovereignty of man?

This way of thinking is now so widely accepted, that it is assumed everyone recognizes its truth.
Colin Wilson:

Is modern man justified in believing in God on the basis of faith? There is, of course, no simple answer to this simple question; in the final analysis it appears to be more a question of emotional motivation than of rational argument.

Ann Jellico:

When I write a play I am trying to communicate with the audience. I do this by every means in my power—I try to get at them through their eyes, by providing visual action; I try to get at them through their ears, for instance by noises and rhythm . . . I am trying to use every possible effect that the theater can offer to stir up the audience—to get at them through their emotions . . . I write this way because—the image everybody has of the rational, intellectual, and intelligent man—I don't believe it's true. I think people are driven by their emotions, and by their fears and insecurities.

☐ The objection does at least admit that Christian beliefs do seem to meet certain human needs we all feel, e.g., the need to find some meaning and purpose in life. But the Christian is not ashamed that these beliefs meet his need any more than he is ashamed to eat food because it meets his physical need. The fact that these beliefs meet a need does not by itself prove they must be false.

☐ The Christian does not deny that heredity and environment have a very important influence on all our beliefs and decisions. But he would deny that these factors (even if we could understand them completely) account for *every* belief and decision. He does so on the basis of his belief that man can make certain genuinely free choices because he bears something of the image of the God who can act in perfect freedom.

☐ Psychological determinism has serious effects on personal relationships. It means that we cannot take other people at face value; instead we are always trying to find out what makes the other person speak and act in the way he does.

☐ If this kind of determinism is completely consistent, then no place is left for free choices or for the free acceptance of any beliefs. But we all live on the assumption that we are genuinely free in certain ways—e.g., we assume we are free to decide whether or not to read to the end of this page. But if all our choices and all our beliefs are determined and programed by factors outside our control, then our feeling of freedom is an illusion. If we then go on living *as if* we have some freedom, we are being inconsistent.

☐ The objector who uses these arguments from psychology to justify his rejection of Christian beliefs must allow the same kind of argument to be used against his own beliefs. This means that his rejection of God is purely and simply an expression of his feelings and his desires. If beliefs are merely the product of the subconscious, then *no one*, believer or non-believer, has the right to claim that his beliefs are true; all one can do is to speak about one's own feelings. But the objector imagines he enjoys a specially privileged position, and has access to objective knowledge denied to the Christian. He "knows" that beliefs are motivated by the unconscious. But how can he possibly "know" if *all* beliefs are motivated by the subconscious? If Christian beliefs are the projection of human desires and feelings, then so are his own. In this case, we must give up hope of finding truth.

Isn't there a basic difference between faith and knowledge? Aren't there many different kinds of knowledge and certainty?

At the risk of oversimplification we may say that the relationship between faith and knowledge can be described in three ways. Each of them can be illustrated diagrammatically.

☐ Scientific knowledge and religious faith are *entirely different*. There is an absolute distinction between them. They belong to completely different worlds.

FAITH
_____
REASON

This position was first stated by Aquinas, and was stated in its most extreme form by Kierkegaard.

Colin Wilson completely accepts this dichotomy between objective and scientific truth on the one hand and subjective, religious truth on the other:

> Our criterion has been this: that any "truth" of religion shall be determinable *subjectively*. When we normally speak of the truth of an idea, we mean that it corresponds with some outside fact. "Truth is subjectivity," Kierkegaard said. That is the Existential concept. "The dog is blue." Is that, *could* it be, a religious truth? No; even if it is objectively true that the dog is blue, it is an objective truth; therefore it could not be a religious truth. "There is a spirit world where we all go when we die." That may be true, in the same sense that the dog is blue; but in that case it is a truth about the external world, and not therefore a religious truth.

☐ Scientific knowledge and personal knowledge are *at different ends of the same scale*. Scientific knowledge has to do with what can be measured, and is articulate knowledge. Some of our knowledge of other people comes into this category. But at the other end of the scale we have the knowledge of persons that is inarticulate. Christian faith is more like personal knowledge; it is knowledge of a Person.

Scientific knowledge—articulate and precise:	Personal knowledge—inarticulate; knowledge through involvement and interest:
e.g., I know that this tree is 30 years old; I know that x is 30 years old and that he wears glasses.	e.g., I know what x is like as a person, because I have lived and worked with him for many years.

John Habgood:

We know different facets of our experience in different ways and with different degrees of precision. There is a hierarchy of knowledge. At one end of the scale there is precise scientific knowledge of those features of experience that can be treated as objects existing independently of us; at the other end, there is the knowledge we have of other persons by our involvement with them, the kind of knowledge we can only have when we *stop* treating them as objects. At one end of the scale we have extreme articulateness; at the other end, extreme inarticulateness. And just as there is an inverse relationship between articulateness and involvement, so there is also a relationship between involvement and interest. When we stop thinking about knowledge in the abstract, we have to admit that what interests us most is what involves us most as persons. Quite apart from every other consideration, a world of which we only had precise scientific knowledge would be appallingly dull.

Religious knowledge belongs to the inarticulate end of the scale and the kind of mystery that should concern it therefore is the mystery of our involvement with persons.

New Dutch Catechism:

Man has difficult steps to take before he arrives at faith . . . The first difficulty is undoubtedly the desire to be master of all things, to subject everything to our will, including man himself. There is no room for admiration or reverence. The one thing we ask is: what is there in it for me? There is no mystery about things to make us pause reverently and ask: where do they come from? We simply work out how we can be safe and try for that. The unexpected or incalculable is taboo.

Our attitude to men is the same . . . We manipulate men and things and are blind to their mystery.

127

. . . Covetousness, cold and hard, often mixed with pride, is a disability that lies deep in all of us, no matter how friendly we may be in our contacts.

This is a threshold we cross when we take the step of really loving . . . We cease to calculate and foresee everything. We now see that the only way to know the other as he is is to let oneself be won over, to give oneself, to trust, to believe. Without belief there is no love. This belief in the other is not a lower form of knowledge but a higher. It is the one way of knowing the greatest thing on earth: another person . . .

If these approaches were to take seriously the comparison between Christian faith and knowledge and love of persons, they would allow a greater place for words and questions and answers in the process of finding out if Christianity is true. The process of getting to know another person—and even the process of falling in love—depends to a considerable extent on listening to what the other person says and asking questions to find out what he feels and thinks. It may be hard in the end to sum up exhaustively in words our knowledge or love of another person. But if we could not use words, we could not hope to arrive at this knowledge or this love in the first place. Personal trust and love are always open to tests of various kinds and are never completely blind.

☐ There are many *different levels of certainty* in any field; but we should think of truth and knowledge as being one and not many. Knowledge in one area is not of a completely different kind from knowledge in another. There should be no fundamental distinction between knowledge and faith. The different levels of certainty in different areas can be illustrated by a series of parallel scales:

CERTAIN	↑ PEOPLE	↑CHRISTIAN FAITH	↑SCIENCE
	that **x** and **y** are legally married; that **x** and **y** are utterly trustworthy and I can trust them implicitly.	that Jesus rose from the dead; that Jesus is wholly trustworthy, and that we can take him at his word.	that when water is heated to a certain temperature at a given pressure, it will boil; that dinosaurs existed.
PROBABLE	that **x** is deeply in love with **y**.	that the resurrection of Jesus is to be dated April, A.D. 30.	that a cure for cancer will be found.

POSSIBLE	that **x** and **y** will have twins; that **x** may let me down in small things.		that a black cock and a black hen will produce a brown chick.
IMPROBABLE	that **x** and **y** will have quadruplets; that **x** will become a millionaire.		that the Loch Ness Monster exists; that there is human life on other planets.

The New Testament refuses to draw a sharp line between faith and knowledge.

> Simon Peter answered him, "Lord, to whom shall we go? You have the words of eternal life; and we have *believed*, and have come to know, that you are the Holy One of God."

> His disciples said, "Ah, now you are speaking plainly, not in any figure! Now we *know* that you know all things, and need none to question you; by this we *believe* that you came from God."

This approach deprives man of his freedom and leads to complacency.

G. E. Lessing:

> What constitutes man's worth is not the truth he possesses, or thinks he possesses; it is the sincerity of the effort he makes to approach it. For it is not the possession of, but the search for, truth which strengthens the forces that contribute to his evergrowing perfection. Possession makes a man easy in his mind, inert, and self-satisfied. If God held the whole truth in his right hand, and in his left, the eternal longing for truth . . . and if he were to bid me choose, humbly I should choose the left, saying "Give me that, Father, for perfect truth is for thee alone."

☐ We must make our own choices and accept the consequences. If we believe that we cannot hope to understand the Riddle of Existence, then we must live with our agnosticism. And many who have tried consistently to live with agnosticism have found that it leads not to a spirit of "glorious adventure" but to profound despair. If we prefer "an eternal longing for the truth" to the truth itself, we must be prepared to feel the terrible pain of a thirst that will never be satisfied.

If, however, we approach the Christian faith with a desire to find the truth about it, we can ask as many questions as we want, and in the end we are utterly free to make our own decision one way or the other. And if we once believe that Christianity has the truth, there should be no complacency, but rather a longing to discover more and more of the truth, to live by it, and to demonstrate it to others.

☐ There is no loss of freedom and no complacency when the believer is able to say with the psalmist:

> Give me understanding, that I may keep thy law
> and observe it with my whole heart.
> Open my eyes, that I may behold
> wondrous things out of thy law.

Many people are not skeptical by nature and are willing to be told what the truth is

☐ It is perfectly true that some people are immediately convinced when they hear the Christian message clearly and simply explained, and when they see evidence for its truth in the lives of other Christians. They may have no desire or no need to "verify" Christian beliefs. But we are not justified in concluding that because *some* come to believe in this way, *all* can or ought to believe in this way.

☐ The real point at issue is whether or not we have the right to ask the question "How can I know if Christianity is true?" This approach is based on the assumption that we *can* and *ought* to ask as many questions as we want to. If the simple Gospel story of the death and resurrection of Jesus convinces a person and speaks to his need, then he will believe without asking further questions. But there are others who want to ask more questions. Like Thomas they say, "Unless . . . I will not believe."

☐ The New Testament writers make it quite plain that when a person becomes a Christian he is meant to grow in his understanding of what he believes.

> Make every effort to supplement your faith with virtue, and virtue with knowledge.

> Brethren, do not be children in your thinking; be babes in evil, but in thinking be mature.

Paul prays in these terms for Christians:

We have not ceased to pray for you, asking that you may be filled with the knowledge of his will in all spiritual wisdom and understanding.

☐ Even if a person never asks "intellectual" questions to satisfy himself before or after he becomes a Christian, he ought at least to be aware of the questions and the possible answers if he wants to be able to give an account of his faith to others.

Always be prepared to make a defense to any one who calls you to account for the hope that is in you, yet do it with gentleness and reverence.

Why so negative? Why deny so many things?

☐ In ordinary everyday speech some negatives make for greater clarity. We can often make clearer what we *do* mean by adding what we do *not* mean. For example, "X lives in the third house on the right; not the first one with the red door, and not the next one with black shutters, but the third one with the bird cage in the front window."

☐ The basic rule of logic (the law of non-contradiction) says that *a* cannot be *non-a*. If I say "This is a book," it cannot be a book and a house at the same time. If we were not able to make distinctions between things, speech would soon cease to mean very much. Negatives, therefore, help to establish that Christian beliefs are rational. We are not moving in a world in which *all* religious beliefs can be right and *none* wrong.

☐ A particular view of truth says in effect that there is no need for any negatives. We need never say No to any beliefs—they can all be true. According to this view you can say,
"Jesus is a revelation of God, and so is Krishna, and so is Buddha."
"God is personal and impersonal; he is kind and cruel."
This is the outlook of Hinduism and of the philosophy that follows Hegel's concept of synthesis (see p. 68).
If the Christian is speaking to those who consciously or unconsciously accept this approach, he must use some negatives if he wants to make himself understood:
"Jesus is a revelation of God; and Krishna and Buddha are not."
"God is personal and not impersonal."

☐ In presenting the Christian faith to the person who really under-

131

stands his own culture, it is essential that the Christian should say what he accepts and what he rejects in that culture.

Bonhoeffer in this significant passage shows how much he seems to accept of the assumptions of the Renaissance and of the Enlightment:

> The movement beginning about the thirteenth century . . . toward the autonomy of man (under which head I place the discovery of the laws by which the world moves and manages in science, social and political affairs, art, ethics, and religion) has in our time reached a certain completion. Man has learned to cope with all questions of importance without recourse to God as a working hypothesis. In questions concerning science, art, and even ethics, this has become an understood thing which one scarcely dares to tilt at any more. But in the last hundred years or so it has been increasingly true of religious questions also: it is becoming evident that everything gets along without "God," and just as well as before. As in the scientific field, so in human affairs generally, what we call "God" is being more and more edged out of life, losing more and more ground.

> On the historical side I should say that there is *one* great development which leads to the idea of the autonomy of the world. In theology it is first discernible in Lord Herbert of Cherbury, with his assertion that reason is the sufficient instrument of religious knowledge. In ethics it first appears in Montaigne and Bodin with their substitution of moral principles for the ten commandments. In politics, Machiavelli, who emancipates politics from the tutelage of morality, and founds the doctrine of "reasons of state." Later, and very differently, though like Machiavelli tending toward the autonomy of human society, comes Grotius, with his international law as the law of nature, a law which would still be valid *etsi deus non daretur*. The process is completed in philosophy. On the one hand we have the deism of Descartes, who holds that the world is a mechanism which runs on its own without any intervention from God. On the other hand there is the pantheism of Spinoza, with its identification of God with nature. In the last resort Kant is a deist, Fichte and Hegel pantheists. All along the line there is a growing tendency to assert the autonomy of man and the world . . .

> There is no longer any need for God as a working hypothesis, whether in morals, politics, or science.

Even if Bonhoeffer does not accept all the developments himself, he is prepared to concede these points to the person who is not a Christian. He refuses to challenge any of these developments as being a rejection of Christian assumptions.

> The attack by Christian apologetic upon the adulthood of the world I consider to be in the first place pointless, in the second ignoble, and in the third un-Christian. Pointless, because it looks to me like an attempt to put a grown-up man back into adolescence, i.e., to make him dependent on things on which he is not in fact dependent any more, thrusting him back into the midst of problems which are in fact not problems for him any more. Ignoble, because this amounts to an effort to exploit the weakness of man for purposes alien to him and not freely subscribed to by him. Un-Christian, because for Christ himself is being substituted one particular stage in the religiousness of man.

Bonhoeffer's refusal to challenge the presuppositions of naturalistic man leads him to present the Christian God in this way:

> God allows himself to be edged out of the world and on to the cross. God is weak and powerless in the world, and that is exactly the way, the only way, in which he can be with us and help us. Matthew 8:17 makes it crystal clear that it is not by his omnipotence that Christ helps us, but by his weakness and suffering . . . Man's religiosity makes him look in his distress to the power of God in the world; he uses God as a *Deus ex machina.* The Bible however directs him to the powerlessness and suffering of God; only a suffering God can help.

To the person who does not already believe, however, this language must sound like the language of symbol. It must seem like an invitation to make a leap of faith for which there are no compelling reasons.

There are right ways, and there are wrong and unkind ways in which to challenge the assumption of the autonomy of man. But if the Christian refuses at crucial points to say *No,* he is likely to find his gospel transformed into something quite different.

☐ It is sometimes suggested that while most Christians are tolerant, it is the biblical Christian who is the most intolerant. But it is only fair to point out that even those whose approach seems to be the most tolerant and all-inclusive feel the need to draw some lines and say "We cannot have this."

Emmanuel Amand de Mendieta:

> We must become more and more "intolerant" of the bigoted sectarian Catholic who is not an Evangelical, and of the bigoted and sectarian Evangelical who is not a Catholic . . . On the other hand, the so-called "moderate" Anglican, who is neither Catholic nor Evangelical, but prefers to follow a kind of practical middle way, which, for our souls' health, ought to be vigorously excluded, is even further from the Anglican vision.

☐ In serious discussion, disagreement and negation can contribute toward better understanding. We often suffer from unjustified fear of controversy. Its ultimate objective is the truth and not mere negation.

Arnold Lunn:

> The prevailing prejudice against controversy is partly due to our English distrust of logical argument and partly to a silly confusion which equates the quarrelsome with the controversial, silly because it is the inability to see another man's point of view which makes people quarrelsome, and the ability to understand the other man's position which makes a good controversialist.

☐ All the negatives in this context are intended to emphasize something very positive. *Peter*, for example, says:

> By the name of Jesus Christ of Nazareth, whom you crucified, whom God raised from the dead, by him this man is standing before you well. This is the stone which was rejected by you builders, but which has become the head of the corner. And there is salvation in no one else, for there is no other name under heaven given among men by which we must be saved.

With some writers who claim to be positive in their approach, one is forced to wonder if they have ever really felt the profound despair and nihilism of many today.

John Wren-Lewis:

> The thing that makes me angriest of all . . . is when people seize joyfully upon the failures of the modern world as occasions for urging a return to the Christian faith, for the

truth is that the real Christian faith is the very thing that
could give and should give us the confidence to press on
with our technological/humanist tasks in the belief that
there is no limit to the possibility of success.

The approach of this book does not mean seizing joyfully upon
the failures of the modern world. It means simply that one
begins with sympathy for those who feel these failures most
keenly. Then he goes on to consider the alternatives.

Simplification distorts the truth and is bound to be superficial

☐ Some kind of simplification is demanded in almost every field.
Bronowski writing about the sciences:

> What we try to reach . . . is the simplest law, that will hold
> together the total complex of our evidence.

Norman Hampson writing about history:

> As always, the historian must choose between generaliza-
> tions, which are never quite true in any specific instance,
> and an incomprehensible anarchy of individual cases.

Aldous Huxley writing about some of the dilemmas of the
modern world in his Preface to *Brave New World Revisited*:

> Life is short and information endless: nobody has time to
> do everything. In practice we are generally forced to choose
> between an unduly brief exposition and no exposition at all.
> Abbreviation is a necessary evil and the abbreviator's busi-
> ness is to make the best of a job which, though intrinsically
> bad, is still better than nothing. He must learn to simplify,
> but not to the point of falsification. He must learn to
> concentrate on the essentials of a situation, but without
> ignoring too many of the reality's qualifying side-issues. In
> this way he may be able to tell not indeed the whole truth
> (for the whole truth about almost any subject is incompat-
> ible with brevity), but considerably more than the danger-
> ous quarter-truths and half-truths which have always been
> the current coin of thought.

☐ A sense of historical perspective will remind us that specialization
and concentration on narrow fields has been forced on us comparatively recently. In the past, men had few suspicions about

the person whose knowledge covered many fields.

Norman Hampson writing about the outlook of the Enlightenment:

> The Enlightenment was, to a remarkable degree, a period when the culture of the educated man was thought to take in the whole of human knowledge . . . In dealing with an age which would have regarded the conception of "two cultures" as equivalent to no culture at all, there is perhaps as much distortion in the specialist investigation of one subject in isolation from its contemporary context, as in the more superficial survey of the period as a whole. I certainly feel that whatever insight into the Enlightenment I have been able to attain is directly due to this kind of synthetic approach.

☐ Simplicity is not necessarily always a mark of naivety or ignorance. Socrates did much of his arguing with people in the market place.

☐ There is a good theological reason for simplicity.
Jesus said:

> Truly, I say to you, whoever does not receive the kingdom of God like a child shall not enter it.

> At that time Jesus declared, "I thank thee, Father, Lord of heaven and earth, that thou hast hidden these things from the wise and understanding and revealed them to babes; yea, Father, for such was thy gracious will. All things have been delivered to me by my Father; and no one knows the Son except the Father, and no one knows the Father except the Son and any one to whom the Son chooses to reveal him. Come to me, all who labor and are heavy laden, and I will give you rest. Take my yoke upon you, and learn from me; for I am gentle and lowly in heart, and you will find rest for your souls. For my yoke is easy, and my burden is light."

Why the mania for consistency?

Aldous Huxley:

> No man is by nature exclusively domiciled in one universe . . . The only completely consistent people are the dead; the living are never anything but diverse. But such is man's pride, such is his intellectually vicious love of system and fixity, such is his terror and hatred of life, that the majority

of human beings refuse to accept the facts. Men do not
want to admit that they are what in fact they are—each one
a colony of separate individuals, of whom now one and now
another consciously lives with the life that animates the
whole organism and directs its destinies. They want, in
their pride and their terror, to be monsters of stiff consistency; they pretend, in the teeth of the facts, that they are
one person all the time, thinking one set of thoughts, pursuing one course of action throughout life.

☐ The concern for consistency is simply part of concern for the
truth. If we give up the hope of being consistent, we give up
hope of finding the truth. And Huxley's starting point is a
profound skepticism. (See p. 84). And it is perhaps not unfair to
ask where this abandonment of any concern for consistency led
him. By 1954, in his *Doors of Perception* he was advocating taking
such drugs as mescaline in order to enjoy experiences that would
reveal something of the truth of the universe. Toward the end
of his life he was still advocating drugs as the only way to solve
the problem of truth. (See p. 85.)

☐ Truth has to do with life, with the everyday business of living,
and not simply with rarified experiences. We have to live in the
world as it is, and if our philosophy of life does not correspond
with life as it is, life must become intolerable to a greater or
lesser extent. The many extracts from *Alice in Wonderland* in this
book are not included to raise a cheap laugh at the expense of
others or to mock the weaknesses of others. They are included
because they show vividly the difficulty of living in a world where
there is no consistency, where people and things do not obey the
usual laws.

John Lehmann:

Alice . . . is the representative of common sense, in a world
gone crazy. This world is inhabited by beings who put logic
before sense and feeling, only the logic happens to be
phoney, upside-down logic . . . I call them nonsense-
intellectuals. These beings—Humpty Dumpty, the March
Hare, the Mad Hatter, the Queen of Hearts, the Gryphon,
and the rest—are forever snubbing, contradicting, bossing
Alice about quite callously, and proving that *they* know best
by arguments which are nonsense but nevertheless satisfy
them. Alice knows in her heart that they are wrong, but she
cannot get the better of them in the argument game. Only
at the end of Alice in Wonderland does Alice at last score

in an argument; in the trial scene, where the King, who is conducting the trial, suddenly notices that Alice is growing larger and larger, and announces "Rule forty-two. All persons more than a mile high to leave the court." Alice immediately points out that, if the rule is the oldest in the book—as the King asserts that it is—then it ought to be rule number one. The King turns pale—and that is really the beginning of the end of the nonsense-intellectuals.

We make our own choice: if we abandon the search for consistency, we must accept the consequences.

Is there really any significant difference between the biblical answer and the others?

The biblical answer is not "Scholastic" (compare Answer 2). To say that Christian beliefs are open to verification does not mean that certain beliefs can be proved by reason apart from God's revelation. It is not a question of laying down certain axioms and then showing that Christian beliefs must necessarily follow from these axioms. This is the Scholastic approach, which lies behind the traditional arguments for the existence of God. To verify Christian beliefs means that we start with the whole system of Christian beliefs; we then test them by seeing how well they fit the facts.

It is not authoritarian (compare Answer 2). The Christian does not need to, and in fact he ought not to, speak from a position of authority. He should not say, "This is the truth and you must accept it simply because I say so, or because the infallible Bible or the infallible Church says so." There should be no suggestion of "'Will you come into my parlor?' said the spider to the fly." When the Christian is talking to the person who does not share his presuppositions, his challenge will take this form: "I am not asking you to believe simply because someone is telling you to believe. I want you to be convinced by yourself of your own free will. If you reject Christian beliefs, do your own beliefs fit the facts any better? You have to live, like anybody else. You have to eat, work, love, and die. You and I are both faced with the business of living. If this is what you believe, do you actually live in this way? Do you really live as if you believe these things to be true? Do your beliefs square with everything else that you know about yourself and about life? If you reach the point at which you realize that your beliefs do not fit the facts, then you may be prepared to think again and consider whether Christian beliefs fit the facts better."

It is not Rationalistic (compare Answer 3). Verifying Christian beliefs does not mean that they must be tailored to fit the presuppositions of every man. Testing Christian beliefs in this way does not mean altering them, or watering them down to make them acceptable to the man who has already ruled God out of his thinking. There will always be the challenge to repentance and faith, but it will not be a blind or unthinking faith. Every man has the right to ask "How can I know if this is true?" and to expect substantial answers. Repentance for the rationalist will mean reaching the point at which he realizes that he has been wrong, because his rationalism does not fit the facts, and when he decides to start with a new set of presuppositions —the Christian presuppositions.

It is not purely Existential (compare Answer 5). Verifying Christian beliefs means that we cannot bypass the question of whether they are true or not. We dare not say that we will stake our lives on these beliefs, regardless of whether or not they are objectively true. And we dare not simply believe them if our reason tells us that they are unconvincing or absurd. If we are convinced that these beliefs are true, and want to become Christians, we will need to take a *step of faith*. But it does not need to be, and ought not to be, a *leap of blind faith*. Becoming a Christian is not like throwing oneself off a cliff, not knowing whether one will land safely at the bottom. It is more like the process of finding out about another person and then knowing him personally and trusting him. Or it is like the process of learning to swim, knowing that, however strange the idea of floating in water may seem, countless other people have learned how to swim. Complete certainty will come after we have taken the step of faith, but we can be reasonably certain of the truth of Christianity even before we take the step.

It is not Mystical (compare Answer 6). We cannot hope to find out whether Christianity is true by switching off our minds and hoping to enjoy a mystical experience that will make everything clear to us. If we are convinced about Christian beliefs and take the step of faith, we will sooner or later *feel* its truth. But we cannot become Christians by trying to induce a mystical experience that bypasses our thinking processes.

139

WHERE DO WE GO FROM HERE?

If the question for you now is the evidence for the person of Jesus himself, the meaning of his death and evidence of his resurrection, turn to Part 3.

If your questions are more basic, going back to an understanding of God, man, and the universe, go on to Part 2.

PART TWO QUESTIONS OF GOD MAN AND THE UNIVERSE

The question about God is a two-part one:

☐ *Who or what is God? (the question of definition)*

☐ *Does he, if we think of him as a personal God, really exist? (the question of his existence)*

In practice, however, we cannot discuss the existence of God without discussing what we mean by the word God.

QUESTION TWO:
WHO OR WHAT IS GOD?
DOES HE EXIST?

William Koechling

There was a time when people in the western world could take it for granted that everyone had basically the same idea of what God is like. But for the vast majority these days are long past.

George Harrison:

> When you say the word *God* people are going to curl up and cringe—they all interpret it in a different way.

Alasdair MacIntyre:

> It is not just that many people no longer believe in God. Many people no longer can understand what is meant.

John Robinson:

> The word *God* is so slippery and the reality so intangible that many today are questioning whether they have reference to anything that can usefully or meaningfully be talked about at all.

The traditional arguments for the existence of God are far from convincing (see Part 1, pp. 37–50). We must therefore study in outline the different answers to the question about God which are live options in the world today, and test them by seeing how they affect beliefs about truth, man and the universe.

WHO OR WHAT IS GOD?
DOES HE EXIST?

God really exists; he is as the Bible describes him.
PAGE 148

We can never know whether or not God exists.
PAGE 167

There is no God.
PAGE 175

There is a God; but he is rather different from the Bible's description.
PAGE 160

There is no God; but the word is useful if we redefine its meaning.
PAGE 181

ANSWER ONE:
BIBLICAL CHRISTIANITY

God really exists; he is
as the Bible describes him.

*We can summarize the Bible's under-
standing of God in the following propositions. These do not exhaust the
meaning of God for the Christian, but
they do lay down certain fundamental
guidelines.*

☐ *God is personal and God is infinite*

☐ *God is the Creator of the universe and
God is the Sustainer of the universe*

☐ *God is loving and God is holy*

☐ *God is one and God is three "persons"
The corresponding propositions in each
pair must be taken closely together to
balance each other.*

For example, it is not enough to say that God is the Creator of the universe, because this says nothing about his relationship to the universe now. So the statement that he is Creator must be paired with the statement that he is the Sustainer of the universe. Similarly, when we say that God is personal, we must immediately add that he is infinite. Although he has something in common with man who is conscious of being a person, he is not subject to the limitations of human personality.

All eight propositions must be held together. If we reject or seriously modify even one of them our whole belief about God will be seriously affected. (See further under Answer 2, pp. 15ff.)

God is personal ·

☐ He is not an impersonal "It," or a force like energy or electricity. Just as men have personal names, so God in the Old Testament gives himself a personal name, Yahweh (probably meaning something like "the One who is," "the One who is there").

> God said to Moses, "I am who I am . . . the Lord (Yahweh)
> . . . this is my name for ever, and thus I am to be remembered throughout all generations . . ."

☐ He has *mind* and can think: he is not in some realm beyond thought or reason:

> For my thoughts are not your thoughts,
>   neither are your ways my ways, says the Lord.
> For as the heavens are higher than the earth,
>   so are my ways higher than your ways
>   and my thoughts than your thoughts.

☐ He has *will* and can decide and make free choices: he is not controlled by any higher power like "Fate":

> I know that the Lord is great,
>   and that our Lord is above all gods.
> Whatever the Lord pleases he does,
>   in heaven and on earth,
>   in the seas and all deeps.

☐ He has *emotions* and can feel. The prophet Hosea describes God as speaking in this way about himself:

> How can I give you up, O Ephraim! . . .
> My heart recoils within me, my compassion grows
>   warm and tender.

☐ Because he is "personal," he can communicate truth and reveal himself to men; he can enter into personal relationships with us, and we can come to know him in a personal way.

> For thus says the high and lofty One
>   who inhabits eternity, whose name is Holy:
> "I dwell in the high and holy place,
>   and also with him who is of a contrite and
>   humble spirit,
> to revive the spirit of the humble,
>   and to revive the heart of the contrite."

> The friendship of the Lord is for those who fear
>   him,
>   and he makes known to them his covenant.

God is infinite

☐ Although he is personal, he does not have the limitations of human personality. He himself was not created by someone greater.

> "You are my witnesses," says the Lord,
>   "and my servant whom I have chosen,
> that you may know and believe me
>   and understand that I am He.
> Before me no god was formed,
>   nor shall there be any after me."

☐ He has always existed and will always exist. He is not limited by time, because he has created both space and time.

> Before the mountains were brought forth
>   or ever thou hadst formed the earth and the
>   · world,
>   from everlasting to everlasting thou art God.

☐ He is not limited by the universe, because he is at work throughout it; he is omnipresent. Nothing in the universe works independently of him.

> Am I a God at hand, says the Lord, and not a God afar off? Can a man hide himself in secret places so that I cannot see him? says the Lord. Do I not fill heaven and earth? says the Lord.

☐ He knows everything; he is omniscient. He knows everything about each individual person, and about the future.

> O Lord, thou hast searched me and known me!
>> Thou knowest when I sit down and when I
>> rise up;
>> thou discernest my thoughts from afar.
> I am God, and there is none like me,
>> declaring the end from the beginning.

☐ He can do anything he wants (though he always acts "in character"); he is omnipotent. There is no Chance or Fate or Luck working independently of God.

> But he is unchangeable and who can turn him?
>> what he desires, that he does.
> For he will complete what he appoints for me;
>> and many such things are in his mind.

☐ In this prayer Habakkuk speaks of God as both personal and infinite:

> Art thou not from everlasting,
>> O Lord my God, my Holy One?

God is the Creator of the universe

☐ The universe of time and space has been brought into existence by him of his own free choice. He did not *have* to create the universe; he was perfectly complete without it.

> In the beginning God created the heavens and
>> the earth . . .
> Praise him, sun and moon,
>> praise him, all you shining stars!
> Praise him, you highest heavens,
>> and you waters above the heavens!
> Let them praise the name of the Lord!
>> For he commanded and they were created.

☐ The universe is completely distinct from God; he is transcendent. The universe is not a part of God or an emanation from God; neither is he a part of it.

> By the word of the Lord the heavens were made,
>> and all their host by the breath of his mouth.
> He gathered the waters of the sea as in a bottle;
>> he put the deeps in storehouses.
> Let all the earth fear the Lord,

let all the inhabitants of the world stand in awe
    of him!
For he spoke, and it came to be;
    he commanded, and it stood forth.

☐ God created the universe "out of nothing"; there was no "raw
material" for God simply to marshal into order.

By faith we understand that the world was created by the
word of God, so that what is seen was made out of things
which do not appear.

☐ God uses the same great power with which he created the world,
to help man in his weakness:

Have you not known? Have you not heard?
    The Lord is the everlasting God,
    the Creator of the ends of the earth.
He does not faint or grow weary,
    his understanding is unsearchable.
He gives power to the faint,
    and to him who has no might he increases
        strength.
Even youths shall faint and be weary,
    and young men shall fall exhausted;
but they who wait for the Lord
    shall renew their strength,
    they shall mount up with wings like eagles,
they shall run and not be weary,
    they shall walk and not faint.

God is the Sustainer of the universe

☐ Not only is the universe created by God, it is also "maintained"
by him. He is immanent within the universe, although he is not a
part of it. He is not merely the First Cause. He is not like the
watchmaker who leaves the watch to run by itself. The universe
could not continue without God.

O Lord my God, thou art very great!
Thou art clothed with honor and majesty,
    who coverest thyself with light as with a
        garment,
who hast stretched out the heavens like a tent . . .
Thou dost cause grass to grow for the cattle,
    and plants for man to cultivate . . .
Thou makest darkness, and it is night . . .

He covers the heavens with clouds,
he prepares rain for the earth,
he makes grass grow upon the hills.
He gives to the beasts their food,
and to the young ravens which cry.

☐ Nehemiah links together the work of God in creating and sustaining the universe:

Thou art the Lord, thou alone; thou hast made heaven, the heaven of heavens, with all their host, the earth and all that is on it, the seas and all that is in them; and thou preservest all of them.

God is loving

☐ The Old Testament speaks in many different ways of the love of God toward man whom he has created in his image:

I have loved you with an everlasting love;
therefore I have continued my faithfulness to
you.

As I live, says the Lord God, I have no pleasure in the death of the wicked, but that the wicked turn from his way and live . . .

Seek the Lord while he may be found,
call upon him while he is near;
let the wicked forsake his way,
and the unrighteous man his thoughts;
let him return to the Lord, that he may have
mercy on him,
and to our God for he will abundantly pardon.

The steadfast love of the Lord never ceases,
his mercies never come to an end;
they are new every morning;
great is thy faithfulness.

☐ In the New Testament the supreme revelation of the love of God is seen in the coming of the eternal Son:

For God so loved the world that he gave his only Son, that whoever believes in him should not perish but have eternal life.

God shows his love for us in that while we were yet sinners Christ died for us.

153

☐Some passages go further and speak of an eternal relationship of love between the Father, the Son and the Spirit. Love is thus part of the character of God: he did not become loving after he created man.

Jesus speaks in this way about the Father:

> For the Father loves the Son, and shows him all that he himself is doing . . .

He prays:

> Father, I desire that they also, whom thou hast given me, may be with me where I am, to behold my glory which thou hast given me in thy love for me before the foundation of the world.

God is holy

☐God is morally perfect; he is utterly good. He is not morally neutral; he is not beyond good and evil or above morality.

> Thou who art of purer eyes than to behold evil
> and canst not look on wrong . . .

> For thou art not a God who delights in wickedness,
> evil may not sojourn with thee.

> Thus says the Lord: "Let not the wise man glory in his wisdom, let not the mighty man glory in his might, let not the rich man glory in his riches; but let him who glories glory in this, that he understands and knows me, that I am the Lord who practice kindness, justice, and righteousness in the earth; for in these things I delight, says the Lord."

☐The moral laws he has revealed to men are an expression of his character. There is an absolute standard for right and wrong in the character of God himself.

> The Lord appeared to Abram, and said to him, "I am God Almighty; walk before me, and be blameless."

> You shall be holy; for I the Lord your God am holy.

> For the Lord is righteous, he loves righteous
> deeds;
> the upright shall behold his face.

> You shall walk before the Lord your God and fear him, and keep his commandments and obey his voice, and you shall serve him and cleave to him . . . You shall purge the evil from the midst of you.

☐ Man's revolt against God is a personal affront to him and a breach of his laws. God cannot simply overlook man's disobedience or behave as if it doesn't matter, or as if it doesn't really exist.

> . . . thou who triest the minds and hearts,
>   thou righteous God . . .
> God is a righteous judge,
>   and a God who has indignation every day.

> How can I pardon you?
>   Your children have forsaken me,
>   and have sworn by those who are no gods.
> When I fed them to the full,
>   they committed adultery
>   and trooped to the houses of harlots.
> They were well-fed lusty stallions,
>   each neighing for his neighbor's wife.
> Shall I not punish them for these things? says
>   the Lord;
>   and shall I not avenge myself on a nation such
>   as this?

> For wicked men are found among my people;
>   they lurk like fowlers lying in wait.
> They set a trap;
>   they catch men.
> Like a basket full of birds,
>   their houses are full of treachery;
> therefore they have become great and rich,
>   they have grown fat and sleek.
> They know no bounds in deeds of wickedness;
>   they judge not with justice
> the cause of the fatherless, to make it prosper,
>   and they do not defend the rights of the needy.
> Shall I not punish them for these things? says
>   the Lord,
>   and shall I not avenge myself on a nation such
>   as this?

☐ In this revelation of the character of God given to Moses we have the love of God and the holiness of God held closely together:

> The Lord passed before him, and proclaimed, "The Lord, the Lord, a God merciful and gracious, slow to anger, and abounding in steadfast love and faithfulness, keeping stead-

fast love for thousands, forgiving iniquity and transgression
and sin, but who will by no means clear the guilty."

Isaiah similarly holds together love and holiness:

> For a brief moment I forsook you,
>   but with great compassion I will gather you.
> In overflowing wrath for a moment I hid my face
>   from you,
>   but with everlasting love I will have compassion
>   on you,
>   says the Lord, your Redeemer.

There is only one God

☐ Other supernatural beings and powers do exist—Satan and the
angels; but they are all created beings, and subordinate to God.
There are not a number of gods, each controlling different parts
of the universe.

> The Lord our God is one Lord; and you shall love the
> Lord your God with all your heart, and with all your soul,
> and with all your might.

☐ Since there is only one God, all men are bound to acknowledge
him:

> I am the Lord, and there is no other,
>   besides me there is no God.
>   I gird you, though you do not know me,
> that men may know, from the rising of the sun
>   and from the west, that there is none besides
>   me;
>   I am the Lord, and there is no other.
> Turn to me and be saved,
>   all the ends of the earth!
>   For I am God, and there is no other.
> By myself I have sworn,
>   from my mouth has gone forth in righteous-
>   ness
>   a word that shall not return:
> "To me every knee shall bow,
>   every tongue shall swear."

There are three "persons" in the one God

The first Christians were orthodox Jews who had been brought
up to believe that God is one. They never abandoned their belief

that God is one. But they gradually came to understand the oneness of God in a new way, and to distinguish between the Father, the Son and the Spirit. This radical reinterpretation of the oneness of God came about because of three things:

☐ Jesus spoke of himself as "the Son" who enjoyed an intimate relationship with "the Father." This relationship had existed before the creation of the world:

> All things have been delivered to me by my Father; and no one knows the Son except the Father, and no one knows the Father except the Son and any one to whom the Son chooses to reveal him.

> And now, Father, glorify thou me in thy own presence with the glory which I had with thee before the world was made.

☐ Jesus spoke about the Holy Spirit as distinct from himself and from the Father:

> When the Counselor comes, whom I shall send to you from the Father, even the Spirit of truth, who proceeds from the Father, he will bear witness to me.

> You shall receive power when the Holy Spirit has come upon you; and you shall be my witnesses . . .

☐ The early Christians experienced God working in their lives in a radically new way, and they understood this to be the work of the Holy Spirit.

> When the day of Pentecost had come, they were all together in one place. And suddenly a sound came from heaven like the rush of a mighty wind, and it filled all the house where they were sitting. And there appeared to them tongues as of fire, distributed and resting on each one of them. And they were all filled with the Holy Spirit and began to speak in other tongues, as the Spirit gave them utterance.

> The fruit of the Spirit is love, joy, peace, patience, kindness, goodness, faithfulness, gentleness, self-control.

What kind of response does this God arouse in the believer?

Worship:

> O come, let us worship and bow down,
> let us kneel before the Lord, our Maker!

Awe and reverence:

> I through the abundance of thy steadfast love
> will enter thy house,
> I will worship toward thy holy temple
> in the fear of thee.

Thanksgiving and wonder:

> I will give thanks to the Lord with my whole
> heart;
> I will tell of all thy wonderful deeds.
> I will be glad and exult in thee,
> I will sing praise to thy name, O Most High.

Joy:

> How lovely is thy dwelling place,
> O Lord of hosts!
> My soul longs, yea, faints
> for the courts of the Lord;
> my heart and flesh sing for joy
> to the living God.

Love:

> I love thee, O Lord, my strength.

Trust:

> The Lord is my strength and my shield;
> in him my heart trusts;
> so I am helped, and my heart exults,
> and with my song I give thanks to him.

HOW THIS UNDERSTANDING OF GOD AFFECTS OUR UNDERSTANDING OF TRUTH, MAN, AND THE UNIVERSE

TRUTH

If God is personal and has something in common with man,
then there is no reason why God should not be able to communicate truth in different ways to the minds of men. There is no reason why he should not be able to communicate truth in words.

If there are three persons within the Godhead,
then there can be communication between them; and it is not
strange to think of this kind of God wanting to communicate
also with man whom he has made in his image.

If there are three persons,
then it becomes possible to think of the Son becoming man in
order to reveal God more fully.

See further Part 1, pp. 5–36.

MAN

If man is a creature of God, created by deliberate choice and not
the product of a chance process, which could easily have produced something different,
then we have at least a starting-point for understanding and
explaining the dignity of man, and finding answers to the questions of man.

See further, pp. 219ff.

THE UNIVERSE

If the universe has been created by God and is even now sustained by God,
then we have a starting-point for understanding its complexity,
order, and beauty, and for finding answers to the basic questions
about the universe.

See further, pp. 335ff.

*Problems and Questions arising out of
biblical Christianity's answer to the
question "Who or what is God? Does
he exist?" are taken up on pp. 197ff.*

ANSWER TWO:
PRIMAL RELIGION AND JUDAISM, ISLAM AND DEISM

There is a God; but he is rather different from the Bible's description.

The concept of God in these religions differs from the Christian concept in certain important respects:

Some have no knowledge of certain aspects of the Christian understanding of God; or they ignore or deny them

*(that God is infinite, for example, or
that there are three persons in one God,
or that he can be known in a personal
way).*

Primal religion

In all the primal religions there is a strong awareness of the
existence of a personal God. Examples are taken from African
religions, which have much in common with primal religions in
other continents.

John Mbiti:

> African knowledge of God is expressed in proverbs, short
> statements, songs, prayers, names, myths, stories and re-
> ligious ceremonies. All these are easy to remember and pass
> on to other people, since there are no sacred writings in
> traditional societies. One should not, therefore, expect long
> dissertations about God. But God is no stranger to African
> peoples, and in traditional life there are no atheists. This is
> summarized in an Ashanti proverb that "no one shows a
> child the Supreme Being." That means that everybody
> knows of God's existence almost by instinct, and even chil-
> dren know Him.

This God, however, has withdrawn himself. He exists, but he
is too distant for any man to enjoy communion with him.

John Mbiti:

> It is particularly as Spirit that God is incomprehensible. So
> the Ashanti rightly refer to Him as "the fathomless Spirit,"
> since no human mind can measure Him, no intellect can
> comprehend or grasp Him . . . Many people readily admit
> that they do not know what God is like, and that they do
> not possess the words of God—since words are vehicles of
> someone's thoughts and to a certain degree they give a
> portrait of the speaker. Some even say that God's proper
> name is unknown; or give Him a name like that of the
> Lunda, which means or signifies "the God of the Un-
> known," or that of the Ngombe which means "the Unex-
> plainable," or of the Maasai which means "the Unknown."
> A person's name in African societies generally has a mean-
> ing descriptive of His personality and being. In the case of
> God, people might know some of His activities and mani-
> festations, but of His essential nature they know nothing. It
> is a paradox that they "know" Him, and yet they do not

"know" Him; He is not a Stranger to them, and yet they are strangers to Him; He knows them, but they do not know Him. So God confronts men as the mysterious and incomprehensible, as indescribable and beyond human vocabulary. This is part of the essential nature of God.

The remoteness and unknowableness of God also calls for different kinds of mediators to put man in touch with the power which controls the universe. In this way the spirits of the ancestors and witch doctors come to play an important role in man's quest for health, happiness and security.

It was once thought that primitive religion as practiced by many tribes all over the world is the nearest thing one can find to the original religion of man. But the evidence is more easily explained by the assumption that this form of religion has developed (or degenerated) from an original worship of the one Creator-God.

Robert Brow:

> Led by Fr. Wilhelm Schmidt of Vienna, anthropologists have shown that the religion of the hundreds of isolated tribes in the world today is not primitive in the sense of being original. The tribes have a memory of a "High God," a benign Creator-Father-God, who is no longer worshiped because he is not feared. Instead of offering sacrifice to him, they concern themselves with the pressing problems of how to appease the vicious spirits of the jungle. The threats of the witch doctor are more strident than the still, small voice of the Father-God.
>
> We see, then, that the evolution of religion from a primitive Animatism can no longer be assumed as axiomatic and that some anthropologists now suggest that Monotheism may be more naturally primitive as a world-view than Animism. Their research suggests that tribes are not animistic because they have continued unchanged since the dawn of history. Rather, the evidence indicates degeneration from a true knowledge of God. Isolation from prophets and religious books has ensnared them into sacrificial bribery to placate the spirits instead of joyous sacrificial meals in the presence of the Creator.

Judaism

The understanding of God in Judaism is based on the Old Testament, and thus has a great deal in common with the Christian understanding.

Roy A. Stewart:

Jew and Christian agree on certain essential characteristics
of God . . . A working basis for the doctrine of God, acceptable at least in outline to either faith, may be posited as
follows. *God is One and unique, eternally existing, endowed with
limitless power and knowledge, present throughout His creation,
throned in unimaginable transcendent splendor, yet close to
every creature, supreme in His decrees, righteous, just, holy and
merciful.*

The only one of the eight propositions which Judaism denies is
that there are three "Persons" in the one God. But this denial
has a profound effect on the interpretation of the other beliefs
about God.

Islam

The Qur'an lays great emphasis on the oneness of God, his
transcendence and power, and his lordship over the whole universe.

Allah: there is no god but Him, the Living, the Eternal
One. Neither slumber nor sleep overtakes Him. His is what
the heavens and the earth contain. Who can intercede with
Him except by His permission? He knows what is before and
behind men. They can grasp only that part of His knowledge which He wills. His throne is as vast as the heavens
and the earth, and the preservation of both does not weary
Him. He is the Exalted, the Immense One.

He is Allah, besides whom there is no other god. He is the
Sovereign Lord, the Holy One, the Giver of Peace, the
Keeper of Faith; the Guardian, the Mighty One, the All-
powerful, the Most High! Exalted be He above their idols!
He is Allah, the Creator, the Originator, the Modeler. His
are the most gracious names. All that is in heaven and
earth gives glory to Him. He is the Mighty, the Wise One.

One result of this emphasis on the sovereignty of God is that
it is very difficult to establish any point of contact between God
and man, and God can hardly be known.

Al-Junayd, the ninth-century mystic:

No one knows God save God Himself Most High, and
therefore even to the best of His creatures He has only
revealed His names in which He hides himself.

This kind of agnosticism about the nature of God has led

many Muslims to move toward the mystical faith of the Sufis. Much of the teaching of Sufism, instead of being rejected as heretical, has been accepted into the mainstream of Islamic thought.

Reynold Nicholson, writing about the Qur'an:

> Are there any germs of mysticism to be found there (in the Koran)? The Koran . . . starts with the notion of Allah, the One, Eternal, and Almighty God, far above human feelings and aspirations—the Lord of His slaves, not the Father of His children; a judge meting out stern justice to sinners, and extending His mercy only to those who avert His wrath by repentance, humility, and unceasing works of devotion; a God of fear rather than of love. This is one side, and certainly the most prominent side, of Mohammed's teaching; but while he set an impassable gulf between the world and Allah, his deeper instinct craved a direct revelation from God to the soul. There are no contradictions in the logic of feeling. Mohammed, who had in him something of the mystic, felt God both as far and near, both as transcendent and immanent. In the latter aspect, Allah is the light of the heavens and the earth, a Being who worked in the world and in the soul of man.

Writing about the development of Islamic theology, he says:

> The champions of orthodoxy had set about constructing a system of scholastic philosophy that reduced God's nature to a purely formal, changeless, and absolute unity, a bare will devoid of all affections and emotions, a tremendous and incalculable power with which no human creature could have any communion or personal intercourse whatsoever. That is the God of Mohammedan theology. That was the alternative to Sufism. Therefore, "all thinking, relious Moslems are mystics," as Professor D. B. Macdonald, one of our best authorities on the subject, has remarked. And he adds: "All, too, are pantheists, but some do not know it."

Another consequence of the Islamic belief about God is that God's attitude toward man tends to be defined in terms of compassion and mercy, rather than love. These, for example, are some of the Ninety-nine Names of God:

> The Merciful; the Compassionate, the Forgiver, the Forgiving; the Clement, the Generous, the Affectionate, the Kind.

If the Muslim ever speaks about the love of God, he thinks not so much of God's love for man, as man's love for God, as the response which is aroused by contemplating the attributes of God.

Ahmad Galwash, a contemporary apologist:

> Rightly to understand the love of God is so difficult a matter that one sect of philosophers have altogether denied that man can love a being who is not of his own species, and they have defined the love of God as consisting merely in obedience to Him. But this is not true . . . The following prayer was taught by the Arabian Prophet to his followers: *"O God, grant me to love Thee and to love those who love Thee, and whatsoever brings me nearer to Thy love, and make Thy love dearer to me than cold water to the thirsty traveler in the desert."*

> We now come to treat love in its essential nature, according to the spiritual Muslim conception. Love may be defined as an inclination to that which is pleasant.

The Muslim is probably forced to speak of the mercy and compassion of God rather than the love of God because love sounds too human a word to apply to God. One could also say that if God is one in the sense that the Muslim understands, it does not make sense, logically, to speak of love as being part of the character of God. Love by definition demands an object, unless it is to become self-love. And if there is no Trinity which allows a relationship of love between the three persons of the godhead, then the only possible object of the love of God can be the universe and man. But this makes it difficult to think of God as sufficient in himself and not dependent on the existence of the universe.

Deism

The Deists of the eighteenth century did not deny the existence of God. They simply denied or ignored certain aspects of the traditional Christian teaching about God. Gradually, however, the idea of God was so emptied of content that hardly anything could be said about him.

Joseph Joubert:

> God has withdrawn within himself and hidden within the bosom of his own being; withdrawn even as the sun, when it hides behind a cloud. The sun of the spirit is visible to them no more . . . With nothing now to wake them to ecstasy, nothing to excite their lofty contemplation, able no

more to gaze upon God, they busy themselves with the world.

Voltaire:

I shall always be convinced that a watch proves a watchmaker, and that a universe proves a God.

I believe in God, not the God of the mystics and the theologians, but the God of nature, the great geometrician, the architect of the universe, the prime mover, unalterable, transcendental, everlasting.

Paul Hazard, writing about the God of the Deists:

God was to remain, but a God so remote, so watered down, so pallid that his presence imposed no constraint on the City of Men. He would neither visit them with his wrath, nor bedazzle them with his glory . . .

Deism had recourse to a sort of filtering process. If we strain off whatever strikes us as superstitious in the Church of Rome, in the Reformed Church, and in every other church and sect, what remains at the conclusion of the process will be God; a God whom we know not, and whom we cannot know. Hardly anything has been left to him save the bare fact of his existence. Of all the possible adjectives, he was awarded the one which was at once the most honorable and the most vague; he was called the Supreme Being.

HOW THIS UNDERSTANDING OF GOD AFFECTS OUR UNDERSTANDING OF TRUTH, MAN, AND THE UNIVERSE

The clearest way of seeing where these different beliefs about God lead—and the problems and questions they raise—is to apply them to the questions of truth (see Part 1, especially pp. 37–85), man (see pp. 243ff.) and the universe (see pp. 350f.).

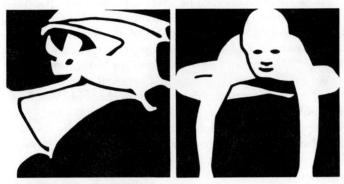

ANSWER THREE:
AGNOSTICISM AND MYSTICISM

We can never know
whether or not God
exists.

*Some of the great European thinkers
join with Hinduism and Buddhism in
returning a "don't know" answer to the
question of the existence of God. (See
also Part 1, pp. 64ff. for further examples and discussion of agnosticism.)*

European thinkers

The Deists of the eighteenth century ignored or denied or modified some of the aspects of the biblical understanding of God
(see pp. 148ff.). It was not long before some took this skepticism
one step further and said: "God *may* exist; but we just do not
know, and we have no way of knowing for sure." (See Part 1, pp.
64ff.)

Thomas Hobbes's agnosticism is summed up in this way by Basil
Willey:

It is, then, the God of deism—first mover and designer of
the world-machine—that Hobbes offers as a substitute for

Zeus or Jehovah. But even to say that he "offers" this is an overstatement. For him the word *God* is really little but a symbol of the philosopher's fatigue. In his quest for truth the investigator at last reaches the limits of human capacity; then, in sheer weariness, he gives over, and says "God" . . . And it is noticeable that in speaking of God his main endeavor is to empty this conception of all content. Of that which has not reached us through the senses we can have no "image," thus we can have no "idea" or "conception" of God. We can only speak of him in a series of negatives, such as "infinite," "immutable," "incomprehensible," or in terms signifying his remoteness from our mortal state, such as "omnipotent," "most high," and the like. All these "attributes" are really "pseudo-statements," that is to say, the reality to which they point is just simply our own pious disposition.

Thomas Carlyle, in the nineteenth century:

The name (of God) has become as if obsolete to the most devout of us; and it is, to the huge idly impious million of writing, preaching, and talking people as if the *fact* too had quite ceased to be certain.

Hinduism

Hinduism starts from a profound agnosticism about the nature of God.

Radhakrishnan:

The Hindu never doubted the reality of the one supreme universal spirit, however much the descriptions of it may fall short of its nature. Whatever the doctrinaires may say, the saints of God are anxious to affirm that much is hidden from their sight. God hideth himself. It is a sound religious agnosticism which bids us hold our peace regarding the nature of the supreme spirit. Silence is more significant than speech regarding the depths of the divine. The altars erected to the unknown gods in the Graeco-Roman world were but an expression of man's ignorance of the divine nature. The sense of failure in man's quest for the unseen is symbolized by them. When asked to define the nature of God, the seer of the Upanishad sat silent, and when pressed to answer exclaimed that the Absolute is silence. The mystery of the divine reality eludes the machinery of speech and symbol. The "Divine Darkness," "That of which nothing can be said," and such other expressions are used by the devout when they attempt to describe their consciousness of direct communion with God.

See further pp. 182ff. for other Hindu definitions of the word *God.*

Buddhism

Christmas Humphreys would not use the word "agnostic" about the Buddhist understanding of God; but his description of the Buddhist position fits more easily into this category than that of the theist or the atheist, and is similar to that of some western mystics like Eckhart:

> As between the theist and atheist positions, Buddhism is atheistic, but it would be more correct to say that it analyzes the complex of conflicting ideas comprised in the term *God* with the same dispassionate care as it analyzes the so-called soul. Such analysis, which all are pressed to make for themselves, proves, say Buddhists, that the Western ideas are inaccurate and inadequate. The Buddhist teaching on God, in the sense of an ultimate Reality, is neither agnostic, as is sometimes claimed, nor vague, but clear and logical. Whatever Reality may be, it is beyond the conception of the finite intellect; it follows that attempts at description are misleading, unprofitable, and waste of time. For these good reasons the Buddha maintained about Reality "a noble silence." If there *is* a Causeless Cause of all Causes, an Ultimate Reality, a Boundless Light, an Eternal Noumenon behind phenomena, it must clearly be infinite, unlimited, unconditioned and without attributes. We, on the other hand, are clearly finite, and limited and conditioned by, and in a sense composed of, innumerable attributes. It follows that we can neither define, describe, nor usefully discuss the nature of *That* which is beyond the comprehension of our finite consciousness. It may be indicated by negatives and described indirectly by analogy and symbols, but otherwise it must ever remain in its truest sense unknown and unexpressed, as being to us in our present state unknowable.

Mysticism

The Mystic generally starts from the same position as the agnostic: he denies the possibility of knowing God with his mind. But he believes that knowledge of God of a different kind *is* possi-

169

ble—and this is a knowledge based purely on the mystical experience of union with God (see Part 1, pp. 110ff.).

Meister Eckhart (?1260–?1327) writes that knowledge of God is only possible through union with him:

> Know'st thou of him anything? He is no such thing, and in that thou dost know of him anything at all thou art in ignorance, and ignorance leads to the condition of the brute; for in creatures what is ignorant is brutish. If thou wouldst not be brutish then, know nothing of the unuttered God.—"What then shall I do?"—Thou shalt lose thy thy-ness and dissolve in his his-ness; thy thine shall be his mine, so utterly one mine that thou in him shalt know eternalwise his is-ness, free from becoming; his nameless nothingness.

The Cloud of Unknowing (an anonymous work of the four-teenth-century) speaks of "love" as a way of knowing God:

> All rational beings, angels and men, possess two faculties, the power of knowing and the power of loving. To the first, to the intellect, God who made them is forever un-knowable, but to the second, to love, he is completely know-able, and that by every separate individual. So much so that one loving soul by itself, through its love, may know for itself him who is incomparably more than sufficient to fill all souls that exist.

> Whoever hears or reads about all this, and thinks that it is fundamentally an activity of the mind, and proceeds then to work it all out along these lines, is on quite the wrong track . . . Do not attempt to achieve this experience intellec-tually. I tell you truly that it cannot come this way . . .

> By "darkness" I mean "a lack of knowing"—just as anything that you do not know or may have forgotten may be said to be "dark" to you, for you cannot see it with your inward eye. For this reason it is called "a cloud," not of the sky, of course, but "of unknowing," a cloud of unknowing between you and your God.

With the Beat movement in America in the 1950s religious mysticism with a Buddhist flavor became the basis for a popular philosophy which is still being worked out in the popular arts.

Jack Kerouac, the Beat movement's chronicler, attempted to describe his experience, in the character of Ray Smith, in *The Dharma Bums*:

And then I thought, later, lying on my bag smoking, "Everything is possible. I am God, I am Buddha, I am imperfect Ray Smith, all at the same time, I am empty space, I am all things. I have all the time in the world from life to life to do what is to do, to do what is done, to do the timeless doing, infinitely perfect within, why cry, why worry, perfect like mind essence and the minds of banana peels," I added laughing remembering my poetic Zen Lunatic Dharma Bum friends of San Francisco whom I was beginning to miss now. And I added a little prayer for Rosie.

Kerouac's advice was reprinted in 1971 in a book of poetry called *Amazing Grace*:

Wait awhile, close your eyes, let your breathing stop three seconds or so, listen to the inside silence in the womb of the world, let the bliss you forgot, the emptiness and essence and ecstasy of ever having been and ever to be the golden eternity. This is the lesson you forgot.

Tom Wolfe wrote about the experience of Ken Kesey and his Merry Pranksters in the early days of Haight-Ashbury in *The Electric Kool-Aid Acid Test*:

Gradually the Prankster attitude began to involve the main things religious mystics have always felt, things common to Hindus, Buddhists, Christians, and for that matter Theosophists and even flying-saucer cultists. Namely, the *experiencing* of an Other World, a higher level of reality. And a perception of the cosmic unity of this higher level. And a feeling of timelessness, the feeling that what we know as time is only the result of a naive faith in causality . . .

There was something so . . . *religious* in the air, in the very atmosphere of the Prankster life, and yet one couldn't put one's finger on it. On the face of it there was just a group of people who had shared an unusual psychological state, the LSD experience—

But exactly! The *experience*—that was the word! and it began to fall into place. In fact, none of the great founded religions, Christianity, Buddhism, Islam, Jainism, Judaism, Zoroastrianism, Hinduism, none of them began with a philosophical framework or even a main idea. They all began with an overwhelming *new experience*, what Joachin Wach called "the experience of the holy," and Max Weber, "possession of the deity," the sense of being a vessel of the divine, of the All-one.

Every vision, every insight of the . . . original . . . circle always came out of the *new experience* . . . the *kairos* . . . and how to tell it! How to get it across to the multitudes who have never had this experience for themselves? *You couldn't put it into words.* You had to create conditions in which they would feel an approximation of *that feeling,* the sublime *kairos.* You had to put them into ecstasy . . . Buddhist monks immersing themselves in cosmic love through fasting and contemplation, Hindus zonked out in Bhakti, which is fervent love in the possession of God, ecstatics flooding themselves with Krishna through sexual orgies or plunging into the dinners of the Bacchanalia, Christians off in Edge City through gnostic onanism or the Heart of Jesus or the Child Jesus with its running sore—or—

THE ACID TESTS

And suddenly Kesey sees that they, the Pranksters, already have the expertise and the machinery to create a mind-blown state such as the world has never seen, totally wound up, lit up, amplified and . . . controlled—plus the most efficient key ever devised to open the doors in the mind of the world: namely, Owlsley's LSD.

The Beatles did a lot to draw both the LSD experience and eastern mysticism together and to express it in their music. The first thing to do is to turn off your mind:

Turn off your mind relax and float
down-stream,
it is not dying, it is not dying,
lay down all thought surrender to the void,
it is shining, it is shining.
That you may see the meaning of within,
it is speaking, it is speaking,
that love is all and love is ev'ryone,
it is knowing, it is knowing.
Without going out of my door.
I can know all things on earth.
Without looking out of my window
I could know the ways of heaven

The Rock musical *Hair* tried to sum up the feeling of moving towards a mystical understanding for everyone:

Harmony and Understanding,
Sympathy and Trust abounding,
No more falsehoods or derisions.
Golden living dreams of visions,
Mystic crystal revelation,
And the mind's true liberation,
This is the dawning of the Age of Aquarius . . .

PROBLEMS
AND QUESTIONS

If we can't know about God, can we be sure we know about anything else?

In most cases, agnosticism about the existence of God or the character of God is closely connected with agnosticism about truth in general.

Albert Camus:

> Contemporary unbelief does not rest on science as it did toward the close of the last century. It denies both science and religion. It is no longer the skepticism of reason in the presence of miracle. It is a passionate unbelief.

Sartre's novel *Nausea:*

> I am beginning to believe that nothing can ever be proved. These are reasonable hypotheses which take the facts into account: but I am only too well aware that they come from me, that they are simply a way of unifying my own knowledge. The question of truth is therefore even more fundamental than the question of God's existence.

See further Agnosticism, Part 1, pp. 64–85.

Is anyone really satisfied with pure agnosticism?

It is very hard for most people to be content with the bare answer of agnosticism. Their restlessness has usually led them *beyond* the point of pure agnosticism.

Baron von Hugel, writing in 1916, sums up in some prophetic words how dissatisfaction with agnosticism would lead many to the answer of pantheism:

> Agnosticism is going, going, gone. Not it, but Pantheism is now and will long be, the danger of religion.

See further, pp. 181ff.

If we do not know, we must act as if God does *not* exist

The agnostic has to live in practice as if there is no God.

Somerset Maugham:

> In religion above all things the only thing of use is an
> objective truth. The only God that is of use is a being who
> is personal, supreme, and good, and whose existence is as
> certain as that two and two makes four. I cannot penetrate
> the mystery. I remain an agnostic, and the practical out-
> come of agnosticism is that you act as though God did not
> exist.

See further Atheism, pp. 175ff. and Question Three, "What is
Man?," pp. 209ff.

ANSWER FOUR:
ATHEISM
There is no God.

Whereas the agnostic says, "God may exist, but we shall never know," (see pp. 167ff.), the atheist says categorically "God does not exist; there is no one there."

Nietzsche, writing in 1882:

Have you not heard of the madman who lit a lamp in broad daylight and ran up and down the market place shouting incessantly, "I'm looking for God! I'm looking for God!" But, because many of the people who were standing there did not believe in God, he aroused a good deal of mirth . . . But the madman thrust in between them and fixed them with his eyes. "Where is God?" he shouted. "I'll tell you! We have killed him—you and I! We are all his murderers! But how have we done it? How could we drink the sea dry? Who gave us the sponge to wipe away the horizon? What did we do when we uncoupled the earth from its sun? Where is the earth moving to now? Where are we moving to? Away from all suns? Are we not running incessantly? Backwards, sideways and forwards, in all directions? Is there still an above and a below? Are we not wandering through an infinite nothing? Is not the void yawning ahead of us? Has it not become colder? Is it not more and more night? Do the lamps not have to be lit during the day? Do we hear nothing of the noise of the gravediggers who are burying God? Do we smell nothing of the decomposition of God? The gods are decomposing! God is dead! God is dead! And we have killed him! . . . I have come too soon! My time has not yet come. This terrible event is still coming."

Matthew Arnold, writing in 1882, speaks of the widespread rejection of Christian beliefs on the Continent of Europe, while most Englishmen were completely unaware of what was happening:

The partisans of traditional religion in this country do not know, I think, how decisively the whole force of progressive and liberal opinion on the Continent has pronounced against the Christian religion.

Martin Esslin, writing about the implications of Nietzsche's atheism in his book *The Theatre of the Absurd*:

Zarathustra was first published in 1883. The number of people for whom God is dead has greatly increased since Nietzsche's day, and mankind has learned the bitter lesson of the falseness and evil nature of some of the cheap substitutes that have been set up to take his place. And so, after two terrible wars, there are still many who are trying to come to terms with the implications of Zarathustra's message, searching for a way in which they can, with dignity, confront a universe deprived of what was once its center and its living purpose, a world deprived of a generally accepted integrating principle, which has become disjointed, purposeless—absurd.

The Theatre of the Absurd is one of the expressions of this search.

Arthur Adamov, the playwright, quoted in *The Theatre of the Absurd*:

The name of God should no longer come from the mouth of man. This word that has so long been degraded by usage no longer means anything . . . To use the word *God* is more than sloth, it is refusal to think, a kind of short cut, a hideous shorthand.

A. J. Ayer:

I do not believe in God. It seems to me that theists of all kinds have largely failed to make their concept of a deity intelligible; and to the extent that they have made it intelligible they have given no reason to think that anything answers to it.

Jean-Paul Sartre, describing the religious atmosphere in which he was brought up and which contributed to his atheism:

My family had been affected by the slow dechristianization which was born in the Voltaire-influenced *haute bourgeoisie* and took a century to spread to every stratum of Society: without this general slackening of faith, Louise Guillemin, a young Catholic lady from the provinces, would have made more fuss about marrying a Lutheran. Naturally, everyone at home believed: for reasons of discretion . . . An atheist was an eccentric, a hot-head whom you did not invite to dinner lest he "create a scandal," a fanatic burdened with taboos who denied himself the right to kneel in church, to marry his daughters or indulge in tears there, who took it on himself to prove the truth of his doctrine by the purity of his conduct, who injured himself and his happiness to the extent of robbing himself of his means of dying comforted, a man with a phobia about God who saw his absence everywhere and who could not open his mouth without saying His name: in short, a Gentleman with religious convictions. The believer had none: for two thousand years the Christian certainties had had time to prove themselves; they belonged to everyone, and they were required to shine in the priest's glance, in the half-light of a church, and to illumine souls, but no one needed to appropriate them to himself; they were the common patrimony. Polite society believed in God so that it need not talk of Him. How tolerant religion seemed! How convenient it was: the Christian could abandon Mass and yet marry his children in church, smile at the religious "art" of the Place Saint-Sulpice and shed tears as he listened to the Wedding March from Lohengrin; he was not obliged to lead an exemplary life or to die in despair, or even to have himself cremated.

In our circle, in my family, faith was nothing but an official name for sweet French liberty; I had been baptized, like so many others, to preserve my independence: in refusing me baptism, they would have been afraid of doing harm to my soul; as a registered Catholic, I was free, I was normal. "Later on," they said, "he can do as he pleases." It was reckoned, at the time, far harder to acquire faith than to lose it.

Deep down, it all bored me to death; I was led to unbelief not through conflicting dogma but through my grandparents' indifference. Yet I believed: in my nightshirt, kneeling on my bed, hands folded, I said my daily prayer but thought less and less often about the good God . . . For several years longer, I kept up public relations with the Almighty; in private, I stopped associating with Him. Only once I had the feeling that He existed. I had been playing with matches and had burnt a mat; I was busy covering up my crime when suddenly God saw me. I felt His gaze inside my head and on my hands; I turned round and round in the bathroom, horribly visible, a living target. I was saved by indignation: I grew angry at such a crude lack of tact, and blasphemed, muttering like my grandfather: *"Sacre nom de Dieu de nom de Dieu de nom de Dieu."* He never looked at me again.

I have just told the story of a missed vocation; I needed God, he was given to me, and I received him without understanding what I was looking for. Unable to take root in my heart, he vegetated in me for a while and then died. Today, when he is mentioned, I say with the amusement and lack of regret of some aging beau who meets an old flame: "Fifty years ago, without that misunderstanding, without that mistake, without the accident which separated us, there might have been something between us."

Nothing happened between us . . .

Atheism is a cruel, long-term business: I believe I have gone through it to the end.

PROBLEMS AND QUESTIONS

How do you know?

It is usually the Christian who is challenged with this question and asked to give a reasonable basis for his belief in God, and he ought to be able to give some solid reasons.

But the Christian has every right to challenge the atheist with the same question and ask: how do *you know for certain* that there is no God? Is there a reasonable basis for your atheism? On what grounds do you base your belief? How do you know that your atheism is true?

The atheist will probably give the answer of the Rationalist (see Part 1, pp. 56–63).

But if he shrinks from defending his belief in this way, he will probably have to take refuge in the answer of Agnosticism (see p. 167 and Part 1, pp. 64–85).

If we don't believe in God, what do we believe about man?

Albert Camus, writing about the significance of Nietzsche's atheism:

> We sense the change of position that Nietzsche makes. With him, rebellion begins at "God is dead" which is assumed as an established fact . . . Contrary to the opinion of certain of his Christian critics, Nietzsche did not form a project to kill God. He found Him dead in the soul of his contemporaries. He was the first to understand the immense importance of the event and to decide that this rebellion among men could not lead to a renaissance unless it were controlled and directed.

Nietzsche believed that atheism opened new horizons:

> The most important of more recent events—that "god is dead," that the belief in the Christian God has become unworthy of belief—already begins to cast its first shadows over Europe . . . In fact, we philosophers and "free spirits" feel ourselves irradiated as by a new dawn by the report that the "old God is dead"; our hearts overflow with gratitude, astonishment, presentiment, and expectation. At last the horizon seems open once more, granting even that it is not bright; our ships can at last put out to sea in face of every danger; every hazard is again permitted to the discerner; the sea, *our* sea, again lies open before us; perhaps never before did such an "open sea" exist.

Michael Harrington writes of those who have passed beyond this exhilaration to a profound pessimism:

> After God died, Man, who was supposed to replace Him,

grew sick of himself. This resulted in a crisis of belief and disbelief which made the twentieth century spiritually empty.

God died in the nineteenth century. Nietzsche announced the event as a fact, not as an argument, and his report has been taken as the starting point of most serious theology ever since . . .

But since God did not have any heir, the funeral has been going on for over a hundred years. The nineteenth century predicted often enough that the modern world would dispel faith. It did not, however, expect that it would subvert anti-faith as well.

Jean-Paul Sartre:

And when we speak of "abandonment"—a favorite word of Heidegger—we only mean to say that God does not exist, and that it is necessary to draw the consequences of his absence right to the end.

The discussion must therefore move from the question of *God* to the question of *man*. See further, Question Three, "What is Man?," pp. 209ff.

ANSWER FIVE:
PANTHEISM AND SOME
MODERN THEOLOGIANS

There is no God; but
the word is useful if
we redefine its
meaning.

> *Certain conclusions seem to follow
> from thoroughgoing atheism or agnos-
> ticism:*
>
> ☐ *What we have in the universe is all
> there is; there is nothing beyond what
> we can see or touch—no unseen super-
> natural world.*
>
> ☐ *Death is the end of the individual;
> there is no life beyond.*
> *But not everyone is prepared to accept
> these conclusions as inevitable, to live*

with the idea that there is nothing beyond appearances, nothing but the present.

Although many are consistent and build their philosophies on these assumptions—e.g. Communism, Existentialism and Humanism (see Man, pp. 255ff.)—others are only too conscious of the vacuum created by the "death" of God and the supernatural. They are anxious to find some belief that will account for their sense of awe and mystery as they look at the universe, and give it some meaning.

Those who take this course tend to retain the word *God* and words such as *divinity* and *transcendence,* but they give them different meanings. This position has many different forms of expression, but they all have certain features in common:

☐ "God" does not mean a Personal Being who is distinct from the universe and was there "before" the universe was created.

☐ "God" is identified in some way with the universe as a whole or with some part or aspect of it (e.g., the spirit or consciousness of man, the "personal" aspect of the universe).

Hindu Pantheism

Hinduism, as we now understand it, sprang from a reaction against the debased polytheistic religion which developed in India before the eighth century B.C.

Robert Brow, writing about the religion which the Aryan invaders took with them to India in the second millennium B.C.:

> If we could look down on the ancient world about 1500 B.C. we would see ordinary men and women still offering animal sacrifices as their normal way of approaching God or the gods. The earliest literature of India, the Sanskrit *Vedas,* picture the nomadic Aryan tribes who fought their way eastwards across the Indus and Ganges plains. The head of the family offered animal sacrifice with the same simplicity as Abraham. When they settled in India the Aryans developed a regular priesthood, and the *Vedas* are the hymns which the priests chanted as the sacrificial smoke ascended to God. Their hymns address God under various names such as "The Sun," "The Heavenly One," and "The Storm," but the interesting thing is that, whatever name they give to God, they worshiped him as the Supreme Ruler of the universe. This practice is called *Henotheism.* God has several

names, just as Christians today have several names for God, but the names do not indicate different gods. They are different facets of the one God. Henotheism changes into Polytheism when the names of God are so personified that various gods are separated, and they begin to disagree and fight among themselves. The later Vedic literature has certainly become polytheistic by, say, 1000 B.C., but the earliest Aryans must have been Monotheists.

Then, after believing in the existence of many gods, someone took the step of identifying "God" more closely with the universe and saying "God is *not different* from or distinct from the universe. God *is* everything there is, and everything there is *is* God."

It is important to realize, however, that not all forms of Pantheism are quite as simple and crude as this. *Robert Brow* distinguishes four variations or refinements on this basic theme:

1. "Everything there is is God." (Absolute Pantheism)
2. "God is the reality or principle behind nature." (Modified Pantheism)
3. "God is to nature as soul is to body." (Modified Monism)
4. "Only God is reality. All else is imagination." (Absolute Monism).

The nearest word to "God" in Hinduism is "Brahman," the Universal Spirit. In the *Upanishads* he is described as the one Divine Being . . .

> hidden in all beings, all-pervading, the self within all beings, watching over all works, dwelling in all beings, the witness, the perceiver, the only one, free from all qualities. He is the one ruler of many who (seem to act, but really) do not act; he makes the one seed manifold.

In the *Bhagavad Gita*, the Brahman "speaks" to Arjuna through Krishna in these words:

> Listen and I shall reveal to thee some manifestations of my divine glory . . .

> I am the soul, prince victorious, which dwells in the heart of all things. I am the beginning, the middle, and the end of all that lives . . .

> Among the sons of light I am Vishnu, and of luminaries the radiant sun. I am the lord of the winds and storms, and of the lights in the night I am the moon.

> Of the Vedas I am the Veda of songs, and I am Indra, the

chief of the gods. Above man's senses I am the mind, and in all living beings I am the light of consciousness.

Among the terrible powers I am the god of destruction . . .

I am time, never-ending time. I am the Creator who sees all. I am death that carries off all things, and I am the source of things to come.

And know, Arjuna, that I am the seed of all things that are; and that no being that moves or moves not can ever be without me . . .

Know thou that whatever is beautiful and good, whatever has glory and power is only a portion of my own radiance.

But of what help is it to thee to know this diversity? Know that with one single fraction of my Being I pervade and support the Universe, and know that I AM.

In the many traditions of Hindu philosophy, "God" may be *either* personal *or* impersonal: or "God" may be *both* personal *and* impersonal.

H. D. Lewis:

All that can be said is that the scriptures provide grist for the mills of both theistic and monistic interpretations which come later in Hindu story, with more grist, perhaps, for the monist than for the theist.

This different understanding of the meaning of "God" means that Hinduism and Christianity are not even starting from the same premises.

Professor Zaehner, writing out of a Hindu background:

To maintain that all religions are paths leading to the same goal, as is so frequently done today, is to maintain something that is not true.

Not only on the dogmatic, but also on the mystical plane, too, there is no agreement.

It is then only too true that the basic principles of Eastern and Western, which in practice means Indian and Semitic, thought are, I will not say irreconcilably opposed; they are simply not starting from the same premises. The only common ground is that the function of religion is to provide release; there is no agreement at all as to what it is that man must be released from. The great religions are talking at cross purposes.

European thinkers

Spinoza's position, summarized by Paul Hazard:

> The *Ethic*, which appeared posthumously in 1667, in-
> troduced us to a sort of palace, a palace wrought of con-
> cepts so aspiring they seem like a vaulted roof soaring up as
> though to mingle with the heavens. Geometrical, no doubt,
> but tremulous throughout with the breath of life itself, the
> *Ethic* is woven of tissues both human and divine, making
> the two a single category, and over its portals are engraven
> the words, God is All and All is God . . . All that is, is in
> God, and nothing can be, or be conceived, apart from God.
> God is thought; God is extension, and man, body, and soul,
> is a mode of Being.

Hegel:

> We define God when we say, that He distinguishes Himself
> from Himself, and is an object for Himself, but that in this
> distinction He is purely identical with Himself, is in fact
> Spirit. This notion or conception is now realized, conscious-
> ness knows this content and knows that it is itself absolutely
> interwoven with this content; in the Notion which is the
> process of God, it is itself a moment. Finite consciousness
> knows God only to the extent to which God knows Himself
> in it; thus God is Spirit, the Spirit of His Church in fact, i.e.,
> of those who worship Him. This is the perfect religion, the
> Notion become objective to itself. Here it is revealed what
> God is; He is no longer a Being above and beyond this
> world, and Unknown, for He has told men what He is, and
> this is not merely in outward history, but in consciousness.

Julian Huxley:

> It is a fact that many phenomena are charged with some
> sort of magic or compulsive power, and do introduce us to
> a realm beyond our ordinary experience. Such events and
> such experiences merit a special designation. For want of a
> better, I use the term *divine*, though this quality of divinity
> is not truly supernatural but *transnatural*—it grows out of
> ordinary nature, but transcends it. The divine is what man
> finds worthy of adoration, that which compels his awe.
> From the specifically religious point of view, the desirable
> direction of evolution might be defined as the divinization
> of existence—but for this to have operative significance, we
> must frame a new definition of "the divine" free from all
> connotation of external supernatural beings.

Religion today is imprisoned in a theistic frame of ideas, compelled to operate in the unrealities of the dualistic world. In the unitary Humanist frame it acquires a new look and new freedom. With the aid of our new vision it has the opportunity of escaping from the theistic impasses and of playing its proper role in the real world of unitary existence.

Some modern theologians

Some of these writers would maintain that they are not *departing from* the historic Christian understanding of God, but are merely *reinterpreting* the traditional ideas in a form that is more intelligible and acceptable today. These restatements, however, seem to come much closer to this general answer than to the biblical answer (pp. 148ff); or else they present an uneasy compromise between the two.

Paul Tillich describes God as "Being Itself" rather than "A Being":

> The God who is *a* being is transcended by the God who is Being itself, the ground and abyss of every being. And the God who is *a* person is transcended by the God who is the Personal—Itself, the ground and abyss of every person.

> God does not exist, He is being—itself beyond essence and existence. Therefore, to argue that God exists is to deny him.

This is how Tillich explains his concept of God in a more popular form:

> The name of this infinite and inexhaustible depth and ground of all being is *God*. That depth is what the word *God* means. And if that word has not much meaning for you, translate it, and speak of the depths of your life, of the source of your being, of your ultimate concern, of what you take seriously without any reservation. Perhaps, in order to do so, you must forget everything traditional that you have learned about God, perhaps even that word itself. For if you know that God means depth, you know much about him. You cannot then call yourself an atheist or unbeliever. For you cannot think or say: Life has no depth! Life is shallow. Being itself is surface only. If you could say this in complete seriousness, you would be an atheist; but otherwise you are not. He who knows about depth knows about God.

Teilhard de Chardin:

As early as in St. Paul and St. John we read that to create, to fulfill and to purify the world is, for God, to unify it by uniting it organically with himself. How does he unify it? By partially immersing himself in things, by becoming "element," and then, from this point of vantage in the heart of matter, assuming the control and leadership of what we now call evolution. Christ, principle of universal vitality because sprung up as a man among men, put himself in the position (maintained ever since) to subdue under himself, to purify, to direct and superanimate the general ascent of consciousness into which he inserted himself. By a perennial act of communion and sublimation, he aggregates to himself the total psychism of the earth. And when he has gathered everything together and transformed everything, he will close in upon himself and his conquests, thereby rejoining, in a final gesture, the divine focus he has never left. Then, as St. Paul tells us, *God shall be in all.* This is indeed a superior form of "pantheism" without trace of the poison of adulteration or annihilation: the expectation of perfect unity, steeped in which each element will reach its consummation at the same time as the universe.

The universe fulfilling itself in a synthesis of centers in perfect conformity with the laws of union. God, the center of centers.

He describes his position as "a superior form of 'pantheism.'" But he identifies God so closely with the universe that it is difficult for him to maintain at the same time that God is transcendent and distinct from the universe:

To put an end once and for all to the fears of "pantheism," as regards evolution, how can we fail to see that, in the case of a *converging universe* . . . the universal center of unification . . . must be conceived as pre-existing and transcendent. A very real "pantheism" if you like (in the etymological meaning of the word) but an absolutely legitimate pantheism—for if, in the last resort, the reflective centers of the world are effectively "one with God," this state is obtained not by identification (God becoming all) but by the differentiating and communicating action of love (God all *in everyone*). And that is essentially orthodox and Christian.

John Robinson seeks to go beyond a mere "restating of traditional orthodoxy":

> I believe we are being called, over the years ahead, to far more than a restating of traditional orthodoxy in modern terms. Indeed, if our defense of the Faith is limited to this, we shall find in all likelihood that we have lost out to all but a tiny religious remnant. A much more radical recasting, I would judge, is demanded, in the process of which the most fundamental categories of our theology—of God, of the supernatural, and of religion itself—must go into the melting.

Like Tillich, he rejects the idea of God as "a Being." In doing so he is not merely rejecting certain caricatures of God (as in Deism), but vital elements of historic Christian belief:

> The conception of God as *a* Being, a Person—like ourselves but supremely above and beyond ourselves—will, I believe, come to be seen as a human projection.

> I believe, with Tillich, that we should give up speaking of "the existence" of God. For it belongs to a way of thinking that is rapidly ceasing to be ours.

> Unless we can represent him (God) in functional rather than ontological terms, he will rapidly lose all reality. As a Being he has no future.

He agrees with some words written by *Julian Huxley* in his book *Religion without Revelation*:

> The sense of spiritual relief which comes from rejecting the idea of God as a superhuman being is enormous.

He vigorously rejects the accusation that he is propounding pantheism. He describes his position by the word "panentheism." Writing about his earlier book *Honest to God* he says:

> I was concerned not to abolish transcendence (for without transcendence God becomes indistinguishable from the world, and so superfluous), but to find a way of *expressing* transcendence which would not tie God's reality to a supernaturalistic or mythological world-view which, if not actually falsifying, was largely meaningless for twentieth century man.

> If one had to find a label to replace that of traditional "theism" I would fall back on one that has a respectable

pedigree but has never quite succeeded in establishing itself in orthodox Christian circles—namely, "panentheism." This is defined by *The Oxford Dictionary of the Christian Church* as "the belief that the Being of God includes and penetrates the whole universe, so that every part of it exists in him, but (as against pantheism), that his Being is more than, and is not exhausted by, the universe." It is the view that God is in everything and everything is in God.

He explains his beliefs in their simplest form by saying that the starting-point of his belief is:

... the awareness of the world as "Thou"—and ... the meeting through it of "the Eternal Thou."

... the overmastering, yet elusive, conviction of the "Thou" at the heart of everything.

This seems to amount to saying: "The universe is not impersonal. There is a kind of personal *x*, a personal quality in the universe over and above matter." He uses the word *God* as a kind of pointer to this feeling that the universe is personal:

To use the famous image of Lao Tzu, it is the hole in the middle that makes the wheel. The word "God" is useful not because it fills in what is in the middle, but precisely because it witnesses to that which can never be filled in. In itself the word is expendable, it "says" nothing. But *something like it* is an indispensable necessity if we are to refer to the hole at all. Since there is in fact nothing quite like it—no word that can replace it as a direct substitute—I am convinced that we must be able to go on using it, if only as shorthand. And this means that we must try to redeem it.

To assert that "*God* is love" is to believe that in love one comes into touch with the most fundamental reality in the universe, that Being itself ultimately has this character.

To affirm that "the Lord is my rock" is to affirm that there is a bottom, an utterly reliable and unshakable basis to living.

God-language does not describe a Thing-in-Itself or even a Person-in-Himself ... It points to an ultimate relatedness in the very structure of our being from which we cannot get away. It is a way of keeping guard over the irreducible, ineffable mystery at the heart of all experience.

John Wren-Lewis:

The first essential step in convincing people that Christianity can be true in spite of Freud is to assert outright that belief based on the projection-mechanism he describes is false, however much it may say "Lord, Lord." It is not enough to describe such beliefs as childish or primitive, for this implies that the truth is *something* like them, even though much more "refined" or "enlightened," whereas in reality *nothing like* the "God" and "Christ" I was brought up to believe in can be true. It is not merely that the Old Man in the Sky is only a mythological symbol for the Infinite Mind behind the scenes, nor yet that this Being is benevolent rather than fearful: the truth is that this whole way of thinking is wrong, and if such a Being did exist, he would be the very devil.

F. C. Happold:

The Something, within and beyond the polarities of human perception, which simply *is* has been called by many names with various shades of meaning. In general terms it is spoken of as Ultimate Reality or Ultimate Truth. Some philosophers call it the Absolute. For the religious it is God. Chinese metaphysicians call it Tao, Plotinus the One. For Hinduism it is the Everlasting Spirit. For others Ultimate Reality is conceived as Mind, though in a much wider sense than our finite minds. Scientists use the concept of Energy, which cannot be known in itself, but only through its effects.

This Something which is the Is-ness of everything, is, however, in its completeness, concealed from human perception. It is the *Unknowable*, the *Inexpressible*, the *Unconditioned*. It is the *Mystery* which can only be known, at least intellectually, as an *image*, a *model*, an *approximation*.

The "Death of God" theologies

This theology is not pure atheism. The following are the main points of this school.

☐ For many, the traditional language about God has become meaningless.

T. J. J. Altizer:

The man who chooses to live in our destiny can neither know the reality of God's presence nor understand the

world as his creation; or, at least, he can no longer respond,
either interiorly or cognitively, to the classical Christian
images of the Creator and the creation.

William Hamilton:

When we speak of the death of God, we do not speak only
of the death of the idols or the falsely objectivized being in
the sky; we speak as well of the death in us of any power to
affirm any of the traditional images of God . . . and wonder
whether God himself has gone.

God is dead. We are not talking about the absence of the
experience of God, but about the experience of the absence
of God. Yet the death of God theologians claim to be
theologians, to be Christians, to be speaking out of a community to a community. They do not grant that their view
is really a complicated sort of atheism dressed in a new
spring bonnet.

☐ This calls for a denial of much that historic Christianity
stands for.

T. J. J. Altizer:

In the presence of a vocation of silence, theology must
cultivate the silence of death. To be sure, the death to
which theology is called is the death of God. Nor will it
suffice for theology to merely accept the death of God. If
theology is truly to die, it must *will* the death of God, must
will the death of Christendom, must freely choose the destiny before it, and therefore must cease to be itself. Everything that theology has thus far become must now be negated; and negated not simply because it is dead, but rather
because theology cannot be reborn unless it passes through,
and freely wills, its own death and dissolution.

☐ The "Death of God" refers to an actual event which has happened in history: i.e., the God who once existed as a God distinct
from the universe actually died at a particular time, and became
incarnate in the world.

T. J. J. Altizer:

To confess the death of God is to speak of an actual and
real event, not perhaps an event occurring in a single moment of time or history, but notwithstanding this reserva-
tion an event that has actually happened both in a cosmic
and in a historical sense . . . The radical Christian proclaims

that God has actually died in Christ, that this death is both a historical and a cosmic event, and as such, it is a final and irrevocable event, which cannot be reversed by a subsequent religious or cosmic movement.

God has fully and totally become incarnate in Christ . . . a dynamic process of the transcendent's becoming immanent.

Only by accepting and even willing the death of God in our experience can we be liberated from a transcendent beyond, an alien beyond which has been emptied and darkened by God's self-annihilation in Christ.

☐ The "Death of God" theologies continue to use the word *God*, as expressing a wistful longing and hope that the death of the supernatural God of Christianity will lead to the rebirth of faith, to a new revelation of "God."

William Hamilton:

There is an element of expectation, even hope, that removes my position from classical atheisms and that even removes from it a large amount of anguish and gloom.

Thus we wait, we try out new words, we pray for God to return, and we seem to be willing to descend into the darkness of unfaith and doubt that something may emerge on the other side . . .

But we do more than play the waiting game. We concentrate our energy and passion on the specific, the concrete, the personal. We turn from the problems of faith to the reality of love.

PROBLEMS
AND QUESTIONS

Why not call a spade a spade and admit that this view is atheistic?

Why keep the name *God*? If there is no personal Being called God, why not dispense with the name altogether? If we still need some name to describe the mystery of the universe, why not find a new and less confusing one?

Peter Dumitriu describes a kind of mystical experience in which he sees that the sense and meaning of the universe is "love." He then wonders what *words* he should use:

What name was I to use? "God," I murmured, "God." How else should I address Him. O Universe? O Heap? O Whole?

As "Father"? or "Mother"? I might as well call Him "Uncle." As "Lord"? I might as well say, "Dear Sir," or "Dear Comrade." How could I say "Lord" to the air I breathed and my own lungs which breathed the air? "My child"? But he contained me, preceded me, created me. "Thou" is His name, to which "God" may be added. For "I" and "me" are no more than a pause between the immensity of the universe which is Him and the very depth of our self, which is also Him.

Dumitriu thinks it is obvious that he should use the name of "God." But is it so obvious and self-evident? Would not words like "O Universe," "O Heap," and "O Whole" be very much more consistent? Is there anything more than convention and sentiment to justify choosing "God"?

Y. Takeuchi, a Japanese Buddhist philosopher, suggests what he sees as the logical conclusion of the desire of many theologians to go beyond the idea of a personal God:

> If we were to transcend the personal God (trinity of God) it would not be toward Being-itself, but rather towards Absolute Nothingness.

Walter Kaufmann similarly asks the question, why the name "God"?

> The atheist can agree with Tillich in his denial of the "existence" of God and the affirmation of "being-itself"—only why name it God?

All these answers, therefore, contain an element of linguistic cheating. There is bound to be an element of deception in continuing to use the word "God"—which most people associate with a personal Being—while denying that any such Being exists. Humanists and Christians are not slow to point this out.

Julian Huxley:

> (Robinson) is surely wrong in making such statements as that "God is ultimate reality." God is a hypothesis constructed by man to help him understand what existence is all about. The God hypothesis asserts the existence of some sort of supernatural person or supernatural being, exerting some kind of purposeful power over the universe and its destiny. To say that God is ultimate reality is just semantic cheating, as well as being so vague as to become effectively meaningless (and when Dr. Robinson continues by saying

"and ultimate reality must exist," he is surely running
round a philosophically very vicious circle.)

Dr. Robinson, like Dr. Tillich and many other modernist
theologians, seems to me, and indeed to any humanist, to
be trying to ride two horses at once, to keep his cake and
eat it. He wants to be modern and meet the challenge of
our new knowledge by stripping the image of God of virtually all its spatial, material, mythological, Freudian, and an-
thropomorphic aspects. But he still persists in retaining the
term *God*, in spite of all its implication of supernatural power and personality; and it is these implications, not the mod-
ernists' fine-spun arguments, which consciously or unconsciously affect the ordinary man and woman. Heads I win,
tails you lose: humanists dislike this elaborate double-talk.

Alasdair MacIntyre, writing about John Robinson's *Honest to
God*:

What is striking about Dr. Robinson's book is first and
foremost that he is an atheist . . . Yet . . . he is unwilling to
abandon the word "God" and a great many kindred theological words. Yet I think that we might well be puzzled by
this strong desire for a theological vocabulary; for the only
reason given for preserving the name "God" is that "our
being has depths which naturalism, whether evolutionary,
mechanistic, dialectical or humanistic, cannot or will not recognize." But this is to say that all atheists to date have described "our being" inadequately . . . His book testifies to the
existence of a whole group of theologies which have retained
a theistic vocabulary but acquired an atheistic substance.

He points out that while the new theologies disown historic
Christianity, they still depend on all the associations which surround the traditional language:

The formulas of the new theology seem to me to derive
both such sense and such emotional power as they have by
reason of their derivation from and association with the
much more substantial faith of the past. Without that derivation and association these formulas, far from providing
modern man with a faith rewritten in terms that he can
understand, would be even more unintelligible than the
theology they seek to correct. Thus the new theologians are
in a fundamentally false position. They in fact depend on
the traditionalism which they proclaim that they discard.

Writing about Paul Tillich:

> Belief in God has been evacuated of all its traditional content. It consists now in moral seriousness and nothing more.

Barbara Wooton:

> The disappearance of a personal deity does not . . . dispose of the riddle of the universe and of man's place therein. Nor can this riddle be solved by such verbal tricks as those which the Bishop of Woolwich proceeds to employ. According to him, "God is by definition ultimate reality. And one cannot argue whether ultimate reality *exists*. One can only ask what ultimate reality is like." Such statements, I submit, are purely semantic exercises, which, strictly interpreted, are devoid of all meaning. If God and ultimate reality are identical, then the statement that God is ultimate reality amounts to neither more nor less than an assertion that ultimate reality is ultimate reality.

Altizer, writing about Teilhard de Chardin:

> It is true that Teilhard occasionally and inconsistently introduces traditional Christian language into the pages of *The Phenomenon of Man*; but this fact scarcely obviates the truth that virtually the whole body of Christian belief either disappears or is transformed in Teilhard's evolutionary vision of the cosmos.

Professor Peter Beyerhaus expresses his fears about the transformation of Christian theology:

> Personally I am most worried by the teaching of theologians who adapt the traditional Christian concepts to the expectations and desires of the new generation.

> Here the language, in contrast to both the old fashioned liberalism and Bultmannian demythologization, sounds more and more orthodox. The doctrine of the Trinity, the two natures of Christ, the redemptive character of his cross, the reality of his resurrection and second coming are reaffirmed. But their authentic content has secretly been changed and replaced by evolutionist concepts. That which euphemistically is called a "theology related to society" or "political theology" is, in its deepest analysis, a camouflaged atheistic humanism, in which the names of God and Christ are simply cyphers for the real nature and destiny of man.

195

In what sense can this answer be true?

This answer is usually based on a particular understanding of truth, and many who give this answer have to a greater or lesser extent accepted the Hindu answer.

Radhakrishnan:

> Hinduism developed an attitude of comprehensive charity instead of fanatic faith in an inflexible creed. It accepted the multiplicity of aboriginal gods and others which originated, most of them, outside the Aryan tradition, and justified them all. It brought together into one whole all believers in God. Many sects professing many different beliefs live within the Hindu fold.

Arnold Toynbee:

> Since I do not believe in a personal god, I don't have a vested interest in any one religion . . . Although, of course, I can't get away from my Judaeo-Christian background, temperamentally I am a Hindu. As a Hindu, I don't have any difficulty in believing in many gods simultaneously, or thinking that a syncretist faith may be the answer for our age. To Hindus, it's of no consequence which road, Siva or Vishnu, one travels—all roads lead to heaven.

In this case, therefore, the discussion must shift from the question about *God* to the question about *truth.* See further the different answers to the question of truth in Part 1: "We can never know for certain" (pp. 64ff.); "We can know only by a leap of faith" (pp. 86ff.); "We can know only through mystical experience" (pp. 110ff.).

How does this understanding of God affect our view of man?

Sooner or later all our "God-talk" must be related to *man,* and it is here that the profound implications of this concept of God become even more apparent. See Question Three: "What is Man?," pp. 209ff.

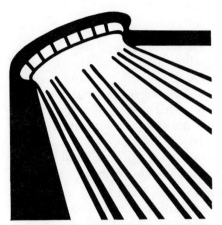

BACK TO ANSWER ONE

God really exists; he is as the Bible describes him.

*Having examined other possible an-
swers to the question, "Who or what is
God? Does he exist?," we return to
option one, the biblical Christian answer, for a closer look at some of the
questions and objections raised.*

**What sort of mental image of God does the Bible
give? Are we supposed to know what he looks
like?**

☐ The Old Testament emphasizes the fact that no one can see God
as he really is, in all his glory. When we read of certain individuals who "saw" God, their description of what they saw is hardly
adequate to convey a clear mental image of what God "looks

like." But it at least conveys the conviction that there really is Someone there and points to certain aspects of his character.

To see Christ as he is and to know his character is to know what God is like.

Moses:

> Moses said, "I pray thee, show me thy glory." And he (God) said, "I will make all my goodness pass before you, and will proclaim before you my name 'The Lord' . . . But . . . you cannot see my face; for man shall not see me and live . . . Behold, there is a place by me where you shall stand upon the rock; and while my glory passes by I will put you in a cleft of the rock, and I will cover you with my hand until I have passed by; then I will take away my hand, and you shall see my back; but my face shall not be seen."
>
> And the Lord descended in the cloud and stood with him there, and proclaimed the name of the Lord. The Lord passed before him, and proclaimed, "The Lord, the Lord, a God merciful and gracious, slow to anger, and abounding in steadfast love and faithfulness, keeping steadfast love for thousands, forgiving iniquity and transgression and sin, but who will by no means clear the guilty . . ."

Isaiah:

> In the year that King Uzziah died I saw the Lord sitting upon a throne, high and lifted up; and his train filled the temple. Above him stood the seraphim; each had six wings: with two he covered his face, and with two he covered his feet, and with two he flew. And one called to another and said:
>   "Holy, holy, holy is the Lord of hosts;
>   the whole earth is full of his glory."
> And the foundations of the thresholds shook at the voice of him who called, and the house was filled with smoke. And I said: "Woe is me! For I am lost; for I am a man of unclean lips, and I dwell in the midst of a people of unclean lips; for my eyes have seen the King, the Lord of hosts!"

Ezekiel:

> Above the firmament over their heads there was the likeness of a throne, in appearance like sapphire; and seated above the likeness of a throne was a likeness as it were of a human form. And upward from what had the appearance of his loins I saw as it were gleaming bronze, like the

appearance of fire enclosed round about; and downward
from what had the appearance of his loins I saw as it were
the appearance of fire . . . Such was the appearance of the
likeness of the glory of the Lord.

☐ To have a clear idea of the *character* of God is far more important, and this can be known through the action of God in
history and through revelation in words.

Jeremiah:

Thus says the Lord: "Let not the wise man glory in his
wisdom, let not the mighty man glory in his might, let not
the rich man glory in his riches; but let him who glories
glory in this, that he understands and knows me, that I am
the Lord who practice kindness, justice, and righteousness
in the earth; for in these things I delight, says the Lord."

☐ When we come to the New Testament, the character of Jesus
gives us the clearest picture we have of what God is like.

John writes:

No one has ever seen God; the only Son, who is in the
bosom of the Father, he has made him known.

He records the following conversation with Philip:

Philip said to him, "Lord, show us the Father, and we shall
be satisfied." Jesus said to him, "Have I been with you so
long, and yet you do not know me, Philip? He who has
seen me has seen the Father; how can you say, 'Show us the
Father'? Do you not believe that I am in the Father and the
Father in me?"

Toward the end of his life John records a vision of the living
Christ in heaven:

Then I turned to see the voice that was speaking to me,
and on turning I saw seven golden lampstands, and in the
midst of the lampstands one like a son of man, clothed with
a long robe and with a golden girdle round his breast; his
head and his hair were white as white wool, white as snow;
his eyes were like a flame of fire, his feet were like bur-
nished bronze, refined as in a furnace, and his voice was
like the sound of many waters; in his right hand he held
seven stars, from his mouth issued a sharp two-edged
sword, and his face was like the sun shining in full strength.
When I saw him, I fell at his feet as though dead.

199

To see Christ as he is and to know his character is to know what God is like.

☐ People who have never seen Jesus but believe in him on the basis of the apostles' testimony can share the same kind of knowledge, the same certainty and joy:

Peter writes:

> Without having seen him you love him; though you do not now see him you believe in him and rejoice with unutterable and exalted joy.

Isn't the idea of "God" simply a projection of the human mind?

Thomas Merton:

> Our ideas of God tell us much more about ourselves than they do about God.

James Mitchell writes about collecting a series of essays for a book entitled *The god I want* (note the 'god' with a small *g*), and about the conclusion he reached:

> The question running through the whole book is: was man created in god's image? Or god in man's?
>
> What kind of a god, if any, would you create if you had the chance?
>
> This whole exercise has forever destroyed for me the possibility that I might again find certitude in religious belief.

Aldous Huxley:

> It is, I take it, generally agreed, that the origin of religion is to be found in the savage's fear of the unknown. All around him the savage sees the operation of forces, thunder and lightning, earthquakes and floods, which he cannot understand, or can understand only if he personifies them. And so he personifies them . . . And being human inventions they bear the stamp of their creators all too visibly on them. Literally they are made in man's image. As man is, so too are his gods, or rather his God, for . . . in the course of time the multitudinous deities of the savage world are unified into a single personage, and Jehovah appears upon the scene.

Albert Einstein:

> I cannot imagine a God who rewards and punishes the

object of his creation, whose purposes are modeled after our own—a God, in short, who is but a reflection of human frailty.

☐ This objection does not take into account the vast *differences* between the ideas of God in the different religions. The ancient Greeks would have acknowledged quite unashamedly that their gods were very much like themselves. They have human virtues and vices, and have the advantage that they are not subject to as many limitations as human beings.

Ernst Cassirer describes the religion of ancient Greece and Rome in this way:

> What man portrays in his gods is himself, in all his variety and multiformity, his turn of mind, his temperament, even his idiosyncracies. But it is not, as in Roman religion, the practical side of his nature that man projects upon the deity. The Homeric gods represent no moral ideals, but they express very characteristic mental ideals. They are not those functional and anonymous deities that have to watch over a special activity of man: they are interested in and favor individual men. Every god and goddess has his favorites who are appreciated, loved, and assisted, not on the ground of a mere personal predilection but by virtue of a kind of mental relationship that connects the god and the man. Mortals and immortals are the embodiments not of moral ideals but of special mental gifts and tendencies.

There is good evidence to believe that this kind of belief developed from a degenerate form of monotheism.

☐ It is not so easy as Huxley suggests to see precisely *how* such indulgent and "human" gods of this kind could be transformed into the righteous and loving God of the Old Testament. It is much easier to trace the possible process of development if we begin with the assumption that men originally worshiped *one* Creator God, and that this belief degenerated into belief in many different gods. (See the quotations from Robert Brow on pp. 162 and 182.)

The uncomfortable thing about the God of the Bible is that he so often cuts across our personal desires and wishes. He does not allow us to be selfish, and always confronts us with an uncompromisingly high standard. This is *not* the kind of God man creates when he sets out to make a god in his own image.

☐ Even if we had a full scientific explanation of the *process* by which a person comes to hold certain beliefs about God, we would still be no nearer to discovering whether or not those beliefs were *true*. The most exact description of the mechanism of the brain when it believes the law of gravity, can not help us know whether the law of gravity is in fact true.

To take another example, a child's ideas of God are built up largely through what he hears from others and through his own experience. He may be told "God is like a father; he loves you, cares for you and provides for your needs as a father does." And he may be taught to pray "Our Father . . ." He therefore naturally attaches to his image of God the qualities which he observes in his father. If he experiences little love and kindness from his father, this will inevitably affect his understanding of God. Now although this kind of explanation may tell us a great deal about *how* a person comes to believe, it still does not tell us whether *what* he believes is true or false.

☐ Agnosticism about God often goes hand in hand with agnosticism or skepticism about the possibility of *any* kind of knowledge. If we say that the idea of God must be the product of the imagination, then the idea of "beauty" may equally be the product of the human mind; there is no objective beauty in what we see—it is simply the name we attach to things that happen to please us. Similarly, we could say that the idea of Cause and Effect, or the laws of science are nothing more than the product of the human mind. They do not tell us the truth about what is there in the natural world, but are simply ideas that we find convenient for describing what we see. This is not mere theorizing. Ever since David Hume challenged the idea of Cause and Effect, others have taken this kind of skepticism quite seriously. And if we are prepared to go all the way with this skepticism, we must eventually conclude, with Sartre's Roquentin, that:

> these are reasonable hypotheses which take the facts into account: but I am only too well aware that they come from me, that they are simply a way of unifying my own knowledge.

(See further Part 1, pp. 64–85.)

Surely some of these beliefs about God are contradictory

How can God be both personal *and* infinite? How can he be both loving *and* holy? How can he be one *and* three?

Ronald Hepburn:

> Recent philosophical studies have not been so much con-
> cerned with evidence for or against God's existence, as with
> the question of the coherence or incoherence of the con-
> cept of God. If the concept is ultimately incoherent, that is
> because theism tries to pack into it a wealth of sublime but
> incompatible elements—God is personal but infinite, is in
> causal contact with the world but not in space and time, is
> impenetrably mysterious yet known beyond doubt in the
> Christian revelation. This is a downfall through excessive
> riches.

☐ Some pairs of words are obviously *mutually exclusive*: e.g. black
and white (if something is black it cannot also be white), personal
and impersonal (if God is personal he cannot also be impersonal—except in the thinking of Hinduism, which allows the laws
of logic to be set aside—see Part 1, pp. 69–74).

☐ In the four pairs of statements about God (p. 148), the words in
each pair do not *exclude* each other, but merely help to *define* or
qualify. When we say, for example, that God is one, but that
there are three persons within that oneness, we are simply defining the kind of unity or oneness we mean. It is not the mathematical or physical oneness of something that is indivisible, but a
oneness that is nearer to the unity of the atom; a oneness which
is a complex unity holding together the Father, the Son and the
Spirit, who share the same nature and enjoy a living relationship.

☐ Similarly with the other pairs: God's love is a holy love and his
holiness is a loving holiness. His infinity is not a philosophical
abstraction: he is personal, but without most of the limitations
that we see in human beings.

How can we talk about the "God of the Bible"? Surely the Bible contains many different ideas of God

☐ If we see a father being angry with his children one day and
kind to them the next, we may think him inconsistent, or we may
go away with two quite different impressions of his character.
But as we get to know him better, we may discover that he had
every reason to be angry: it is *because he cares* for his children
that he must sometimes discipline them.

The same holds true in the relationship between God and
man. The many different pictures of God in the Bible may seem

203

inconsistent, until we realize their underlying unity. Each is an expression of the same holy and loving God in his relationship with men in many different situations.

To take the analogy one stage further: a father may often scold his children, but only occasionally tell them that he loves them. If he really loves his children it will show in action more than in words. Similarly, God does not have to keep saying he loves us: sooner or later we come to realize that everything he says and does springs from his holy love.

☐ The Bible claims to record a *progressive* revelation of God. It is vital to notice that according to the biblical account, one of the results of the Fall was banishment from the presence of God, and therefore, we must assume, an increasing ignorance about him. Thus Cain says:

> "Behold, thou hast driven me this day away from the ground; and from thy face I shall be hidden; and I shall be a fugitive and a wanderer on the earth . . ." . . . Then Cain went away from the presence of the Lord.

This is how the writer of Genesis describes the condition of man before the Flood:

> The Lord saw that the wickedness of man was great in the earth, and that every imagination of the thoughts of his heart was only evil continually.

If this is a true account of the state of alienation which man had reached as a result of his rebellion, God would have to begin by revealing himself gradually. Therefore, in studying the course of this progressive revelation, we must ask ourselves: does this new revelation *complement* and *add to* what has already been revealed, or does it *contradict* it? If we understand truth as the writers of the Bible understood it, we can see how the apparently different pictures of God complement each other, taking their place in the context of the whole revelation.

☐ We can see how this principle works out by taking one specific objection which is often raised: how can we reconcile the God of love in the New Testament with the God of wrath in the Old? Surely the earlier revelation of God in the Old Testament as one who is wrathful and seeking vengeance must be superseded by the God of love revealed in the life and teaching of Jesus.

☐ This objection rests partly on a misunderstanding of phrases like "the wrath of God." The Bible does not use expressions like this

to mean that God is losing his temper; there is no suggestion
that his wrath is petty or selfish or vindictive in the way that
human anger often is. These expressions are used simply to
describe God's opposition to sin and evil. They emphasize that
God is not morally neutral, and that he cannot allow sin to have
a permanent place in his universe. Thus the writer of Proverbs
says:

> There are six things which the Lord hates,
>   seven which are an abomination to him:
> haughty eyes, a lying tongue,
>   and hands that shed innocent blood,
> a heart that devises wicked plans,
>   feet that make haste to run to evil,
> a false witness who breathes out lies,
>   and a man who sows discord among
>   brothers.

Stephen Neill:

> The best way to understand the doctrine of the wrath of
> God is to consider the alternatives. The alternative is not
> love; since rightly considered, love and wrath are only the
> obverse and reverse of the same thing . . . The alternative
> to wrath is neutrality—neutrality in the conflict of the
> world . . . To live in such a world would be a nightmare. It
> is only the doctrine of the wrath of God, of his irreconcil-
> able hostility to all evil, which makes human life tolerable in
> such a world as ours.

☐ This objection is also based on a very selective reading of the
Bible. The Old Testament has much to say about the love of
God, while the New Testament speaks as much as the Old
Testament about the wrath of God—perhaps even more. The
following passages are from two of the prophets who are reveal-
ing the mind of God.

Jeremiah:

> "I have loved you with an everlasting love;
>   therefore I have continued my faithfulness
>   to you."

Isaiah:

> "For a brief moment I forsook you,
>   but with great compassion I will gather you.

205

> In overflowing wrath for a moment I hid my face
>   from you,
> but with everlasting love I will have compassion
>   on you,
>   says the Lord, your Redeemer."
> "Can a woman forget her sucking child,
>   that she should have no compassion on the
>   son of her womb?"
> Even these may forget, yet I will not forget you.
> Behold, I have graven you on the palms of my
>   hands.

Jesus had much to say about the love of God; but he also spoke in the strongest language about the awfulness of the judgment on those who refused to recognize him and follow his teaching:

> And when he drew near and saw the city he wept over it, saying, "Would that even today you knew the things that make for peace! But now they are hid from your eyes. For the days shall come upon you, when your enemies will cast up a bank about you and surround you, and hem you in on every side, and dash you to the ground, you and your children within you, and they will not leave one stone upon another in you; because you did not know the time of your visitation."

> Then he (the Son of man) will say to those at his left hand, "Depart from me, you cursed, into the eternal fire prepared for the devil and his angels; for I was hungry and you gave me no food, I was thirsty and you gave me no drink, I was a stranger and you did not welcome me, naked and you did not clothe me, sick and in prison and you did not visit me." . . . And they will go away into eternal punishment, but the righteous into eternal life.

Paul saw no difficulty in holding together the wrath of God and the love of God and speaking of them in the same breath:

> God shows his love for us in that while we were yet sinners Christ died for us. Since, therefore, we are now justified by his blood, much more shall we be saved by him from the wrath of God.

John, similarly, holds the love and the wrath of God together; the word *propitiation* contains the idea of turning away wrath:

In this is love, not that we loved God, but that he loved us
and sent his Son to be the propitiation for our sins.

One of the most striking expressions of the wrath of God is in
the phrase "the wrath of the Lamb," which is found in the book
of Revelation, where John is describing his vision of the day of
judgment:

Then the kings of the earth and the great men and the
generals and the rich and the strong, and every one, slave
and free, hid in the caves and among the rocks of the
mountains, calling to the mountains and rocks, "Fall on us
and hide us from the face of him who is seated on the
throne, and from the wrath of the Lamb; for the great day
of their wrath has come, and who can stand before it?"

The phrase "the wrath of the Lamb" combines the thought of
the love and the wrath of God. In the first place we immediately
think of the weakness and gentleness of a young lamb. Then
further we are reminded of John's description of Jesus as "The
Lamb of God, who takes away the sins of the world." The Lamb,
therefore, has done all in his power to *save* men from this
terrifying judgment, if only they will turn to him. He has a right
to our love and trust because of who he is and what he has
done; and where his love is rejected, there can be no neutrality,
only wrath.

Certain vital questions are being asked today, and are likely to be asked more and more in the future—questions which focus on the individual, on the meaning and purpose of life, on choice, on relationships, on coming to terms with suffering and evil. The answer we give to the question "What is man?" directly affects these more specific and personal questions. For this reason each of the three basic answers is outlined in turn and tested for its effect in these five major areas.

QUESTION THREE
WHAT IS MAN?

William Koechling

THE INDIVIDUAL

Who am I?

Harold Pinter, the dramatist, puts the question into the mouth of
one of his characters:

> The point is, who are you? Not why or how, not even what.
> I can see what, perhaps, clearly enough. But who are you?
> It's no use saying you know who you are just because you
> tell me you can fit your particular key into a particular slot
> which will duly receive your particular key because that's
> not foolproof and certainly not conclusive.

Am I in any sense "free"?
Am I a self or a machine?

Jacob Bronowski:

> This is where the fulcrum of our fears lies: that man as a
> species and we as thinking men, will be shown to be no
> more than a machinery of atoms. We pay lip service to the
> vital life of the amoeba and the cheese mite; but what we
> are defending is the human claim to have a complex of will
> and thoughts and emotions—to have a mind.
>
> . . . the crisis of confidence . . . springs from each man's
> wish to be a mind and a person, in the face of the nagging
> fear that he is a mechanism. The central question I ask is
> this: Can man be both a machine and a self?

The question of the freedom of the individual is also forced
upon us because of the vast concentrations of power in the
hands of individuals in government, industry and the mass me-
dia.

Thomas Mann:

> The whole question of the human being and what we think
> about him is put to us today with a life-and-death serious-
> ness unknown in times that were not so stern as ours. For
> everybody, but most particularly for the artist, it is a matter
> of spiritual life or spiritual death; it is to use the religious
> terminology, a matter of salvation. I am convinced that the
> writer is a lost man who betrays the things of the spirit by

211

refusing to face and decide for himself the human problem, put, as it is today, in political terms.

Aldous Huxley:

How can we control the vast impersonal forces that now
menace our hard-won freedoms?

MEANING

What do I mean? What is the meaning of my life?

Somerset Maugham:

If . . . one puts aside the existence of God and the possibility of survival as too doubtful to have any effect on
one's behavior, one has to make up one's mind what is the
meaning and use of life. If death ends all, if I have neither
to hope for good to come nor to fear evil, I must ask
myself what I am here for, and how in these circumstances
I must conduct myself.

Tolstoy:

What is life for? To die? To kill myself at once? No, I am
afraid. To wait for death till it comes? I fear that even
more. Then I must live. *But what for?* In order to die? And
I could not escape from that circle. I took up the book,
read, and forgot myself for a moment, but then again, the
same question and the same horror. I lay down and closed
my eyes. It was worse still.

Adam Schaff, the Polish Marxist philosopher, asks questions
about the meaning and value of man in his book *A Philosophy of
Man.* Communism has generally refused to admit that these are
genuine questions, and its philosophy has never attempted to
include answers. But he insists that they are real questions, and
that Communists can no longer pretend that they do not exist:

"Vanity, vanity, all is vanity!" These words, repeated in
various forms in all the philosophies of the East, seem to
appeal to many who in old age begin to reflect on life and
death. It is possible to shrug this off with a compassionate
smile as nonsense, and yet the words echo a problem which
simply cannot be ignored. Nor can the questions "Why?,"
"What for?," which force their way to the lips of people
tired of the adversities and delusions of life. This applies
still more to the compulsive questions which come from

reflection upon death—why all this effort to stay alive if we are going to die anyway? It is difficult to avoid the feeling that death is senseless—avoidable, accidental death especially. Of course we can ask: senseless from what point of view? From the point of view of the progress of nature death is entirely sensible. But from the point of view of a given individual death is senseless and places in doubt everything that he does . . . Attempts to ridicule this do not help . . .

"What is the meaning of life?" "What is man's place in the universe?" It seems difficult to express oneself scientifically on such hazy topics. And yet if one should assert ten times over that these are typical pseudo-problems, problems would remain.

VALUES

How am I to make choices?

Nietzsche:

As soon as . . . no thinker can any longer relieve his conscience with the hypothesis "God or eternal values," the claim of the lawgiver to determine new values rises to an awfulness which has not yet been experienced.

Arthur Koestler speaks of the moral dilemma that must have faced Scott during his return from the South Pole in 1912. Either he must take the sick Owens along with him and accept the risks of delay, or he must leave him behind in the hope of saving his own life and the lives of the other three in the party.

This dilemma . . . symbolizes the eternal predicament of man, the tragic conflict inherent in his nature. It is the conflict between expediency and morality . . . This conflict is at the root of our political and social crisis, . . . it contains in a nutshell the challenge of our time . . .

That both roads end as blind alleys is a dilemma which is inseparable from man's condition; it is not an invention of the philosophers, but a conflict which we face at each step in our daily affairs . . . The more responsible the position you hold, the sharper you feel the horns of the dilemma. When a decision involves the fate of a great number of people, the conflict grows proportionately. The technical progress of our age has enormously increased the range and consequence of man's actions, and has thus amplified his inherent dilemma to gigantic proportions. This, there-

fore, is the reason for our acute awareness of a crisis. We
are like the patient who for the first time hears in a loud-
speaker the irregular ticking of his heart.

Albert Camus:

When man submits God to moral judgment, he kills Him in
his own heart. And then what is the basis of morality? God
is denied in the name of justice but can the idea of justice
be understood without the idea of God?

Jean-Paul Sartre:

Any morality which does not present itself explicitly as
impossible today contributes to the mystification and alienation of man. The moral "problem" arises from the fact that
morals are *for us* both unavoidable and impossible. Action
must give itself its ethical norms in this climate of un-
surmountable impossibility. It is in this light, for example,
that one should consider the problem of violence or that of
the relation between the means and the end.

I do not present these contradictions to condemn Christian
morals: I am too deeply convinced that *any* morals are both
impossible and necessary.

RELATIONSHIPS

What hope is there for communication and love?

John Russell Taylor, in his comments on a play by Harold Pinter,
speaks of the doubt about knowing the truth about other people:

The technique of casting doubt upon everything by match-
ing each apparently clear and unequivocal statement with
an equally clear and unequivocal statement of its contrary
. . . is one which we shall find used constantly in Pinter's
plays to create an air of mystery and uncertainty . . . in
these ordinary surroundings lurk mysterious terrors and
uncertainties—and by extension, the whole external world
of everyday realities is thrown into question. Can we ever
know the truth about anybody or anything? Is there any
absolute truth to be known?

Bertrand Russell, speaking of the obstacles which stand in the
way of human progress:

What stands in the way? Not physical or technical obstacles, but only the evil passions in human minds; suspicion, fear, lust for power, intolerance . . .

The root of the matter is a very simple and old-fashioned thing, a thing so simple that I am almost ashamed to mention it, for fear of the derisive smile with which wise cynics will greet my words. The thing I mean—please forgive me for mentioning it—is love, Christian love, or compassion . . .

Thomas Mann ends his novel *The Magic Mountain* with the question:

Out of this universal feast of death, out of this extremity of fever, kindling the rain-washed evening sky to a fiery glow, may it be that Love one day shall mount?

SUFFERING AND EVIL

How can I live with suffering and evil?

Ionesco:

Shortly after my arrival in my second homeland, I saw a man, still young, big and strong, attack an old man with his fists and kick him with his boots . . . I have no other images of the world except those of evanescence and brutality, vanity and rage, nothingness or hideous, useless hatred. Everything I have since experienced has merely confirmed what I had seen and understood in my childhood: vain and sordid fury, cries suddenly stifled by silence, shadows engulfed forever in the night.

Aldous Huxley:

In the form in which men have posed it, the Riddle of the Universe requires a theological answer. Suffering and enjoying, men want to know why they enjoy and to what end they suffer. They see good things and evil things, beautiful things and ugly, and they want to find a reason—a final and absolute reason—why these things should be as they are.

Adam Schaff:

The fact alone of some agnostics undergoing deathbed conversions gives much food for thought. Philosophy must take the place of religion here. It must tackle a number of diverse questions which have remained from the wreck of the religious view of life—the senselessness of suffering, of broken lives, of death, and many other questions relating to the fate of the living, struggling, suffering and dying individuals. Can this be done scientifically, that is in a way that is communicable and subject to some sort of verification?

Albert Camus:

The certainty of the existence of a God who would give meaning to life has a far greater attraction than the knowledge that without him one could do evil without being punished. The choice between these alternatives would not be difficult. But there is no choice, and that is where the bitterness begins.

Confronted with this evil, confronted with death, man from the very depths of his soul cries out for justice.

WHAT IS MAN?

Man is a creature created in the image of God—the God of the Bible.
PAGE 219

Man is a creature created by God—but this is not the God of the Bible.
PAGE 238

Man is not the creation of God because there is no personal Creator.
PAGE 255

ANSWER ONE:
BIBLICAL CHRISTIANITY

Man is a creature
created in the image
of God—the God of
the Bible.

The Christian teaching on man can be summarized as follows:

☐ *Man has been created in the image and likeness of God.*

☐ *Man is now a rebel against his Creator.*

☐ *Man can become a "son" of God.*

MAN IS A CREATURE CREATED IN THE IMAGE OF GOD

☐ The Bible recognizes that man in his physical make-up has a great deal in common with the animals; the writer of Genesis speaks of man being made "of dust from the ground" like the animals. But the basic difference between man and the animals is that man is in some ways *like* God:

> Then God said, "Let us make man in our image, after our likeness . . ." So God created man in his own image, in the image of God he created him; male and female he created them.

The following passage later in the book of Genesis makes it clear that the "image and likeness" is to be understood quite naturally as resemblance:

> When God created man, he made him in the likeness of God. Male and female he created them, and he blessed them and named them Man and they were created. When Adam had lived a hundred and thirty years, he became the father of a son in his own likeness, after his image.

☐ To say that man is *like* God means that:

Just as God is personal, *so* man is personal.

Just as God has mind and can think and communicate, *so* man has a mind and can think and communicate; he is rational.

Just as God has will and can decide and make free choices, *so* man has a will and can make certain free choices; he is responsible and accountable.

Just as God has emotions and can feel, *so* man has emotions and can feel.

☐ Man, however, is clearly *unlike* God in certain respects:

God is infinite, unlimited by space and time: man is not.

God is Spirit and has no body: man has a physical body with all its limitations.

God has absolute knowledge and absolute power: man does not.

☐ As he was originally created, man "was perfect":

> And God saw everything that he had made, and behold, it was very good.

☐ Although man is no longer perfect, he is still God's creation, bearing his image. The likeness has been spoiled, but not obliterated completely. Man still has something in common with God, and it is this which gives him his greatness and dignity. So however much the writers of the Bible may stress man's fallen state, they never lose sight of the fact that he is the crown of God's creative work in the universe.

When I look at thy heavens, the work of thy
     fingers,
  the moon and the stars which thou hast
     established;
what is man that thou art mindful of him,
   and the son of man that thou dost care for him?
Yet thou hast made him little less than God,
   and dost crown him with glory and honor.
Thou hast given him dominion over the works of
     thy hands,
   thou hast put all things under his feet,
all sheep and oxen, and also the beasts of the field,
the birds of the air, and the fish of the sea,
   whatever passes along the paths of the sea.

☐ I am a created being, and I have to accept that fact. I have to
acknowledge my own imperfections and limitations and weaknesses:

Woe to him who strives with his Maker,
   an earthen vessel with the potter!
Does the clay say to him who fashions it, "What
     are you making?"?
   or "Your work has no handles"?
Woe to him who says to a father, "What are you
     begetting?"
   or to a woman, "With what are you in travail?"

☐ Once I reach this point of acceptance I can have a deep sense of
confidence and joy in the one who has made me and knows me
so completely:

For thou didst form my inward parts,
   thou didst knit me together in my mother's womb.
I praise thee, for thou are fearful and wonderful.
   Wonderful are thy works!
Thou knowest me right well;
   my frame was not hidden from thee,
when I was being made in secret,
   intricately wrought in the depths of the earth.
Thy eyes beheld my unformed substance;
   in thy book were written, every one of them,
the days that were formed for me,
   when as yet there was none of them.
How precious to me are thy thoughts, O God!

> Thy hands have made and fashioned me;
>> give me understanding that I may learn thy
>> commandments.

MAN IS NOW A REBEL AGAINST HIS CREATOR

☐ The human race is now in a state of rebellion against its Creator. Men may recognize that God exists. They may even try to worship him in different ways. But they fail to love him as he deserves. They fail to live up to his standards.

☐ Man was not *created* a rebel; he has *become* a rebel. When Adam was created, he was given a choice: either to depend on God and obey him, or to be independent.

God plainly warned what the consequences of disobedience would be:

> You may freely eat of every tree of the garden; but of the tree of the knowledge of good and evil you shall not eat, for in the day that you eat of it you shall die.

☐ The effects of Adam's rebellion and sin were transmitted to the whole human race:

> Sin came into the world through one man and death through sin, and so death spread to all men because all men sinned.

☐ Man's rebellion against God at the present time thus consists in a refusal to live according to God's revealed laws.

John defines sin in terms of lawlessness:

> Every one who commits sin is guilty of lawlessness; sin is lawlessness.

Paul defines sin as man's refusal to acknowledge the truth that he knows about God:

> The wrath of God is revealed from heaven against all ungodliness and wickedness of men who by their wickedness suppress the truth. For what can be known about God is plain to them, because God has shown it to them. Ever since the creation of the world his invisible nature, namely, his eternal power and deity, has been clearly perceived in the things that have been made. So they are without excuse; for although they knew God they did not honor him as God or give thanks to him, but they became futile in their thinking and their senseless minds were darkened.

☐ Those who have not had the fuller revelation of God through the Bible and through Jesus Christ are in the same state of rebellion against God. *Paul* writes that although they have not had the fuller revelation, they have set certain standards for themselves and others, and have failed to live up to them:

> Therefore you have no excuse, O man, whoever you are, when you judge another; for in passing judgment upon him you condemn yourself, because you, the judge, are doing the very same things. We know that the judgment of God rightly falls upon those who do such things. Do you suppose, O man, that when you judge those who do such things and yet do them yourself, you will escape the judgment of God?

This means that men who have never heard the fuller revelation of God recorded in the Bible will be judged on the basis of whether or not they have lived up to the standards they have set for themselves and others. And on this basis, there is no one who is innocent before God.

> . . . all men, both Jews and Greeks, are under the power of sin.

> . . . all have sinned and fall short of the glory of God.

☐ God's reaction to this situation cannot be neutral. He cannot pretend that disobedience does not matter or that it can be passed over or forgiven lightly. The prophets give many examples of situations in which God is compelled to act in judgment:

> I was ready to be sought by those who did not ask
> for me;
> I was ready to be found by those who did not
> seek me.
> I said, "Here am I, here am I," to a nation that did
> not call on my name.
> I spread out my hands all the day to a rebellious
> people,
> who walk in a way that is not good, following
> their own devices;
> a people who provoke me to my face continually . . .
> Behold, it is written before me:
> "I will not keep silent, but I will repay,
> yea, I will repay into their bosom their iniquities
> and their fathers' iniquities together, says
> the Lord."

The Bible uses the word *wrath* to describe God's reaction to man's rebellion:

> . . . we all once lived in the passions of our flesh, following the desires of body and mind, and so we were by nature children of wrath . . .

Paul speaks in this way about the final consequences of man's rebellion, if there is no repentance and turning to God:

> They shall suffer the punishment of eternal destruction and exclusion from the presence of the Lord and from the glory of his might.

☐ But this punishment is not inevitable. God offers forgiveness, if only rebel man will seek it:

> Come now, let us reason together, says the Lord:
> Though your sins are like scarlet,
>   they shall be as white as snow;
> though they are red like crimson,
>   they shall become like wool.

MAN CAN BECOME A "SON" OF GOD

☐ Although man is a rebel by nature and under the judgment of God, God has taken the initiative and done something to restore the broken relationship.

> While we were yet helpless, at the right time Christ died for the ungodly. Why, one will hardly die for a righteous man—though perhaps for a good man one will dare even to die. But God shows his love for us in that while we were yet sinners Christ died for us . . . We also rejoice in God through our Lord Jesus Christ, through whom we have now received our reconciliation.

☐ Jesus is the "Son of God" in a special and unique sense. But those who put their trust in him and accept the reconciliation which is offered on the basis of his death (see Part 3, Question Six, "What is the meaning of the death of Jesus?"), are born into the family of God to become "sons":

> To all who received him, who believed in his name, he gave power to become children of God; who were born, not of blood nor of the will of the flesh nor of the will of man, but of God.

☐Peter speaks in this way about the transforming process which
can go on in the life of the Christian here and now—even to the
point of "sharing the divine nature":

> His divine power has granted to us all things that pertain to
> life and godliness, through the knowledge of him who
> called us to his own glory and excellence, by which he has
> granted to us his precious and very great promises, that
> through these you may escape from the corruption that is
> in the world because of passion, and become partakers of
> the divine nature.

THE ANSWER
THIS APPROACH
GIVES TO THE
BASIC QUESTIONS
ABOUT MAN

THE INDIVIDUAL

Job has a frightening sense of God's awareness of every individual. In his suffering he even wishes that God were *less* concerned
about him:

> What is man, that thou dost make so much of him,
>   and that thou dost set thy mind upon him,
> dost visit him every morning,
>   and test him every moment?
> How long wilt thou not look away from me
>   nor let me alone till I swallow my spittle?
> If I sin, what do I do to thee, thou watcher of men?
>   Why hast thou made me thy mark?
>   Why have I become a burden to thee?
> Why dost thou not pardon my transgression
>   and take away my iniquity?
> For now I shall lie in the earth;
>   thou wilt seek me, but I shall not be.

At other times Job takes comfort from the knowledge that God
knows him and deals with him as an individual:

> But he knows the way that I take;
>   when he has tried me, I shall come forth as gold.

Ezekiel emphasizes that every individual is held responsible by
God for his own choices, and cannot blame his parents or anyone else:

225

The word of the Lord came to me again: "What do you
mean by repeating this proverb concerning the land of
Israel, 'The fathers have eaten sour grapes, and the children's teeth are set on edge'? As I live, says the Lord God,
this proverb shall no more be used by you in Israel. Behold, all souls are mine; the soul of the father as well as the
soul of the son is mine: the soul that sins shall die . . . The
son shall not suffer for the iniquity of the father, nor the
father suffer for the iniquity of the son; the righteousness
of the righteous shall be upon himself, and the wickedness
of the wicked shall be upon himself."

Jesus speaking about the value of the individual to God:

Are not five sparrows sold for two pennies? And not one of
them is forgotten before God. Why, even the hairs of your
head are all numbered. Fear not; you are of more value
than many sparrows.

This belief in the value of the individual provides a compelling reason for fighting for the rights of the individual.

Leslie Newbigin:

During World War II, Hitler sent men to the famous Beth-
el Hospital to inform Pastor Bodelschwingh, its director,
that the State could no longer afford to maintain hundreds
of epileptics who were useless to society and only constituted a drain on scarce resources, and that orders were
being issued to have them destroyed. Bodelschwingh confronted them in his room at the entrance to the Hospital
and fought a spiritual battle which eventually sent them
away without having done what they were sent to do. He
had no other weapon for the battle than the simple affirmation that these were men and women made in the
image of God and that to destroy them was to commit a sin
against God which would surely be punished. What other
argument could he have used?

MEANING

What gives meaning and significance to man's life is the fact that
God himself seeks to enter into a relationship with him:

". . . I am the Lord . . . and I will take you for my people,
and I will be your God; and you shall know that I am the
Lord your God . . ."

The individual can know that God has a plan and purpose for his life. God says to *Jeremiah* the prophet:

> Before I formed you in the womb I knew you,
> and before you were born I consecrated you;
> I appointed you a prophet to the nations.

Paul writes in this way about the plan of God which embraces the whole of our universe:

> Blessed be the God and Father of our Lord Jesus Christ, who has blessed us in Christ with every spiritual blessing in the heavenly places, even as he chose us in him before the foundation of the world, that we should be holy and blameless before him. He destined us in love to be his sons through Jesus Christ, according to the purpose of his will, to the praise of his glorious grace which he freely bestowed on us in the Beloved. In him we have redemption through his blood, the forgiveness of our trespasses, according to the riches of his grace which he lavished upon us. For he has made known to us in all wisdom and insight the mystery of his will, according to his purpose which he set forth in Christ as a plan for the fullness of time, to unite all things in him, things in heaven and things on earth.

The simplest and clearest description of the meaning of man's existence is given in the words of the *Westminster Shorter Catechism*:

> Man's chief end is to glorify God, and to enjoy him for ever.

VALUES

The ultimate standard of what is right and good is the character of God himself. What is in accordance with his character is right and what is contrary to his character is wrong.

> . . . the Lord appeared to Abram, and said to him, "I am God Almighty; walk before me, and be blameless . . ."

> . . . as he who called you is holy, be holy yourselves in all your conduct; since it is written, "You shall be holy, for I am holy."

The *Ten Commandments* revealed to Moses give an outline of the standards which God sets for men:

> You shall have no other gods before me . . .

You shall not make yourself a graven image . . .
you shall not bow down to them or serve them . . .
You shall not take the name of the Lord your
God in vain . . .
Remember the sabbath day, to keep it holy . . .
Honor your father and your mother . . .
You shall not kill.
You shall not commit adultery.
You shall not steal.
You shall not bear false witness against your neighbor.
You shall not covet . . .

The prophets were constantly exposing injustice and corruption
in personal and public life, applying the commandments in particular situations:

For I the Lord love justice,
I hate robbery and wrong . . .

Then I will draw near to you for judgment; I will be a swift
witness against the sorcerers, against the adulterers, against
those who swear falsely, against those who oppress the
hireling in his wages, the widow and the orphan, against
those who thrust aside the sojourner, and do not fear me,
says the Lord of hosts.

Jesus extended some of these commandments to cover the
thought life as well as outward actions, and he gave his own
summary of the Law of the Old Testament by bringing together
two verses from different books:

You shall love the Lord your God with all your heart, and
with all your soul, and with all your mind. This is the great
and first commandment. And a second is like it, You shall
love your neighbor as yourself. On these two commandments depend all the law and the prophets.

In the New Testament the meaning of love for others is
revealed much more clearly in the example of the love of Christ.
The character and teaching of Jesus thus becomes the clearest
demonstration of what Christian values are supposed to be:

Put to death . . . what is earthly in you: immorality, impuri-
ty, passion, evil desire, and covetousness, which is idolatry.
On account of these the wrath of God is coming. In these
you once walked, when you lived in them. But now put
them all away: anger, wrath, malice, slander, and foul talk

from your mouth. Do not lie to one another, seeing that
you have put off the old nature with its practices and have
put on the new nature, which is being renewed in knowledge after the image of its creator. . . . Put on then, as
God's chosen ones, holy and beloved, compassion, kindness,
lowliness, meekness, and patience, forbearing one another
. . . forgiving each other; as the Lord has forgiven you, so
you also must forgive. And above all these put on love,
which binds everything together in perfect harmony . . .

While the Christian, therefore, does not have ready-made
solutions to all moral problems, he at least has a firm starting-
point. And where there is doubt in particular situations, he can
rely on the leading of the Holy Spirit who can make his conscience sensitive to the mind of Christ.

. . . try to learn what is pleasing to the Lord . . . do not be
foolish, but understand what the will of the Lord is. And
do not get drunk with wine, for that is debauchery; but be
filled with the Spirit . . .

RELATIONSHIPS

There is a possibility of real communication between men because man still bears the image of the three-in-one God.

The Bible recognizes the deep *un*truthfulness in fallen human
nature, and reminds us that no deception can be hidden from
God:

The heart is deceitful above all things,
    and desperately corrupt;
    who can understand it?
"I the Lord search the mind and try the heart,
    to give to every man according to his ways,
        according to the fruit of his doings."
O Lord, thou hast searched me and known me!
Thou knowest when I sit down and when I rise up;
    thou discernest my thoughts from afar.
Thou searchest out my path and my lying down,
    and art acquainted with all my ways.
Even before a word is on my tongue,
    lo, O Lord, thou knowest it altogether.

Living in the light of God's presence and being a member in
the "body" of those who believe are real incentives to truthfulness:

229

If we walk in the light, as he is in the light, we have
fellowship with one another, and the blood of Jesus his Son
cleanses us from all sin.

Therefore, putting away falsehood, let every one speak the
truth with his neighbor, for we are members one of another.

Similarly, there is the possibility of love between people because man is made in the image of the God who *is* love, in his
very nature. Thus all relationships can be restored and guided
by the love that Christ has shown in practice:

Let all bitterness and wrath and anger and clamor and
slander be put away from you, with all malice, and be kind
to one another, tenderhearted, forgiving one another, as
God in Christ forgave you. Therefore be imitators of God,
as beloved children. And walk in love, as Christ loved us
and gave himself up for us.

Paul goes on to say in the same letter that within the marriage
relationship there can be a deep belonging and loving, not only
because man and woman become "one flesh," but because the
Christian has, in the sacrificial and self-giving love of Christ, a
pattern of what love can be in marriage:

Wives, be subject to your husbands, as to the Lord . . .
Husbands, love your wives, as Christ loved the church and
gave himself up for her.

Within this relationship there can be a deep sense of mutual
belonging:

I am my beloved's and my beloved is mine.

SUFFERING AND EVIL

The Christian is bound to feel this problem intensely. His belief
in the goodness of God is bound to accentuate the question of
"*why* suffering and evil?"

My God, my God, why hast thou forsaken me?
   why art thou so far from helping me, from the
      words of my groaning?
O my God, I cry by day, but thou dost not answer;
   and by night, but find no rest.

Thou who art of purer eyes than to behold evil
   and canst not look on wrong,
why dost thou look on faithless men,

> and art silent when the wicked swallows up the
>   man more righteous than he?
> Righteous art thou, O Lord, when I complain
>   to thee;
>   yet I would plead my case before thee.
> Why does the way of the wicked prosper?
>   Why do all who are treacherous thrive?
> Thou plantest them, and they take root;
>   they grow and bring forth fruit . . .

The Bible does not present a complete and systematic explanation of suffering and evil, but it does give some clues to this great mystery.

The origin of suffering and evil

At the start, everything in the universe was good:

> And God saw everything that he had made, and behold, it was very good.

Evil and suffering as we now know them are described as an intrusion as far as the human race is concerned. Man disobeyed God at the suggestion of the Serpent, who in other parts of the Bible is interpreted as the mouthpiece of Satan—a created supernatural being, less powerful than God, who has rebelled against him and is doing his utmost to spoil God's universe. Human suffering is very closely connected with man's rebellion; for God says to the woman after her disobedience:

> I will greatly multiply your pain in childbearing;
>   in pain you shall bring forth children . . .

And to the man:

> In the sweat of your face you shall eat bread till you return to the ground, for out of it you were taken; you are dust, and to dust you shall return.

Jesus saw the activity of Satan behind much suffering. For example, he describes a woman who has been paralyzed for eighteen years as one "whom Satan bound."

The Bible makes a distinction between suffering where there is an element of human responsibility, and suffering where the sufferer is in no sense responsible.

Suffering where there is an element of human responsibility. If man is free to do good, he is also free to do evil. This is part of the real

231

freedom God has given to man. *Moses* here reminds the children
of Israel about the laws of God for their national life; he tells
them that, as a general principle, disobedience will bring suffering:

> All these blessings shall come upon you and overtake you,
> if you obey the voice of the Lord your God. Blessed shall
> you be in the city, and blessed shall you be in the field.
> Blessed shall be the fruit of your body, and of your
> ground, and the fruit of your beasts.

But on the other hand:

> If you are not careful to do all the words of this law which
> are written in this book, that you may fear this glorious and
> awful name, the Lord your God, then the Lord will bring
> upon you and your offspring extraordinary afflictions, af-
> flictions severe and lasting, and sickness grievous and last-
> ing.

Jesus on one occasion suggested a possible connection between
a man's suffering and his sin. The man had been ill for thirty-
eight years, and after Jesus had healed him, he said:

> See, you are well! Sin no more, that nothing
>   worse befall you.

There are times when we realize we have brought suffering
on ourselves; the blame is ours. Then we may be able to say with
the Psalmist:

> It is good for me that I was afflicted,
>   that I might learn thy statutes . . .
> I know, O Lord, that thy judgments are right,
>   and that in faithfulness thou hast afflicted me.
> Let thy steadfast love be ready to comfort me
>   according to thy promise to thy servant.

Suffering where the sufferer has no responsibility. The book of *Job*
deals with the problem of the suffering of the innocent. Job is
portrayed as a God-fearing man (though not perfect or sinless),
who suffers bereavement, the loss of his possessions and finally
an intensely painful and unpleasant illness. The prologue of the
book makes it clear that Job's suffering is not in any way connected with any sin or disobedience, but is brought about by the
malicious activity of Satan. Job's friends do not know what has

happened "behind the scenes" in heaven. They argue that Job's
suffering is a direct result of his sin, or that it comes from God
to teach him some lesson. But Job is naturally impatient with
these half-truths which do not meet his need or explain his
particular suffering.

At the end of the book, God breaks into the discussion and
speaks to Job as the Sovereign Creator and Sustainer of the
universe. What he says to Job in effect is this: "I am the Creator
of the universe and you are a creature. I am infinite, and know
the answers to the questions about your suffering; but you are
finite and cannot expect to know all the answers. If you did, you
would be God. But look around you at the universe which I have
created and which I still control. Can't you see enough evidence
there to convince you that I am still in control? Can't you go on
trusting me as Creator, even though you do not understand the
reason for your suffering?"

After this Job reaches the point of surrendering himself to
God in trust and humility:

> I know that thou canst do all things,
>   and that no purpose of thine can be thwarted . . .
> Therefore I have uttered what I did not under-
>   stand,
>   things too wonderful for me, which I did not
>   know . . .
> I had heard of thee by the hearing of the ear,
>   but now my eye sees thee;
> therefore I despise myself,
>   and repent in dust and ashes.

At the conclusion of the book we are told that Job's reaction
to his suffering—with all its despair and angry questioning—is
much nearer to the truth about his suffering than the inadequate
half-truths his comforters have expressed:

> After the Lord had spoken these words to Job, the Lord
> said to Eliphaz the Temanite: "My wrath is kindled against
> you and against your two friends; for you have not spoken
> of me what is right, as my servant Job has . . ."

Jesus' attitude to suffering and evil

His mission included relieving suffering and fighting evil. At the
beginning of his public ministry Jesus applied some words of
Isaiah to himself—words which have been described as the "Nazareth Manifesto":

The Spirit of the Lord is upon me,
   because he has anointed me to preach good
     news to the poor.
He has sent me to proclaim release to the captives
and recovering of sight to the blind,
to set at liberty those who are oppressed,
to proclaim the acceptable year of the Lord.

He described himself as the one who is stronger than Satan, and has come to undo the ravages of Satan:

. . . if it is by the finger of God that I cast out demons, then the kingdom of God has come upon you. When a strong man, fully armed, guards his own palace, his goods are in peace; but when one stronger than he assails him and overcomes him, he takes away his armor in which he trusted, and divides his spoil.

When he stood before the grave of Lazarus his friend, we read:

When Jesus saw (Mary) weeping, and the Jews who came with her also weeping, he was deeply moved in spirit and troubled . . .

The word that is used here suggests that Jesus was moved not only with sorrow, but also with indignation—indignation over the terrible power of death. When he raised Lazarus from death, he was showing his determination and his power to overcome death and break its power.

There is something worse than physical suffering. Alongside this determination to fight suffering and evil, there is the reminder that there is something very much worse than physical suffering in this life:

There were some present at that very time who told him of the Galileans whose blood Pilate had mingled with their sacrifices. And he answered them, "Do you think that these Galileans were worse sinners than all the other Galileans, because they suffered thus? I tell you, No; but unless you repent you will all likewise perish. Or those eighteen upon whom the tower of Siloam fell and killed them, do you think that they were worse offenders than all the others who dwelt in Jerusalem? I tell you, No; but unless you repent you will all likewise perish."

I tell you, my friends, do not fear those who kill the body,
and after that have no more that they can do. But I will
warn you whom to fear: fear him who, after he has killed,
has power to cast into hell; yes, I tell you, fear him!

The meaning of his own suffering. Jesus endured suffering himself,
and fully identified himself with suffering humanity. After recording some of his healing miracles, Matthew says of Jesus:

This was to fulfil what was spoken by the prophet
    Isaiah,
"He took our infirmities and bore our diseases."

The writer of the letter to the Hebrews speaks of the significance of the suffering of Jesus in this way:

The children of a family share the same flesh and blood;
and so he too shared ours, so that through death he might
break the power of him who had death at his command,
that is, the devil; and might liberate those who, through
fear of death, had all their lifetime been in servitude . . .
And therefore he had to be made like these brothers of his
in every way, so that he might be merciful and faithful as
their high priest before God, to expiate the sins of the
people. For since he himself has passed through the test of
suffering, he is able to help those who are meeting their test
now.

Thus when Jesus the eternal Son suffered and died a cruel
death which he did not deserve, it was as if he was saying to
men: "I know what it means to suffer and I am prepared to
share the worst human suffering. But your greatest problem is
not suffering, it is sin and evil. And I am going through suffering and death now in order to break their power."

The certainty of an end to suffering and evil
One of the basic convictions of the Old Testament writers is that
God will one day judge the world, right wrongs, and act in such
a way that justice is done and seen to be done.

Let the heavens be glad, and let the earth rejoice;
    let the sea roar, and all that fills it;
    let the field exult, and everything in it!
Then shall all the trees of the wood sing for joy
    before the Lord, for he comes,

for he comes to judge the earth.
He will judge the world with righteousness,
and the peoples with his truth.

This "coming" has been partially fulfilled in the coming of the
Son among men. One of the "Servant Songs" in Isaiah emphasizes that the coming of God's Servant must lead to the
establishing of justice "in the earth":

Behold my servant, whom I uphold,
my chosen, in whom my soul delights . . .
He will not fail or be discouraged
till he has established justice in the earth.

If this bringing of justice has begun in the coming of Jesus, the
disciples of Jesus bear a heavy responsibility to see that it is
worked out in practice in society. These words of Isaiah emphasize the priority of justice even over "religious" duties:

Is not this the fast that I choose:
to loose the bonds of wickedness,
to undo the thongs of the yoke,
to let the oppressed go free,
and to break every yoke?
Is it not to share your bread with the hungry,
and bring the homeless poor into your
house . . . ?

The book of the Revelation speaks of the judgment of God on
evil beginning to be worked out in history. But the final goal is
the new heaven and the new earth:

Then I saw a new heaven and a new earth; for the first
heaven and the first earth had passed away, and the sea was
no more. And I saw the holy city, new Jerusalem, coming
down out of heaven from God, prepared as a bride
adorned for her husband; and I heard a great voice from
the throne saying, "Behold the dwelling of God is with
men. He will dwell with them, and they shall be his people,
and God himself will be with them; he will wipe away every
tear from their eyes, and death shall be no more, neither
shall there be mourning nor crying nor pain any more, for
the former things have passed away."

☐ The Christian answer to the problem of suffering and evil has
something to say to the *sufferer himself*.

Michel Quoist:

"It is not I, your God, who has willed suffering, it is men
. . . Sin is disorder, and disorder hurts . . . But I came, and
I took all your sufferings upon me, as I took all your sins. I
took them and suffered them before you."

☐ It also has something to say to *those who are thinking about* the
problem. Look again at the quotation from *C. E. M. Joad* on pp.
33–34 of Part 1.

☐ It provides *a strong motive for fighting suffering and evil* here and
now. They are seen to be intruders in God's universe. Jesus
committed himself to fighting them. And our present struggle
against them will contribute to their final overthrow.

Stephen Neill:

It is only the doctrine of the wrath of God, of his irrecon-
cilable hostility to all evil, which makes life tolerable in such
a world as ours.

*Problems and Questions arising out of
biblical Christianity's answer to the
question "What is man?" are taken up
on p. 312.*

ANSWER TWO:
PRIMAL RELIGION AND JUDAISM, ISLAM AND DEISM

Man is a creature
created by God—
but this is not the God
of the Bible.

The concepts of man in the different religions have a certain amount in common with the Christian concept. But the differences are significant and have far-reaching consequences.

Adopting the three main points of the Christian answer (p. 219), we can pinpoint some of the major points of difference:

☐ *Man the creature: all these religions think of man as God's creation. Judaism (and to some extent Islam) teaches that man has been made in the image of God. But since the concept of God is different, this is bound to be understood in a different way.*

☐ *Man the rebel: the non-Christian religions do not have the same sense of the serious consequences of man's disobedience towards God, and of the deep corruption of human nature.*

☐ *Man the son: if man is ever thought of as a son of God, it is usually in the general sense, meaning little more than "God's creature."*

Primal religion

In the different tribal religions of Africa, for example, man feels himself to be a creature of God. But at the same time he is very aware of many other supernatural powers which are at work in the universe and affect his everyday life.

Leopold Senghor, writing about the way in which the African tends to think of man and his place in the universe:

> Let us . . . consider the Negro African as he faces the object to be known, as he faces the Other: God, man, animal, tree or pebble, natural or social phenomenon. In contrast to the classic European, the Negro African does not draw a line between himself and the object; he does not hold it at a distance, nor does he merely look at it and analyze it. After holding it at a distance, after scanning it at a distance without analyzing it, he takes it vibrant in his hands, careful

239

not to kill or fix it. He touches it, feels it, *smells* it . . . Thus the Negro African *sympathizes*, abandons his personality to become identified with the Other, dies to be reborn in the Other. He does not assimilate; he is assimilated. He lives a common life with the Other; he lives in a symbiosis. To use Paul Claudel's expression, he "knows the Other." Subject and object are dialectically face to face in the very act of knowledge. It is a long caress in the night, an embrace of joined bodies, the act of love . . . The Negro African could say, "I feel, I dance the Other; I am." To dance is to discover and to recreate, especially when it is a dance of love. In any event it is the best way to know. Just as knowledge is at once discovery and creation—I mean, re-creation and recreation, after the model of God.

Writing about the African's unique way of looking at man, he says:

The Negro will have contributed, with other peoples, to reforging the unity of man and the world: linking flesh to the spirit, man to fellow men, the pebble to God.

Judaism

Judaism tends to have a more optimistic estimate of man's present condition than Christianity and denies the Christian belief that the individual inherits a sinful nature.

Dr. Isidore Epstein:

The divine relationship with man is indestructible. It can be strained or marred but cannot be severed entirely and broken beyond repair, not even by transgression and sin . . . If by erring from the right path man yields to temptation and lapses into sin, regret and penitence can repair the ravages of his sin and restore perfect harmony to this relationship.

Judaism rejects the idea of human proneness to sin. A natural tendency to evil would be a contradiction to the fundamental command of holiness, a contradiction to the holiness of God which man is called upon to reproduce in himself . . . Sin lieth at the door, not within man himself, and this is followed by "and thou shalt rule over him."

Dr. Hertz outlines the Jewish "doctrine of salvation" in this way:

Note that the initiative in atonement is with the sinner. He cleanses himself on the Day of Atonement by fearless self-

examination, open confession, and the resolve not to repeat
the transgressions of the past year. When our Heavenly
Father sees the abasement of the penitent sinner, He sprin-
kles, as it were, the clean waters of pardon and forgiveness
upon him.

On the Day of Atonement the Israelites resemble the
angels, without human wants, without sins, linked together
in love and peace. It is the only day of the year on which
the accuser Satan is silenced before the throne of Glory,
and even becomes the defender of Israel . . . The closing
prayer begins: "Thou givest a hand to transgressors, and
Thy right hand is stretched out to receive the penitent.
Thou hast taught us to make confession unto Thee of all
our sins, in order that we may cease from the violence of
our hands and may return unto Thee who delightest in the
repentance of the wicked." These words contain what has
been called "the Jewish doctrine of salvation."

Islam

The Qur'an has much to say about the dignity of man as God's
creature:

Your Lord said to the angels: "I am creating man from
clay. When I have fashioned him and breathed of My Spirit
into him, kneel down and prostrate yourselves before him."

The angels all prostrated themselves except Satan, who was
too proud, for he was an unbeliever.

"Satan," said Allah, "why do you not bow to him whom My
own hands have made? Are you too proud, or do you think
he is beneath you?"

Satan replied: "I am nobler than he. You created me from
fire, but him from clay."

. . . your Lord said to the angels: "I am placing on the
earth one that shall rule as My deputy" . . .

But in Islamic theology, the emphasis on the "otherness" of
God has tended to create a qualitative difference between God
and man.

H. A. R. Gibb:

In . . . setting man as it were face to face with God, without
any mediating spiritual or personal elements, Islam necessarily emphasized the contrast between them. In spite of
the passages of mystical intuition in the Koran, the dogmat-

241

ic derived from it could not but start from the postulate of
the opposition between God and man, and (as a necessary
corollary) the equality of all men in their creaturely relation
to God. In this stark contrast lies the original tension of
Islam.

C. C. Adams, writing about the attitude of Mohammed Abduh,
the nineteenth-century apologist, to the attributes of God:

> The orthodox position . . . is reaffirmed: although they may
> be similar in name to attributes and qualities ascribed to
> human beings, they are in reality not the same in nature.
> "God does not resemble any of His creatures, and there is
> no relation between them and Him, except that He is the
> one who brought them into existence, and they belong to
> Him and will return to Him."

The Qur'an has a different emphasis from the Bible's in its
story of Adam and his sin:

> "Adam," we said, "Satan is an enemy to you and to your
> wife. Let him not turn you out of Paradise and plunge you
> into affliction. Here you shall not hunger or be naked; you
> shall not thirst, or feel the scorching heat."

> But Satan whispered to him, saying: "Shall I show you the
> Tree of Immortality and an everlasting kingdom?"

> They both ate of its fruit, so that they beheld their naked-
> ness and began to cover themselves with leaves. Thus Adam
> disobeyed his Lord and went astray.

> Then his Lord had mercy on him; He relented towards
> him and rightly guided him.

Deism

Deism ignores or denies certain aspects of the Christian understanding of man.

Carl Becker, summarizing typical beliefs about man in the
eighteenth century:

1. Man is not natively depraved;
2. The end of life is life itself, the good life on earth
   instead of the beatific life after death;
3. Man is capable, guided solely by the light of reason and
   experience, of perfecting the good life on earth; and
4. The first essential condition of the good life on earth is
   the freeing of men's minds from the bonds of ignorance

and superstition, and of their bodies from the arbitrary oppression of the constituted social authorities.

The Deists of this period were often well aware of the end to which a more complete denial of Christian beliefs about God and man could go.

Paul Hazard:

> The Deism which we meet with in the writings of the period attenuates the idea of God, but does not annihilate it. It makes God the object of a belief vaguely defined, perhaps, yet positive none the less, and intentionally so. It sufficed at all events to endow its adherents with a sense of superiority over their godless brethren; it enabled them to pray and to worship; it prevented them from feeling that they were alone in the world, lost and fatherless . . . It is no easy matter to be an Atheist and brutally to crush out belief in the divine; it is incomparably easier to be a Deist . . . "A Deist," Bonald will one day be telling us, "is simply a man who hasn't had time to become an Atheist." "A man who doesn't want to be an Atheist," would be much nearer the mark.

THE ANSWER THIS APPROACH GIVES TO THE BASIC QUESTIONS ABOUT MAN

The quotations in this section are selective: we have not attempted to give the answer of *every* religion to *every* question.

THE INDIVIDUAL
Belief in any kind of personal God is likely to give the individual some feeling of uniqueness and significance in his relationship with his Creator. But in some cases the sense of individuality may be called in question or severely modified.

Islam
The problem for the individual is that the greatness and sovereignty of God can be stressed to the point where the individual no longer feels that he has any freedom, because all his actions have already been determined by God.

This is an admonition to all men: to those among you that have the will to be upright. Yet you cannot will except by the will of Allah, the Lord of the Creation.

Mohammed Abduh outlines the orthodox teaching in this way:

All . . . Muslim sects believe that they have a share of free choice in their actions which they call "acquisition" (*kasb*), and this is the basis of reward and punishment in the opinion of all of them.

At the same time he admits that, in practice, this balance has not always been held:

We do not deny that in the thought of the common people in Muslim lands this article has been contaminated with traces of the belief in compulsion, and this perhaps has been the cause of some of the misfortunes that have befallen them in past generations.

The Qur'an stresses that the individual stands alone before God:

There is none in the heavens or the earth but shall return to Him in utter submission. He has kept strict count of all His creatures, and one by one they shall approach Him on the Day of Resurrection. Invoke no other god with Allah. There is no god but He. All things shall perish except Himself. He is the judgment, and to Him you shall return.

However, the emphasis on the sovereignty of God is such that there is always the danger of the individual being swallowed up in the presence of the all-powerful God. And in some forms of Sufi mysticism, the sense of the individual is in danger of being lost completely.

Nicholson:

Does personality survive in the ultimate union with God? If personality means a conscious existence distinct, though not separate, from God, the majority of advanced Moslem mystics say "No!" As the rain-drop absorbed in the ocean is not annihilated but ceases to exist individually, so the disembodied soul becomes indistinguishable from the universal Deity.

Deism

The Deist's God has made the universe work according to its own fixed laws. But if the universe as a whole seems to work according to these laws, then man also must work in the same way. He cannot think that he is exempt from the working of these mechanical laws.

Norman Hampson describes how this problem was felt in the eighteenth century:

> The general direction of scientific thought combined . . . with a more pessimistic view of Providence to drive mid-century writers towards an unwilling choice between complete skepticism and rigorous determinism.

> The great mass of the population of western Europe continued to accept the literal truth of the Bible and the existence of a Christian order. But those in the forefront of the new scientific and intellectual movements had come to recognize that Moses was an unreliable historian. Alienated from a Church that insisted on the literal truth of Revelation, natural religion no longer afforded them acceptable proof of a providential order. Only two attitudes seemed to remain: to follow Hume in denying man's access to objective knowledge of any kind, or to accept d'Holbach's conception of a universe of matter in motion, in which everything happened of necessity and the answer to every question was "because it cannot be otherwise."

Charles Darwin, who came to call himself an agnostic, expresses the dilemma of the Deist who feels the difficulty of holding on to the significance of the individual:

> Believing as I do that man in the distant future will be a far more perfect creature than he now is, it is an intolerable thought that he and all other sentient beings are doomed to complete annihilation after such long-continued progress.

MEANING

Primal religion

John Mbiti describes the African world-view of man and his ultimate hopes of the future:

> According to African religions and philosophy, the grave is the seal of everything, even if a person survives and continues to exist in the next world. There is an accelerated rhythm from death through the state of personal immortality (as the living-dead) to the state of collective immortality (as ordinary spirits). This final "beat" of the rhythm may or

may not have an end. There is, however, nothing to hope
for, since this is the destiny of everybody; though older
people do not seem to fear, and may even long for, the
"departure" from this to the next world. There is no resurrection for either the individual or mankind at large . . .
The departed do not grow spiritually towards or like God,
though some may act as intermediaries between men and
God and may have more power and knowledge than
human beings. Such is the anthropocentric view of the
destiny of man, and as far as traditional African concepts
are concerned, death is death and the beginnings of a
permanent ontological departure of the individual from
mankind to spirithood. Beyond that point, African religions
and philosophy are absolutely silent, or at most extremely
vague. Nothing can reverse or halt that process, and death
is the end of real and complete man.

African religions have their own mythology about the origins of
the human race; but they can hold out little hope for the individual as he faces death:

Yet behind these fleeting glimpses of the original state and
bliss of man, whether they are rich or shadowy, there lie
the tantalizing and unattained gift of the resurrection, the
loss of human immortality and the monster death. Here
African religions and philosophy must admit a defeat: they
have supplied no solution. This remains the most serious
cul-de-sac in the otherwise rich thought and sensitive feeling of our peoples.

Islam

The Qur'an emphatically agrees with Christianity that "man's
chief end is to glorify God . . .":

"I created mankind and the jinn in order that they might
worship Me."

Many passages speak of the hope of Paradise which is held out
to believers:

For the unbelievers We have prepared fetters and chains,
and a blazing fire. But the righteous shall drink of a cup
tempered at the Camphor Fountain, a gushing spring at
which the servants of Allah will refresh themselves: they
who keep their vows and dread the far-spread terrors of
Judgment-day; who for love of Allah give sustenance to the

poor man, the orphan, and the captive, saying: "We feed
you for Allah's sake only; we seek of you neither recom-
pense nor thanks: for we fear from Him a day of anguish
and of woe."

Allah will deliver them from the evil of that day and make
their countenance shine with joy. He will reward them for
their steadfastness with robes of silk and the delights of
Paradise. Reclining there upon soft couches, they shall feel
neither the scorching heat nor the biting cold. Trees will
spread their shade around them, and fruits will hang in
clusters over them . . .

They shall be arrayed in garments of fine green silk and
rich brocade, and adorned with bracelets of silver. Their
Lord will give them a pure beverage to drink.

Thus you shall be rewarded; your high endeavors are grati-
fying to Allah.

Many Muslims would not interpret passages such as these in a
literal way. But when every allowance has been made for metaphor and symbol, the Muslim cannot hold out the hope of
enjoying a personal relationship with God. He may point to the
mystic's hope of union with God, but this has to be understood
in terms of absorption into God. So that although he can speak
of man's goal as being "to glorify God," he cannot consistently
add with the Christian, "and to enjoy him for ever."

Deism

The God of Deism offers little consolation to man in his search
for meaning.

Diderot:

O God, I do not know if you exist . . . I ask nothing in this
world, for the course of events is determined by its own
necessity if you do not exist, or by your decree if you
do . . . Here I stand, as I am, a necessarily organized part
of eternal and necessary matter—or perhaps your own creation.

Martin Esslin, quoting and explaining some words from Samuel Beckett's *Waiting for Godot:*

"Given the existence . . . of a personal God . . . outside time
without extension who from the heights of divine apathia
divine athambia divine aphasia loves us dearly with some

247

exceptions for reasons unknown . . . and suffers . . . with those who for reasons unknown are plunged in torment . . ." Here again we have the personal God, with his divine apathy, his speechlessness (aphasis), and his lack of the capacity for terror or amazement (athambia), who loves us dearly—with some exceptions, who will be plunged into the torments of hell. In other words, God, who does not communicate with us, cannot feel for us, and condemns us for reasons unknown.

VALUES

Primal religion
God tends to have little to do with the standards or values adopted by any society.

John Mbiti, writing about African religions:

> Even if . . . God is thought to be the ultimate upholder of the moral order, people do not consider Him to be immediately involved in the keeping of it. Instead, it is the patriarchs, living-dead, elders, priests, or even divinities and spirits who are the daily guardians or police of human morality. Social regulations of a moral nature are directed towards the immediate contact between individuals, between man and the living-dead and the spirits. Therefore, these regulations are on the man-to-man level, rather than the God-to-man plane of morality.

Judaism
The moral values of Judaism are derived, with varying strictness, from the Old Testament law. In many cases they differ from Christian values because they are affected by Judaism's more optimistic diagnosis of man's present condition.

Roy Stewart:

> The Christian view of sin and atonement is sterner, more realistic, and more inward than the Jewish one. Its outward rules are fewer, less related to specific circumstance, centered in greater measure in the intangible realm of the human heart—which makes its canons loftier and more difficult for the observer. Much of what the Christian regards as sin might be redefined as insufficiency of love, God-ward or manward . . . It follows from this that a Jew may sometimes feel a satisfaction with his life and conduct

which is impossible for the Christian . . . If ever a Jew looks
for some divine reward for his virtues, a Christian can look
only for divine pardon for his sins.

Herbert Danby, writing about an article by Ahad ha-Am (Asher
Ginzberg):

The Christian "golden rule" is "Do unto others what you
would that men should do unto you." Judaism has the
same, or what seems to be the same rule in the negative
form: "What is hateful to thyself, do not do unto thy
neighbor." And Ahad ha-Am believes that in these two
forms lies the ethical difference in the two religions: egotism is the mark of Jewish ethics; but Christian altruism, he
insists, is merely inverted egotism, the substitution of *other*
for *self.*

Ahad ha-Am is not content to leave the matter at that. To
make an apparently abstruse point clear as daylight he
quotes the following case from the Talmud:

Imagine two men traveling in the desert; only one of them
has a bottle of water; if both drink they will both die before
their journey's end; if only one drinks he will reach safety,
but his companion will certainly die. What should the man
with the bottle of water do? Rabbi Akiba decided (and
Ahad ha-Am fully agrees that the decision counts as a
fundamental principle of Jewish morality)—R. Akiba decided that the man with the water should keep it and drink
it all himself; because *both* of them could not survive, it is
more *just,* more in accord with God's righteousness, that a
man should save himself rather than that he should save his
neighbor and so lose his own life. Other things being equal,
says Jewish morality, you have no right to assume that your
neighbor's affairs are of more worth in God's eyes than
your own affairs. Certainly Judaism approves of the laying
down of life to fulfill a religious idea (sanctification of the
name of God, martyrdom); but it condemns the man who
will suppress himself for the sake of his fellow. Christianity,
on the contrary, teaches: "Greater love hath no man than
this, that a man lay down his life for his friends."

Ahad ha-Am maintains that this, the basic difference between Jewish and Christian ethics, shows the superiority of
Jewish ethics, in that it replaces the illogical Christian doctrine of self-sacrifice, self-renunciation, by the *absolute rule of
justice.*

249

Islam

The word *holy* is applied to God, but it occurs only once in the Qur'an:

> He is Allah, besides whom there is no other god. He is the Sovereign Lord, the Holy One, the Giver of Peace, the Keeper of Faith, the Guardian, the Mighty One, the All-Powerful, the Most High! Exalted be He above their idols!

This holiness, however, is not defined in terms of moral purity or perfection, but in terms of transcendence:

Baidawi, the great Moslem commentator on the Qur'an of the thirteenth century writes:

> Holy means the complete absence of anything that would make Him less than He is.

Al-Ghazzali writes in this way about the justice of God:

> Allah's justice is not to be compared with the justice of men. For a man may be supposed to act unjustly by invading the possession of another, but no injustice can be conceived on the part of God. It is in His power to pour down upon men torments, and if He were to do it, His justice could not be arraigned. Yet he rewards those that worship Him for their obedience on account of His promise and beneficence, not of their merit or of necessity, since there is nothing which He can be tied to perform; nor can any injustice be supposed in Him nor can He be under any obligation to any person whatsoever.

Thus, since God is not holy in the biblical sense, the moral law for man cannot be based on the character of God—what he *is* by nature. It has to be based on the commands or decrees of God. And the Five Pillars of Islam express the most important things in the life of the Moslem: Recital of the Creed, Prayer, Fasting, Almsgiving, Pilgrimage.

J. N. D. Anderson:

> It is these Five Pillars, and particularly the profession of the Creed and the performance of prayer and fasting, which chiefly make up the practice of Islam to the average Muslim. He who acknowledges the Unity and Transcendence of God, pays Him His due in prayer and fast, and accepts Muhammed as the last and greatest of the Prophets, may well, indeed, have to taste the Fire, but hopes that he will

not, like the infidel, remain in it for ever—through the timely intercession of the Prophet. The most heinous sins are polytheism, apostasy, skepticism and impiety, besides which social sins and all subtler forms of evil pale into comparative insignificance.

Deism

The eighteenth-century Deists believed that Nature and Reason pointed to certain basic, self-evident values and truths. Any reasonable person therefore should be able instinctively to recognize these values for himself.

John Locke:

> The state of Nature has a law of Nature to govern it, which obliges every one, and reason, which is that law, teaches all mankind who will but consult it, that being all equal and independent, no one ought to harm another in his life, health, liberty or possessions.

Hooke:

> There is in all men a general benevolence and freely given goodness . . . Thus there is no duty that is not commended to us, not only by reason, but even by appetite.

This attitude to Reason and Nature, however, eventually led many toward profound moral skepticism, as soon as they realized the impossibility of establishing agreed values on this basis.

Basil Willey writing about William Wordsworth:

> By the summer of 1795 the effort to rise superior to "infirmities of nature, time and place" had landed him in moral skepticism, and he reached "the crisis of that strong disease" in which he "yielded up moral questions in despair" . . . His own experience had taught him that the process of dragging all precepts to the bar of reason led to moral chaos.

RELATIONSHIPS

Two basic questions we need to ask are these:

☐ Do these religions supply a compelling reason for truthfulness and love in personal relationships?

☐ If one cannot speak of God as being "love" in his very nature, does it make sense to speak of the "love of God" as a guide in our understanding of human love?

251

Primal religion

John Mbiti writes about the closely-knit tribal society:

> Within this tightly knit corporate society where personal
> relationships are so intense and so wide, one finds perhaps
> the most paradoxical areas of African life. This corporate
> type of life makes every member of the community danger-
> ously naked in the sight of other members. It is paradoxi-
> cally the center of love and hatred, of friendship and enmi-
> ty, of trust and suspicion, of joy and sorrow, of generous
> tenderness and bitter jealousies. It is paradoxically the
> heart of security and insecurity, of building and destroying
> the individual and the community. Everybody knows every-
> body else: a person cannot be individualistic, but only cor-
> porate. Every form of pain, misfortune, sorrow or suffer-
> ing; every illness and sickness; every death whether of an
> old man or of the infant child; every failure of the crop in
> the fields, of hunting in the wilderness or of fishing in the
> waters; every bad omen or dream: these and all the other
> manifestations of evil that man experiences are blamed on
> somebody in the corporate society.

The love of God is taken for granted, but is seldom made
explicit:

> As for the love of God, there are practically no direct
> sayings that God loves. This is something reflected also in
> the daily lives of African peoples, in which it is rare to hear
> people talking about love. A person shows his love for
> another more through action than through words. So, in
> the same way, people experience the love of God in con-
> crete acts and blessings; and they assume that He loves
> them, otherwise He would not have created them.

Islam

The following are some of the passages of the Qur'an which
speak about the obligation to love:

> Such is Allah's promise to true believers who do good
> works. Say: "For this I demand of you no recompense. I
> ask you only to love your kindred. He that does a good
> deed shall be repaid many times over. Allah is forgiving
> and bounteous in His rewards."

> By one of His signs He created you from dust; you became
> men and multiplied throughout the earth. By another sign

He gave you wives from among yourselves that you might
live in joy with them, and planted love and kindness in
your hearts. Surely there are signs in this for thinking men.

It may well be that Allah will put good will between you
and those with whom you have hitherto been at enmity.
Allah is mighty. He is forgiving and merciful.

Allah does not forbid you to be kind and equitable to those
who have neither made war on your religion nor driven
you from your homes. Allah loves the equitable. But he
forbids you to make friends with those who have fought
against you on account of your religion and driven you
from your homes or abetted others to do so. Those that
make friends with them are wrongdoers.

SUFFERING AND EVIL

Primal religion

John Mbiti describes how suffering and evil are understood in
African tribal society:

> By this ("natural evil") I mean those experiences in human
> life which involve suffering, misfortune, diseases, calamity,
> accidents and various forms of pain. In every African soci-
> ety these are well known. Most of them are explainable
> through "natural" causes. But . . . for African peoples noth-
> ing sorrowful happens by "accident" or "chance": it must all
> be "caused" by some agent (either human or spiritual) . . .
> In some societies it is thought that a person suffers because
> he has contravened some regulation, and God or the spirits,
> therefore, punish the offender. In that case, the person
> concerned is actually the cause of his own suffering . . . But
> in most cases, different forms of suffering are believed to be
> caused by human agents who are almost exclusively witches,
> sorcerers and workers of evil magic . . . They are . . .
> "responsible" for "causing" what would be "natural evil," by
> using incantations, mystical power, medicines, by sending
> secondary agents like flies and animals, by using their "evil
> eye," by wishing evil against their fellow man, by hating or
> feeling jealous, and by means of other "secret" methods
> . . . In the experience of evil, African peoples see certain
> individuals as being intricately involved, but wickedly, in the
> otherwise smooth running of the natural universe.

In African villages, disease and misfortune are religious
experiences, and it requires a religious approach to deal

with them. The medicine-men are aware of this, and make
attempts to meet the need in a religious (or quasi-religious)
manner—whether or not that turns out to be genuine or
false or a mixture of both . . .

Suffering, misfortune, disease and accident, are all "caused"
mystically, as far as African peoples are concerned. To
combat the misfortune or ailment the cause must also be
found, and either counteracted, uprooted or punished.
This is where the value of the traditional medicine-man
comes into the picture. So long as people see sickness and
misfortune as "religious" experiences, the traditional medicine-man will continue to exist and thrive.

Islam

Everything, both good and evil, is determined by the Will of
God, although man is not completely absolved from his responsibility.

Allah does not change a people's lot unless they change
what is in their hearts. If he seeks to afflict them with a
misfortune, none can ward it off. Besides Him, they have
no protector.

Whatever good befalls you, man, it is from Allah: and
whatever ill from yourself.

While the problem of suffering and evil must remain an inscrutable mystery, the Qur'an on the one hand emphasizes the
need to create a just society here and now, and on the other
points forward to the day of judgment when evil will be overcome. The crucial difference between this and the Christian
answer is that Islam has no place for Jesus as the suffering
Savior who defeated evil by experiencing its full horrors and
going through death.

ANSWER THREE:
HUMANISM, EXISTENTIALISM, COMMUNISM, AND EASTERN RELIGIONS

Man is not the creation
of God because there
is no personal Creator.

After many centuries of Christian the-
ism, the "Western mind" has rejected
the Creator and the supernatural, and
proclaimed the autonomy of man. In
consequence:

□ *Man is now "forlorn," he is on his
own.*

□ *The question "What is man?" becomes
almost unanswerable. We can no
longer hope to explain what we are.*

□ *The autonomy of man's thinking about
himself has brought him to a "complete
anarchy of thought."*

Albert Camus:

Up till now, man derived his coherence from his Creator.
But from the moment that he consecrates his rupture with
Him, he finds himself delivered over to the fleeting moment, to the passing days, and to wasted sensibility. Therefore he must take himself in hand.

Jean-Paul Sartre:

If God does not exist . . . man is in consequence forlorn,
for he cannot find anything to depend upon, either within
or outside himself.

Christopher Dawson:

The Western mind has turned away from the contemplation of the absolute and eternal to the knowledge of the
particular and the contingent. It has made man the measure of all things and has sought to emancipate human life
from its dependence on the supernatural. Instead of the
whole intellectual and social order being subordinated to
spiritual principles, every activity has declared its independence, and we see politics, economics, science, and art
organizing themselves as autonomous kingdoms which owe
no allegiance to any higher power.

Hannah Arendt:

The problem of human nature . . . seems unanswerable in
both its individual psychological sense and its general philosophical sense. It is highly unlikely that we, who can know,
determine, and define the natural essences of all things
surrounding us, which we are not, should ever be able to
do the same for ourselves . . . The conditions of human

existence—life itself, natality and mortality, worldliness, plurality, and the earth—can never "explain what we are." . . .

Ernst Cassirer, writing about the legacy of thinkers like Nietzsche, Freud and Marx:

> Owing to this development our modern theory of man lost its intellectual center. We acquired instead a complete anarchy of thought . . . An established authority to which one might appeal no longer existed. Theologians, scientists, politicians, sociologists, biologists, psychologists, ethnologists, economists all approached the problem from their own viewpoints . . . Every author seems in the last count to be led by his own conception and evaluation of human life.

He quotes *Max Scheler:*

> In no other period of human knowledge has man become more problematical to himself than in our own days . . . We no longer possess any clear and consistent idea of man.

Humanism

Humanism is defined in *The Glossary of Humanism* as follows:

> In broad terms contemporary Humanism subscribes to a view of life that is centered on man and his capacity to build a worthwhile life for himself and his fellows here and now. The emphasis is placed on man's own intellectual and moral resources, and the notion of supernatural religion is rejected.

> One of the most important trends in modern Humanism is its reliance on the application of scientific inquiry and its evaluation of truth, reality and morals in purely human terms.

We may take each of these main elements and illustrate them in turn.

The autonomy of man.
Blackham:

> Humanism proceeds from the assumption *that* man is on his own and this life is all and an assumption *of* responsibility for one's own life and for the life of mankind.

> The simple theme of humanism is self-determination, for persons, for groups and societies, for mankind together.

257

Edmund Leach:

Men have become like gods. Isn't it about time that we understood our divinity? Science offers us total mastery over our environment and over our destiny, yet instead of rejoicing we feel deeply afraid . . . All of us need to understand that God, or Nature, or Chance, or Evolution, or the Course of History, or whatever you like to call it, can't be trusted any more. We simply must take charge of our own fate . . . It has ceased to be true that nature is governed by inevitable laws external to ourselves. We ourselves have become responsible.

Progress and improvement of man's condition.
Lord Willis:

Humanism is a faith, a faith by which it is possible to live. To sum it up very briefly, I believe that this life is the only one of which we have any knowledge, and it is our job to improve it.

Reliance on reason.
Geoffrey Scott:

Humanism is the effort of men to think, to feel, and to act for themselves, and to abide by the logic of results . . . A new method is suddenly apprehended, tested, and carried firmly to its conclusion. Authority, habit, orthodoxy, are disregarded or defied. The argument is pragmatic, realistic, human. The question, "Has this new thing a value?" is decided directly by the individual in the court of his experience; and there is no appeal. That is good which is seen to satisfy the human test, and to have brought an enlargement of human power.

A. J. Ayer:

I do not like to think of Humanism as a religion because one of its great merits, one of the things that has attracted me to it and caused me to become a Humanist, is its lack of dogma. One of the fundamental positions taken by Humanists is that men should have freedom to think out for themselves how they ought to live, to think out their own principles.

H. J. Blackham:

Each must think and decide for himself on important ques-

tions concerning the life he has and his conduct of it; and,
most general, that nothing is exempt from human question.
This means that there is no immemorial tradition, no revelation, no authority, no privileged knowledge (first principles, intuitions, axioms) which is beyond question because
beyond experience and which can be used as a standard by
which to interpret experience. There is only experience to
be interpreted in the light of further experience, the sole
source of all standards of reason and value, for ever open
to question. This radical assumption is itself, of course,
open to question, and stands only in so far as it is upheld
by experience.

Reliance on science.
  Julian Huxley:

> This new idea-system, whose birth we of the mid twen-
> tieth-century are witnessing, I shall simply call *Humanism*,
> because it can only be based on our understanding of man
> and his relations with the rest of his environment . . .

> Science has attained a new and very real unity and firmness
> of organization and is giving us a scientifically-based picture
> of human destiny and human possibilities. For the first time
> in history, science can become the ally of religion instead of
> its rival or its enemy, for it can provide a "scientific" theolo-
> gy, a scientifically-ordered framework of belief, to whatever
> new religion emerges from the present idealogical disorder.

Existentialism

It is impossible to give a precise definition of Existentialism,
because it is not a precise philosophy. One of its basic ideas is
that there can be no complete philosophical system which answers all our questions. It insists that instead of talking about
"objective truth," which can never be obtained, we should begin
with the actual individual and his experience as a human being—with his freedom, his despair and his anguish. The following extracts give some idea of what Existentialism stands for.

  E. L. Allen defines it as:

> the attempt to philosophize from the standpoint of the
> actor rather than from that of the detached spectator.

  Karl Heim:

> A proposition or truth is said to be *existential* when I cannot

259

apprehend or assent to it from the standpoint of a mere
spectator but only on the ground of my total existence.

The Humanist Glossary, under Existentialism:

Kierkegaard and Heidegger, who are religious existentialist
philosophers, and Sartre, who is an atheist, all share certain
fundamental ideas. The starting point of their philosophy is
the plight of the individual, thrust, as it were, into a world
without authority, system of values, of law or human nature. Their basic tenet is that there is an inescapable tension
between thought and existence; existence cannot be
thought and thought departs from existence into abstraction. Man, being both thinker and in existence, has to live
this tension, which he can never resolve once for all. Similarly, there are other oppositions which man has to live and
cannot resolve because they make the human condition, e.g.
faith and reason, the other and myself as persons. Human
beings are always finding ways to escape from instead of
living by, the conditions of the human situation.

Sartre:

Existentialism is nothing else but an attempt to draw the
full conclusions from a consistently atheistic position.

Atheistic existentialism, of which I am a representative,
declares with greater consistency that if God does not exist
there is at least one being whose existence comes before its
essence, a being which exists before it can be defined by
any conception of it. That being is man or, as Heidegger
has it, the human reality. What do we mean by saying that
existence precedes essence? We mean that man first of all
exists, encounters himself, surges up in the world—and
defines himself afterwards. If man as the existentialist sees
him is not definable, it is because to begin with he is
nothing . . . Man is nothing else but that which he makes of
himself. That is the first principle of existentialism.

The first effect of existentialism is that it puts every man in
possession of himself as he is, and places the entire responsibility for his existence squarely upon his own shoulders.
And, when we say that man is responsible for himself, we
do not mean that he is responsible only for his own individuality, but that he is responsible for all men.

H. J. Blackham:

> The peculiarity of existentialism . . . is that it deals with the separation of man from himself and from the world, which raises the questions of philosophy . . . The main business of this philosophy therefore is not to answer the questions which are raised but to drive home the questions themselves until they engage the whole man and are made personal, urgent, and anguished . . . Existentialism goes back to the beginning of philosophy and appeals to all men to awaken from their dogmatic slumbers and discover what it means to become a human being . . .

> The second business of philosophy . . . is to cure the mind of looking for illusory objective universal answers, and to aid the person in making himself and getting his experience.

Communism

The particular aspects of Communism which concern us here are not its political and economic theory, but rather its basic humanism.

John Lewis, writing about Karl Marx:

> We must not consider Marx as an economist . . . but as a sociologist, a philosopher . . . His thought remains that of a philosopher. Beyond the economic "appearances" it plunges into the human reality that causes them. For the *factual* view of things, Marx substitutes a profound insight into human needs. His is a new humanism, new because it is incarnate.

> Humanism, the *philosophy of humanism*, rather than economics, is the basic character and positive contribution of Marxian thought.

> Marxism is humanism in its contemporary form . . . And the Marxist has this to convince the disinherited, whether in the great industrial cities of the West or the fields and mines of the colonial countries, that their very oppression could be the instrument of their emancipation, their entrance into an earthly paradise of material plenty and human justice.

> It is not sufficiently understood that Marx's own thinking was basically humanist. He recognized the worth of the individual personality, he blazed with indignation at social injustice; there was prophetic fire in his passion for righteousness . . .

Behind the whole philosophy of Marxism there is a passionate opposition to all relations, all conditions in which
man is a humiliated, enslaved, despised creature. That is
why Marxism is a humanism.

Guy Wint, writing about Communism in East Asia:

Communism, seen in one light, is an effort by a group of
the intelligentsia, inspired by moral ideas borrowed from
the West . . . to end or lessen the exploitation, to see that
more justice is done to the mass of the people, and to open
to them the opportunities of better life made possible by
science.

Richard Crossman, in the introduction to his book *The God
That Failed* (essays by six people who were all at one time members of the Communist Party or very sympathetic to it) writes:

The only link . . . between these six very different personalities is that all of them—after tortured struggles of conscience—chose Communism because they had lost faith in
democracy and were willing to sacrifice "bourgeois liberties"
in order to defeat Fascism. Their conversion, in fact, was
rooted in despair—a despair of western values.

Eastern religions

Hinduism. The clue to all eastern thinking about man is
contained in one of the most significant sayings of Hinduism:
"Thou art That"—i.e. the individual soul is to be identified with
the Brahman, the all-pervading God.

K. M. Sen:

The *Upanishads* point out that the *Brahman* and the *Atman*
are the same. The Supreme has manifested Himself in
every soul, and the student of religion is dramatically told
in the *Upanishads*, "Thou art That" (*tat tvam asi*). This idea
provides the core of most Hindu religious thought and is
developed later by Samkara into his doctrine of *advaita* (lit.
non-duality). This is a monistic doctrine, which denies the
existence of the world as separate from God.

W. Cantwell Smith, writing about the sentence "Thou art
That":

The phrase . . . consists of three Sanskrit words, generally
regarded in India as the most important sentence that that

country has ever pronounced; the succinct formulation of a
profound and ultimate truth about man and the universe.
The phrase is: *tat tvam asi*. *Tat* means "that"; *tvam* means
"thou"; and *asi* is the second person singular of the verb "to
be." "That thou art"; *tat tvam asi*. It means, thou art that
reality, thou art God. The same truth is expressed in other
ways; for instance, in the famous equation "*atman* equals
Brahman"—or the soul of man is God, or the Ultimate
Reality, with a very large capital U and capital R; the really
real. The individual self is the world soul. The soul of man
equals the ultimate of the universe. "Thou," or to use our
more colloquial term, "you"—each one of you reading this
book—are in some final, cosmic sense the total and transcendent truth that underlies all being, *Brahman* who precedes and transcends God himself, the Infinite and Absolute Reality beyond all phenomena, beyond all apprehension and beyond all form.

Buddhism. Buddhism accepts the same starting-point as Hinduism, and looks forward to the state of Nirvana, in which man
becomes one with the universe.

Christmas Humphreys:

At the heart of the Universe is the One Reality of which the
universe as we know it is but a periodic manifestation. This
is the only Supreme Deity known to Indian thought, for the
Upanishadic philosophy, like Buddhism, "revolts against the
deistic conception of God." (Radhakrishnan) . . .

The quintessence of Indian thought may be summed up by
saying that the Atman of man and the Atman of the universe are one.

Nirvana . . . is not the goal of escapism, a refuge from the
turning Wheel; it *is* the Wheel, and he who realizes himself
in this discovery makes his daily life divine. For him all
things are Suchness, and he sees but the Suchness of things.
His *Citta*, or inmost heart and mind, is one with the Universe; he *is* Mind Only.

In spite of the many differences between Humanism, Existentialism, Communism, and the Eastern religions, they all share the
same basic starting point in their attitude to man. They therefore
also share many of the same dilemmas.

263

THE ANSWER
THIS APPROACH
GIVES TO THE
BASIC QUESTIONS
ABOUT MAN

THE INDIVIDUAL

If I am not a creature created in the image of God and therefore having meaning and value as an individual, what reason do
I have for holding on to the feeling that my personality is
unique and individual? The following extracts are from writers
who have felt the problem in different ways.

Pearl Buck sees no difficulty in asserting the freedom and
uniqueness of the individual:

> I believe we are born free—free of inheritance in that we
> can by our wills determine to be free of it, free of environ-
> ment because no environment can shape one who will not
> be shaped. We are born free, in other words, of every sort
> of predestination. In each of us there is a little germ of
> individual being, compounded, it may be, of everything,
> inheritance, environment and all else, but the compound
> itself is new. It is forever unique. This *I* is never *You* or *He.*
> And this *I* is free, if I only know it and act upon that
> freedom.
>
> Does this make a philosophy? Such as it is, it is all I have.

E. M. Forster feels the problem more keenly, but has the
optimistic hope that the individual can hold on to the feeling of
his own individuality:

> These are the reflections of an individualist and a liberal
> who has found liberalism crumbling beneath him and at
> first felt ashamed. Then, looking around, he decided there
> was no special reason for shame, since other people, what-
> ever they felt, were equally insecure. And as for individual-
> ism—there seems no way out of this, even if one wants to
> find one . . .
>
> Until psychologists and biologists have done much more
> tinkering than seems likely, the individual remains firm and
> each of us must consent to be one, and to make the best of
> the difficult job.

Colin Wilson describes the problem as it is felt by "The Outsider," and is not as confident as Forster about the security of
the individual:

Their problem is the unreality of their lives. They become acutely conscious of it when it begins to pain them, but they are not sure of the source of the pain. The ordinary world loses its values, as it does for a man who has been ill for a very long time. Life takes on the quality of a nightmare, or a cinema sheet when the screen goes blank. These men who had been projecting their hopes and desires into what was passing on the screen suddenly realize they are in a cinema. They ask: Who are we? What are we doing here? With the delusion of the screen identity gone, the causality of its events suddenly broken, they are confronted with a terrifying dream. In Sartre's phrase, they are "condemned to be free." Completely new bearings are demanded; a new analysis of this real world of the cinema has to be undertaken. In the shadow world on the screen, every problem had an answer; this may not be true of the world in the cinema. The fact that the screen world has proved to be a delusion arouses the disturbing possibility that the cinema world may be unreal too. "When we dream that we dream, we are beginning to wake up!" Novalis says. Chuang Tzu had once said that he had dreamed he was a butterfly, and now wasn't sure if he was a man who dreamed he was a butterfly or a butterfly dreaming he was a man.

Eugene Ionesco writes of the problem of the individual as he expresses it in his plays:

> Two fundamental states of consciousness are at the root of all my plays . . . These two basic feelings are those of evanescence on the one hand, and heaviness on the other; of emptiness and of an overabundance of presence; of the unreal transparency of the world, and of its opaqueness . . . The sensation of evanescence results in a feeling of anguish, a sort of dizziness. But all of this can just as well become euphoric; anguish is suddenly transformed into liberty . . . This state of consciousness is very rare, to be sure . . . I am most often under the dominion of the opposite feeling: lightness changes to heaviness, transparence to thickness; the world weighs heavily; the universe crushes me. A curtain, an insuperable wall, comes between me and the world, between me and myself. Matter fills everything, takes up all space, annihilates all liberty under its weight . . . Speech crumbles.

Harold Pinter expresses the despair of one who does not know who he is himself, and is enraged at the complacency of others who think they do know:

> Occasionally I believe I perceive a little of what you are, but that's pure accident. Pure accident on both our parts, the perceived and the perceiver. It's nothing like an accident, it's deliberate, it's a joint pretense. We depend on these contrived accidents, to continue . . . What you are, or appear to be to me, or appear to be to you, changes so quickly, so horrifyingly, I certainly can't keep up with it and I'm damn sure you can't either. But who you are I can't even begin to recognize, and sometimes I recognize it so wholly, so forcibly, I can't look, and how can I be certain of what I see? You have no number. Where am I to look, where am I to look, what is there to locate, so as to have some surety, to have some rest from this whole bloody racket? You're the sum of so many reflections. How many reflections? Is that what you consist of? What scum does the tide leave? What happened to the scum? When does it happen? I've seen what happens. But I can't speak when I see it. I can only point a finger. I can't even do that. The scum is broken and sucked back. I don't see where it goes, I don't see when, what do I see, what have I seen? What have I seen, the scum or the essence? What about it? Does all this give you the right to stand there and tell me you know who you are? It's a bloody impertinence.

Aldous Huxley, in *Brave New World Revisited* is aware of the problem of the freedom of the individual even in the so-called "free world" of the west:

> Meanwhile there is still some freedom left in the world. Many young people, it is true, do not seem to value freedom. But some of us still believe that, without freedom, human beings cannot become human and that freedom is therefore supremely valuable. Perhaps the forces that now menace freedom are too strong to be resisted for very long.

Virginia Woolf's novels reflect a kind of disintegration of personality. Her declared aim is to:

> record the atoms as they fall upon the mind in the order in which they fall, tracing the pattern, however disconnected and incoherent in appearance, which each sight or incident scores upon the consciousness.

This attitude is interpreted by *C. E. M. Joad* as the effect of a particular kind of psychological theory:

> Under the influence of psychology there is today a widespread belief that personality is a myth. A man is not a continuing entity; he is a series of separate psychological states. The ego, the thread upon which the states used to be strung like beads on a necklace, has disappeared. This disintegration of the *person* is bound up with the discrediting of reason, for it was reason that gave the background of cohesion and continuity to the essentially discontinuous series of moods and feelings. If reason is dismissed as unimportant, a human being becomes not a personality enduring through change, but a succession of changing moods. A man, on this view, is like a cinematographic man; that is to say, he is like a series of separate momentary men, succeeding one another with such rapidity as to create the illusion of continuity. The truth about a man so conceived will be the truth about the separate states; it will be a collection of accounts of successive little pieces of him, the tiny physical acts, the fleeting psychological moods, the semiconscious wishes, the memories half-evoked. And in order to get as close as possible to this succession of little pieces, one writes a succession of little pictures, matching the discontinuity of life with a discontinuity of style. By this means, it is thought, the essential reality of life will be captured, its essence distilled into one's pages.

Jean-Paul Sartre's novel *Nausea* expresses these feelings about the individual in the experience of the main character, Roquentin:

> Now when I say "I," it seems hollow to me. I can no longer manage to feel myself, I am so forgotten. The only real thing left in me is some existence which can feel itself existing. I give a long, voluptuous yawn. Nobody. Antoine Roquentin exists for Nobody. That amuses me. And exactly what is Antoine Roquentin? An abstraction. A pale little memory of myself wavers in my consciousness. Antoine Roquentin . . . And suddenly the I pales, pales, and finally goes out . . .

Many are aware of the possibility of losing the individual completely, and therefore see the individual as being absorbed in some greater entity such as "the race" or "the universe."

267

H. G. Wells:

I think Man may be immortal, but not men.

Our individuality is, so to speak, an inborn obsession from which we shall escape as we become more intelligent.

Julian Huxley sees the individual as involved in the evolution of the whole human race:

In the light of the evolutionary vision the individual need not feel just a meaningless cog in the social machine, nor merely the helpless prey and sport of vast impersonal forces. He can do something to develop his own personality, to discover his own talents and possibilities, to interact personally and fruitfully with other individuals, to discover something of his own significance. If so, in his own person he is realizing an important quantum of evolutionary possibility: he is contributing his own personal quality to the fulfillment of human destiny; and he has assurance of his own significance in the vaster and more enduring whole of which he is a part.

Aldous Huxley describes the experience of the mystics who lose consciousness of their individuality and personality, and feel themselves part of "an impersonal spiritual reality underlying all being."

They find that their visions disappear, that their awareness of a personality fades, that the emotional outpourings which were appropriate when they seemed to be in the presence of a person, become utterly inappropriate and finally give place to a state in which there is no emotion at all . . .

This new form of experience—the imageless and emotionless cognition of some great impersonal force—is superior to the old and represents a closer approach to ultimate reality.

Buddhism tries to be utterly consistent, and looks forward to the state of Nirvana, in which the individual no longer exists as a separate individual.

Christmas Humphreys:

Nirvana is the extinction of the not-Self in the completion of the Self. It is, therefore, to the limited extent that we can understand it, a concept of psychology, a state of consciousness. As such it is, as Professor Radhakrishnan points out, "the goal of perfection and not the abyss of annihilation. Through the destruction of all that is individual in us, we enter into communion with the whole universe, and become an integral part of the great purpose. Perfection is then the sense of oneness with all that is, has ever been and can ever be. The horizon of being is extended to the limits of reality." It is therefore not correct to say that the dewdrop slips into the Shining Sea; it is nearer to the truth to speak of the Shining Sea invading the dewdrop. There is here no sense of loss but of infinite expansion when, "Foregoing self, the Universe grows I."

D. T. Suzuki explains the doctrine of "non-ego" in Buddhism:

The doctrine of non-ego not only repudiates the idea of an ego-substance but points out the illusiveness of the ego-idea itself. As long as we are in this world of particular existences we cannot avoid cherishing the idea of an individual ego. But this by no means warrants the substantiality of the ego. Modern psychology has in fact done away with an ego-entity.

Problems and questions arising out of this answer in relation to the individual are raised on p. 305.

MEANING

If there is no Creator-God who gives man meaning and value, one immediate reaction is to say that the question about meaning in life is itself meaningless.

Arthur Koestler, writing about the crucial change in the thinking of many in the west in the seventeenth century:

Before the shift, the various religions had provided man with explanations of a kind which gave everything that happened to him meaning in the wider sense of transcendental causality and transcendental justice. But the explanations of the new philosophy were devoid of meaning in this wider sense . . . In a word, the old explanations, with all their arbitrariness and patchiness, answered the question after "the meaning of life" whereas the new explanations, with all their precision, made the question of meaning itself meaningless.

Another reaction is to say that we cannot hope to know the meaning of life.
Albert Camus:

> I do not know whether this world has a meaning that is beyond me. But I know that I am unaware of this meaning and that, for the time being, it is impossible for me to know it. What can a meaning beyond my condition mean to me? I can understand only in human terms. I understand the things I touch, things that offer me resistance.

The vast majority of writers who are vocal on the subject have reached a pessimistic answer:
Somerset Maugham:

> If one puts aside the existence of God and the possibility of survival as too doubtful to have any effect on one's behavior, one has to make up one's mind what is the meaning and use of life. If death ends all, if I have neither to hope for good to come nor to fear evil, I must ask myself what I am here for, and how in these circumstances I must conduct myself. Now the answer to one of these questions is plain, but so unpalatable that most men will not face it. There is no reason for life, and life has no meaning.

Bertrand Russell:

> That man is the product of causes which had no prevision of the end they were achieving; that his origin, his growth, his hopes and fears, his loves and his beliefs, are but the outcome of accidental collocations of atoms: that no fire, no heroism, no intensity of thought and feeling, can preserve an individual life beyond the grave; that all the labor of the ages, all the devotion, all the inspiration, all the noonday brightness of human genius, are destined to extinction in the vast death of the solar system, and that the whole temple of man's achievement must inevitably be buried beneath the debris of a universe in ruins—all these things, if not quite beyond dispute, are yet so nearly certain, that no philosophy which rejects them can hope to stand. Only within the scaffolding of these truths, only on the firm foundation of unyielding despair, can the soul's habitation henceforth be safely built.

H. J. Blackham, who is an optimistic humanist, starts from the position of "recognizing the pointlessness of it all":

There is no end to hiding from the ultimate end of life,
which is death. But it does not avail. On humanist assumptions, life leads to nothing, and every pretense that it does
not is a deceit. If there is a bridge over a gorge which spans
only half the distance and ends in mid-air, and if the bridge
is crowded with human beings pressing on, one after another they fall into the abyss. The bridge leads to nowhere,
and those who are pressing forward to cross it are going
nowhere. It does not matter where they think they are
going, what preparations for the journey they may have
made, how much they may be enjoying it all . . . such a
situation is a model of futility.

Francis Bacon:

Man now realizes that he is an accident, that he is a completely futile being, that he has to play out the game without reason. I think that even when Velasquez was painting,
even when Rembrandt was painting, they were still, whatever their attitude to life, slightly conditioned by certain
types of religious possibilities, which man now, you could
say, has had canceled out for him. Man now can only
attempt to beguile himself for a time, by prolonging his
life—by buying a kind of immortality through the doctors.
You see, painting has become—all art has become—a game
by which man distracts himself. And you may say that it
always has been like that, but now it's entirely a game.

Martin Esslin, writing about the Theatre of the Absurd:

The Theatre of the Absurd . . . can be seen as the reflection of what seems to be the attitude most genuinely representative of our own time.

The hallmark of this attitude is its sense that the certitudes
and unshakable basic assumptions of former ages have been
swept away, that they have been tested and found wanting,
that they have been discredited as cheap and somewhat
childish illusions.

Eugene Ionesco:

Absurd is that which is devoid of purpose . . . Cut off from
his religious, metaphysical, and transcendental roots, man is
lost; all his actions become senseless, absurd, useless.

Martin Esslin, writing about Samuel Beckett:

271

Language in Beckett's plays serves to express the break-down, the disintegration of language. Where there is no certainty, there can be no definite meanings—and the impossibility of ever attaining certainty is one of the main themes of Beckett's plays. Godot's promises are vague and uncertain. In *Endgame*, an unspecified something is taking its course, and when Hamm anxiously asks, "We're not beginning to . . . to . . . mean something?" Clov merely laughs. "Mean something! You and I mean something!"

Sartre's novel *Nausea* conveys the feeling of meaninglessness in the experience of Roquentin:

His judgment pierced me like a sword and called in question my very right to exist. And it was true, I had always realized that: I hadn't any right to exist. I had appeared by chance, I existed like a stone, a plant, a microbe. My life grew in a haphazard way and in all directions. Sometimes it sent me vague signals; at other times I could feel nothing but an inconsequential buzzing.

I was just thinking . . . that here we are, all of us, eating and drinking, to preserve our precious existence, and that there's nothing, nothing, absolutely no reason for existing.

Allen Ginsberg:

I feel as if I am at a dead
end and so I am finished.
All spiritual facts I realize
are true but I never escape
the feeling of being closed in
and the sordidness of self,
the futility of all that I
have seen and done and said.

Many who reach the point of saying that human life is meaningless find it difficult, if not impossible, to *live* with this conclusion. They feel compelled to cast around for a way to create at least some measure of meaning somewhere.

Some attempts to create meaning

"Say a defiant 'yes' to life in spite of its absurdity."
George Eliot:

The "highest calling and election" is to *do without opium,*

and live through all our pain with conscious, clear-eyed
endurance.

Bertrand Russell:

Brief and powerless is man's life; on him and all his race
the slow, sure doom falls pitiless and dark. Blind to good
and evil, reckless of destruction, omnipotent matter rolls on
its relentless way; for man, condemned today to lose his
dearest, tomorrow himself to pass through the gate of
darkness, it remains only to cherish, ere yet the blow fall,
the lofty thoughts that ennoble his little day; disdaining the
coward terrors of the slave of Fate, to worship at the shrine
that his own hands have built; undismayed by the empire
of chance, to preserve a mind free from the wanton tyranny that rules his outward life; proudly defiant of the irresistible forces that tolerate, for a moment, his knowledge and
his condemnation, to sustain alone, a weary but unyielding
Atlas, the world that his own ideals have fashioned despite
the trampling march of unconscious power.

Nietzsche:

The kind of *experimental philosophy* which I am living, even
anticipates the possibility of the most fundamental Nihilism,
on principle: but by this I do not mean that it remains
standing at a negation, at a *no*, or at a will to negation. It
would rather attain to the very reverse—to a *Dionysian
affirmation* of the world, as it is, without subtraction, exception, or choice . . .

To overcome pessimism effectively and, at last, to look with
the eyes of a Goethe full of love and goodwill.

Nikos Kazantzakis, the Greek novelist, author of *Zorba the
Greek*, writing to a friend in 1947:

To conquer illusion and hope, without being overcome by
terror: this has been the whole endeavor of my life these
past twenty years; to look straight into the abyss without
bursting into tears, without begging or threatening, calmly,
serenely preserving the dignity of man; to see the abyss and
work as though I were immortal . . .

"Live with the absurd."
Maurice Friedman:

Today meaning can be found, if at all, only through the

attitude of the man who is willing to *live* with the absurd, to remain open to the mystery which he can never pin down.

Jean-Paul Sartre in his autobiographical work *Words*:

I felt superfluous so I had to disappear. I was a sickly bloom under constant sentence of extinction. In other words, I was condemned, and the sentence could be carried out at any time. Yet I rejected it with all my strength: not that my life was dear to me—quite the contrary, for I did not cling to it: the more absurd life is, the less tolerable death.

For many, the only way to *live* with the absurd is to *write* about it. The very fact that one feels the meaninglessness of life and yet is able to give artistic expression to it is a kind of defiance.

André Malraux:

The greatest mystery is not that we have been flung at random among the profusion of the earth and the galaxy of the stars, but that in this prison we can fashion images of ourselves sufficiently powerful to deny our nothingness.

Arthur Adamov:

Everything happens as though I were only one of the particular existences of some great incomprehensible and central being. . . . Sometimes this great totality of life appears to me so dramatically beautiful that it plunges me into ecstasy. But more often it seems like a monstrous beast that penetrates and surpasses me and which is everywhere, within me and outside me . . . And terror grips me and envelops me more powerfully from moment to moment . . . My only way out is to write, to make others aware of it, so as not to have to feel all of it alone, to get rid of however small a portion of it.

Jean-Paul Sartre:

My retrospective illusions are in pieces. Martyrdom, salvation, immortality: all are crumbling; the building is falling in ruins. I have caught the Holy Ghost in the cellars and flung him out of them. Atheism is a cruel, long-term business: I believe I have gone through it to the end. I see

clearly, I am free from illusions . . . I have renounced my
vocation, but I have not unfrocked myself. I still write.
What else can I do?

"Just live—life itself is the only value."
   Colin Wilson, writing about Ernest Hemingway:

> The key sentence, "Most men die like animals, not like
> men," is his answer to the humanist notion of the perfect-
> ibility of man . . . There is nothing that man cannot lose.
> This doesn't mean that life is of no value; on the contrary,
> life is the only value; it is ideas that are valueless.

Rebecca West:

> The living philosophy which really sustains us, which is our
> basic nourishment, more than any finding of the mind, is
> simply the sensation of life, exquisite when it is not painful.

Santayana:

> To love, to live just as we do, that is the purpose and the
> crown of living . . . The worth of life lies in pursuit, not in
> attainment; therefore everything is worth pursuing, and
> nothing brings satisfaction—save the endless destiny itself.

Lin Yutang:

> Great wisdom consists in not demanding too much of
> human nature, and yet not altogether spoiling it by in-
> dulgence. One must try to do one's best, and at the same
> time, one must, when rewarded by partial success or con-
> fronted by partial failure, say to himself, "I have done my
> best." That is about all the philosophy of living that one
> needs.

Albert Camus:

> It is plain that absurdist reasoning . . . recognizes human
> life as the single necessary good, because it makes possible
> that confrontation, and because without life the absurdist
> wager could not go on. To say that life is absurd, one must
> live. How can one, without indulging one's desire for com-
> fort, keep for oneself the exclusive benefits of this argu-
> ment? The moment life is recognized as a necessary good,
> it becomes so for all men.
>
> . . . the living warmth that gives forgetfulness of all . . .

H. J. Blackham rejects the pessimism and despair he sees in Francis Bacon and Jean-Paul Sartre, and believes that these are "distorted and immature forms of humanist expression." He then goes on to ask:

> But can humanism really and justifiably maintain equanimity in the face not only of probable ultimate annihilation but also of actual human suffering and stupidity and brutality on the present scale? Is there any satisfaction at all to be found in the general behavior of mankind or in the trends and tendencies that can be discerned? There is no answer to such a question, or no general answer, for there is no general behavior of mankind. Everybody must balance his own account here. In any such reckoning, the ready money of daily cheerfulness and unalloyed pleasures is not too small to count. One dimension of finality is here and now. On the public fronts, defeatism may sometimes be the part of reason acting as prudence, but who will responsibly say that the time is not? So long as there are better or worse possibilities there is time for action. Today the better and the worse are better and worse than they have ever been. That is the summons to humanists and the summons of humanism.

"Evolution gives meaning to life." While there may be little or no meaning in the life of the individual by himself, there *is* some meaning to life when it is seen in the context of the evolution of the human race as a whole.

Julian Huxley believes that a philosophy based on evolution can meet man's need for a new religious system:

> The evolutionary vision is enabling us to discern, however incompletely, the lineaments of the new religion that we can be sure will arise to serve the needs of the coming era. Just as stomachs are bodily organs concerned with digestion, and involving the biochemical activity of special juices, so are religions psychological organs concerned with the problems of human destiny, and involving the emotion of sacredness and the sense of right and wrong. Religion of some sort is probably necessary. But it is not necessarily a good thing.

Colin Wilson diagnoses the problem in this way:

> He (man) is not yet a "spiritual being," for spiritual, in its ultimate sense, means capable of exercising freedom, and

freedom is meaningless without ultimate purpose . . . The
one thing that is required to complete the transition from
ape to man is the birth of a new kind of purpose *inside*
man. Sir Julian Huxley is right in calling this sense of
evolutionary purpose a "new religion."

He suggests as his answer what he calls "evolutionary phenomenology":

What has been suggested is that the answer is to be sought
in the idea of evolution, as described by Shaw, Wells, or Sir
Julian Huxley . . . What if science *could* replace that sense
of individual meaning, the feeling of having a direct telephone line to the universal purpose? For this is precisely
the aim of evolutionary phenomenology: to change man's
conception of himself and of the *interior forces* he has at his
command, and ultimately to establish the new evolutionary
type, foreshadowed by the "outsiders."

"Man has meaning only as he is absorbed into the universe." Life has
meaning only as the individual sees himself as part of the universe and looks forward to a more complete absorption in it.

Henry Miller:

I see that behind the nobility of (man's) gestures there lurks
the specter of the ridiculousness of it all . . . he is not only
sublime, but absurd. Once I thought that to be human was
the highest aim man could have, but I see now that it was
meant to destroy me. Today I am proud to say that I am
inhuman, that I belong not to men and governments, that I
have nothing to do with creeds and principles. I have nothing to do with the cracking machinery of humanity—I belong to the earth! . . . If I'm unhuman it is because my
world has slopped over its human bounds, because to be
human seems like a poor, sorry, miserable affair, limited by
the senses, restricted by moralities and codes, defined by
platitudes and isms . . . It may be that we are doomed, that
there is no hope for us, any of us, but if that is so then let
us set up a last agonizing, blood-curdling howl, a screech of
defiance, a war-whoop! Away with lamentations! Away with
elegies and dirges! Away with biographies and histories,
and libraries and museums! Let the dead eat the dead. Let
us living ones dance about the rim of the crater, a last
expiring dance. But a dance! . . . The great incestuous wish
is to flow on, one with time, to merge the great image of

the beyond with the here and now. A fatuous, suicidal wish that is constipated by words and paralyzed by thought.

Rabindranath Tagore, writing against a Hindu background:

Dark is the future to her, and the odor cries in
    despair,
  "Ah me, through whose fault is my life so
    unmeaning?
  Who can tell me, why I am at all?"
Do not lose heart, timid thing!
The perfect dawn is near when you will mingle
    your life with all life and know at last your
    purpose.

Problems and questions arising out of this answer in relation to meaning are raised on pp. 307.

VALUES

If I am not a creature subject to the moral law of God, I cannot look beyond myself for values by which to live.

Pete Townshend:

I'm happy when life's good, and when it's bad I cry.

I've got values but I don't know how or why.

Jean-Paul Sartre:

If I have excluded God the Father, there must be some-body to invent values.

The "death" of God thus creates a kind of moral vacuum.
Proust's character Oriane in the novel *Remembrance* gives an example of the kind of situation in which this moral vacuum shows itself:

Placed for the first time in her life in the presence of two duties as different as whether to leave by car and dine in town, or to show pity to a man who was going to die, she saw nothing in her code which told her which choice to make, and not knowing where her preference should be directed, she decided to pretend that the second option had not been presented to her, which would allow her to follow

the first course of action and demanded less effort, thinking
that the best way of resolving the conflict was to deny it.

Arthur Koestler:

The logic of expediency leads to the atomic disintegration
of morality; a kind of radioactive decay of all values.

Donald Kalish, writing about the present state of moral philosophy:

There is no system of philosophy to spin out. There are no
ethical truths, there are just clarifications of particular ethical problems. Take advantage of these clarifications and
work out your own existence. You are mistaken to think
that anyone ever had the answers. There are no answers.
Be brave and face up to it.

Gerald Emanuel Stern, writing about Marshall McLuhan:

McLuhan's ideas are not susceptible to the rigid formalism
of genteel discussion; the question of right or wrong ("categories, categories") is, in many ways, irrelevant.

George Eliot, writing about McLuhan:

It is easy to see why McLuhan is listened to so eagerly:
With the highest of intellectual credentials, he sounds like a
Future-salesman assuring us that there are great days ahead
and that what seems to be so terrible now arises only from
resistance to change. What if admen do use TV as a way to
spread lies and distortions and idiocy? It doesn't matter
much anyway: The medium is the message, and a medium
is neither moral nor immoral.

Edmund Leach points out the dangers involved in any so-called
morality, and the impossibility of saying whether one code or
another is right:

The question I am asking is: can scientists and politicians
who have acquired god-like power to alter our way of life
be restrained by the application of moral principles? If so,
what moral principles? And the sort of answer that seems
to be coming up is this: "Beware of moral principles . . ."
When we elevate other people's behavior we do so according to a code which we have been taught. The code is
arbitrary. It changes as we move across the map from one

279

place to another, or through time from one generation to another . . . The old start to denounce the young for their immorality because the code is changing, and they can no longer interpret the signals. But it is still all a question of interpretation; there is no way of saying what the facts really are. In their own estimation the psychedelic hippies with their marijuana and their LSD are primitive Christians proclaiming the brotherhood of man; in the eyes of many of their seniors their activities are a close approximation to witchcraft and the Black Masses. Either may be right.

Faced with this moral vacuum, then, what can we do about it? There are in principle only five possible answers.

Ways of dealing with the moral vacuum

"Live as if there are absolutes." We cannot be sure whether there are any moral standards. But we can at least act on the assumption that they do exist.

Sartre describes French Radicalism toward the end of the nineteenth century, holding on to traditional values long after their basis had dissolved:

Towards 1880, when the French professors endeavored to formulate a secular morality, they said something like this: God is a useless and costly hypothesis, so we will do without it. However, if we are to have morality, a society and a law-abiding world, it is essential that certain values should be taken seriously; they must have an *a priori* existence ascribed to them. It must be considered obligatory *a priori* to be honest, not to lie, not to beat one's wife, to bring up children and so forth; so we are going to do a little work on this subject, which will enable us to show that these values exist all the same, inscribed in an intelligible heaven although, of course, there is no God. In other words—and this is, I believe, the purport of all that we in France call radicalism—nothing will be changed if God does not exist; we shall rediscover the same norms of honesty, progress and humanity and we shall have disposed of God as an out-of-date hypothesis which will die away quietly of itself.

Arthur Koestler, writing in the 1940s:

I am not sure whether what the philosophers call the ethical absolutes exist, but I am sure that we have to act as if they existed.

J. B. Priestley:

> We can try to feel and think and behave, to some extent, *as
> if* society were already beginning to be contained by reli-
> gion, as if we were certain that Man cannot even remain
> Man unless he looks beyond himself, as if we were finding
> our way home again in the universe.

*A problem arising from this way of
dealing with the moral vacuum is
raised on pp. 309f.*

"Find a new absolute." Many attempts have been made to find
some new absolute, some new principle which would provide a
standard by which all moral values and judgments could be
tested. For example, people have pointed to "Nature" or "Happiness" or "Love" as the ultimate criterion by which to decide
values.

1. NATURE. The Deists of the eighteenth century believed
that "Nature" and "Reason" could combine to point to moral
standards which would be evident and acceptable to all thinking
people. This idea is still held by some.

Lin Yutang, developing Taoist ideas:

> I believe that the only kind of religious belief left for the
> modern man is a kind of mysticism in the broadest sense of
> the word, such as preached by Lao-tse. Broadly speaking, it
> is a kind of reverence and respect for the moral order of
> the universe, philosophic resignation to the moral order,
> and the effort to live our life in harmony with this moral
> order. The *tao* in Taoism exactly means this thing. It is
> broad enough to cover the most advanced present and
> future theories of the universe. It is, for me, the only
> antidote against modern materialism.

Somerset Maugham:

> What then is right action? For my part the best answer I
> know is that given by Fray Luis de León. To follow it does
> not look so difficult that human weakness quails before it as
> beyond its strength. With it I can end my book. The beauty
> of life, he says, is nothing but this, that each should act in
> conformity with his nature and his business.

BUT: "Nature" is incapable of teaching us values.

T. H. Huxley:

> The thief and the murderer follow nature just as much as
> the philanthropist. Cosmic evolution may teach us how the
> good and the evil tendencies of man may have come about;
> but, in itself, it is incompetent to furnish any better reason
> why what we call good is preferable to what we call evil
> than we had before.

2. HAPPINESS. The Utilitarian Principle of J. S. Mill says
that an action is right if it promotes the greatest happiness of the
greatest number. Many modern humanists hold a similar position, and claim that we can derive a system of values by the
scientific study of life as it is actually lived.

H. J. Blackham:

> The humanist's system of morality is a consecration of the
> actual facts of life as men live it. He proceeds in the reverse
> direction from that taken by the super-humanist; for, in-
> stead of passing from the arbitrary imperative to the cor-
> responding fantastic indicative, he moves from the indica-
> tive of the observed and experienced facts to the imperative
> of a realistic morality and a rational legislation.

Adam Schaff asks the question "What is the aim of life?" and
gives the answer:

> Marxist theory . . . leads to the general position that may be
> called "social hedonism"—the view that the aim of human
> life is to secure the maximum happiness for the broadest
> mass of the people, and that only within the compass of this
> aim can personal happiness be reached.

BUT: happiness is generally a by-product of action pursued
for other reasons than the attainment of happiness.

J. S. Mill himself recognized this later in life:

> I never, indeed, wavered in the conviction that happiness is
> the test of all rules of conduct, and the end of life. But now
> I thought that this end was only to be attained by not
> making it the direct end. Those only are happy (I thought)
> who have their minds fixed on some subject other than
> their own happiness; on the happiness of others, on the
> improvement of mankind, even on some art or pursuit,
> followed not as a means, but as itself an ideal end. Aiming
> thus at something else, they find happiness by the way.

A second objection is that it is not possible, logically, to derive an "ought" statement from an "is" statement.

We cannot move from a simple statement about a state of affairs (how things actually are) to make a further statement about an obligation (how things ought to be). If we say "people *do in fact act* like this . . ." we have no right to base a moral judgment on this and say "therefore people *ought to act* as follows . . ." For example, not even the most exhaustive study of the sexual habits and customs of a particular society would enable us to say what customs people ought to accept or reject.

3. "LOVE." It is often suggested that the ultimate principle by which all moral values should be decided is the principle of "Love." It is usually assumed that in every situation it is self-evident what the principles of love would point to.

John Wren-Lewis speaks of love as:

> . . . the concrete ultimate good.

John Robinson:

> Assertions about God are in the last analysis assertions about Love . . .

> Life in Christ Jesus . . . means having no absolutes but his love . . . And this utter openness in love to the "other" for his own sake is equally the only absolute for the non-Christian . . .

> Love alone, because, as it were, it has a built-in moral compass, enabling it to "home" intuitively upon the deepest need of the other, can allow itself to be directed completely by the situation . . . It is the only ethic which offers a point of constancy in a world of flux and yet remains absolutely free for, and free over, the changing situation . . .

BUT: It is not obvious and self-evident in *every* situation what the demands of love are. This argument assumes that the person who makes "love" the absolute moral principle will know the right thing to do. But in practice people have widely differing views of what love demands in particular situations. "Love" cannot help us to define moral standards any more than "Reason" or "Nature" or "Happiness."

Nor is it possible, logically, to move from statements of fact to statements of value (see above). It is obvious that every person *does* show love to others to a greater or lesser extent. But why *should* we love? How can we move from the fact that men *do* love to build on this the moral command that men *ought* to love? This is a logical fallacy.

4. THE VALUES OF SCIENCE. *Bronowski* believes that science can actually "create" values:

> The values of science derive neither from the virtues of its members, nor from the finger-wagging codes of conduct by which every profession reminds itself to be good. They have grown out of the practice of science, because they are the inescapable conditions for its practice . . .

> Like the other creative activities which grew from the Renaissance, science has humanized our values. Men have asked for freedom, justice, and respect precisely as the scientific spirit has spread among them . . .

> The inspiration of science . . . has created the values of our intellectual life and, with the arts, has taught them to our civilization.

These are some of the values which he believes have been "created" by science:

> Independence and originality, dissent and freedom and tolerance: such are the first needs of science; and these are the values which, of itself, it demands and forms . . .

> In societies where these values do not exist, science has had to create them.

> From these basic conditions, which form the prime values, there follows step by step a range of values: dissent, freedom of thought and speech, justice, honor, human dignity, and self-respect.

> Our values since the Renaissance have evolved by just such steps.

This, therefore, is the principle which he puts forward as the scientific basis for values: *We OUGHT to act in such a way that what IS true can be verified to be so.*

Arthur Koestler:

> Can science heal the neurotic flaw in us? If science cannot, then nothing can. Let us stop pretending. There is no cure in high moral precepts . . . The insight of science is not different from that of the arts. Science will create values, I

believe, and discover virtues, when it looks into man; when
it explores what makes him man and not an animal, and
makes his societies human and not animal packs.

BUT: making scientific values our "absolute" creates some
problems. In the first place, it is a confusion of language to say
that science can "create" values. Science is a human activity
pursued by individual scientists. "Science" cannot create values
any more than other human activities like art or sport. Science
may proceed more effectively if scientists recognize certain
values; but the values which are said to have been created by
science were recognized and practiced long before the development of modern science.

Second, there are certain values which have little or nothing
to do with science.

Bronowski admits in the Preface to the later edition of his
book, that there are some values

> which are not generated by the practice of science—the
> values of tenderness, of kindliness, of human intimacy and
> love.

Third, when it comes to particular moral problems, it will
always be particular scientists or groups of scientists who will
have to make the choices and point out the values. The tyranny
of scientists could be just as frightening as the tyranny of
soldiers or politicians.

Koestler, although he holds this view, shows elsewhere that he
is well aware of the possible consequences:

> Within the foreseeable future, man will either destroy him-
> self or take off for the stars . . .

> Our hypnotic enslavement to the numerical aspects of real-
> ity has dulled our perception of non-quantitative moral
> values; the resultant end-justifies-the-means ethic may be a
> major factor in our undoing.

He describes science as

> . . . the new Baal, lording it over the moral vacuum with his
> electronic brain.

5. "DHARMA." Values in Hinduism are based on the concept
of *dharma.*
Radhakrishnan:

> Dharma is right action. In the *Rg Veda, rta* is the right

order of the universe. It stands for both the *satya* or the
truth of things as well as the dharma or the law of evolution. Dharma formed from the root *dhr*, to hold, means
that which holds a thing or maintains it in being. Every
form of life, every group of men has its dharma, which is
the law of its being. Dharma or virtue is conformity with
the truth of things; adharma or vice is opposition to it.
Moral evil is disharmony with the truth which encompasses
and controls the world.

This concept of *dharma* comes close to the concept of "Nature" (see p. 281). In practice, Hinduism teaches a strict code
based on the traditions of society:

Radhakrishnan:

Hinduism is more a way of life than a form of thought.
While it gives absolute liberty in the world of thought it
enjoins a strict code of practice. The theist and the atheist,
the skeptic and the agnostic may all be Hindus if they
accept the Hindu system of culture and life.

In Buddhism there is the similar concept of *karuna*, love.

D. T. Suzuki:

Karuna corresponds to love. It is like the sands of the
Ganges: they are trampled by all kinds of beings: by ele-
phants, by lions, by asses, by human beings, but they do not
make any complaints. They are again soiled by all kinds of
filth scattered by all kinds of animals, but they just suffer
them all and never utter a word of ill-will. Eckhart would
declare the sands on the Ganges to be "just," because "the
just have no will at all: whatever God wishes it is all one to
them, however great the discomfort may be."

Christmas Humphreys quotes some words of Radhakrishnan to
the effect that good and evil are ultimately merely different
aspects of one great reality:

The antitheses of cause and effect, substance and attribute,
good and evil, truth and error, are due to the tendency of
man to separate terms which are related. Fichte's puzzle of
self and not-self, Kant's antinomies, Hume's opposition of
facts and laws, can all be got over if we recognize that the
opposing factors are mutually complementary elements
based on one identity.

In practice the Buddhist code of morals is summed up in
what is known as "The Eight-fold Path": Right Belief, Right
Thought, Right Speech, Action, Means of Livelihood, Exertion,
Remembrance, and Meditation. And the essence of Buddhism is
summed up in the words:

> "To cease from all sin,
> To get virtue,
> To purify the heart."

BUT: If good and evil are both aspects of the One Great
Reality, ultimately there is no sure way of deciding between what
is good and what is evil.

Francis Schaeffer relates the following incident to illustrate this
dilemma:

> One day I was talking to a group of people in the digs of a
> young South African in Cambridge. Among others, there
> was present a young Indian who was of Sikh background
> but a Hindu by religion. He started to speak strongly
> against Christianity, but did not really understand the prob-
> lems of his own beliefs. So I said, "Am I not correct in
> saying that on the basis of your system, cruelty and non-
> cruelty are ultimately equal, that there is no intrinsic differ-
> ence between them?" He agreed. The people who listened
> and knew him as a delightful person, an "English gen-
> tleman" of the very best kind, looked up in amazement. But
> the student in whose room we met, who had clearly under-
> stood the implications of what the Sikh had admitted,
> picked up his kettle of boiling water with which he was
> about to make tea, and stood with it steaming over the
> Indian's head. The man looked up and asked him what he
> was doing and he said, with a cold yet gentle finality,
> "There is no difference between cruelty and non-cruelty."
> Thereupon the Hindu walked out into the night.

"The individual must decide for himself." *Rousseau* rejects reason as
a reliable guide for morals, and looks instead to conscience and
feelings:

> Whatever I feel to be right is right. Whatever I feel to be
> wrong is wrong. The conscience is the best of all casuists
> . . . Reason deceives us only too often and we have acquired
> the right to reject it only too well but conscience never
> deceives.

287

Charles Darwin:

> A man who has no assured and ever present belief in the
> existence of a personal God or of a future existence with
> retribution and reward, can have for his rule of life, as far
> as I can see, only to follow those impulses and instincts
> which are the strongest or which seem to him the best ones.

Albert Camus believes that man's natural impulse to rebellion
should be the source from which values can be derived:

> The controversial aspect of contemporary history compels
> us to say that rebellion is one of man's essential dimensions.
> It is our historical reality. Unless we ignore reality, we must
> find our values in it. Is it possible to find a rule of conduct
> outside the realm of religion and absolute values? That is
> the question raised by revolt . . .
>
> Rebellion is the common ground on which every man bases
> his first values. I *rebel*—therefore we *exist*.

The excesses to which rebellion has led in the last few centuries, he argues, point to certain "limits" or a new "law of
moderation." It is up to the individual to perceive what these
limits are, because they should be almost self-evident.

> We know at the end of this long inquiry into rebellion and
> nihilism that rebellion with no other limits but historical
> expediency signifies unlimited slavery. To escape this fate,
> the revolutionary mind, if it wants to remain alive, must
> therefore return again to the sources of rebellion and draw
> its inspiration from the only system of thought which is
> faithful to its origins; thought which recognizes limits.

Sartre believes that freedom is the foundation of all values:

> Dostoievsky once wrote, "If God did not exist, everything
> would be permitted"; and that, for existentialism, is the
> starting point. Everything is indeed permitted if God does
> not exist, and man is in consequence forlorn, for he cannot
> find anything to depend upon either within or outside
> himself. He discovers forthwith, that he is without excuse.
> For if indeed existence precedes essence, one will never be
> able to explain one's action by reference to a given and
> specific human nature; in other words, there is no deter-
> minism—man is free, man *is* freedom. Nor, on the other
> hand, if God does not exist, are we provided with any
> values or commands that could legitimize our behavior.

Thus we have neither behind us, nor before us in a lumi-
nous realm of values, any means of justification or excuse.
We are left alone, without excuse. That is what I mean
when I say that man is condemned to be free.

My freedom is the unique foundation of values. And since
I am the being by virtue of whom values exist, nothing—
absolutely nothing—can justify me in adopting this or that
value or scale of values. As the unique basis of the existence
of values, I am totally unjustifiable. And my freedom is in
anguish at finding that it is the baseless basis of values.

This freedom does not mean that the individual can be irresponsible; on the contrary it places on man an even heavier
burden of responsibility. "In fashioning myself," says Sartre, "I
fashion man."

This means, in practice, that the individual must "create" his
values. His freedom is similar to the free creativity of the artist:

Moral choice is comparable to the construction of a work of
art.

We are in the same creative situation. We never speak of a
work of art as irresponsible . . . There is this in common
between art and morality, that in both we have to do with
creation and invention. We cannot decide *a priori* what it is
that should be done.

BUT: to follow this out consistently could lead to a position in
which all morals are arbitrary. If we cannot point to any firm
standard of values, we have no right to protest when each
individual *does* decide what is right for himself. If we are completely free in this sense, we have no right to expect others to
accept our values, no right to say, "You *ought* to do this . . ." or
"You *ought not* to do that."

To the ordinary reader Sartre's position sounds like this summary by *Colin Wilson*:

His philosophy of "commitment" . . . is only to say that
since all roads lead nowhere, it's as well to choose any of
them and throw all the energy into it . . .

. . . Any purpose will do, provided it is altruistic.

John D. Wild, writing about the weaknesses of the existential
understanding of man, speaks of:

the supposed arbitrariness of human choice, and the lack of

any firm grounds. For Sartre, the whole effort to justify an act is a cowardly abandonment of freedom and responsibility, the turning of myself into a thing. Whether I decide to die for justice or drink at a bar, the matter is indifferent.

In practice this approach means that the individual has to rely on his own instincts. *Sartre* himself makes this admission:

If values are uncertain, if they are still too abstract to determine the particular, concrete case under consideration, nothing remains but to trust in our instincts.

One can never hope to *know* for certain whether one's values are good or bad. His extreme agnosticism becomes evident at this point:

Who, then, can prove that I am the proper person to impose, by my own choice, my conception of man upon mankind? I shall never find any proof whatever; there will be no sign to convince me of it. If a voice speaks to me, it is still I myself who must decide whether the voice is or is not that of an angel. If I regard a certain course of action as good, it is only I who choose to say that it is good and not bad.

No state can function on a philosophy of complete freedom. Here Sartre himself is inconsistent. As *Adam Schaff* points out, Sartre the existentialist is committed to total freedom, while Sartre the Communist sympathizer pays tribute to a political system that restricts the freedom of the individual in the interests of the state:

Does the individual create society, by choosing the manner of his behavior in complete spontaneity and freedom of choice? Or is it society that creates the individual and determines his mode of behavior?—These questions lie at the heart of the antagonism between Existentialism and Marxism.

There is a contradiction between the Sartre who clings to traditional Existentialism and the Sartre who pays tribute to the philosophy of Marxism. The contradiction can be overcome only by abandoning one or other of the two antagonistic views he now holds.

"Find values based on agreement." The solution proposed by many humanists today is to find values by studying how people actually live and by agreeing on basic principles.

H. J. Blackham:

Only too obviously, there is precious little agreement in the world outside the province of the natural sciences—and perhaps less inside than is popularly supposed. Nevertheless, agreement is the ultimate criterion for values as well as for facts, some humanists would hold, and at any rate for rules which concern everybody in a society . . .

All humanists want to see a consensus on the secular *foundations* of society fully prevail.

Edmund Leach, summing up some basic ideas in his Reith Lectures of 1966, stakes his hopes on the value of tolerance:

I suppose the idea underlying them all was this problem of: How can we arrive at a moral consensus throughout society? . . . I do not feel that we could reach a moral consensus, but I did suggest that if we could only introduce the value of tolerance, that if we could only lead people to expect that other people within your own society might think differently from yourself, we might perhaps to some extent get over this problem—that in a changing society it's impossible for everybody to have an agreed moral consensus.

But in saying this, as *Alasdair MacIntyre* points out in reply, Leach—while insisting that *all* moral codes are relative—is himself insisting that there are some things which are right—absolutely right:

You are in effect saying that to be tolerant is clearly and absolutely right and to be intolerant and too hasty is wrong.

BUT: the problem is to decide what the "agreed principles" are. Furthermore, quite apart from the inconsistency in declaring dogmatically what the agreed principles must be, there is the difficulty of seeing how agreement could ever be the ultimate criterion of values. One could hardly hope for 100 percent agreement on a code of values. Failing such a consensus, what kind of majority vote would be acceptable—80 percent or 51 percent? In many situations, a society would be at the mercy of individual experts who would claim to *know* what is best for society. And in this case the concept of agreement cannot mean "agreement of the majority" but rather "agreement of the experts."

"Let some powerful authority decide what is right." If we cannot allow each individual to work out his own values, then powerful individuals or groups are at liberty to impose their values on society. It hardly needs saying that this "solution" is in itself a problem, which can lead to all the horrors of the totalitarian state.

Norman Hampson describes how this dilemma appeared to thoughtful minds at the time of the Enlightenment in the eighteenth century:

> The escape from moral anarchy was already beginning to point toward a new totalitarian nightmare.

> An attempt to base a code of ethics on purely human values was likely to lead, not to the emancipation of the individual, but to his immolation on the altar of society.

Dostoievsky:

> Starting from unlimited liberty, I arrive at unlimited despotism.

C. S. Lewis, writing about the implications of the bold claims about the powers of modern man:

> The power of Man to make himself what he pleases means . . . the power of some men to make other men what *they* please . . . the man-molders of the new age will be armed with the powers of an omnicompetent state and an irresistible scientific technique: we shall get at last a race of conditioners who really can cut out all posterity in what shape they please.

C. E. M. Joad, writing in 1942:

> Christianity preached the virtues of kindliness, gentleness, humanity, tolerance, justice, charity and respect for the personality of others. Its virtues, we doubt, were rarely practiced; but they were at least professed. It will be a long time yet before the practice of mankind squares with its profession, but the first step is for its profession to condemn its practice. That step Christianity has taken.

> In the philosophies of the Fascist people this step has been reversed; the Christian virtues are condemned as the weakness of cowards and half-wits, unable to meet, as good men should, the challenge of the hard world, and the contrary (Christian) vices of arrogance, ruthlessness and ferocity,

combined with a professed determination to treat one's
neighbors as inferior, are held in honor. The result of this
substitution of one code of values for another is all too
visible before us.

Leslie Paul, writing about the practical morality of Communist
revolutionaries:

> If moral indignation is the motivator of Marxist parties in
> opposition, it disappears from their baggage once they at-
> tain power. There is a clear conflict between this morality in
> opposition and the immorality in power which has nothing
> to do with the ordinary process of corruption by office . . .

> It was the moral passion of Marxism, and its principal
> child, Communism, which commended Marxism to so many
> social consciences in the interwar years and it was the disil-
> lusion with its moral consequences which has done so much
> to tarnish its image since. All over the world it has behaved
> with a moral indifference to human rights and sufferings.
> Its penal camps in Russia, which operated over at least a
> generation, probably succeeded in killing as many people as
> the Nazi extermination camps for the Jews. In lying, terror,
> secrecy, judicial murder, there has been little to choose
> between Nazi and Communist dictatorships.

RELATIONSHIPS

Communication

Many modern writers express what they feel is an almost complete breakdown of communication.

Dramatist *Harold Pinter:*

> I feel that instead of any inability to communicate there is a
> deliberate evasion of communication. Communication itself
> between people is so frightening that rather than do that
> there is continual cross-talk, a continual talking about other
> things, rather than what is at the root of their relationship.

Martin Esslin, writing about Samuel Beckett's plays:

> The experience expressed in Beckett's plays is of a far
> more profound and fundamental nature than mere autobi-
> ography. They reveal his experience of temporality and
> evanescence; his sense of the tragic difficulty of becoming
> aware of one's own self in the merciless process of renova-

tion and destruction that occurs with change in time; of the
difficulty of communication between human beings; of the
unending quest for reality in a world in which everything is
uncertain and the borderline between dream and waking is
ever shifting; of the tragic nature of all love relationships
and the self-deception of friendship . . .

BUT: they have to use words to show the impossibility of
conveying meaning in words.

Martin Esslin shows Beckett's awareness of this tension:

When Gessner asked him about the contradiction between
his writing and his obvious conviction that language could
not convey meaning, Beckett replied, *"Que voulez-vous, Mon-
sieur? C'est les mots; on n'a rien d'autre."*

John Wild points out a similar tension in much existentialist
thinking. One of the weaknesses of the existentialist theory of
man is

its failure to account for human communication. According
to Heidegger, my ordinary mode of being with others is
impersonal, debased, and unauthentic. He briefly refers to
the possibility of authentic communication between persons,
but nowhere explains how this is possible or even reconcil-
able with his picture of the genuine person who has broken
from his fellows to live alone with himself in a world of his
own choice. The more authentic we become, the more
isolated we seem to be. Jaspers has struggled with this
problem, but his rejection of universal concepts and judgments makes an intelligible solution impossible. In Sartre,
this weakness emerges with brutal clarity. When two persons meet, each tries to absorb the other as an object into
his world. Communication is thus restricted to conflict.
Love, friendship, and devoted cooperation for common
ends are excluded *a priori*.

Love

Many writers profoundly question the possibility of love; yet if it
is possible, it may become the *only* thing that can make life worth
living.

Cyril Connolly in conversation with *Jonathan Miller*:

Would it be a fair summary of your position to say that in
this universe—which presumably you regard, as I do, as a
deserted universe—friendship perhaps is the only solace,

and that some sort of exercise of belief in the nature of friendship is perhaps the most important thing that one can spend one's time on?

I think friendship is one form of love; there is also sexual love; there is also marriage. Love is the prime source of communication between these lonely human organisms.

Camus speaks of friendship, and love between a man and a woman, as perhaps the only thing that can have meaning in an otherwise absurd universe:

If there is one thing one can always yearn for, and sometimes attain, it is human love.

Sartre's picture of love is much blacker. In *Nausea*, Roquentin speaks of his disgust at the way in which a man and a woman are behaving with each other—disgust simply because there is no such thing as love any more:

I stop listening to them: they annoy me. They are going to sleep together. They know it. Each of them knows that the other knows it. But as they are young, chaste, and decent, as each wants to keep his self-respect and that of the other, and as love is a great poetic thing which mustn't be shocked, they go several times a week to dances and restaurants, to present the spectacle of their ritualistic, mechanical dances . . .

After all, you have to kill time. They are young and well built, they have another thirty years in front of them. So they don't hurry, they take their time, and they are quite right. Once they have been to bed together, they will have to find something else to conceal the enormous absurdity of their existence. All the same . . . is it absolutely necessary to lie to each other? I look around the room. What a farce!

BUT: at this point it is in order to ask: If you don't *believe* in love, what happens when you find yourself falling in love?

Francis Schaeffer takes the example of lovers on the left bank of the Seine in Paris, who fall in love and then cry because they do not believe love exists:

If I met any of these I would put my hand gently on their shoulders and say, ". . . at this moment you understand something real about the universe. Though your system may say love does not exist, your own experience shows

that it does." They have not touched the personal God who
exists, but, for a fleeting moment, they have touched the
existence of true personality in their love. This is indeed an
objective reality . . .

SUFFERING AND EVIL

The answer to this question usually amounts to one of four
things: despair, resignation, optimism, or rebellion.

Despair

D. R. Davies, writing about his despair in the 30s as he came to
understand the significance of what was happening in Europe:

> As the significance of each group . . . of events became
> clear to my mind, my whole being underwent a most pain-
> ful process of disintegration. I became oppressed with a
> dreadful sense of futility. As I came to realize the failure to
> establish peace; as the utter irrationality of the whole eco-
> nomic life of Europe gradually broke in upon me; and the
> meaning of Fascism gradually dawned upon me; and final-
> ly, as the illusion of Russia broke in upon me, I suffered a
> despair I had never previously known.

> *W. E. Hocking:*

> What we see is the moment-to-moment boundary of our
> being, the nothingness that completes itself in death, our
> own and that of the race: in such a world, riddled the while
> with horror-filled actualities, how can a being aspiring and
> infinite be other than condemned to frustration? And in
> this world we are nevertheless condemned to engage and to
> act as men: is it possible?

If this despair does not lead to resignation, it may lead to
complete anarchy and destructiveness.

Aldous Huxley, writing in 1936, foresees what such an anarchic
revolution might be like:

> The time is not far off when the whole population and not
> merely a few exceptionally intelligent individuals will con-
> sciously realize the fundamental unlivableness of life under
> the present regime. And what then? . . . The revolution
> that will then break out will not be communistic—there will
> be no need for such a revolution . . . and besides, nobody
> will believe in the betterment of humanity or in anything
> else whatever. It will be a nihilist revolution. Destruction for

destruction's sake. Hate, universal hate, and an aimless and therefore complete and thorough smashing up of everything.

Resignation

If the individual feels that life is full of suffering that he can do little to alleviate, he tends to resign himself to the thought that lasting happiness is hardly attainable, and see good and evil as purely relative terms. This has generally been the attitude of the Eastern religions.

Radhakrishnan, writing about Hinduism:

> Evil, error, and ugliness are not ultimate. Evil has reference to the distance which good has to traverse. Ugliness is half-way to beauty. Error is a stage on the road to truth. They have all to be outgrown. No view is so utterly erroneous, no man is so absolutely evil as to deserve complete castigation . . . In a continuously evolving universe evil and error are inevitable, though they are gradually diminishing.

Christmas Humphreys, writing about Buddhism:

> Nothing can be manifested in a finite world without its opposite. Light implies darkness, else it would not be known as light, and breathing could not be sustained unless we breathed both in and out. Like the double action of the human heart, the heartbeat of the universe implies duality, a cosmic pulse, an alternation of in-breathing and out-breathing, of manifestation and rest. To the Buddhist good and evil are relative and not absolute terms. The cause of evil is man's inordinate desire for self. All action directed to selfish separative ends is evil; all which tends to union is good.

John Robinson rejects the pantheism of the east, but his view of evil is not every different from that of the eastern religions. He does not regard evil as something distinct from God which he hates and fights. He writes of his sympathy with the outlook of Peter Dumitriu's book, *Incognito*:

> It is the ability to take up *evil* into God and transform it that is the most striking—and shocking—feature of this theology . . .
> God is everything and everything is in God—literally everything material and spiritual, evil as well as good.

God is not outside evil any more than he is outside anything else, and the promise is that he "*will* be all in all" *as
love.*

BUT: this resigned attitude has far-reaching practical consequences.

G. T. Manley describes the results of Hinduism in India:

A man's life consists of actions, good and bad, each bearing
fruit, and when he dies there is an accumulation of *karma,*
merit and demerit, remaining to be worked off. This determines his status in the next life which may be that of a god,
a Brahman, an outcaste, a woman, a dog, a plant, and so
on. Once again he is caught up in the round of desire,
action and consequences, as the water in the water-wheel is
passed from one plate to the next, and finds no release.

This doctrine gives an easy explanation for all the differences in human life. Bad and good fortune, health or
sickness, poverty or riches, are all ascribed to *karma.* Not
only every calamity of the world, but the caste system itself
is explained by this doctrine. It also accounts to a great
extent for the pessimism found in Hindus today, and largely explains the apparent callousness towards suffering. A
man's moral and spiritual state are not really under his
control since it is the result of a former life.

Leslie Newbigin:

It cannot be denied that the main thrust of the teaching of
the ancient Asian religions has been away from a concern
to change the world. Their dominant teaching has been
that the wise man is he who seeks to be content with the
world, to be released from attachment to it, but not to seek
to change it. The idea of total welfare for all men as a goal
to be pursued within history is foreign to the Asian religions, and modern Indian writers such as Sarma and Pan-
nikar have no hesitation in acknowledging that, so far as
India is concerned, it is part of the western invasion of the
last few centuries.

Optimism

Those who refuse to despair or become resigned about the
present suffering state of mankind, adopt a more optimistic
outlook.

H. W. Van Loon:

> I prefer to concentrate my powers upon that which is within my reach to do: to make this world with its tremendous, with its incredible potentialities for beauty and happiness—a place in which every man, woman, and child will be truly able to say, "We are grateful that we are alive, for life is good!"

> Today that sounds like mocking blasphemy. A hundred centuries hence, it will make sense. For by then man will have acquired the courage necessary to see himself as he really is—as a being equipped with a power of intellect which will eventually allow him to penetrate into every secret of nature until he will truly be the master of all he surveys, and endowed with such a complete freedom of will that he himself—and no one else—is the true master of his fate and therefore dependent for his ultimate happiness upon no one but *himself*.

This optimism about the future of man may be based on political action, on the sciences, or on philosophy.

Hope based on political action.
Bertrand Russell:

> I think we may hope that liberation from the load of fear, private economic fear and public fear of war, would cause the human spirit to soar to hitherto undreamt of heights. Men, hitherto, have always been cramped in their hopes and aspiration and imagination by the limitations of what has been possible . . . There is no need to wait for Heaven. There is no reason why life on earth should not be filled with happiness. There is no reason why imagination should have to take refuge in a myth. In such a world as men could now make, it could be freely creative within the framework of our terrestrial existence . . . If our present troubles can be conquered, Man can look forward to a future immeasurably longer than his past, inspired by a new breadth of vision, a continuing hope perpetually fed by a continuing achievement. Man has made a beginning creditable for an infant—for, in a biological sense, man, the latest of the species, is still an infant. No limit can be set to what he may achieve in the future. I see in my mind's eye, a world of glory and joy, a world where minds expand, where hopes remain undimmed, and what is noble is no

longer condemned as treachery to this or that paltry aim.
All this can happen if we let it happen. It rests with our
generation to decide between this vision and the end de-
creed by folly.

Franz Fanon writes as an Algerian who is very conscious of the
crimes of Europe as well as its profession of humanism. He looks
to the "Third World" to produce a new humanism:

Come, then, comrades . . . Leave this Europe where they
are never done talking of Man, yet murder men everywhere they find them . . . Let us decide not to imitate Europe; let us combine our muscles and our brains in a new
direction. Let us try to create the whole man, whom Europe
has been incapable of bringing to triumphant birth . . . The
Third World today faces Europe like a colossal mass whose
aim should be to try to resolve the problems to which
Europe has not been able to find the answers . . .

It is a question of the Third World starting a new history of
Man, a history which will have regard to the sometimes
prodigious theses which Europe has put forward, but which
will also not forget Europe's crimes, of which the most
horrible was committed in the heart of man, and consisted
of the pathological tearing apart of his functions and the
crumbling away of his unity. And in the framework of the
collectivity there were the differentiations, the stratifications
and the bloodthirsty tensions fed by classes; and finally, on
the immense scale of humanity, there were racial hatreds,
slavery, exploitation, and above all the bloodless genocide
which consisted in the setting aside of fifteen thousand
millions of men . . .

For Europe, for ourselves and for humanity, comrades, we
must turn over a new leaf, we must work out new concepts,
and try to set afoot a new man.

Hope based on science.
Arthur Koestler diagnoses the problem of man in this way:

When one contemplates the streak of insanity running
through human history, it appears highly probable that
homo sapiens is a biological freak, the result of some remark-
able mistake in the evolutionary process . . . somewhere
along the line of his ascent something has gone wrong.

The cause underlying these pathological manifestations is
the split between reason and belief—or more generally,

insufficient co-ordination between the emotive and discriminating faculties of the mind . . . between instinct and
intellect, emotions and reason.

He believes that science alone can provide a solution:

Biological evolution has let us down; we can only hope to
survive if we develop techniques which supplant it by in-
ducing the necessary changes in human nature.

He believes that a "New Pill" could be developed which could
change human nature by acting as a mental stabilizer:

The psycho-pharmacist cannot *add* to the faculties of the
brain—but he can, at best, *eliminate* obstructions or block-
ages which impede their proper use. He cannot aggrandize
us—but he can, within limits, normalize us; he cannot put
additional circuits into the brain, but he can, again within
limits, improve the coordination between existing ones, at-
tenuate conflicts, prevent the blowing of fuses, and ensure a
steady power supply. That is all the help we can ask for—
but if we were able to obtain it, the benefits to mankind
would be incalculable; it would be the "Final Revolution" in
a sense opposite to Huxley's—the break-through from ma-
niac to man.

Hope based on evolution.
Julian Huxley believes that the course of evolution itself will
lead to a better future for mankind:

Evolution . . . is the most powerful and the most comprehensive idea that has ever risen on earth. It helps us to
understand our origins, our own nature, and our relations
with the rest of nature. It shows us the major trends of
evolution in the past and indicates a direction for our
evolutionary course in the future.

From the specifically religious point of view, the desirable
direction of evolution might be defined as the divinization
of existence—but for this to have operative significance, we
must frame a new definition of "the divine," free from all
connotations of external supernatural beings.

This new point of view that we are reaching, the vision of
evolutionary humanism, is essentially a religious one, and
. . . we can and should devote ourselves with truly religious
devotion to the cause of ensuring greater fulfillment for the
human race in its future destiny.

301

Hope based on "A New Humanism."
John Wren-Lewis:

> The Renaissance failed precisely in so far as society failed
> to push the revolt against the traditional outlook right
> through, and here too it seems to me that we are today
> witnessing the gradual emergence of a new vision which
> fulfills the Renaissance promise because it *does* complete the
> revolution. We are witnessing, that is to say, the emergence
> of a deeper humanism based on a positive vision of human
> good in concrete experience, and it springs from the same
> discipline of psychological analysis that has exposed the
> neurotic character of mankind's traditional moral and social
> orientations.
>
> Just what practical expression can be given to this faith is
> something which still remains to be worked out.

Thomas Mann looks forward to a "new humanity":

> I believe in the coming of a new, a third humanism, dis-
> tinct, in complexion and fundamental temper, from its
> predecessors. It will not flatter mankind, looking at it
> through rose-colored glasses, for it will have had experi-
> ences of which the others knew not. It will have a stout-
> hearted knowledge of man's dark, daemonic, radically "nat-
> ural" side; united with reverence for his superbiological,
> spiritual worth.

BUT: all these different kinds of optimism are based on a
"leap of faith." There is not, in fact, a great deal to justify these
utopian hopes. And it is hardly any encouragement to be told,
"If you look far enough ahead, all will be well."

Some of the writers already quoted express their own fears as
well as their hopes:

Michael Harrington speaks of the "weary pessimism" which is
found in *Thomas Mann* alongside his optimism:

> Of all the great writers of the Devil's Party, Mann is the
> most relevant to a study of the contemporary decadence.
> He lived through the unnerving transitions of the period:
> the turn of the century, World War I, the stultification of
> the German middle class, the rise of fascism, World War II
> and the Cold War. Not only did he write of these incredible
> times; the times wrote his life as if it were one of his
> novels . . .

He died undecided, hesitating between a desperate optimism and a weary pessimism.

Bertrand Russell, in an interview with Ved Mehta, confesses:

I have to read at least one detective book a day to drug myself against the nuclear threat.

Arthur Koestler's novel *Darkness at Noon* was based on his knowledge of people involved in the Moscow Trials in the early 30s. The main character, Rubashov, has been condemned to death for crimes against the state and at any moment he expects the final summons. His feelings express the reaction of those who are not content to pin their hopes on a glorious future which they themselves will never see, and of which they see little evidence at the present time. The book ends with these words:

What happened to those masses, to this people? For forty years it had been driven through the desert, with threats and promises, with imaginary terrors and imaginary rewards. But where the Promised Land?

Did there really exist any such goal for this wandering mankind? That was a question to which he would have liked an answer before it was too late. Moses had not been allowed to enter the land of promise either. But he had been allowed to see it, from the top of the mountain, spread at his feet. Thus it was easy to die, with the visible certainty of one's goal before one's eyes. He, Nicolai Salmanowitch Rubashov, had not been taken to the top of a mountain; and wherever his eye looked, he saw nothing but desert and the darkness of night.

Rebellion

This attitude faces the absurdity of suffering and evil and a profound despair. In its determination to protest and rebel and fight suffering and evil it comes nearer than the rest to the Christian answer.

Albert Camus, addressing a Christian audience:

I share with you the same horror of evil. But I do not share your hope, and I continue to struggle against this universe where children suffer and die.

Writing in *The Rebel*:

303

The words which reverberate for us at the confines of this long adventure of rebellion, are not formulae for optimism, for which we have no possible use in the extremities of our unhappiness, but words of courage and intelligence which, on the shores of the eternal seas, even have the qualities of virtue.

No possible form of wisdom today can claim to give more. Rebellion indefatigably confronts evil, from which it can only derive a new impetus. Man can master, in himself, everything that should be mastered. He should rectify in creation everything that can be rectified. And after he has done so, children will still die unjustly even in a perfect society. Even by his greatest effort, man can only propose to diminish, arithmetically, the sufferings of the world. But the injustice and the suffering of the world will remain and, no matter how limited they are, they will not cease to be an outrage. Dmitri Karamazov's cry of "Why?" will continue to resound through history; art and rebellion will only die with the death of the last man on earth.

Camus' novel *The Plague* gives a vivid picture of what this rebellion in the face of suffering must mean. Rieux, the doctor, sees his work in the plague as "fighting against creation as he found it."

I have no idea what's awaiting me, or what will happen when all this ends. For the moment I know this; there are sick people and they need curing. Later on, perhaps, they'll think things over; and so shall I. But what's wanted now is to make them well. And I defend them as best I can, that's all . . .

Have you ever heard a woman scream "Never!" with her last gasp? Well, I have. And then I saw that I could never get hardened to it. I was young then, and I was outraged by the whole scheme of things, or so I thought. Subsequently, I grew more modest. Only, I've never managed to get used to seeing people die. That's all I know . . .

At this moment he suffered with Grand's sorrow, and what filled his breast was the passionate indignation we feel when confronted by the anguish all men share.

BUT: this rebellion means fighting against the order of things without knowing why, and without hope.

Rieux, the doctor in Camus' *Plague*, expresses this dilemma:

> For nothing in the world is it worth turning one's back on
> what one loves. Yet that is what I'm doing—though *why* I
> do not know . . . That's how it is . . . and there's nothing to
> be done about it. So let's recognize the fact, and draw the
> conclusions . . . a man can't cure and *know* at the same time.
> So let's cure as quickly as we can. That's the more urgent
> job.

> He knew that the tale he had to tell could not be one of a
> final victory. It could be only the record of what had had to
> be done, and what assuredly would have to be done again
> in the never-ending fight against terror and its relentless
> onslaughts, despite their personal afflictions, by all who,
> while unable to be saints but refusing to bow down to
> pestilences, strive their utmost to be healers.

> And, indeed, as he listened to the cries of joy rising from
> the town, Rieux remembered that such joy is always imper-
> iled.

PROBLEMS
AND QUESTIONS

With regard to the individual; whatever we may think, we have to live here and now as if he is real.

Dostoievsky writes:

> Man's whole business is to prove that he is a man and not a
> cog-wheel . . .

Aldous Huxley is well aware of the dilemma of the person who
says that the individual does not matter or is unreal. We can only
deny the individual by going against all our normal experience
of life.

> Even if it were not so difficult to arrive at the vision of what
> philosophers and mystics assure us . . . to be the Truth;
> even if it were easy for us to pass in the spirit from the
> world of distinctions and relations to that of infinity and
> unity, we should be no nearer to being able to *live* in that
> higher world. For we live with our bodies; and our bodies
> grossly refuse to be anything but distinct and relative.
> Nothing can induce the body to admit its own illusoriness.

> Our separateness is not wholly an illusion. The element of
> specifity in things is a brute fact of experience. Diversity

cannot be reduced to complete identity even in scientific and philosophical theory, still less in life which is lived with bodies, that is to say, with particular patternings of the ultimately identical units of energy.

A consistent denial of the individual must lead to a philosophy of total negation and meaninglessness.

C. E. M. Joad spells out the logical conclusion of the Eastern religions:

A condition in which I shall cease to think, to feel as an individual or, indeed to *be* an individual, is a condition in which *I* shall cease to be at all. Now why should I hope or seek to realize such a condition, unless I take my individual personality to be of no account?

Christmas Humphreys is convinced that Buddhism allows for the freedom of the will; but the rest of the Buddhist system hardly leaves room for this confident assertion:

The Buddhist fails to see any conflict between the hypotheses of freewill and predestination, for karma and freewill are two facets of the same spiritual truth. "Buddhism," Ananda Coomaraswamy says, "is fatalistic in the sense that the present is always determined by the past; but the future remains free. Every action we make depends on what we have come to be at the time, but what we are coming to be at any time depends on the direction of the will."

Is there a guarantee that the larger entity of which the individual is supposed to be a part, has meaning?

Aldous Huxley:

Individual salvation can have no real sense if existence in the cosmos is itself an illusion. In the monistic view the individual soul is one with the Supreme, its sense of separateness an ignorance, escape from the sense of separateness and identity with the Supreme its salvation. But who then profits by this escape? Not the Supreme Self, for it is supposed to be always and inalienably free, still, silent, pure. Not the world, for that remains constantly in the bondage and is not freed by the escape of any individual soul from the universal illusion. It is the individual soul itself which effects its supreme good by escaping from the sorrow and the division into the peace and the bliss. There would seem then to be some kind of reality of the individual soul as distinct from the world and from the Supreme even in the event of freedom and illumination. But for the illusionist the individual soul is an illusion and non-existent except in the inexplicable mystery of maya. Therefore we arrive at the escape of an illusory soul from an illusory non-existent bondage in an illusory non-existent world as the supreme good which that non-existent soul has to pursue! . . .

The principle of negation prevails over the principle of affirmation and becomes universal and absolute. Thence arise the great world-negating religions and philosophies.

On the question of meaning: can anyone live with a philosophy of total meaninglessness?

Nietzsche tried perhaps harder than any person to *live* his philosophy of meaninglessness to the end. This is how H. J. Blackham describes his attempt:

> In his own case, he provided himself with no means of getting out of the nihilism into which he plunged himself, precisely because it was a deliberate plunge over the edge. He tried to say at the same time: nihilism must be surmounted; nihilism cannot be surmounted; nihilism is good, nihilism is best. He imprisoned himself within the chalked circle of his own metaphysical assumptions.

Colin Wilson describes what the philosophy of meaninglessness meant for some in the nineteenth century:

> Most of these poets of the late nineteenth century were only "half in love with easeful death"; the other half clung very firmly to life and complained about its futility. None of them, not even Thomson, goes as far as Wells in *Mind at the End of Its Tether*. But follow their pessimism further, press it to the limits of complete sincerity, and the result is a completely life-denying nihilism that is actually a danger to life. When Van Gogh's "Misery will never end," is combined with Evan Strowde's "Nothing is worth doing," the result is a kind of spiritual syphilis that can hardly stop short of death or insanity. Conrad's story *Heart of Darkness* deals with a man who has brought himself to this point; he dies murmuring: "The horror, the horror." Conrad's narrator comments: ". . . I wasn't arguing with a lunatic either . . .

His intelligence was perfectly clear; concentrated . . . upon
himself with a horrible intensity, yet clear . . . But his soul
was mad. Being alone in the Wilderness, it had looked
within itself, and . . . it had gone mad: he had summed up;
he had judged: the Horror."

Albert Camus points out the contradiction in the absurdist
position:

I proclaim that I believe in nothing and that everything is
absurd, but I cannot doubt the validity of my own proclamation and I am compelled to believe, at least, in my own
protest.

If life as a WHOLE has no meaning, why should we think that PARTS of life may have some meaning?

Aldous Huxley, writing in the 30s speaks of how some of his
contemporaries accepted a philosophy of meaninglessness, but
then went on to reintroduce meaning in different ways. It was
the results of this thinking in practice and in history which
forced Huxley to reconsider the truth of the philosophy:

Meaning was reintroduced into the world, but only in
patches. The universe as a whole still remained meaningless, but certain of its parts, such as the nation, the state,
the class, the party, were endowed with significance and the
highest value. The general acceptance of a doctrine that
denies meaning and value to the world as a whole, while
assigning them in a supreme degree to certain arbitrarily
selected parts of the totality, can only have evil and disastrous results . . .

It was the manifestly poisonous nature of the fruits that
forced me to reconsider the philosophical tree on which
they had grown.

How can one create meaning out of meaninglessness?

Many of these attempts to create meaning, in spite of their
seriousness and intensity of feeling, sound very much like the
attempt of the King in *Alice in Wonderland* to make sense of
some nonsensical verses of poetry:

"That's the most important piece of evidence we've heard
yet," said the King, rubbing his hands; "so now let the
jury——"

"If any one of them can explain it," said Alice (she had grown so large in the last few minutes that she wasn't a bit afraid of interrupting him), "I'll give him sixpence. *I* don't believe there's an atom of meaning in it."

The jury all wrote down on their slates, "*She* doesn't believe there's an atom of meaning in it," but none of them attempted to explain the paper.

"If there's no meaning in it," said the King, "that saves a world of trouble, you know, as we needn't try to find any. And yet I don't know," he went on, spreading out the verses on his knee, and looking at them with one eye; "I seem to see some meaning in them, after all . . ."

With regard to values: how can one hold on to Christian values when the beliefs on which they are based are no longer accepted?

Nietzsche pours scorn on those who reject Christian beliefs about God but at the same time want to hold on to Christian values:

They have got rid of the Christian God, and now feel obliged to cling all the more firmly to Christian morality: that is *English* consistency, let us not blame it on little blue-stockings *à la* Eliot. In England, in response to every little emancipation from theology one has to reassert one's position in a fear-inspiring manner as a moral fanatic. That is the *penance* one pays there.—With us it is different. When one gives up Christian belief one thereby deprives oneself of the *right* to Christian morality. For the latter is absolutely *not* self-evident: one must make this point clear again and again, in spite of English shallowpates. Christianity is a system, a consistently thought out and *complete* view of things. If one breaks out of it a fundamental idea, the belief in God, one thereby breaks the whole thing to pieces: one has nothing of any consequence left in one's hands. Christianity presupposes that man does not know, *cannot* know what is good for him and what is evil: he believes in God, who alone knows. Christian morality is a command: its origin is transcendental; it is beyond all criticism, all right to criticize; it possesses truth only if God is truth—it stands or falls with the belief in God.—If the English really do believe they know, of their own accord, "intuitively," what is good and evil; if they consequently think they no longer have need of Christianity as a guarantee of morality; that is merely the *consequence* of the ascendancy of the Christian

evaluation and an expression of the *strength* and *depth* of
this ascendancy: so that the origin of English morality has
been forgotten, so that the highly conditional nature of its
right to exist is no longer felt. For the Englishman morality
is not yet a problem.

But morality is very much of a problem—even for the English!

C. E. M. Joad, writing in 1942, when he was still an agnostic,
was well aware of the difficulty, even the dishonesty, of the
position Nietzsche scorned:

> I have been led to place a new value upon the Christian
> code of ethics and the way of life that is based on their
> acceptance, and to see that this value remains, even if the
> metaphysical foundations upon which Christianity bases the
> codes are thought to be dubious or dismissed as untenable.
> But then comes the question: "Can the code endure with-
> out the supernatural foundation, any more than a flower
> can endure that is cut from its roots?" That the Christian
> code and the Christian way of life may so endure *for a time*
> is clear. Plato has an interesting passage about the substitu-
> tion of habit for principle in a society. He gives a vivid
> description of the power of habit, describing how men and
> women will continue to cultivate certain virtues and practice
> restraints, when the principles which would alone have jus-
> tified the cultivating and the practicing have ceased to be
> held. They may do so, he points out, for a time, even, if the
> times are quiet, for a long time, in ignorance that the basis
> of principle is no longer there; but the structure of habit
> lacking foundation collapses at the first impact of adversity.
>
> Is it not doing so now? Is it well that it should do so? And
> if it is not well, is it wise to continue to erode the founda-
> tions in history and metaphysics upon which the Christian
> faith is based? If we can't accept them ourselves, may it not,
> nevertheless, be well that we should at least pretend, re-
> membering in our emergency Plato's hint about the social
> beneficence of the useful lie?

Sartre:

> When we speak of "abandonment"—a favorite word of
> Heidegger—we only mean to say that God does not exist,
> and that it is necessary to draw the consequences of his
> absence right to the end. The existentialist is strongly op-

posed to a certain type of secular moralism which seeks to
suppress God at the least possible expense. The existentialist, on the contrary, finds it . . . embarrassing that God does
not exist, for there disappears with Him all possibility of
finding values in an intelligible heaven. There can no longer be any good *a priori*, since there is no infinite and
perfect consciousness to think it. It is nowhere written that
"the good" exist, that one must be honest or must not lie,
since we are now upon the plane where there are only men.

BACK TO ANSWER ONE

"Man is a creature created in the image of God—the God of the Bible."

PROBLEMS AND QUESTIONS

Having examined other possible answers to the basic question, "What is man?" we return to option one, the biblical Christian answer, for a closer look at some of the questions and objections raised.

Doesn't calling man a "creature" rob him of his dignity?

Colin Wilson associates belief in creation with a submissive passivity. He believes that religion gives

> the sense of being a mere creature whose only business is passive obedience to a master.

Lord Willis, speaking as a humanist, sees belief in God and the divinity of Jesus as signs of weakness:

> I disbelieve in them actively, I am afraid. In fact I would regard it as a weakness to believe in them. I do not believe they are necessary. I respect very much indeed the need that some people have for this particular belief and would not dream of attacking them in any way, but for myself I do not need this belief and I would regard it as an affront to my dignity as a human being to put my faith in something supernatural.

☐ It has to be admitted that Christians have at times held a view of man which makes him much less than the Bible's picture of him.

The Psalmist's words "I am a worm and no man" (Psalm 22:6) have been used to give the impression that man is little more than an insignificant worm. But these words in their context express the feelings of a man in the depths of his suffering and humiliation, and cannot be taken as a summary of the whole biblical view of man.

☐ The Bible regards man's status as a created being, far from *degrading* man, as being the very thing that gives him his *dignity and greatness*. What kind of a creature is this who is created, not like the plants and the trees "after their kind," but in the image and likeness of God himself? In the two passages where the Old Testament writers ask the question "what is man . . .?" (Psalm 8:3–8 and Job 7:17–21, quoted on pp. 221 and 225) the basic thought is: "O God, what is man that you *make so much of him?*"

☐ What happens if man is *not* regarded as a creature created in God's likeness? It may seem that the idea of the dignity and worth of every human being is so obvious and self-evident, that no one in his senses would ever deny it. But the history of the last three centuries shows that it is far from self-evident, and we cannot guarantee that this belief will continue indefinitely if it has no firm foundation. (See pp. 255ff.)

How can man be created and free at the same time?

I.e., doesn't the very idea of creation rule out the possibility that the created thing can be free and responsible? If God creates man in a certain way, how can he hold him responsible for his choices?

☐ We *all* behave in practice *as if* we have a certain measure of freedom and responsibility. However much a person doubts or denies the possibility of man's freedom in making choices, he cannot in fact live as if he has no freedom. Any discussion of determinism and freewill must start with this fact of our experience, not simply with our philosophy.

Jacob Bronowski describes the kind of freedom which is an essential part of being human:

> When I say that I want to be myself, I mean as the existentialist does that I want to be *free* to be myself. This implies that I too want to be rid of constraints (inner as well as outward constraints) in order to act in unexpected ways. Yet I do not mean that I want to act either at random or unpredictably. It is not in these senses that I want to be free but in the sense that I want to be allowed to be different from others. I want to follow my own way—but I want it to be a way, recognizably my own, and not a zig-zag. And I want people to recognize it: I want them to say, "How characteristic!"

He believes that the analogy of the machine—even the most sophisticated machine—is inadequate for describing human experience:

> Until we find a concept of what a machine is which follows fundamentally different laws from any that we know now, my self contains a part that is certainly not a machine in any known sense.

☐ If we agree that a measure of freedom is an essential part of the human condition, what actually happens when a choice or decision is made?

Professor Donald Mackay, a brain scientist, approaches the problem by saying: "Just suppose for the sake of argument that we could predict a person's actions with 100 percent accuracy—what would it prove?" He argues that it doesn't prove the case of the determinist, because there would still be an unknown element: will the person concerned believe what is predicted about himself or will he not?

> It follows that even if the brain were as mechanical as clockwork, no completely detailed present or future description of a man's brain can be equally accurate whether the man believes it or not. (a) It may be accurate *before* he believes it, and then it would automatically be rendered out of date by the brain-changes produced by his believing it; or (b) it might be possible to arrange that the brain-changes

produced by his believing it would bring his brain into the state it describes, in which case it must be inaccurate *unless* he believes it, so he would not be in error to *disbelieve* it.

In either case, the brain-description lacks the "take it or leave it" character of scientific descriptions of the rest of the physical world, since its validity depends precisely upon whether the subject takes it or leaves it! True, any number of detached observers could predict whether the subject will "take it" or "leave it"; but this prediction in turn, though valid for the observers in detachment, would lack any "take it or leave it" validity for the subject. It would still be true that for such brain-states, and future events causally dependent upon them, no *universally valid (pre) determination exists*: no complete and certain prediction waits undiscovered upon which the subject and his observers would be correct to agree . . .

I suggest . . . that the question whether all human brain activity has a mechanistic explanation is one we can peacefully leave open for future investigation, no matter how high a view we take of man's power of decision and its moral and religious significance. A complete mechanistic explanation of the brain would not eliminate our freedom, and those who urge mechanistic behaviorism so as to abolish moral and spiritual categories seem to be pursuing an illusion.

☐Mackay also suggests that there is a similarity between the problem of determinism and responsibility on the human level and the relation between *God*'s sovereignty and man's responsibility. He claims that just as there need be no antithesis between (possibly) mechanistic explanations and human responsibility, so in the same way there is no logical antithesis between divine sovereignty and human responsibility. It is possible for man to be created and at the same time to make choices for which he is responsible. Professor Mackay uses the analogy of the author and the story he creates.

It may help our thinking if we look first at the logical relation between the "predestined course" of a human novel, and what the people in the story would have been correct to believe. The human author is sovereign over the whole of their created history, which for him is one coherent spatio-temporal fact. No event appears in it that he has not ordained, and we can share his complete knowledge of every decision made by his creatures. This does not mean that we know *in advance* an event still in the future for us, nor are the events over which the author is sovereign ahead of *him* in (his) time; so for us and him the prefix "fore-" in such terms as "fore-known" and "fore-ordained" would be inappropriate. All events in the synthetic history, from beginning to end, are for us not prospects but data.

Suppose now that we ask what the people in the story would be correct to believe about the events in their future. John, let us suppose, makes up his mind to ask Mary rather than Jane to marry him. Mary eventually decides to turn him down. Can we say that before either of these decisions was taken, the outcomes were already foreordained and therefore inevitable for John and Mary? Can we say that Mary was not really free to make up her mind, and that she was forced by her author to reject John?

Fortified by our earlier discussions, we can easily see that no such conclusion need follow. No doubt the author *could* write a story in which the characters were mindless puppets, but this is not our story. If John and Mary have been conceived by their author as normal human people, then their decisions will depend upon their cognitive processes in just the way we have already analyzed, with the same logical consequences. Not even the author himself can produce a prediction of the outcome which John and Mary would be correct to accept as inevitable before they make up their minds; for no such prediction exists. On such matters our "predestinarian" knowledge generates nothing definitive for them to know until they make up their minds—and then of course without our help! . . .

So their author's creative sovereignty and "fore-knowledge," complete though it is, does not imply that while they are making up their minds, there exists a secret prediction of their decision, already known to their author, which they would be correct to believe as certain whether they liked it or not, and which thus proves the outcome to be inevitable for them; nor are they *forced* by their author to make the decisions they do, nor is their responsibility for them in any way reduced. But it does imply that although their author may be unknowable by them, they owe their whole existence and that of their world to him, since he decrees every fact of their history—including the fact that they themselves are free agents.

If there is this element of freedom in the relationship between God and man, God can address man and hold him responsible for his response.

> Dialogue . . . is a relationship in which the parties necessarily know one another as undetermined agents. If then our Creator has chosen to offer Himself to us in that relationship, *even He must know us as free and responsible beings.* So in any discussion of the relationship between ourselves and God, we must sharply distinguish between what may be logically applicable to "God-in-dialogue" and to "God-in-eternity" respectively, just as we would have to do if we were speaking of a human author who had created a history in which he himself was one of the characters . . . Logically, we can depend for our existence upon the "creative" will of God-in-eternity, and still be answerable for our response as free beings to the "normative" will of God-in-dialogue. Whatever our attitude to the twin doctrines of divine sovereignty and human responsibility, no logical antithesis can be sustained between them in their biblical form.

☐ If we reject the Christian answer (or any kind of theistic answer), we still have the problem of *accounting for* our freedom. We are faced with a dilemma:

either we must say "we know *that* we have some freedom, but we cannot hope to be able to explain *how* we have evolved in this way";

or we must deny that we have any freedom, and say that our feeling of being free is an illusion.

Thus, if there is a problem in understanding how divine creation can be reconciled with human freedom and responsibility, the problem is very much *more acute* for the agnostic or the atheist. (See pp. 264ff. for some illustrations of this dilemma.)

Is belief in a historic Adam an essential part of Christian beliefs about man?
The following are the main reasons why the biblical Christian generally holds that belief in a historic Adam *is* an essential part of Christian beliefs:

☐ It is the basic principle in interpreting the Bible that we must always ask: "What did the original writer intend?" When we ask

317

this question about the early chapters of Genesis, we find an important clue in the phrase "these are the generations of. . . ." This phrase is repeated in different forms eleven times in the course of the book, and its meaning is: "This is the genealogy, or genealogical history, of. . . ." For example,

> These are the generations of the heavens and the
> earth (2:4)
>
> This is the book of the generations of Adam (5:1)
>
> These are the generations of Noah (6:9)
>
> These are the generations of the sons of Noah, Shem,
> Ham, and Japheth (10:1)

The writer thinks of Adam in the same way as all the other characters who come after him—i.e., as real historical characters. If the writer had wanted to convey the idea that Adam stands for "Everyman" and that the story represents an existential myth about universal human experience, he would hardly have included Adam in this framework of genealogies and spoken of the "descendants of Adam."

☐ The Jews always understood that the creation account referred to a single pair, and *Jesus* clearly accepted this view without question.

> Pharisees came up to him and tested him by asking, "Is it lawful to divorce one's wife for any cause?" He answered, "Have you not read that he who made them from the beginning made them male and female, and said, 'For this reason a man shall leave his father and mother and be joined to his wife, and the two shall become one'?"

Luke traces the genealogy of Jesus back to Adam, the first man:

> Jesus, when he began his ministry, was about thirty years of age, being the son (as was supposed) of Joseph, the son of Heli . . . the son of Enos, the son of Seth, the son of Adam, the son of God.

Paul assumes that Adam was the first man, the one through whom sin entered the world. His whole argument in the following passage about the effects of the death and resurrection of Jesus depends on the assumption that the fall of Adam was just as much a historical event as the death and resurrection of Jesus:

. . . sin came into the world through one man and death through sin, and so death spread to all men because all men sinned . . . If many died through one man's trespass, much more have the grace of God and the free gift in the grace of that one man Jesus Christ abounded for many. And the free gift is not like the effect of that one man's sin. For the judgment following one trespass brought condemnation, but the free gift following many trespasses brings justification. If, because of one man's trespass, death reigned through that one man, much more will those who receive the abundance of grace and the free gift of righteousness reign in life through the one man Jesus Christ.

Then as one man's trespass led to condemnation for all men, so one man's act of righteousness leads to acquittal and life for all men. For as by one man's disobedience many were made sinners, so by one man's obedience many will be made righteous.

☐ Rejection of the belief in a historic Adam creates far more problems than it solves. If the early chapters of Genesis have nothing to do with *origins*—the origin of the universe, of man and sin and suffering—then a host of very vital questions are left completely unanswered: e.g., what does it mean to say that man was "created in the image of God"? Did man grow into the image of God, and did the divine likeness in man evolve gradually? Was man created perfect, or was he created in the same condition as he is now? Was man always a sinner and a rebel by nature?

> *John Habgood:*
>
> Even if we believe, as most theologians now do, that the stories of Adam and Eve are profound myths and not literal history, some difficulties remain. The doctrines of the Fall and of the uniqueness of man are not just forced upon Christians because they happen to be there in Genesis 1:3. They are essential pieces of Christian theology, interlocking with the whole of the rest of theology, which cannot be removed without putting the whole structure in jeopardy.

Is creation compatible with evolution?

Our answer to this question must depend on the answers we give to the following questions:

How do we define "creation" and "evolution"?

How do we understand the relation between science and revelation?

How do we interpret the scientific evidence?

How far are we influenced by other assumptions which have nothing to do with science?

How do we define "creation" and "evolution"? One of the opening scenes of de Laurentii's film *The Bible* shows Adam literally being formed out of dust—a heap of dust is transformed into a living man before our eyes in a few seconds. The text of Genesis, however, does *not* demand an interpretation of this kind. Nor does it demand the interpretation that man was created in an instant "out of nothing."

The writer of Genesis reserves the word "create" for three decisive stages in the creation of the universe:

> In the beginning God created the heavens and the earth . . .
>> (the initial creation of the "raw material" of the universe, 1:1)
>
> God created the great sea monsters and every living creature that moves, with which the waters swarm . . . and every winged bird . . .
>> (the creation of animal life, 1:21)
>
> God created man in his own image . . .
>> (the creation of man, 1:27)

In the first of these stages the word *create* must imply "created out of nothing." But in the other two stages, it is not a creation out of nothing, but rather a creation through working on matter that is already there:

> And God said, "Let the waters bring forth swarms of living creatures . . ." (1:20)
>
> The Lord God formed man of dust from the ground, and breathed into his nostrils the breath of life; and man became a living being . . . (2:7)

Thus, when the writer speaks of God creating man, he speaks of it as a decisively new stage in the unfolding process of creation. But he does not define precisely *how* God created man; and we must be careful not to read into the text ideas that are not there. If we are careful to distinguish between what the Bible *does say* and what it *does not say*, we can afford to have a more open mind over the process by which God created man.

The difficulty in defining "evolution" arises from the fact that the word is used in at least three different senses:

☐ Used in a very *general sense*, it means little more than "development," and describes the process whereby animals and plants change in such a way that new varieties are formed. In this case it normally refers to development within limited areas, and nothing is implied about "natural selection."

☐ Used in the *technical sense*, it refers to the biological theory formulated by Charles Darwin, and is applied to all living things from the amoeba to man.

Professor W. R. Thompson, in the Introduction to the latest Everyman edition of *The Origin of Species,* summarizes Darwin's theory of evolution and the view of most representative modern Darwinians in this way:

> . . . natural selection, leading to the survival of the fittest, in populations of individuals of varying characteristics and competing among themselves, has produced in the course of geological time gradual transformations leading from the simple primitive organism to the highest form of life, without the intervention of any directive agency or force . . . Purposeless and undirected evolution, says J. S. Huxley, eventually produced, in man, a being capable of purpose and of directing evolutionary change.

Those who believe that creation is compatible with evolution in this sense are forced to make a drastic reinterpretation of Genesis; for if the human race has evolved gradually without any special "break," there cannot have been a single "Adam." They are also faced with the problem of how God is able to work purposefully through a process which, by definition, works by chance. Darwin himself spoke of "a Creator," and may have thought that the idea of creation was not incompatible with his theory of evolution. But it was not long before he rejected the Christian belief in creation, and most of his modern followers find the theory a convincing reason for rejecting Christian beliefs:

Professor W. R. Thompson:

> The doctrine of evolution by natural selection as Darwin formulated, and as his followers still explain it, has a strong anti-religious flavour. This is due to the fact that the intricate adaptations and co-ordinations we see in living things, naturally evoking the idea of finality and design and, therefore, of an intelligent providence, are explained, with what

321

seems to be a rigorous argument, as the result of chance
. . . It is clear that in the *Origin* evolution is presented as an
essentially undirected process. For the majority of its readers, therefore, the *Origin* effectively dissipated the evidence
of providential control.

☐ In many cases "evolution" is understood to be *not only a biological
theory but also a philosophical theory* which can be applied in many
other fields and rules out the existence of God.

Julian Huxley writes of evolution as an all-embracing philosophy:

All reality is evolution . . . it is a one-way process in time;
unitary, continuous; irreversible; self-transforming, and
generating variety and novelty during its transformations.

How do we understand the relation between science and revelation?
When this general question is related to the particular question
of evolution, there are basically four different answers that can
be given.

1. "Accept the principle of evolution without question and
revise our interpretation of Genesis accordingly."

This means that we accept the probability that man has
evolved gradually from ape-like ancestors. There cannot have
been one Adam, as Genesis describes him, and the early chapters
of Genesis cannot be understood as speaking about the origin of
the human race.

The difficulty with this view is that it demands such a drastic
reinterpretation of the book of Genesis and of the Bible as a
whole. For the biblical Christian, belief in a single Adam is a vital
part of his Christian beliefs, and rejection of this belief creates
more problems than it solves (see "Man," pp. 317ff.).

2. "Reject the principle of evolution completely and refuse to
allow any scientific evidence to affect our understanding of the
Bible."

In this case we keep science completely separate from revelation, and are unwilling even to consider modifying our interpretation of what the Bible says in the light of the findings of the
sciences.

The weakness of this view is that it creates a dichotomy of
truth by making a total separation between the truth of revelation and the truth of science. If God is the author of *all* truth,
truth must be *one*, and it must be possible to relate the truth of
revelation to the truth of science. Another weakness of this view
is that it refuses to make any distinction between the *authority* of

the Bible itself and the authority of a particular *interpretation.* It allows only one way of interpreting the book of Genesis and gives to this particular interpretation the same authority as to the text of the Bible itself.

3. "Be discriminating in interpreting the scientific evidence, but keep science and revelation completely separate."

If we adopt this approach, we refuse to accept evolution as a dogma which cannot be challenged, and we may be critical of some aspects of evolutionary theory. But we also say that, whatever our views about evolution, we must realize that the scientist and the writer of Genesis are approaching the question of the origin of man from completely different standpoints. They are presenting two different views of man which are not necessarily incompatible, but rather complementary. Science is concerned with the "how?" of creation, whereas the Bible is concerned with the "why?" Both viewpoints are valid within their own sphere, and must be examined separately in the way that is most appropriate to each.

There is of course a great deal of truth in this, but the problem with this view is that it tends to put science and revelation in two apparently separate, water-tight compartments, and therefore makes it very difficult for the scientist or the non-Christian to examine the truth of Christian beliefs about the origin of man. If there are no points of contact between science and revelation, Christian beliefs have to be accepted "by faith," and the questioner inevitably wonders how he is to find his "way in" to the Christian faith.

4. "Be discriminating in interpreting the scientific evidence, but try as far as possible to reconcile or harmonize science and revelation."

This is the approach most consistent with the biblical understanding of truth outlined in Part 1 (pp. 9ff.). It means that we are willing to accept the vulnerability of the Christian faith at this point: if Christian beliefs about man are open to verification, they are also open to falsification. Thus, if we find that there is no possible way of reconciling science and revelation, we must have grave doubts about the truth of these Christian beliefs.

How does this work out in practice?

We have to be *aware of the tentative nature of most scientific theories.* It is only too easy for the scientist to dogmatize about his theories, but then to find that they have to be revised radically in a few years time in the light of new knowledge. If we remember how confidently certain scientific theories were advanced, say fifty years ago, and how much they have had to be revised since then, we shall be less inclined to have an unjustifiable confidence in the theories which are propounded as certain today.

We have to be *willing to revise our interpretation of what the Bible means.* We must acknowledge that we may not always have understood the meaning which the author intended to convey. Revising our *interpretation* of the Bible, however, does not demand a change in our estimate of its *authority.*

We have to be *prepared to suspend judgment* when we find that we cannot make sense of all the different pieces of evidence. This means that we may have to say, "Yes, there *is* a problem here, and we cannot *at present* see a solution to it. We are not running away from the evidence, and it *is* conceivable that compelling evidence would tell against Christian beliefs at this point and make us reject them. But the evidence is not so decisive as to make us abandon our understanding of the Bible's teaching. We must therefore simply suspend judgment now, and hope to be able to see a solution at some future date." Far from being an escape or an excuse for lazy minds, this attitude can be a genuine expression of Christian and scientific humility.

Derek Kidner, writing in his Commentary on Genesis about his understanding of the relation between the story of Adam and science:

> The exploratory suggestion is only tentative, as it must be, and it is a personal view. It invites correction and a better synthesis; meanwhile it may serve as a reminder that when the revealed and the observed seem hard to combine, it is because we know too little, not too much . . .

How are we to interpret the scientific evidence about the origin of man? The problem here is that while one does not need to be a trained historian in order to study the documents concerning the life of Jesus, the vast majority of us find ourselves out of our depth when faced with the intricacies of biological and anthropological studies. The layman also finds that while there may be widespread acceptance of the *theory* of evolution, there are significant gaps in the *data* which ought to support the theory.

Julian Huxley speaks as if we can be reasonably certain about the stages by which man has evolved:

> We can distinguish . . . three stages in the physical evolution of man. First . . . pre-men . . . Next came the proto-men . . . The broad picture of their prehistory which emerges from modern discoveries is something like this . . . And then we reach the fully human phase—man in the proper sense of the word.

Romer, in his book *Man and the Vertebrates* is more cautious
about the origins of man:

> When he (*Homo sapiens*) came is a question to which we
> have as yet no satisfactory answer . . . Nor can we be dog-
> matic as to his pedigree.

David Lack, an ornithologist:

> New species of animals normally arise from isolated popu-
> lations, not individuals. But it is theoretically possible for
> one pair to give rise to a new species, and this may well
> have happened in various land animals that have found
> their way to remote islands. Hence on biological grounds it
> is not at all impossible, though it would be unusual, if the
> population ancestral to man were at one time reduced to a
> single pair through mortality, or more probably,
> emigration . . .

> The available biological and fossil evidence would allow the
> unity of the human race . . . At the same time, the evidence
> is so scanty that nearly all biologists . . . would prefer to
> leave the question open.

Professor W. R. Thompson:

> Darwin himself considered that the idea of evolution is
> unsatisfactory unless its mechanism can be explained. I
> agree, but since no one has explained to my satisfaction
> how evolution could happen I do not feel impelled to say
> that it has happened. I prefer to say that on this matter our
> information is inadequate.

> There is a great divergence of opinion among biologists,
> not only about the causes of evolution but even about the
> actual process. This divergence exists because the evidence
> is unsatisfactory and does not permit any certain conclu-
> sion. It is therefore right and proper to draw the attention
> of the non-scientific public to the disagreement about evo-
> lution. But some recent remarks of evolutionists show that
> they think this unreasonable. This situation, where scientific
> men rally to the defense of a doctrine they are unable to
> define scientifically, much less demonstrate with scientific
> rigor, attempting to maintain its credit with the public by
> the suppression of criticism and the elimination of difficul-
> ties, is abnormal and undesirable in science.

How far are we influenced by other assumptions which have nothing at all to do with science? If the purely scientific evidence is not decisive one way or the other, it may well be that our general assumptions about God and man enter far more fully than we realize into our thinking about creation and evolution—and this is probably true for the non-Christian as much as for the Christian.

Julian Huxley, for example, confuses purely scientific knowledge and his own philosophical assumptions when he makes the following claim:

> Supernatural creation runs counter to the whole of our scientific knowledge . . . To postulate a divine interference with these exchanges of matter and energy at a particular moment in the earth's history is both unnecessary and illogical.

Professor D. S. M. Watson, who was himself a biologist, suggested that the consensus that accepts the theory of evolution (in the third sense noted above) may not be based on purely scientific evidence:

> Evolution has been accepted by scientists, not because it has been observed to occur or proved by logical coherent evidence to be true, but because the only alternative, special creation, is clearly unacceptable.

If our general assumptions play such an important part in this question of evolution and creation, we must emphasize again that what is at stake is not simply the question of whether or not man is descended from the apes, but our total view of man. The person who uses evolutionary theory to reject divine creation has not solved all his problems: in fact they are only just beginning, because he is faced with other more personal questions—about the individual and the meaning of life, about values, relationships, and suffering and evil. (See further Part 1, pp. 23–27; and "Man," pp. 255ff.).

Can we therefore say if creation is compatible with evolution in any sense?

John Stott gives a personal view:

> It seems perfectly possible to reconcile the historicity of Adam with at least some (theistic) evolutionary theory. Many biblical Christians in fact do so, believing them to be not entirely incompatible. To assert the historicity of an original pair who sinned through disobedience is one thing; it is quite another to deny all evolution and to assert the

separate and special creation of everything, including both subhuman creatures and Adam's body. The suggestion (for it is no more than this) does not seem to me to be against Scripture and therefore impossible that when God made man in His own image, what He did was to stamp His own likeness on one of the many "hominids" which appear to have been living at the time.

Speaking hesitatingly as a non-scientist, the extraordinary homogeneity of the human race (physiological and psychological) has always appealed to me as the best available scientific evidence of our common ancestry.

The chief problem in the reconciliation of Scripture and science regarding the origins of mankind concerns the antiquity of Adam. If Adam and Eve were a historical pair, when do you date them? There are two main alternatives.

The first is that they were very early indeed, many thousands of years B.C., so that all the cave-drawing, tool-making hominids were descended from them. The difficulty here is that we would then have to postulate immense gaps in the Genesis story and genealogies.

The second alternative is that they were comparatively recent, even as late as 5 or 10,000 B.C. This reconstruction begins with the biblical witness that the dawn of civilization, adumbrated in Genesis 4:17–22, almost immediately follows the Fall. If this is correct, then even the fairly advanced (although prehistoric) cave-drawing hominids were pre-Adamic. The difficulty here is the claimed scientific evidence that true humans were living in some parts of the world long before this period. But were they Adamic? Anatomically they may have been virtually indistinguishable from modern man; but by what criteria can we judge if they bore the image of God in a biblical sense?

It may be that we shall not be able to solve this problem until we know more precisely what "the image of God" means, and how much cultural (and even primitive religious!) development may have been possible to pre-Adamic hominids who nevertheless did not possess the divine likeness.

The basic question here is this:

☐ *Has the universe been created by some supernatural Being, or is it an "uncreated" universe?*

QUESTION FOUR:
WHAT KIND OF UNIVERSE
DO WE LIVE IN?

John Chao

Fred Hoyle:

> The universe being what it is the creation issue simply
> cannot be dodged.

Julian Huxley:

> Science has removed the obscuring veil of mystery from
> many phenomena, much to the benefit of the human race;
> but it confronts us with a basic and universal mystery—the
> mystery of existence in general, and of the existence of
> mind in particular. Why does the world exist?

Following on from the basic question are three further important questions which we should ask:

CAN WE BE SURE THE UNIVERSE IS REALLY THERE?

Bertrand Russell, in his book the *Problems of Philosophy* explains the
problem in this way:

> Is there a table which has a certain intrinsic nature, and
> continues to exist when I am not looking, or is the table
> merely a product of my imagination, a dream-table in a
> very prolonged dream? This question is of the greatest
> importance . . . If we cannot be sure of the independent
> existence of objects, we shall be left alone in a desert—it
> may be that the whole outer world is nothing but a dream,
> and that we alone exist.

COSMOS OR CHAOS? DESIGN OR CHANCE?

C. E. M. Joad voices a question vital in the development of
modern science.

> Has the universe . . . any design, or is it merely a fortuitous
> concourse of atoms?

IS THERE SUCH A THING AS BEAUTY?

Is beauty something which is "there" in the universe? Or is it
merely the name which we give to things that please us? Our
answer to this question will affect our whole approach to art.

Art historian *H. R. Rookmaaker* writes about aesthetics, the
theory of beauty and art:

It was first developed in the same Greece that conceived classical art . . . the purpose of art was to reveal the ideal, beauty in the highest form. Where this beauty was to be found and how the artist was to realize it were the great questions in aesthetics.

Before the eighteenth century . . . both the artist and the public judged with the same criteria. Since the Enlightenment, this has changed.

In the pages that follow, we take the three basic answers to the question "What kind of universe do we live in?" and then see where each leads in relation to the three supplementary questions.

WHAT KIND OF UNIVERSE DO WE LIVE IN?

A universe created and sustained by God—the God of the Bible.
PAGE 335

A universe which is not the work of any Creator God.
PAGE 352

A universe created by God—but not the God of the Bible.
PAGE 344

ANSWER ONE:
BIBLICAL CHRISTIANITY

The universe was
created and is
sustained by God—the
God of the Bible.

THE UNIVERSE WAS CREATED BY GOD

The universe has been brought into existence by God. It is not
eternal.

God created the universe of his own free choice. He was not
under any compulsion to create the universe. He was not incom-
plete without it.

The universe is completely distinct from God; God is transcendent. The universe is not a part of God or an emanation
from God, nor is God a part of the universe.

God created the universe "out of nothing"; there was no raw
material already there which he simply brought into order.

All these propositions can be derived from the first chapter of
the Bible:

> In the beginning God created the heavens and the earth.
> The earth was without form and void, and darkness was

upon the face of the deep; and the Spirit of God was
moving over the face of the waters.

And God said, "Let there be light"; and there was light.
And God saw that the light was good; and God separated
the light from the darkness . . .

"God created" implies that he created "out of nothing."

"God said . . ." implies that the creation of the universe was a
free act, a free choice of God.

"God saw . . ." implies that the universe is distinct from God.
The writer of the letter to the Hebrews:

Now faith is the assurance of things hoped for, the conviction of things not seen . . . By faith we understand that the
world was created by the word of God, so that what is seen
was made out of things which do not appear.

THE UNIVERSE IS SUSTAINED BY GOD

The universe was not only created by God; it is also sustained by
him all the time. The universe could not exist without God.

God sustains the universe according to certain "laws"; but
these laws do not work independently of him. Both the normal
and the abnormal ordering of natural phenomena are the work
of God. God is able to work miracles at any time in his own
universe for a particular purpose.

God is responsible for what we *do* know about the universe as
well as for what we *do not* know. He is not simply the "God of
the gaps," brought in to account for the areas of life we do not
yet understand.

☐ The Psalmist speaks of the activity of God in the regular and
"natural" processes of nature:

Thou makest springs gush forth in the valleys;
    they flow between the hills,
they give drink to every beast of the field;
    the wild asses quench their thirst.
By them the birds of the air have their habitation;
    they sing among the branches.
From thy lofty abode thou waterest the
        mountains;
    the earth is satisfied with the fruit of thy work.
Thou dost cause the grass to grow for the cattle,
    and plants for man to cultivate,

that he may bring forth food from the earth,
   and wine to gladden the heart of man,
oil to make his face shine,
   and bread to strengthen man's heart.

□Many writers do not draw any sharp line between God's work in creation and sustaining; they are aspects of the same activity.

It is he who made the earth by his power,
   who established the world by his wisdom,
and by his understanding stretched out the
     heavens.
When he utters his voice there is a tumult of
     waters in the heavens,
   and he makes the mist rise from the ends of
     the earth.
He makes lightnings for the rain,
   and he brings forth the wind from his store-
     houses.

□Several passages in the New Testament speak of the work of the eternal Son in the creation and sustaining of the universe.

He is the image of the invisible God, the first-born of all creation; for in him all things were created, in heaven and on earth, visible and invisible, whether thrones or dominions or principalities or authorities—all things were created through him and for him. He is before all things, and in him all things hold together.

. . . for us there is one God, the Father, from whom are all things and for whom we exist, and one Lord, Jesus Christ, through whom are all things and through whom we exist.

In the beginning was the Word, and the Word was with God, and the Word was God. He was in the beginning with God; all things were made through him, and without him was not anything made that was made.

□As originally created, the universe was "very good":

And God saw everything that he had made, and behold, it was very good.

□The fall of Adam in some ways affected even the physical universe:

And to Adam he (God) said,

"Because you have listened to the voice of your
    wife,
   and have eaten of the tree
of which I commanded you,
   'You shall not eat of it,'
cursed is the ground because of you;
   in toil you shall eat of it all the days of your life;
thorns and thistles it shall bring forth to you."

Paul speaks of the whole creation being "subjected to futility."

☐ The person who believes the universe to be created and sustained in this way can respond with amazement, worship, and joy:

Bless the Lord, O my soul!
O Lord my God, thou art very great!
Thou art clothed with honor and majesty,
   who coverest thyself with light as with a
      garment,
who hast stretched out the heavens like a tent . . .

☐ This way of thinking about the universe is not inconsistent with the outlook of the modern scientist.

Professor D. M. Mackay, himself a scientist, explains what is meant by the biblical concept of creation and "upholding":

What sense can we make of this unfamiliar idea of "holding in being"? . . .

An imaginative artist brings into being a world of his own invention. He does it normally by laying down patches of paint on canvas, in a certain special order (or disorder!). The *order* in which he lays it down determines the *form* of the world he invents. Imagine now an artist able to bring his world into being, not by laying down paint on canvas, but by producing an extremely rapid succession of sparks of light on the screen of a television tube. (This is in fact the way in which a normal television picture is held in being.) The world he invents is now not static but dynamic, able to change and evolve at will. Both its form and its laws of change (if any) depend on the way in which he orders the sparks of light in space and time. With one sequence he produces a calm landscape with quietly rolling clouds; with another, we are looking at a vigorous cricket match on a village green. The scene is steady and unchanging just for as long as he wills it so; but if he were to cease his activity, his invented world would not become chaotic; it would simply cease to be . . .

Creation in the biblical sense is the "willing into reality" of the *whole* of our space-time: future, present and past.

THE ANSWER THIS APPROACH GIVES TO OTHER QUESTIONS ABOUT THE UNIVERSE

CAN WE BE SURE THE UNIVERSE IS REALLY THERE?

We can be sure that it is really there because God has created the universe "outside of" himself. It exists outside of God, and is not part of his mind or of his "dreaming."

> Praise him, sun and moon,
> praise him, all you shining stars!
> Praise him, you highest heavens,
> and you waters above the heavens!
> Let them praise the name of the Lord!
> for he commanded and they were created.
> And he established them for ever and ever;
> he fixed their bounds which cannot be passed.

COSMOS OR CHAOS? DESIGN OR CHANCE?

The universe is not the product of chance, but of the purpose and design of God. It is God who is responsible for the "natural" laws of the universe.

After the Flood, God says to Noah,

> "While the earth remains, seedtime and harvest, cold and heat, summer and winter, day and night, shall not cease."

The Psalmist speaks of the stability and reliability of the universe as the work of God:

> Thou didst set the earth on its foundations,
> so that it should never be shaken.
> Thou didst cover it with the deep as with a
> garment;
> the waters stood above the mountains.
> At thy rebuke they fled;
> at the sound of thy thunder they took to flight.

339

> The mountains rose, the valleys sank down
> to the place which thou didst appoint for them.
> Thou didst set a bound which they should not
> pass,
> so that they might not again cover the earth.

Belief in the fundamental stability of the universe contributed significantly to the rise of modern science. We may say that the birth of modern science depended on:

the geometry developed by the Greeks;

the accumulation of astronomical knowledge from the classical period onward;

the development of arithmetic and algebra among the Arabs;

the rejection of the Greek approach to science which relied on deduction from first principles rather than observation and experiment;

belief in the regularity of nature, the rationality of God, and the certainty that the universe is there;

the linking of the rational and the empirical, the combination of thought and fact.

Professor Hooykaas in his book *Religion and the Rise of Science*:

The confrontation of Graeco-Roman culture with biblical religion engendered, after centuries of tension, a new science. This science preserved the indispensable parts of the ancient heritage (mathematics, logic, methods of observation and experimentation), but it was directed by different social and methodological conceptions, largely stemming from a biblical world view. Metaphorically speaking, whereas the bodily ingredients of science may have been Greek, its vitamins and hormones were biblical.

C. F. Von Weizacker, a German physicist, summarizes his argument about the connection between modern science and Christian beliefs:

The concept of strict and generally valid laws of nature could hardly have arisen without the Christian concept of creation. Matter in the Platonic sense, which must be "prevailed upon" by reason, will not obey mathematical laws exactly: matter which God has created from nothing may

well strictly follow the rules which its Creator had laid down
for it. In this sense I called modern science a legacy, I
might even have said a child, of Christianity.

Professor Donald Mackay writes of how the biblical outlook
provides a solid basis for the activity of the scientist today:

> The biblical doctrine . . . provides a more stable, rather
> than a less stable, foundation for our normal scientific ex-
> pectations, in the stability of the will of a God who is always
> faithful.

> We are emerging from a period of confused conflict during
> which the biblical doctrine of divine activity seems to have
> become largely distorted or forgotten. It is in this doctrine,
> untrimmed by any concessions to the spirit of our age, that
> I see the basis of the deepest harmony between Christian
> faith and the scientific attitude. There could be no higher
> guarantee of our scientific expectations than the rationality
> and faithfulness of the One who holds in being the stuff
> and pattern of our world.

IS THERE SUCH A THING AS BEAUTY?

The natural starting-point for the biblical answer to this question
is contained in the words of Genesis:

> And God saw everything that he had made, and behold it
> was very good.

The word *saw* implies that the universe is distinct from God; and
the words that follow give God's description of the universe as
he created it: "it was very good." Thus the "goodness" is something inherent in the universe: it is not merely a feeling in the
mind of God or of man. The word *good* cannot refer to moral
goodness and must imply at least that there was order and
beauty in the universe.

The Christian believes, therefore, that beauty is not simply an
idea in his own mind. Beauty is a quality of things as they are; *it
is there*—even if we find it hard to define what beauty is or have
different opinions about what is beautiful.

H. R. Rookmaaker discusses how the Christian's starting-point
affects his understanding of art:

> We may now ask: what is Christian art? It is clear that this
> term cannot mean only art with biblical or ecclesiastical
> subject matter. It is quite possible for a painting of a cruci-

fixion, for example, to have an unbiblical content or even be anti-Christian. And it must be clear that the inherent Christian qualities are not bound to one specific style—just as a sermon can be preached in different languages without losing its integrity. Yet it may be true that one style is better suited to "do the truth" than another—just as Christianity when it enters into the cultural life of people, alters their language and adds new elements to it, and may eliminate certain peculiarities. In a way, the real Christian quality cannot be found by looking for specific elements. In a way, just the opposite is the case. When things are in accordance with God's created possibilities and His will for His world, they are just "normal." When love reigns in a community, that community is not strange but healthy. Problems, strangeness, conflicts, tensions, etc. always arise only from sin and its results. In a way, it is, therefore, perhaps even better to speak, not of Christian art, but of truthful art, art that is art in the fullness of the meaning as God intended it to be. Perhaps a still-life of a man like Heda (who worked in the Netherlands in the early seventeenth century) is more intrinsically "Christian" than a crucifixion by El Greco.

Christian art is not to be defined as art made by a Christian. Christians can sin; they can make (even with the best of intentions) ugly, silly, or shallow works of art. And a non-Christian can make beautiful and truthful ones. The criterion is the inherent truth of the work. This fact gives rise to another question: how can such truthful works of art come into being? The answer is that they can be made by man where the artist is fully human and true to his calling. This may happen anywhere and at any time, when man acts out of his created humanness. As soon as sinful elements, or tendencies not in accord with God's will as laid down in His creation, enter into the production of the work of art, its integrity is challenged and . . . ugliness, and mannerisms enter in.

Our being cannot be satisfied unless the thirst for Beauty is quenched. This is why the child of God fights for Beauty and Holiness, because at the Creation man was absolutely beautiful. The beautiful and the good for which Plato was searching will come when the Lord returns.

We must be fully aware that the truth is at stake, the question of whether God's creation is good, whether life is

beautiful and worth the living of it, or whether evil is sin
and a result of sin. It is the question of whether human life
has value, whether our work has meaning, and the question
of whether there is meaning outside God and Jesus Christ.
It is not an academic question to ask what are the results of
over-stepping the first and second commandments, refusing
to acknowledge God, refusing to love our neighbor and
dragging him through the mire because we do not recognize him in his humanness.

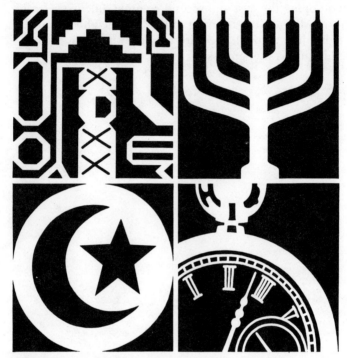

ANSWER TWO:
PRIMAL RELIGION AND JUDAISM, ISLAM AND DEISM

The universe is created
by God—but not the
God of the Bible.

It is not enough to say that the universe is created by God. We must also define what we mean by the word God. Different concepts of God are bound to lead to different ways of thinking about the universe.

*The following are some of the main
points in which these different religions
differ from the biblical understanding:*

☐ *some deny that the creation is good;*

☐ *others see God's relationship with the
universe in terms of that between a
mechanic and his machine;*

☐ *some set the "natural" over against the
"supernatural," seeing them as two distinct spheres.*

Primal religion

John Mbiti describes how the African sees the universe:

> It emerges clearly that for African peoples, this is a re-
> ligious universe. Nature in the broadest sense of the word is
> not an empty impersonal object or phenomenon: it is filled
> with religious significance. Man gives life even where natu-
> ral objects and phenomena have no biological life. God is
> seen in and behind these objects and phenomena: they are
> His creation, they manifest Him, they symbolize His being
> and presence. The invisible world is symbolized or mani-
> fested by these visible and concrete phenomena and objects
> of nature. The invisible world presses hard upon the visi-
> ble: one speaks of the other, and African peoples "see" that
> invisible universe when they look at, hear, or feel the visible
> and tangible world.

Judaism

Because they are based on the Old Testament, Jewish beliefs can
come close to the Christian understanding. (See pp. 335ff.)

Islam

Some of the most beautiful verses of the Qur'an are about the
creative work of God in the universe.

> We spread out the earth and set upon it immovable moun-
> tains. We brought forth in it all kinds of delectable plants.
> A lesson and an admonition to penitent men.

> We send down blessed water from the sky with which We
> bring forth gardens and the harvest grain, and tall palm-

trees laden with clusters of dates, a sustenance for men; thereby giving new life to some dead land.

We have decked the heavens with constellations and guarded them from all accursed devils. Eavesdroppers are pursued by fiery comets.

We have spread out the earth and set upon it immovable mountains. We have planted it with every seasonable fruit, thus providing sustenance for man and beast. We hold the store of every blessing and send it down in appropriate measure. We let loose the fertilizing winds and bring down water from the sky for you to drink; its stores are beyond your reach.

Deism

In order to understand how Deism developed it is important to see how Christian ideas about the universe were gradually contaminated by Greek ideas.

Hooykaas describes the difference between the biblical view of the universe and that of the ancient Greeks:

There is a radical contrast between the deification of nature in pagan religion and, in a rationalized form, in Greek philosophy, and de-deification of nature in the Bible. By contrast with the nature-worship of its neighbors, the religion of Israel was a unique phenomenon. The God of Israel, by his word, brings forth all things out of nothingness. He is truly all-powerful: He was not opposed by any matter that had to be forced into order, and He did not have to reckon with eternal Forms; His sovereign will alone created and sustains the world. In the first chapter of Genesis it is made evident that absolutely nothing, except God, has any claim to divinity; even the sun and the moon, supreme gods of the neighboring peoples, are set in their places between the herbs and the animals and are brought into the service of mankind. The personal god of the Greeks had an origin, in spite of their immortality. The God of the Bible is the only god who is immutable and eternal, unlike all created things which are liable to change and final destruction. Nothing else has divine power, not even by delegation: "The Lord is one; there is no one but He."

The New Testament proclaims again the message that there is no eternal cycle of nature or cycle of history. The history

of the world moves towards its final destination and heaven
and earth are destined to fall back into the nothingness
from which they once emerged. Not only the creating, but
also the upholding of the world belongs to God alone; that
is to say, Jahveh is not a deistic supreme being who, after
the creative act, leaves everything to the innate laws of
nature, and He does not withdraw, like a platonic demi-
urge, into "the way of being that belongs solely to Him."
He remains for ever the will and power behind all events
. . . In total contradiction to pagan religion, nature is not a
deity to be feared and worshiped, but a work of God to be
admired, studied, and managed. When we compare pagan
and biblical religions, we find a fundamental contrast between the ideas concerning God and man which have
emerged. In the Bible God and nature are no longer both
opposed to man, but God and man together confront nature. The denial that God coincides with nature implies the
denial that nature is god-like.

Some of these ideas from pagan religions were carried over
into the thinking of many Christians in the Middle Ages.

Nature was considered as a semi-independent power, and
when things happened according to nature, this meant that
they followed a pattern that seemed rational to the human
mind, one which had been discovered by Aristotle . . . In
the Middle Ages . . . the biblical view was only superim-
posed on, and did not overcome, the Aristotelian conception. The regular order of nature was considered to be
something instituted by God, but liable to be over-ruled by
Him in a *super*-natural way (the term is significant) when
performing a miracle. Thomas Aquinas considered one of
the useful functions of natural philosophy to be to enable
us to distinguish that which belongs only to God (for example miracles, or the origin of things) from that which belongs to nature.

The lengths to which the devaluation of the natural universe
could go is illustrated in these words from a medieval church-
man, *Lallemant*:

We should marvel at nothing in Nature except the redeeming death of Christ.

This is a thoroughly *un*-Christian sentiment, and we are not
surprised to learn that these words contain the essence of what

Nietzsche detested about Christian sainthood.

Combined with this was the belief that the material universe is somehow part of the Satanic order.

Basil Willey, speaking of the medieval idea of science as "the forbidden knowledge":

> The Faustus legend testifies to the strength of the fascinated dread with which the Middle Ages had thought of natural science . . . "Nature" had, in quite a special sense, been consigned to the Satanic order.
>
> For practical purposes . . . we may perhaps take the later fifteenth and the sixteenth centuries as the epoch of the rebirth of confidence in "Nature" . . .
>
> This recrudescence of confidence in Nature was immensely strengthened by the scientific movement of the Renaissance, which reclaimed the physical world from its traditional association with Satan.

When we come to the seventeenth century, we find that as the Creator recedes more and more into the background, "Nature" itself becomes almost like a god.

Basil Willey, writing about John Locke:

> Locke's deity, in a word, is that of the contemporary reconcilers of science and religion, such as Glanvill or Boyle, and that of the eighteenth century as a whole—a Deity to be approached by demonstration, and whose existence, proclaimed by the spacious firmament on high, is as well attested as any proof in Euclid. This phase of religious thought, with which the term *Deism* is often associated, was rendered possible largely by the completeness with which the findings of seventeenth-century science, up to that date, could be made to fuse with the inherited religious certainties. Newton's Great Machine needed a Mechanic, and religion was prepared ahead with that which could serve this purpose. Everywhere that science had so far disclosed was nothing but "order, harmony, and beauty"; and finally the incomparable Newton had linked the infinitely great and the infinitely little in one inspired synthesis. The mighty maze was not without a plan, and Locke could declare with perfect candor that "the words of Nature in every part of them sufficiently evidence a Deity."

Shaftesbury in the seventeenth century addressed "Nature" in this way:

O Glorious *Nature!* supremely Fair, and sovereignly Good!
All-loving and All-lovely, All-divine! . . . Whose every single
Work affords an ampler scene, and is a nobler Spectacle
than all which ever Art presented! O mighty *Nature!* Wise
Substitute of Providence! impower'd *Creatress!* Or Thou im-
powering Deity, supreme Creator! Thee I invoke, and Thee
alone adore. To Thee this solitude, this place, these Rural
Meditations are sacred . . .

Basil Willey comments on the significance of Shaftesbury:

Thus far . . . had the divinization of Nature proceeded a
hundred years before Wordsworth. Already the injunction
"First follow Nature" had passed beyond the region of
ethics and poetics, and the Wordsworthian nature-religion
can be regarded, less as something wholly new, than as the
culmination of a process which had been implicit in the
"humanist" tradition ever since the Renaissance.

Ever since the Renaissance the Creation had been steadily
gaining in prestige as the "art of God," the universal divine
Scripture which "lies expans'd unto the eyes of all." The
emotion of the numinous formerly associated with super-
nature, had become attached to Nature itself; and by the
end of the eighteenth century the divinity, the sacredness
of nature was, to those affected by this tradition, almost a
first datum of consciousness.

Wordsworth's understanding of God and his relation to the
universe is summed up in this passage from *Mark Rutherford,*
writing about the effect which Wordsworth's Lyrical Ballads had
on him:

God is nowhere formally deposed, and Wordsworth would
have been the last man to say that he had lost his faith in
the God of his fathers. But his real God is not the God of
the Church, but the God of the hills, the abstraction Nature, and to this my reverence was transferred.

Charles Darwin at the time when he wrote *The Origin of Species*
(published in 1859) described himself as a theist:

When thus reflecting, I feel compelled to look to a First
Cause having an intelligent mind in some degree analogous
to that of man; and I deserve to be called a Theist.

But disbelief gradually crept over him, and in his *Autobiography* (written in 1876) he wrote:

> The mystery of the beginning of all things is insoluble to
> us; and I for one must be content to remain an Agnostic.

THE ANSWER
THIS APPROACH
GIVES TO OTHER
QUESTIONS ABOUT
THE UNIVERSE

Other questions on the universe are not too difficult for those
who believe in a personal Creator. But for the Deist they may
become real problems as God recedes into the background.

HOW CAN WE BE SURE
THE UNIVERSE IS REALLY THERE?

The existence of a personal Creator is generally held to guarantee that the tangible world is real.

Descartes, however, with his principle of systematic doubt was
forced to question the existence of the external universe. The
only way in which he could solve the problem for himself was to
say that we all feel that the material world really exists outside of
ourselves. And it is inconceivable that God should give us this
feeling if it is not in accordance with the truth, since God would
not deceive us. Therefore, the external world must exist. So
Descartes uses God as a guarantee that our convictions about the
universe are true.

COSMOS OR CHAOS? DESIGN OR CHANCE?

Those who believe in the existence of a Creator usually believe
there is design and order in the universe.

But the vaguer the belief in the existence of God, the more
doubtful the concept of design and order, as *Charles Darwin*
shows:

> My theology is a simple muddle; I cannot look at the
> universe as the result of blind chance, yet I can see no
> evidence of beneficent design, or indeed of design of any
> kind, in details.

IS THERE SUCH A THING AS BEAUTY?

The Deist believes that the creation is the handiwork of God,
and therefore that its beauty is something given to it by God.
But as the relationship between "Nature" and God becomes

more and more tenuous, beauty becomes less and less dependent
on God.

Wordsworth found that his experience of ecstasy over Nature
did not last. He could not find lasting peace and satisfaction
through his attitude to Nature, and finally he was forced to turn
to other things for inspiration.

Basil Willey writes:

> In the later life of our greatest "Nature" poet . . . there is a
> steady retreat towards the religious sources of his mysti-
> cism, and grace supplants the visionary gleam.

> It is significant that Wordsworth to some extent abandoned
> Nature himself, as if he had discovered its inadequacy;
> abandoned it first for "Duty" and then for Faith.

It would seem that beauty divorced from the God who has
created beautiful things cannot long remain real and satisfying.

Charles Darwin, in his *Autobiography*, speaks of how in later
years he began to lose some of his appreciation of beauty. This
may have been partly the effect of old age and sickness; but
there is probably also some connection with his general understanding of the universe.

> My mind seems to have become a kind of machine for
> grinding general laws out of large collections of facts, but
> why this should have caused the atrophy of that part of the
> brain alone, on which the higher tastes depend, I cannot
> conceive.

> In my Journal I wrote that whilst standing in the midst of
> the grandeur of a Brazilian forest, "it is not possible to give
> an adequate idea of the higher feelings of wonder, admira-
> tion, and devotion which fill and elevate the mind." I well
> remember my conviction that there is more in man than
> the mere breath of his body; but now the grandest scenes
> would not cause any such conviction and feelings to arise in
> my mind. It may be truly said that I am like a man who has
> become color-blind.

ANSWER THREE:
HINDUISM, EUROPEAN THINKERS, AND SOME MODERN THEOLOGIANS

The universe is not the work of any Creator God.

Hinduism

Radhakrishnan, writing in *the Hindu View of Life* is content to remain agnostic about the origin of the universe:

> The hypothesis of creation is a weak one, and it assumes that God lived alone for some time and then suddenly it occurred to him to have company, when he put forth the world. The theory of manifestation is not more satisfying, for it is difficult to know how the finite can manifest the infinite. If we say that God is transformed into the world, the question arises whether it is the whole of God that is transformed or only a part. If it is the whole, then there is no God beyond the universe and we lapse into the lower pantheism. If it is only a part, then it means that God is capable of being partitioned. We cannot keep one part of God above and another part below. It would be like taking half the fowl for cooking, leaving the other half for laying

eggs. Samkara believes that it is not possible to determine logically the relation between God and the world. He asks us to hold fast both ends. It does not matter if we are not able to find out where they meet.

The history of philosophy in India as well as Europe has been one long illustration of the inability of the human mind to solve the mystery of the relation of God to the world. The greatest thinkers are those who admit the mystery and comfort themselves by the idea that the human mind is not omniscient. Samkara in the East and Bradley in the West adopt this wise attitude of agnosticism. We have the universe with its distinctions. It is not self-sufficient. It rests on something else, and that is the Absolute. The relation between the two is a mystery.

He rejects an extreme form of pantheism, but there is still no possibility of the existence of a personal Creator God.

The Hindu view rebels against the cold and formal conception of God who is external to the world, and altogether remote and transcendent. The natural law of the world is but a working of God's sovereign purpose. The uniformity of nature, the orderliness of the cosmos, and the steady reaching forward and upward of the course of evolution proclaim not the unconscious throbbing of a soulless engine, but the directing mind of an all-knowing spirit. The indwelling of God in the universe does not mean the identity of God with the universe. According to the latter view God is so immanent in everything that we have only to open our eyes to see God in it, but also there is nothing of God left outside the whole of things. God lies spread out before us. The world is not only a revelation, but an exhaustive revelation of God. Hindu thought takes care to emphasise the transcendent character of the Supreme. "He bears the world but is by no means lost in it." The world is in God and not God in the world. In the universe we have the separate existence of the individuals. Whether the divine spark burns dimly or brightly in the individual, the sparks are distinct from the central fire from which they issue.

European thinkers

Ernst Cassirer describes how new ways of thinking in the fifteenth century called in question the traditional Christian belief:

All this is suddenly called into question by the new cosmology. Man's claim to being the center of the universe has lost its foundation. Man is placed in an infinite space in which his being seems to be a single and vanishing point. He is surrounded by a mute universe, by a world that is silent to his religious feelings and to his deepest moral demands.

He quotes some words of *Montaigne* which, he says, give the clue to the whole subsequent development of the modern theory of man.

"Let man . . . make me understand by the force of his reason, upon what foundation he has built those great advantages he thinks he has over other creatures. Who has made him believe that this admirable notion of the celestial arch, the eternal light of those luminaries that roll so high over his head, the wondrous and fearful motions of that infinite ocean, should be established and continue so many ages for his service and convenience? Can anything be imagined so ridiculous, that this miserable and wretched creature, who is not so much as master of himself, but subject to the injuries of all things, should call himself master and emperor of the world, of which he has not power to know the least part, much less to command the whole?

"Whoever shall represent to his fancy, as in a picture, the great image of our mother nature, portrayed in her full majesty and luster; whoever in her face shall read so general and so constant a variety, whoever shall observe himself in that figure, and not himself but a whole kingdom, no bigger than the least touch of a pencil, in comparison of the whole, that man alone is able to value things according to their true estimate and grandeur."

Montaigne's words give us the clue to the whole subsequent development of the modern theory of man. Modern philosophy and modern science had to accept the challenge contained in these words. They had to prove that the new cosmology, far from enfeebling or obstructing the power of human reason, establishes and confirms this power. Such was the task of the combined efforts of the metaphysical systems of the sixteenth and seventeenth centuries. These systems go different ways, but they are all directed toward one and the same end. They strive, so to speak, to turn the apparent curse of the new cosmology into a blessing.

354

Julian Huxley:

In the evolutionary pattern of thought there is no longer
either need or room for the supernatural. The earth was
not created: it evolved. So did all the animals and plants
that inhabit it, including our human selves, mind and soul
as well as brain and body. So did religion.

All aspects of reality are subject to evolution, from atoms
and stars to fish and flowers, from fish and flowers to
human societies and values—indeed . . . all reality is a single process of evolution.

A. J. Ayer:

While I believe that there can be an explanation in mundane terms for anything that happens within the world, I
do not think it makes sense or ask for an explanation of the
existence to characteristics of the world as a whole.

Jacob Bronowski indicates some of the assumptions of much
scientific thinking today:

We have to accept the subtle but closely woven evidence
that man is not different in kind from other forms of life;
that living matter is not different in kind from dead matter;
and therefore that a man is an assembly of atoms that obeys
natural laws of the same kind that a star does . . .

The atoms in the brain as much as those in the body
constitute a mechanism, which ticks with the same orderly
regularity, and abides by similar laws, as any other in-
terlocking constellation of atoms. Men have uneasily pushed
this thought out of their heads because they wanted to
avoid the conflict with their rooted conviction that man is a
free agent who follows only the promptings of his own will.
But we cannot hide this contradiction for ever.

My fundamental assumption . . . is that man is a part of
nature.

This simple proposition seems innocent enough, and neutral. Nearly all educated men accept it now . . . In the latter
half of the twentieth century, it seems self-evident to say
that man is a part of nature, in the same sense that a stone
is, or a cactus, or a camel . . . Yet this bland proposition
contains the explosive charge which in this century has split
open the self-assurance of western man.

355

We sense that there is no break in the continuity of nature. At one end of her range, the star has been linked with the stone; and at the other end, man has been put among the animals . . . An unbroken line runs from the stone to the cactus and on to the camel, and there is no supernatural leap in it. No special act of creation, no spark of life was needed to turn dead matter into living things.

D. H. Lawrence expresses his dissatisfaction with an arid naturalism:

Give me the mystery! And let the world live again for me!

The universe is dead for us, and how is it to come alive again? "Knowledge" has killed the sun, making it a ball of gas with spots; "Knowledge" has killed the moon—it is a dead little earth fretted with extinct craters as with smallpox; the machine has killed the earth for us . . . How, out of all this, are we to get back the grand orbs of the soul's heavens, that fill us with unspeakable joy? How are we to get back Apollo, and Attis, Demeter, Persephone, and the halls of Dis? We've got to get them back, for they are the world our soul, our great consciousness, lives in. The world of reason and science . . . this is the dry and sterile little world the abstracted mind inhabits . . . Two ways of knowing, for man, are knowing in terms of apartness, which is mental, rational, scientific, and knowing in terms of togetherness, which is religious and poetic.

Albert Camus, especially in his earlier works, writes freely of his sensations in enjoying nature:

The world is beautiful and, outside it, there is no salvation.

There is but one love in this world. To embrace a woman's body is also to retain, close to one, that strange joy which descends from the sky to the sea . . . I love this life with abandon and I want to speak of it freely; it fills me with pride at my human fate.

Some modern theologians

Teilhard de Chardin's thought is completely dominated by the concept of evolution, which he regards not simply as a biological principle, but as an all-inclusive philosophy. Although he speaks of God as Creator, it would seem that even God is in a sense subject to this same law of evolution.

One might well become impatient or lose heart at the sight of so many minds (and not mediocre ones either) remaining today still closed to the idea of evolution, if the whole of history were not there to pledge to us that a truth once seen, even by a single mind, always ends up by imposing itself on the totality of human consciousness. For many, evolution is still only transformism, and transformism is only an old Darwinian hypothesis as local and dated as Laplace's conception of the solar system or Wegener's Theory of Continental Drift. Blind indeed are those who do not see the sweep of a movement whose orbit infinitely transcends the natural sciences and has successively invaded and conquered the surrounding territory—chemistry, physics, sociology, and even mathematics and the history of religions. One after the other all the fields of human knowledge have been shaken and carried away by the same under-water current in the direction of the study of some *development.* Is evolution a theory, a system, or a hypothesis? It is much more: it is a general condition to which all theories, all hypotheses, all systems must bow and which they must satisfy henceforward if they are to be thinkable and true. Evolution is a light illuminating all facts, a curve that all lines must follow.

If as a result of some interior revolution, I were successively to lose my faith in Christ, my faith in a personal God, my faith in the Spirit, I think I would continue to believe in the World. The World (the value, the infallibility, the goodness of the World); that, in the final analysis, is the first and last thing in which I believe.

John Robinson seems to reject not only popular distortions of Christian beliefs, but the whole supernaturalism of historic Christianity:

A dualist model of the universe is out. Whether looked at from the outside or the inside, reality for us is all of a piece. As Van Peursen puts it, "There is no supernatural reality, high and lofty, above us. There is only that reality which concerns us directly concretely." There is no second story to the universe, no realm of the divine over and above or behind the processes of nature and history which perforates this world or breaks it up by supernatural intervention.

What he puts in place of the historic Christian belief is the concept of a "personalizing" universe:

The doctrine of creation *ex nihilo* does not exist to assert
that there was a time or a state in which a Being called God
was there alone and that "out of nothing" he made the
world—though he might not have done. That is to indulge
in a tissue of mythopoeic speculation. What it asserts is that
there is nothing in the whole range of experience which
cannot be interpreted in terms of God or which requires
any other ground. That is to say, there is no aspect of
nature or history, however resistant to personal categories,
that is not *ultimately* to be seen in terms of spirit, freedom,
love. From the start, affirms the believer, this is a "personalizing" universe, in the sense that the whole is to be understood as a process making for personality and beyond.

What essentially the Christian faith is asserting is that in
and through all the processes of nature and history there is
a personal outcome to be traced and a love to be met which
nothing can finally defeat.

God is to be met in, with, and under, not apart from,
response to the world and the neighbor.

He vigorously rejects the accusation that he is propounding
pantheism, or that he is seeking to abolish transcendence. But
what he does, in effect, is simply to reinterpret the meaning of
the word *transcendence* in accordance with the belief he has outlined.

The implication of this is not the abolition of the transcendent in pure naturalism: it is an apprehension of the
transcendent as given in, with, and under the immanent.
"The beyond" is to be found always and only "in the
midst," as a function and dimension of it. This is a shot-silk
universe, spirit and matter, inside and outside, divine and
human, shimmering like aspects of one reality which cannot
be separated or divided.

John Wren-Lewis:

The first thing to be said about this doctrine [of God as
Creator of the world *ex nihilo*] is that it is in no sense . . .
the starting-point of Christian belief . . .

If . . . the idea of God originated from the experience of
creative love in personal life (a conclusion much more in
line with the findings of modern anthropology), then Ten-
nyson's question "Are God and nature then at strife?" arises

at once, for the system of nature as we ordinarily experience it has no place for such personal values as love, beauty, or justice. Against this background, the assertion that nothing exists apart from God's creative action becomes *a supreme declaration of faith in man's ability to change the world if he acts upon it in the power of love*: there is no *thing*, no systematic order, apart from personal action—only potentiality.

THE ANSWER THIS APPROACH GIVES TO OTHER QUESTIONS ABOUT THE UNIVERSE

CAN WE BE SURE THE UNIVERSE IS REALLY THERE?

The eastern religions do not believe in a personal Creator God, and for them this is a very real question. Their general answer has been to say that we *cannot* be sure that there is anything there. We cannot be sure that our senses are not deceiving us.

Arthur Koestler:

> The traditional Eastern way of looking at things is to deny that there *are* things independently from the act of looking. The objects of consciousness cannot be separated from the conscious subject; observer and observed are a single, indivisible, fluid reality, as they are at the dawn of consciousness in the child, and in the culture dominated by magic. The external world has no existence in its own right; it is a function of the senses; but that function exists only in so far as it is registered by consciousness, and consequently has no existence in its own right.

In *Sartre*'s novel *Nausea*, Roquentin describes one aspect of his Nausea—the awareness of the bare existence of everything.

> So this is the Nausea: this blinding revelation? To think how I've racked my brains over it! To think how much I've written about it! Now I know: I exist—the world exists— and I know that the world exists. That's all. But I don't care. It's strange that I should care so little about everything: it frightens me. It's since that day when I wanted to play ducks and drakes. I was going to throw that pebble, I looked at it and that was when it all began; I felt that it

359

existed. And then, after that, there were other Nauseas; every now and then objects start existing in your hand.

But these things lose their names and their identity, and everything appears with a "frightening, obscene nakedness":

Things have broken free from their names. They are there, grotesque, stubborn, gigantic, and it seems ridiculous to call them seats or say anything at all about them: I am in the midst of Things, which cannot be given names. Alone, wordless, defenseless, they surround me, under me, behind me, above me. They demand nothing, they don't impose themselves, they are there . . .

All of a sudden, there it was, as clear as day: existence had suddenly unveiled itself . . . the diversity of things, their individuality, was only an appearance, a veneer. This veneer had melted, leaving soft, monstrous masses, in disorder—naked, with a frightening, obscene nakedness.

Lewis Carroll in *Through the Looking Glass* conveys the same frightening sense of things losing their identity in the account of Alice as she enters the wood where things lose their names.

"This must be the wood," she said thoughtfully to herself, "where things have no names. I wonder what'll become of *my* name when I go in? I shouldn't like to lose it at all."— She was rambling on in this way when she reached the wood: it looked very cool and shady. "Well, at any rate it's a great comfort," she said as she stepped under the trees, "after being so hot, to get into the—into the—into *what?*" she went on, rather surprised at not being able to think of the word. "I mean to get under the—under the—under *this*, you know!" putting her hand on the trunk of the tree. "What *does* it call itself? I do believe it's got no name—why, to be sure it hasn't!"

She stood silent for a minute, thinking: then she suddenly began again. "Then it really *has* happened, after all! And now, who am I? I *will* remember, if I can! I'm determined to do it!" But being determined didn't help her much, and all she could say, after a great deal of puzzling, was "L, I *know* it begins with L!"

Just then a Fawn came wandering by: it looked at Alice with its large gentle eyes, but didn't seem at all frightened. "Here then! Here then!" Alice said, as she held out her hand and tried to stroke it; but it only started back a little, and then stood looking at her again.

"What do you call yourself?" the Fawn said at last. Such a soft, sweet voice it had!

"I wish I knew!" thought poor Alice. She answered, rather sadly, "Nothing just now."

"Think again," it said. "That won't do."

Alice thought, but nothing came of it. "Please, would you tell me what *you* call yourself?" she said timidly. "I think that might help a little."

"I'll tell you, if you'll come a little further on," the Fawn said. "I can't remember here."

So they walked on together through the wood, Alice with her arms clasped lovingly round the soft neck of the Fawn, till they came out into another open field, and here the Fawn gave a sudden bound into the air, and shook itself free from Alice's arms. "I'm a Fawn!" it cried out in a voice of delight. "And, dear me, you're a human child!"

Alice Through the Looking Glass ends with Alice trying to discuss a vital question with the kitten. For many this is not mere fantasy; it is a very real and serious question: how can we be sure that we are not dreaming all the time? How can we be sure that we are not a part of someone else's dream?

"So I wasn't dreaming, after all," she said to herself, "unless—unless we're all part of the same dream. Only I do hope it's *my* dream, and not the Red King's. I don't like belonging to another person's dream," she went on in a rather complaining tone.

"Now, Kitty, let's consider who it was that dreamed it all. This is a serious question, my dear, and you should *not* go on licking your paw like that—as if Dinah hadn't washed you this morning! You see, Kitty, it *must* have been either me or the Red King. He was part of my dream, of course —but then I was part of his dream, too! *Was* it the Red King, Kitty? You were his wife, my dear, so you ought to know—Oh, Kitty, *do* help me to settle it! I'm sure your paw can wait!" But the provoking kitten only began on the other paw, and pretended it hadn't heard the question.

Which do *you* think it was?

Life, what is it but a dream?

Francis Schaeffer describes the following conversation with an atheist who realized he had no reason for believing that anything is there outside of himself:

> He was an atheist, and when he found out I was a pastor he anticipated an evening's entertainment, so he started in. But it did not go quite that way. Our conversation showed me that he understood the implications of his position and tried to be consistent concerning them. After about an hour I saw that he wanted to draw the discussion to a close, so I made one last point which I hoped he would never forget, not because I hated him, but because I cared for him as a fellow human being. I noticed that he had his lovely little Jewish wife with him. She was very beautiful and full of life and it was easy to see, by the attention he paid to her, that he really loved her.

> Just as they were about to go to their cabin, in the romantic setting of the boat sailing across the Mediterranean and a beautiful full moon shining outside, I finally said to him, "When you take your wife into your arms at night, can you be sure she is there?"

> I hated to do it to him, but I did it knowing that he was a man who would really understand the implications of the question and not forget. His eyes turned, like a fox caught in a trap, and he shouted at me, "No, I am not always sure she is there," and walked into his cabin.

COSMOS OR CHAOS? DESIGN OR CHANCE?
If there is no Creator God who gives order to the universe, it is far from self-evident that the universe is an ordered system.

Bertrand Russell:

> Academic philosophers, ever since the time of Parmenides, have believed that the world is a unity . . . The most fundamental of my beliefs is that this is rubbish . . . I think the universe is all spots and jumps, without unity, without continuity, without coherence or orderliness.

Jules Romanes:

> I find it difficult to say anything certain or even plausible on the subject (of God). It can at most be suggested that the God of traditional metaphysics, perfect, infinite, creator, and all-powerful ruler of the universe, is highly improbable. The probability continues to decrease as our knowledge of

the universe grows and becomes richer. The crude, for-tuitous, elements of the universe, its intolerable contradic-tions, the frightful, gratuitous waste inherent in it—to cite only a few shortcomings among many—scarcely make it seem possible that an intelligence has from the beginning been in perfect control of the cosmos in all its respects.

Colin Wilson:

For the bourgeois, the world is fundamentally an orderly place, with a disturbing element of the irrational, the terri-fying, which his preoccupation with the present usually permits him to ignore. For the Outsider, the world is not rational, not orderly. When he asserts his sense of anarchy in the face of the bourgeois' complacent acceptance, it is not simply the need to cock a snook at respectability that provokes him; it is a distressing sense *that truth must be told at all costs,* otherwise there can be no hope for an ultimate restoration of order. Even if there seems no room for hope, the truth must be told.

Jacob Bronowski believes that modern science has gone beyond the concept of a thoroughly ordered cosmos. But he believes that the concept of chance may provide the clue which will deliver us from despair:

The statistical concept of chance may come . . . to unify the scattered pieces of science in the future . . . We are on the threshold of another scientific revolution. The concept of natural law is changing. The laws of chance seem at first glance to be lawless. But I have shown . . . that they can be formulated with as much rigor as the laws of cause. Cer-tainly they can be seen already to cover an infinitely wider field of human experience in nature and in society . . . Chance has a helpless ring in our ears. But the laws of chance are lively, vigorous, and human, and they may give us again that forward look which in the last half century has so tragically lowered its eyes.

Von Weizacker points out the strange irony in the fact that modern science, while it owes its existence partly to Christian beliefs about the universe, has now discarded some of these beliefs.

I called modern science a legacy, I might even have said a child of Christianity. But then I had to show how science

363

lost contact with its parental home. Children can experience the death of their parents.

It is one thing to speak of chance as a theory in science. It is quite different when chance invades the life of the individual. In *Sartre's Nausea*, Roquentin experiences the feeling that there are no fixed natural laws: "anything could happen."

It is out of laziness, I suppose, that the world looks the same day after day. Today it seemed to want to change. And in that case, *anything, anything* could happen.

The idiots. It horrifies me to think that I am going to see their thick, self-satisfied faces again. They make laws, they write Populist novels, they get married, they commit the supreme folly of having children. And meanwhile, vast, vague Nature has slipped into their town, it has infiltrated everywhere, into their houses, into their offices, into themselves. It doesn't move, it lies low, and they are right inside it, they breathe it, and they don't see it, they imagine that it is outside, fifty miles away. I *see* it, that Nature, I *see* it . . . I know that its submissiveness is laziness, I know that it has no laws, that what they consider its constancy doesn't exist. It has nothing but habits and it may change those tomorrow.

An absolute panic took hold of me. I no longer knew where I was going. I ran along the docks, I turned into the deserted streets of the Beauvoisis district: the houses watched my flight with their mournful eyes. I kept saying to myself in anguish: "Where shall I go? Where shall I go? *Anything* can happen."

Martin Esslin speaks of the "terrible stability of the world" as seen in *Samuel Beckett's* plays, where time loses all meaning.

Waiting is to experience the action of time, which is constant change. And yet, as nothing real ever happens, that change is in itself an illusion. The ceaseless activity of time is self-defeating, purposeless, and therefore null and void. The more things change, the more they are the same. That is the terrible stability of the world. "The tears of the world are a constant quantity. For each one who begins to weep, somewhere else another stops." One day is like another, and when we die, we might never have existed.

IS THERE SUCH A THING AS BEAUTY?

Many are not conscious of any problem here simply because they are still living off the legacy of Christian beliefs.

C. E. M. Joad, writing in the days when he was still an agnostic, speaks of how he thinks of beauty and its significance.

> If . . . beauty means something, yet we must not seek to interpret the meaning. If we glimpse the unutterable, it is unwise to try to utter it, nor should we seek to invest with significance that which we cannot grasp. Beauty in terms of our human meanings *is* meaningless. It does not mean that the universe is good, that life has a purpose, that God is in heaven, or even that the human and the friendly conditions and underlies the alien and the brutal . . .

> But we still look for meaning in life and above all for meaning in beauty, meaning that we can somehow relate to ourselves . . . To realize . . . the vast indifference of the universe to man, is the beginning of the wisdom of an adult mind.

Somerset Maugham for some years believed that it is beauty alone which gives meaning to life, but later came to reject this belief:

> The work of art, I decided, was the crowning product of human activity, and the final justification for all the misery, the endless toil, and the frustrated strivings of humanity. So that Michelangelo might paint certain figures on the ceiling of the Sistine Chapel, so that Shakespeare might write certain speeches and Keats his odes, it seemed to me worth while that untold millions should have lived and suffered and died. And though I modified this extravagance later by including the beautiful life among the works of art that alone gave a meaning to life, it was still beauty that I valued. All these notions I have long since abandoned.

He sees beauty not as something objective and lasting, but as relative and temporary.

> The only conclusion is that beauty is relative to the needs of a particular generation, and that to examine the things we consider beautiful for qualities of absolute beauty is futile. If beauty is one of the values that give life significance it is something that is constantly changing and thus cannot be analyzed, for we can as little feel the beauty our ancestors felt as we can smell the rose they smelled.

For many today, however, there is no longer any such thing as beauty. In *Sartre*'s *Nausea* Roquentin has repeated experiences of nausea. He cannot speak about "beauty," since for him there is no such thing as "beauty"; there can only be things which produce a pleasant sensation in him.

> I went out and walked along the streets as usual . . . And then, all of a sudden, as I was pushing open the gate of the municipal park, I had the impression that something was signaling me. The park was bare and empty. But . . . how shall I put it? It didn't have its usual look, it was smiling at me. I stayed for a moment leaning against the gate, and then, suddenly, I realized it was Sunday. It was there in the trees, on the lawns, like a faint smile.

Henry Moore's conception of his work is summed up in this way by *Herbert Read*. The old ideal of beauty is rejected.

> The modern artist has dared—and no one has been more explicit than Moore about his intentions in this respect—to abandon the ideal of beauty and to establish in its place the ideal of vitality. But vitality is but a provisional word which serves to disguise the fact that we do not know and cannot measure the nature of life. Beauty is no mystery: it can be presented in geometrical formulas, by calculated proportions. But the vital process is intangible, and can be represented only in symbolic forms—forms symbolic of the essential nature of living organisms and forms symbolic of the racial experiences that have left an impress on our mental condition—the archetypal patterns of birth and death, of social conflict and tragic drama.

Marc:

> I found man to be ugly—animals are much more beautiful . . . but in them too I discovered so much that I felt to be appalling and ugly that my representations of them instinctively, out of inner necessity, became increasingly more schematic, more abstract. Each year trees, flowers, the earth, everything showed me aspects that were more hateful, more repulsive, until I came at last to a full realization of the ugliness, the uncleanness of nature.

Karel Appel:

> I do not paint, I hit.
> Painting is destruction.

Lucebert, the Dutch poet:

Beauty has burned its face.

Professor H. R. Rookmaaker, an art historian, speaks of the consensus in much modern art and the way in which it is interpreted by many critics.

Modern art, in a very direct and special way, speaks of the same things as Existentialist Philosophy. It is antinomian or gnostic and often preaches an anarchistic mysticism. Its expressions are often strange and not understandable at first encounter. In a way this is fortunate, for then at least a number of people just pass by. On the other hand it is not so fortunate; for if men turn all laws upside-down, beauty and the possibility of communication fall out. But we must not deceive ourselves. The strange situation in which art says "A" and its critic says it means "B"—a diluted, detached, euphemistic rendering of the actual message—still does not make it impotent. Quite the contrary. Because the spiritual struggle is avoided, a great many of the real issues are blurred. Nevertheless this art communicates something, even if it is only that there is nothing beautiful or sensible to say.

According to Eastern ways of thinking about the universe, beauty is something that is purely relative.

Rabindranath Tagore writes of the tradition in Hinduism which believes that ultimately there is no difference between beauty and its opposite:

According to some interpretations of the Vedanta doctrine Brahman is the absolute Truth, the impersonal It, in which there can be no distinction of this and that, the good and the evil, the beautiful and its opposite, having no other quality except its ineffable blissfulness in the eternal solitude of its consciousness utterly devoid of all things and all thoughts.

D. T. Suzuki in his book on *Mysticism, Christian and Buddhist* speaks of the difference in the understanding of art between the West and the East. This difference springs from a different way of thinking about the natural universe and its beauty.

I often hear Chinese or Japanese art critics declare that Oriental art consists in depicting spirit and not form. For they say that when the spirit is understood the form creates itself; the main thing is to get into the spirit of an object which the painter chooses for his subject. The west on the other hand, emphasizes form, endeavors to reach the spirit by means of form. The East is just the opposite: the spirit is all in all. And it thinks that when the artist grasps the spirit, his work reveals something more than colors and lines can convey. A real artist is a creator and not a copyist. He has visited God's workshop and has learned the secrets of creation—creating something beautiful out of nothing . . .

How does the painter get into the spirit of the plant, for instance, if he wants to paint a hibiscus as Mokkei (Mu-chi) of the thirteenth century did in his famous picture, which is now preserved as a national treasure in Daitokuji temple in Kyoto? The secret is to become the plant itself. But how can a human being turn himself into a plant? Inasmuch as he aspires to paint a plant or an animal, there must be in him something which corresponds to it in one way or another. If so, he ought to be able to become the object he desires to paint.

The discipline consists in studying the plant inwardly with his mind thoroughly purified of its subjective, self-centered contents. This means to keep the mind in unison with the "Emptiness" or Suchness, whereby one who stands against the object ceases to be the one outside that object but transforms himself into the object himself. This identification enables the painter to feel the pulsation of one and the same life animating both him and the object. This is what is meant when it is said that the subject is lost in the object, and that when the painter begins his work it is not he but the object itself that is working and it is then that his brush, as well as his arm and his fingers, become obedient servants to the spirit of the objects. The object makes its own picture. The spirit sees itself as reflected in itself. This is also a case of self-identity.

It is said that Henri Matisse looked at an object which he intended to paint for weeks, even for months, until its spirit began to move him, to urge him, even to threaten him, to give it an expression.

BACK TO ANSWER ONE

The universe was created and is sustained by God— God of the Bible.

PROBLEMS AND QUESTIONS

Having examined other possible answers to the basic question "What kind of universe do we live in?" we return to option one, the biblical Christian answers, to look at some of the questions and objections raised.

How are we to reconcile cruelty in the animal kingdom and natural disasters with belief in a loving Creator?

Cruelty. Many animals prey on each other, and it is not very realistic to imagine that animals do not feel pain. It is probably true that they do not have the same horror and dread of death as most human beings do. But this does not remove the problem: were things always like this in the universe of which we are told, "And God saw everything that he had made, and behold, it was very good" (Genesis 1:31)?

Natural disasters. Here again we are bound to ask: could earthquakes and tornados which can take such a toll of human life really be part of a universe which is "very good"?

In answering these questions we need to look for clues in several different parts of the Bible:

☐ After the fall of Adam, God tells him some of the results of his disobedience, and some of these affect the physical world:

> And to Adam he said,
> "Because you have listened to the voice of your
>   wife,
>   and have eaten of the tree of which I com-
>   manded you,
>   'You shall not eat of it,'
> cursed is the ground because of you;
>   in toil you shall eat of it all the days of your life;
> thorns and thistles it shall bring forth to you;
>   and you shall eat the plants of the field . . ."

☐ The Bible does not give us a clear picture of the state of the natural world before the fall. But some of the prophets speak about a future restoration of nature.

> *Isaiah:*

> The wolf shall dwell with the lamb,
>   and the leopard shall lie down with the kid,
> and the calf and the lion and the fatling together,
>   and a little child shall lead them.
> The cow and the bear shall feed;
>   their young shall lie down together;
> and the lion shall eat straw like the ox.
> The sucking child shall play over the hole of
>   the asp,
>   and the weaned child shall put his hand on the
>   adder's den.
> They shall not hurt or destroy
>   in all my holy mountain;
> for the earth shall be full of the knowledge of the
>   Lord
>   as the waters cover the sea.

If this is a picture of how things will be in a restored universe, it may also give some idea of how things were before sin entered into the world.

☐ Paul speaks of "the whole creation" being caught up in the bondage and futility to which man is subject. Similarly, "the whole creation" will be affected when God's plan for the human race is brought to completion:

> The creation waits with eager longing for the revealing of the sons of God; for the creation was subjected to futility, not of its own will but by the will of him who subjected it in hope; because the creation itself will be set free from its bondage to decay and obtain the glorious liberty of the children of God. We know that the whole creation has been groaning in travail together until now; and not only the creation, but we ourselves, who have the first fruits of the Spirit, groan inwardly as we wait for adoption as sons, the redemption of our bodies.

In the light of these different aspects of the Bible's teaching, the Christian should feel the full force of the objection and admit that these features of the universe as it is now do *not* seem to be marks of the creation of a good and loving God. They must be seen as evidence of the abnormal state of the universe resulting from man's sin, and they are not likely to be present in the "new heavens and the new earth" to which we look forward.

How original is the Genesis account of creation?

How is the Genesis story of creation related to the many other creation stories and myths of the ancient Near East? Is there not some evidence to suggest that the Hebrews may have borrowed their story from their neighbors—for example in Babylon?

Alan Millard, a lecturer on the languages of the ancient Near East writes:

> Genesis 1 and 2 consist of a general account of the creation of the heavens and the earth, followed by a more detailed description of the making of man. Stories of cosmic and of human creation, either separately or as unities, are numerous, and many have several points in common: pre-existent deity; creation by divine command; man the ultimate creature; man formed from the earth as a pot is made; man in some way a reflection of deity. Almost all polytheistic faiths possess family-trees of their gods which can figure in creation stories. A primal pair or even a single self-created and

self-propagating god heads the divine family, all of whose members represent or control natural elements and forces.

For some peoples, the physical universe or a basic element such as water or earth always existed, and the gods arose from it. For others it was the handiwork of a god or gods. These are simple concepts based on observation and elementary logic. For example, man as "dust" is easily deduced from the cycle of death and decay.

However, common ideas need not share a common origin; it is misleading to reduce differing stories from all over the world to their common factors in order to claim that they do. A single source for all, or large numbers, of different stories is improbable.

Nevertheless, it is quite in order to set Genesis beside other accounts from the world of the Old Testament. When we do so, we find that few of the ancient creation stories share more than one or two basic concepts—such as the separation of heaven and earth, and the creation of man from clay. The Babylonian literature, however, affords some striking resemblances. In the century since one was first translated into English, the Babylonian accounts have been cited as the ultimate source of the Hebrew's beliefs. Recently, the recovery of more texts and the re-assessment of those long known has shown that many of the accepted similarities are in fact illusory.

The famous *Babylonian Genesis*, usually linked with the Hebrew creation story, is one of several, and was neither the oldest nor the most popular. Written late in the 2nd millennium B.C. to honor Marduk, god of Babylon, who is its hero, it begins with a watery mother-figure, Tiamat, from whom the gods are born. (The name is related to the Hebrew word for "the deep" through the prehistoric linguistic connections between Babylonian and Hebrew.) She is killed by Marduk in a battle with her children whose noise had angered her, and her corpse is formed into the world. Man is made to relieve the gods of the toil of keeping the earth in order, so the gods have rest.

There are clear indications that this story was made up from older ones, and earlier compositions have been found which contain some of these features. Only one theme recurs often, the relief of the gods from their labor by the making of man with a divine ingredient. The battle of the gods in the *Babylonian Genesis* has no Old Testament equivalent, despite attempts by many scholars to discover underlying references to it in the text of Genesis 1:2 and other passages which speak of God's power over the waters.

WHERE DO WE GO FROM HERE?

If the question for you now is the evidence for the person of Jesus himself, the meaning of his death, and the evidence of his resurrection, turn to Part 3.

If you still question the whole approach underlying this presentation of Christian beliefs about God, man and the universe, turn back again to Part 1—How can I know if Christianity is true?

PART THREE QUESTIONS ABOUT JESUS CHRIST

If we can assume that Jesus was a real historical figure, was he anything more than an ordinary man? If he was related to God in some special way, how are we to describe this relationship? The main evidence we have to consider in the four Gospel accounts concerns his birth, his character, his claims about himself, and his miracles.

QUESTION FIVE:
WHAT WAS JESUS'
RELATIONSHIP TO GOD?

Randy Birkey

HIS BIRTH

Two of the Gospels begin with an account of the birth of Jesus.
His birth is described as a perfectly natural birth, but his conception as the work of the Holy Spirit.

Matthew describes the events from the point of view of *Joseph*,
who was at this time engaged to Mary:

> Now the birth of Jesus Christ took place in this way. When
> his mother Mary had been betrothed to Joseph, before they
> came together she was found to be with child of the Holy
> Spirit; and her husband Joseph, being a just man and
> unwilling to put her to shame, resolved to divorce her
> quietly. But as he considered this, behold, an angel of the
> Lord appeared to him in a dream, saying, "Joseph, son of
> David, do not fear to take Mary your wife, for that which is
> conceived in her is of the Holy Spirit; she will bear a son,
> and you shall call his name Jesus, for he will save his people
> from their sins." . . . When Joseph awoke from sleep, he
> did as the angel of the Lord commanded him; he took his
> wife, but knew her not until she had borne a son; and he
> called his name Jesus.

Luke describes the events from the point of view of *Mary*:

> In the sixth month the angel Gabriel was sent from God to
> a city of Galilee named Nazareth, to a virgin betrothed to a
> man whose name was Joseph, of the house of David; and
> the virgin's name was Mary. And he came to her and said,
> "Hail, O favored one, the Lord is with you! . . . Do not be
> afraid, Mary, for you have found favor with God. And
> behold, you will conceive in your womb and bear a son, and
> you shall call his name Jesus . . ." And Mary said to the
> angel, "How shall this be, since I have no husband?" And
> the angel said to her, "The Holy Spirit will come upon you,
> and the power of the Most High will overshadow you;
> therefore the child to be born will be called holy, the Son of
> God."

HIS CHARACTER

At least four features stand out clearly: compassion and anger,
humility and goodness.

Compassion

Jesus' compassion shows in his attitude toward the crowds:

They went away in the boat to a lonely place by themselves.
Now many saw them going, and knew them, and they ran
there on foot from all the towns, and got there ahead of
them. As he went ashore he saw a great throng, and *he had
compassion on them*, because they were like sheep without a
shepherd; and he began to teach them many things.

—toward children:

They were bringing children to him, that he might touch
them; and the disciples rebuked them. But when Jesus saw
it he was indignant, and said to them, "Let the children
come to me, do not hinder them; for to such belongs the
kingdom of God . . ." And he took them in his arms and
blessed them, laying his hands upon them.

—toward the sick:

And a leper came to him beseeching him, and kneeling said
to him, "If you will, you can make me clean." *Moved with
pity*, he stretched out his hand and touched him, and said
to him, "I will; be clean." And immediately the leprosy left
him and he was made clean.

—toward the bereaved:

As he drew near to the gate of the city, behold, a man who
had died was being carried out, the only son of his mother,
and she was a widow; and a large crowd from the city was
with her. And when the Lord saw her, *he had compassion* on
her and said to her, "Do not weep." And he came and
touched the bier, and the bearers stood still. And he said,
"Young man, I say to you, arise." And the dead man sat
up, and began to speak.

—toward the socially unacceptable:

Now the tax collectors and sinners were all drawing near to
hear him. And the Pharisees and the scribes murmured,
saying, "This man receives sinners and eats with them."

Anger

☐ Jesus had many angry words to say to the religious leaders who,
by their teaching and behavior, were distorting or denying the
truth for which Jesus had such deeply-felt concern:

Well did Isaiah prophesy of you hypocrites . . . You leave
the commandment of God, and hold fast the tradition of

men . . . You have a fine way of rejecting the commandment of God, in order to keep your tradition!

Woe to you, scribes and Pharisees, hypocrites! because you
shut the kingdom of heaven against men; for you neither
enter yourselves, nor allow those who would enter to go in . . .

Woe to you, blind guides . . . you blind fools!

Woe to you, scribes and Pharisees, hypocrites! for you
cleanse the outside of the cup and of the plate, but inside
they are full of extortion and rapacity . . . You . . .
outwardly appear righteous to men, but within you are full
of hypocrisy and iniquity.

He entered the temple and began to drive out those who
sold and those who bought in the temple, and he over-
turned the tables of the money-changers and the seats of
those who sold pigeons; and he would not allow any one to
carry anything through the temple. And he taught, and
said to them, "Is it not written, 'My house shall be called a
house of prayer for all the nations'? But you have made it a
den of robbers."

☐ The reaction of Jesus to the death of his friend, Lazarus, reveals
both compassion and anger in the face of death:

When Jesus saw her weeping, and the Jews who came with
her also weeping, he was deeply moved in spirit and
troubled; and he said, "Where have you laid him?" They
said to him, "Lord, come and see." Jesus wept. So the Jews
said, "See how he loved him!"

Humility
☐ Jesus' humility before God:

I can do nothing on my own authority . . . I seek not my
own will but the will of him who sent me.

I have come down from heaven, not to do my own will, but
the will of him who sent me.

☐ His humility before men. Luke describes this incident at the Last
Supper:

A dispute also arose among them, which of them was to be
regarded as the greatest. And he said to them, "The kings
of the Gentiles exercise lordship over them; and those in
authority over them are called benefactors. But not so with
you; rather let the greatest among you become as the

youngest, and the leader as one who serves. For which is the greater, one who sits at table, or one who serves? Is it not the one who sits at table? But I am among you as one who serves."

After the supper, he demonstrated in action something of what he meant by the outlook of the servant:

Jesus, knowing that the Father had given all things into his hands, and that he had come from God and was going to God, rose from supper, laid aside his garments, and girded himself with a towel. Then he poured water into a basin, and began to wash the disciples' feet, and to wipe them with the towel with which he was girded . . .

When he had washed their feet, and taken his garments and resumed his place, he said to them, "Do you know what I have done to you? You call me Teacher and Lord; and you are right, for so I am. If I then, your Lord and Teacher, have washed your feet, you also ought to wash one another's feet. For I have given you an example, that you also should do as I have done to you."

Goodness

☐ People acknowledged the positive goodness of what Jesus was doing:

And they were astonished beyond measure, saying, "He has done all things well; he even makes the deaf hear and the dumb speak."

☐ He himself claimed to be without sin:

Which of you convicts me of sin?

☐ His disciples claimed that he was sinless:

He committed no sin; no guile was found on his lips. When he was reviled, he did not revile in return; when he suffered, he did not threaten; but he trusted to him who judges justly.

If we say we have no sin, we deceive ourselves . . . He appeared to take away sins, and in him there is no sin.

HIS CLAIMS ABOUT HIMSELF

His claim to be the Son

He spoke of himself as "the Son" and of God as "the Father" or "my Father."

Of that day or that hour [the day of judgment] no one
knows, not even the angels in heaven, nor *the Son*, but only
the Father.

All things have been delivered to me by *my Father*; and no
one knows *the Son* except *the Father*, and no one knows *the
Father* except *the Son* and any one to whom *the Son* chooses
to reveal him.

Whoever does the will of *my Father* in heaven is my brother.

The Son of man is to come with his angels in the glory of
his Father.

I and *the Father* are one.

The Father judges no one, but has given all judgment to
the Son, that all may honor *the Son*, even as they honor *the
Father*. He who does not honor *the Son* does not honor *the
Father* who sent him.

No one comes to *the Father*, but by me. If you had known
me, you would have known *my Father* also.

His claim to be the fulfillment of the Old Testament

The time is fulfilled [i.e. the time spoken about by the
prophets], and the kingdom of God is at hand.

The Son of man also came . . . to serve, and to give his life
as a ransom for many.

  (These are allusions to the Son of man described in
Daniel 7 and the Suffering Servant in Isaiah 42–53.)

This is my blood of the covenant, which is poured out for
many.

  (An allusion to the blood of the Old Testament sacrifices,
the covenant God made with the nation at Sinai, and the
"new covenant" spoken of by Ezekiel and Jeremiah.)

The high priest asked him, "Are you the Christ, the Son of
the Blessed?" And Jesus said, "I am; and you will see the
Son of man seated at the right hand of Power, and coming
with the clouds of heaven."

  (Another reference to the Son of man in Daniel.)

He opened the book and found the place where it was
written, "The Spirit of the Lord is upon me . . ." And he

began to say to them, "Today this scripture has been fulfilled in your hearing."

(He was reading from a passage in Isaiah.)

Everything written about me in the law of Moses and the
prophets and the psalms must be fulfilled . . . Thus it is
written, that the Christ should suffer and on the third day
rise from the dead.

The scriptures . . . bear witness to me.

If you believed Moses, you would believe me, for he wrote
of me.

His indirect claims

Jesus claimed to be able to do things which, according to Jewish
belief, only God could do.

☐ He forgave sins:

Jesus . . . said to the paralytic, "My son, your sins are forgiven." Now some of the scribes were sitting there, questioning in their hearts, "Why does this man speak thus? It is
blasphemy! Who can forgive sins but God alone?" And . . .
Jesus . . . said . . . ". . . the Son of man has authority on
earth to forgive sins."

☐ He claimed to be able to give eternal life:

As the Father raises the dead and gives them life, so also
the Son gives life to whom he will.

I am the resurrection and the life; he who believes in me,
though he die, yet shall he live.

☐ He claimed to teach the truth with authority:

You have heard that it was said to the men of old, "You
shall not kill. . . ." But I say to you . . .

Heaven and earth will pass away, but my words will not
pass away.

For this I have come into the world, to bear witness to the
truth. Every one who is of the truth hears my voice.

☐ He said he would one day judge the world:

When the Son of man comes in his glory, and all the angels
with him, then he will sit on his glorious throne. Before
him will be gathered all the nations, and he will separate

384

them one from another as a shepherd separates the sheep
from the goats.

The Father judges no one, but has given all judgment to
the Son, that all may honor the Son, even as they honor the
Father.

☐ He claimed to be able to satisfy the deepest needs of men, and
he invited them to follow him and give him their allegiance:

Come to me, all who labor and are heavy laden, and I will
give you rest. Take my yoke upon you, and learn from me;
for I am gentle and lowly in heart, and you will find rest
for your souls.

If any one comes to me and does not hate his own father
and mother . . . and even his own life, he cannot be my
disciple.

If any one thirst, let him come to me and drink.

This is the work of God, that you believe in him whom he
has sent.

Believe in God, believe also in me.

HIS MIRACLES

Three different kinds of miracle are recorded.

☐ Nature miracles: e.g. stilling the storm (Mark 4:35–41); feeding
the 5,000 with five loaves and two fishes (Mark 6:30–44); walking
on the water (Mark 6:45–52); changing the water into wine
(John 2:1–11).

☐ Healing miracles: e.g. healing of fever, leprosy, blindness,
demon possession, etc.

☐ Raising from death: e.g., the son of the woman of Nain (Luke
7:11–17); Lazarus of Bethany (John 11:1–53).

The Gospels record Jesus' motives in performing the miracles.

☐ Compassion:

As they went out of Jericho, a great crowd followed him.
And behold, two blind men sitting by the roadside, when
they heard that Jesus was passing by, cried out, "Have
mercy on us, Son of David!" . . . Jesus stopped and called
them, saying, "What do you want me to do for you?" They
said to him, "Lord, let our eyes be opened." And Jesus *in
pity* touched their eyes, and immediately they received their
sight and followed him.

In those days, when again a great crowd had gathered, and
they had nothing to eat, he called his disciples to him, and
said to them, "*I have compassion* on the crowd, because they
have been with me now three days, and have nothing to
eat . . ."

☐ The glory of God. Many of the miracles led people to give glory
to God:

. . . so that the throng wondered, when they saw the dumb
speaking, the maimed whole, the lame walking, and the
blind seeing; and they glorified the God of Israel.

☐ Evidence to support his claims:

And immediately Jesus, perceiving in his spirit that they
thus questioned within themselves, said to them, "Why do
you question thus in your hearts? Which is easier, to say to
the paralytic 'Your sins are forgiven,' or to say, 'Rise, take
up your pallet and walk'? But *that you may know that the Son
of man has authority* on earth to forgive sins"—he said to the
paralytic—"I say to you, rise, take up your pallet and go
home.' And he rose, and immediately took up the pallet
and went out before them all . . .

When John heard in prison about the deeds of the Christ,
he sent word by his disciples and said to him, "Are you he
who is to come, or shall we look for another?" And Jesus
answered them, "Go and tell John what you hear and see:
the blind receive their sight and the lame walk, lepers are
cleansed and the deaf hear, and the dead are raised up,
and the poor have good news preached to them."

If I am not doing the works of my Father, then do not
believe me; but if I do them, even though you do not
believe me, believe the works, *that you may know and understand* that the Father is in me and I am in the Father.

There were times, however, when people pressed him to work
miracles not out of a genuine desire to be convinced, but out of
a defiant skepticism. And on these occasions, Jesus refused to
work miracles to order:

The Pharisees came and began to argue with him, seeking
from him a sign from heaven, to test him. And he sighed
deeply in his spirit, and said, "Why does this generation
seek a sign? Truly, I say to you, no sign shall be given to
this generation." And he left them.

Matthew's version of this saying (Matthew 12:39–40) adds an exception that points forward to the resurrection as the one and only sign he would give to these proud Pharisees.

PEOPLE'S REACTIONS

How did people react to the man Jesus? These are some of the earliest reactions to Jesus, as recorded by Mark:

> . . . they were astonished at his teaching, for he taught them as one who had authority . . . (1:22)

> . . . they were all amazed and glorified God, saying, "We never saw anything like this!" (2:12)

> . . . they said, "He is beside himself." (3:21)

> . . . they were filled with awe, and said to one another, "Who then is this, that even wind and sea obey him?" (4:41)

> . . . they were afraid . . . and they began to beg Jesus to depart from their neighborhood. (5:15, 17)

> . . . many who heard him were astonished, saying, "Where did this man get all this? What is the wisdom given to him? What mighty works are wrought by his hands! Is not this the carpenter, the son of Mary and brother of James and Joses and Judas and Simon, and are not his sisters here with us?" (6:2–3)

> . . . they were astonished beyond measure, saying, "He has done all things well; he even makes the deaf hear and the dumb speak." (7:37)

In our study of the evidence about Jesus, we have to get beyond these initial reactions and make up our minds about the deeper issue: what was the relationship of this man Jesus to God? Our answer will depend not only on how we interpret the evidence of the Gospels, but also on our assumptions about the meaning of the word *God*.

Anyone who believes in the existence of a personal God will probably find little difficulty in accepting the following assumptions about the meaning of the word *God*:

that he is a being who exists;

that he is personal and infinite;

that he is the Creator and Sustainer of the universe;

that he is loving and holy;

387

that he is one (the precise nature of this oneness does not need to be defined at this stage; it can be left an open question for the time being).

If we cannot accept these assumptions, or if we cannot even accept them for the time being as a working hypothesis, then we should consider first the other possible answers to the question about God. There is little point in discussing Jesus' relationship with "God" if we do not have at least some measure of agreement about the meaning of the word *God* (see further Part 2, pp. 143).

WHAT WAS JESUS' RELATIONSHIP TO GOD?

He was both man and God; he was the Son of God.
PAGE 391

He was a created being from heaven.
PAGE 396

He was only a man—but also a revelation of "God."
PAGE 418

He was a man and nothing more.
PAGE 412

He was a prophet sent by God.
PAGE 401

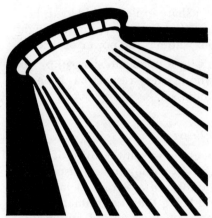

ANSWER ONE:
BIBLICAL CHRISTIANITY

He was both man and
God; he was the Son
of God.

He was fully human and fully divine.
He was a real human being; but at the
same time he was God the Son, the
second person of the Trinity, who had
existed with the Father and the Spirit
from eternity.

The first disciples could not have expressed their beliefs about
Jesus in these terms *during* his lifetime. But they spoke of him as
God's Messiah, i.e., God's Anointed Agent for working out his
purposes in the world. And they used words and titles for him
that a Jew would reserve exclusively for the one true God:

   Peter said: "You are the Christ." (Mark 8:29)
   Thomas said: "My Lord and my God!" (John 20:28)
   The disciples said: "We have believed and have come to know,

that you are the Holy One of God." (John 6:69) "We believe that you came from God." (John 16:30)

The words which they used *after* his lifetime do not go beyond these claims. They identify him fully *both* with man *and* with God:

> Since therefore the children share in flesh and blood, he himself likewise partook of the same nature, that through death he might destroy him who has the power of death.

> We have not a high priest who is unable to sympathize with our weaknesses, but one who in every respect has been tempted as we are, yet without sin.

> . . . the Lord of glory . . .

> . . . the . . . man . . . from heaven . . .

> . . . Christ Jesus, who, though he was in the form of God, did not count equality with God a thing to be grasped, but emptied himself, taking the form of a servant, being born in the likeness of men. And being found in human form he humbled himself and became obedient unto death, even death on a cross. Therefore God has highly exalted him and bestowed on him the name which is above every name, that at the name of Jesus every knee should bow, in heaven and on earth and under the earth, and every tongue confess that Jesus Christ is Lord, to the glory of God the Father.

HOW DOES THIS ANSWER MAKE SENSE OF THE EVIDENCE?

Christ's birth

The narratives make perfect sense if the baby was human and divine at the same time. If his conception had been totally natural, he could not in any sense have been anything other than, or more than, a human being.

His character

Jesus' compassion can be seen as something more than ordinary human compassion; it becomes a demonstration in practice of the love of God for man.

His anger is not the purely human feeling of rage, which results from frustration, or wounded pride, or selfish indignation; it becomes an expression of the hatred of the holy God towards anything that denies him, or distorts the truth, or degrades man.

His humility is the humility of the Son who has humbled himself before the Father to become man and to live as a man; and because he is utterly humble before the Father and is empty of self, he can be humble before men.

His goodness is not an inevitable or automatic perfection. As a real man he experienced all kinds of temptations, but he relied on the power of the Holy Spirit and was obedient to the word of the Father.

His claims

Jesus' claims about himself are not the ravings of a megalomaniac or the subtle deceptions of a man who wants to gain power; they simply express the closest possible personal relationship between Jesus and the Father.

His miracles

Jesus' miracles make sense as demonstrations of the love and compassion of God that would lead men to give all the credit and the glory to God. And they also provide further evidence to substantiate his claims to have come from God and to be doing the work of God.

SOME IMPLICATIONS OF THIS ANSWER

☐ If Jesus is both God and man, *he can be a perfect revelation of God to men.* He can reveal God adequately because he himself is fully divine:

> No one has ever seen God; *the only Son, who is in the bosom of the Father*, he has made him known.

This revelation is in a form that can be grasped fully by men; they can perceive it through hearing, through sight, and through touch:

> That which was from the beginning, which we have *heard,* which we have *seen* with our eyes, which we have *looked upon* and *touched with our hands*, concerning the word of life—the life was made manifest, and we *saw* it, and testify to it, and proclaim to you the eternal life which was with the Father and was made manifest to us—that which we have *seen* and *heard* we proclaim also to you, so that you may have fellowship with us . . .

☐ If Jesus is both God and man, *he is in a position to deal with the moral problem of man.* As a man, he lived a life of complete obedience to the Father, and he was obedient right to the point of death.

His life of obedience can therefore be the reversal of the disobedience of Adam. His complete obedience has the effect of undoing the consequences of the sin of Adam:

> . . . sin came into the world through one man and death through sin, and so death spread to all men because all men sinned . . . But the free gift is not like the trespass. For if many died through one man's trespass, much more have the grace of God and the free gift in the grace of *that one man Jesus Christ* abounded for many. . . . If, because of one man's trespass, death reigned through that one man, much more will those who receive the abundance of grace and the free gift of righteousness reign in life through *the one man Jesus Christ*. Then as one man's trespass led to condemnation for all men, so *one man's act of righteousness* leads to acquittal and life for all men. For as by one man's disobedience many were made sinners, so by *one man's obedience* many will be made righteous.

Because he himself is fully divine, what *he* does, *God* does in him:

> All is from God, who through Christ reconciled . . . the world to himself . . . *in Christ God was* reconciling the world to himself, not counting their trespasses against them . . .

Because he is fully human, he can identify himself with men and the guilt of their sin:

> There is one God, and there is one mediator between God and men, *the man Christ Jesus*, who gave himself as a ransom for all . . .

☐ The fact that Jesus is both divine and human *can mean something in the present experience of the Christian.* Jesus is still fully human in heaven. He did not discard his humanity as if it were a garment he could take off. There is therefore no need for any further mediator (such as Mary or the saints). There can be no one in heaven who is "more human" and tender and compassionate than Jesus himself.

> He had to be made like his brethren in every respect, so that he might become a merciful and faithful high priest in the service of God . . . For because he himself has suffered and been tempted, he is able to help those who are tempted.

We have not a high priest who is unable to sympathize with
our weaknesses, but one who in every respect has been
tempted as we are, yet without sin. Let us then with
confidence draw near to the throne of grace, that we may
receive mercy and find grace to help in time of need.

☐ When the Christian puts his faith in Jesus Christ as the one who
is fully God and fully man, *he is united with him in the closest
possible union.* It is not a union in which the believer is absorbed
into God, but a union in which he retains his identity and even
experiences the love that there is between the Father and the
Son. This was the kind of union for which Jesus prayed before
his arrest. It is possible because Jesus is perfectly one *both* with
God *and* with man.

I do not pray for these only, but also for those who are to
believe in me through their word, that they may all be one;
even as thou, Father, art in me, and I in thee, that they also
may be in us, so that the world may believe that thou hast
sent me. The glory which thou hast given me I have given
to them, that they may be one even as we are one, I in
them and thou in me, that they may become perfectly one,
so that the world may know that thou hast sent me and hast
loved them even as thou hast loved me. Father, I desire
that they also, whom thou hast given me, may be with me
where I am, to behold my glory which thou hast given me
in thy love for me before the foundation of the world. O
righteous Father, the world has not known thee, but I have
known thee; and these know that thou hast sent me. I have
made known to them thy name, and I will make it known,
that the love with which thou hast loved me may be in them
and I in them.

If this answer is the one you would give, go on to consider the
meaning of the death of Jesus, pp. 445ff.

ANSWER TWO:

He was a created being from heaven.

This is to say, Jesus was more than an ordinary man; but he was not God in any sense. He was the "Son of God" in the sense that he was a supernatural being from heaven—but a created being.

This answer has taken several different forms throughout the course of history. It was, for example, the teaching of *Arius of Alexandria* in the fourth century.

In our own day, *Jehovah's Witnesses* teach that Jesus was a created spirit from heaven:

That Jesus might save his people from their sin, it was necessary that the Son of God be born as a human creature and grow to become "the man Christ Jesus" . . . None of Adam's offspring being sinless or having the right life to offer as a redemptive price, it was necessary for the Son of God to lay aside his spirit existence and become the needed

perfect man, no more, no less. Thus Jesus could die, not as
a spirit creature, but as a perfect human creature, for
humankind needing redemption. For these and other reasons Jesus was not a "God-man," for that would be more
than the required price of redemption. Had he been immortal God or an immortal soul he could not have given
his life. According to the Scriptural facts, he was mortal on
earth . . .

The primary purpose of the Son of God in coming to earth
was to meet and decisively answer Satan's false charge that
God cannot put on earth a creature who will keep his
integrity and abide faithful till death under the test of
persecution from the Devil and his demons . . .

They believe that Jesus was appointed to be the Son of God at
the time of his baptism:

John heard God's voice announcing Jesus as His Son. This
proves that God there begot Jesus by his Spirit or active
force, by virtue of which Jesus now became the spiritual
Son of God, possessing the right to spirit life in heaven.
God so begot him, because Jesus' right to human life was
henceforth to be dedicated to redeeming humankind . . . .

God's prophecy, at Psalm 2:7, was directed to Jesus: "Thou
art my Son; this day I have begotten thee." When Jehovah
begot the baptized Jesus and made him the spiritual Son of
God with right to life in the heavenly spirit realm, Jesus
became a "new creature."

He thus became immortal after his death on the cross:

In due time, after proving his faithfulness to death and
providing redemption from sin, the Son was rewarded with
immortality.

POINTS
TO CONSIDER
ABOUT THIS
ANSWER

*This answer is based on a very selective reading of the New
Testament.* It makes use of verses that speak of Jesus'
dependence on the Father and his humility before the Father.
But it ignores all the other evidence that points to a much
closer relationship with the Father.

The verses used to support this interpretation can hardly bear the weight that is put on them; as the three following examples show.

> The Father is greater than I.

These words must be understood in the light of all the other sayings of Jesus in John's Gospel, for example:

> I and the Father are one.

> He who has seen me has seen the Father; how can you say, "Show us the Father"? Do you not believe that I am in the Father and the Father in me?

These words therefore point to the way in which the eternal Son humbled himself before the Father, for the work of revelation and salvation. Paul writes about the humbling and self-emptying of the Son in this way:

> . . . Christ Jesus . . . though he was in the form of God, did not count equality with God a thing to be grasped, but emptied himself, taking the form of a servant, being born in the likeness of men . . .

> Why do you call me good? No one is good but God alone.

Jesus gave this answer in reply to the person who asked him:

> Good Teacher, what shall I do to inherit eternal life?

Jesus was probably testing the man to see whether his words were a casual compliment, or whether he had realized who Jesus was. Or he could be saying, "If you think I am no more than an ordinary human teacher, why do you call me good?" Whatever the exact interpretation of these words, Jesus goes on to make a very big claim for himself. He does not argue with the man when he claims that he has kept all the commandments. Instead he takes it upon himself to tell the man where he is still falling short, and tells him to become a disciple:

> One thing you still lack. Sell all that you have and distribute to the poor, and you will have treasure in heaven; and come, follow me.

> He is the image of the invisible God, the first-born of all creation . . .

The remaining verses of this passage show that the writer did *not* believe that Jesus was a created being. On the contrary, *everything* both in heaven and on earth was created through him:

> He is the image of the invisible God, the first-born of all
> creation; for in him all things were created, in heaven and
> on earth, visible and invisible, whether thrones or domin-
> ions or principalities or authorities—all things were created
> through him and for him. He is before all things, and in
> him all things hold together. . . .

C. F. D. Moule explains the two possible interpretations of the
word *first-born*:

> (i) Translate the "first-" as a *time-metaphor* . . . Translated
> thus, it may allude to Christ's priority to the created world:
> he was born (or, as more considered theology would say,
> begotten, not born) before any created thing . . .
>
> (ii) Take "firstborn" not as a temporal term so much as in
> the sense of *supreme*— "the one who is supreme over all
> creation" . . . If one must choose, there is, perhaps, a little
> more to be said in favor of (ii) . . . But possibly (i) and (ii)
> are to be combined: "prior to and supreme over."

*Other passages of the New Testament expressly reject this kind of
interpretation.* The writer of the letter to the Hebrews, for example, was aware of beliefs which made Jesus an exalted being, but
a being created by God. He emphasizes the gulf which separates
Jesus, the Son, from all the created angels in heaven:

> In many and various ways God spoke of old to our fathers
> by the prophets; but in these last days he has spoken to us
> by a Son, whom he appointed heir of all things, through
> whom also he created the world. He reflects the glory of
> God and bears the very stamp of his nature, upholding the
> universe by his word of power. When he had made purifi-
> cation for sin, he sat down at the right hand of the Majesty
> on high, having become as much superior to angels as the
> name he has obtained is more excellent than theirs.

*If you give this kind of answer, you must think of Jesus as a mediator
who is less than God.* Being less than God, he cannot do anything
more than reveal messages from God, and he cannot deal with
the guilt of man before the holy God. He can act to some extent
on behalf of men if he is fully man, but he cannot take it upon
himself to forgive sin. Since it is God himself who has been
wronged, and God himself whose laws have been broken, *only
God* can forgive the wrong and the disobedience. If Jesus were

less than God, he could not act on behalf of God in dealing with the moral problem of man.

This answer is usually based not only on a selective reading of the New Testament, but also on certain assumptions about God and man.

It is assumed that the gulf between God and man is so great that Godhead and humanity cannot possibly be combined in a single personality.

It is also assumed that God is one in the strictly literal sense, so that there cannot possibly be any kind of diversity within the unity. This is the assumption behind the teaching of Jehovah's Witnesses: Jehovah is, by definition, "one" in the most literal sense:

> If Jesus had been Almighty God Jehovah he could not save his people from their sin, by his blood, because Jehovah God is immortal, "from everlasting to everlasting." . . .
> Almighty God cannot die, but Jesus could die and did die, as testified by the Scriptures; hence he could not be God his Father, but was God's mortal Son.

See further, Part 2, Question Two, "Who or what is God?" and Question Three, "What is man?"

ANSWER THREE:

He was a prophet sent by God.

Many Jews recognize that Jesus was a godly man who brought a real message from God to his fellow men. Islam goes further and affirms that Jesus was one of the great prophets sent by God.

In the first few centuries after the death of Jesus, although most Jews did not recognize Jesus as Messiah, they were not totally unsympathetic to him. Later, however, more critical attitudes were expressed.

Herbert Danby, writing about the Jewish traditions recorded in the *Talmud:*

> Here is the sum-total of all that the Talmud is *alleged* (sometimes rightly, but more often wrongly) to say of Christianity's Founder:

> A certain Yeshu, called the Notsri, or the Son of Stada, or the Son of Pantera, was born out of wedlock. His mother was called Miriam. She was a woman's hairdresser (the

word here is *M'gadd'la*, a pun on the name Mary Mag-
dalen). Her husband was Pappus, the son of Yehudah, and
her paramour a Roman soldier, Pantera. She is said to have
been the descendant of princes and rulers. This Yeshu had
been to Egypt, whence he brought back the knowledge of
many tricks and sorcery. He was just a sorcerer, and so
deceived and led astray the people of Israel; he sinned and
caused the multitude to sin. He made a mock of the words
of the learned men and was excommunicated. He was
tainted with heresy. He called himself God and said that he
would go up to heaven. He was tried before the Court at
Lud on a charge of being a deceiver and teacher of apostasy. Evidence was produced against him by concealing witnesses to hear his statements, and a lamp was so placed that
his face could be seen, but so that he could not see the
witnesses. He was executed in Lud on the Eve of Passover,
which fell on the eve of a Sabbath. During forty days a
herald proclaimed that Yeshu was to be stoned, and evidence was invited in his favor, but none was forthcoming.
He was stoned and hanged. Under the name of Balaam he
was put to death by "Pinhas the Robber" (supposed to refer
to Pontius Pilate). At the time he was thirty-three years old.
He was punished in Gehenna by means of boiling scum. He
was "near to the kingdom" (whatever that may mean). He
had five disciples: Mattai, Naqai, Netser, Buni and Today.
Under the name of Balaam he was excluded from the
world to come.

The following articles from the *Jewish Encyclopedia* sum up the
attitude of many Jews in the twentieth century to Jesus.
His birth:

The supernatural in the life of Jesus according to the Gospels is restricted to the smallest dimensions, consisting
mainly of incidents and characteristics intended to support
these prophecies (from the Old Testament) and the dogmatic positions of Christianity. This applies especially to the
story of the virgin-birth, a legend which is common to
almost all folk-heroes as indicating their superiority to the
rest of their people.

His claims:

The Prophets spoke with confidence in the truth of their
message, but expressly on the ground that they were de-

claring the word of the Lord. Jesus adopted equal confidence, but he emphasized his own authority apart from any vicarious or deputed authority from on high. Yet in doing so he did not—at any rate publicly—ever lay claim to any authority as attaching to his position as Messiah.

The most striking characteristic of the utterances of Jesus, regarded as a personality, were the tone of authority adopted by him and the claim that spiritual peace and salvation were to be found in the mere acceptance of his leadership. Passages like Matt. 11:29; 8:35; 25:40 indicate an assumption of power which is certainly unique in Jewish history, and indeed account for much of modern Jewish antipathy to Jesus, so far as it exists. On the other hand, there is little in any of these utterances to show that they were meant by the speaker to apply to anything more than personal relations with him; and it might well be that in his experience he found that spiritual relief was often afforded by simple human trust in his good-will and power of direction.

This . . . raises the question whether Jesus regarded himself as in any sense a Messiah or spiritual ruler; and there is singularly little evidence in the synoptic Gospels to carry out this claim. These assert only that the claim was made to some of the disciples, and then under a distinct pledge of secrecy. In the public utterances of Jesus there is absolutely no trace of the claim (except possibly in the use of the expression "Son of man"). Yet it would almost appear that in one sense of the word Jesus regarded himself as fulfilling some of the prophecies which were taken among contemporary Jews as applying to the Messiah. In other words, Jesus regarded himself as typically human, and claimed authority and regard in that respect.

His miracles:

It is difficult to estimate what amount of truth exists in the accounts of these cures, recorded about forty years after their occurrence; but doubtless the mental excitement due to the influence of Jesus was often efficacious in at least partial or temporary cures of mental illness. This would tend to confirm the impression, both among those who witnessed the cures and among his disciples, of his possession of supernatural powers. He himself occasionally deprecated the exaggeration to which such cures naturally led.

Other Jews have expressed a considerably more sympathetic
attitude.

Claude Montefiore:

> The most important Jew who ever lived, one who exercised
> a greater influence upon mankind and civilization than any
> other person, whether within the Jewish race or without
> it . . . A Jew whose life and character have been regarded
> by almost all the best and wisest people who have heard or
> read of his actions and his words, as the greatest religious
> exemplar of every age.

> God's nearness was felt by Jesus directly with a vivid inten-
> sity unsurpassed by any man.

Sholem Asch:

> What was quite new in the teaching of Jesus was that for
> the first time there appeared in Israel a teacher who, while
> in agreement with the law of Moses, did not derive his
> authority from that law . . . He appealed to an authority
> which had been entrusted to his keeping . . . The Jews were
> bound to the authority which had been given to Moses on
> Sinai, and which they had recognized with their promise of
> obedience. They could not pass to the new authority with-
> out the sign which should proclaim that the old had been
> cancelled and the new one validated . . . The first coming
> of the Messiah was not for us but for the Gentiles.

It is only right to admit that it was the shameful way in which
Christians began to treat the Jews that made Jews take a more
hostile attitude to Jesus. It is Christians who are largely responsible for preventing Jews from getting a fair and accurate picture
of Jesus.

Herbert Danby:

> We are forced to the conclusion that so long as Pharisaic
> Judaism (which, we must remember, was the only form of
> Judaism which survived the destruction of Jerusalem)—so
> long as it records personal or almost personal reminiscence
> of our Lord, the surviving record is not viciously hostile (as
> later became the case); but the farther the Jews were re-
> moved from the time of our Lord's earthly life, and the
> more dependent they became for knowledge of Jesus upon
> later generations of *Christians*, then so much worse became
> the Jewish characterization of Jesus.

Writing about the Jewish Talmud:

> In the main the Jews had already begun the process which
> has characterized a great part of Judaism even to the pres-
> ent day—the process of slamming the door, and locking,
> barring and bolting his mind against the whole subject of
> Christianity.

POINTS TO CONSIDER ABOUT THIS ANSWER

Some of these observations (particularly in the Jewish Encyclopedia*)
are hardly consistent with the Gospels as we have them.* How could
orthodox Palestinian Jews introduce elements from pagan
legends to describe the birth of Jesus, knowing that by doing
so they denied the most fundamental article of their faith, the
one-ness of God?

Is it really true to say that Jesus never claimed any
authority deputed by the Father? What of his claims to be
"the Son"?

Granted that he did not claim openly to be *the Messiah*; did
he not make many other direct and indirect claims in which
he identified himself with *God himself*?

How could a Jew invite fellow Jews to find comfort in
personal relations with him by using language which associated
him so closely with God, and which ignored the difference
between the creature and the Creator?

*This answer is usually based on the assumption that the Gospels
cannot be an objective or reliable account of what Jesus said and did.*

> Because the Gospels, while containing valuable material, are
> all written in a polemical spirit and for the purpose of
> substantiating the claim of the Messianic spirit and super-
> human character of Jesus, it is difficult to present an impar-
> tial story of his life.

If there can be no agreement about the Gospel evidence, the
discussion must turn on assumptions about God and man. If, for
example, you approach the Gospels with your mind already
made up that God is one in the strictly literal sense, and if no
amount of evidence will persuade you to revise your understanding of what this one-ness means, then you must consider some of

the problems involved in this concept of the one-ness of God.
(See Part 2, Question Three, "Who or what is God?", pp. 142ff.)

ISLAM

The Qur'an has its own accounts of the different aspects of the
life of Jesus, who is known as "Esa, son of Mary."
   His birth:

> "I am the messenger of your Lord," he (Gabriel) replied,
> "and have come to give you a holy son." "How shall I bear
> a child," she answered, "when I am a virgin, untouched by
> man?"

> "Such is the will of your Lord," he replied. "This is no
> difficult thing for Him. 'He shall be a sign to mankind,' says
> the Lord, 'and a blessing from Ourself. That is Our
> decree.'" Thereupon she conceived . . .

> And remember the angel's words to Mary. He said: "Allah
> has chosen you. He has made you pure and exalted you
> above all women . . ."

   His character:
There are many references to Jesus, but it is not possible to
build up any picture of his character. Islam, however, seems to
share the belief that Jesus was sinless. Although it speaks of the
sins of all the other great prophets, Adam, Noah, Abraham,
Moses, and Mohammed, it nowhere attributes any sin to Jesus.
This conclusion is expressed in one of the *Traditions*:

> Every child born of Adam is touched by Satan the day his
> mother is delivered of him with the exception of Mary and
> her son.

   His claims:
None of Jesus' claims for himself are quoted. But the Qur'an
gives the following titles to Jesus:

"the Messiah"
"the Word of God"
"the Sure Saying"
"a spirit sent from God"
"the Messenger of God," or "the Apostle of God"
"the Servant of God"
"the Prophet of God"

The Messiah, Jesus the son of Mary, was no more than Allah's apostle and His Word which he cast to Mary: a spirit from Him.

To these titles we can add two further claims made about Jesus in the *Traditions*:

He will be an Intercessor in heaven. The Qur'an says of Jesus "God took him to himself," implying that Jesus is now alive in heaven. Another verse describes Jesus as "worthy of regard in this world and in that to come."

Baidawi, an authoritative commentator, interprets these words in this way:

In this world as Prophet, in the next as an Intercessor.

He will be a judge.

There is no doubt that the Son of Mary, on whom be blessing and peace, shall descend in the midst of you as a righteous judge.

His miracles:

☐ Jesus, while still a baby, defends his mother against those who think she has been immoral and had a child out of wedlock:

Then she took her child to her people, who said to her: "This is indeed a strange thing! Sister of Aaron, your father was never a wicked man, nor was your mother a harlot."

She made a sign to them, pointing to the child. But they replied: "How can we speak with a new-born infant?"

Whereupon he spoke and said: "I am the servant of Allah. He has given me the Gospel and ordained me a prophet. His blessing is upon me wherever I go, and He has commanded me to be steadfast in prayer and to give alms to the poor as long as I shall live . . ."

☐ This miracle of the table spread with food sent from heaven contains echoes of the miracle of the feeding of the 5,000 as recorded in the Gospels:

"Jesus, son of Mary," said the disciples, "can Allah send down to us from heaven a table spread with food?"

He replied: "Have fear of Allah, if you are true believers."

"We wish to eat of it," they said, "so that we may reassure

our hearts and know that what you said to us is true, and that we may be witnesses of it."

"Lord," said Jesus, the Son of Mary, "send to us from heaven a table spread with food, that it may mark a feast for us and our sustenance; You are the best Giver."

Allah replied: "I am sending one to you. But whoever of you disbelieves hereafter shall be punished as no man has ever been punished."

☐ This summary of his miracles refers to the story, found also in one of the apocryphal gospels, of Jesus making clay birds come to life:

Allah will say: "Jesus, son of Mary, remember the favor I have bestowed on you and on your mother: how I strengthened you with the Holy Spirit, so that you preached to men in your cradle and in the prime of manhood; how I instructed you in the Scriptures and in wisdom, in the Torah and in the Gospel; how by My leave you fashioned from clay the likeness of a bird and breathed into it so that, by My leave, it became a living bird; how, by My leave, you healed the blind man and the leper, and by My leave restored the dead to life; how I protected you from the Israelites when you brought them veritable signs: when the unbelievers among them said: 'This is nothing but plain magic'; how when I enjoined the disciples to believe in Me and in my Apostle they replied: 'We believe; bear witness that we submit to You utterly.'"

POINTS TO CONSIDER ABOUT THIS ANSWER

From the above passages it is obvious that the Qur'an puts Jesus in a unique position. This is a position not shared by any of the other prophets, not even by Mohammed who is said to be the last and greatest of the prophets:

☐ The birth of Jesus was a miraculous virgin birth; the words of annunciation addressed to Mary are not paralleled by any similar words addressed to Amina, the mother of Mohammed.

☐ No sin of any kind is attributed to Jesus; but all the other five great prophets need to seek forgiveness from God.

☐Of the titles given to Jesus, some are exactly the same as the titles given to Mohammed: "the Messenger of God," "the Servant of God," "the Prophet of God." But the other titles given to Jesus are given to no other prophet: "the Messiah," "the Word of God," "the Sure Saying," "a spirit sent from God." Whereas Jesus can be thought of as an intercessor, Mohammed explicitly disclaims the right to intercede for sinners before God. And whereas Jesus is said to have been raised to heaven, Mohammed is dead and has not yet been raised to be with God in heaven.

☐Later traditions attributed miracles to Mohammed. But according to the Qur'an, he consistently disclaimed power to work miracles. When he was challenged to produce his credentials and to prove that he was a prophet sent from God, he pointed to the Qur'an as being sufficient miracle in itself.

But why is Jesus so unique if Mohammed is the greatest prophet and the final messenger from God?

And what of the many questions left unanswered in the Qur'an? Why is Jesus called "the Messiah"? Why his miraculous birth? What precisely was his Message, his Ingil? The Jesus of the Qur'an remains something of an enigma.

Henri Michaud in his study of Jesus according to the Qur'an:

> After having tried to understand what the Qur'an says about Jesus, we shall ask our brothers of Islam with very great anxiety: "Is this indeed what you believe about Jesus?" If there is a reply without ambiguity, then an irenical dialogue can be begun.

If you accept the Qur'an as a reliable source of evidence about Jesus, but are not satisfied with the incompleteness of this picture, are you willing to *supplement* it with the fuller picture of Jesus in the Gospels? And are you willing to consider how the Gospels answer these questions? (See pp. 376ff.)

The Qur'an's rejection of the Christian understanding of Jesus is based to some extent on a misunderstanding.

It may be that the Trinity which Mohammed rejected was a Trinity consisting of the Father, Jesus and Mary:

> Then Allah will say: "Jesus, son of Mary, did you ever say to mankind: 'Worship me and my Mother as gods beside Allah?'"

The relationship between the Father and the Son is thought of as a purely physical relationship:

He is the Creator of the heavens and the earth. How
should He have a son when he had no consort?

Never has Allah begotten a son, nor is there any other god
beside him.

The Christian rejects these ideas as vigorously as the Moslem.
Therefore, if you reject the Christian understanding of Jesus on
these grounds, you are simply rejecting a misunderstanding
which the Christian rejects as strongly as you do.

*It may be, however, that in the end we must move from the details of the
picture of Christ in the Qur'an and the Gospels and talk about fundamental assumptions.*

☐ The original disciples of Jesus were as firmly convinced as any
Moslem that God is one. This was their basic creed, their basic
assumption. However, through their contact with Jesus over a
period of three years they were gradually forced by what they
saw and heard and experienced to *revise* their understanding of
the oneness of God. They did not *reject* it; they simply revised
their idea of "oneness" in the light of the inescapable evidence
which confronted them. If you are not willing even to consider
the possibility of revising your assumption about the oneness of
God in the light of the evidence of the life of Jesus, then the
discussion must turn on some of the problems involved in insisting on the literal oneness of God. (See further Part 2, Question
Two, "Who or what is God?")

☐ If you accept the Qur'an as the Word of God, you will not be
willing simply to *supplement* the Qur'an's picture of Jesus with
what the Gospels say about him, because the Qur'an contains
many explicit *rejections* of the divinity of Jesus:

Unbelievers are those that say: "Allah is the Messiah, the
son of Mary." For the Messiah himself said: "Children of
Israel, serve Allah, my Lord and your Lord." He that wor-
ships other gods besides Allah shall be forbidden Paradise
and shall be cast into the fire of Hell. None shall help the
evil-doers.

Unbelievers are those that say: "Allah is one of three."
There is but one God. If they do not desist from so saying,
those of them that disbelieve shall be sternly punished.

Will they not turn to Allah in repentance and seek forgiveness of Him? He is forgiving and merciful.

The Messiah, the son of Mary, was no more than an apos-

tle: other apostles passed away before him. His mother was
a saintly woman. They both ate earthly food.

See how We make plain to them Our revelations. See how
they ignore the truth.

The discussion at this point, therefore, must turn on the
question: How do we know what is the word of God? How can
we know whether the Qur'an or the Bible is the Word of God?
(See further Part 1, especially pp. 9–35 and 37–50.)

ANSWER FOUR:
He was a man and
nothing more.

This is to say, Jesus was simply a man. He was not divine in the sense that he shared the nature of a supernatural God. And he was not a created being from heaven. He may have been a very exceptional person, and he may help us to find the meaning of life. But he was not in any sense more than an ordinary human being.

Hugh Schonfield explains the Christian belief as being the result of

> . . . the intrusion into early Christianity of a pagan assessment of his worth in terms of deity.

In spite of this he is able to see some deeper meaning in the person of Jesus:

> We find in him the symbol both of the martyrdom and the aspirations of man, and therefore we must cling to him as

the embodiment of an assurance that our life has meaning and purpose.

Paul van Buren interprets the life of Jesus through the concept of "freedom":

Jesus of Nazareth was a singular individual. His characteristics seem to have impressed his followers so that he stands out as a remarkably free man in the records of remembered parable, saying, or incident, and in the way in which the early Christian community spoke of him . . .

He followed the religious rites and obligations of his people, but he also felt free to disregard them. In miracle stories he is even presented mythologically as being free from the limitations of natural forces.

He was called rabbi, teacher, but his teaching broke down the limitations of this title . . . He simply spoke and acted with the authority of a singular freedom.

The content of his teaching reveals this same freedom . . . Perhaps the most radical expression of this freedom is found in an incident in which Jesus forgave a sick man his sins, and then demonstrated his right to do so by healing him . . . His freedom, finally, is evident in his making no claims for himself. He seems to have been so free of any need for status that he was able to resist all attempts by others to convey status on him . . .

If we would define Jesus by his freedom, however, we must emphasize its positive character. He was free from anxiety and the need to establish his own identity, but was above all free for his neighbor . . . He was free to be compassionate for his neighbor, whoever that neighbor might be, without regard to himself . . .

We have summed up the characteristics of Jesus around the one concept, freedom . . .

POINTS TO CONSIDER ABOUT THIS ANSWER

If you give this kind of answer, you are still faced with the further question: how was it that the early Christians came to believe that he was more than an ordinary man?

413

☐If the Gospels do give a substantially reliable account of his life, what do you make of his claims about himself? In the final analysis there are only two possible answers:

either   he was *deceived* and *misled* about his own identity; he was wrong about his claims, but did not know it. Therefore, at best he was mentally unbalanced, at worst he was out of his mind, completely mad.

or   he *deceived* and *misled* others consciously and deliberately; he was wrong about his claims, and he knew it; but he spoke and acted in this way to get people to believe in his teaching and in what he stood for. Therefore, at best he was a teacher with ideals, who used unscrupulous methods; at worst he was a dishonest rogue.

☐If the Gospels are not a reliable account of the life of Jesus, how are we to account for the distortion? The first Gospel was probably written thirty to forty years after the death of Jesus; and the process of distortion must already have begun at this stage. There are three possible answers:

either   the disciples and/or the writers were *deceived* and *misled*; they completely misunderstood Jesus themselves, and passed on their misunderstanding to others.

BUT: are we to imagine that Jesus spent the best part of three years with the disciples and allowed them to misunderstand him so completely?

And how can we explain this misunderstanding in the light of the vast difference between Jewish beliefs about the one God and pagan beliefs about many gods? The first disciples were all Palestinian Jews; is it likely that they would make Jesus out to be a demigod?

or   the disciples and/or the writers were *deceiving* and *misleading* their readers deliberately, although they may have had the best of motives. Somewhere along the line there were those who knew that Jesus was an ordinary man, but they made him out to be more than a man in order to convince others of the importance of his message.

BUT: how could a religion based on a lie, or even on an "honest" deception make so much of truthfulness and honesty?

And what possible motive could they have had?

Jews would find it very difficult to accept a new understanding of the oneness of God. And non-Jews would
not easily accept the claims about the uniqueness of
Jesus.

or   the disciples and/or the writers were not misled or
misleading; it is *we* who are misled if we read the
Gospels as a straightforward account of what Jesus
said and did. The Gospels tell us about the inward
experience and *faith* of the first disciples, and cannot be
taken as reliable evidence about the *events* behind that
faith.

BUT: if we are to be agnostic about what it was that
created the faith of the disciples, Christian faith ceases to be
faith in the Jesus of history, and becomes faith in the faith
of the first disciples. And why not carry the agnosticism one
stage further and be agnostic about the *faith* of the disciples
as well as the *events*?

*Sooner or later the discussion must turn on basic assumptions rather
than on detailed points of interpretation.* One of the basic assumptions evident in answers of this kind is that a "God-man" is
inconceivable and incredible.

Hugh Schonfield sets out to examine the evidence about Jesus
without any bias or prejudice. In his Introduction to *The Passover
Plot* he begins with a claim to be unbiased and unprejudiced:

Most books about him [Jesus] have been devotional, apologetic, or polemical, and I wished mine to be none of these.
What I aimed at was to shed all dispositions to make use of
Jesus and allow him from his own time to explain himself
to me.

But on the very next page he writes:

The traditional portraiture no longer satisfies; it is too baf-
fling in its apparent contradiction of the terms of our
earthly existence. The God-man of Christianity is increasingly incredible, yet it is not easy to break with centuries of
authoritative instruction and devout faith, and there remains embedded deep in the subconscious a strong sense of
the supernatural inherited from remote ages.

One of his basic assumptions, therefore, is that the Christian
interpretation of Jesus can be safely ruled out from the start

415

because it no longer satisfies and appears increasingly incredible.

Joel Carmichael, in his book *The Death of Jesus*, begins with a claim to be objective:

> My attitude throughout is purely historical.

But a little later he declares his presuppositions:

> The international cultic transformation of perspective in-
> volved in the magnification of Jesus was accompanied by
> the external, historical change of perspective due to the
> growing and ultimately unbridged schism between the new
> sect and Judaism.

> This theme is basic in any study of Christian origins . . .

> This will give us our cardinal criterion:

> *Anything that conflicts with this transformation or perspective is*
> *likely to be true.*

> That is, any fragment we can manage to isolate that runs
> counter to the prevailing Gospel tendency of exalting Jesus,
> or preaching his universality, and of emphasising his origi-
> nality, will be regarded as *ipso facto* probable (other things,
> of course, being equal).

Even as a historian he cannot approach the inquiry without any assumptions. In this case he declares that it was the Christians who made Jesus God; therefore none of the evidence of the New Testament can be taken at its face value.

Paul van Buren indicates that he begins his study accepting the basic assumptions of "secular man." His interpretation is deter-mined by the methods of linguistic analysis:

> How can the Christian who is himself a secular man under-
> stand his faith in a secular way? . . . The answer will be
> reached by analyzing what a man means when he uses the
> language of faith, when he repeats the earliest Christian
> confession: "Jesus is Lord."

> The question is whether a Christian is to be distinguished
> from an "unbeliever" by a different logic or thinking . . .
> We shall conduct this study on the assumption that "being a
> Christian" does not deny one's involvement in the secular
> world and its way of thinking. This assumption will govern
> our attempt to understand the Christian conviction that
> "Jesus is Lord."

He admits that Jesus is not unique in having freedom:

Having spoken of him as an exceptionally liberated individual, we should point out that we might say this of
other men.

If you approach the Gospels with assumptions of this kind, no
amount of detailed study of the Gospels is likely to make you
change your mind. It is the assumption itself which needs to be
tested and challenged. (See further Part 2, Question Two, "Who
or what is God?" and Question Three, "What is man?")

ANSWER FIVE:

He was only a man—but also a revelation of "God."

This is to say, he was an ordinary man; he was not related personally to a supernatural God, for no such God exists. However, if we redefine the word God, we can see in Jesus a revelation of the true meaning of "God."

F. C. Happold:

What the early Christians saw in Jesus, implicitly if not explicitly, was a full and perfect pattern of divinity, so far as divinity could be shown forth in man. This divinity, moreover, was inherent in each one of them. For Jesus was Representative Man, Archetypal Man, Man as he might be if he could become that which in his essential nature he really is: or, as a Hindu would put it, if he could realize his Greater Self.

John Robinson:

Jesus himself said in so many words, "If I claim anything for myself, do not believe me."

It is, indeed, an open question whether Jesus ever claimed to be the Son of God, let alone God . . .

We cannot be sure what titles Jesus claimed . . .

Jesus makes no claims for himself in his own right and at the same time makes the most tremendous claims about what God is doing through him and uniquely through him . . .

Jesus never claims to be God, personally: yet he claims to bring God, completely.

It is in Jesus, and Jesus alone, that there is nothing of self to be seen, but solely the ultimate, unconditional love of God. It is as he emptied himself utterly of himself that he became the carrier of "the name which is above every name," and that glory is simply Love.

For it is in making himself nothing, in his utter self-surrender to others in love, that he discloses and lays bare the Ground of man's being as Love.

What is Christ for us today?

Jesus is "the man for others," the one in whom Love has completely taken over, the one who is utterly open to, and united with, the Ground of his being . . . For at this point, of love "to the uttermost," we encounter *God*, the ultimate "depth" of our being, the unconditional in the conditioned. This is what the New Testament means by saying that "God was in Christ" and that "what God was the Word was." Because Christ was utterly and completely "the man for others," because he *was* love, he was "one with the Father," because "God is love."

POINTS TO CONSIDER ABOUT THIS ANSWER

These answers are based on assumptions about the meaning of the word God *which are clearly expressed. F. C. Happold begins with an understanding of the meaning of the word* God *which is very different from the Christian understanding. He assumes* that all the religions have basically the same vision of "God" and "man," even though they use different words and symbols.

> Eternal and essential God-man-unity; this is what these men saw and what they were determined to express, even though, with their inherited idea of God, it seemed to involve contradictions. In doing so they expressed the supreme significance of the Christian revelation. For the Incarnation of Jesus Christ was not only a diaphany of the Divine, but also a diaphany of the human.

> Though they express it in different ways according to their different theologies and philosophies, the mystics of all religions are at one in asserting the inherent divinity of man's real self. This inner deity is, however, hidden. It exists at the level of human existence as a potentiality. For it to become an actuality a "divine birth" must take place in the soul, so that a man is raised to a higher state of consciousness. In Christianity this divine birth is thought of as the birth of Jesus Christ, the eternal Son or Logos (Word) of God, in the center of the soul.

John Robinson shows clearly that his starting-point is the assumption that "God" is not to be thought of as a supernatural being:

> As long as God and man are thought of as two "beings," each with distinct natures, one from "the other side" and one from "this side," then it is impossible to create out of them more than a God-man, a divine visitant from "out there" who chooses in every respect to live like the natives. The supernaturalist view of the Incarnation can never really rid itself of the idea of the prince who appears in the guise of the beggar. However genuinely destitute the beggar may be, he *is* a prince; and that in the end is what matters.

If you begin with assumptions of this kind, the details of the Gospel narratives will be irrelevant. The discussion must therefore hinge on the meaning of the word *God*. (See further Part 2, Question Two, "Who or what is God?")

These answers are based on the assumption that the truth about Jesus can be expressed in many different ways, depending on the standpoint of the individual. F. C. Happold believes that statements of Christian belief, like statements of any kind of belief, express intuitions arising out of personal experience:

> What may not be able to be established as either scientifically or historically true, may be regarded as *mythically* and *dogmatically* true.

> When examined objectively, dogma is seen to be a complex of mythological, symbolic, metaphysical, psychological, mystical and, in the Christian creeds, historical elements. It is a translation into the terms of the intellect of intuitions which have been apprehended mystically, psychologically, and intuitively. It is thus a particular sort of truth demanding a particular sort of language, which, like every other sort of language, has to be learned, if it is to be rightly understood.

John Robinson understands the language of the New Testament in terms of "myth":

> But suppose the whole notion of "a God" who "visits" the earth in the person of "his Son" is as mythical as the prince in the fairy story? Suppose the Christian myth (the invasion of "this side" by "the other side")—as opposed to the Christmas history (the birth of the man Jesus of Nazareth)—has to go? Are we prepared for that? Or are we to cling here to this last vestige of the mythological or metaphysical world-view as the only garb in which to clothe the story with power to touch the imagination? Cannot perhaps the supernaturalist scheme survive at least as part of the "magic" of Christmas?

> Yes, indeed, it can survive—as myth. For myth has its perfectly legitimate, and indeed profoundly important, place. The myth is there to indicate the significance of the events, the divine depth of the history.

Assumptions of this kind must be discussed on their own, for they have nothing to do with the Gospel accounts of the life of Jesus. What is at stake is our understanding of what truth is. (See further Part 1.)

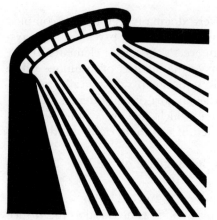

BACK TO ANSWER ONE:
He was both man and God: he was the Son of God.

PROBLEMS AND QUESTIONS

Having examined other possible answers to the basic question, we must now return to option one, the biblical Christian answer, and look at some of the main questions and objections raised.

Can we be really certain that Jesus actually lived?

The following are the four main witnesses outside the New Testament to the historicity of Jesus.

Pliny, a Roman pro-consul in Bithynia (Asia Minor), writing to the Emperor Trajan in A.D. 110 about the way in which he has been dealing with Christians:

> This is the course that I have adopted in the case of those brought before me as Christians. I ask them if they are

Christians. If they admit it I repeat the question a second
and a third time, threatening capital punishment; if they
persist I sentence them to death. For I do not doubt that,
whatever kind of crime it may be to which they have confessed, their pertinacity and inflexible obstinacy should certainly be punished. There were others who displayed a like
madness and whom I reserved to be sent to Rome, since
they were Roman citizens.

Thereupon the usual result followed: the very fact of my
dealing with the question led to a wider spread of the
charge, and a great variety of cases were brought before
me. An anonymous pamphlet was issued, containing many
names. All who denied that they were or had been Christians I considered should be discharged, because they called
upon the gods at my dictation and did reverence, with
incense and wine, to your image which I had ordered to be
brought forward for this purpose, together with the statues
of the deities; and especially because they cursed Christ, a
thing which, it is said, genuine Christians cannot be in-
duced to do. Others named by the informer first said that
they were Christians and then denied it; declaring that they
had been but were so no longer, some having recanted
three years or more before and one or two as long ago as
twenty years. They all worshiped your image and the statues of the gods and cursed Christ. But they declared that
the sum of their guilt or error had amounted only to this,
that on an appointed day they had been accustomed to
meet before daybreak, and recite a hymn antiphonally to
Christ, as to a god, and to bind themselves by an oath, not
for the commission of any crime but to abstain from theft,
robbery, adultery and breach of faith, and not to deny a
deposit when it was claimed. . . .

Tacitus, the Roman historian, writing in about A.D. 115 about
Nero's persecution of Christians in the year A.D. 64:

But all the endeavors of men, all the emperor's largesse
and the propitiations of the gods, did not suffice to allay the
scandal or banish the belief that the fire had been ordered.
And so, to get rid of this rumor, Nero set up as the culprits
and punished with the utmost refinement of cruelty a class
hated for their abominations, who are commonly called
Christians. Christus, from whom their name is derived, was
executed at the hands of the procurator Pontius Pilate in

423

> the reign of Tiberius. Checked for the moment, this perni-
> cious superstition again broke out, not only in Judaea, the
> source of the evil, but even in Rome, that receptacle for
> everything that is sordid and degrading from every quarter
> of the globe, which there finds a following.

Suetonius, the Roman historian, writing in about A.D. 120 in
his *Life of Claudius* (the Emperor from 41–54). It is probable that
"Chrestus" is a confusion of "Christus" (Christ).

> Since the Jews were continually making disturbances at the
> instigation of Chrestus, he (Claudius) expelled them from
> Rome.

This probably refers to quarrels between Jew and Christian
teachers about Jesus.

Josephus, the Jewish historian, writing about A.D. 93 or 94 in
his *Antiquities of the Jews* (this version is based on the Greek text,
which dates from the fourth century):

> About this time there arose Jesus, a wise man, if indeed it
> be lawful to call him a man. For he was a doer of wonder-
> ful deeds, and a teacher of men who gladly receive the
> truth. He drew to himself many both of the Jews and of the
> Gentiles. He was the Christ; and when Pilate, on the indict-
> ment of the principal men among us, had condemned him
> to the cross, those who loved him at the first did not cease
> to do so, for he appeared to them again alive on the third
> day, the divine prophets having foretold these and ten
> thousand wonderful things about him. And even to this day
> the race of Christians, who are named after him, has not
> died out.

Josephus was not a Christian, and some scholars have argued
that some clauses (e.g. "he was the Christ") could not have been
written by Josephus, and must have been interpolated in an early
text by a Christian. But others, including scholars who have no
Christian bias, see no reason for doubting that Josephus could
have written these words. They argue that this is exactly how a
slightly cynical Jew might refer to Christian beliefs about Jesus.

Further light has been shed on this text by Professor Shlomo
Pines of the Hebrew University in Jerusalem, who has discovered
an Arabic version of the same text which he believes to be older
than the Greek one. It was found in a church history written by
Bishop Agapius, an Arab Bishop in Baghdad. This is what the
Arabic text says:

At this time there was a wise man who was called Jesus.
And his conduct was good and (he) was known to be vir-
tuous. And many people from among the Jews and from
the other nations became his disciples. Pilate condemned
him to be crucified and to die.

And those who had become his disciples did not abandon
his discipleship. They reported that he had appeared to
them three days after his crucifixion and that he was alive.
Accordingly he was perhaps the Messiah of whom the prophets have recounted wonders.

Professor Pines believes that medieval Christian censorship was
probably responsible for the differences between the two ver-
sions:

The Arabic version is less Christian in character than the
traditional Greek one. Because of this it may be an earlier
version than the traditional one.

In another passage in the *Antiquities*, Josephus writes about the
martyrdom of James, the brother of Jesus:

(Ananus) assembled the sanhedrin of the judges, and
brought before them the brother of Jesus, who was called
Christ, whose name was James, and some others, and when
he had formed an accusation against them as breakers of
the law, he delivered them to be stoned.

Roderic Dunkerley, in his book *Beyond the Gospels*, examines all
the evidence about Jesus from contemporary sources outside the
New Testament and comes to this conclusion:

In none of these various testimonies to the fact of Christ is
there any slightest hint or idea that he was not a real
historical person . . . Indeed it has been argued—and I
think very rightly—that myth theories of the beginnings of
Christianity are modern speculative hypotheses motivated
by unreasoning prejudice and dislike. "It would never enter
anyone's head," says Merezhovsky, "to ask whether Jesus
had lived, unless before asking the question the mind had
been darkened by the wish that he had not lived."

Why is there so little about the virgin birth in the rest of the New Testament?

The only direct evidence for belief in the virgin birth in the New
Testament is contained in the two passages from Luke and

425

Matthew. If the belief is important, why do the other Gospels not record the story? And if no other book in the New Testament speaks of it, does this not mean that the belief was not well known in the early period?

☐ From the very nature of the case, we would not expect the story to be common knowledge in the early days of the church.

At first only Mary and Joseph would have known the circumstances of the conception of Jesus. They would hardly be likely to tell the story to others inside or outside the family.

Joseph must have died at some time before Jesus began his public ministry. Mary would have no compelling motive for publishing the story, since she herself seems to have had doubts about him during this period. Luke gives the impression that Mary kept the secret to herself, and that he heard the story about Jesus' birth and childhood from her own mouth:

> . . . and all who heard it wondered at what the shepherds told them. But Mary kept all these things, pondering them in her heart.

> And he [Jesus] went down with them and came to Nazareth, and was obedient to them; and his mother kept all these things in her heart.

In the early days of the church, the story of the death and resurrection of Jesus would have overshadowed the story of his birth. The story might therefore have remained a secret tradition, known only to a small number.

☐ There are hints in other parts of the New Testament that something was known about the unusual circumstances of his birth.

When the Jews objected to the way in which Jesus called himself "the Son," they taunted him with these words:

> We were not born of fornication; we have one Father, even God.

The implication may well be "We were not born of fornication—*as you were.*"

Paul speaks of the entrance of Jesus into the world in these words:

> When the time had fully come, God sent forth his Son, born of woman, born under the law . . .

☐ There are two possible conclusions we can draw from the scarcity of references to the virgin birth:

426

either   the story was invented as a way of adding to the
dignity of Jesus, but it was not widely known or accepted, or regarded as important in the early days.

or   it could simply underline the general impression we
get from the rest of the New Testament that Mary is
completely overshadowed by Jesus and that the circumstances of his death and resurrection were regarded as being far more important than his birth.

What is the rightful place of Mary in Christian faith and devotion?

If Mary played such a significant role in the coming of Jesus into
the world and in his early life, what place should she have in
Christian faith and devotion today?

Nicholas Zernov, writing about Eastern Orthodox beliefs:

Among these saints a unique place is reserved for the
Mother of God—the Virgin Mary. The long process of
purification and enlightenment of the Jewish race so vividly
described in the Old Testament reached its culmination in
the Theotokos (Mary). In her the faith and heroism of
many generations of the Chosen People found fulfillment.
She accepted with humility the challenge of the Annunciation. During the lifetime of her Son she kept in the background, but she presided over the assembly of apostles on
the day of Pentecost, when the new period in the history of
mankind was inaugurated by the descent of the Holy Spirit.
"Warm Veneration of the Theotokos is the soul of Orthodox piety," writes Fr. Bulgakov. Her name is constantly
invoked in both liturgical and personal prayers, she is
loved, not only as the Mother of Christ, but also as the
Mother of mankind, for she embraces in her charity the
entire human family of which her Son is the sole Redeemer.

☐ The first thing to note is how Mary was addressed by the angel
at the time of his visitation, and how she thought of herself. The
angel addressed her in these words:

Hail, O favored one, the Lord is with you! . . . Do not be
afraid, Mary, for you have found favor with God. And
behold, you will conceive in your womb and bear a son, and
you shall call his name Jesus . . . (Revised Standard Version)

427

Greetings, most favored one . . . (New English Bible)

Rejoice, so highly favored! . . . (Jerusalem Bible)

There is no justification for the translation "full of grace," or for the idea that Mary is a means by which God gives grace to men. The greeting is explained by the later sentence, "You have found favor with God."

Mary responded to the angel's message:

Behold I am the handmaid of the Lord; let it be to me according to your word.

☐ Some incidents are recorded in which Jesus seems to play down the human and physical relationship between himself and his mother:

And his mother and his brothers came; and standing outside they sent to him and called him. And a crowd was sitting about him; and they said to him. "Your mother and your brothers are outside, asking for you." And he replied, "Who are my mother and my brothers?" And looking around on those who sat about him, he said, "Here are my mothers and my brothers! Whoever does the will of God is my brother, and sister, and mother."

A woman in the crowd raised her voice and said to him, "Blessed is the womb that bore you, and the breasts that you sucked!" But he said, "Blessed rather are those who hear the word of God and keep it!"

At the wedding at Cana, Mary seems to be wanting to impress her will on Jesus and he replies:

O woman, what have you to do with me?

When he hung on the cross, he committed Mary to the care of John the disciple:

. . . he said to his mother, "Woman, behold your son!"

Then he said to the disciple, "Behold your mother!"

In these last two incidents he addressed her as "woman," which would not have been an insult, but a title of respect. If, however, he had wanted to emphasize the mother-son relationship, it would have been very natural for him to address her as "mother." It seems that Jesus had to make it clear to Mary—

gently but firmly—that the relationship between them could not always be the ordinary mother-son relationship.

☐ The only other reference to Mary outside the Gospels is in Acts, where she is described as joining with the other disciples in prayer:

> All these with one accord devoted themselves to prayer, together with the women and Mary the mother of Jesus, and with his brothers.

There is no suggestion that Mary was presiding over the gathering, as Zernov claims. In the context of the early chapters of Acts this can only mean that Mary joined with the other disciples in prayer to God *through* the risen Jesus, or *to* the risen Jesus himself.

☐ One further point. In the book of Revelation, in which John describes his vision of heaven there is no reference to Mary. There is no suggestion that Mary has already received a place of special honor in heaven, or that she is in any sense to be regarded as a mediator between men and God.

So perhaps we come nearest to the mind of Mary herself, and of Jesus, if we give her the simple but honorable title she herself used—"the handmaid of the Lord."

Why is there so little in the Gospels about the early life of Jesus?

The Jewish Encyclopedia:

> Perhaps the most remarkable thing about the life of Jesus as presented in the Gospels is the utter silence about its earlier phases.

☐ The only details given in the Gospels are these.

Joseph and Mary took Jesus to Egypt while he was still a baby because of the threat to his life from Herod. After the death of Herod, they returned to Nazareth, and it was here that he was brought up (Matthew 2:13–15).

Jesus had brothers and sisters who were born to Mary and Joseph (this is the most natural and obvious interpretation of the references to the "brothers" of Jesus):

> Many who heard him (Jesus) were astonished, saying, "Where did this man get all this? . . . Is not this the carpenter, the son of Mary and brother of James and Joses and Judas and Simon, and are not his sisters here with us?"

429

Similarly, Paul speaks of

> . . . James, the Lord's brother . . .

The interpretation that the "brothers" were in fact cousins
and not blood-brothers first appears in Christian writings in the
third century. This tradition seems to have been associated with
the belief that Mary remained a virgin after her marriage to
Joseph and after the birth of Jesus; but there is no basis for this
belief in the New Testament itself.

Jesus first visited Jerusalem at the age of twelve. After a long
search his parents found him "in the temple, sitting among the
teachers, listening to them and asking them questions" (Luke
2:41–51).

Joseph, his foster-father, was a carpenter, and it appears that
Jesus learned this trade from him. Joseph must have died
before Jesus left home for his public ministry. Being the eldest
son, Jesus would have had the responsibility for the home
(Matthew 13:55).

☐ Our only other source of information about the early life of
Jesus is the so-called apocryphal Gospels.

Roderic Dunkerley:

> As regards the conventionally called "apocryphal Gospels"
> . . . it does not take very much examination to convince us
> that they are almost entirely fiction not fact. They deal
> mostly with the nativity and boyhood of Jesus on the one
> hand, and with his passion and resurrection on the other.
> Many fantastic miracles are attributed to the child Jesus, as
> for example that he made birds of clay and then they flew
> away, and again that another boy who accidentally ran
> against him dropped down and died . . .

> But we cannot rule out the possibility that here and there
> some small points of authentic tradition may have survived
> amidst all the fiction and fantasy . . . Dean Farrar in his
> *Life of Christ* quoted the following charming little tale and
> thought it might be based on fact:

>> Now in the month of Adar, Jesus assembled the boys as
>> if he were their king; they strewed their garments on the
>> ground and he sat upon them. Then they put on his
>> head a crown wreathed of flowers and like attendants
>> waiting on a king they stood in order before him on his
>> right hand and on his left. And whoever passed that way
>> the boys took him by force saying, Come hither and
>> adore the King and then proceed upon thy way.

430

This is quite different from the usual grotesque narratives and is something that might quite easily have happened— and been remembered and retold. But it cannot be more than an interesting possibility.

☐ If we ask why the writers of the Gospels do not tell us more about the early life of Jesus, the simplest answer is that they were not intending to write full biographies of Jesus. Their main concern was with his public ministry, his death, and resurrection.

How trustworthy are reports of the character of Jesus which were written by his friends and admirers?

The point raised is that reports about his character are bound to be prejudiced because they were written by admirers who idolized him, and who would not have been able to see his faults.

☐ The Gospels say that the disciples were with Jesus for the best part of three years. And these Gospels were written either by some of the disciples or by others who were acquainted with them. We are dealing therefore with the testimony of men who knew him intimately, and not with casual acquaintances. John claims, for example, to be writing about someone he knew very well:

> That which was from the beginning, which we have heard, which we have seen with our eyes, which we have looked upon and touched with our hands . . .

☐ The disciples would have been brought up to believe that *all* men are sinners:

> God looks down from heaven
>   upon the sons of men
> to see if there are any that are wise,
>   that seek after God.
> They have all fallen away;
>   they are all alike depraved;
> There is none that does good,
>   no, not one.
> All we like sheep have gone astray;
>   we have turned every one to his own way . . .

The disciples would have had to have some very good reason for claiming that Jesus was an exception to this rule.

☐ None of the New Testament writers goes out of his way to paint an impressive picture of the character of Jesus. All that we learn

431

about his character is from his actions and his words; there are
no passages which set out to describe what kind of person he
was. In the two cases where they speak of his sinlessness, they do
so almost as an aside:

.... Christ also suffered for you, leaving you an example,
that you should follow in his steps. He committed no sin;
no guile was found on his lips. When he was reviled, he did
not revile in return . . .

You know that he appeared to take away sins, and in him
there is no sin.

☐ The Gospel writers also attempt to give some idea of what Jesus'
critics and enemies thought of him. These were some of the
accusations they brought against him:

blasphemy:
Who can forgive sins but God alone?

keeping bad company:
Why does he eat with tax collectors and sinners?

*that his disciples were not strict enough in their religious ob-
servances:*
Why do your disciples not fast?

that his disciples broke the sabbath:
Why are they [the disciples] doing what is not lawful on the
sabbath? [They were going against a ruling of the scribes,
but not against the Old Testament itself.]

The Gospel writers make no deliberate attempt to defend Jesus
from any of these charges. They simply leave their accounts of
his actions and words to speak for themselves.

☐ If the disciples and the writers *were* conscious of weaknesses or
faults in his character, they have been very clever in suppressing
them—and very much cleverer than the followers and admirers
of other great men have been.

☐ None of the founders and leaders of the great religions—e.g.
Mohammed or Buddha or Confucius—ever claimed that he was
perfect, or sinless; and their followers generally have never made
this claim for them.

Why did Jesus appear at times to conceal his identity?

Why was he so indirect in his claims about himself? If he really

was God the Son, why did he not say so directly and openly
from the beginning, so as to leave no shadow of doubt in people's minds? When some *did* think of him as "the Christ" or as
"the Son of God," why did he tell them not to tell others?

> And whenever the unclean spirits beheld him, they fell
> down before him and cried out, "You are the Son of God."
> And he strictly ordered them not to make him known.

> And he [Jesus] asked them [the disciples], "But who do you
> say that I am?" Peter answered him, "You are the Christ."
> And he charged them to tell no one about him.

☐ *A political reason:* Jesus would have been well aware of the confused and misleading ideas about the Messiah which were circu-
lating at the time (e.g., the idea of the warrior king who would
lead the Jews to drive out the Romans, or the heavenly Son of
man who would descend from the clouds in glory). If he had
repeatedly used titles like "Messiah," he would have identified
himself in the eyes of the people and the Roman authorities with
the extreme nationalists, and he might well have been taken as a
purely political figure.

☐ *A theological reason:* Jesus would also have been aware of the
Jewish emphasis on the oneness of God: "The Lord our God is
one Lord . . ." If he had made direct and unmistakable claims
from the beginning, his hearers might not have been willing
even to give him a hearing. A certain indirectness would force
people to think for themselves and to come gradually to understand the full implications of what he claimed. However, we
must add, that although the claims of Jesus may seem very
indirect and subtle to us today, they would have sounded *less* so
to the well-taught Jew who heard him. No Jew would fail to see
what was implied when Jesus claimed authority to forgive sins—
he would immediately accuse him of blasphemy.

☐ *A moral reason:* when Jesus spoke indirectly about himself, he was
not simply encouraging his hearers to think with their minds. He
was at the same time presenting a challenge to their wills and
their consciences. On one occasion he refused to be more direct
simply because he could see that his questioners were ignoring
the moral challenge in what they already knew.

> As he was walking in the temple, the chief priests and the
> scribes and the elders came to him, and they said to him,
> "By what authority are you doing these things, or who gave
> you this authority to do them?" Jesus said to them, "I will

ask you a question; answer me, and I will tell you by what authority I do these things. Was the baptism of John from heaven or from men? Answer me." And they argued with one another, "If we say, 'From heaven,' he will say, 'Why then did you not believe him?' But shall we say, 'From men'?"—they were afraid of the people, for all held that John was a real prophet. So they answered Jesus, "We do not know." And Jesus said to them, "Neither will I tell you by what authority I do these things."

☐ *The time factor:* when the disciples came to realize that he was the Christ, the Son of God, he told them not to tell anyone openly:

And he asked them, "But who do you say that I am?" Peter answered him, "You are the Christ." And he charged them to tell no one about him.

And he began to teach them that the Son of man must suffer many things . . . and be killed, and after three days rise again.

Very soon after this three of the disciples witnessed the transfiguration, and Jesus gave a similar command:

As they were coming down the mountain, he charged them to tell no one what they had seen, until the Son of man should have risen from the dead. So they kept the matter to themselves, questioning what the rising from the dead meant.

This suggests that Jesus expected that what was hidden and obscure *during* his lifetime would be proclaimed openly to all *after* his death and resurrection.

☐ *Direct answers:* on some occasions when he was presented with a direct question, he gave a direct answer:

The high priest said to him, "I adjure you by the living God, tell us if you are the Christ, the Son of God." Jesus said to him, "You have said so . . ." [or "the words are yours," New English Bible] . . . Then the high priest tore his robes, and said, "He has uttered blasphemy . . ."

Are all the miracle stories equally important and relevant?

Should we not distinguish between the different kinds of miracles, and be prepared to admit that some are less unlikely than others? For example, is it not easier to believe some of the healing miracles because of what we are now finding out about the power of mind over body? This kind of miracle presents fewer problems to the scientific mind than the feeding of the 5,000.

☐ This approach still leaves us with the questions: how are we to define what is a "likely" or "credible" or "suitable" miracle, and what would be "unlikely," or "incredible" or "inappropriate"? It is very hard to draw these dividing lines, and once we start drawing them the critic has every right to say, "Why do you stop there? Why don't you exclude more?"

☐ Everything depends on our assumptions about God and the universe: is he or is he not the Creator and Sustainer of the universe? Is he or is he not the infinite and personal God who wants to demonstrate his existence and his character, and to act in order to meet the needs of men? If we begin with the assumption that he exists, and that this is what he is like, then our question about the miracles becomes: is this miracle story consistent with this idea of God—or is it not? If we reject this assumption, or if we refuse to commit ourselves to it explicitly, our discussion should turn on assumptions rather than on the miracle stories themselves. (See further Part 2, Question Two, "Who or what is God?" and Question Four, "What kind of universe do we live in?")

☐ This question is often based on the assumption that if we do not insist that all the miracles really happened, then it will be easier for the doubter to believe. But it is hard to reconcile this assumption with the realism of the Gospels, which suggest that there was little difference between the effects of the "extraordinary" miracles and the "more ordinary" ones. Many of them played an important part in bringing individuals and groups to believe in Jesus and accept his claims about himself. But there is no suggestion that they persuaded vast numbers of people; and sometimes we are given no idea of whether or not they led the people concerned to believe. All the Gospels speak of the suspicion and ill-feeling and opposition aroused by some of the miracles. And one miracle, the raising of Lazarus from death, led to the final plot to kill Jesus.

Mark shows that right from the beginning the miracles of Jesus aroused opposition:

> And he looked around at them with anger, grieved at their
> hardness of heart, and said to the man, "Stretch out your

hand." He stretched it out, and his hand was restored. The Pharisees went out, and immediately held counsel with the Herodians against him, how to destroy him.

John notes the effects of six of the seven miracles he records:
—Turning the water into wine:

> This, the first of his signs, Jesus did at Cana in Galilee, and manifested his glory; and his disciples believed in him.

—The healing of the son of the official at Capernaum:

> He [the father] himself believed, and all his household.

—The healing of the paralyzed man at the pool in Jerusalem:

> This was why the Jews sought all the more to kill him, because he not only broke the sabbath, but also called God his Father, making himself equal with God.

—The feeding of the 5,000:

> When the people saw the sign which he had done they said, "This is indeed the prophet who is to come into the world!" Perceiving then that they were about to come and take him by force and make him king, Jesus withdrew again.

In the discussion that followed when the crowd found Jesus the next day, he made some very big claims for himself—e.g., "I am the bread which came down from heaven." This was the reaction:

> Many of his disciples, when they heard it, said, "This is a hard saying; who can listen to it?" . . . After this many of his disciples drew back and no longer went about with him.

—The healing of the man blind from birth:

> They [the religious authorities] cast him out. Jesus heard that they had cast him out, and having found him he said, "Do you believe in the Son of man?" He answered, "And who is he, sir, that I may believe in him?" Jesus said to him. "You have seen him, and it is he who speaks to you." He said, "Lord, I believe"; and he worshiped him.

—The raising of Lazarus from the dead:

> Many of the Jews therefore, who had come with Mary and had seen what he did, believed in him; but some of them went to the Pharisees and told them what Jesus had done.

So the chief priests and the Pharisees gathered the council,
and said, "What are we to do? For this man performs many
signs. If we let him go on thus, everyone will believe in
him . . ." So from that day on they took counsel how to put
him to death.

☐ The contrast between the miracles recorded in the Gospels and
the miracles recorded in the apocryphal Gospels and the Qur'an
(see pp. 407, 408) is very significant.

The Gospel of Thomas includes the following stories in which
the boy Jesus works miracles largely to get himself out of awkward situations:

> Now on a day, when Jesus climbed up upon an house with
> the children, he began to play with them: but one of the
> boys fell down through the door out of the upper chamber
> and died straightway. And when the children saw it they
> fled all of them, but Jesus remained alone in the house.
> And when the parents of the child which had died came
> they spake against Jesus saying: Of a truth thou madest
> him fall. But Jesus said: I never made him fall: nevertheless
> they accused him still. Jesus therefore came down from the
> house and stood over the dead child and cried with a loud
> voice, calling him by his name: Zeno, Zeno, arise and say if
> I made thee fall. And on a sudden he arose and said: Nay,
> Lord. And when his parents saw this great miracle which
> Jesus did, they glorified God, and worshiped Jesus.

> And when Jesus was six years old, his mother sent him to
> draw water. And when Jesus was come unto the well there
> was much people there and they brake his pitcher. But he
> took the cloak which he had upon him and filled it with
> water and brought it to Mary his mother. And when his
> mother saw the miracle that Jesus did she kissed him and
> said: Lord, hearken unto me and save my son.

How could a single personality
be both human and divine?

It is one thing to conceive of God as a personal Being; but it is
very difficult, if not impossible, to conceive of this God uniting
himself in any way with human nature. And if a man has a fully
human personality, how can he at the same time be fully divine?

☐ Everything here depends on our assumptions about God and
man. The Christian believes that man has been created in the
image and likeness of God:

> Then God said, "Let us make man in our image, after our
> likeness . . ."
>
> When God created man, he made him in the likeness of
> God. Male and female he created them, and he blessed
> them, and named them Man when they were created . . .
> Adam . . . became the father of a son in his own likeness,
> after his image, and named him Seth . . .

The image of God in man has been marred and spoiled by
man's rebellion against God, but it has not been obliterated or
defaced completely. Even fallen man is *like God* in certain respects. There is not a total discontinuity between God and man.
Godhead and humanity are not opposites. If we begin with this
assumption, then we may be prepared to believe that Jesus could
be both human and divine *provided* the detailed evidence for it is
compelling.

If, on the other hand, we believe that God is "the Wholly
Other," who is remote and completely different from man, then
there can hardly be any point of contact between them. The gulf
between deity and humanity becomes too great to be bridged in
a single personality.

If we interpret the oneness of God as a strictly literal oneness,
no amount of detailed evidence will make us revise our ideas of
what oneness could be. We may allow that in the physical world
there can be different kinds of unity, like the complex unity of
the atom. And we may allow that husband and wife are "a unity"
(as the writer of Genesis says). But if we insist on sticking to our
assumption of a literal oneness, then it will always be inconceivable that Jesus could be anything more than a man in close
touch with God.

☐ If we approach the question from a purely biblical point of view,
we find that the enigma of humanity and deity combined in a
single personality is already implicit in Daniel's visions of the
"son of man." Every Jew was brought up to believe the statement
Jesus used to refute Satan (Matthew 4:10): "You shall worship
the Lord your God, and him only shall you serve." Daniel's
vision of the son of man must therefore have sounded strange, if
not incredible to Jewish ears:

> I saw in the night visions,
> and behold, with the clouds of heaven
>   there came one like a son of man,

and he came to the Ancient of Days
   and was presented before him.
And to him was given dominion and glory
and kingdom,
   that all peoples, nations, and languages
should serve him;
his dominion is an everlasting dominion,
   which shall not pass away,
and his kingdom one that shall not be destroyed.

We may well ask: who can this "son of man" be who is worshiped by people of all nations and languages? How can God give him the "dominion and glory and kingdom" which belong exclusively to himself? When Jesus adopted the title "son of man," he probably took it from these passages in Daniel.

☐ As far as the New Testament is concerned we need to look at the problem from the standpoint of the first disciples. When they first met Jesus, they were confronted by a man who was every bit as human as they were. Nothing in their experience of him during the three years of his ministry can have made them doubt his real humanity. Even when they saw his miracles, they saw them as the work of a man: "*What sort of man* is this, that even winds and sea obey him?" (Matthew 8:27). At the same time, the combined evidence of his character, his claims, and his miracles forced them to associate him more and more closely with God.

Obviously they could not have arrived at this position in an instant; and when they did, they would not have wanted (or been able) to formulate any philosophical concept of a God-man. All they could do was to say in effect, "All the evidence points to the fact that this man Jesus is truly one of us; he is *one with us.* He must also be *one with God*, and in some sense must be God." The New Testament writers therefore do not try to explain philosophically how a single personality could be divine and human; they simply paint a portrait of Jesus as they knew him, and use every title they can think of to identify him *both* with God *and* with man.

What is the meaning of the term "Son of God"?

If a person who believes in Jesus can be called a "son of God" (see Part 2, pp. 224, 225) in what sense can Jesus be called "*the* Son of God"?

☐ *The Old Testament background.* In the Old Testament the metaphor of the father-son relationship is used in different ways

to refer to those who have a special relationship of some kind
with God.

For example, *Job* speaks of the angels as sons of God:

> Where were you when I laid the
> foundation of the earth? . . .
> On what were its bases sunk,
> or who laid its cornerstone,
> when the morning stars sang together,
> and all the sons of God shouted for joy?

Hosea says of the people of Israel:

> When Israel was a child, I loved him,
> and out of Egypt I called my son.

Israel's king is described in these words:

> Thus says the Lord of hosts [to David], I took you from the
> pasture, from following the sheep, that you should be
> prince over my people Israel . . . When your days are ful-
> filled and you lie down with your fathers, I will raise up
> your offspring after you, who shall come forth from your
> body, and I will establish his kingdom . . . I will be his
> father, and he shall be my son. When he commits iniquity,
> I will chasten him with the rod of men . . .

☐ *Jesus' use of the father-son metaphor* (see the references on pp. 382,
383). In all these sayings Jesus speaks of a relationship of deep
intimacy with God. And when he makes a sharp distinction
between "my Father" and "your Father," he implies that there is
something unique about his sonship; he is not merely an ordinary man who is very conscious of God.

☐ *The main ideas implied in the metaphor.* The phrase is not used to
say anything about the *origin* of Jesus, the eternal Son, but
rather to say something about his *relationship* with God. It does
not tell us "where he came from," because the eternal Son has
always been with the Father and the Spirit; it simply tells us
about his relationship with the Father. There seem to be at least
three main ideas associated with the father-son relationship in
the Bible:
—Likeness ("like father, like son"). In this case, the idea is that
Jesus is supremely "like God"; his character bears the closest
possible resemblance to the character of God. When a person
becomes a Christian, he becomes a "son of God" or a "child of

God" in a derived sense. And the family likeness is meant to be evident in the Christian. *John* writes:

> See what love the Father has given us, that we should be called children of God; and so we are. The reason why the world does not know us is that it did not know him. Beloved, we are God's children now; it does not yet appear what we shall be, but we know that when he appears we shall be like him, for we shall see him as he is.

—Knowledge. One might say that in an ordinary family, the better the father, the better he will know his son, and the better the son will know his father. This knowledge should be mutual with father and son understanding and knowing each other intimately. This is the idea expressed in these words of Jesus:

> I thank thee, Father, Lord of heaven and earth, that thou hast hidden these things from the wise and understanding and revealed them to babes; yea, Father, for such was thy gracious will. All things have been delivered to me by my Father; and no one knows the Son except the Father, and no one knows the Father except the Son and any one to whom the Son chooses to reveal him . . .

> If I glorify myself, my glory is nothing; it is my Father who glorifies me, of whom you say that he is your God. But you have not known him; I know him. If I said, I do not know him, I should be a liar like you; but I do know him and I keep his word.

—Obedience. Life in a family is impossible unless there is a real measure of willingness on the part of the child to listen to his father and respect his wishes. It can never be a total obedience and it is for a limited period. The writer of Proverbs speaks in this way about this relationship of obedience:

> My son, do not forget my teaching,
>   but let your heart keep my commandments.

> Hear, O sons, a father's instruction,
>   and be attentive, that you may gain insight;
> for I give you good precepts:
>   do not forsake my teaching.
> When I was a son with my father,
>   tender, the only one in the sight of my mother,
> he taught me . . .

441

When applied to Jesus the idea of sonship points to his complete obedience to God the Father. This submission springs out of love:

> The Son can do nothing of his own accord, but only what he sees the Father doing; for whatever he does, that Son does likewise. For the Father loves the Son, and shows him all that he himself is doing.

Weren't there many myths about gods coming to earth and about virgin births? And what is the difference between the incarnation of Jesus and the incarnations of Hindu gods?

Is there really anything unique about the belief that Jesus is a God-man? Was it not a common idea at the time? Is it not obvious that the early Christians took over the idea from pagan sources around them?

☐ The background to the stories of gods coming to earth is always polytheistic. They arise out of the belief that there are many gods with different functions and powers, and with a special interest in particular people or places. This is very different from the biblical idea of the one Creator-God who is "the Lord of all the earth." In Hinduism, the concept of "God" as the "universal Spirit" is very different from the Christian understanding of the infinite, personal God. (See Part 2, pp. 168, 169 and 148ff.).

☐ Many of the ancient myths about gods coming to earth were associated with the mystery religions or the fertility cults, whose rituals were intended to assist the annual cycle of nature. (See further pp. 547ff.).

Thomas Boslooper concludes a comparative study of such stories by underlining the vast difference in outlook between the biblical account and the other stories:

> The story of the virgin birth is as different from pagan "analogies" as monotheism is from polytheism, as different as biblical ideas of the relationship between God and man are from the mythological activities of gods in human affairs, and as different as the polygamous and incestuous pagan society was from the Christian teaching on morals and marriage. Primitive Christianity as opposed to Gentile thought (Greek, Roman, Egyptian, Babylonian, and Persian) believed in marriage as over against asceticism and monogamy as over against polygamy. Over against early Catholic Christianity (as reflected in apocryphal tradition)

and Buddhist thought, it believed that sex in itself was not sinful and that moral order could result from the human process of birth. Furthermore, primitive Christianity did not project its hope for a new society into the life of the gods, i.e., into suprahuman speculation. Its hope for humanity lay in reflection on him who was the first in a new order within society.

Professor Zaehner, who himself writes out of a Hindu background, emphasizes the vast difference between Christian assumptions and Hindu assumptions. The incarnation of Jesus, therefore, has little or no connection with Hindu incarnations of "God."

> . . . to maintain that all religions are paths leading to the same goal, as is frequently done today, is to maintain something that is not true.

> Not only on the dogmatic, but also on the mystical plane, too, there is no agreement.

> It is then only too true that the basic principles of Eastern and Western, which in practice means Indian and Semitic, thought are, I will not say irreconcilably opposed; they are simply not starting from the same premises. The only common ground is that the function of religion is to provide release; there is no agreement at all as to what it is that man must be released from. The great religions are talking at cross purposes.

> It is therefore foolish to discuss either Hinduism or Buddhism in Christian terms; and it is at least as foolish to try to bring the New Testament into harmony with the Vedanta. They do not deal with the same subject matter. Even Indian theism is not comparable with Christianity in a way that, for example, Zoroastrianism and Islam are; nor are the various avatars of Vishnu really comparable to the Christian doctrine of the Incarnation.

Does the death of Jesus mean anything more than the death of any other historical figure? Did it achieve anything?

Our answers to these questions will depend partly on our general assumptions about Jesus, and partly on our interpretation of the Old Testament and the Gospel accounts.

QUESTION SIX:
WHAT IS THE MEANING
OF THE DEATH OF JESUS?

Randy Birkey

THE OLD TESTAMENT BACKGROUND

The teaching of the Old Testament formed the background of the thinking of Jesus and the disciples. The following are some of the basic truths which they would have learned from the Old Testament.

The relationship between God and man

The Old Testament speaks of both the *personal* aspect and the *legal* aspect of the relationship between God and man. God deals with men in a fully personal way; but at the same time he is the one who has given man the law and who judges man by that law.

☐ *The personal aspect.* Many of the writers of the Bible describe the relationship between God and man in incredibly personal·and human terms.

Hosea the prophet speaking on behalf of God:

When Israel was a child, I loved him . . .
The more I called them,
   the more they went from me;
they kept sacrificing to the Baals,
   and burning incense to idols.
Yet it was I who taught Ephraim to walk,
   I took them up in my arms;
   but they did not know that I healed them.
I led them with the cords of compassion,
   with the bands of love,
and I became to them as one
   who eases the yoke on their jaws,
   and I bent down to them and fed them.

☐ *The legal aspect.* This is how Moses speaks about the laws which God has given to the nation:

All the commandments which I command you this day you shall be careful to do, that you may live and multiply, and go in and possess the land which the Lord swore to give to your fathers . . . So you shall keep the commandments of the Lord your God, by walking in his ways and by fearing him . . . Take heed lest you forget the Lord your God, by not keeping his commandments and his ordinances and his

447

statutes, which I command you this day . . . And if you forget the Lord your God and go after other gods and serve them and worship them, I solemnly warn you this day that you shall surely perish. Like the nations that the Lord makes to perish before you, so shall you perish, because you would not obey the voice of the Lord your God.

God's attitude to man the sinner

God is both loving and holy. This means that he loves the sinner and longs for the very best for him; but at the same time he cannot accept man's rebellion lightly. He is not morally neutral, and he cannot simply forgive the sin of those who persist in their rebellion against him and refuse to accept their guilt before him. He cannot turn a blind eye or act as if nothing had happened. Man's sin is a personal affront to God; but it is also at the same time a violation of his laws. And when the laws are broken, the sanctions must be applied. Thus God's reaction to man in his sin can be summed up in two words: love and wrath.

This is what God reveals to *Moses* about his own character:

The Lord, the Lord, a God merciful and gracious, slow to anger, and abounding in steadfast love and faithfulness, keeping steadfast love for thousands, forgiving iniquity and transgression and sin, but who will by no means clear the guilty . . .

These are the words of *Jeremiah* speaking on behalf of God:

How can I pardon you?
Your children have forsaken me,
and have sworn by those who are no gods.
When I fed them to the full,
they committed adultery
and trooped to the houses of harlots.
They were well-fed lusty stallions,
each neighing for his neighbor's wife.
Shall I not punish them for these things?
says the Lord.

These are the words of *Ezekiel* speaking on behalf of God:

Have I any pleasure in the death of the wicked, says the Lord God, and not rather that he should turn from his way and live?

The connection between sin and death

The book of Genesis speaks of death as an intruder in the

human race, and as something closely tied up with man's rebellion against God. It tells how God tested the obedience of Adam and Eve:

> The Lord God commanded the man, saying, "You may freely eat of every tree of the garden; but of the tree of the knowledge of good and evil you shall not eat, for in the day that you eat of it you shall die."

Adam and Eve chose to disobey because they wanted to become gods themselves and to cease being dependent on their Creator. These were some of the consequences of their disobedience:

> more acute physical suffering;

> physical death (although we are not told what human life would have been like if they had not been disobedient);

> they forfeited the possibility of living in constant fellowship and communion with God.

This Old Testament teaching about the inseparable connection between sin and death is summarized by *Paul* and *James* in these words:

> Sin came into the world through one man and death through sin, and so death spread to all men because all men sinned.

> The wages of sin is death . . .

> . . . desire when it has conceived gives birth to sin; and sin when it is full-grown brings forth death.

Dealing with sin and its consequences

The sacrificial system points to a way of "bearing sin." The New Testament writers were familiar with all the sacrifices of the Old Testament period. And they regarded them as part of a system instituted by God himself to teach fundamental truths about his dealings with men.

☐ The expression "to bear sin (or sins)" means "to be responsible for sin and to bear the consequences of it."

For instance, when a person breaks the laws of God governing social life and worship, it is said of him:

> He shall *bear his iniquity.*

> He shall *bear his sin.*

This amounts to saying, "He shall be responsible for the wrong he has done; and he shall bear the punishment his wrongdoing deserves."

☐In one case we read that one person can bear the sins of another person:

> He shall *bear her iniquity.*

In the sacrificial system certain animals are said to "bear sin":

> The sin offering . . . has been given to you [the sons of Aaron, the priests] that you may *bear the iniquity* of the congregation.

☐On the Day of Atonement each year Aaron was to confess the sins of the people as he laid his hands on the head of the goat, and . . .

> the goat shall *bear all their iniquities* upon him to a solitary land.

These sacrifices were intended to bring home to the Jew in a vivid and dramatic way certain basic truths:

> that sin and guilt have to be punished;

> that if men bear the consequences of their sin and guilt, it means death;

> that forgiveness is available to men, not because God turns a blind eye to sin and acts as if it does not exist, but because the full responsibility and consequences of it can be borne by another;

> that the sacrifices were not simply the expression of homage of man the creature to his Creator, but also of man the sinner to the God against whom he had sinned;

> that there is a way by which the guilty party can be acquitted and forgiven without setting aside or annulling the law of God.

☐The prophet *Isaiah* speaks not of an animal bearing sin, but of *a person* who will bear sins. He is speaking about someone whom he calls "the Servant of the Lord," and these are some of the things which he says about him:

> He was wounded for our transgressions,
>   he was bruised for our iniquities;
> upon him was the chastisement that made
>   us whole,
>   and with his stripes we are healed . . .
> The Lord has laid on him the iniquity of us all.

He shall *bear their iniquities.*

He *bore the sin* of many.

Yet it was the will of the Lord to bruise him;
    he has put him to grief;
when he makes himself an offering for sin,
    he shall see his offspring, he shall prolong
    his days.

The identity of the Servant of the Lord is left open. Isaiah can
hardly be speaking of himself or of any known person or of the
nation as a whole when he speaks about him "bearing sins."

The death penalty

Under the Old Testament law *the death penalty* was prescribed for
various offenses:

Whoever curses his God shall bear his sin. He who blas-
phemes the name of the Lord shall be put to death.

A hanged person was regarded as being *under a curse from God*:

If a man has committed a crime punishable by death and
he is put to death, and you hang him on a tree, his body
shall not remain all night upon the tree; but you shall bury
him the same day, for a hanged man is accursed by God.

JESUS' OWN TEACHING ABOUT HIS DEATH

Mark records three predictions which Jesus made of his approaching death:

And he began to teach them that the Son of man must
suffer many things, and be rejected by the elders and the
chief priests and the scribes, and be killed, and after three
days rise again. And he said this plainly.

They went on from there and passed through Galilee. And
he would not have any one know it; for he was teaching his
disciples, saying to them, "The Son of man will be delivered
into the hands of men, and they will kill him; and when he
is killed, after three days he will rise."

And they were on the road, going up to Jerusalem, and
Jesus was walking ahead of them; and they were amazed,
and those who followed were afraid. And taking the twelve
again, he began to tell them what was to happen to him,
saying, "Behold, we are going up to Jerusalem; and the Son

of man will be delivered to the chief priests and the scribes, and they will condemn him to death, and deliver him to the Gentiles; and they will mock him, and spit upon him, and scourge him, and kill him; and after three days he will rise."

Jesus did not give a detailed explanation of why he was going to die. But he gave certain important indications or clues as to what it would mean.

Jesus as the suffering Servant

Jesus identified himself with the suffering Servant of Isaiah. In his predictions of his sufferings there are echoes of the description of the suffering of the Servant. Compare, for example, Mark 8:31, "The Son of man must suffer many things, and be rejected . . . and be killed . . ." with Isaiah 53:3,8, "He was despised and rejected by men. . . . By oppression and judgment he was taken away. . . ." And Mark 10:15, "The Son of man . . . came not to be served but to serve, and to give his life as a ransom for many" with Isaiah 53:10, "It was the will of the Lord to bruise him . . . he makes himself an offering for sin" ("ransom" is another possible translation for "offering for sin" here).

Good news

Jesus saw his death as part of the good news to be spread throughout the world. At a party in Bethany a short time before his death a woman anointed Jesus with expensive ointment, and there were complaints about the waste:

> But Jesus said, "Let her alone; why do you trouble her? She has done a beautiful thing to me . . . She has done what she could; she has anointed my body beforehand for burying. And truly, I say to you, wherever the gospel is preached in the whole world, what she has done will be told in memory of her."

Connection with the Passover

Jesus connected the meaning of his death with the Passover. When he celebrated the Passover with his disciples, just before his arrest—commemorating the deliverance of Israel from Egypt—he gave some parts of the meal a new significance:

> And as they were eating, he took bread, and blessed, and broke it, and gave it to them, and said, "Take; this is my body." And he took a cup, and when he had given thanks

he gave it to them, and they all drank of it. And he said to
them, "This is my blood of the covenant, which is poured
out for many. Truly, I say to you, I shall not drink again of
the fruit of the vine until that day when I drink it new in
the kingdom of God."

God's judgment on sin

Jesus connected his death with the judgment of God on human
sin. He thought of the suffering and death before him as "a cup"
held out to him by the Father:

And going a little farther he fell on his face and prayed,
"My Father, if it be possible, let this cup pass from me;
nevertheless, not as I will, but as thou wilt."

Again, for the second time, he went away and prayed, "My
Father, if this cannot pass unless I drink it, thy will be
done."

There is an echo here of the many passages in the Old Testament which speak of the cup of the wrath of God—for example:

For in the hand of the Lord there is a cup,
    with foaming wine, well mixed;
and he will pour a draught from it,
    and all the wicked of the earth
    shall drain it down to the dregs.

Thus the Lord, the God of Israel, said to me: "Take from
my hand this cup of the wine of wrath, and make all the
nations to whom I send you drink it. They shall drink and
stagger and be crazed because of the sword which I am
sending among them."

Rouse yourself, rouse yourself,
    stand up, O Jerusalem,
you who have drunk at the hand of the Lord
    the cup of his wrath,
who have drunk to the dregs
    the bowl of staggering.

THE CIRCUMSTANCES OF HIS DEATH

Jesus' last week is reported in all four Gospels in much greater
detail than any other period of his life. This suggests that the
writers saw a great deal of significance in the actual events
leading up to his death. If we put the four accounts together,
certain points stand out clearly.

453

☐ He went to his death voluntarily. The words and actions of Jesus provoked opposition from the religious authorities at an early stage in his ministry. When Jesus made his final journey to Jerusalem he knew that he was going to die.

He must have known what was involved in scourging and execution at the hands of the Romans. They would use a flagellum, a whip of leather thongs, to which small pieces of metal or bone were tied. People sometimes died under the scourge. The procedure for crucifixion was this: the two hands were nailed to the cross-beam while the victim was still on the ground; the cross-beam would then be drawn up by ropes and fastened to the upright part of the cross. The feet would then be nailed to the upright. The victim rarely died in less than thirty-six hours, but could be put out of his misery at any time by having his legs broken with a hammer, which would soon lead to suffocation; or his side could be pierced by a sword.

Right up to the moment before his arrest, Jesus was aware that he could avoid this kind of death if he wanted to. He did not believe that he was caught in a trap from which he could not escape.

> They went to a place which was called Gethsemane . . . And he took with him Peter and James and John, and began to be greatly distressed and troubled. And he said to them, "My soul is very sorrowful, even to death . . ." And going a little farther, he fell on the ground and prayed that, if it were possible, the hour might pass from him. And he said, "Abba, Father, all things are possible to thee; remove this cup from me; yet not what I will, but what thou wilt."

☐ It is significant also that he had done nothing to deserve the death penalty. The Jewish authorities realized that their own charge of blasphemy would mean nothing according to Roman law. They therefore handed him over to Pilate, the Roman Governor, on a charge of treason against the state. They accused him of claiming to be "the king of the Jews" and thereby posing a threat to the authority of Caesar:

> And Pilate asked him, "Are you the King of the Jews?" And he answered him, "You have said so." . . . Pilate again said to them, "Then what shall I do with the man you call the King of the Jews?" And they cried out again, "Crucify him." And Pilate said to them, "Why, what evil has he done?" But they shouted all the more, "Crucify him." So Pilate, wishing to satisfy the crowd, released for them

Barabbas; and having scourged Jesus, he delivered him to
be crucified.

Pilate tried in three ways to avoid passing the sentence of
death which the Jewish authorities wanted him to pass:

he tried to pass the responsibility over to Herod, the puppet
king;

he offered to punish Jesus simply with a flogging and then to
release him;

and finally he offered to release Jesus as a gesture of goodwill
during the Passover feast.

But the Jewish authorities and the crowd were not satisfied, and
in the end Pilate passed the sentence of death on Jesus simply to
satisfy their demands and avoid a riot.

It was obvious to at least four people that he had done
nothing to deserve the death penalty:

Pilate:

I find no crime in him.

Herod:

Nothing deserving death has been done by him.

One of the criminals crucified with him:

We are receiving the due reward of our deeds; but this
man has done nothing wrong.

The *Roman centurion* who watched him dying:

Certainly this man was innocent!

Jesus' last recorded words

And when they came to the place which is called The Skull,
there they crucified him, and the criminals, one on the
right and one on the left. And Jesus said, "Father forgive
them; for they know not what they do."

When Jesus saw his mother, and the disciple whom he
loved standing near, he said to his mother, "Woman, behold your son!" Then he said to the disciple, "Behold your
mother!"

455

One of the criminals being crucified beside Jesus began mocking him, but later came to change his mind about him:

> And he said, "Jesus, remember me when you come into your kingdom." And he said to him, "Truly, I say to you, today you will be with me in Paradise."

> At the ninth hour Jesus cried with a loud voice, "Eloi, Eloi, lama sabachthani?" which means, "My God, my God, why hast thou forsaken me?"

> Then Jesus, crying with a loud voice, said, "Father, into thy hands I commit my spirit!"

> After this Jesus, knowing that all was now finished, said (to fulfill the scripture), "I thirst." A bowl full of vinegar stood there; so they put a sponge full of the vinegar on hyssop and held it to his mouth. When Jesus had received the vinegar, he said, "It is finished"; and he bowed his head and gave up his spirit.

WHAT IS THE MEANING OF THE DEATH OF JESUS?

His death achieved something—he was bearing our sins.
PAGE 459

He died as an example—his death shows us something about God and man.
PAGE 469

His death has no special meaning.
PAGE 474

The cross is merely a symbol—any interpretation is "myth."
PAGE 477

ANSWER ONE:
BIBLICAL CHRISTIANITY

His death achieved
something—he was
bearing our sins.

*This is to say, Jesus was bearing the
guilt and consequences of human sin.
He was dying in our place and enduring what we deserve for our proud rebellion against our Creator. His death
can deal with the guilt of our past, and
can bring us into a new relationship
with God in the present. We can enjoy
increasing deliverance from the power
of sin in our lives and all the other
positive benefits of his death.*

Almost every writer of the New Testament gives an explanation
of *how* the death of Jesus achieved something. They take as their

starting-point that the death of Jesus deals with the sin of men:
John records John the Baptist's description of Jesus:

> Behold, the Lamb of God, who *takes away* [i.e. bears] *the sin* of the world.

> . . . Jesus Christ the righteous; and he is the *expiation for our sins*, and not for ours only but also for the sins of the whole world.

Luke records some of the last words of Jesus before his ascension:

> Thus it is written, that the Christ should suffer and on the third day rise from the dead, and that repentance and *forgiveness of sins* should be preached in his name to all nations . . .

Peter:

> He himself *bore our sins* in his body on the tree.

> Christ . . . *died for sins* once for all, the righteous for the unrighteous, that he might bring us to God.

Paul:

> Christ died *for our sins.*

The writer to the Hebrews:

> . . . he . . . *made purification for sins* . . .

POINTS TO CONSIDER ABOUT THIS ANSWER

This answer makes sense of the Old Testament background.

☐ It takes seriously both the *personal* aspect of the relationship between God and man, and also the *legal* aspect. There is, through the cross, both forgiveness for the personal injury to God and for the disobedience to his laws:

> And you, who were dead in trespasses and the uncircumcision of your flesh, God made alive together with him, having forgiven us all our trespasses, having canceled the bond which stood against us with its legal demands; this he set aside, nailing it to the cross.

☐It does justice both to the *wrath* of God and to the *love* of God toward the sinner. It is the love of God which turns aside the wrath of God and all its consequences:

> God shows his love for us in that while we were yet sinners Christ died for us. Since, therefore, we are now justified by his blood, much more shall we be saved by him from the wrath of God.

> In this is love, not that we loved God but that he loved us and sent his Son to be the propitiation for our sins.

The word propitiation conveys the idea of turning aside the wrath of God.

☐It fits in with the close connection the Old Testament sees between *sin* and *death*.

> The death he died he died to sin, once for all, but the life he lives he lives to God.

> The wages of sin is death, but the free gift of God is eternal life in Christ Jesus our Lord.

☐It explains how the system of sacrifices, which were said to "bear sin," has been fulfilled:

> When Christ had offered for all time a single sacrifice for sins, he sat down at the right hand of God, then to wait until his enemies should be made a stool for his feet. For by a single offering he has perfected for all time those who are sanctified. . . . Where there is forgiveness . . . there is no longer any offering for sin.

☐ It explains the sense in which Jesus could be under a *curse* from God as he hung on the cross:

> Christ redeemed us from the curse of the law, having become a curse for us—for it is written, "Cursed be every one who hangs on a tree" . . .

It makes sense of Jesus' own teaching about his death.
☐It explains why he identified himself with the Servant of the Lord in the book of Isaiah.

Thus, when *Peter* writes about the meaning of the death of Jesus there are very definite echoes of the passages about the Servant who bears sins:

> He committed no sin; no guile was found on his lips (1

461

Peter 2:22) / He had done no violence, and there was no deceit in his mouth (Isaiah 53:9)

He was reviled (1 Peter 2:23) / He was despised and rejected by men (Isaiah 53:3)

He himself bore our sins (1 Peter 2:24) / He bore the sin of many (Isaiah 53:12)

By his wounds you have been healed (1 Peter 2:24) / With his stripes we are healed (Isaiah 53:5)

You were straying like sheep (1 Peter 2:25) / All we like sheep have gone astray (Isaiah 53:6)

☐ It explains how he could think of his death as being part of the good news for all men. For if his death is connected with God's forgiveness, then his death is part of the good news that must be spread to all men.

Thus, *Jesus* explains to the disciples after his resurrection:

Then he opened their minds to understand the scriptures, and said to them, "Thus it is written, that the Christ should suffer and on the third day rise from the dead, and that repentance and forgiveness of sins should be preached in his name to all nations, beginning from Jerusalem . . ."

☐ It explains why he connected his death with the Passover. We can begin to understand the intention of Jesus when we notice the significance of the first Passover. On the night before the Israelites' deliverance from Egypt, each household killed a lamb and sprinkled some of the blood on the two doorposts and on the lintel. The flesh was cooked and eaten with bread and herbs. This was the meaning of the ceremony:

It is the Lord's passover. For I will pass through the land of Egypt that night, and I will smite all the first-born in the land of Egypt, both man and beast . . . The blood shall be a sign for you, upon the houses where you are; and when I see the blood, I will pass over you, and no plague shall fall upon you to destroy you, when I smite the land of Egypt.

This is how the children of Israel were commanded to commemorate each year the deliverance from Egypt:

Observe the month of Abib, and keep the passover to the Lord your God; for in the month of Abib the Lord your God brought you out of Egypt by night. And you shall offer the passover sacrifice to the Lord your God, from the

flock or the herd . . . seven days you shall eat it with un-
leavened bread, the bread of affliction . . . that all the days
of your life you may remember the day when you came out
of the land of Egypt.

Jesus' death achieved a new deliverance for men. Thus *Paul*
writes:

Christ, our paschal lamb, has been sacrificed.

Peter:

You know that you were ransomed from the futile ways
inherited from your fathers, not with perishable things such
as silver or gold, but with the precious blood of Christ, like
that of a lamb without blemish or spot.

☐ It explains how he connected his death with the judgment of
God on human sin. If Jesus bore our sins, he has also borne the
condemnation that we deserve.

Thus *Paul* writes:

There is therefore now no condemnation for those who are
in Christ Jesus. For the law of the Spirit of life in Christ
Jesus has set me free from the law of sin and death. For
God has done what the law, weakened by the flesh, could
not do: sending his own Son in the likeness of sinful flesh
and for sin, he condemned sin in the flesh . . .

It makes sense of the circumstances of his death.

☐ It accounts for Jesus' willingness to go through suffering and
death, which he could easily have avoided if he had wanted to.
Thus, when Peter starts to fight to defend Jesus:

Jesus said to Peter, "Put your sword in its sheath; shall I
not drink the cup which the Father has given me?"

☐ It makes sense of some of his last words: "Father forgive them
. . ." His attitude towards those who killed him is a demonstration of the willingness of God to forgive. One of the criminals
asked Jesus to remember him when he came in his kingly power.
Jesus answered, "Today you will be with me in Paradise." He
thus pointed to the victory and royal triumph which would
immediately be won by his death.

"My God, my God, why hast thou forsaken me?" If we are
prepared to take these words at their face value, we must recog-

nize that Jesus was *not* saying, "O God, I feel as if you have forsaken me—although I trust that you must still be with me." What he was saying, rather, was something much more profound and horrifying: "My God, my God, *you have forsaken me. Why?*" These words begin to make sense if we understand that Jesus was actually bearing the judgment of God on man's sin.

"It is finished." These words suggest that Jesus was conscious of something that had been achieved by all his suffering and agony. He was conscious not only that his life was ending, but also that he had accomplished something permanent.

This interpretation also makes sense of the many different metaphors used by the New Testament writers to describe what Jesus achieved by his death. It also shows how these different metaphors are related to each other, because it provides a basic link that binds them together.

☐ The metaphor of *justification* comes from the law court and means simply "acquittal." If Jesus was bearing the judgment of God on human sin, then for those who believe in Jesus and accept for themselves the benefits of his death, there is complete acquittal before God. The verdict of "guilty" no longer stands against them, and they can now enjoy fellowship with God without fear or shame.

> Therefore, since we are justified by faith, we have peace with God through our Lord Jesus Christ . . . God shows his love for us in that while we were yet sinners Christ died for us.

☐ The metaphor of *redemption* or *ransom* comes from the Old Testament idea of the kinsman redeemer and from the slave-market, where a person could be redeemed through the payment of a fee. This metaphor, therefore, emphasizes that the forgiveness God offers on the basis of the death of Jesus cost him something. There was no simple announcement of forgiveness. It shows that if it costs men something to forgive each other, the cost for God in forgiving rebellious man is infinitely greater.

> You know that you were ransomed from the futile ways inherited from your fathers, not with perishable things such as silver or gold, but with the precious blood of Christ . . .

☐ The metaphor of *victory* emphasizes that in the death of Jesus a decisive victory was won over sin and death and over the supernatural powers of evil that lie behind the rebellion of the human race against God. By this victory he had liberated men who were held prisoners of sin, death, and the devil. If Jesus was bearing the sins of men when he died on the cross, we have an explanation as to *why* and *how* Jesus was able to gain the victory over the devil.

> . . . You, who were dead in trespasses and the uncircumcision of your flesh, God made alive together with him, having forgiven us all our trespasses, having canceled the bond which stood against us with its legal demands; this he set aside, nailing it to the cross. He disarmed the principalities and powers and made a public example of them, triumphing over them in him.

☐ The metaphor of *reconciliation* stresses that man has broken off relations with God, and also that God cannot turn a blind eye to man's rebellion against him and act as if nothing had happened. If we understand that Jesus was dying in our place on the cross, this metaphor stresses that God himself has taken the initiative in doing something to win men back into fellowship with himself.

> God shows his love for us in that while we were yet sinners Christ died for us . . . For if while we were enemies we were reconciled to God by the death of his Son, much more, now that we are reconciled, shall we be saved by his life. Not only so, but we also rejoice in God through our Lord Jesus Christ, through whom we have now received our reconciliation.

☐ The metaphor of *salvation* comes from the many occasions in the Old Testament when the children of Israel were delivered or saved from a desperate situation. If we think of the death of Jesus as the remedy for the guilt and power of sin, then the word *salvation* stresses the completeness of the deliverance from the consequences and power of sin available through the death of Christ. If Christ was bearing sins on the cross, this is the means by which the deliverance has been achieved.

> Since, therefore, we are now justified by his blood, much more shall we be saved by him from the wrath of God.

This answer provides us with a starting point from which we can go on to see what the death of Jesus must mean in the experience of the individual Christian. To say that Jesus was bearing the sins of men when he died on the cross by no means exhausts all that can or should be said about the death of Jesus. But without this basic starting point, anything else that we may say lacks an adequate foundation and leaves many questions unanswered.

☐ The way Jesus reacted to undeserved abuse and suffering is an example the Christian is bound to follow:

> Christ . . . suffered for you, leaving you an example, that you should follow in his steps. He committed no sin; no guile was found on his lips. When he was reviled, he did not revile in return; when he suffered, he did not threaten; but he trusted him who judges justly.
>
> . . . rejoice in so far as you share Christ's sufferings, that you may also rejoice and be glad when his glory is revealed.

☐ The way Jesus renounced self-interest and went to the cross for the sake of others shows the Christian that he too must say no to his self-centeredness and be willing to be closely identified with Jesus in the eyes of the world. He must also be prepared to receive the same kind of treatment that Jesus received.

> If any man would come after me, let him deny himself and take up his cross daily and follow me . . . For whoever is ashamed of me and of my words, of him will the Son of man be ashamed when he comes in his glory and the glory of the Father and of the holy angels.

This is how *Paul* longs to be identified fully with Jesus; he wants to receive his righteousness, to share his sufferings, and be like him in his denial of self in death:

> . . . whatever gain I had, I counted as loss for the sake of Christ. Indeed I count everything as loss because of the surpassing worth of knowing Christ Jesus my Lord. For his sake I have suffered the loss of all things, and count them as refuse, in order that I may gain Christ and be found in him, not having a righteousness of my own, based on law, but that which is through faith in Christ, the righteousness from God that depends on faith; that I may know him and the power of his resurrection, and may share his sufferings, becoming like him in his death. . . .

Jesus' willingness to die to self when he went to the cross is the strongest possible plea that we should die to self and live for him and not ourselves:

> . . . the love of Christ controls us, because we are convinced

that one has died for all; therefore all have died. And he
died for all, that those who live might live no longer for
themselves but for him who for their sake died and was
raised.

The way Jesus went willingly to death, the death of the worst
kind of criminal, is a powerful incentive to an attitude of humility:

Have this mind among yourselves, which you have in Christ
Jesus, who, though he was in the form of God, did not
count equality with God a thing to be grasped, but emptied
himself, taking the form of a servant, being born in the
likeness of men. And being found in human form he humbled himself and became obedient unto death, even death
on a cross . . .

Jesus' death for all men must affect our attitude to others as
we realize their value before God. We are not to despise any
individual, for he is

. . . the brother for whom Christ died.

When the Christian shares the suffering of Christ, he can also
experience the comfort and consolation of Christ. And this in
turn can be shared with all Christ's people:

Blessed be the God and Father of our Lord Jesus Christ,
the Father of all mercies and God of all comfort, who
comforts us in all our affliction, so that we may be able to
comfort those who are in any affliction, with the comfort
with which we ourselves are comforted by God. For as we
share abundantly in Christ's sufferings, so through Christ
we share abundantly in comfort too. If we are afflicted, it is
for your comfort and salvation; and if we are comforted, it
is for your comfort, which you experience when you patiently endure the same sufferings that we suffer. Our hope
for you is unshaken; for we know that as you share in our
sufferings, you will also share in our comfort.

☐ Death is no longer to be feared, because it brings us into the
presence of Christ. Christ's death has taken the "sting" out of
death for us.

The sting of death is sin, and the power of sin is the law.
But thanks be to God, who gives us the victory through our
Lord Jesus Christ.

. . . to me to live is Christ, and to die is gain.

The Christian is not afraid, if necessary, to die for his faith. John speaks of the victory of believers, who, in their own lives in the world are able to defeat Satan through the power of Jesus' death:

> And I heard a loud voice in heaven, saying, "Now the salvation and the power and the kingdom of our God and the authority of his Christ have come, for the accuser of our brethren has been thrown down, who accuses them day and night before our God. And they have conquered him by the blood of the Lamb and by the word of their testimony, for they loved not their lives even unto death. Rejoice then, O heaven and you that dwell therein! . . ."

If you give this answer about the meaning of the death of Jesus, you should go on to consider the question of the resurrection.

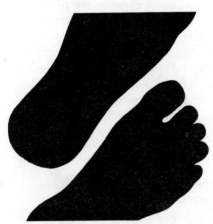

ANSWER TWO:

He died as an example—his death shows us something about God and man.

The meaning of Christ's death is to be seen primarily in what it teaches us and in how it influences us. His death is an example of self-sacrifice, of non-resistance in the face of evil and injustice, and of patient endurance of undeserved suffering. His attitude and behavior in facing death give a demonstration of the love of God, and give us an example to follow when we face suffering ourselves.

In this view, it is not important to ask whether Jesus actually achieved anything at the time when he died on the cross; his death achieves something only when it moves me here and now. In his life he proclaimed the willingness of God to forgive sin; and his death is simply a further demonstration of the love of God, because it shows us the lengths to which Jesus was prepared to go to win us back to God. His death is also a demonstration of the sinfulness of man, because it exposes the pride and selfishness of human nature. Evil is shown up in its true colors when it comes face to face with the holy Son of God.

The message of the death of Jesus, therefore, is this: "This is what God is like—look how far love was prepared to go for us. And this is what human nature is like—look and see what you are by nature." As we look at the crucified Jesus, therefore, we ought to be moved to turn to him in repentance and faith. We ought to come to God to ask for forgiveness and to put our faith in Jesus as the one who shows us that we are accepted by God.

J. W. C. Wand explains what theologians have called the "Exemplarist Theory" of the atonement:

> This is the view that we are changed in conformity with the example of Jesus. That example is so beautiful, so overwhelming in its beauty, that it has the power to transform anyone who sincerely considers it and is prepared to yield to it. "We needs must love the highest when we see it," and living it be changed by it.

> The typical illustration of this divine alchemy is the incident of the penitent thief on Calvary. In the midst of his sufferings he had evidently been so moved by the patience and calmness of the Person who hung between him and his blaspheming fellow bandit that he attained some kind of belief in the crucified Messiah and prayed to be taken into his kingdom. The contrast between the two robbers has stirred the imagination of Christians all down the ages, and change in the penitent thief has always been taken as an indication of what the example of Christ can do.

David Edwards:

> The Creator of the universe was willing to suffer everything in order that the nails which harpooned and bloodily smashed the human life in which he was expressing himself might also pin down our wandering thoughts and stab our consciences awake.

**POINTS
TO CONSIDER
ABOUT THIS
ANSWER**

☐This answer contains many important aspects of the first answer (pp. 459ff.), but it leaves many important questions unanswered. For example, *how* and *why* can the death of Jesus on a criminal's cross become a demonstration of the love of God? One could make out a good case for seeing it as a demonstration not so much of the love of God, but of the cruelty or callousness or weakness of God. For how could God the Father "stand by" and do nothing while God the Son was being tortured to death? If a man stands by and does nothing while he watches his wife being beaten to death, this does not prove his love either for his wife or for anyone else.

The problem therefore can be stated in this way: how can the death of Jesus be a demonstration of the love of God unless it actually *achieves* something? If a woman is in danger of drowning in a river and a man jumps in at considerable risk to save her, he is certainly demonstrating his concern for her. But if he fails to rescue her, the mere demonstration of his concern doesn't help her at all. The death of Jesus certainly shows the self-sacrifice, the humility, and the courage of Jesus, and it may move men to pity and repentance. But how can we speak about the cross as a demonstration of the love of God if we can give no clues as to *how* or *why* it rescues men from their terrible condition?

☐This answer has nothing to say to the person who is not in the least moved by imagining Jesus dying a cruel death on a cross. If the picture of Jesus being slowly tortured to death doesn't appeal to him or move him, he may say, "It leaves me cold; I don't see what it has to do with me or with anyone else." This answer could be open to the charge that it uses the death of Jesus to make a purely emotional appeal. And if this is so, the skeptic has every right to say, "Why are you trying to pull at my heart strings in this way? Of course there is something repulsive and revolting about his death. But so what? What does it prove? Even if he is the Son of God, why should his death by itself move me to repentance any more than the deaths of other innocent people who have died even more horribly?"

☐Whenever the New Testament writers speak of the cross as a demonstration of the love of God, they give a clue as to *why* this is so. They speak of the death of Christ as God's way of dealing with sin, and averting the consequences of sin:

> God so *loved* the world that he gave his only Son, that whoever believes in him *should not perish* but have eternal life.

> God is *love*. In this the love of God was made manifest among us, that God sent his only Son into the world, so that we might live through him. In this is love, not that we loved God but that he loved us and sent his Son to be *the expiation for our sins.*

> God shows his *love* for us in that while we were yet sinners Christ died for us. Since, therefore, we are now justified by his blood, much more shall we be *saved by him from the wrath of God.*

Peter speaks of the example that Christians can see in the way Jesus faced suffering and death. But while he sees this as *part* of the meaning of the death of Jesus, he does not see it as the *only* meaning, or as the heart of its meaning. For in the same paragraph he goes on to speak about the death of Jesus as God's way of dealing with sin.

> For what credit is it, if when you do wrong and are beaten for it you take it patiently? But if when you do right and suffer for it you take it patiently, you have God's approval. For to this you have been called, because Christ also suffered for you, leaving you an example, that you should follow in his steps. He committed no sin; no guile was found on his lips. When he was reviled, he did not revile in return; when he suffered, he did not threaten; but he trusted to him who judges justly. He himself bore our sins in his body on the tree, that we might die to sin and live to righteousness. By his wounds you have been healed . . .

☐ The root of the difficulty may well be that this answer rests on the assumption that man's basic problem is his ignorance about himself and God, and his lack of feeling towards God and Christ. What we need therefore is not someone to deal with our guilt, but rather someone to show us the truth and to melt our hard hearts. And this assumption is different in certain important respects from the biblical assumption that man's most fundamental need is for his guilt before a holy God to be dealt with. (See further Part 2, Question Three, "What is man?", pp. 219ff.)

For many, an answer like this may prove to be the starting point for genuine Christian faith. But it is hardly adequate as a

complete answer, because it leaves many questions unanswered.
If you can go one step further and believe that Jesus died as a
sin-bearer, then there is an adequate answer to these questions.
(See pp. 459ff.) And it becomes clear why the hymn-writer could
say:

> Were the whole realm of nature mine,
> That were an offering far too small;
> Love so amazing, so divine,
> Demands my soul, my life, my all.

ANSWER THREE:

His death has no special meaning.

This answer takes a number of different forms.

He died as a martyr; his death was not unique. In this view, the meaning of Christ's death is simply that it shows us how far he was prepared to go to uphold his cause. He was willing to suffer and die a cruel death rather than deny what he stood for. Just as people have died for social and political causes, so in the same way Jesus died as a martyr in his own cause. His willingness to die in this way shows how sincerely he believed in his message, and how concerned he was that others should know it.

BUT: what precisely was the cause that he died for? Did he die merely to uphold the ideal of an unselfish life or the idea of the brotherhood of man? Did he die merely to convince others that it is a good thing to love one's neighbor?

The Gospels make it clear that what the Jews objected to was not the moral teaching of Jesus, but rather his claims about himself and his relationship with God the Father. If Jesus had died merely as a martyr advocating love, it is difficult to see how the cross could ever have come to be regarded as "good news."

The view that Jesus died as a martyr ignores a great deal of the evidence about how Jesus thought about his death, and how his disciples came to interpret it. In the interests of truth, it is only fair to ask those who hold it to look carefully at the detailed evidence of the New Testament.

If you are not interested in discussing the details of the New Testament picture, it is likely that the real problem lies further back—in questions about God and man (Part 2) or about truth (Part 1).

Certain other answers that have been given by Christians come into this category, because they play down or deny the unique significance of his *death*.

The incarnation (i.e., the Son of God becoming man in the person of Jesus Christ), *not the death of Christ, is the heart of the Christian message.* The mere fact that God became man and lived the kind of life he lived reveals what God is like. There was no need or necessity for Jesus to die on the cross; his incarnation and life are themselves an adequate revelation of the character of God. The way he died does not add anything to what his life achieved.

BUT: it is difficult to reconcile this answer with the teaching of the New Testament as a whole. The main center of interest in both the Gospels and the Epistles is the crucifixion and resurrection.

This answer is sometimes based on the assumption that the material world is somehow infected with sin and needs to be redeemed. But this is contrary to the biblical view of the universe.

It is not the laying down of Christ's life in death which was the significant factor in procuring salvation for men, but rather his offering of his risen life to the Father in heaven. We are saved in so far as we participate in his present offering of his life to the Father.

BUT: the New Testament nowhere suggests that Jesus continues to offer any sacrifice in heaven—even the sacrifice of his life. On the contrary it stresses the finality and completeness of Jesus' sacrifice.

> When Christ had offered for all time a single sacrifice for sins, he sat down at the right hand of God, then to wait until his enemies should be made a stool for his feet. For by a single offering he has perfected for all time those who are sanctified.

This idea of Jesus offering his risen life to the Father is based on the assumption that in the sacrificial system of the Old Testament it was the *offering of the blood* of the animal to God that was the important thing, because the offering of the blood signified the *offering of the life* of the animal. However, the way in which the word *blood* is used throughout the Bible would suggest rather that it signifies not so much the life that is offered to God but rather the life that is laid down in death. The offering of life cannot deal with the guilt of sin; it can only be dealt with when life is surrendered in death, which is the ultimate penalty for sin.

It was not the death of Jesus as such that saves men, but his "repentance" on our behalf. Jesus felt our sins *as if* they were his own, and was able to repent for them on our behalf. The sympathetic or vicarious repentance of Christ and its influence on men therefore enables God to forgive men.

BUT: however sympathetically Jesus could enter into our condition, how could he repent for sins which he had not committed?

According to this view, our forgiveness and salvation are dependent on our own repentance and faith. Our repentance and faith become the *grounds* on which God forgives us. In this way we can be said to earn our salvation through repentance and faith. But the New Testament writers speak about what God has already done in the death of Jesus; and they invite us to repent and believe on these grounds. In this way our repentance and faith are our response to what God has done.

Peter writes:

> You know that you were ransomed from the futile ways inherited from your fathers, not with perishable things such as silver or gold, but with the precious blood of Christ, like that of a lamb without blemish or spot . . . Through him you have confidence in God, who raised him from the dead and gave him glory, so that your faith and hope are in God.

ANSWER FOUR:

The cross is merely a symbol—any interpretation is "myth."

This is to say, Jesus did not actually achieve anything when he died on the cross. We must look at the cross from our own standpoint, and see it as a symbol of what is true in human experience or what is true for us as individuals.

Rudolph Bultmann puts all the emphasis on what the cross must mean in the experience of the individual:

> To believe in the cross of Christ does not mean to concern ourselves with a mythical process wrought outside of us and our world, or even an objective event turned by God to our advantage, but rather to make the cross of Christ our own, to undergo crucifixion with him. . . . The cross is not just

an event of the past which can be contemplated in detachment, but the eschatological event in and beyond time, for
as far as its meaning—that is, its meaning for faith—is
concerned, it is an ever-present reality.

The cross and passion are ever-present realities . . . The
abiding significance of the cross is that it is the judgment of
the world, the judgment and the deliverance of man . . .
The real meaning of the cross is that it has created a new
and permanent situation in history. The preaching of the
cross as the event of redemption challenges all who hear it
to appropriate this significance for themselves, to be willing
to be crucified with Christ.

For us the cross cannot disclose its own meaning; it is an
event of the past. We can never recover it as an event in
our lives.

Cross and resurrection form a single, indivisible cosmic
event which brings judgment to the world and opens up
for men the possibility of authentic life.

According to Bultmann, the language of the New Testament
about Jesus dying for our sins is mythological language. What we
must do, therefore, is to translate it into existential language
which will mean something to modern man. The preaching of
the cross in this way becomes a challenge to existential decision.
And if we respond to the challenge in the appropriate way, we
gain a deep understanding of ourselves and of the human predicament. We can begin to enjoy authentic existence.

Colin Wilson:

The need for God I could understand, and the need for
religion; I could even sympathize with the devotees like
Suso or St. Francis, who weave fantasies around the Cross,
the nails, and all the other traditional symbols. But ultimately I could not accept the need for redemption by a
Savior. To pin down the idea of salvation to one point in
space and time seemed to me a naive kind of anthropomorphism.

Dietrich Bonhoeffer sees the cross as a symbol of "the suffering
of God in the life of the world" and of "the participation in the
powerlessness of God in the world."

The God who makes us live in this world without using him
as a working hypothesis is the God before whom we are

ever standing. Before God and with him we live without
God.

God allows himself to be edged out of the world and on to
the cross. God is weak and powerless in the world, and that
is exactly the way, the only way, in which he can be with us
and help us. Matthew 8:17 makes it crystal clear that it is
not by his omnipotence that Christ can help us, but by his
weakness and suffering. This is the decisive difference between Christianity and all religions. Man's religiosity makes
him look in his distress to the power of God in the world;
he uses God as a *deus ex machina*. The Bible, however,
directs him to the powerlessness and suffering of God; only
a suffering God can help.

Paul van Buren interprets the death of Jesus in accordance
with his understanding of existential "freedom":

What can it mean to say, "He *died* for our sins"? The
emphasis is on his death, but we need to remember that
theology, as well as the New Testament, speaks of the
"cross" or the death of Jesus as the consequence of his life.
"The cross" and other references to Jesus' death became
summary ways of speaking of his whole history, as indeed
his end seemed to his disciples, after the fact, to have been
foreshadowed in all of his life. Since his life was one of
solidarity with men, compassion for them, mercy towards
their weakness and wrong, it is not surprising that his
death, which was the consequence of his freedom to be
related to men in this way, was spoken of as a death "for
us." His death . . . was regarded as the measure of the
freedom for which he set other men free. The man for
whom the history of Jesus and his liberation of his disciples
on Easter is a discernment situation of prime importance
will say, "He died for me, for my forgiveness and freedom." When the New Testament says that he died not only
for "our" sins, "but also for the sins of the whole world," it
reflects the fact that Jesus was free for every man, those
who did not acknowledge him as well as those that did, and
it articulates a perspective by which all men, not just believers, are seen.

David Edwards:

The cross is the Christian symbol not only because it
marked the end of the public life of Jesus of Nazareth, but
also because it stands for truths of continuing experience.

479

As examples of these truths of experience he mentions "inevitable suffering," "the evil corruption of our very ideals," "the great suffering of the innocent individual."

Nikos Kazantzakis' novel *Christ Recrucified* describes the life of a village as it prepares to perform a Passion Play. The events of the year turn out to be a strange re-enactment of the events leading to the death of Jesus, and towards the end the Christ-figure, Manolios, is killed.

> He (Pope Fotis) extended his hand and tenderly caressed the face of Manolios.

> "Dear Manolios, you'll have given your life in vain," he murmured; "they've killed you for having taken our sins upon you; you cried: 'It was I who robbed, it was I who killed and set things on fire; I, nobody else!' so that they might let the rest of us take root peacefully in these lands . . . In vain, Manolios, in vain will you have sacrificed yourself . . ."

> Pope Fotis listened to the bell pealing gaily, announcing that Christ was coming down on earth to save the world . . . He shook his head and heaved a sigh: "In vain, my Christ, in vain," he muttered; "two thousand years have gone by and men crucify You still. When will you be born, my Christ, and not be crucified any more, but live among us for eternity?"

Thomas Mann writes this about the Kazantzakis novel:

> The novel *Christ Recrucified* is without doubt a work of high artistic order formed by a tender and firm hand and built up with strong dynamic power. I have particularly admired the poetic tact in phrasing the subtle yet unmistakable allusions to the Christian Passion story. They give the book its mythical background which is such a vital element in the epic form of today.

POINTS TO CONSIDER ABOUT THIS ANSWER

☐ This answer hardly does justice to the *whole* of the New Testament teaching. For the New Testament writers it was not a case of *either* an event which achieved something in the past *or* a truth of present experience. It was rather a case of *both/and.* The death

of Jesus meant something to them in present experience because
it had really achieved something for them in the first place.

☐ Is there any criterion for deciding the meaning of symbols? To
some the very ambiguity of symbols commends them as a means
of religious communication:

> *F. C. Happold:*
>
> The religious symbol when examined is seen to have an
> ambivalent quality. It is an indefinite expression which con-
> veys different meanings to different people. People react to
> religious symbols in different ways, according to their par-
> ticular mental and psychological make-ups. The symbols
> point to something beyond themselves which is not intellec-
> tually definable, and therefore cannot be fully rationally
> known or described. They make perceptible what is in-
> visible, ideal and transcendent, giving it a sort of objectivity,
> and so allowing it to be better apprehended.

If you treat the cross in this way, therefore, you are in effect
saying, "If the cross means something to you and something
completely different to me, then it doesn't matter—because its
truth is indefinable, and cannot properly be described in words.
There is no such thing as 'the true interpretation' of the death of
Jesus; any interpretation can be true if it is true to me." This
comes very close to saying—if we may adapt the saying of
Humpty Dumpty—"When I use a symbol, it means just what I
choose it to mean—neither more nor less."

This answer therefore is based on an understanding of truth
which is different in certain important respects from the biblical
understanding of truth. And the discussion must turn on what
we mean by truth, rather than on the details of the New Testament interpretation of the death of Jesus. (See Part 1, especially
pp. 86ff.)

☐ Those who do not share or do not understand the basic assumptions about truth on which this answer is based, tend to react to
the language of symbols with indifference or impatience:

> *C. E. M. Joad:*
>
> I have never been able to make anything of symbolism. A
> symbol I understand to be a sign for something else. Either
> the symbolist knows what the something else is, in which
> case I cannot see why he should not tell us what it is
> straight out, instead of obscurely hinting at it in symbols, or
> he does not, in which case not knowing what the symbols

stand for he cannot expect his readers to find out for him. Usually, I suspect, he does not, and his symbolism is merely a device to conceal his muddled thinking.

☐If we regard the death of Jesus on the cross as merely a symbol, we cannot at the same time claim that it is unique. Why should we not attach the same significance to the deaths of great men like Socrates or Gandhi?

☐If salvation has not been worked out in history at a particular place and at a particular time, then the Christian message ceases to be good news about what God *has done* for man. If the saving work of Christ is extracted from history and made completely independent of history, Christian faith changes its character completely.

J. Gresham Machen outlines the alternatives in this way:

If the saving work of Christ were confined to what He does now for every Christian, there would be no such thing as a Christian gospel—an account of an event which put a new face on life. What we should have left would be simply mysticism, and mysticism is quite different from Christianity . . .

If religion be made independent of history there is no such thing as a gospel. For "gospel" means "good news," tidings, information about something that has happened. A gospel independent of history is a contradiction in terms.

☐Sometimes this answer is based on assumptions about God and man which are clearly stated.

Rudolph Bultmann:

How can the guilt of one man be expiated by death of another who is sinless—if indeed we may speak of a sinless man at all? What primitive notions of guilt and righteousness does this imply? And what primitive idea of God? The rationale of sacrifice in general may of course throw some light on the theory of the atonement, but even so, what a primitive mythology it is, that a divine Being should become incarnate, and atone for the sins of men through his own blood! . . . Moreover if the Christ who died such a death was the pre-existent Son of God, what could death mean for him? Obviously very little, if he knew that he would rise again in three days!

John Robinson:

The doctrine of the Atonement is not—as in the supranatu-
ralistic way of thinking—a highly mythological, and often
rather dubious, transaction between two parties, "God" on
the one hand and "man" on the other, who have to be
brought together . . .

Even when it is Christian in content, the whole scheme of a
supernatural Being coming down from heaven to "save"
mankind from sin, in the way that a man might put his
finger into a glass of water to rescue a struggling insect, is
frankly incredible to man "come of age," who no longer
believes in such a *deus ex machina.*

If your answer is based on assumptions of this kind about
God and man, see further Part 2, Question Two, "Who or what
is God?" and Question Three, "What is man?"

BACK TO ANSWER ONE

His death achieved
something—he was
bearing our sins.

PROBLEMS
AND QUESTIONS

*Having examined other possible an-
swers to the basic question, we must
now return to option one, the biblical
Christian answer, and look at some of
the main questions and objections
raised.*

Is there any evidence outside the New Testament to confirm its account of the trial and death of Jesus?

The procedure of the trial of Jesus as described in the Gospels
does not seem to be consistent with what we know of Jewish legal
procedure of that time (for example, the fact that the trial was
held at night). Is there any way of confirming whether or not the
Gospels are reliable in their details?

The Jewish Encyclopedia:

> Nothing corresponding to a Jewish trial took place, though it was by the action of the priests that Jesus was sent before Pontius Pilate.

☐ There are only two references to the trial of Jesus outside the New Testament, but they are so general that they hardly confirm or deny any of the details of the Gospel accounts:

Tacitus, the Roman historian (see pp. 423, 424):

> . . . Christ . . . was executed in the reign of Tiberius by the Procurator Pontius Pilate . . .

The Talmud:

> On the eve of Passover they hanged Yeshu of Nazareth, and the herald went before him for forty days saying, Yeshu of Nazareth is going forth to be stoned in that he hath practiced sorcery and beguiled and led astray Israel. Let everyone knowing aught in his defense come and plead for him. But they found naught in his defense and hanged him on the eve of the Passover.

☐ The reliability of the Gospel writers in *other* areas, where we *can* test them, gives a fair indication as to their general reliability. For example, Luke, the writer of the Gospel and of Acts, shows an intimate knowledge of Roman law, and Acts contains accounts of Paul's encounters with Roman officials in many different places. The accurate detail of the Acts account has been confirmed at many points. If Luke's knowledge of Roman law can be relied on, it is highly likely that he took equal care to give a correct account of the events leading up to the death of Jesus. He specifically claims to have investigated all that he had heard and to have set down an ordered and accurate account.

☐ There are two possible reasons for the discrepancies between the Gospel accounts of the trial and what we know of Jewish procedure of the period.

either   the Gospel writers have deliberately given a distorted and misleading account of what happened;

or   the Jewish leaders were so determined to get rid of Jesus that they were prepared to break some of their own rules in order to sentence Jesus quickly and hand him over to the Romans.

Why do we need to have an "explanation" of the death of Jesus?

Why do we need to discuss *theories* about the meaning of the death of Jesus? Can we not be satisfied with the *story*, and leave it to communicate its own message and make its own impact? If we insist on an explanation, aren't there a number of possible explanations, rather than just one?

☐ The New Testament writers were not satisfied with simply telling the story of what happened.

Mark records this saying of Jesus about the meaning of his death:

> The Son of man . . . came . . . to give his life as a ransom for many.

Some of the events he records can only be understood as pointers to the meaning of the death of Jesus:

> And Jesus uttered a loud cry, and breathed his last. And the curtain of the temple was torn in two, from top to bottom.

Peter was an eyewitness of the sufferings of Christ, and he does not hesitate to interpret the meaning of his sufferings:

> Christ also died for our sins, once and for all. He, the just, suffered for the unjust, to bring us to God.
>
> He himself bore our sins in his body on the tree.

Paul, in 1 Corinthians 15, one of the earliest passages of the New Testament, combines a statement of the bare fact of the death of Jesus ("Christ died . . .") with an interpretation of the fact (". . . for our sins"). There is good reason to believe that he is here quoting from a summary of the gospel which he had received from the first Christians.

> Therefore, if we refuse to interpret the meaning of the death of Jesus, we are being very much more agnostic than the New Testament writers.

☐ No single theory about the death of Jesus can hope to exhaust its meaning. An element of mystery will inevitably remain. But we cannot discount the meaning which Jesus and the New Testament writers clearly attached to it. Most modern hesitation about interpreting the death of Jesus starts with a reluctance or an unwillingness to accept the clear indications that are offered in the New Testament.

☐ If we refuse to interpret the meaning of the death of Jesus, then
we must allow people to interpret it in any way they wish. The
Hindu, the humanist, the existentialist and the Communist will
interpret it in the light of their own ways of thinking. Many of
these interpretations will have little or nothing to do with the
New Testament. They will often be incompatible with the New
Testament and with each other. And there will be no way of
deciding which interpretation is the *true* one; each one will be
"true" for the individual person. This is an approach based on a
particular understanding of what truth is. (See further Part 1,
especially pp. 64–118.)

☐ The New Testament writers certainly speak about the death of
Jesus in a great variety of ways. But if we put them all together,
and compare them, is there any *basic idea* which they all have in
common, and which links together the many different expressions they use? We should not be content with partial and fragmentary insights if we can find an explanation which takes us
right to the heart of its meaning and embraces all the different
word pictures.

The answer outlined on pp. 459ff. suggests that there *is* such a
basic idea, and that it is to be found in the idea of Jesus dying to
"bear sins." The phrase "bear sins" is not simply another metaphor; it means quite literally "to bear the consequences of sins."
And all the different metaphors used in the New Testament
spring from this basic idea: that Jesus in his death dealt with
human sin by bearing its consequences and its guilt in our place.

Why the obsession with sin?

Lin Yutang:

What repels me particularly in religion is its emphasis on
sin. I have no consciousness of sin and no feeling of being
damned.

A. J. Ayer:

I regard the idea of original sin as morally repulsive, and
indeed am inclined to reject the whole concept of sin as a
theological survival which can find no place in any scientific
study of human psychology.

Albert Camus:

There are words that I have never quite understood, such
as sin.

☐ The Christian should be no more obsessed with sin than a doctor is obsessed with disease. A doctor is concerned to restore and maintain health; and the Christian is concerned with sin simply because he believes it to be the basic problem of man which prevents him from knowing God and enjoying him and his universe. The Bible sees forgiveness of sin not as an end in itself, but as leading to something very positive.

Zechariah, speaking about the work of John the Baptist, links forgiveness with the knowledge of God:

> You will go before the Lord to prepare his ways, to give knowledge of salvation to his people in the forgiveness of their sins . . . (to . . . lead his people to salvation through knowledge of him, by the forgiveness of their sins, New English Bible).

☐ It is true that some Christians do place an unhealthy emphasis on sin. The following extract from the biography of D. L. Moody, the famous nineteenth-century American evangelist, shows how he was brought to abandon a wrong emphasis on sin and the wrath of God through hearing the preaching of a young Englishman named Harry Moorhouse:

> Moorhouse announced his text: "John 3:16: God so loved the world, that he gave his only begotten Son, that whosoever believeth in him should not perish but have everlasting life." Instead of dividing the text into firstly, secondly, thirdly in ministerial manner, Moody noted, "he went from Genesis to Revelation giving proof that God loves the sinner, and before he got through, two or three of my sermons were spoiled." Moody's teaching that it was the sinner God hates, the sinner as well as the sin, lay shattered at his feet. "I never knew up to that time that God loved us so much. This heart of mine began to thaw out; I could not keep back my tears."
>
> Moody turned in his ways, to become from that time forth an apostle of the love of God . . .

☐ Our understanding of the word *sin* depends entirely on our own idea of God. The concept is bound to be meaningless if there is no awareness of the *God* against whom we have sinned. (See further Part 2, Question Two, "Who or what is God?")

How can God be a God of love and a God of law at the same time?

Behind this question lies the belief that love and law are incompatible. If God is a God of love he cannot at the same time be a lawgiver and judge. If God deals with men in a personal way, there cannot be any element of legalism in the relationship.

Kenneth Barnes:

> You cannot have it both ways. Either God is a law-maker or he is the *fons et origo* of tenderness, mutuality, involvement, responsibility. For me God is in no sense a law-maker. Laws and morals are made by human beings . . . .

This objection is based on an unrealistic understanding of human love. Far from being incompatible with love, law can sometimes be an expression of it.

In the family, for example, a father makes certain rules for his children and expects them to be kept. There is no inconsistency between law and love in this case. It is the father's love for his children which makes him set certain standards for them.

Similarly, the love a husband and wife have for each other will lead them to agree certain points, simply because there are some things they will not want to do to one another. To reach an understanding of this kind is in a sense to agree about certain rules. And such an agreement is not incompatible with love; it is itself an expression of love. For love demands that they should together recognize certain limits.

If, therefore, we can say that law and love are not necessarily incompatible in personal relationships between human beings in the family, there is no reason why they should be incompatible in the relationship between God and man. The Bible refuses to drive a wedge between law and love; for the love of God towards men is a holy love. It seeks the very best for man and must set certain standards.

Why can't God forgive us as easily as we forgive one another?

If we can forgive other people when they apologize for the wrong they have done, why isn't it enough for us to repent and say to God, "I'm sorry for the wrong I've done. Please forgive me."

☐ In the first place, it isn't always that simple to forgive other people. If someone hurts you in a small way and apologizes, it is easy to accept the apology. But the greater the wrong or the injury, the harder it is to forgive. If a husband is unfaithful to his wife but comes back and asks forgiveness, she may be willing to forgive; but the forgiveness will not be an easy or casual thing.

It will cost a great deal. It will hurt. For the essence of forgiveness is that you accept the wrong or the injury that has been done to you; you bear the consequences of it without retaliation and without being bitter or resentful.

☐ There are some circumstances in which a person can *not*, or should not, simply forgive another person, however much he may want to.

For example, a father makes certain rules for his children and expects them to be kept. If they are broken, for the child's own good there must be some kind of punishment. The father may dislike punishing his children, and his natural instinct may be to let them off every time. But if he refuses to punish in any way, and lets the children off every time they break the rules, they are not likely to take the rules (or their father) very seriously. The end result of this indulgence is likely to be a weakening rather than a strengthening of character.

A judge in a court of law is there to administer the laws of the society. If someone has broken the laws certain sanctions must be applied. The judge may lighten the sentence; but he cannot simply forgive the offender and treat him as if the law does not exist. If this is true in human society, it is also true of the relations between God and man. If we have broken God's law, we should not imagine that we can be forgiven lightly. If the laws mean anything at all, the sanctions must be applied.

☐ If God is the Creator to whom we owe our existence, we can hardly expect him to treat us in exactly the same way as we treat our fellow creatures. The Creator-creature relationship is bound to be different in some respects from the creature-creature relationship. For example, God is himself the source and standard of what is right and good; and he has given us the law. I and my neighbor are creatures subject to the law of God, and when I wrong God, I am wronging the one whose character is utterly holy. But when I wrong my neighbor, I am wronging a fellow creature who is also a sinner.

The need for mediation or atonement arises, therefore, because man's sin—his infringement on God's laws and standards —is more serious than the injury done to a human being. It is injury to God, and a breach of his laws. It is this which makes it more difficult and costly for God to forgive man than for human beings to forgive one another.

From man's side the problem is: how can I get right with God? If I have affronted him and broken his laws, how can I make my peace with him? How can the relationship be restored?

From God's side (if we can speak in these terms) the problem is: how to uphold the laws (which God must do if he is not to deny his nature—light cannot abide darkness) and at the same time acquit the sinner. How can God forgive *and* remain just? How can he forgive (as he longs to do) and at the same time register his hatred and condemnation of everything that spoils his universe?

This is the dilemma which Paul is thinking of in Romans 3:26 where he speaks about the cross:

> . . . it was to prove at the present time that he himself is righteous and that he justifies him who has faith in Jesus . . .

B. B. Warfield sums up the problem and the need for atonement in this way:

> It is the distinguishing characteristic of Christianity . . . not that it preaches a God of love, but that it preaches a God of conscience. A benevolent God, yes: men have framed a benevolent God for themselves. But a thoroughly honest God, perhaps never. That has been left for the revelation of God himself to give us. And this is the really distinguishing characteristic of the God of revelation: he is a thoroughly honest, a thoroughly conscientious God—a God who deals honestly with himself and us, who deals conscientiously with himself and with us. And a thoroughly conscientious God, we may be sure, is not a God who can deal with sinners as if they were not sinners. In this fact lies the deepest ground of the necessity of the Atonement.

The old concept of punishment is out of favor today. How can we accept an explanation which relies in any way on this theory?

People generally no longer believe in the idea of punishment as a penalty that the offender *deserves* for what he has done. Can we seriously consider an interpretation of the death of Jesus that makes use of this discredited idea?

☐ There are three basic theories of punishment:

that it is retributive: i.e., that certain crimes deserve certain punishments. If a person does *x*, then he deserves *y*. The punishment may help to reform the offender or to deter others from committing similar crimes; but these results should be considered as secondary, and as following from the fact that the punishment fits the crime.

that it is a deterrent: i.e., that any punishment is intended to deter others from doing the same thing.

that it is remedial: i.e., that any punishment or penalty is intended to benefit the offender and to enable him to change his ways.

In the past the first of these theories has generally been regarded as the most important of the three. Today, however, it is very widely rejected, and emphasis is put on the other two. Punishment is not regarded as retributive, because the idea of retribution is too close to legalized revenge; and revenge is always wrong, whether it is taken by an individual or by the state. Thus punishment comes to be thought of basically as a way of reforming the criminal and protecting society.

What is the reason for this widespread rejection of the idea of retribution? It arises from genuine concern for the well-being of the offender, and from revulsion against the way in which laws have often been applied in the past. But it usually goes much deeper than this, and is often based on assumptions such as these:

that there is no God, and no absolute moral standards;

that even if there is a God, moral standards have little or nothing to do with him; laws are simply social agreements arrived at by popular consensus.

These assumptions are discussed in Part 2, Question Three, "What is man?" especially pp. 255ff.

☐ There are certain serious weaknesses in the other two theories, if it is claimed that they exclude the idea of retributive punishment.

If punishment is basically a *deterrent,* what justification is there for punishment in cases where the punishment does *not* seem to deter? In these cases, punishment loses all justification and becomes arbitrary.

If, however, punishment is considered as retributive, it is something the offender deserves for what he has done. And the unpleasantness of the suffering may well have the effect of discouraging others from committing the same offenses. But the deterrent effect is in a sense a by-product; for it springs from the way in which the punishment fits the crime.

If punishment is basically *remedial,* what grounds are there for punishing a person who seems incapable of being reformed or unwilling to be reformed? As soon as it becomes evident that the

offender is incapable of responding, or is deliberately refusing to
respond, then the punishment becomes something arbitrary, or
else it must be abandoned altogether. Sooner or later we arrive
at the situation in which the offender is at the mercy of those
who wish to reform him—the policeman, the judge or the psy-
chiatrist.

If, on the other hand, punishment is basically retributive, the
offender is aware that if he does *x* he will receive *y*. He therefore
knows where he stands, and the law can even act as a kind of
safeguard, protecting him from the whims of those who think
they know what is good for him. And when the sentence has
been paid, the offender is entitled to a fresh start.

☐ The idea that we deserve to be punished for wrong-doing is
basic to the teaching of the whole Bible.

At the beginning of the Bible, God says to Adam:

> You may freely eat of every tree of the garden; but of the
> tree of the knowledge of good and evil you shall not eat,
> for in the day that you eat of it you shall die.

There is no suggestion here that physical death would come in
order to reform Adam if he was disobedient, or to deter him
from further sin. Death would simply be what he *deserved* for his
disobedience to his Creator.

The form in which all the laws are given in the Old Testament suggests that for each crime or offense there is an appropriate—a just—penalty:

> Whoever strikes his father or his mother shall be put to
> death.

> Whoever steals a man, whether he sells him or is found in
> possession of him, shall be put to death.

> When men strive together, and hurt a woman with child, so
> that there is a miscarriage, and yet no harm follows, the
> one who hurt her shall be fined, according as the woman's
> husband shall lay upon him; and he shall pay as the judges
> determine. If any harm follows, then you shall give life for
> life, eye for eye, tooth for tooth, hand for hand, foot for
> foot, burn for burn, wound for wound, stripe for stripe.

These penalties sound horrifying to modern ears, but they were
in fact intended to set a limit to personal vengeance. It was an
eye for an eye, and *no more*. There is also a clear distinction
between punishment for offenses against people (which are

493

severe) and offenses against property (which are much lighter),
stressing the value of even the humblest individual.

Jesus condemned the desire for personal revenge (as did the
Old Testament law); but he clearly did not believe that there was
never any case for punishment as a deserved penalty. When he
predicted the destruction of Jerusalem, he spoke of it as a
judgment that would come on the nation simply *because* it had
refused to recognize and acknowledge God's Messiah. And he
spoke these words not in a fit or temper, but with tears:

> And when he drew near and saw the city he wept over it,
> saying, "Would that even today you knew the things that
> make for peace! But now they are hid from your eyes. For
> the days shall come upon you, when your enemies will cast
> up a bank about you and surround you, and hem you in on
> every side, and dash you to the ground, you and your
> children within you, and they will not leave one stone upon
> another in you; *because* you did not know the time of your
> visitation."

Animal sacrifice is unintelligible and revolting to the modern mind. How can we accept any theory about the death of Jesus that is based on it?

Although most people in the Western world have never seen an
animal being killed in sacrifice, the very idea of offering such
sacrifices to any god seems either quite meaningless, or to imply
primitive and unworthy ideas of God. It conveys the idea that
God is angry with men and needs to be placated with offerings.

☐ In the long run it is no help to say that it does not matter
whether or not we understand what animal sacrifices were all
about, because these ideas play such a large part in the way in
which Jesus and the early Christians interpreted the meaning of
his death. If we exclude all ideas connected with animal sacrifice,
we may be in danger of arriving at an interpretation that has
little or no connection with the thinking of Jesus and the early
Christians.

Leon Morris outlines the ideas associated with sacrifice in the
Old Testament:

> Throughout the world of antiquity sacrifice was the almost
> universal religious rite. Among the Jews the procedure was
> as follows. A man would take along an animal to the altar,
> lay his hands on its head and then solemnly kill it. The
> priest would collect the blood, sprinkle some of it in a
> prescribed manner and pour the rest of it at the base of the

altar. Then he would take certain prescribed parts of the
animal (the whole of it in the case of the burnt sacrifice)
and offer it to God in the flames of the altar. Finally the
priest would dispose of the rest of the carcase according to
the rules governing the particular sacrifice being offered.
Sacrifice might express homage to God, or fellowship before God with other worshipers, or it might be concerned
with the expiation of sin.

☐ When we do understand the idea of animal sacrifice in the Old
Testament, we may discover that the real reason why we find it
repulsive is that it is associated with certain assumptions we do
not *like*. We may not like the idea that our proud independence
of God, or our rebellion against him and his standards, call forth
a certain reaction from him. We may not like the idea that, since
we have grown up saying "No!" to him in this life and refusing
to accept him, we deserve to forfeit fellowship with him. We
would like to believe that our refusal to love him and obey him is
not as serious as the Bible would make us believe, and that we
do not deserve such treatment from him. We may not *like* these
assumptions very much; but we can hardly say that we do not
understand them when they are clearly explained. Death *is* repulsive. The sacrifices serve as a visual aid in helping us to understand the death of Jesus.

Isn't the idea of someone dying in our place unjust?

Lord Byron:

> The basis of your religion is injustice; the Son of God, the
> pure, the immaculate, the innocent is sacrificed for the
> guilty. This proves *His* heroism; but no more does away
> with *man's* guilt than a schoolboy's volunteering to be
> flogged for another would exculpate the dunce from neg-
> ligence or preserve him from the rod.

☐ This objection rests partly on a misunderstanding. The New
Testament never suggests that God the Father "used" Jesus as an
unwilling victim in order to vent his fury and rage on him
instead of on the whole human race. There is no suggestion that
God is like a teacher who is confronted with a disobedient class,
and because he cannot punish the whole class, picks out one
innocent person and punishes him. The New Testament writers
stress that the whole process of reconciliation from start to finish
was motivated by the love of God (i.e., of God the Father, God

495

the Son and God the Holy Spirit). And when God the Son willingly went to the cross, this was God's way of expressing his hatred of sin and his love for the sinner at the same time. When we say, therefore, that Jesus bore our sins, we are saying that *God himself* has borne the consequences of our sins. There is no unwilling third party who is used as a scapegoat.

Paul shows how closely he related the work of Jesus to the work of God the Father when he speaks of

> the church of God which he (i.e. God) purchased with his own blood.

☐ The objection may in some cases spring from human pride. Even admitting our need to be saved from the judgment of God, we would naturally prefer to find our own way of making our peace with him, a way by which we could take most of the credit for ourselves, or a way which would not cost us a great deal. It is therefore humiliating for us to be told that we cannot save ourselves, and that only God can save us.

☐ If we look at the alternatives, they are even less acceptable:

either   we must hope that God will not after all give us what we deserve, or that he will disregard his laws;

or   we must be prepared to remain guilty and bear the full consequences ourselves.

How can the death of one man in the first century deal with the sins of the whole human race?

That is to say:

How can the death of *one* man have this effect for *all* men?

How can *suffering and death* deal with *sin*?

How can his death *then* deal with my sins *now*?

☐ The answer to the first part of the question lies in the *identity* of the person who died. The death of an ordinary man could not have this effect for all men. But when the person who dies is the eternal Son of God, his death is unique and has unique effects. For if Jesus was the eternal Son of God, then what *Jesus* did, *God* did. We must not think of Jesus merely as a neutral third party coming between God and man. This is why Paul links God the Father so closely with Christ when he says:

> God was in Christ reconciling the world to himself, not counting their trespasses against them . . .

The biblical understanding of the solidarity of the human race helps further to explain how the action of Jesus can affect all men. Adam is seen as the first man and the "head" of the human race. All his descendants are thought of as being "in Adam," and inherit his fallen human nature. Jesus, on the other hand, is seen as the "second Adam" who reverses the effects of Adam's disobedience. All who believe in Christ are now no longer "in Adam" and doomed to condemnation, but are "in Christ" and enjoy a new relationship with God. And just as the disobedience of the *one* man Adam affected *all* men, so the obedience of the *one* man Jesus affects *all* who trust in him. This is how Paul draws out the parallel between Adam and Christ:

> . . . sin came into the world through one man and death through sin, and so death spread to all men because all men sinned . . . But the free gift is not like the trespass. For if many died through one man's trespass, much more have the grace of God and the free gift in the grace of that one man Jesus Christ abounded for many. And the free gift is not like the effect of that one man's sin. For the judgment following one trespass brought condemnation, but the free gift following many trespasses brings justification. If, because of one man's trespass, death reigned through that one man, much more will those who receive the abundance of grace and the free gift of righteousness reign in life through the one man Jesus Christ.

☐ The answer to the second question similarly hinges on the *identity* of the man who suffered and died. It was not the *intensity* of the suffering that had the effect of dealing with sin, but its quality and value. It was not *how much* he suffered which makes the difference; it is rather *who* suffered, and the fact that death is so closely associated with sin in the Bible. (See pp. 448, 449.)

Moreover, the suffering and death of Jesus must not be isolated from his whole life. Sin came into the world through the *disobedience* of Adam, and the consequences of this disobedience could therefore only be undone through *obedience*—obedience exemplified not only in an isolated act, but throughout a life. In this way the willingness of Jesus to go to the cross is seen as the climax of a life utterly obedient to God. Paul writes:

> Then as one man's trespass led to condemnation for all men, so one man's act of righteousness leads to acquittal and life for all men. For as by one man's disobedience many were made sinners, so by one man's obedience many will be made righteous.

497

☐We must not think of the death of Jesus simply as a transaction carried out in the past. The New Testament writers speak of something that was accomplished when Jesus died on the cross. But the benefits of what he achieved do not pass to us automatically; we have to receive them by a conscious and deliberate act of faith. The fact that Jesus died so many years ago is hardly relevant; all that is relevant is that he died at a particular time in history, and that his death achieved salvation once and for all. His death does not need to be repeated in each generation, even if it could be.

> He has appeared once for all at the end of the age to put away sin by the sacrifice of himself.

> When Christ had offered for all time a single sacrifice for sins, he sat down at the right hand of God . . . For by a single offering he has perfected for all time those who are sanctified.

What Jesus achieved in the past has to be appropriated by each person in the present; and it is simply faith and trust in Jesus that makes the connection between the death and resurrection of Jesus in the past and our experience in the present. Paul writes:

> Since we are justified by faith, we have peace with God through our Lord Jesus Christ. Through him we have obtained access to this grace in which we stand, and we rejoice in our hope of sharing the glory of God.

Isn't it inconceivable that a prophet sent from God should suffer and die in this way?

If a man is sent from God as a prophet, he has the authority of God behind him, and he represents God to the people. Is it conceivable that God should allow his messenger to undergo such humiliation and rejection? Surely God would intervene to save his representative from such a degrading fate.

This was probably *Peter's* feeling when he protested at the suggestion of Jesus having to suffer and die:

> And Peter took him and began to rebuke him, saying, "God forbid, Lord! This shall never happen to you."

Judaism has generally reacted in precisely the same way as Peter did, finding it inconceivable that God should have a "'Son," or that he should allow him to be killed without intervening.

The Jewish Encyclopedia:

> "My God, my God . . ." which showed that even his resolute
> spirit had been daunted by the ordeal. This last utterance
> was in all its implications itself a disproof of the exaggerat-
> ed claims made for him after his death by his disciples. The
> very form of his punishment would disprove those claims in
> Jewish eyes. No Messiah that Jews could recognize could
> suffer such a death; for "He that is hanged is accursed of
> God" (Deut. 21:23), "an insult to God" (Targum, Rashi).

Hans Joachim Schoeps:

> It is an impossible article of belief, which detracts from
> God's sovereignty and absolute otherness—an article which,
> in fact, destroys the world . . . It is the same passionate
> belief which can be heard in an admittedly late homiletical
> midrash: "It is not permitted a human mouth to say, 'The
> Holy One—blessed be he—has a son.' If God could not
> look on in anguish while Abraham sacrificed his son, would
> he then have suffered his own son to be killed, without
> destroying the entire world?"

☐ It is clear from the Gospels that *Jesus* himself felt the full force
of this kind of thinking. He must have felt its attraction very
keenly, but rejected it because he knew that it was a purely
human way of thinking that was not in accordance with the mind
of God. He answered Peter very sternly:

> Then Jesus turned and said to Peter, "Away with you,
> Satan; you are a stumbling-block to me. You think as men
> think, not as God thinks."

When Jesus realized what kind of death lay ahead of him, he
knew that it was possible for him to appeal to God for deliverance; but he firmly rejected the idea:

> Now is my soul troubled. And what shall I say, "Father,
> save me from this hour"? No, for this purpose I have come
> to this hour . . .

When Peter began using a sword to protect Jesus, Jesus rebuked him and explained why he rejected the use of force to
defend himself and why he refused to ask for a miraculous
deliverance:

> Then Jesus said to him, "Put your sword back into its place;
> for all who take the sword will perish by the sword. Do you

think that I cannot appeal to my Father, and he will at once send me more than twelve legions of angels? But how then should the scriptures be fulfilled, that it must be so?"

After his resurrection Jesus explained to the disciples that it was *necessary* for him to suffer in this way:

> "O foolish men, and slow of heart to believe all that the prophets have spoken! Was it not necessary that the Christ should suffer these things and enter into his glory?" And beginning with Moses and all the prophets, he interpreted to them in all the scriptures the things concerning himself.

> Then he opened their minds to understand the scriptures, and said to them, "Thus it is written, that the Christ should suffer and on the third day rise from the dead, and that repentance and forgiveness of sins should be preached in his name to all nations . . ."

The many Old Testament passages from which Jesus explained the need for his suffering and death must have been the main source of understanding for the New Testament writers.

Islam. It is probably this same assumption that God could not allow his prophet to suffer and die in this way that lies behind the *Qur'an's* statements about the death of Jesus:

> They denied the truth and uttered a monstrous falsehood against Mary. They declared: "We have put to death the Messiah Jesus the son of Mary, the apostle of Allah." They did not kill him, nor did they crucify him, but they thought they did.

> Those that disagreed about him were in doubt concerning his death, for what they knew about it was sheer conjecture; they were not sure that they had slain him. Allah lifted him up to his presence; He is mighty and wise.

We need to be clear as to what precisely the Qur'an denies and what it does not deny:

It does *not deny* that men wanted to kill Jesus.

It does *not deny* that Jesus was willing to suffer and die.

It *does deny* that Jesus was finally killed on the cross.

Dr. Kenneth Cragg explains the background to this belief, and the traditional interpretations in Islam:

The context of controversy and dispute here referred to
may reflect certain docetic tendencies in early heretical
Christianity which, for various mainly metaphysical reasons,
questioned the possibility of the Messiah being literally and
actually a sufferer. The attitudes of Islam reproduce many
of these misgivings and may derive from them historically . . .

The prevailing view is that at some point, undetermined, in
the course of the final events of Christ's arrest, trial and
sentence, a substitute person replaced Him while Jesus
Himself was, in the phrase, raised or raptured into Heaven
from whence, unscathed and uncrucified, He returned to
His disciples in personal appearances in which He commissioned them to take His teachings out into the world. The
Gospel they were thus to preach was a moral law only and
not the good tidings of a victorious, redemptive encounter
with sin and death. Meanwhile, the substitute sufferer bore
the whole brunt of the historical crucifixion, having been
sentenced and condemned *as if he were the Christ.*

☐ The Moslem argues that the death of Jesus is unthinkable because it is *unnecessary* from God's point of view. The Christian
answer must therefore be to seek to explain as far as possible *why*
it was necessary for Christ to die (see pp. 445ff). Some further
points are worth making here:
   —Forgiveness by its very nature involves suffering. The essence of forgiveness is that you accept an injury or an offense
without wanting to punish or to fight back. You simply bear the
injury and accept all the consequences. If this is true on the
human level, the Christian would say that it is also true when we
think about God forgiving men. When he forgives men the
wrongs and injuries they have done to him, he himself is bearing
the personal affront. In a sense he is taking the consequences
upon himself. The Moslem, on the other hand, feels that God's
forgiveness has little in common with forgiveness between men,
and is more like the pardon extended by an all-powerful ruler to
his subjects.
   —If we can say that "Christ . . . died for sins once for all . . .
that he might bring us to God . . ." (1 Peter 3:18), then it is
possible to be *sure* that if we repent, we have been forgiven.
Assurance of forgiveness is therefore based on what Jesus has
already accomplished through his death. According to the Moslem way of thinking forgiveness depends entirely on our repentance and on God's mercy, which in turns depends on what

happens on the Day of Judgment, when our good deeds are weighed in the balance against our bad deeds. This means we cannot be sure, here and now, of God's forgiveness, or of our final acceptance by him.

—If Jesus did not die, then he ceased to be identified with men at the point which men fear and dread most of all. And if Jesus did not die, he could not in any sense defeat and overcome death. If there was no death, there can have been no resurrection. Yet the writer of the letter to the Hebrews speaks in the clearest terms of Jesus destroying the power of death through his own death:

> Since . . . the children share in flesh and blood he himself likewise partook of the same nature, that through death he might destroy him who has the power of death, that is, the devil, and deliver all those who through fear of death were subject to lifelong bondage.

The question we are asking here is a question about historical fact. Did Jesus rise from the dead or did he not? Did the resurrection really happen?

The evidence in the Gospels rests on the accounts of the empty tomb and of the appearances of the risen Jesus, and on the existence of the Christian church.

QUESTION SEVEN:
DID JESUS RISE FROM THE DEAD?

Randy Birkey

THE ACCOUNTS OF THE EMPTY TOMB
Christ's death
Jesus was nailed to the cross at about 9 A.M. on Friday. Many
were present when he died at about 3 P.M. (Mark 15:21–37).
John (19:31–37) records that a Roman soldier "stabbed his side
with a lance, and at once there was a flow of blood and water."

His burial
Soon after he died, Joseph of Arimathea, a member of the
Jewish Council, received permission from Pilate, the Roman
Governor, to take the body off the cross. He and Nicodemus
(also a member of the Council) wrapped it with spices in strips of
linen cloth and laid it in Joseph's unused tomb, which had been
cut out of the rock in a garden very close to the site of the
crucifixion. The women who had followed Jesus watched all this
being done (Mark 15:40–47; John 19:38–42).

The guard
On Saturday morning, the chief priests and Pharisees went to
Pilate to ask him to have the tomb guarded, in case the disciples
stole the body. Pilate agreed to this, and the tomb was then
sealed and guarded by Roman soldiers (Matthew 27:62–66).

The women at the tomb
Very early on Sunday morning some of the women came to the
tomb bringing more spices to anoint the body of Jesus, and they
found that the stone had been rolled away from the entrance to
the tomb. When they went inside they saw two angels who
explained that Jesus had risen from the dead, and told them he
would meet them again in Galilee (Mark 16:1–8; Luke 24:1–11).

The disciples at the tomb
The women hurried back to tell the disciples, and Peter and
John ran to the tomb to see for themselves. John records that
they saw "the linen cloths lying, and the napkin, which had been
on his head, not lying with the linen cloths but rolled up in a
place by itself" (John 20:1–10).

THE ACCOUNTS OF THE APPEARANCES
OF THE RISEN JESUS
☐ Mary returned to the tomb with Peter and John, and remained

507

there after they had gone back. She stooped to look into the tomb again, and after speaking to the two angels, she turned around and saw Jesus, though at first she did not recognize him. He told her not to cling to him and gave her a message for the disciples (John 20:11–18).

☐ On the same day, when two of the disciples were on their way to a village called Emmaus, about seven miles from Jerusalem, "Jesus himself drew near and went with them. But their eyes were kept from recognizing him." They talked with him about all that had happened and invited him to spend the night with them. As he broke the bread at table, "they recognized him; and he vanished out of their sight." They immediately returned to Jerusalem to tell the other disciples (Luke 24:13–33).

☐ When they got back to the disciples, they were told that Jesus had appeared to Peter, and they gave their account of how Jesus had appeared to them on the road (Luke 24:34–35).

☐ While they were talking about all this, "Jesus himself stood among them. But they were startled and frightened and supposed that they saw a spirit. And he said to them, 'Why are you troubled, and why do questionings rise in your hearts? See my hands and my feet, that it is I myself; handle me, and see; for a spirit has not flesh and bones as you see that I have.'" They were still unconvinced, and to give them further evidence he took a piece of fish and ate it in front of them (Luke 24:36–49).

☐ On the following Sunday he appeared to them again in the upper room. Thomas had not been present the previous week and was still skeptical about what the others told him; but now he was with them. "The doors were shut, but Jesus came and stood among them." He invited Thomas to touch his hands and his side (John 20:24–29).

☐ Some time later he appeared to the disciples beside the Lake of Galilee, where he had spent much of the three years of his ministry. He had prepared a charcoal fire at the lakeside and had breakfast with them (John 21:1–9).

☐ He appeared to them on another occasion on a mountain in Galilee, and gave them the commission, "Go therefore and make disciples of all nations" (Matthew 28:16–20).

☐ During this period also "he appeared to more than 500 brethren at one time . . . then he appeared to James, then to all the apostles" (1 Corinthians 15:3–8; Paul writing in about A.D. 57).

☐The last occasion on which the disciples saw him was on the Mount of Olives in Jerusalem, about forty days after the resurrection (Acts 1:6–11).

This is Luke's summary (in Acts 1:3) of the period after the resurrection:

> He showed himself to these men after his death, and gave ample proof that he was alive: over a period of forty days he appeared to them and taught them about the kingdom of God.

THE EXISTENCE OF THE CHRISTIAN CHURCH

The writer of the Acts of the Apostles describes the origin and spread of the Christian church. According to his account, the very fact that Christianity became a separate religion is part of the evidence for the resurrection.

The transformation of the disciples

When Jesus was arrested at night in the Garden of Gethsemane, the disciples all forsook him and fled. Peter followed at a distance while Jesus was led away for trial, and disowned him three times; he was apparently too ashamed or too afraid to be identified with Jesus now that he was being tried as a criminal. After the public execution of Jesus, the disciples all hid for a time in a locked room in Jerusalem, because they were still afraid of the Jewish authorities.

Seven weeks after the death of Jesus, however, a dramatic change came over the disciples. They were now no longer ashamed to be identified with Jesus, but were speaking about him boldly in public. When this brought them into open conflict with the Jewish authorities, they were prepared to be imprisoned and flogged rather than be forced to disown Jesus or to keep quiet about him (Acts 2–4).

The separation of Christianity from Judaism

When *the disciples* first began to speak boldly about Jesus on the Day of Pentecost, they laid special emphasis on the resurrection and its implications. They never ceased to think of themselves as Jews, but it was their persistent teaching of this message about Jesus and the resurrection that led to persecution from the Jewish authorities (Acts 4:1–22).

This same pattern was repeated in the life of *Paul*, who had been brought up as a devout Jew and thoroughly trained in the school of the Pharisees. He took an active part in the persecution of Christians, but in about A.D. 34 or 35 he himself became a Christian and his preaching about Jesus and the resurrection soon brought him into conflict with the Jewish authorities.

Luke, the author of Acts, was writing for a Roman called Theophilus, who probably wanted to know how Christianity had come into being, how it differed from Judaism, and in particular why Paul was on trial in Rome. He therefore describes in considerable detail how he came to be a prisoner in Rome, and in doing so illustrates the final breach between Christianity and Judaism.

He tells us that in many places Jews opposed Paul and his message and often actively persecuted him. Eventually some of them plotted to murder him, and were about to kill him during a disturbance in the Temple area in Jerusalem, when he was rescued by Roman soldiers. The Roman authorities arranged for him to be tried before the Jewish Council, the same Council that had condemned Jesus and handed him over for execution about thirty years before. In the course of the trial he argued (Acts 23:6):

> The true issue in this trial is our hope of the resurrection of the dead.

What he was saying to them in effect was this: "Those of you who are Pharisees believe in the future resurrection; and you who are Sadducees say that the resurrection is impossible. We Christians believe in a future resurrection, and we also believe that Jesus has already been raised from the dead. The basic issue in this trial therefore is simply this: did it happen or did it not? Was Jesus raised from the dead or was he not?"

Luke clearly wanted his readers to understand that it was belief in the resurrection of Jesus that was the basic issue dividing Christianity from Judaism, and for which Paul was on trial (Acts 21:27–28:31).

Luke also tells us (Acts 17:16–32) that it was Paul's insistence on the resurrection that roused the curiosity and the scorn of the philosophers in Athens:

> Some said, "What would this babbler say?" Others said, "He seems to be a preacher of foreign divinities"—because he preached Jesus and the resurrection . . . Now when they heard of the resurrection of the dead, some mocked; but others said, "We will hear you again about this."

Since we are asking a historical question (did Jesus rise from the dead or did he not?), we need to approach the above evidence in the same way as we would for other historical questions.

But since we are dealing with something unique, it is essential to be aware of our own assumptions. It is not quite so simple as a Sherlock Holmes detective case. Our assumptions will play an important part in our estimate of what is possible or impossible in history. If we approach the evidence with our minds *already made up* that miracles *cannot* happen, no amount of evidence will convince us that the resurrection *did* happen. If on the other hand we are prepared to believe that there is a God who can work miracles in the universe he has made, then we may be willing to be convinced—provided, of course, the evidence is good enough.

DID JESUS RISE FROM THE DEAD?

It is reasonably certain.
PAGE 515

It is possible.
PAGE 519

It is improbable.
PAGE 525

It is impossible.
PAGE 529

We don't know.
PAGE 533

*We don't know
—and it doesn't
matter.*
PAGE 535

ANSWER ONE:
BIBLICAL CHRISTIANITY

It is reasonably certain
that Jesus rose from
the dead.

*This is to say, although we cannot ob-
jectively prove the resurrection with
100 percent certainty, we have sufficient evidence to be reasonably certain
that it did happen. There are good
grounds for believing that Jesus rose
from the dead.*

If you give this answer, the next obvious step is to consider what
the resurrection means. If the event has no significance there is
no point in pursuing the inquiry any further. We might just as
well conclude that it did not happen.

These are some of the conclusions the early Christians drew
from the resurrection:

It provides conclusive evidence about the identity of Jesus. All that Jesus had claimed about himself is vindicated by the resurrection.

Peter speaking to the crowds in Jerusalem on the Day of Pentecost:

> This Jesus God raised up, and of that we all are witnesses . . . Let all the house of Israel therefore know assuredly that God has made him both Lord and Christ, this Jesus whom you crucified.

It vindicates the work of Jesus and demonstrates that his death achieved something. If he had not been raised from death, his death would have been evidence of the failure of his mission. This is how the risen Jesus himself interpreted the meaning of his death:

> These are my words which I spoke to you, while I was still with you, that everything written about me in the law of Moses and the prophets and the psalms must be fulfilled . . . Thus it is written, that the Christ should suffer and on the third day rise from the dead, and that repentance and forgiveness of sins should be preached in his name to all nations.

It makes Jesus the perfect mediator who brings us into fellowship with the Father. The risen Christ gives us the right to come to the Father with boldness and confidence.

> Through him (Jesus) we . . . have access in one Spirit to the Father.

> He is able for all time to save those who draw near to God through him, since he always lives to make intercession for them.

It can mean something in everyday experience. For the Christian the resurrection is not simply an event in the past to which he looks back. It also has implications for the present.

The person who puts his trust in Jesus is united with him;* and this union and identification with him offers a real deliverance from the power of sin, and an opportunity of enjoying here and now a "newness of life" that flows from Christ's own risen life. If we are now "in Christ" and are willing to die to self as he did, all the benefits of his death and resurrection are available to us.

We were buried therefore with him by baptism into death, so that as Christ was raised from the dead by the glory of the Father, we too might walk in newness of life. For if we have been united with him in a death like his, we shall certainly be united with him in a resurrection like his. We know that our old self was crucified with him so that the sinful body might be destroyed, and we might no longer be enslaved to sin. For he who has died is freed from sin. But if we have died with Christ, we believe that we shall also live with him. For we know that Christ being raised from the dead will never die again; death no longer has dominion over him. The death he died he died to sin, once for all, but the life he lives he lives to God. So you also must consider yourselves dead to sin and alive to God in Christ Jesus.

I count everything as loss because of the surpassing worth of knowing Christ Jesus my Lord. For his sake I have suffered the loss of all things, and count them as refuse, in order that I may gain Christ . . . that I may know him and the power of his resurrection, and may share in his sufferings, becoming like him in his death, that if possible I may attain the resurrection from the dead.

None of us lives to himself, and none of us dies to himself. If we live, we live to the Lord, and if we die, we die to the Lord; so then, whether we live or whether we die, we are the Lord's. For to this end Christ died and lived again, that he might be Lord both of the dead and of the living.

The power by which God raised Jesus from death is available still. In desperate situations the Christian can have confidence that God is still able to work in the same dynamic way. Paul makes it plain that this confidence is no mere wishful thinking:

. . . we do not want you to be ignorant, brethren, of the affliction we experienced in Asia; for we were so utterly, unbearably crushed that we despaired of life itself. Why, we felt that we had received the sentence of death; but that was to make us rely not on ourselves but on God who raises the dead; he delivered us from so deadly a peril, and he will deliver us; on him we have set our hope that he will deliver us again.

It means that Jesus has triumphed over death. The believer will share this victory, and even now can enjoy the confidence and peace which this gives:

Our Savior Christ Jesus . . . abolished death and brought
life and immortality to light through the gospel.

Blessed be the God and Father of our Lord Jesus Christ!
By his great mercy we have been born anew to a living
hope through the resurrection of Jesus Christ from the
dead.

Since . . . the children share in flesh and blood, he himself
likewise partook of the same nature, that through death he
might destroy him who has the power of death, that is, the
devil, and deliver all those who through fear of death were
subject to lifelong bondage.

Lo! I tell you a mystery. We shall not all sleep, but we shall
all be changed, in a moment, in the twinkling of an eye, at
the last trumpet. For the trumpet will sound, and the dead
will be raised imperishable, and we shall be changed. For
this perishable nature must put on the imperishable, and
this mortal nature must put on immortality. When the
perishable puts on the imperishable, and the mortal puts on
immortality, then shall be brought to pass the saying that is
written: "Death is swallowed up in victory." "O death,
where is thy victory? O death, where is thy sting?"

If you believe that it is probable or reasonably certain that
Jesus was raised from the dead, and that these are some of the
implications of the resurrection, then you should go on to consider what it means to be a Christian and to enter into a personal
relationship with the living Christ. (See further "Where do we go
from here?" pp. 552ff.)

ANSWER TWO:
It is possible that Jesus
rose from the dead.

*This is to say, we cannot rule out the
possibility that the resurrection happened; we just cannot be certain.*

If you think that the resurrection *could* possibly have happened,
but are still unable to decide definitely for yourself one way or
the other, then your final answer will probably depend on
further examination of the evidence. You can sift the evidence
by asking such questions as these and considering all the possible
answers.

How are we to account for
the story of the empty tomb?
The following are all the theories that have been suggested:

Jesus was not really dead. The theory goes that Jesus was not really
dead when he was taken down from the cross. Some time after
being placed in the cool tomb he revived and got out of the
tomb.

BUT: after being scourged and hanging on the cross for six hours, Jesus would have needed considerable medical treatment. Is it likely that a person in such a condition (with his back lacerated by a scourging that often proved fatal, with wounds in his hands and feet and a sword-thrust in his side) could appear to people who had known him well, *and* give the impression that he had been raised from death?

We are told that the body of Jesus was wrapped in long pieces of cloth and covered with a large amount of spices. He would have had to extricate himself from these graveclothes, roll aside the heavy stone which several women feared they would be unable to move, and escape the notice of the guard.

If he didn't really die at this time, what happened to him afterwards? How did he finally die?

The women went to the wrong tomb. It is argued that in the dim light of the early morning the women went to a different tomb, which was empty.

BUT: we are told that the women watched Joseph and Nicodemus taking the body and putting it in the tomb on the Friday evening.

The disciples went to the tomb after hearing the report of the women; are we to assume that they were all misled, and that they did nothing to check up on the facts?

When Joseph of Arimathea heard the rumors about the resurrection, wouldn't he have taken the trouble to check the facts for himself, since he had put the corpse in his own tomb in his private garden?

What about the detailed description of the way the graveclothes were lying? Must we assume this was invented?

The body could have been stolen.

BUT: who would have stolen it? And what motive could there be?

☐ It could have been the Roman authorities or the guards: but what possible motive could they have? It was in their own interests to see that the Jesus affair was closed.

☐ It could have been the Jewish authorities: but again, what was the motive? If they knew (as Matthew tells us) that Jesus had prophesied that he would rise from the dead, they would want to insure that the body did *not* disappear from the tomb, in case the disciples might claim that he had risen. Indeed, Matthew tells us that it was the Jewish authorities who asked for the guard to be placed at the tomb.

☐ It could have been an unknown person or group of people: but what was the motive? If the body was stolen by anyone who was not a disciple, could he not have produced the remains of the body as soon as the Christians began preaching about the resurrection? If he couldn't produce the remains, could he not at least come forward and provide enough evidence to convince many people that there was a perfectly natural explanation for what the disciples were talking about? Or must we fall back on the suggestion that it was done by an unknown person without any particular motive; that he let no one know what he had done, and left Jerusalem soon after stealing the body? No one can deny that this is a possible explanation; but is it likely?

☐ It could have been the disciples or some friends of Jesus (e.g., Joseph of Arimathea); but what possible motive was there? And does this tally with the rest of the account which tells us that the disciples were not expecting anything to happen? Would they not be putting themselves in a dangerous position with the authorities, who might give them the same treatment they had given Jesus? And if one or more of the friends of Jesus stole the body, how could they have concealed it from the others? If those who stole it remained Christians for the rest of their lives, their whole faith would have been based on a lie. We would also have to say that the other disciples were extraordinarily gullible in believing the story of the resurrection without checking up on the facts for themselves, and in being prepared to die for this incredible story.

The story has been exaggerated. On this theory, something miraculous may have happened, and the story may have some basis in fact. But we cannot accept all the details of the story, since there must have been some elaboration somewhere along the line.

BUT: how are we to decide what is fact and what is fiction in the accounts? By what principles are we to decide what really happened and what was added later on? Most of the suggested rules are very subjective and the dividing line is bound to be very delicate. The skeptic will naturally want to say, "Why do you draw the line here? If you reject so much, why do you stop here and not reject some more?"

No vast period of time elapsed between the death of Jesus and the first written record that speaks about the resurrection— i.e., Paul's letter to the Corinthians, which was written about twenty-six years after the events.

It is natural to assume that the disciples and followers of Jesus would have gone to the tomb to check up on the rumors for themselves. And the more eyewitnesses there are to any event, the greater the safeguard against individuals elaborating the story.

The story was not passed on through a large number of people between the original eyewitnesses and the writers. It is not a fair comparison to say, "Look how much a story can get twisted and distorted when it passes from mouth to mouth. It comes out very different by the time it reaches the fiftieth person."

When the first accounts were written, many of the original eyewitnesses would still have been alive, and could easily have confirmed the details of the story or cast doubt on them and discredited them. Luke, for one, specifically claims to have obtained information directly from eyewitnesses (Luke 1:2).

The whole story has been invented. Nothing like this ever happened, so the argument goes. The body remained in the tomb, and the first disciples knew it. However, in the course of time they, and/or other Christians, came to express their faith in Jesus in terms of a story describing events. The story was not intended to be an historical account of what happened, but was merely intended as a way of expressing their beliefs about Jesus. Some would say that the stories were invented deliberately and consciously to convince others about the identity of Jesus. Others say that there was nothing dishonest about what they did, and that it would have been very natural for them to express their personal beliefs and experiences in this way.

BUT: if there was no event that led the disciples to their faith in the victory of Jesus over death, how did they come to believe this in the first place? If it was the faith of the early Christians which produced the story of the empty tomb, what gave them that faith?

One can imagine a person composing a myth to teach something or to stir the imagination; but why compose such a story (even with the best of motives) and present it as sober fact rather than as pure fantasy?

Even if the disciples had the very best motives in inventing the story, would they really be prepared to go on teaching it to others as simple fact when they found that it led to ridicule, persecution and suffering?

If the early Christians who used the story of the empty tomb understood it simply as myth and nothing more, why should anyone want to oppose their message?

What about the question of honesty? When is a lie not a lie?

At some stage in the process there would inevitably have been many Christians (followers of one who claimed to be "the truth") who knew perfectly well that the story of the empty tomb was not true, but went on telling the story which led others to believe that something objective really did happen.

The documents are reliable. If the theories outlined above seem unconvincing, there remains only one alternative—that the New Testament documents are reliable. They give us an account (though not an exhaustive one) of what the disciples actually witnessed.

How are we to account for the stories of the appearances of the risen Jesus?

Hallucination. There was never anyone there; the disciples were simply experiencing some kind of hallucination.

BUT: although individuals can experience hallucination, a group of people who have very different personalities normally do not. It is virtually unheard of for 500 people to experience the same kind of hallucination at the same time.

These experiences were reported over a period of seven weeks and were not confined to one day; and they occurred at different places and at different times of the day.

Hallucination often takes the form of seeing things one would like to see; but there is no evidence that the disciples were expecting or looking for these appearances.

Exaggeration. There was something there, but the details have been exaggerated.

BUT: as before (see p. 521), how are we to decide what happened? How are we to pare away the additions from the accounts as they stand?

Nothing really happened. Nothing actually happened in the objective world; the disciples either *saw visions* communicated to them by God or had *purely subjective experiences.* Eventually they came to express these experiences and their new beliefs about Jesus in terms of stories about seeing, hearing, and touching the risen Jesus. They were so conscious of the continuing influence of his personality and teaching, that they came to express this in terms of "myth"—i.e., the stories looked as if they were about real events in the external world, but in fact they were merely a convincing way of expressing personal beliefs about Jesus.

BUT: exactly the same problems arise as before (see p. 521 above).

The accounts are factual and reliable. The documents together give us an account of *what the disciples* actually witnessed—what they saw with their eyes, heard with their ears, and touched with their hands. The accounts are not exhaustive; they do not tell us, for instance, what the risen Christ was wearing. But they are detailed enough to rule out the idea that the appearances were purely inward, subjective experiences, or that the disciples were merely seeing some kind of ghost.

How are we to account for the existence of the Christian church?

If we discount the evidence of the New Testament about the origin of the Christian church, how did it come into existence?

How are we to explain the transformation of the small group of frightened disciples?

How are we to account for the separation of Christianity from Judaism?

According to the Gospels and Acts, it was the resurrection which transformed the disciples. Because of their conviction about the risen Christ, they had the courage to abandon their defensive position and to tell the world the good news of his death and resurrection. The records imply that if they had been content to speak about Jesus simply as a good man or a prophet or teacher, they would never have brought on themselves such fierce opposition and suffering. The Jews would never have had any reason to persecute the Christians, and they would probably have remained as a small sect within Judaism. In this case, Christianity would never have become a separate religion.

For each of these questions you must simply decide for yourself which answer best fits the facts. This kind of examination of the evidence should therefore lead you to one of the other possible answers:

reasonably certain (p. 515)

improbable (p. 525)

don't know (p. 533)

ANSWER THREE:

It is improbable that Jesus rose from the dead.

This is to say, it is not impossible that something extraordinary happened, but the evidence is far from convincing. There are other possible and far more plausible explanations of what is recorded in the Gospels.

The Jewish Encyclopedia suggests that the belief in the resurrection is

> . . . due to two psychic forces that never before had come so strongly into play: (1) the great personality of Jesus, which had so impressed itself upon the simple people of Galilee as to become a living power to them even after his death; and (2) the transcendentalism, or other-worldliness, in which those penance-doing, saintly men and women of the common classes, in their longing for godliness, lived . . .

In an atmosphere of such perfect naiveté the miracle of the Resurrection seemed as natural as had been the miracle of the healing of the sick.

Hugh Schonfield has put forward his theory of the "Passover Plot." He suggests that Jesus planned secretly with a few friends (but not with his disciples) that he should be taken down from the cross before he died, so that he could be revived later. They were to give the impression, however, that he was really dead. In the event, the plot failed; for although he was not completely dead when he was taken down from the cross, he died soon afterwards before he could be revived. In spite of the failure of the plot, Schonfield sees a profound meaning in these events:

> He had schemed in faith for his physical recovery, and what he expected had been frustrated by circumstances quite beyond his control. Yet when he sank into sleep, his faith was unimpaired, and by an extraordinary series of contributory events, partly resulting from his own planning, it proved to have been justified. In a manner he had not forseen resurrection had come to him . . .

> . . . Whenever mankind strives to bring in the rule of justice, righteousness and peace, there the deathless presence of Jesus the Messiah is with them.

Ronald Gregor Smith believes that the historical evidence for the resurrection is altogether unconvincing; but he goes on to say that this does not destroy Christian faith:

> So far as historicity is concerned, . . . it is necessary to explain: we may freely say that the bones of Jesus lie somewhere in Palestine.

> Christian faith is not destroyed by this admission. On the contrary, only now, when this has been said, are we in a position to ask about the meaning of the resurrection as an integral part of the message concerning Jesus.

POINTS TO CONSIDER ABOUT THIS ANSWER

☐ If you give this kind of answer, you still have to account for the very strong *belief* in the resurrection among the early Christians. If you believe that nothing like the resurrection took place, you still ought to work out some theory to explain how it was that the disciples were misled, *or* how they came to be misleading others, *or* how we today (and the majority of Christians in the past) are misled when we read these stories as if they are an account of events which actually happened.

Many of those who say that the story is highly improbable refuse to work out a *detailed* alternative. But some who do, recognize how tentative it must be.

Hugh Schonfield:

> We are nowhere claiming for our reconstruction that it represents what actually happened, but that on the evidence we have it may be fairly close to the truth . . .

> Naturally it cannot be said that this is a solution to the puzzle (about the alleged appearances of Jesus after his death). . . . There is room for other theories, such as that the man concerned (i.e., the man who collaborated with Jesus in the Passover Plot), if there was one, was a medium, and that Jesus, rising from the dead into the After Life in the spiritualist sense, spoke through him in his own voice which enabled his presence to be recognized . . . Too little is told, and that little quickly became too legendary, and too contradictory, for any assured conclusion. The view taken here does seem to fit the requirements and is in keeping with what has been disclosed of the Passover Plot. The planning of Jesus for his expected recovery created the mystery of the empty tomb.

☐ If you give this kind of answer you ought to be completely consistent and draw the appropriate conclusions about Jesus (as the first writer does): that he was an ordinary man whose career was ended by a cruel death, and that he is no more "alive" today than Socrates or Confucius or any other historical character.

You may want to say that Jesus' outlook on life is an appropriate one for people today to have. But there is nothing unique about making this kind of claim for a historical character. A nationalist in South America could speak in exactly the same way about Che Guevara, and a Chinese Communist might think in these terms about Mao Tse Tung. If you use the word *resurrection* to describe the influence of Jesus and his life and teaching on you, you are confusing the issue. For you are giving the word a completely different meaning from the usual Christian one.

If you use the word *resurrection*, most people will automatically think of someone being raised from death. But this is not what you mean by the word, and there is bound to be an element of deception or misunderstanding if you continue to use the word. You ought in all fairness to find a different one (compare the similar problems in the ambiguous use of "God," Part 2, pp. 181ff.)

☐ The *meaning* of the resurrection can hardly survive without the *event* of the resurrection. If the resurrection did not happen, you cannot ask what the resurrection means. And to say that the meaning can survive without the event is rather like the story in Alice in Wonderland where the grin of the Cheshire Cat survives even after the Cat himself has slowly disappeared:

> "All right," said the Cat; and this time it vanished quite slowly, beginning with the end of the tail, and ending with the grin, which remained sometime after the rest of it had gone.

> "Well! I've often seen a cat without a grin," thought Alice; "but a grin without a cat! It's the most curious thing I ever say in all my life!"

In the end there may be little point in arguing about the details of the historical events. For your estimate of what is probable or improbable in history will be determined by your understanding of God and the universe. (See further Part 2, Questions Two and Four, "Who or what is God?" and "What kind of universe do we live in?")

ANSWER FOUR:
It is impossible for Jesus to have risen from the dead.

This is to say, it is inconceivable that any human being should be raised from death. In the light of all that science has discovered about the workings of the universe, it is simply not possible for a dead man to be raised to life.

David Hume, the eighteenth-century Scottish philosopher, gave this kind of answer, and many answers given today are simply a restatement of his argument in a different form.

A miracle is a violation of the laws of nature; and as a firm and unalterable experience has established these laws, the proof against a miracle from the very nature of the fact, is as entire as any argument from experience can possibly be imagined. . . . It is a miracle, that a dead man should come to life; because that has never been observed in any age or country. There must therefore be a uniform experience against every miraculous event, otherwise the event would not merit that appellation. And as a uniform experience amounts to proof, there is here a direct and full *proof*, from the nature of the fact, against the existence of any miracle; nor can such a proof be destroyed, or the miracle rendered credible, but by an opposite proof, which is superior.

The plain consequence is . . . that no testimony is sufficient to establish a miracle, unless the testimony be of such kind, that its falsehood would be more miraculous, than the fact, which it endeavors to establish . . . When anyone tells me that he saw a dead man restored to life, I immediately consider with myself, whether it be more probable, that this person should either deceive or be deceived, or that the fact, which he relates, should really have happened. I weigh the one miracle against the other; and according to the superiority, which I discover, I pronounce my decision, and always reject the greater miracle.

After discussing the evidence for certain miracles outside the Bible, but without discussing in detail the evidence for the resurrection, he concludes:

Upon the whole, then, it appears, that no testimony for any kind of miracle has ever amounted to a probability, much less to a proof; and that even supposing it amounted to a proof, it would be opposed by another proof . . . We may establish it as a maxim, that no human testimony can have such force as to prove a miracle, and make it a just foundation for any such system of religion.

His argument can be summarized in these stages:

The uniformity of natural causes within a closed system is an established fact.

No testimony about any miracle has ever been sufficiently convincing.

Therefore miracles *cannot* happen.

Therefore miracles *do not* happen, and the resurrection did not happen.

Hume draws the obvious conclusion that Christianity cannot be true.

C. S. Lewis summarizes Hume's argument in this way:

> Ever since Hume's famous *Essay* it has been believed that historical statements about miracles are the most intrinsically improbable of all historical statements. According to Hume, probability rests on what may be called the majority vote of our past experiences. The more often a thing has been known to happen, the more probable it is that it should happen again; and the less often the less probable. Now the regularity of Nature's course, says Hume, is supported by something better than the majority vote of past experiences: it is supported by their unanimous vote, or, as Hume says, by "firm and unalterable experience." There is, in fact, "uniform experience" against Miracle; otherwise, says Hume, it would not be Miracle. A Miracle is therefore the most improbable of all events. It is always more probable that the witnesses were lying or mistaken than that a Miracle occurred.

POINTS TO CONSIDER ABOUT THIS ANSWER

☐ You still have to account for the strong *belief* in the resurrection among the early Christians. If you believe that the resurrection could not have happened, you still ought to find some way of explaining how it was that the disciples were misled, *or* how they came to be misleading others, *or* how we today (and the majority of Christians in the past) have been misled in assuming that these stories were intended to be taken at their face value as accounts of things that happened.

☐ In the end the real argument will not be about the details of the New Testament accounts, but about basic assumptions. If you approach the evidence with your mind already made up that no human being could ever be raised from death, then no amount of historical evidence will convince you.

C. E. M. Joad, writing at the time when he did not believe in the resurrection, explains how his presuppositions prevented him from taking the detailed evidence seriously:

> The question at issue is . . . for me not so much a question of proving that the Christian record of fact is false or that the Christian revelation in the matter of the Resurrection cannot be substantiated; to a mind awake to the new knowl-

edge of science these time-honored claims you continue to make seem to be those of a man talking in his sleep.

To ascribe a central position to Jesus in the history of mankind may have accorded well enough with the narrow world picture of the Middle Ages, with its few thousand years of human history and its expectation of Christ's Return in the comparatively near future to put an end to the universe. But to me and to any modern this whole way of thinking is as unintelligible as it is impertinent. The framework of assumptions required for an understanding of the modern universe has been so widened that the old Christian hypothesis is lost sight of. And that, I suppose, is why, to return to your oft-reiterated complaint, we simply cannot be bothered to give the Christian hypothesis the attention which you seem to think it still deserves.

If therefore you would give an answer of this kind, you should consider some of the implications of this view of the universe. (See further Part 2, Questions Two and Four, "Who or what is God?" and "What kind of universe do we live in?")

ANSWER FIVE:

We don't know
whether or not Jesus
rose from the dead.

*This is to say, we cannot be sure one
way or the other. We simply do not
know for certain.*

**POINTS
TO CONSIDER
ABOUT THIS
ANSWER**

☐ If it is a question of the *amount* of evidence available, how much
more evidence would you demand before making up your mind?
Are you demanding a degree of certainty you would never
dream of asking for other events supposed to have happened in
the past? The resurrection of a dead man is obviously an extraordinary event; and you have every right to ask for convincing evidence before you commit yourself to believing that it
happened. But are you asking for an impossible kind of historical proof?

533

☐ What *kind* of evidence do you think could be found which would enable you to give a more definite answer? Suppose, for example, a document were found which was written by a Roman or a Greek or a Jew, and which said that Jesus had been raised from death; what would it prove? It would prove that some people (perhaps including non-Christians) believed that Jesus did rise from death. But would it prove anything more than this? And in any case, would you not be able to find an easier way of explaining this evidence—by saying, for example, that the document could have been a forgery, written by Christians to provide independent evidence?

The well-known passage from Josephus' *Antiquities* comes into this very category; since Josephus, the Jewish historian, was not a Christian. (See pp. 424 and 545.)

☐ Even supposing (for the sake of argument) that there were no evidence outside the New Testament for the resurrection, what would it prove? It could mean:

either   that the whole story was invented by Christians;

or   that of those who believed that it did happen, some became Christians and were content to believe the testimony of the eyewitnesses who were still alive, while others saw no significance in the event and saw no reason to write about it.

☐ If, after a detailed study of the evidence, you continue to give this answer, you should consider some of the consequences of consistent agnosticism (see Part 1, pp. 64ff.)

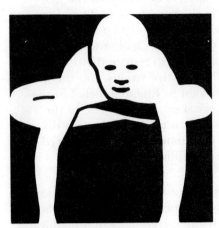

ANSWER SIX:

We don't know
whether or not Jesus
rose from the dead—
and it doesn't matter.

*This is to say, it is impossible to be
certain whether the resurrection happened or not; but in any case, it doesn't
really matter. Faith in Jesus Christ
does not depend on the results of historical inquiry. For it is a personal faith,
independent of questions about what
actually happened.*

To this way of thinking, therefore, in spite of the uncertainty,

either   we accept the resurrection by a leap of faith, knowing
that it is contrary to reason;

or   we accept the resurrection as symbol or myth;

or   we remain content simply to experience what "resurrection" means in our own lives.

Rudolph Bultmann:

The resurrection is not an event of past history. All that
historical criticism can establish is the fact that the first
disciples came to believe in the resurrection. The historian
can perhaps to some extent account for that faith from the
personal intimacy which the disciples had enjoyed with
Jesus during his earthly life, and so reduce the resurrection
appearances to a series of subjective visions. But the historical problem is scarcely relevant to Christian belief in the
resurrection. For the historical event of the rise of the
Easter faith means for us what it meant to the first disciples, namely, the self-manifestation of the risen Lord, the
act of God in which the redemptive event of the cross is
completed.

The resurrection of Jesus cannot be a miraculous proof by
which the skeptic might be compelled to believe in Christ.
The difficulty is not simply the incredibility of a mythical
event like the resuscitation of a corpse—for that is what the
resurrection means . . . Nor is it merely the difficulty of
establishing the objective historicity of the resurrection no
matter how many witnesses are cited, as though once it was
established it might be believed beyond question and might
have its unimpeachable guarantee. No; the real difficulty is
that the resurrection is itself an article of faith, and you
cannot establish one article of faith because it is far more
that the resuscitation of a corpse—it is an eschatological
event. And so it cannot be a miraculous proof.

The resurrection is not a mythological event adduced in
order to prove the saving efficacy of the cross, but an article
of faith just as much as the meaning of the cross itself.
Indeed, faith in the resurrection is really the same thing as
faith in the saving efficacy of the cross, faith in the cross as
the cross of Christ.

The real purpose of myth is not to present an objective
picture of the world as it is, but to express man's understanding of himself in the world in which he lives. Myth
should be interpreted not cosmologically, but anthropologi-
cally, or better still, existentially.

Harvey Cox is prepared to accept the assumptions of naturalistic science—i.e., the universe is a system in which there can be no
divine intervention. He therefore admits that on these assump-

tions, the resurrection is not possible. He believes, however, that
Christian faith can survive in spite of this contradiction:

> We will have to live the rest of our lives both with the
> affirmation that in some way the Christ lives among us and
> with the gnawing doubt that this really isn't possible. If we
> want to escape this kind of ambiguity, we are looking for a
> perfection which will not be available in this life.

> I personally do not believe that we shall have any *personal*
> experience of the deep mystery . . . (of the resurrection)
> until we are ready to identify our lives with these people
> (the poor, the rejected, the despised, the sick, and the hurt)
> in our time. Then and only then I think do we have the
> kind of experience on the basis of which we can talk about
> the reality of the resurrection.

Paul van Buren:

> As historians, and indeed as proper users of the English
> language, we would prefer not to speak of the Easter event
> as a "fact" at all, not in the ordinary sense of the word. We
> can say something about the situation before Easter, and we
> can say other things about the consequences of the Easter
> event, but the resurrection does not lend itself to being
> spoken of as a "fact," for it cannot be described. We can say
> that Jesus died and was buried, and that his disciples were
> then discouraged and disappointed men. That was the situ-
> ation before Easter . . . On the other side of Easter, we can
> say that the disciples were changed men. They apparently
> found themselves caught up in something like the freedom
> of Jesus himself, having become men who were free to face
> even death without fear. Whatever it was that lay between,
> and which might account for this change, is not open to
> our historical investigation. The evidence is insufficient. All
> we can say is that something happened.

John Wren-Lewis:

> The important thing about a myth or a fiction is the direc-
> tion in which it points us, and for me the Christian myth of
> resurrection is important because it represents a vision of the
> possibility of building a world where love shall be all in all.

> There is a real possibility . . . that the idea of resurrection
> might well be an expression of the ultimate achievements of
> technology.

POINTS
TO CONSIDER
ABOUT THIS
ANSWER

☐ If you give this kind of answer, how do you justify your historical skepticism? Are you just as skeptical about other documents
of the period—e.g., the writings of Roman historians and Josephus, the Jewish historian? Or is it merely the extraordinary
content of the New Testament documents that makes you believe
that they cannot be taken as straightforward records of what
happened?

And why do you not carry your skepticism one stage further?
What answer can you give to the person who refuses even to
believe that the first disciples came to believe in the resurrection?
How do you decide where to draw the line between what can be
established by historical criticism and what must be left open?

☐ This kind of answer depends on certain assumptions, either
about the nature of faith or about the universe:

Eduard Schweitzer declares the assumption that only "faith" can
create faith:

> Even if we had the best film of a Jerusalem newsreel of the
> year A.D. 30 (or whatever it was), it would not help us much
> since it could not show us what really happened on that
> day. Only Easter, the revelation of the Spirit, shows what
> really happened . . . Historical facts never create faith, only
> faith creates faith.

> Proof cannot be given of Jesus' resurrection . . . God ex-
> poses himself to skepticism, doubt, and disbelief, renounc-
> ing anything that would compel men to believe.

> The immediate effect of this conclusion is extremely liberat-
> ing. The earliest Christians obviously cared astonishingly
> little about all the details of the Easter event—the where
> and how of it. But this means that the Easter faith does not
> depend on our success in believing in the possibility and
> historicity of all kinds of remarkable happenings, like the
> ability of the risen Lord to eat. It means, furthermore, that
> our assurance of Jesus' resurrection does not wax or wane
> depending on how precisely we read these accounts and on
> what new sources are discovered. But if there are no guar-
> antees for Easter faith, on what is our assurance based? . . .

> When . . . assurance grows out of life with the word of the
> risen Lord and in obedience to him, the historical details of

what happened at Easter become incidental. For faith no
longer needs the guarantees of proof. To faith, the empty
tomb will be a sign of what has taken place. It will not,
however, fight for the empty tomb as for an article of faith,
because the truth of Easter does not in fact depend on the
empty tomb. What is important is whether the believer has
such faith in the risen Lord that he will live under his
dominion, will hold fast to the lordship of Jesus even when
it leads him to his death. Only then will he find out
whether he really relies on him "who raises the dead" (2
Cor. 1: 8–9). And so the disciples, too, had to learn to
understand what really took place at Easter through years
of service under the living Christ, by living under his dominion and letting him show them what his resurrection really
meant.

Rudolph Bultmann defines faith as

. . . an understanding of existence . . . Existential self-
understanding can be appropriated only existentially. In my
existential self-understanding, I could not learn what existence means in the abstract, but I understand in my concrete here and now, in my concrete encounters.

In answer to one of his critics, he confesses that he finds it hard
to think in terms of enjoying a personal relationship with the
living Christ:

I must confess . . . that the language of personal relationships with Christ is just as mythological as the other imag-
ery you favor.

Gunther Bornkam, a disciple of Bultmann:

Certainly faith cannot and should not be dependent on the
change and uncertainty of historical research.

Van Buren declares his assumptions about the nature of the
universe:

If we speak of Easter as a fact, we shall have to be able to
give a description of it. To take the latter tradition as a
description of the appearances, however, raises far more
problems than it solves. Because of the influence of the
natural sciences, especially biology, on our thinking today,
we can no more silence the questions concerning the
changes in cells at death which spring to the mind when we

read the Easter story of the Gospels, than we can deny that
we live in the twentieth century.

J. S. Bezzant exposes the assumptions behind Bultmann's concept of faith, shared by many of these writers:

> It is even said (by Bultmann) that Christ crucified and risen
> meets us in the word of preaching and nowhere else. Faith
> in the word of preaching is sufficient and absolute . . .
> Believe the message and it has saving efficacy. But what is
> the ground for believing? The answer given is Jesus' dis-
> ciples' experience of the resurrection. But this is not, he
> holds, a historical confirmation of the crucifixion as the
> decisive saving event because the resurrection is also a mat-
> ter of faith only, i.e., one act of faith has no other basis
> than another act of faith. And what is the resurrection?
> Another theologian who accepts the historical skepticism of
> Bultmann says "the resurrection is to be understood neither
> as outward nor inward, neither mystically nor as a supernat-
> ural phenomenon nor as historical." If this has any mean-
> ing it can only be that the resurrection is not to be under-
> stood in any sense. No intelligent person desires to substi-
> tute prudent acceptance of the demonstrable for faith; but
> when I am told that it is precisely its immunity from proof
> which secures the Christian proclamation from the charge
> of being mythological, I reply that immunity from proof
> can "secure" nothing whatever except immunity from
> proof, and call nonsense by its proper name. Nor do I
> think that anything like historical Christianity can be re-
> lieved of objections by making the validity of assertions
> depend upon the therapeutic function it plays in healing
> fractures in the souls of believers, or understand how it can
> ever have this healing function unless it can be believed to
> be true.

This answer is therefore open to the same objections as the
belief that the *meaning* of the resurrection can survive independently of the *event* (see pp. 525ff.). See Part 1, pp. 86–
109, for a further discussion of this understanding of "faith."

BACK TO ANSWER ONE

It is reasonably certain that Jesus rose from the dead.

Having examined other possible answers to the basic question, we must now return to option one, the biblical Christian answer, and look at some of the main questions and objections raised.

What was the resurrection body of Jesus like?

These are the only indications given in the accounts:

He was able to appear in a locked room (John 20:19).

He insisted that he was not a spirit or a ghost, but that his body was tangible. The disciples therefore were able to perceive the risen Christ through three of their senses—they could see him, touch him, and hear his words (Luke 24:36–43).

541

He was recognizable by those who had known him before his death. It is true that he was not always recognized immediately (e.g., by Mary and by the disciples on the road to Emmaus). But this apparent inconsistency is understandable, since they did not expect Jesus to be raised from the dead. And if the whole story had been invented, an awkward detail like this would hardly have been included.

According to the accounts, therefore, there was some real continuity between his physical body during his lifetime and his body after the resurrection. But his resurrection body did not have all the limitations of a human body; it was not merely a resuscitated corpse.

But does the resurrection body have to be a *physical* body? Can we not believe in a *spiritual* resurrection, i.e., that Jesus survived death in a unique way, but without a visible and tangible body?

This idea runs counter to the whole way of thinking of the disciples. As Jews they would *already* have believed in a vague kind of spiritual survival beyond death in Sheol; and they would have believed in a future resurrection. But that resurrection was by definition a physical resurrection. A purely "spiritual" resurrection without a physical body of some kind would not have made sense to a Jew; the disciples would not have spoken of it in these terms.

We can only interpret the accounts in this way if we assume that the writers were not claiming to write accounts of what actually happened, and that they did not expect the intelligent reader to understand them literally. But this assumption is based on a particular understanding of truth, which is different from the biblical understanding. (See Part 1.)

Don't the different accounts contradict one another?

There are certainly some differences in the four accounts; but they hardly amount to contradictions. It does not require much ingenuity to suggest ways in which they can be fitted together. For example:

☐ *Who came to the tomb first?*

> *Mark* 16:1–2: "Mary of Magdalene, and Mary the mother of James, and Salome . . . went to the tomb . . ."

> *Luke* 23:55: "the women who had come with him from Galilee . . ."

Matthew 28:1: "Mary Magdalene and the other Mary."

John 20:1: "Mary Magdalene came to the tomb . . ."

These accounts would be contradictory if, and only if, they claimed to be exhaustive accounts; i.e., if John said, for example, that Mary of Magdala came *alone* to the tomb.

It is hardly reasonable to discount a report of an incident simply on the grounds that it is selective and records the incident from the point of view of *one* of those who were involved.

☐ *What did the women and the disciples see at the tomb?*

Mark 16:5: "a young man . . . dressed in a white robe . . ."

Luke 24:4: "two men . . . in dazzling apparel . . ."

Matthew 28:2: "an angel of the Lord . . ."

John 20:12: "two angels in white . . ."

This is not an insuperable difficulty if we remember that Mark and Luke were writing for a Roman audience, who might not be familiar with the idea of angels from the Old Testament.

The difference in the number of the angels would amount to a contradiction only if Mark and Matthew spoke of "one and only one." If one acts as spokesman for the two, we can hardly blame an eyewitness for mentioning that one only.

☐ *Why did Jesus tell Mary not to touch him, but invite Thomas to touch him?*

John 20:17: "Jesus said to her, 'Do not hold me, for I have not yet ascended to the Father . . .'"

John 20:27: "Then he said to Thomas, 'Put your finger here, and see my hands; and put out your hand, and place it in my side . . .'"

Mary was wanting to cling to Jesus in a physical way, and therefore Jesus had to say to her, "Don't cling to me, because I am soon to ascend to the Father; and in this new relationship you will not be able to see me or touch me any more." With Thomas, however, the position was different. Thomas had said, "Unless I see in his hands the print of the nails, and place my finger in the mark of the nails, and place my hand in his side, I will not believe" (John 20:25). When Jesus invited Thomas to touch him, therefore, he was simply wanting to give him the firm and tangible evidence he wanted before he would believe that Jesus was alive from the dead.

543

If we really want to press this kind of apparent inconsistency, we are in effect saying, "We would be more prepared to believe the documents if they agreed in every small detail." But if the documents did agree in every small detail, would this not raise even *more* doubts in our minds and suggest that there had been some collusion amongst the writers?

And even if the documents do appear to contradict each other, what does it prove? The different accounts of an automobile accident or of a football game show that eyewitness reports can differ enormously. But the differences only remind us that the four different people saw the event from their own standpoint. They hardly lead us to conclude that *nothing* of the kind happened. The uncertainty about some of the events surrounding the assassination of President Kennedy in 1963 only proves that we shall probably never have an exhaustive account of what happened. No one would use the uncertainty to suggest that Kennedy was not assassinated.

> *Arnold Lunn:*
>
> Do please apply to the Resurrection narratives the same "commonsense standards" that you would apply to any historical event. If we had two accounts of the landing of William the Conqueror we should not reject *both* because the first made him land in England with his left foot first and the second with his right foot first.

Why doesn't Paul mention the story of the empty tomb?

In his first letter to the Corinthians, which is the earliest record of the resurrection (A.D. 56), Paul does not actually mention the story of the empty tomb. It is sometimes argued from this that Paul did not know the story, which must therefore be of later origin.

☐ In the passage in question—1 Corinthians 15—Paul is reminding the Corinthian Christians of the gospel he preached to them when he was with them. He is therefore simply reminding them of something they already knew, and not speaking to them as if they had never heard the story before. He introduces his summary with the words:

> Now I would remind you, brethren, in what terms I preached to you the gospel . . . For I delivered to you as of first importance what I also received, that Christ died for our sins in accordance with the scriptures, that he was

buried, that he was raised on the third day in accordance with the scriptures, and that he appeared to Cephas, then to the twelve. . . .

There is good reason to believe that Paul uses for his summary here an early Christian hymn or confession.

☐ The most obvious meaning of the words "he was buried . . . he was raised on the third day" is that the body of Jesus was buried *in a tomb* and was raised *from the tomb* on the third day.

☐ Paul shows very clearly in the rest of the chapter that he believed in a physical resurrection. His understanding of the resurrection body which all men will receive was based on his understanding of the resurrection body of Jesus. He describes the resurrection body as a "spiritual body" in the sense that it is not identical with our present physical bodies, but is immortal and imperishable.

> But some one will ask, "How are the dead raised? With what kind of body do they come?" You foolish man! What you sow does not come to life unless it dies. And what you sow is not the body which is to be, but a bare kernel, perhaps of wheat or of some other grain . . . So it is with the resurrection of the dead. What is sown is perishable, what is raised is imperishable. It is sown in dishonor, it is raised in glory. It is sown in weakness, it is raised in power. It is sown a physical body, it is raised a spiritual body . . .

> For the trumpet will sound, and the dead will be raised imperishable, and we shall be changed. For this perishable nature must put on the imperishable, and this mortal nature must put on immortality . . .

Is there any evidence for the resurrection outside the New Testament?

There are several pieces of evidence from outside the New Testament which have an indirect bearing on the resurrection.

☐ *Josephus*, the Jewish historian, writing in *The Antiquities of the Jews*:

The Greek Version:

> When Pilate, on the indictment of the principal men among us, had condemned him to the cross, those who loved him at the first did not cease to do so, for he appeared to them again alive on the third day . . .

The Arabic Version:

Pilate condemned him to be crucified and to die. And those who had become his disciples did not abandon his discipleship. They reported that he had appeared to them three days after his crucifixion and that he was alive.

See further pp. 424, 425.

☐ The following *inscription*, found at Nazareth, records an edict of the Emperor Claudius (A.D. 41–54) or the Emperor Tiberius (A.D. 14–37) about the robbing of graves:

> Ordinance of Caesar. It is my pleasure that graves and tombs remain undisturbed in perpetuity for those who have made them for the cult of their ancestors or children or members of their house. If however any man lay information that another has either demolished them, or has in any other way extracted the buried, or has maliciously transferred them to other places in order to wrong them, or has displaced the sealing of other stones, against such a one I order that a trial be instituted, as in respect of the gods, so in regard to the cult of mortals. For it shall be much more obligatory to honor the buried. Let it be absolutely forbidden for anyone to disturb them. In case of contravention I desire that the offender be sentenced to capital punishment on charge of violation of sepulture.

Obviously we cannot be certain any connection exists between this inscription and the disappearance of the body of Jesus from the tomb. But it does suggest, at the very least, that reports had reached the Emperor about bodies being removed from tombs, perhaps in Palestine itself. This edict could possibly represent the official reaction to these reports.

☐ In 1945 the following two *inscriptions* on ossuaries (bone-caskets) were found in a burial chamber at Talpioth, a suburb of Jerusalem. They were found by Professor E. L. Sukenik, a Jewish archaeologist, and can be dated with certainty to between A.D. 40 and 50.

Ihco c|ıɔ

i.e., ᾿Ιησους ᾿ιου —which probably means "Jesus woe!" or "Jesus, help!" (i.e., a short prayer addressed to Jesus).

Ihcoʹ|ı ᴧᴧwθ

i.e., ᾿Ιησους αλωθ —which probably means "Jesus, let him (who rests here) arise!"

These two inscriptions suggest that even at this early date Christians were praying to Jesus; and looking forward to a future resurrection.

☐ The *earliest Jewish writings that speak about Jesus* nowhere deny that the tomb was empty. It is reasonable to suppose that Jewish tradition would have handed down any suggestions that the tomb of Jesus had never been touched and that the body remained in the tomb. But there is no such suggestion. The Jewish traditions agreed that the tomb was empty, but explained this by saying that the disciples stole the body (this apparently despite the guard of soldiers they themselves set—Matthew 27:62–66).

Didn't many religions at this time have beliefs about immortality and stories about gods rising from the dead?

☐ A belief in the survival of the individual seems to have been universal in primitive societies.

S. H. Hooke:

The archaeological evidence of primitive funerary practices shows that early man believed that his dead continued to exist in some form, and could be affected by his behavior toward them, and could also exercise a power over him that might be either malign or benificent.

☐ The idea of resurrection is found in many of the myths of the ancient world, and is always connected with the annual cycle of agriculture (winter—death: spring—resurrection).

S. H. Hooke:

The idea of resurrection, as distinct from survival after death, or the return of the spirits or ghosts of the dead to trouble the living, appears in the mythology of both Egypt and Babylon. In Egypt we find the cult-myth of Osiris, slain and dismembered by Set, and revivified by Isis and Nepthys by means of magic spells. In Sumer and Babylon we have the myth of Tammuz, the god who dies and descends in the underworld, and is brought back to life by his sister and wife Ishtar, who descends into the underworld in search of him. Both of these myths belong to the cult pattern of an agricultural civilization. They arise out of the observation of the annual death and rebirth of vegetation, and are connected with rituals intended to secure the annual renewal of the life of nature.

☐ In these myths resurrection is only for the *gods* and not for *men*:

S. H. Hooke:

> It must be remarked that in all these forms of the myth it is aways gods who die and rise again. There is no suggestion that men may share in the resurrection of the gods. This is confirmed by the Babylonian epithet for the underworld, "the land of no-return." There are, however, two interesting points to be noted which suggested the possibility that in some way man might share in or benefit by the death and resurrection of a god. The first is that in the Egyptian funerary cult the dead person for whom the mummification rituals are performed is thereby identified with Osiris, and his salvation in the after-life secured. The other is that in Babylonian *puhu* or substitution rituals dealing with certain forms of sickness, it was possible for the sick man to be symbolically identified with the death of Tammuz and thereby to be freed from his sickness. These faint adumbrations of what was to be developed in the pattern of revelation form part of the background of our study.

☐ The intention behind these myths and rituals was that the individual should obtain salvation; but this salvation bears little resembalance to the Christian understanding of salvation.

C. K. Barrett:

> The object of the mystery cults was to secure salvation for men who were subject to moral and physical evil, dominated by Destiny, and unable by themselves to escape from the corruption that beset the material side of their nature. Salvation accordingly meant escape from Destiny, release from corruption and a renewed moral life. It was affected by what may broadly be called sacramental means. By taking part in prescribed rites the worshiper became united with God, was enabled in this life to enjoy mystical communion with him, and further was assured of immortality beyond death. This process rested upon the experiences (generally including the death and resurrection of a Savior-God, the Lord (*kurios*)) of his devotees. The myth, which seems often to have been cultically represented, rested in many of these religions upon the fundamental annual cycle of agriculture fertility; but rites which probably were in earlier days intended to secure productiveness in field and flock were now given an individual application and effect.

☐ Against this background we can understand how, when the
Christian message of the resurrection was proclaimed, some
thought it ridiculous that there could be any kind of physical
resurrection for the individual. But others gladly embraced the
Christian gospel because it contained something *new*, and
brought the fulfillment of their hopes and longings for a life
with meaning and purpose beyond the grave.

Do contemporary physics and psychic research make it any easier to believe in the resurrection?

In other words do recent developments in physics and in psychic
research make it easier to believe in the possibility of the resurrection of a dead man?

A. M. Ramsay:

The trend of modern science and psychology seems to have
features in common which confirm the credibility of the
Pauline doctrine . . . Today there is in physics the tendency
to regard material objects as the organization of energy
particles in particular forms, and to hold that the persist-
ence of a body lies not in the immutability of its physical
constituents but in their continual organization in accordance with the principle of the body's self-identity.

Leslie Weatherhead believes that psychic research sheds much
light on the resurrection of Jesus:

Basing my summary on religious truth and what seems to
me the authentic findings of psychical research, I believe
that for everyone the actual experience of dying is one of
great happiness, of immediate union with loved ones on the
other side, and of tender, welcoming care from ministering
spirits. Indeed, loved ones seem to attend the dying before
death happens. Their presence has often been commented on.

The body in which we manifest ourselves immediately after
death will I think *appear to us* to be still material, and
indeed, may consist of highly attenuated matter on a different scale of vibration. There may be a form of "matter"
which lies between the physical as we know it and the
psychical. This may account for the difficulty some newly-
dead people have of realizing that they are what we call
"dead." They wonder why the living do not respond when
they speak, and yet they find they can pass through closed
doors. One communicator tells how "for fun" he rushed at
a door only to find he could pass right through it.

549

☐ In many cases, these arguments do not help a person to believe in the resurrection unless he is *already* convinced on other grounds.

  David Edwards:

  It would seem that this sort of scientific (or pseudo-scientific) research may help those who already believe in the resurrection of Jesus by providing foretastes and comparisons congenial to modern minds. But it gives us little or no help in answering the question: *did* Jesus rise from the dead?

☐ Sometimes, however, physics and psychic research force people to question their materialistic assumptions and to open their minds to the possibility that some phenomena cannot be explained adequately in traditional scientific terms. Then, if there is a willingness to believe that the resurrection *may* or *could* have happened, a thorough study of the evidence is still needed to show whether or not it *did* happen.

The question we have been asking all along is simply this:

Is Christianity true?

That is, when we have discovered the basic Christian beliefs about God, man, and the universe, and about Jesus Christ, do we consider that these beliefs are really true?

When we put the question as simply and baldly as this, some may see the issue as a simple choice—"Yes" or "No." But in fact there are other possible answers.

WHERE DO WE GO FROM HERE?
IS CHRISTIANITY TRUE?

Randy Birkey

WHERE DO WE GO FROM HERE?
IS CHRISTIANITY TRUE?

Yes, it is true.
PAGE 557

I am not sure.
PAGE 563

It is true in parts.
PAGE 566

We don't know —and it is impossible to know—but it can still "become true."
PAGE 571

We don't know —and it is not possible to know.
PAGE 569

No, it is not true.
PAGE 573

ANSWER ONE:

Yes, Christianity is true.

> *This is to say, "I believe—*
> ☐ *that Christian beliefs are true in the*
> *sense that they tell us the truth about*
> *God and man and the universe" (see*
> *further Part 1);*
> ☐ *that God is personal and infinite*
> *the Creator of the universe and its*
> *Sustainer*
> *loving and holy*
> *one God and three persons";*
> ☐ *that man is a creature created in the*
> *image of God and is now a rebel*
> *against God, but capable of becoming*
> *a 'son' of God";*
> ☐ *that the universe is created and sus-*
> *tained by God" (see further Part 2).*

"I believe—

☐ *that Christian beliefs about Jesus are true in the sense that they give us a true account of who he was and is, and of what he achieved":*

☐ *that he was both man and God, the Son of God in a unique sense";*

☐ *that he bore our sins in his death";*

☐ *that he rose from the dead and is now alive."*

☐ The New Testament writers invite us to *believe that* certain things are true about God and about Jesus Christ:

> Whoever would draw near to God must believe *that* he exists and *that* he rewards those who seek him.

> If you confess with your lips *that* Jesus is Lord and believe in your heart *that* God raised him from the dead, you will be saved.

Believing that certain things are true should lead us to *believing in* Jesus Christ, and trusting him in a personal way.

> Now Jesus did many other signs in the presence of the disciples, which are not written in this book; but these are written that you may believe that Jesus is the Christ, the Son of God, and that believing you may have life in his name.

> He came to his own home, and his own people received him not. But to all who received him, who believed in his name, he gave power to become children of God.

Intellectual belief and personal trust are therefore vital elements of Christian faith. Intellectual convictions are inadequate in themselves; but without them there can hardly be a basis for a genuine personal trust.

☐ At some stage in the process of coming to faith, we need to consider exactly what it means to be a Christian. Jesus himself was very anxious that those who followed him should realize the total claims he made upon them, and that they should consider the cost carefully. At a time when large crowds were following him, he stressed the importance of counting the cost of true discipleship:

> Now great multitudes accompanied him; and he turned and said to them, "If any one comes to me and does not hate his own father and mother and wife and children and brothers and sisters, yes, and even his own life, he cannot be my disciple. Whoever does not bear his own cross and come after me, cannot be my disciple. For which of you, desiring to build a tower, does not first sit down and count the cost, whether he has enough to complete it? Otherwise, when he has laid a foundation, and is not able to finish, all who see it begin to mock him, saying, 'This man began to build, and was not able to finish.' Or what king, going to encounter another king in war, will not sit down first and take counsel whether he is able with ten thousand to meet him who comes against him with twenty thousand? And if not, while the other is yet a great way off, he sends an embassy and asks terms of peace. So therefore, whoever of you does not renounce all that he has cannot be my disciple."

This means in practice that we must ask ourselves questions like these:

Am I prepared to die to myself and my own ambitions, and to put Christ first in every part of my life—my thinking and my feeling; my work, my personal relationships, my marriage, and my leisure?

Am I prepared to be identified with Christ in the eyes of others?

Am I prepared to face the same sort of treatment that he received from others—scorn, persecution, death?

Am I prepared for the sacrifice of home and comfort, wealth and reputation for the sake of sharing with Christ in working out his will among men?

Am I prepared to be identified with other Christians, and to belong to a particular body of Christians?

While emphasizing the need to count the cost, however, Jesus also pointed out that the sacrifice involved is not a joyless or barren sacrifice:

> Truly, I say to you, there is no one who has left house or
> brothers or sisters or mother or father or children or lands,
> for my sake and the gospel, who will not receive a hun-
> dredfold now in this time, houses and brothers and sisters
> and mothers and children and lands, with persecutions, and
> in the age to come eternal life.

☐ If then, I have counted the cost and want to go the whole way
with Jesus, how exactly do I take the step of *becoming* a Christian? For many people, it involves a step of faith which is as
simple and natural as meeting a person for the first time and
establishing a friendship. They don't need to be told *how* to enter
into a personal relationship of faith with God through Christ;
when they hear the good news and believe it, they simply find
themselves praying to Christ, and soon become aware that he has
become a part of their lives.

For others, however, it means a more conscious process of
coming to God as Creator, and of affirming a personal trust in
Jesus as the Son of God who accepts us as we are and gives us
the gift of the Holy Spirit.

We may take this step on our own, in secret, or with others.
But sooner or later there will need to be some public profession
of it—in baptism and by word of mouth.

☐ When we take the step of belief in Christ and commitment to
him we receive the Holy Spirit. These are some of the things the
Holy Spirit will do in us:

He will give us the inward certainty that we are now children
of God:

> You have received the spirit of sonship. When we cry,
> "Abba! Father!" it is the Spirit himself bearing witness with
> our spirit that we are children of God, and if children, then
> heirs . . .

He will make the living Christ real to us, and help us to
appreciate the extent of his love. Paul prays in these terms:

> I bow my knees before the Father . . . that . . . he may
> grant you to be strengthened with might through his Spirit
> in the inner man, and that Christ may dwell in your hearts
> through faith; that you, being rooted and grounded in love,
> may have power to comprehend with all the saints what is
> the breadth and length and height and depth, and to know
> the love of Christ which surpasses knowledge, that you may
> be filled with all the fullness of God.

He will guide and direct us:

All who are led by the Spirit of God are sons of God.

He will work in our personality and make us more like Jesus. Paul writes about the qualities which the Spirit can produce:

The fruit of the Spirit is love, joy, peace, patience, kindness, goodness, faithfulness, gentleness, self-control . . .

He will help us to understand the teaching of Christ and the whole Bible. Jesus spoke these words to his disciples on the night of his arrest:

I have yet many things to say to you, but you cannot bear them now. When the Spirit of truth comes, he will guide you into all the truth; for he will not speak on his own authority, but whatever he hears he will speak, and he will declare to you the things that are to come. He will glorify me, for he will take what is mine and declare it to you.

☐ The Holy Spirit works within us in the context of the group of Christians or the church to which we belong. Simply by being a Christian, one belongs to the body of Christ. And this belonging is to be expressed and worked out in association with other Christians. The writer to the Hebrews urges:

Let us hold fast the confession of our hope without wavering, for he who promised is faithful; and let us consider how to stir up one another to love and good works, not neglecting to meet together, as is the habit of some, but encouraging one another, and all the more as you see the Day drawing near.

☐ This is how John describes his vision of "a new heaven and a new earth" which is prepared for those who have trusted in Jesus Christ:

Then I saw a new heaven and a new earth; for the first heaven and the first earth had passed away, and the sea was no more. And I saw the holy city, new Jerusalem, coming down out of heaven from God, prepared as a bride adorned for her husband; and I heard a great voice from the throne saying, "Behold, the dwelling of God is with men. He will dwell with them, and they shall be his people, and God himself will be with them; he will wipe away every tear from their eyes, and death shall be no more, neither shall there be mourning nor crying nor pain any more, for the former things have passed away."

And he who sat upon the throne said, "Behold, I make all things new" . . . "To the thirsty I will give water without price from the fountain of the water of life. He who conquers shall have this heritage, and I will be his God and he shall be my son . . ."

ANSWER TWO:

I am not sure.

This is to say, "It may be true, but I am not sure. I cannot make up my mind."

☐ Some people give this answer because they feel that they don't yet know enough about the Christian faith. And it is obvious that we cannot be pushed into believing something that we know very little about. In this case, it may simply be a problem of time. If this is how you feel, and you are in earnest, you need to be prepared to think and search until you arrive at the truth.

☐ Others give this answer because they think that this kind of presentation gives insufficient basis for any final commitment. If this is so, *how much more* would you want to know before making up your mind? Is it really the lack of evidence which makes you uncertain, or are you in fact unwilling to be convinced? Jesus himself stressed the need for this willingness:

> My teaching is not mine, but his who sent me; if any man's will is to do his will (God's), he shall know whether the teaching is from God or whether I am speaking on my own authority.

563

This willingness to be convinced does not mean that we assume that Christianity is true and then look for reasons to confirm our assumption. It simply means that we approach all the evidence with open minds, in this frame of mind: "I am not sure if Christianity is true. But I am prepared to consider the possibility that it *may* be true. And I am willing to believe, provided I am convinced that it is true . . . O God, if you really are there, show me the truth about yourself, and about Jesus, and show me the truth about myself." If you cannot approach the inquiry in this spirit, you are in virtually the same position as the person who concludes that Christianity is true only in parts (see p. 566), or that we cannot know (p. 569) or that it is not true at all (p. 573).

☐Others give this answer because, while basically they believe, they still have many questions about Christian beliefs and about what is involved in the Christian life. But this is hardly a good enough reason for holding back. A man and a woman do not know everything about each other when they fall in love; and they do not make final detailed decisions about how to conduct their married life before they become engaged. The lesser problems of Christian belief and the details of Christian living can only be worked out in the Christian life as we live in relationship with God. Jesus understood perfectly the element of honest uncertainty in the mind of one who came to ask him to help "if he could"; and this did not deter him from meeting his need:

> Jesus said to him, "If you can! All things are possible to him who believes." Immediately the father of the child cried out and said, "I believe; help my unbelief!" And . . . Jesus . . . rebuked the unclean spirit, saying to it, "You dumb and deaf spirit, I command you, come out of him, and never enter him again."

☐If you give this answer because you want to evade the challenge of Christ at this particular moment in your life, you may simply be playing for time. The Bible gives some examples of people whose procrastination prevented them from coming to know the truth.

We read of Herod:

> Herod feared John, knowing that he was a righteous and holy man, and kept him safe. When he heard him, he was much perplexed; and yet he heard him gladly.

Herod knew that he was hearing the truth about himself from John the Baptist; but he lost his opportunity to hear more of the truth from him, because at a banquet he made a rash oath to Herodias' daughter, and was forced to have John beheaded.

> And the king was exceedingly sorry; but because of his oaths and his guests he did not want to break his word to her.

Herod hoped that he might have another opportunity to hear the truth from Jesus himself. But Jesus was probably all too aware that Herod's curiosity would not take him any further in discovering the truth. After Pilate had examined Jesus, he passed him over to Herod:

> When Herod saw Jesus, he was very glad, for he had long desired to see him, because he had heard about him, and he was hoping to see some sign done by him. So he questioned him at some length; but he made no answer.

Felix, the Roman Procurator who kept Paul in prison at Caesarea seems to have been intellectually curious about the Christian faith, but unwilling to face the moral challenge it involved for him. He hoped to postpone making a final decision; but it seems that the further opportunity never came:

> He sent for Paul and heard him speak upon faith in Christ Jesus. And he argued about justice and self-control and future judgment. Felix was alarmed and said, "Go away for the present; when I have an opportunity I will summon you."

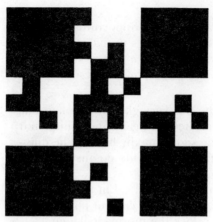

ANSWER THREE:

It is true in parts.

> *This is to say, "I accept some Christian beliefs, but not others." For example:*
>
> ☐ *I believe that there is a God, but I don't entirely accept the Bible's description of what he is like.*
>
> ☐ *or, I accept Christian moral teaching, Christian values and standards; but I don't believe everything that the New Testament says about Christ.*
>
> ☐ *or, I accept the form of words of Christian beliefs, but I don't accept the traditional interpretation of them, and feel free to reinterpret them in a different way.*

☐ If you claim to be able to know for certain that some Christian beliefs are true, and some are not, what is your criterion for deciding what is true and what is false? In most cases you have to judge by the standard of reason and/or feelings. But this approach leaves you wide open to all the dangers of the answer of Rationalism and Romanticism. (See Part 1, pp. 51–63.)

☐ Have you any compelling reasons for holding on to the parts of Christianity that you *do* believe to be true? You may be convinced that these beliefs are self-evident (e.g., the dignity of man), and that you can go on holding Christian values without Christian beliefs. But can you be so confident that your children and the next generation will be as easily convinced? And what do you have to say to those who go one step farther than you yourself are prepared to go, and reject the *whole* system of Christian beliefs, including its values? In many cases it is little more than feeling or tradition or prejudice which makes a person hold on to his semi-Christian beliefs and yet be appalled at those who are more consistent and discard them altogether.

☐ This kind of answer is based on the assumption that Christianity is a storehouse of insights and beliefs from which we can pick and choose as we please. But Christian beliefs need to be taken together because they form a structure like a building. If you begin to take away pieces here and there, the whole structure is weakened; and if the process goes on, the building itself may well collapse.

The Sermon on the Mount gives a good example of the way in which Christian beliefs are linked with each other. It contains much straightforward moral teaching; but interwoven with this are the startling claims which Jesus makes for himself:

> Not every one who says to me, "Lord, Lord," shall enter the kingdom of heaven, but he who does the will of my Father who is in heaven. On that day many will say to me, "Lord, Lord, did we not prophesy in your name, and cast out demons in your name, and do many mighty works in your name?" And then I will declare to them, "I never knew you; depart from me, you evildoers."

Similarly, in the passage in which Jesus speaks about feeding the hungry, welcoming the stranger, clothing the naked and visiting the sick, he claims that *he himself* is going to judge all men at the day of judgment according to the way in which they have acted on this teaching:

When the Son of man comes in his glory, and all the angels
with him, then he will sit on his glorious throne. Before
him will be gathered all the nations, and he will separate
them one from another as a shepherd separates the sheep
from the goats, and he will place the sheep at his right
hand, but the goats at the left. Then the King will say to
those at his right hand, "Come, O blessed of my Father,
inherit the kingdom prepared for you from the foundation
of the world; for I was hungry and you gave me food, I
was thirsty and you gave me drink . . . As you did it to one
of the least of these my brethren, you did it to me." Then
he will say to those at his left hand, "Depart from me, you
cursed, into the eternal fire prepared for the devil and his
angels; for I was hungry and you gave me no food, I was
thirsty and you gave me no drink . . . As you did it not to
one of the least of these, you did it not to me."

If you accept *parts* of the teaching of Jesus, are you prepared
for the possibility that you may come under the judgment of the
whole of his teaching?

ANSWER FOUR:
We don't know—and it
is not possible to know.

*This is to say, "It is impossible to
know 'the truth' about Christianity—or
about any religion or philosophy. With
our finite minds we cannot hope to
know the truth about the universe as a
whole. If there is any such thing as
'objective truth,' it is impossible to arrive at it."*

Michael Harrington, writing in *The Accidental Century*:

Once destiny was an honest game of cards which followed
certain conventions, with a limited number of cards and
values. Now the player realizes in amazement that the hand
of his future contains cards never seen before and that the
rules of the game are modified by each player.

The whole world has become a dialectical nightmare; there
are no more certainties.

☐If you give this kind of answer, no amount of "evidence" or persuasion is likely to convince you about Christian beliefs. The discussion must turn on the implications of your agnosticism. You may *feel* and *believe* in this total uncertainty; but do you, or can you *live* permanently with it? The more consistently you live with your belief in total uncertainty, the more intolerable your present life will be. (See further, Part 1, pp. 64–85.)

☐If your total uncertainty is not justified, and if Christianity is true, the despair of being finally rejected by God will be even more profound than the despair of living in a world without any certainties.

☐In practice, you are living as if Christianity is *not true*. It is not that you still have an open mind and are prepared to accept the possibility that it might really be true. You are in effect acting on the assumption that it is *not true*. (See pp. 573ff.).

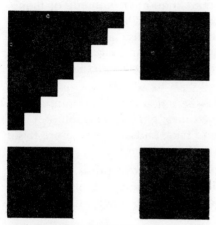

ANSWER FIVE:
We don't know—and it is impossible to know—but it can still "become true."

> *This is to say, "We can never hope to know for certain if Christianity is true; but it can still be 'true for me' in my own experience."*

Wilfred Cantwell Smith:

Religions are not propositions and therefore cannot be true and false in that particular sense of those terms. However, this is not the only sense in which truth is to be conceived. The propositional notion of truth and falsehood, as attributes of statements, has tended to dominate Western thought since the Enlightenment. The re-awakening, however, of our awareness that faith is not a belief in theories, that God has given to us for our salvation not a doctrinal system, should have alerted us more effectively than has sometimes been the case, to a deeper understanding also of truth itself . . . Impersonal truth perhaps lends itself to statement form, but personal truth appears in another quality.

The religion of one Christian may be more true, or more false, at a given moment than at another moment, or than the religion of another Christian . . . The religion of one Muslim may be more true, or more false, at a given moment than at another moment, or than the religion of another Muslim. This must be conceded, must be grasped in all its terrifying and its life-giving quality.

Once it is grasped, a vital issue follows. The question of serious significance then becomes: may the religion of a particular Christian be more true, and may it be more false, than the religion of a particular Muslim?

Rather than what is in general, religious truth is, I suggest, a matter of what is in actuality; and therefore, also, of what has been, and what will be. The future religious history of mankind is open.

Even those who like to think that religions have been false in the past, should hope that they will become true in the future.

This answer is more than a protest against a purely intellectual assent to Christian beliefs, and it falls far short of genuine Christian faith. It denies the possibility of being able to give any genuine intellectual assent, and asserts that the *only* real kind of truth is the truth of experience.

This kind of answer is becoming more and more popular today; but it presents perhaps the most serious and the most subtle challenge to historic Christianity. It suffers from the weaknesses of the agnosticism on which it is based (see Part 1, pp. 64–85) and of the Existentialist and Mystic answers to the question of truth. (See Part 1, pp. 86–109 and pp. 110–118.)

ANSWER SIX:
No, it is not true.

This is to say, "Christian beliefs about God, man, and the universe are not true. Jesus was not the Son of God; his death has no special meaning, and he did not rise from the dead. The whole of Christianity, its moral values, and its way of life must also be rejected; for since the foundation (i.e., the beliefs about God and about Jesus) is not true, what is built on that foundation (i.e., the moral teaching) cannot be true either."

☐ This answer does at least assume that some things are true and some are not. And it is therefore closer to the Christian understanding of truth than the answer that says that Christianity is neither true nor false, or that it is impossible to know for certain.

573

It means that we can at least still talk in terms of verification and falsification. (See Part 1, pp. 9–36.)

☐ Sometimes this answer is based entirely on the impression made by the lives of Christians in the past or the present. For some, the verdict is simple and clear-cut.

Lord Boothby:

> The history of the Christian churches has been one of such atrocious cruelty. All of them have done untold harm to the world . . . The traditions of the Christian churches, for centuries, can be summarized as "Dogma, persecution, secession, hatred, destruction and fire." In fact, everything that Jesus loathed and denounced.

A person who is examining Christianity has every right to look at the record of the Christian church to see if it bears out the truth of Christian beliefs, just as a person examining the claims of Communism should look at the record of Communist countries. But many people think that when they have discovered something doubtful or discreditable in the church's record in the past or the present, they can safely reject the whole of Christianity as untrue. The danger in this approach is that our interpretation of the record of the church is bound to be influenced by the assumptions with which we approach the subject. The Christian therefore has to say: "You have every right to look at us to see if our lives produce any evidence to suggest that what we believe is true. But at the same time, remember that we don't claim to be perfect, and we are ashamed of many of the things which have been done in the name of Christ. If Christianity is true, you will be judged in the end not by what you think of the Christian church, but by what you think of your Creator and of Jesus Christ."

Even those who oppose Christianity would be prepared to concede that not everyone who claims to be a Christian is a Christian at heart. In some societies there has been a Christian consensus and everyone has been regarded as a Christian, at least in name. But this has never meant that each individual was fully convinced of Christian beliefs or fully committed to live in obedience to Christ. Jesus said, "By their fruits ye shall know them." And if a person's behavior is far from Christian, we have good reason to doubt the genuineness of his Christianity.

The fact that perversions of Christianity exist is not necessarily an adequate reason for rejecting Christian beliefs. In his correspondence with Arnold Lunn, C. E. M. Joad cannot refrain

from ridiculing things that Christians have done and said. This is
Arnold Lunn's reply:

> It is pleasant to remain young, and I am impressed by the
> boyish glee with which you collect newspaper cuttings to
> show up Christianity in a bad light. The love of God is a
> fine emotion and, like all fine emotions, capable of being
> degraded and vulgarized. It would be just as easy to ridi-
> cule human love by a collection of extracts from cheap
> novelists as to expose the love of God with the aid of your
> religious scrap book. As easy, and as futile.

Granting that perversions exist, and that much harm has been
done in the name of Christ, is there any religion or philosophy
that has a similar record of solid, lasting *good*?

☐ If you believe that Christianity is not true, this does not mean
that there is no more that the Christian can say. There are still
many areas open for discussion even when there is no agreement
about God and about Jesus Christ. We can continue to talk about
man and about our common experience of what it means to be
human. In this discussion the Christian, provided he has really
listened and understood what the issues are, is entitled to press
gently but firmly by asking questions such as these:

*How far are you prepared to go with others who have tried to be
consistent and have taken this rejection to its logical conclusion?*

Nietzsche:

> Vast upheavals will happen in the future, as soon as men
> realize that the structure of Christianity is only based on
> assumptions . . . I have tried to deny everything.

Jean-Paul Sartre:

> Atheism is a cruel, long-term business; I believe I have
> gone through it to the end.

If you dislike or disagree with the conclusions men like these
have arrived at, where do you think they have gone wrong? You
may feel at many points that although you share the same
starting point, you do not agree with the *conclusions* at which they
have arrived. There are bound to be differences in the conclusions, and differences in the degrees of consistency with which
they are lived out. But if these are possible conclusions which
follow from the initial assumptions, what is there that prevents
you from following the same road and accepting the same con-

clusion? Can you appeal to some firm principle to show why the
conclusion is wrong or unnecessary? Or do you hold back because you are relying simply on habit, or the force of tradition,
or a consensus of opinion, or "common sense" or pure sentiment?

*Can you in practice be thoroughly consistent in your belief and at the
same time live in the world as it is?*

Many writers who are not Christians are very well aware of
the problem of living with their beliefs.

David Hume:

> Thus the skeptic still continues to reason and believe,
> though he asserts that he cannot defend his reason by
> reason, and by the same rule, he must assent to the princi-
> ple concerning the existence of the body, though he cannot
> pretend by any argument of philosophy to maintain its
> veracity.

Kathleen Knott, writing about Hume's inconsistency:

> Among great philosophers, Hume, who hung his nose as
> far as any over the nihilistic abyss, withdrew it sharply when
> he saw the psychological risks involved and advised dilution
> of metaphysics by playing backgammon and making merry
> with his friends. The conclusion of Hume's philosophizing
> was indeed a radical scepticism, which left no convincing
> logical grounds for believing anything natural, let alone
> supernatural, was there at all, and he saved his "reason" or,
> as we might say, his "philosophical personality" . . . by re-
> fusing to take the implications of his philosophy to heart.

Paul Hazard, writing about the skeptics of the eighteenth century:

> Peculiar people, psychologically, these scholars. They will
> set a fuse to the most daring ideas, apparently unaware or
> regardless of what they are doing. It is their successors
> who, in the fullness of time, realize the implications of their
> legacy. Meanwhile, they themselves still cling to tradition.

H. J. Blackham, writing about Nietzsche:

> His thinking was ancillary to the real philosophic task he set
> himself of experimentally *living* all the valuations of the
> past, together with the contraries, in order to acquire the
> right to judge them . . . There are positions which can be

thought but not lived, there are exploratory ventures from which there is no return. Nietzsche's thoughts were fascinated by unexplored forbidden regions of abysses, glaciers, and mountain peaks. One can look down into the bottom of an abyss refusing the possibility of throwing oneself over the edge, but one cannot explore the possibility by a tentative jump. One can examine in thought the possibility of nihilism (as an irresolvable conflict between human valuations and cosmic facts) and try to show that it is not the truth; but if one is determined to will and to live the possibility of nihilism, then one no longer has any independent standpoint under one's feet; worse than Kierkegaard "out upon the seventy thousand fathoms of water," one is actually sucked down and engulfed: what from the independent standpoint of responsible freedom was regarded as the unavoidable ambiguity of good and evil in the world becomes, first, the ambiguity of one's own will, and then its abandonment to the eternal destruction and the eternal return and the dionysian ecstasy. No more than skepticism can be overcome by doubting it can nihilism be overcome by willing it.

Albert Camus:

What matters . . . is not to follow things back to their origins, but, the world being what it is, to know how to live in it.

Lazare Bickel:

Intelligence is our faculty for not developing what we think to the very end, so that we can still believe in reality.

These different kinds of inconsistency are what *Francis Schaeffer* describes as the "point of tension"—the tension being between the logical conclusions of a person's belief and the direction in which the real world draws him. The Christian therefore feels that he must seek to expose the hidden defenses which prevent a person from feeling the keenness of his inconsistency.

At the point of tension the person is not in a place of consistency in his system and the roof is built *as a protection against the blows of the real world*, both internal and external. It is like the great shelters built upon some mountain passes to protect vehicles from the avalanches of rock and stone which periodically tumble down the mountain. The avalanche, in the case of the non-Christian, is the real and the abnormal fallen world which surrounds him. The Christian, lovingly and with true tears, must remove the shelter and allow the truth of the external world and of what man is to beat upon him. When the roof is off, each man must stand naked and wounded before the truth of what is.

The truth that we let in first is not a dogmatic statement of the truth of the Scriptures but the truth of the external world and the truth of what man himself is. This is what shows him his need. The Scriptures then show him the nature of his lostness and the answer to it.

Is it possible that your rejection of Christian beliefs is based on personal rather than intellectual reasons?

The Christian has no right to assume that *all* intellectual problems are a kind of smoke-screen and therefore do not deserve a thorough and honest answer. He is putting a real stumbling-block in the way of many doubters and questioners if he tries to reduce every intellectual question to a moral question.

At the same time, however, the Gospels show that *some* people refused to become followers of Christ, not because they were unconvinced in their minds, but because they considered the cost too great in practical terms:

The *rich young ruler* refused to follow Jesus because he was so attached to his wealth:

> And Jesus looking upon him loved him, and said to him, "You lack one thing; go, sell what you have, and give to the poor, and you will have treasure in heaven; and come, follow me." At that saying his countenance fell, and he went away sorrowful; for he had great possessions.

Jesus told the parable of the *banquet* to pin-point certain excuses to do with business, other interests, and the family:

> They all alike began to make excuses. The first said to him, "I have bought a field, and I must go out and see it; I pray you, have me excused." And another said, "I have bought five yoke of oxen, and I go to examine them; I pray you, have me excused." And another said, "I have married a wife, and therefore I cannot come."

The *Pharisees* would not commit themselves because of the effect it would have on their reputation. Jesus said to them:

How can you believe, who receive glory from one another and do not seek the glory that comes from the only God?

Are you willing to think again, and to reconsider the Christian answers with an open mind, and if necessary admit that you have been wrong?

Aldous Huxley, writing about his earlier beliefs:

It was the manifestly poisonous nature of the fruits that forced me to consider the philosophical tree on which they had grown.

An obviously untrue philosophy of life leads in practice to disastrous results.

He speaks about

. . . the point where we realize the necessity of seeking an alternative philosophy that shall be true and therefore fruitful of good.

The Christian is bound to feel that Huxley's earlier dissatisfaction with his position never led him to consider Christian faith as such an "alternative philosophy" which would be true and therefore "fruitful of good." He will want to point to the "poisonous nature" of Huxley's later position. But the method he outlines here of seeking an alternative answer goes some way towards explaining what repentance means.

C. E. M. Joad thought again, and it eventually led him to Christian faith. His correspondence with Arnold Lunn, published first in 1932, was carried out on the assumption that it is possible and essential to find out "the truth" about Christianity. He was at least willing to be convinced. And in 1942, in a new preface to the correspondence, he wrote about the way in which he had been forced to think again and change some of his ideas:

For some years . . . my own views have been insensibly changing, and the change has reflected, indeed it has been occasioned by the deepening tragedy of the contemporary world.

When he later abandoned his agnosticism and became a Christian, he wrote the following words about his change of mind:

There is such a thing as the pride of the intellect, a pride in which throughout my life I have been continuously proud. There are certain writers—Shaw is one of them, Swift an-

other and Bertrand Russell another—from whom I derive
an enormous intellectual stimulation. Borne aloft on the
wings of their intellects, I feel myself raised to an eminence
from which I look down upon the past and the present of
my species, and, as momentarily I perceive through Shaw's
eyes or through Russell's, I observe, with amused detachment, its manifold follies, follies from which, while the
moment of exaltation lasts, I fondly believe myself exempt.
I am suffused with a feeling of immense superiority, as I
thank God that I am not as other men.

*If it turns out that Christianity is true, and you have rejected
it—what then?* What you are doing amounts to this: you are
rejecting the God who has made you and the universe, the God
who has given you your body and mind and feelings, and is the
source of everything you enjoy. You are not simply rejecting one
of the great world religions, or a particular outlook on life. You
are saying "No!" to your Creator, and "No!" to the one who
came to reveal the Creator more fully and to reconcile you to
him.

You will not be able to claim in the end, "I had no opportunity to find out the truth. I had no convincing clues to point to the
truth." You will be held responsible for your choice, because you
rejected the clear indications you had, however small they were—
in the universe, in your conscience, in the Bible and in Jesus.

Are you prepared to accept the consequences of your choice,
here in this life and in the life beyond death? When we have
made every allowance for the metaphorical language of Jesus
and other writers in the New Testament, we must realize that
this language is meant to describe as honestly and clearly as
possible the despair and agony of being cut off from God—a
despair which is deeper than any despair we can know in this
life:

> Then the kings of the earth and the great men and the
> generals and the rich and the strong, and every one, slave
> and free, hid in the caves and among the rocks of the
> mountains, calling to the mountains and the rocks, "Fall on
> us and hide us from the face of him who is seated on the
> throne, and from the wrath of the Lamb; for the great day
> of their wrath has come, and who can stand before it?"

These warnings of judgment are not intended by the writers
as cruel threats to compel a terrified and blind surrender. They

are rather urgent appeals, in the light of what is to happen, to think again about the truth.

> For God so loved the world that he gave his only Son, that whoever believes in him should not perish but have eternal life. For God sent the Son into the world, not to condemn the world, but that the world might be saved through him. He who believes in him is not condemned; he who does not believe is condemned already, because he has not believed in the name of the only Son of God. And this is the judgment, that the light has come into the world, and men loved darkness rather than light, because their deeds were evil. For everyone who does evil hates the light, and does not come to the light, lest his deeds should be exposed. But he who does what is true comes to the light, that it may be clearly seen that his deeds have been wrought in God.

In this inquiry, we have been putting Christianity "on trial." But if Christianity is true, *I* am the one who is on trial. The issues are clear-cut; and how each one of us responds to the love of God is a matter of life and death.

REFERENCES
PART ONE

PAGE vii
Thomas Sherlock, *The Trial of the Witness of the Resurrection of Jesus*, London, 1729; in Paul Hazard, *The European Mind 1680-1715* (London: Penguin, 1964), pp. 96, 97.

PAGE viii
Bishop Butler, Advertisement to first edition of *The Analogy;* in Basil Willey, *The Eighteenth Century Background* (London: Chatto and Windus, 1946), p. 82.

PAGE ix
J. S. Mill, *Autobiography*, World's Classics (London: Oxford University Press, 1924), p. 36.
Nietzsche's Letter to his friend Von Gersdorff; in Colin Wilson, *The Outsider* (London: Pan, 1967), p. 132.
Mahatma Gandhi, Address on Christmas Day, 1931; in A. R. Vidler, *Objections to Christian Belief* (London: Pelican, 1963), pp. 50, 51.
Colin Wilson, *Religion and the Rebel* (London: Gollancz, 1957), p. 29.

PAGE x
James Mitchell, *The God I Want* (London: Constable, 1967), p. 2.
C. E. M. Joad, *Is Christianity True?* (London: Eyre and Spottiswoode, 1943), p. 14.
Henri Barbusse, *L'Enfer*, tr. John Rodker (London: Joiner and Steele, 1932), p. 9.
Michael Harrington, *The Accidental Century* (London: Pelican, 1967), p. 116.
Joad, *Christianity*, p. 20.
Margaret Cole, Essay in *What I Believe* (London: Allen and Unwin, 1966), pp. 74, 75.

PAGE 10
Psalm 19:1-4; Job 26:8, 9, 14; Romans 1:18-20.
Richard Wurmbrand, *Tortured for Christ* (London: Hodder and Stoughton, 1967), p. 23.

PAGE 12
Romans 2:1, 14, 15; Exodus 33:11.

PAGE 13
Amos 3:7; Exodus 24:3, 4; Jeremiah 1:9-11; 36:4; Psalm 119; Hebrews 1:1, 2; 2 Peter 1:21.

PAGE 14
Matthew 5:17-19; John 10:34-36; 5:39; Mark 12:35, 36: Matthew 19:3-5; Luke 24:44, 45.

PAGE 15
John 14:26; 16:12, 13; 1 Corinthians 2:12, 13; Galatians 1:6-9; 2 Timothy 1:13, 14; Matthew 11:27.

PAGE 16
John 14:6-10; 1:17, 18; Hebrews 1:1, 2; Deuteronomy 29:29; 1 Corinthians 13:12; 2:12, 13; 14:37; Genesis 15:5-8ff.

PAGE 18
Exodus 4:1-9; 7:17; 14:4, 18; Deuteronomy 4:9-13.

PAGE 19
1 Kings 18:21, 23, 24, 36-39; Deuteronomy 18:21, 22.

PAGE 20
Isaiah 41:20; 48:3-5; *e.g.,* Ezekiel 6:7.

PAGE 21
John 6:68; 2:11; 20:26-28; Acts 2:22-36.

PAGE 22
1 Corinthians 15:3-8; Luke 1:1-4.

PAGE 23
Jacob Bronowski, *Science and Human Values* (London: Penguin, 1964), pp. 33-34; 38-40; 66, 72.

PAGE 24
John Wren-Lewis, "Does Science Destroy Christian Belief?", in *Fact, Faith and Fantasy*, ed. C. F. D. Moule (London: Collins, 1964), pp. 14, 20.

PAGE 26
Bronowski, *Science and Values*, pp. 49; 52-53; 57.

PAGE 27
Aldous Huxley, *Do What You Will*, Essays (London: Watts and Co., 1937), p. 195.

PAGE 28
Pieter Geyl, *Napoleon: For and Against* (London: Penguin, 1965), pp. 15-18.

PAGE 29
C. S. Lewis, *Surprised by Joy* (London: Collins Fontana, 1959), pp. 178, 179.

PAGE 30
Frank Morison, *Who Moved the Stone?* (London: Faber and Faber, 1944), pp. 11, 12.
N. P. Williams (and W. Sanday), *Form and Content in the Christian Tradition*, 1916; in A. R. Vidler, *Twentieth Century Defenders of the Faith* (London: SCM Press, 1965), p. 90.
Joad, *Christianity*, p. 97.

PAGE 31
C. E. M. Joad, *The Book of Joad* (London: Faber and Faber, 1944), p. 213.
Bertrand Russell, *The Problems of Philosophy*, Home University Library (New York: H. Holt and Co., 1967), pp. 9, 10.
Alasdair MacIntyre, *Difficulties in Christian Belief* (London: SCM Press, 1959), p. 31.

PAGE 32
Bertrand Russell, *Human Knowledge: Its Scope and Limitations* (London: Allen and Unwin, 1948), pp. 448; 148.

PAGE 33
C. E. M. Joad, *The Recovery of Belief* (London: Faber and Faber, 1952), pp. 13-14; 16; 46; 63.

PAGE 35
Psalm 34:8; 50:14, 15; Malachi 3:10; Matthew 11:28-30; Psalm 34:4.

PAGE 36
Psalm 116:1, 2; John 6:66-69; 1:14-16; 20:27, 28; 1 John 1:1-4.

PAGE 37
Thomas Aquinas, *Summa Theologica*, 1, Question 1; in *Historical Selections in the Philosophy of Religion*, ed. Ninian Smart (London: SCM Press, 1962), p. 62.

PAGE 39
H. Denzinger, *Enchiridion Symbolorum* (Documents of the First Vatican Council); in Colin Brown, *Philosophy and the Christian Faith* (London: Tyndale Press, 1969), p. 163.

Cardinal J. C. Heenan, *Our Faith* (London: Nelson, 1956), pp. 82, 83.

PAGES 40-42
The Koran, tr. N. J. Dawood (London: Penguin, 1964), Sura 29:50, p. 195; 2:2-4, 23-24, pp. 324, 325; 13:27-28, p. 142; 42:35, p. 153; 3:2-3, p. 395; 46:7-9, p. 124; 7:203-204, p. 256; 3:7-8, p. 395.

PAGE 43
Bronowski, *Science and Values*, p. 44.
Francis Bacon, *Novum Organum*, 1:LXV; in Basil Willey, *The Seventeenth Century Background* (London: Chatto and Windus, 1934), p. 32.
Francis Bacon, *De Augmentis*, IX; in Willey, *Seventeenth Century*, pp. 32, 33.

PAGE 44
Thomas Browne, *Religio Medici*, 1:X; 1:XLVIII; in Willey, *Seventeenth Century*, p. 59.
John Locke, *An Essay Concerning Human Understanding*, 2 vol., ed. Alexander C. Fraser (Dover, 1894), 4:XVIII:2.
Willey, *Seventeenth Century*, pp. 33, 34.
Lord Herbert of Cherbury, *De la Vérité*, pp. 51f.; in Willey, *Seventeenth Century*, p. 114.

PAGE 45
Willey, *Seventeenth Century*, pp. 118-120.
Essay, "What Is Dogma?"; in Vidler, *Defenders of the Faith*, pp. 51-53.

PAGE 46
H. J. Blackham, *Objections to Humanism* (London: Penguin, 1963), p. 28.
George Harrison, interview in *Melody Maker* (December 16, 1967).

PAGE 47
Fyodor Dostoievsky, *The Brothers Karamazov*, Vol. 1 (London: Penguin, 1958), pp. 288-311.

PAGE 48
Emil Brunner, *The Christian Doctrine of Creation and Redemption* (Guildford: Lutterworth, 1952), pp. 240-241.
Anonymous, "Don't Crush the Little Faith I Have," *Eternity* (Vol. 16, Number 12: December, 1965).

PAGE 50
W. Cantwell Smith, *Questions of Religious Truth* (London: Gollancz, 1967), pp. 48, 49.

PAGE 52
Ernst Cassirer, *The Renaissance Philosophy of Man* (Chicago: University of Chicago Press, 1948), pp. 10, 11.
Hazard, *European Mind*, pp. 8, 9.
Ibid., pp. 159, 160.

PAGE 53
Ibid., pp. 499-502.

PAGE 54
René Descartes, *A Discourse on Method*, 15, Everyman Library (London: Dent, 1912) (three quotations).

PAGES 54, 55
John Locke, *An Essay Concerning Human Understanding*, 2:IX:1; in Willey, *Seventeenth Century*, p. 259; John Locke, 4:I:1; 4:XVIII:2.
John Locke, in Willey, *Eighteenth Century*, p. 32.

John Locke, *An Essay Concerning Human Understanding*, 4:XIX:4.

PAGE 55
Hazard, *European Mind*, pp. 278, 282–283.

PAGE 56
G. R. Cragg, *The Church and the Age of Reason (1648–1789)* (London: Pelican, 1960), p. 75.
Norman Hampson, *The Enlightenment* (London: Pelican, 1968), pp. 186–187.

PAGE 58
Willey, *Eighteenth Century*, p. 107.
Jacob Bronowski and Bruce Mazlish, *The Western Intellectual Tradition* (London: Penguin, 1963), p. 330
Samuel Taylor Coleridge, *Biographia Literaria*; in Basil Willey, *Nineteenth Century Studies* (London: Chatto and Windus, 1949), p. 43.

PAGE 59
James Thurber, Essay in *What I Believe*, p. 138.
Blackham, *Objections to Humanism*, p. 11.
H. J. Blackham, in *Prism* (October, 1963).
G. R. Cragg, *The Church and the Age of Reason* (London: Hodder and Stoughton, 1962), p. 76.
G. R. Cragg, *Reason and Authority in the Eighteenth Century* (London: Cambridge University Press, 1964), p. 13.

PAGE 60
Mark Pattison; in Cragg, *Church and Reason*, p. 76.
Willey, *Seventeenth Century*, p. 73.

PAGE 61
Willey, *Eighteenth Century*, p. 83.
D. F. Strauss, *Life of Jesus*, tr. Marian Evans, Vol 1 (London: SCM Press, 1846), p. 71 (two quotations).
Willey, *Eighteenth Century*, p. 237.

PAGE 62
Hazard, *European Mind*, pp. 139; 274.

PAGE 63
Thomas Carlyle; in Willey, *Nineteenth Century*, pp. 120–122.

PAGE 64
A. J. Ayer, Essay in *What I Believe*, p. 14.

PAGE 65
A. Huxley, *Do What You Will*, pp. 2–3; 218–219; 234–235.
Jacquetta Hawkes, in *What I Believe*, p. 137.

PAGE 66
Rebecca West, in *What I Believe*, p. 176.
Albert Einstein, in *What I Believe*, p. 27.
Barbara Wooton, in *What I Believe*, p. 205.
Blackham, *Objections to Humanism*, p. 13.

PAGE 67
David Hume, *Treatise of Human Nature*, 1:II:6; in Willey, *Eighteenth Century*, p. 113.
Hume, *Treatise of Human Nature* (London: Collins Fontana, 1962), 1:III:12.
Hume, *An Abstract of a Treatise of Human Nature*; in Bronowski and Mazlish, *Western Tradition*, p. 528.

PAGE 68
Bernard M. Reardon, *Religious Thought in the Nineteenth Century* (London: Cambridge University Press, 1946), Introduction to the chapter on Kant.

Smith, *Questions of Religious Thought*, p. 74.

PAGE 69
Sarvepalli Radhakrishnan, *The Hindu View of Life* (London: Allen and Unwin, 1927), p. 38.
K. M. Sen, *Hinduism* (London: Penguin, 1969), p. 37.
Christmas Humphreys, *Buddhism* (London: Penguin, n.d.), p. 122.
Leopold Sedar Senghor, *On African Socialism*, tr. Mercer Cook (London: Praeger, 1964), pp. 41; 123.

PAGE 70
Jacob Bronowski, *The Identity of Man* (London: Penguin, 1965), p. 62.
A. Huxley, *Do What You Will*, pp. 31, 37.

PAGE 71
Paul Tillich, "On the Boundary Line," *Christian Century* (December 6, 1960), pp. 1435–1436.
Teilhard de Chardin, source unknown.
John Robinson, *Exploration into God* (London: SCM Press, 1967), pp. 139–141.

PAGE 72
Smith, *Questions of Religious Truth*, pp. 57; 34–35; 37.
MacIntyre, *Difficulties in Belief*, p. 27.

PAGE 73
Lewis Carroll, *Alice in Wonderland* (London: Macmillan, 1966), pp. 88–89; 165; 180–181.

PAGE 74
Voltaire; in Hampson, *Enlightenment*, p. 76.
Hannah Arendt, *The Human Condition* (Chicago: University of Chicago Press, 1969), p. 252.

PAGE 75
Wilson, *Outsider*, pp. 23–24.
Harrington, *Accidental Century*, p. 45.
Bronowski, *Science and Values*, p. 50.

PAGE 76
Hume, *Treatise of Human Nature*, 1:IV:2; 1:IV:7.
Maurice Friedman, *To Deny Our Nothingness* (London: Gollancz, 1967), pp. 223–224.

PAGE 77
Joad, *Book of Joad*, p. 103.
Time Magazine (April 26, 1968), p. 106
Harold Pinter, Programme Note for Royal Court Production of *The Room* and *The Dumb Waiter*; in John Russell Taylor, *Anger and After* (London: Penguin, 1963), pp. 300–301.

PAGE 78
Eric Rhode, "Poor Cow," *Listener* (December 14, 1967), p. 769.
Simon Hoggart, *Guardian Weekly* (December 26, 1968).

PAGE 79
Bronowski, *Science and Values*, pp. 36–37.
Wren-Lewis, *Fact and Fantasy*, p. 24.
Douglas Spanner; in *The Church of England Newspaper* (March 31, 1967).

PAGE 80
C. S. Lewis, *Miracles* (London: Fontana, 1960), p. 110.
G. J. Warnock, *English Philosophy Since 1900*; in Leslie Paul, *Alternatives to Christian Belief* (London: Hodder and Stoughton, 1967), p. 139.

Paul, *Alternatives*, pp. 150, 151.

PAGE 81
George Eliot, *Letters* (1862); in Willey, *Nineteenth Century*, p. 249.
Gotthold E. Lessing, *Nathan the Wise*, Act III, Scene 7; Summary from Brown, *Philosophy and Faith*, p. 89.

PAGE 82
William James, *Pragmatism, A New Way for Some Old Ways of Thinking*, 1907; in Brown, *Philosophy and Faith*, p. 146.
Thomas Arnold, *Introductory Lectures on Modern History* (1842); in Willey, *Nineteenth Century*, p. 71.
J. B. Priestley, in *Literature and Western Man*; quoted by Calder-Marshall in *What I Believe*, p. 68.
Andre Gide, in Richard Howard Crossman, *The God That Failed, Six Studies in Communism* (London: Hamish Hamilton, 1950), p. 198.
George Orwell, *1984* (London: Penguin, 1968), p. 220.

PAGE 83
Arthur Koestler, *The Ghost in the Machine* (London: Hutchinson, 1967), p. 262.
Ignazio Silone, *The God That Failed*, p. 109.
Nikita Struve, *Christians in Contemporary Russia* (London: Collins, 1967), p. 288.

PAGE 84
Carroll, *Alice*, p. 124.
John Lehmann, "Alice at the Sorbonne," *Listener* (September 22, 1966).

PAGE 85
Aldous Huxley, *Doors of Perception and Heaven and Hell* (London: Penguin, 1969), pp. 23–25.

PAGE 87
Brunner, *Christian Doctrine of Creation and Redemption*, p. 27.
Paul Tillich, *Shaking of the Foundations* (London: Penguin, 1962), pp. 163–164.

PAGE 88
Paul Tillich, *The Courage to Be* (London: Fontana, 1962), p. 185.
Rudolph Bultmann, *Kerygma and Myth*, ed. H. W. Bartsch, tr. Reginald H. Fuller (London: SPCK, 1953), p. 26; 1:X.
Smith, *Questions of Religious Truth*, pp. 68–69.

PAGE 89
Teilhard de Chardin, *The Phenomenon of Man* (London: Fontana, 1966), pp. 252; 256–257.
John Robinson, *Honest to God* (London: SCM Press, 1967), pp. 48–49.

PAGE 90
Robinson, *Exploration into God*, p. 68 (two quotations).
Alan Richardson, *Science and Existence* (London: SCM Press, 1957), p. 28.

PAGE 91
Rosemary Haughton in *What I Believe*, p. 114.
Paul, *Alternatives to Belief*, pp. 204–205.

PAGE 92
The New Dutch Catechism (London: Burns and Oates, 1967), pp. 261–262; 269.
Blaise Pascal, *Pensées*, tr. Martin Turnell (London: Harvill Press, 1962), p. 163.

PAGE 93
Bronowski and Mazlish, *The Western Tradition,* pp. 276; 278.
Soren Kierkegaard, *Journals* (1854); in H. Diem, *Kierkegaard's Theology of Existence* (Edinburgh: Oliver and Boyd, 1959), p. 202.
Soren Kierkegaard, *Journals,* selected and tr. Alexander Dru (London: Fontana, 1958), p. 44.

PAGE 94
Kierkegaard; in Diem, *Kierkegaard's Theology,* p. 49.
Kierkegaard, *Philosophical Fragments,* tr. David F. Swenson (Princeton, NJ: Princeton University Press, 1936), p. 87.
Kierkegaard, *Philosophical Fragments* (Princeton: Princeton University Press, 1957 edition), title page.
Kierkegaard, *Concluding Unscientific Postscript* (Princeton: Princeton University Press, 1944), pp. 500; 503.
Kierkegaard; in Diem, *Kierkegaard's Theology,* p. 49.
Kierkegaard, *Philosophical Fragments,* pp. 358–359.
Kierkegaard, *Journals,* ed. A. Dru, pp. 185–186.
Kierkegaard, *The Last Years: Journals 1853–1855,* ed. and tr. Ronald Gregor Smith (London: Collins, 1965), pp. 99–100.
Herbert Read, Review of the above in *The Listener.*

PAGE 96
Karl Barth, *God, Grace and Gospel;* in T. F. Torrance, *Karl Barth; An Introduction to His Early Theology* (London: SCM Press, 1962), pp. 38; 49; 44–45; 143.

PAGE 98
Torrance, *Karl Barth,* p. 82.

PAGE 100
Torrance, *Karl Barth,* pp. 44; 120–121; 87; 148.
Karl Barth, *Anselm: Fides Quaerens Intellectum* (London: SCM Press, 1960), pp. 69; 161; 71.

PAGE 101
Barth, *Anselm,* p. 11.
Barth, *The Doctrine of the Word of God, Church Dogmatics* (Edinburgh: T & T Clark, 1936), 1:1, p. 31.
Torrance, *Karl Barth,* pp. 164; 87; 111.

PAGE 102
H. J. Blackham, *Six Existential Thinkers* (London: Routledge and Kegan Paul, 1965), p. 4.

PAGE 104
Stephen Neill, *The Interpretation of the New Testament 1861–1961* (London: Oxford University Press, 1964), p. 208 footnote.
William Warren Bartley, *The Retreat to Commitment* (London: Chatto and Windus, 1964), pp. 63; 219.
Joad, *Christianity,* p. 20.

PAGE 105
Beatrice Webb, in *What I Believe,* p. 162.
Wilson, *Religion and the Rebel,* pp. 138–139.
Carroll, *Alice,* pp. 220, 221.

PAGE 106
T. W. Fowle, *Nineteenth Century Opinion,* ed. Michael Goodwin (London: Pelican, 1951), p. 117.

PAGE 107
Wilson, *Outsider,* p. 224.
Margharita Laski, "God and the Universe," *Week-end Telegraph* (December 16, 1966).

Bartley, *Retreat to Commitment,* pp. 35–36.

PAGE 108
Leslie Newbigin, *Honest Religion for Secular Man* (London: SCM Press, 1966), p. 10.
J. S. Bezzant, in *Objections to Belief,* p. 78.
T. J. J. Altizer and William Hamilton, *Radical Theology and the Death of God* (London: Penguin, 1968), p. 135.

PAGE 109
Ninian Smart, *World Religions: A Dialogue* (London: Penguin, 1966), p. 88.
Carroll, *Alice,* p. 206.

PAGE 110
David Knowles, *What is Mysticism?* (London: Burns and Oates, 1967), n. p.
F. C. Happold, *Religious Faith and Twentieth Century Man* (London: Penguin, 1966), pp. 172; 106.

PAGE 111
H. R. Rookmaaker, *Modern Art and the Death of a Culture* (Downers Grove, IL: Inter-Varsity Press, 1970), p. 202.

PAGE 112
Albert Ayler, in J. Marks, *Rock and Other Four-Letter Words* (New York: Bantam, 1968); see also Brian Wilson in the same, n. pp.
From the BBC TV *Man Alive* program "Eastern Promise" (May 31, 1972).
Aldous Huxley, *Ends and Means* (London: Chatto and Windus, 1937), p. 286.

PAGES 112, 113
Brian Wilson, Larry Ramos and Peter Townsend in Marks, *Rock and Other Words,* n. pp.

PAGE 113
Humphreys, *Buddhism,* pp. 180, 185–186.

PAGE 114
Dionysius the Areopagite, *The Mystical Theology,* Shrine of Wisdom Press; in Happold, *Religious Faith,* p. 112.

PAGE 115
A. Huxley, *Ends and Means,* pp. 289–290.
Nicholas of Cusa, *The Vision of God,* tr. E. G. Salter; in Happold, *Religious Faith,* p. 45.
Simone Weil, article in *Theology.*

PAGE 116
Happold, *Religious Faith,* pp. 51–52; 149; 152.

PAGES 116, 117
Ibid., pp. 124; 68.

PAGE 117
Joad, *Book of Joad,* pp. 72–73.

PAGE 118
Happold, *Religious Faith,* p. 172.
Joad, *Recovery of Belief,* pp. 97–98.

PAGE 119
Renan; in G. Galloway, *Philosophy of Religion,* International Theological Library (New York: Scribner and Sons, 1920), p. 324.

PAGE 120
S. T. Coleridge, *Aids to Reflection;* in Willey, *Nineteenth Century,* p. 49.
Ronald Knox, *Letter to Lady Acton,* 1956; in Evelyn Waugh, *Ronald Knox* (London: Fontana, 1962), pp. 283–284.
H. E. Root, "What Is the Gospel?", *Theology* (June, 1963).

PAGE 121
A. R. Vidler, Review of Clyde S. Kilby, *The Christian World of C. S. Lewis* in *Book Week.*
Review in *Honey* (January, 1967).

PAGE 122
Constance Padwick, *Temple Gairdner of Cairo* (London: SPCK, 1929), pp. 148–149; 158.

PAGE 123
Brunner, *The Christian Doctrine of Creation and Redemption,* n.p.
Freud, *New Introductory Lectures on Psycho-Analysis,* ed. James Strachey, tr. W. J. H. Sprott (New York: W. W. Norton and Co., Inc., 1965), p. 168.

PAGE 124
Paul, *Alternatives to Belief,* pp. 133–134.
Wilson, *Religion and the Rebel,* p. 177.
Ann Jellico, Interview in *New Theatre Magazine;* in Taylor, *Anger and After,* pp. 69–70.

PAGE 126
Wilson, *Outsider,* p. 296.

PAGE 127
John Habgood, *Religion and Science* (London: Mills and Boon, 1964), pp. 141–142.
New Dutch Catechism, pp. 236–237.

PAGE 129
John 6:68, 69; 16:29, 30.
Gotthold E. Lessing, *Eine Duplik;* in Hazard, *European Thought in the Eighteenth Century* (New York: Peter Smith, n.d.), p. 495.

PAGE 130
Psalm 119:34; 119:18; 2 Peter 1:5, 6; 1 Corinthians 14:20.

PAGE 131
Colossians 1:9; 1 Peter 3:15.

PAGE 132
Dietrich Bonhoeffer, *Letters and Papers from Prison* (London: Fontana, 1959), p. 189.

PAGE 133
Ibid., pp. 146–147; 164.

PAGE 134
Emmanuel Amand de Mendieta, Essay in *The Anglican Synthesis,* ed. W. R. F. Browning (New York: Peter Smith, 1964), pp. 155–156.
Arnold Lunn and C. E. M. Joad, *Christianity,* p. 310.
Acts 4:10–12.
John Wren-Lewis, in *What I Believe,* p. 235.

PAGE 135
Bronowski, *Identity of Man,* p. 45.
Hampson, *Enlightenment,* p. 129.
Aldous Huxley, *Brave New World Revisited* (London: Chatto and Windus, 1959), Introduction.

PAGE 136
Hampson, *Enlightenment,* p. 11.
Mark 10:15; Matthew 11:25–30.
A. Huxley, *Do What You Will,* pp. 185–186.
Lehmann, "Alice at the Sorbonne," *Listener* (September 22, 1966), pp. 424f.

PART TWO

PAGE 145
George Harrison, *Beatles* Magazine (February, 1968).
Alasdair MacIntyre; in *The Listener* (February 15, 1968), p. 194.
Robinson, *Exploration into God,* p. 46.

PAGE 149
Exodus 3:14–15; Isaiah 55:8–9;
Psalm 135:5–6; Hosea 11:8.

PAGE 150
Isaiah 57:15; Psalm 25:14; Isaiah
43:10; Psalm 90:2; Jeremiah
23:23–24.

PAGE 151
Psalm 139:1–2; Isaiah 46:9–10;
Job 23:13–14; Habakkuk 1:12;
Genesis 1:1; Psalms 148:3–5;
33:6–9.

PAGE 152
Hebrews 11:3; Isaiah 40:28–31;
Psalm 104:1–2, 14, 20.

PAGE 153
Psalm 147:8–9; Nehemiah 9:6;
Jeremiah 31:3; Ezekiel 33:11;
Isaiah 55: 6–7; Lamentations
3:22–23; John 3:16; Romans
5:8.

PAGE 154
John 5:20; 17:24; Habakkuk 1:13;
Psalm 5:4; Jeremiah 9:23–24;
Genesis 17:1; Leviticus 19:2;
Psalm 11:7; Deuteronomy
13:4–5.

PAGE 155
Psalm 7:9, 11; Jeremiah 5:7–9;
5:26–29; Exodus 34:6–7.

PAGE 156
Isaiah 54:7–8; Deuteronomy 6:4–
5; Isaiah 45:5–6, 22–23.

PAGE 157
Matthew 11:27; John 17:5; 15:26;
Acts 1:8; 2:1–4; Galatians 5:22–
23; Psalm 95:6.

PAGE 158
Psalms 5:7; 9:1–2; 84:1–2; 18:1;
28:7.

PAGE 161
John Mbiti, African Religions and
Philosophy (London: Heinemann,
1969), pp. 29, 35.

PAGE 162
Robert Brow, Religion, Origins and
Ideas (London: Tyndale Press,
1966), pp. 10–11.

PAGE 163
Roy A. Stewart, Rabbinic Theology
(Edinburgh: Oliver and Boyd,
1961), p. 20.
The Koran, tr. N. J. Dawood (Lon-
don: Penguin, 1964), Sura
2:255, p. 349; 59:23–24, p. 263.
Al-Junayd, in Samuel M. Zwemer,
A Moslem Seeker After God (Al-
Ghazzali) (Old Tappan, N.J: Re-
vell, 1920), p. 182.

PAGE 164
Reynold Nicholson, The Mystics of
Islam (Beirut: Khayyats reprint,
1966), pp. 21–22; 22–23.

PAGE 165
Ahmad A. Galwash, The Religion
of Islam, Vol. 2 (Cairo: The Supreme Council for Islamic Affairs, 1966), pp. 341–342.
Joseph Joubert, Les Cahiers de Joseph Joubert; in Hazard, European
Thought in the Eighteenth Century,
p. 288.

PAGE 166
Voltaire, Letter of 1741, in
Brown, Philosophy and Faith, p.
85.
Voltaire; in Cragg, Church and
Reason, p. 237.
Hazard, European Thought in the
Eighteenth Century, p. 128.

PAGE 167
Willey, Seventeenth Century, pp.
106–107.

PAGE 168
Thomas Carlyle; in Froude,
Carlyle's Life in London (1884);
in Willey, Seventeenth Century, p.
134.
Radhakrishnan, Hindu View, p.
20.

PAGE 169
Humphreys, Buddhism, pp. 79–80.

PAGE 170
Meister Eckhart, tr. C. de B.
Evans; in D. T. Suzuki, Mysti-
cism, Christian and Buddhist
(New York: Collier Books,
1962), pp. 43–44.
The Cloud of Unknowing, tr. Clifton
Wolters (London: Penguin,
1971), pp. 55; 57–58.
Jack Kerouac, The Dharma Bums
(St. Albens, Herts: Granada
Panther Books, 1972), n. p.

PAGE 171
Tom Wolfe, The Electric Kool-Aid
Acid Test (New York: Bantam,
1971), pp. 143, 127 and 128;
130.

PAGE 172
The Beatles' Illustrated Lyrics (London: Macdonald, 1969), n. p.

PAGE 173
Albert Camus, Cahiers du Sud,
April 1943; in Camus, A Collec-
tion of Critical Essays, ed. Ger-
maine Bree (Englewood Cliffs,
NJ: Prentice-Hall, 1965), p. 70.
Jean-Paul Sartre, Nausea, tr. Rob-
ert Baldick (London: Penguin,
1965), p. 26.
Baron von Hugel; in Michael de la
Bedoyere, Baron von Hugel
(London: Dent, 1951), p. 291.

PAGE 174
Somerset Maugham, The Summing
Up (London: Penguin, 1963), p.
179.

PAGE 175
Friedrich Nietzsche, The Joyful
Wisdom; in Robert Adolfs, The
Grave of God (London: Burns
and Oates, 1967), pp. 13–14.

PAGE 176
Matthew Arnold, Letters; in Willey,
Nineteenth Century, pp. 275–276.
Martin Esslin, The Theatre of the
Absurd (London: Penguin,
1968), p. 389.

PAGE 177
Arthur Adamov, L'Aveu; in Esslin,
Theatre of the Absurd, p. 90.
Jean-Paul Sartre, Words (London:
Penguin, 1967), pp. 62–65.

PAGE 179
Albert Camus, The Rebel (London:
Penguin, 1967), pp. 59–60.
Nietzsche, The Joyful Wisdom
No. 343; in Brown, Philosophy
and Faith, p. 139.
Harrington, Accidental Century, p.
115.

PAGE 180
Jean-Paul Sartre, Existentialism and
Humanism, tr. Philip Mairet
(London: Methuen, 1968), pp.
32–33.

PAGE 182
Brow, Origins and Ideas, pp. 37,
13–14.

PAGE 183
Ibid., p. 84.
Sen, Hinduism, p. 53.
The Bhagavad Gita, tr. Juan Mas-
caro (London: Penguin, 1965),
pp. 85–88.

PAGE 184
H. D. Lewis, The Study of Religions
(London: Penguin, 1966), p. 56.

Professor Zaehner, Foolishness to
the Greeks; in H. D. Lewis and R.
L. Slater, The Study of Religions
(London: Penguin, 1969), p.
145.

PAGE 185
Hazard, European Mind, pp. 170–
171.
Hegel, in The Philosophy of Reli-
gion, Vol 2, ed. Ninian Smart
(London: SCM Press, n.d.), p.
327.
Julian Huxley, "The New Divini-
ty," in Essays of a Humanist
(London: Penguin, 1966), p.
227.
J. Huxley, "The Humanist
Frame," in Essays of a Humanist,
p. 117.

PAGE 186
Paul Tillich, Biblical Religion and
the Search for Ultimate Reality
(Chicago: University of Chicago
Press, 1955), pp. 82–83.
Tillich, Systematic Theology, Vol. 1
(Chicago: University of Chicago
Press, 1951), p. 227.
Tillich, Shaking of the Foundations,
pp. 63–64.

PAGE 187
Teilhard de Chardin, The Phenomenon of Man, pp. 322; 338.

PAGE 188
Robinson, Honest to God, p. 7.
Robinson, Exploration into God, pp.
36; 39; 41.
J. Huxley, Essays of a Humanist, p.
223.
Robinson, Exploration into God, pp.
23; 83–84; 127; 15.

PAGE 189
Ibid., p. 58.
Robinson, Honest to God, p. 53.
Robinson, Exploration into God, pp.
134; 72.

PAGE 190
John Wren-Lewis, They Became
Anglicans; in Robinson, Honest to
God, pp. 42–43.
Happold, Religious Faith, p. 51.
Altizer, Radical Theology, p. 102.

PAGE 191
William Hamilton, The New Essence of Christianity (New York:
Association Press, 1961), pp.
58–59.
William Hamilton, Radical Theology, p. 40.
Altizer, Radical Theology, p. 30.
T. J. J. Altizer, The Gospel of Christian Atheism (London: Collins,
1967), p. 103; 106 and 136.

PAGE 192
Hamilton, Radical Theology, p. 53.
Ibid., p. 58.
Peter Dumitriu, Incognito; in Rob-
inson, Exploration into God, p. 89.

PAGE 193
Y. Takeuchi, Essay "Buddhism
and Existentialism"; in Religion
and Culture, Essays in Honour of
Paul Tillich, ed. Walter Leibricht
(New York: Harper, 1959), p.
304.
Walter Kaufmann, Critique of Reli-
gion and Philosophy (London:
Faber and Faber, 1959), p. 128.
J. Huxley, Essays of a Humanist,
pp. 225–226.

PAGE 194
Alasdair MacIntyre, "God and the
Theologians"; in The Honest to
God Debate, ed. David L. Ed-
wards (London: SCM Press,
1963), pp. 215–216.
MacIntyre; in The Listener (Febru-
ary 15, 1968).

PAGE 195
MacIntyre, "God and the Theologians"; in *The Honest to God Debate*, p. 220.
Barbara Wooton; in *What I Believe* pp. 205–206.
Altizer, *Radical Theology*, p. 131.
Professor Peter Beyerhaus, Paper for Islington Clerical Conference, June 1972, Bulletin of EFAC (Evangelical Fellowship in the Anglican Communion) (July, 1972).

PAGE 196
Radhakrishnan, *Hindu View, p. 28.*
Arnold Toynbee; in Ved Mehta, *Fly and Fly Bottle* (London: Penguin, 1965), p. 124.

PAGE 198
Exodus 33:18–23; 34:5–7; Isaiah 6:1–5; Ezekiel 1:26–28.

PAGE 199
Jeremiah 9:23–24; John 1:18; 14:8–10; Revelation 1:12–17.

PAGE 200
1 Peter 1:8.
Thomas Merton, "New Seeds of Contemplation"; in H. A. Williams, *Objections to Christian Belief* (London: Constable, 1963), p. 32.
Mitchell, *God I Want*, pp. 1, 9.
A. Huxley, *Do What You Will*, pp. 54–55.
Albert Einstein; in *What I Believe*, pp. 28–29.

PAGE 201
Ernst Cassirer, *An Essay on Man* (New Haven, CT: Yale University Press, 1963), pp. 98–99.

PAGE 202
Sartre, *Nausea*, p. 26.

PAGE 203
Ronald Hepburn; in Vidler, *Objections to Christian Belief*, p. 31.

PAGE 204
Genesis 4:14, 16; 6:5.

PAGE 205
Proverbs 6:16–19.
Stephen C. Neill, "The Wrath of God and the Peace of God"; in Max Warren, *Interpreting the Cross* (London: SCM Press, 1966), pp. 22–23.
Jeremiah 31:3; Isaiah 54:7–8.

PAGE 206
Isaiah 49:15–16; Luke 19:41–44; Matthew 25:41–43, 46; Romans 5:8–9.

PAGE 207
1 John 4:10 (Revised Version); Revelation 6:15–17.

PAGE 211
Harold Pinter; in Taylor, *Anger and After*, p. 308.
Bronowski, *Identity of Man*, pp. 7–9.
Thomas Mann; in *What I Believe*, p. 88.

PAGE 212
A. Huxley, *New World Revisited*, p. 156.
Maugham, *Summing Up*, pp. 181–182.
Leo Tolstoy, *Memoirs of a Madman;* in Wilson, *Outsider*, p. 164.
Adam Schaff, *A Philosophy of Man* (London: Lawrence and Wishart, 1963), p. 34.

PAGE 213
Nietzsche, *The Will to Power;* in Blackham, *Existentialist Thinkers*, p. 31.

Arthur Koestler, "What the Modern World is Doing to the Soul of Man," essay in *The Challenge of Our Time* (London: Percival, Marshall, 1948), pp. 15–17.

PAGE 213
Camus, *Rebel*, p. 57.
Jean-Paul Sartre, *Saint-Genet;* in *Sartre, A Collection of Critical Essays*, ed. Edith Kern (Englewood Cliffs, NJ: Prentice-Hall, 1962), p. 87.
Ibid., p. 211.
Taylor, *Anger and After.* p. 287.
Bertrand Russell, *The Impact of Science on Society* (London: Allen and Unwin, 1952), p. 114.

PAGE 215
Thomas Mann, *The Magic Mountain* (London: Penguin, 1967), p. 716.
Eugene Ionesco, *"L'orsque j'écris . . .";* in Esslin, *Theatre of the Absurd, p. 132.*
A. Huxley, *Do What You Will*, p. 189.
Schaff, *Philosophy of Man*, p. 35.

PAGE 216
Albert Camus, *The Myth of Sisyphus;* in Esslin, *The Theatre of the Absurd,* p. 416.
Camus, *Rebel*, p. 267.

PAGE 220
Genesis 1:26–27; 5:1–3; 1:31.

PAGE 221
Psalm 8:3–8; Isaiah 45:9–10; Psalm 139:13–17.

PAGE 222
Psalm 119:73; Genesis 2:16–17; Romans 5:12; 1 John 3:4; Romans 1:18–21.

PAGE 223
Romans 2:1–3; 3:9; 3:23; Isaiah 65:1–7.

PAGE 224
Ephesians 2:3; 2 Thessalonians 1:9; Isaiah 1:18; Romans 5:6–11; John 1:12–13.

PAGE 225
2 Peter 1:3–4; Job 7:17–21; 23:10.

PAGE 226
Ezekiel 18:1–4, 20; Luke 12:6–7.
Leslie Newbigin, *Honest Religion for Secular Man* (London: SCM Press, 1966), p. 62.
Exodus 6:6–7.

PAGE 227
Jeremiah 1:5; Ephesians 1:3–10; Genesis 17:1; 1 Peter 1:15–16; Exodus 20:3–17.

PAGE 228
Isaiah 61:8; Malachi 3:5; Matthew 22:37–40; Colossians 3:5–14.

PAGE 229
Ephesians 5:10, 17–18; Jeremiah 17:9–10; Psalm 139:1–4.

PAGE 230
1 John 1:7; Ephesians 4:25; 4:31—5:2; Ephesians 5:22, 25; Song of Solomon 6:3; Psalm 22:1–2; Habakkuk 1:13.

PAGE 231
Jeremiah 12:1–2; Genesis 1:31; 3:16; 3:19; Luke 13:16.

PAGE 232
Deuteronomy 28:2–4, 58–59; John 5:14; Psalm 119:71, 75–76.

PAGE 233
Job 42:2–6; 42:7.

PAGE 234
Luke 4:18–19; 11:20–22; John 11:33; Luke 13:1–5.

PAGE 235
Luke 12:4–5; Matthew 8:17; Hebrews 2:14–18 (NEB); Psalm 96:11–13.

PAGE 236
Isaiah 42:1, 4; 58:6–7; Revelation 21:1–4.

PAGE 237
Michel Quoist, *Prayers of Life* (Dublin: Gill, 1965), p. 66.
Joad, *Recovery of Belief*, p. 63.
Neill, "The Wrath of God and the Peace of God"; in Warren, *Interpreting the Cross*, pp. 22–23.

PAGE 239
Senghor, *African Socialism*, p. 72.

PAGE 240
Ibid., p. vii, footnote.
Dr. Isidore Epstein, *Judaism* (London: Epworth Press, 1939), p. 80; in J. N. D. Anderson, *The World's Religions* (London: IVF Press, 1965), p. 32.
Epstein, *Judaism*, p. 82.
Dr. Hertz, *The Pentateuch and the Haftorahs;* in Anderson, *World's Religions*, p. 32.

PAGE 241
Hertz, *Pentateuch*, pp. 523–524.
Sura 38:71–72, p. 280; 2:30, p. 326.
H. A. R. Gibb, *Mohammedanism* (London: Oxford University Press, 1964), p. 70.

PAGE 242
C. C. Adams, *Islam and Modernism in Egypt, A Study of the Modern Reform Movement Inaugurated by Mohammad Abduh* (London: Oxford University Press, 1933), p. 147.
Sura 20:117–122, p. 225.
Carl Becker, *The Heavenly City of the Eighteenth Century Philosophers;* in Blackham, *Objections to Humanism,* p. 10.

PAGE 243
Hazard, *European Mind*, pp. 295–296.

PAGE 244
Sura 81:27–29, p. 17.
Mohammad Abduh; in Adams, *Islam and Modernism*, p. 153 (two quotations).
Sura 19:93–95, p. 37; 28:88, p. 81.
Nicholson, *Mystics of Islam*, pp. 167–168.

PAGE 245
Hampson, *Enlightenment*, pp. 94–95.
Charles Darwin, *Autobiography*, chapter 3.
Mbiti, *African Religions*, pp. 165; 99.

PAGE 246
Sura 51:56, p. 118; 76:4–22, p. 18.

PAGE 247
Diderot; in Hampson, *Enlightenment*, pp. 95–96.
Esslin, *Theatre of the Absurd*, p. 55.

PAGE 248
Mbiti, *African Religions*, pp. 213–214.
Stewart, *Rabbinic Theology*, pp. 173–174.

PAGE 249
Herbert Danby, *The Jew and Christianity* (London: Sheldon Press, 1927), pp. 83–85.

PAGE 250
Sura 59:23, p. 263.
Baidawi; in Samuel Zwemer, *The Moslem Doctrine of God* (New York: American Tract Society, 1905), pp. 58–59.

586

Al-Ghazzali; in *Ibid.*, pp. 55–56.
Anderson, *World's Religions*, p. 85.

PAGE 251
John Locke, *On Civil Government*, Book II, chapter 11; in Hazard, *European Mind*, p. 325.
Hooke; in Hampson, *Enlightenment*, p. 155.
Willey, *Eighteenth Century*, p. 254.

PAGE 252
Mbiti, *African Religions*, pp. 209; 38.
Sura 42:23, p. 152; 30:20–21, p. 188; 60:7–9, p. 260.

PAGE 253
Mbiti, *African Religions*, pp. 214–215; 169–170.

PAGE 254
Sura 13:11, p. 140; 4:79, p. 363.

PAGE 256
Camus, *Rebel*, p. 47.
Sartre; in *Ibid.*, p. 269.
Christopher Dawson, "Christianity and the New Age," in *Essays in Order*, 1931; in Willey, *Seventeenth Century*, p. 16.
Arendt, *Human Condition*, pp. 12–13.

PAGE 257
Cassirer, *Essay on Man*, pp. 21–22.
Glossary of Humanism, under Humanism.
H. J. Blackham, *Humanism* (London: Penguin, 1968), pp. 13; 19.

PAGE 258
Edmund Leach; in *The Listener* (November 16, 1967).
Lord Willis; in *An Inquiry into Humanism*, (BBC, 1966), p. 21.
Geoffrey Scott, *The Architecture of Humanism*; in Blackham, *Objections to Humanism*, p. 8.
A. J. Ayer; in *An Inquiry into Humanism*, p. 2.
Blackham, *Objections to Humanism*, p. 11.

PAGE 259
J. Huxley, "The Humanist Frame," in *Essays of a Humanist*, pp. 77, 107.
E. L. Allen, *Existentialism from Within;* in Brown, *Philosophy and Faith*, pp. 181–182.
Karl Heim; in A. R. Vidler, *The Church in an Age of Revolution* (London: Penguin, 1961), p. 211.

PAGE 260
Humanist Glossary, under Existentialism.
Sartre, *Existentialism and Humanism*, pp. 56; 27–28, 29.

PAGE 261
Blackham, *Existentialist Thinkers*, pp. 151–152.
John Lewis, *Marxism and the Open Mind*, 1957, pp. 33–34; 161; 144–146; in Lester DeKoster, "Pretense of Humanism: The New Face of Marxism," in *Christianity Today* (October 26, 1962).

PAGE 262
Guy Wint, *Spotlight on Asia* (London: Penguin, 1955), pp. 211–212.
Crossman, *God That Failed*, pp. 9–10.
Sen, *Hinduism*, p. 19.
W. Cantwell-Smith, *The Faith of Other Men* (London: Mentor, 1965), pp. 25–26.

PAGE 263
Humphreys, *Buddhism*, pp. 85; 157.

PAGE 264
Pearl Buck; in *What I Believe*, p. 24–25.

E. M. Forster; in *What I Believe*, p. 50.
Wilson, *Outsider*, pp. 71–72.

PAGE 265
Eugene Ionesco, *Le Point du Départ;* in Esslin, *Theatre of the Absurd*, p. 155.

PAGE 266
Harold Pinter; in Taylor, *Anger and After*, p. 308.
A. Huxley, *New World Revisited*, p. 164.
Virginia Woolf; in Joad, *Book of Joad*, p. 112.

PAGE 267
Joad, *Book of Joad*, p. 116.
Sartre, *Nausea*, p. 241.

PAGE 268
H. G. Wells; in *What I Believe*, pp. 170–171.
J. Huxley, *Essays of a Humanist*, p. 89.
A. Huxley, *Ends and Means*, pp. 290–291.
Humphreys, *Buddhism*, p. 128.

PAGE 269
Suzuki, *Mysticism*, pp. 35–36.
Arthur Koestler, *The Sleepwalkers* (London: Penguin, 1968), p. 540.

PAGE 270
Camus; in *Camus, A Collection of Critical Essays*, p. 116.
Maugham, *Summing Up*, pp. 181–182.
Bertrand Russell, "A Free Man's Worship," in *Why I Am Not A Christian* (New York: Simon and Schuster, 1966), p. 107.
Blackham, *Humanism*, p. 116.

PAGE 271
Francis Bacon; in John Russell, *Francis Bacon* (London: Methuen, 1965); in H. R. Rookmaaker, *Modern Art and the Death of a Culture* (London: IVF Press, 1970), p. 174.
Esslin, *Theatre of the Absurd*, pp. 22–23.
Eugene Ionesco; in *Ibid.*, p. 23.
Esslin, *Theatre of the Absurd*, p. 85.

PAGE 272
Sartre, *Nausea*, pp. 123–124; 162.
Allen Ginsberg; in Steve Turner, "Some Notes from the Underground," *Voice* Magazine (London: IVF Press, 1972), p. 6.
George Eliot, *Cross's Life;* in Willey, *Nineteenth Century*, p. 247.

PAGE 273
Bertrand Russell, "A Free Man's Worship," in *Why I Am Not A Christian*, pp. 115–116.
Nietzsche, *The Will to Power* 1041; in Blackham, *Existentialist Thinkers*, p. 33; and 1031, p. 36.
Nikos Kazantzakis; in Helen Kazantzakis, *A Biography Based on His Letters* (New York: Simon and Schuster, 1968), p. 473.
Maurice Friedman, *The Problematic Rebel* (New York: Random House, 1963), p. 468.

PAGE 274
Sartre, *Words*, pp. 61–62.
Andre Malraux, "The Walnut Trees of Altenberg"; in Maurice Friedman, *To Deny Our Nothingness* (London: Gollancz, 1967), p. 17.
Arthur Adamov, "L'Aveu"; in Esslin *Theatre of the Absurd*, pp. 89–90.
Sartre, *Words*, p. 157.

PAGE 275
Wilson, *Outsider*, p. 38.
Rebecca West; in *What I Believe*, p. 189.

George Santayana, *Three Philosophical Poets;* in Blackham, *Objections to Humanism*, pp. 111–112.
Lin Yutang; in *What I Believe*, p. 76.
Camus, *Rebel*, p. 14.
Camus, *The Plague*, tr. Stuart Gilbert (London: Penguin, 1966), n.p.

PAGE 276
Blackham, *Humanism*, pp. 211–212.
J. Huxley, *Essays of a Humanist*, pp. 91–92.
Colin Wilson, *Beyond the Outsider* (Guildford: Baker, 1965), pp. 62; 165.

PAGE 277
Henry Miller, *Tropic of Cancer;* in Rookmaaker, *Modern Art and the Death*, p. 146.

PAGE 278
Rabindranath Tagore, *Fruit Gathering* (New York: Macmillan, 1922), pp. 82–83.
Pete Townshend, *The Seeker;* in Turner, "Some Notes from the Underground," *Voice*, p. 7.
Sartre, *Existentialism and Humanism*, p. 54.
Proust; in Harrington, *Accidental Century*, p. 154.

PAGE 279
Koestler, "What the Modern World is Doing . . . ," in *Challenge of Our Time*, p. 15.
Donald Kalish, "What (If Anything) To Expect from Today's Philosophers," *Time* Magazine, January 7, 1966; in Paul, *Alternatives*, p. 159.
McLuhan Hot and Cool, ed. Gerald Emanuel Stern (London: Penguin, 1968), p. 18.
George Eliot; in *Ibid.*, p. 90.
Edmund Leach; in *The Listener* (December 7, 1967).

PAGE 280
Sartre, *Existentialism and Humanism*, p. 33.
Koestler, "What the Modern World is Doing, . . . ," in *Challenge of Our Times*, pp. 16–19.

PAGE 281
Priestley, *Literature and Western Man;* in Arthur Calder-Marshall, essay in *What I Believe*, p. 68.
Lin Yutang, essay in *What I Believe*, p. 83.
Maugham, *Summing Up*, p. 203.

PAGE 282
T. H. Huxley, *Evolution and Ethics and Other Essays*, Romanes Lecture, 1893 (New York: D. Appleton, 1905), p. 80.
Blackham, *Humanism*, pp. 58–59.
Schaff, *Philosophy of Man*, p. 60.
J. S. Mill, *Autobiography*, 1873 World's Classics (London: Oxford University Press, 1924), n. p.

PAGE 283
Wren-Lewis; in Moule, *Fact and Fantasy*, p. 32.
Robinson, *Honest to God*, pp. 114–115.

PAGE 284
Bronowski, *Science and Values*, pp. 66, 77, 80, 68; and 70, 75, 63.
Koestler, *Ghost in the Machine*, pp. 153–154.

PAGE 285
Bronowski, *Science and Values*, p. 8.
Koestler, *Sleepwalkers*, pp. 552; 553.

587

PAGES 285, 286
Radhakrishnan, *Hindu View,* pp. 56; 55.

PAGE 286
Suzuki, *Mysticism,* p. 58.
Humphreys, *Buddhism,* p. 122.

PAGE 287
Francis Schaeffer, *The God Who Is There* (London: Hodder and Stoughton, 1968), p. 101.
Rousseau; in Hampson, *Enlightenment,* p. 195.

PAGE 288
Charles Darwin, *The Descent of Man* (London: John Murray, 1888), n. p.
Camus, *Rebel,* pp. 27–28.
Ibid., pp. 258–260.
Sartre, *Existentialism and Humanism,* pp. 33–34.

PAGE 289
Sartre; in *Sartre, A Collection of Critical Essays,* p. 167.
Sartre, *Existentialism and Humanism,* pp. 47–49.
Wilson, *Outsider,* p. 39.
John D. Wild; in *Sartre, A Collection of Critical Essays,* p. 145.

PAGE 290
Sartre, *Existentialism and Humanism,* pp. 36, 31.
Schaff, *Philosophy of Man,* pp. 24; 16.

PAGE 291
Blackham, *Objections to Humanism,* pp. 15–18.
Edmund Leach; in *The Listener* (January 11, 1968).
Alasdair MacIntyre; in *Ibid.*

PAGE 292
Hampson, *Enlightenment,* pp, 124; 127.
Dostoievsky; in Harrington, *Accidental Century,* p. 123.
C. S. Lewis, *The Abolition of Man* (London: Oxford University Press, 1944), p. 30.
Joad, *Christianity,* n.p.

PAGE 293
Paul, *Alternatives.* pp. 60; 66.
Harold Pinter; in Esslin, *Theatre of the Absurd,* p. 274.
Esslin, *Theatre of the Absurd,* pp. 69; 84.

PAGE 294
Wild; in *Sartre, A Collection of Critical Essays,* p. 146.
Cyril Connolly and Jonathan Miller; in *The Listener* (November 3, 1966).

PAGE 295
Camus, *Plague,* p. 249.
Sartre, *Nausea,* pp. 160–161.
Schaeffer, *God Who Is There,* p. 29.

PAGE 296
D. R. Davies, *On to Orthodoxy* (London: Hodder and Stoughton, 1939), p. 61.
W. E. Hocking, "Tentative Outlook for the State and Church," in *This Is My Philosophy,* ed. W. Burnett (London: Allen and Unwin, 1958), pp. 304–305.
A. Huxley, *Do What You Will,* p. 180.

PAGE 297
Radhakrishnan, *Hindu View,* p. 88.
Humphreys, *Buddhism,* p. 123.
Robinson, *Exploration into God,* pp. 89; 88; 110.

PAGE 298
G. T. Manley; in Anderson, *The World's Religions,* p. 65.
Newbigin, *Honest Religion,* p. 27.

PAGE 299
H. W. Van Loon; in *What I Believe,* pp. 153–154.
Bertrand Russell, *Has Man a Future?* (London: Penguin, 1961), pp. 126–127.

PAGE 300
Franz Fanon, *The Wretched of the Earth* (London: Penguin, 1967), pp. 251–255.
Koestler, *Ghost in the Machine,* pp. 267; 336; 335; 335–336.

PAGE 301
J. Huxley, *Essays of a Humanist,* pp. 130; 117; 252.

PAGE 302
Wren-Lewis; in Moule, *Fact and Fantasy,* p. 44.
Thomas Mann; in *What I Believe,* pp. 89–90.
Harrington, *Accidental Century,* pp. 35–36.

PAGE 303
Bertrand Russell; in Mehta, *Fly and Fly Bottle,* p. 41.
Koestler, *Darkness at Noon* (London: Jonathan Cape, 1940), pp. 253–254.
Camus, "Actuelles"; in *Camus, A Collection of Critical Essays,* p. 56.
Camus, *Rebel,* pp. 266–267.

PAGE 304
Camus, *Plague,* pp. 107–108; 214.

PAGE 305
Ibid., pp. 170–171; 251–252.
Dostoievsky; in Wilson, *Outsider,* p. 175.
A. Huxley, *Do What You Will,* p. 50.
A. Huxley, *Ends and Means,* p. 298.

PAGE 306
Joad, *Recovery of Belief,* p. 174.
Humphreys, *Buddhism,* p. 123.
A. Huxley, *Ends and Means,* n. p.

PAGE 307
Nietzsche; in Blackham, *Existentialist Thinkers,* p. 40.
Wilson, *Outsider,* p. 119.

PAGE 308
Camus, *Rebel,* p. 16.
A. Huxley, *Ends and Means,* pp. 274–275.
Lewis Carroll, *Alice in Wonderland* (London: Macmillan, 1964), pp. 127–128.

PAGE 309
Nietzsche, *Twilight of the Idols,* tr. R. J. Hollingdale (London: Penguin, 1968), pp. 69–70.

PAGE 310
Joad, *Christianity,* pp. ix–xx.
Sartre, *Existentialism and Humanism,* pp. 32–33.

PAGE 312
Wilson, *Beyond the Outsider,* p. 164.

PAGE 313
Lord Willis, *Inquiry into Humanism,* BBC, p. 24.

PAGE 314
Bronowski, *Identity of Man,* pp. 14–15.
Professor Donald Mackay, *Freedom of Action in a Mechanistic Universe* (Cambridge: Cambridge University Press, 1967), pp. 11–12.

PAGE 315
Ibid., pp. 36–37; 30–33; 33–34.

PAGE 318
Matthew 19:3–5; Luke 3:23, 38.

PAGE 319
Romans 5:12–19.

Habgood, *Religion and Science,* pp. 69–70.

PAGE 321
Professor W. R. Thompson. Introduction to *The Origin of Species,* Everyman Library No. 811 (London: Dent, 1956).

PAGE 322
J. Huxley, *Essays of a Humanist,* n. p.

PAGE 324
Derek Kidner, *Genesis* (London: Tyndale Press, 1967), p. 30.
J. Huxley, *Evolution in Action* (London: Chatto and Windus, 1953), pp. 136–137.

PAGE 325
A. S. Romer, Man and the Vertebrates, Vol. 2 (London: Penguin, 1963), p. 236. (new title: *Vertebrate Story*)
David Lack, *Evolutionary Theory and Christian Belief: The Unresolved Conflict* (London: Methuen, 1957), passim.
Thompson, Introduction to *The Origin of Species,* n.p.

PAGE 326
J. Huxley, *Essays of a Humanist,* pp. 24–25.
Professor D. S. M. Watson; in Joad, *Recover of Belief,* p. 21.
John R. W. Stott; in *The Church of England Newspaper* (June 7, 1968).

PAGE 331
Fred Hoyle, *The Nature of the Universe* (Oxford: Blackwell, 1960), p. 90.
J. Huxley, *Essays of a Humanist,* p. 112.
Bertrand Russell, *The Problems of Philosophy,* Home University Library (London: Thornton Butterworth, 1932), pp. 26–27.
Joad, *Book of Joad,* p. 213.
H. R. Rookmaaker, *Art and the Public Today* (Switzerland: L'ABRI Fellowship, 1968), pp. 13–14.

PAGE 335
Genesis 1:1–4.

PAGE 336
Hebrews 11:1–3; Psalm 104:10–15.

PAGE 337
Jeremiah 51:15–16; Colossians 1:15–17; 1 Corinthians 8:6; John 1:1–3; Genesis 1:31; 3:17–18.

PAGE 338
Psalm 104:1–2.
Professor Donald Mackay, *Science and Christian Faith Today* (London: CPAS, 1970), pp. 9–10; 14.

PAGE 339
Psalm 148:3–6; Genesis 8:22; Psalm 104:5–9.

PAGE 340
R. Hooykaas, *Religion and the Rise of Modern Science* (Edinburgh: Scottish Academic Press, 1972), pp. 161–162.
C. F. Von Weizacker, *The Relevance of Science* (London: Collins, 1964), p. 163.

PAGE 341
Mackay, *Science and Faith Today,* pp. 18–19; 20.
Rookmaaker, *Art and the Public,* pp. 50–51; 19–20.

PAGE 345
Mbiti, *African Religions,* pp. 56–57.
Sura 50:7–11, p. 119; 15:16–22, p. 236.

PAGE 346
Hooykaas, *Religion and Modern Science*, pp. 7–9; 12–13.

PAGE 347
Lallemant; in Wilson, *Outsider*, p. 149.

PAGE 348
Willey, *Seventeenth Century*, pp. 35; 37–39.
Shaftesbury; in Willey, *Eighteenth Century*, pp. 65–66.

PAGE 349
Willey, *Eighteenth Century*, pp. 67; 267.
Mark Rutherford, *Autobiography*; in Willey, *Eighteenth Century*, pp. 275–276.
Charles Darwin, *Life and Letters of Charles Darwin*, Vol. 3 (London: John Murray, 1888), pp. 312–313. (also available: reprint, Finch Press, 1969).

PAGE 350
Ibid., p. 313.
Charles Darwin, Letter to D. Hooker, 1870; *More Letters*, Vol. 1, p. 85.

PAGE 351
Willey, *Eighteenth Century*, p. 277.
Darwin, *Autobiography* (New York: Harcourt, Brace, 1958), chapters 2 and 3.

PAGE 352
Radhakrishnan, *Hindu View*, pp. 48–49; 51.

PAGE 353
Cassirer, *Essays on Man*, pp. 13–14.

PAGE 354
Ibid., pp. 14–15.

PAGE 355
J. Huxley, *Essays of a Humanist*, pp. 82–83; 78.
A. J. Ayer; in *What I Believe*, p. 14.
Bronowski, *Identity of Man*, pp. 8; 2–4.

PAGE 356
D. H. Lawrence, *A Propos of Lady Chatterley's Lover*; in Willey, *Nineteenth Century*, p. 36.
Camus, "Noces"; in Camus, *A Collection of Critical Essays*, p. 66.
Teilhard de Chardin, *Phenomenon of Man*, p. 241.

PAGE 357
T. de Chardin; in H. de Lubac, *The Faith of Teilhard de Chardin* (London: Collins, 1967), p. 136.
Robinson, *Exploration into God*, pp. 78; 97; 107; 127; 79.

PAGE 358
Wren-Lewis, *Fact and Fantasy*, p. 40.

PAGE 359
Koestler, *The Lotus and the Robot*; in Senghor, *African Socialism*, p. 73.
Sartre, *Nausea*, pp. 176; 180–183.

PAGE 360
Lewis Carroll, *Through the Looking Glass* (London: Macmillan, 1966), pp. 180–182.

PAGE 361
Ibid., pp. 284–285.

PAGE 362
Schaeffer, *God Who Is There*, p. 64.
Bertrand Russell, *The Scientific Outlook*; in Abel Jones, *In Search of Truth* (London: Nelson, 1945), p. 150.
Jules Romanes, essay in *What I Believe*, p. 113.

PAGE 363
Wilson, *Outsider*, pp. 13–14.

Bronowski, *The Common Sense of Science* (London: Penguin, 1966), p. 101.
Von Weizacker, *Relevance of Science*, p. 163.

PAGE 364
Sartre, *Nausea*, pp. 113–114; 225; 115.
Esslin, *Theatre of the Absurd*, p. 51.

PAGE 365
Joad, *Book of Joad*, pp. 281–219.
Maugham, *Summing Up*, pp. 19., 196.

PAGE 366
Sartre, *Nausea*, p. 63.
Henry Moore, *A Study of His Life and Work* (London: Thames and Hudson, 1965), p. 257.
Marc; in Rookmaaker, *Modern Art and the Death*, p. 110.
Karel Appel; in Rookmaaker, *Modern Art and the Death*, p. 160.

PAGE 367
Lucebert; in Rookmaaker, *Art and the Public*, p. 44.
Rookmaaker, *Art and the Public*, p. 18
Rabindranath Tagore, *The Religion of Man* (London: Allen and Unwin, 1931), p. 127.
Suzuki, *Mysticism*, pp. 30–31.

PAGE 370
Genesis 3:17–18; Isaiah 11:6–9.

PAGE 371
Romans 8:19–23.
Alan Millard, *Lion Handbook to the Bible* (Herts: Lion Publishing, 1973), pp. 129–130.

PART 3

PAGE 379
Matthew 1:18–25; Luke 1:26–35.

PAGE 380
Mark 6:32–34; 10:13–16; 1:40–42; Luke 7:12–15; 15:1–2; Mark 7:6, 8, 9.

PAGE 381
Matthew 23:13, 16, 17, 25, 28; Mark 11:15–17; John 11:33–36; 5:30; 6:38; Luke 22:24–27.

PAGE 382
John 12:3–5, 12–15; Mark 7:37; John 8:46; 1 Peter 2:22; 1 John 1:8; 3:5.

PAGE 383
Mark 13:32; Matthew 11:27; 12:50; 16:27; John 10:30; 5:22–23; 14:6–7; Mark 1:15; 10:45; 14:24; 14:61–62; Luke 4:17–21.

PAGE 384
Luke 24:44, 46; John 5:39; 5:46; Mark 2:5–10; John 5:21; 11:25; Matthew 5:21–22; Mark 13:31; John 18:37; Matthew 25:31–32.

PAGE 385
John 5:22–23; Matthew 11:28–29; Luke 14:26; John 7:37; 6:29; 14:1; Matthew 20:29–34.

PAGE 386
Mark 8:1–2; Matthew 15:31; Mark 2:8–12; Matthew 11:2–5; John 10:37–38; Mark 8:11–13.

PAGE 392
Hebrews 2:14; 4:15; James 2:1; 1 Corinthians 15:47; Philippians 2:6–11.

PAGE 393
John 1:18; 1 John 1:1–3.

PAGE 394
Romans 5:12–19; 2 Corinthians 5:18–19; 1 Timothy 2:5–6; Hebrews 2:17–18.

PAGE 395
Hebrews 4:15; John 17:20–26.

PAGE 396
The Truth Shall Make You Free (New York: Watchtower Society, 1943), pp. 248–250.

PAGE 398
John 14:28; 10:30; 14:9–10; Philippians 2:5–7; Luke 18:19; 18:18; 18:22; Colossians 1:15ff.

PAGE 399
C. F. D. Moule, *Colossians and Philemon*, Cambridge New Testament Commentary (London: Cambridge University Press, 1957), p. 64. Hebrews 1:1–4.

PAGE 400
Truth Shall Make You Free, p. 254.

PAGE 401
Herbert Danby, *The Jew and Christianity* (London: Sheldon Press, 1927), pp. 8–9.

PAGE 402
The Jewish Encyclopedia, Vol. VII, Isidore Singer, ed. (London: Funk and Wagnalls Co.), pp. 161, 163.

PAGE 403
Ibid., pp. 163–164; 162.

PAGE 404
Claude Montefiore; in Danby, *Jew and Christianity*, p. 79.
Sholem Asch, *My Personal Faith* (London: Routledge, 1942), pp. 106–107.
Danby, *Jew and Christianity*, p. 23.

PAGE 405
The Jewish Encyclopedia, Vol. VII, p. 166.

PAGE 406
Sura 19:19–22, p. 33; 3:42, p. 398.
Tradition; in M. Goldsack, *Christ in Islam* (Christian Literature Society of India, 1905), p. 32.

PAGE 407
Sura 4:169, p. 371.
Traditions; in Goldsack, *Christ in Islam*, p. 25, 41.

PAGES 407–408
Sura 5:112–115, p. 386; 19:26–31, pp. 33–34; 5:112–115, pp. 386–387; 5:110–111, p. 386.

PAGE 409
Henri Michaud, *Jésu selon le Coran*, p. 10; in Geoffrey Parrinder, *Jesus in the Qur'an* (London: Faber and Faber, 1965), p. 166.

PAGES 409–411
Sura 5:116, p. 387; 6:101, p. 421; 23:91, p. 218; 5:72–75, pp. 382–383.

PAGE 412
Hugh Schonfield, *The Passover Plot* (London: Hutchinson, 1965), pp. 10–11.

PAGE 413
Paul van Buren, *The Secular Meaning of the Gospel* (London: Penguin, 1963), pp. 126–127.

PAGE 415
Schonfield, *Passover Plot*, pp. 9–10.

PAGE 416
Joel Carmichael, *The Death of Jesus* (London: Penguin, 1962), pp. 8, 10.
van Buren, *Secular Meaning*, pp. 16, 30.

PAGE 418
Happold, *Religious Faith,* p. 150.

PAGE 419
Robinson, *Honest to God,* pp. 72–76.
Happold, *Religious Faith,* pp. 145, 124.

PAGE 420
Robinson, *Honest to God,* p. 67.
Happold, *Religious Faith,* pp. 52–53.

PAGE 421
Robinson, *Honest to God,* p. 68.

PAGE 422
Pliny; in *Documents of the Christian Church,* ed. Henry Bettenson (London: Oxford University Press, 1946), pp. 3–5.

PAGE 423
Tacitus; in *Ibid.,* p. 2.

PAGE 424
Suetonius; in *Ibid.,* p. 3.
Josephus; Professor Shlomo Pines, in *Journal of Israeli Academy of Science and Humanities,* 1973; quoted by Peter-Allen Frost, *Church of England Newspaper* (August, 1973).

PAGE 425
Josephus, *Antiquities of the Jews;* in Roderic Dunkerley, *Beyond the Gospels* (London: Penguin, 1957), p. 34.
Dunkerley, *Beyond the Gospels,* pp. 29–30.

PAGE 426
Luke 2:18–19; 2:51; John 8:41; Galatians 4:4.

PAGE 427
Nicholas Zernov, *Eastern Christendom, A Study of the Origin and Development of the Eastern Orthodox Church* (Herts: Weidenfeld and Nicholson, 1961), p. 234.
Luke 1:28, 30–31.

PAGE 428
Luke 1:38; Mark 3:31–35; Luke 11:27–28; John 2:4; 19:26–27.

PAGE 429
Acts 1:14.
Jewish Encyclopedia, Vol. VII, p. 161.
Mark 6:2–3.

PAGE 430
Galatians 1:19.
Dunkerley, *Beyond the Gospels,* pp. 97–98.

PAGE 431
1 John 1:1; Psalm 53:2–3; Isaiah 53:6.

PAGE 432
1 Peter 2:21–23; 1 John 3:5; Mark 2:7; 2:16; 2:18; 2:24.

PAGE 433
Mark 3:11–12; 8:29–30; 11:27–33.

PAGE 434
Mark 8:29–31; 9:9–10; Matthew 26:63–65.

PAGE 435
Mark 3:5–6.

PAGE 436
John 2:11; 4:53; 5:18; 6:14–15; 6:60, 66; 9:34–38; 11:45–53.

PAGE 437
The Gospel of Thomas; in *The Apocryphal New Testament,* tr. M. R. James (London: Oxford University Press, 1924), pp. 62–63.

PAGE 438
Genesis 1:26; 5:1–3; Daniel 7:13–14.

PAGE 440
Job 38:4–7; Hosea 11:1; 2 Samuel 7:8–14.

PAGE 441
1 John 3:1–3; Matthew 11:25–27; John 8:54–55; Proverbs 3:1; 4:1–4.

PAGE 442
John 5:19–20.
Thomas Boslooper, *The Virgin Birth* (London: SCM Press, 1962), p. 186.

PAGE 443
Professor Zaehner; in Lewis, *Study of Religions,* p. 145.

PAGE 447
Hosea 11:1–4; Deuteronomy 8:1, 6, 11, 19–20.

PAGE 448
Exodus 34:6–7; Jeremiah 5:7–9; Ezekiel 18:23.

PAGE 449
Genesis 2:16–17; Romans 5:12; 6:23; James 1:15.

PAGE 450
Numbers 30:15; Leviticus 10:17; 16:22; Isaiah 53:5–6.

PAGE 451
Isaiah 53:11; 53:12; 53:10; Leviticus 24:15–16; Deuteronomy 21:22–23; Mark 8:31–32; 9:30–31; 10:32–34.

PAGE 452
Mark 14:6–10; 14:22–25.

PAGE 453
Matthew 26:39; 26:42; Psalm 75:8; Jeremiah 25:15–16; Isaiah 51:17.

PAGE 454
Mark 14:32–36; 15:2–15.

PAGE 455
John 18:38; Luke 23:15; 23:41; 23:47; 23:33–34; John 19:26–27.

PAGE 456
Luke 23:42–43; Mark 15:34; Luke 23:46; John 19:28–30.

PAGE 460
John 1:29; 1 John 2:1–2; Luke 24:46–47; 1 Peter 2:24; 3:18; 1 Corinthians 15:3; Hebrews 1:3; Colossians 2:13–14.

PAGE 461
Romans 5:8, 9; 1 John 4:10 (Revised Version); Romans 6:10; 6:23; Hebrews 10:12–14, 18; Galatians 3:13.

PAGE 462
Luke 24:45–47; Exodus 12:11–13; Deuteronomy 16:1–3.

PAGE 463
1 Corinthians 5:7; 1 Peter 1:18–19; Romans 8:1–3; John 18:11.

PAGE 464
Romans 5:1, 8; 1 Peter 1:18.

PAGE 465
Colossians 2:13–15; Romans 5:8, 10–11; 5:9.

PAGE 466
1 Peter 2:21–23; 4:13; Luke 9:23–26; Philippians 3:7–10; 2 Corinthians 5:14–15.

PAGE 467
Philippians 2:5–8; 1 Corinthians 8:11; 2 Corinthians 1:3–7; 1 Corinthians 15:56–57; Philippians 1:21.

PAGE 468
Revelation 12:10–12.

PAGE 470
J. W. C. Wand, *The Atonement* (London: SPCK, 1963), p. 12.
David Edwards, *God's Cross in Our World* (London: SCM Press, 1963), p. 41.

PAGE 472
John 3:16; 1 John 4:8–18; Romans 5:8–9; 1 Peter 2:20–24.

PAGE 475
Hebrews 10:12–14.

PAGE 476
1 Peter 1:18–21.

PAGE 477
Rudolph Bultmann, *Kerygma and Myth,* tr. R. H. Fuller, ed. H. W. Bartsch, Vol. I (London: SCM Press, 1953), pp. 36–39. (Vol. II pub. in 1962.)

PAGE 478
Colin Wilson, *Religion and the Rebel* (London: Gollancz, 1957), p. 29.
Dietrich Bonhoeffer, *Letters and Papers from Prison* (London: Collins Fontana, 1959), p. 164.

PAGE 479
van Buren, *Secular Meaning,* pp. 154–155.
Edwards, *God's Cross,* pp. 37 ff.

PAGE 480
Nikos Kazantzakis, *Christ Recrucified* (London: Faber and Faber, 1968), pp. 466–467.
Thomas Mann; quoted on the cover of Kazantzakis, *Christ Recrucified.*

PAGE 481
Happold, *Religious Faith,* p. 172.
Joad, *Christianity,* pp. 72–73.

PAGE 482
J. Gresham Machen, *Christianity and Liberalism* (Eastbourne, Sussex; Victory Press, 1923), pp. 120–121.
Bultmann, *Kerygma and Myth,* Vol. I, pp. 7–8.

PAGE 483
Robinson, *Honest to God,* p. 78.

PAGE 485
Jewish Encyclopedia, Vol. VII, p. 166.
Tacitus; in *Documents of the Church,* p. 2.
Talmud; in Dunkerley, *Beyond the Gospels,* p. 50.

PAGE 486
Mark 10:45; 15:37–38; 1 Peter 3:18; 2:24.

PAGE 487
Lin Yutang; in *What I Believe,* p. 80.
Ayer; in *What I Believe,* p. 16.
Camus; in *Camus, A Collection of Critical Essays,* p. 68.

PAGE 488
Luke 1:76.
J. C. Pollock, *Moody Without Sankey* (London: Hodder and Stoughton, 1963), p. 73.

PAGE 489
Kenneth Barnes; in *What I Believe,* n.p.

PAGE 491
B. B. Warfield, "Modern Theories of the Atonement," in *The Person and Work of Christ* (Nutley, NJ: Presbyterian and Reformed Publishing Co., 1950), p. 386.

PAGE 493
Genesis 2:16–17; Exodus 21:15–16, 22–25.

PAGE 494
Luke 19:41–44.

Leon Morris, *Glory in the Cross* (London: Hodder and Stoughton, 1966), pp. 76–77.

PAGE 495
Lord Byron; in Willey, *Nineteenth Century*, p. 75.

PAGE 496
Acts 20:28; 2 Corinthians 5:19.

PAGE 497
Romans 5:12, 15–17, 18–19.

PAGE 498
Hebrews 9:26; 10:12, 14; Romans 5:1–2; Matthew 16:22.

PAGE 499
Jewish Encyclopedia, Vol. VII, p. 167.
Hans Joachim Schoeps, *The Jewish Christian Argument* (London: Faber and Faber, 1965), p. 23.
Matthew 16:23 (NEB); John 12:27; Matthew 26:52–54.

PAGE 500
Luke 24:25–27; 24:45–47.
Sura 4:156–157, p. 370.
Kenneth Cragg; in M. Kamel Hussein, *City of Wrong*, tr. Kenneth Cragg (Amsterdam: Djambatan, 1959), pp. x–xi.

PAGE 502
Hebrews 2:14–15.

PAGE 509
Acts 1:3 (NEB).

PAGE 516
Acts 2:32; Luke 24:44–47; Ephesians 2:18; Hebrews 7:25.

PAGE 517
Romans 6:4–11; Philippians 3:8–11; Romans 14:7–9; 2 Corinthians 1:8–10.

PAGE 518
2 Timothy 1:10; 1 Peter 1:3; Hebrews 2:14–15; 1 Corinthians 15:51–55.

PAGE 525
Jewish Encyclopedia, Vol. IV, p. 51.

PAGE 526
Schonfield, *Passover Plot*, p. 7.
Ronald Gregor Smith, *Secular Christianity* (London: Collins, 1966), p. 103.
PAGE 527
Schonfield, *Passover Plot*, pp. 172, 180.

PAGE 528
Lewis Carroll, *Alice in Wonderland* (London: Macmillan, 1966), p. 60.

PAGE 529
David Hume, *An Enquiry Concerning Human Understanding*, Section X, *Of Miracles*, ed. L. A. Selby Bigge (Chicago: Open Court, 1924 reprint), pp. 210–212, 222–223.

PAGE 531
C. S. Lewis, *Miracles* (London: Bles, 1947), pp. 122–123.

Joad, *Christianity*, pp. 269–270.

PAGE 536
Bultmann, *Kerygma and Myth*, Vol. I, pp. 42–43.
Harvey Cox, "A Dialogue on Christ's Resurrection"; in *Christianity Today* (April 12, 1968), p. 9.

PAGE 537
van Buren, *Secular Meaning*, pp. 132–133.
Wren-Lewis; in *What I Believe*, p. 236.
Wren-Lewis, "Does Science Destroy Belief?"; in Moule, *Fact and Fantasy*, p. 43.

PAGE 538
Eduard Schweitzer, *Jesus* (London: SCM Press, 1971), pp. 49–51.

PAGE 539
Bultmann, *Kerygma and Myth*, Vol. I, pp. 202, 203, 109.
Gunther Bornkam; in Brown, *Philosophy and Faith*, n.p.
van Buren, *Secular Meaning*, n.p.

PAGE 540
J. S. Bezzant; in Vidler, *Objections to Christian Belief*, pp. 90–91.

PAGE 544
Arnold Lunn; in Joad, *Christianity*, p. 259.
1 Corinthians 15:1–5.

PAGE 545
1 Corinthians 15:35–37, 42–44, 52–53.
Josephus; see pages 424–425, Part 3.

PAGE 546
Ordinance of Claudius; in *The New Testament Background, Selected Documents*, ed. C. K. Barrett (London: SPCK, 1961), p. 15.
E. L. Sukenik; in Berndt Gustafson, *New Testament Studies*, pp. 65–66.

PAGE 547
S. H. Hooke, *The Resurrection of Christ* (London: Darton, Longman and Todd, 1967), p. 1.

PAGES 547 AND 548
Hooke, *Resurrection of Christ*, pp. 2–3.

PAGE 548
Barrett, *New Testament Background*, pp. 92–93.

PAGE 549
A. M. Ramsey, *The Resurrection of Christ* (London: Bles, 1945), p. 112.
Leslie Weatherhead, *The Christian Agnostic* (London: Hodder and Stoughton, 1965), p. 238.

PAGE 550
Edwards, *God's Cross*, p. 144.

PAGE 558
Hebrews 11:6; Romans 10:9; John 20:30–31; 1:11–12.

PAGE 559
Luke 14:25–33.

PAGE 560
Mark 10:29–30; Romans 8:15–16; Ephesians 3:14–19.

PAGE 561
Romans 8:14; Galatians 5:22; John 16:12–14; Hebrews 10:23–25; Revelation 21:1–7.

PAGE 563
John 7:16–17.

PAGE 564
Mark 9:23–25; 6:20.

PAGE 565
Mark 6:26; Luke 23:8–9; Acts 24:24–27.

PAGE 567
Matthew 7:21–23.

PAGE 568
Matthew 25:31–46.

PAGE 569
Harrington, *Accidental Century*, p. 11.

PAGE 571
Smith, *Questions of Religious Truth*, pp. 68–69.

PAGE 574
Lord Boothby; in *What I Believe*, p. 4.

PAGE 575
Arnold Lunn; in Joad, *Christianity*, n.p.
Nietzsche; in Wilson, *Outsider*, p. 133.
Sartre, *Words*, tr. Irene Clephane (London: Penguin, 1964), p. 157.

PAGE 576
Hume, *Treatise on Human Nature* (London: Collins Fontana, 1962), I.IV.I.
Kathleen Knott; in Blackham, *Objections to Humanism*, p. 62.
Hazard, *European Thought*, p. 82.
Blackham, *Existentialist Thinkers*, p. 41.

PAGE 577
Camus, *Rebel*, p. 12.
Lazare Bickel; in Camus, *Rebel*, pp. 258–259.
Schaeffer, *God Who Is There*, p. 129.

PAGE 578
Mark 10:21–22; Luke 14:18–20.

PAGE 579
John 5:44.
A. Huxley, *Ends and Means*, pp. 275, 284.
Joad, *Christianity*, Introduction.
Joad, *Recovery of Belief*, p. 28.

PAGE 580
Revelation 6:15–17.

PAGE 581
John 3:16–21.

593